Staging Gay Lives

Staging Gay Lives

An Anthology of Contemporary Gay Theater

edited by

JOHN M. CLUM

Foreword by Tony Kushner

WestviewPress

A Division of HarperCollinsPublishers

Copyright © 1996 by Westview Press, Inc., A Division of HarperCollins Publishers, Inc.

Published in 1996 in the United States of America by Westview Press, Inc., 5500 Central Avenue,
Boulder, Colorado 80301-2877, and in the United Kingdom by Westview Press, 12 Hid's Copse Road,
Cumnor Hill, Oxford OX2 9JJ

Library of Congress Cataloging-in-Publication Data
Staging gay lives : an anthology of contemporary gay theater / edited
by John M. Clum.
    p. cm.
  ISBN 0-8133-2504-8 (hardcover).—ISBN 0-8133-2505-6 (pbk.)
  1. American drama—20th century. 2. Gay men's writings, American.
3. Gay men's writings, English. 4. English drama—20th century.
5. American drama—Men authors. 6. English drama—Men authors.
7. Gay men—Drama. I. Clum, John M.
PS627.H67S73   1996
812'.540809206642—dc20   95-23652
                                                              CIP

The paper used in this publication meets the requirements of the American National Standard for
Permanence of Paper for Printed Library Materials Z39.48-1984.

10   9   8   7   6   5   4   3   2   1

Contents

Porcelain

Men on the Verge of a His-panic Breakdown

In the Heart of America

Foreword:
Notes Toward a Theater of
the Fabulous

TONY KUSHNER

Queer Nation, a group born out of ACT UP and the AIDS militant movement but concerned primarily with issues of lesbian and gay enfranchisement and power, used to have a slogan: We're here, we're queer, we're fabulous, get used to it. *Fabulous* became a popular word in the queer community—well, it was never *un*popular, but for a while it became a battle cry of a new queer politics, carnival and camp, aggressively fruity, celebratory and tough like a streetwise drag queen: "*FAAAAABULOUS!*" *Fabulous* was roughly the gay equivalent of that indefinable, ineffable thing young African Americans used to identify as *soul*, and later perhaps as *badness* and *def* and *phat*, and which Jews identify as *menschlichkeit*. If you possess it, you don't need to ask what it is. When you attempt to delineate it, you move away from it. *Fabulous* is one of those words that provide a measure of the degree to which a person or event manifests a particular, usually oppressed, subculture's most distinctive, invigorating features.

What are the salient features of Fabulousness? Irony. Tragic history. Defiance. Gender-fuck. Glitter. Drama. It is not butch. It is not hot. The cathexis surrounding Fabulousness is not necessarily erotic. The Fabulous is not delimited by age or beauty. Style has a dialectical relationship to physical reality. The body is the Real. Style is Theater. The raw materials are reworked into illusion. For style to be truly fabulous, one must completely triumph over tragedy, age, physical insufficiencies—and just as importantly, one's audiences must be made aware of the degree of transcendence, of triumph; must see both the triumph and that over which the triumph has been made. (In this the magic of the Fabulous is precisely the magic of the theater. The wires show. The illusion is always incomplete, inadequate; the work behind the magic is meant to be appreciated.)

Gay theater artists, including the talented writers of this volume, are collectively shaping the next chapter in the history of American gay theater, which has at times been inseparable from the history of American theater in its entirety and which is now becoming increasingly distinct. Our great antecedent is Charles Ludlam, who died of AIDS in the early '80s and who was, in addition to being the funniest man who ever lived and a brilliant consumer and regurgitator of theatrical style and legend, the founder and chief arbitrator of the Theater of the Ridiculous.

The Ridiculous as a category is brilliantly defined by Ludlam in his "Manifesto: Ridiculous Theatre, Scourge of Human Folly," with such maxims as "If one is not a living mockery of one's own ideals, one has set one's ideals too low." The Ridiculous, with its roots stretching back into the 1950s, became the first openly gay aesthetic. Perhaps its defining moment was not a theatrical one but rather the political act that began the modern gay liberation movement, the Stonewall riots, which took place on the night of Judy Garland's funeral in 1969 and which began in a spirit of both rage and parody as drag queens, consciously and with considerable irony, hurled bricks and abuse at cops in imitation, even parodic imitation, of the Black Panthers, chanting "Gay is good!" as the queer version of "Black is beautiful!" At the threshold of community, of liberation, at the threshold of transforming closet drama from tragedy into comedy—a step beyond Genet because it's funnier—homosexuals learned the essential strategy of divesting ourselves of furtiveness. We dragged and I do mean dragged the trappings of the underworld, the demimonde, onto the avenues in broad daylight. And yet—and yet we hadn't fully arrived at being capable of seeing ourselves as subjects. We were, by our own self-report, the Ridiculous, perhaps a mirror of the larger ridiculousness that is the world, but still inescapably Ridiculous, not yet able, I think, to take ourselves quite seriously enough. Certain locutions are forbidden the Ridiculous because they collapse the distance irony provides between pain and its articulate expression, a distance that can only be safely collapsed after coming into real power, when the hope, even the remote hope, of the redressing of injustice is at hand.

The tensions between the comic and the serious are fraught with peril. Taking ourselves *too* seriously, we cease to be gay. Becoming subjects cannot mean becoming unfabulous. Becoming people must mean becoming *gay* people, not straightmen. Becoming humorless, we lose connection to the most vital parts of our culture. The Fabulous incorporates the Ridiculous. It is the next step, not a rejection. It is a necessary corrective to the dead earnestness of the butch, corporate, Gay Republican assimilationist camp, if you'll pardon the expression. The Fabulous is the assertively Camp camp, the rapturous embrace of difference, the discovering of self not in that which has rejected you but in that which makes you unlike, and disliked, and Other.

The Fabulous is the recovery of the power of the Bakhtinian, the magic of the grotesque, the carnivalesque—politics as carnival, as Halloween, as theater. You can see this in the amphibious nature of the gay pride parade, a form our community invented, simultaneously angry demonstration, identity assertion, and Mardi Gras. In part Fabulousness is a bestowing of power by merely believing in it: If I dress like a nun I become invested. And this is true. I would rather be blessed by Sister Dementia Praecox than by Cardinal O'Connor. This is also true of Art; Art is like that: There may be nothing there, but that nothing has power; it grows to something of great constancy, but howsoever strange and admirable.

If we are moving from a Theater of the Ridiculous to a Theater of the Fabulous (and I propose such a development purely for the fun of doing so, unsure and even skeptical of its use value), I would guess that this movement also has something to do with telling stories, of having arrived as a community with a history—of both oppression and liberation. One of the gifts of liberation, of even an incomplete liberation such as the one we now enjoy, twenty-six years after Stonewall, is an expanding, more detailed, more coherent collective memory. The past is liberated as well as the present. We are now fabulous in part because we are *fabulists,* fabled, organized and powerful enough to have the luxury to begin to examine the past and interpret it, and to pass it along to our descendants openly. For homosexuals to work to create a history is for us to say that there will be those who come after, to say to the straight world: Some of your children will be queer.

The Fabulous, or whatever one chooses to call the new queer theater, seems to be interested in exploring magic, the spirit, the soul, which the iron irony of the Ridiculous could do only in sidelong glances. In part this magic has the same pedigree as Shakespeare's, as Brecht's, as Marx's, in the uneasy, slippery relationship between the Real and the Imaginary, in which human activity plays a mediational role between the material and the ideal. Marx writes, "We ground consciousness in life activity, in social being," all too familiar an idea to closet cases and proud drag queens alike. Marx also writes, "In direct contrast to German philosophy, which descends from heaven to earth (Hegel), here we ascend from earth to Heaven." Which is DIVINE!

The Millennium is at hand, after all, and the time has come for an identity-based political movement such as ours, for a political movement of gender and sexuality, and for all progressive movements to reconsider the hyper-rationalist bases of our political theories. We must not leap dumbly into some ersatz New Age. But the time has come to begin to explore the role of faith, prayer, and soul in a politics that is concerned, as ours must be, with irreparable loss; with community and with the sacrifices community entails; and with the most difficult and necessary thing of all, hope.

Preface

Staging Gay Lives offers some of the best recent theatrical writing by and about gay men. In a sense it is a companion volume to my historical and critical book *Acting Gay: Male Homosexuality in Modern Drama.*[1] Some of the plays collected here are discussed in that book; others, produced since *Acting Gay* was published, continue the history that book traces. This is the first American appearance in print for all of the works in this anthology (*Mean Tears* and *A Madhouse in Goa* have been published in England) and the debut appearance in print of the younger playwrights. All of the works printed here have been successfully produced in England and/or the United States.

These American and British plays and theater pieces represent the work of white, African-American, Asian, and Hispanic playwrights. All but one of the works are by gay male playwrights; the exception, Naomi Wallace, is one of a number of extraordinary women writers who offer powerful, insightful depictions of the place of gay men in American gender politics. Also represented here are two generations of gay theater artists: from Martin Sherman and Peter Gill, who are scions of gay theater in the United States and England (Gill was one of the first directors of Joe Orton's work in the 1960s, and Sherman's *Bent* [1979] is a central work in the gay dramatic canon), to the exciting young generation of playwrights and performance artists who have emerged in the "gay nineties." I have chosen work that demonstrates the diversity of contemporary gay experience and represents a variety of theatrical forms, including musical, drama, and performance art.[2] These plays also offer a dramatized history of gay life over the past decade, from the shock, grief, and anger of AIDS dramas to plays that place the experience of gay men within a larger cultural critique.

This collection is evidence that the most vibrant drama being written in English today is being written by gay playwrights and that our playwrights no longer have to write of gay experience in code or heterosexualize their experience for audiences not willing to see the validity or commonality of gay experience. The honor roll of major American (and, more and more, English) playwrights also happens to be a list of gay playwrights. Gay writers have the stage by default, and gay drama flourishes not only on Broadway, where Tony Kushner's *Angels in America* and Terrence McNally's *Love! Valour! Compassion!* were among the most celebrated plays in decades, or London's West End, where Kevin Elyot's *My Night with Reg* and Jonathan Harvey's *Beautiful Thing* received critical acclaim, but also in smaller venues such as the Manhattan Theater Club, where Terrence McNally and Christopher Durang had hit plays, and London's most distinguished fringe theaters, where Naomi Wallace's *In the Heart of America* and Patrick Wilde's *What's*

Wrong with Angry? were the best of a number of fine gay plays that were staged. And many American cities, from San Francisco to Chicago to Durham, North Carolina, have a gay theater or gay theater festival. Bill Kaiser's *On the Purple Circuit* directory contains scores of gay producing organizations, playwrights, and performance artists.

What accounts for the explosion of gay theater? In an era in which serious drama no longer attracts large mainstream audiences, the theater is the only place where gay men can see their experience played out. Therefore, gay men need the theater as the theater now needs gay men. Television is still skittish about homosexuality. A top-rated television situation comedy can be produced and written by gay men and have gay-featured actors but still only occasionally recognize the existence of gay men. Would not *Frasier,* which boasts a gay producer, a gay writer, and at least one openly gay cast member, be funnier and more honest if Frasier and Niles were a gay couple? They talk and act like one! The one gay character on a popular nighttime soap opera is the only character in the series denied any romance and therefore denied any plot line. And PBS caved in to right-wing noise and canceled participation in the sequel to the highly popular and critically acclaimed miniseries *Tales of the City.* Hollywood can only provide the blandness of a film like *Philadelphia,* in which the hero is allowed a death scene but not a victory.

So we need the stage to show us our lives. It can also be said that more gay playwrights than straight ones still feel a commitment to theater despite the small likelihood of their receiving any remuneration for their labors. The Broadway commercial theater is no longer a place for serious drama of any kind. Tony Kushner's *Angels in America,* with all its rave reviews and awards and a run of over eighteen months, lost money for its producers and backers, a sure sign that the economics of Broadway has made producing anything but an Andrew Lloyd Webber musical spectacular impossible. Serious playwrights now write for love and the hope of a film sale. One of the ironies of this book is that the majority of the plays written by playwrights born in or living in the United States had their success in London, the only city left with a thriving theater culture.

Gay playwrights and theaters that produce gay work face political problems as well. Gay theater still meets with resistance from cultural conservatives wary of the arts and eager to stop all efforts of lesbians and gay men to be recognized as full citizens onstage and off. A 1993 Marietta, Georgia, production of Terrence McNally's *Lips Together, Teeth Apart,* a gentle satire of homophobia set on Fire Island, where the play's heterosexual characters feel very much in the minority, became the pretext for a virulent antigay feeding frenzy that led the Cobb County Council to pass an antigay resolution and withdraw all county arts funding. Fortunately, the local and national controversy engendered by the Cobb County Council's actions showed that a growing number of Americans accept what Tony Kushner's Prior Walter says at the end of *Angels in America*: "The world only spins forward. We will be citizens. The time has come."[3]

England, too, has seen signs of a cultural backlash. The new gay visibility on the

London stage has inspired some grumbling from more conservative critics. A September 30, 1994, column in the conservative *Evening Standard* bore the headline "Stop the Plague of Pink Plays." In the column critic Milton Shulman laments that "in 1994 more than half of all new plays in London were concerned with characters who had gay or lesbian tendencies." Shulman clearly does not believe that a gay play can have the universality of a play by and about heterosexuals and ends his column with an exhortation: "It is time managements encouraged playwrights to concern themselves with the complex permutations of love and tears among heterosexuals." The use of the word *complex* assumes that love and tears among homosexuals are simpler, more superficial. Nor does Shulman believe that gay experience has any common bonds with heterosexual experience. Fortunately, Shulman is in the minority of London critics.

What the plays and theater pieces in this book have in common, beyond depictions of the experiences of gay men, is what the components of any collection of fine plays share: a commitment to the possibilities of theater as the most vibrant means of reflecting and commenting on human experience and a gift for creating rich characters and arresting dramatic narratives. Above all, the work on offer here has considerable variety. This collection is an argument against any monolithic definition of contemporary gay drama or contemporary gay experience. The playwrights here have unique individual visions and voices.

Is there anything these works share that defines them as gay theater? I would say a certain kind of adventurousness, a playing with the possibilities of theater. When discussing gay theater, I am always reminded of Blanche DuBois's proclamation: "I don't want realism. I want magic!!" It is the sense of theater as a magical space mirroring life but larger than life and the sense that theater best mirrors the performance of gender and the awareness of performativity that have historically been part of the gay experience. These plays all take their audiences and their readers to surprising places. There is no way in which we could refer to these plays as "straight" plays. Gay playwrights, even at their most serious moments, remind their audiences of the many meanings of the word *play*. What does gay theater mean if not joyous, camp, liberating, magical? It is *not* somber, literal, or naturalistic.

I teach my students that what makes a particular drama unique or artistically successful is not the originality of its story (even William Shakespeare borrowed most of his stories) or characters, but its mastery of the verbal and visual languages of the stage. Plays must have powerful, unique visions and voices. The visions are often provided by directors, designers, and actors, but the voice is the playwright's. The plays on offer here have unique, challenging, exciting voices. Moreover, they are about characters who move from domination by an oppressive language to liberation through the finding of their own gay voice. Chay Yew calls his most recent play *A Language of Their Own*. This book shows gay men fighting for a language of their own within societies out to define, limit, and sometimes defeat them. Often these plays show gay men achieving poetry in a prosaic world as they strive for self-definition and self-assertion. Many of the plays also dramatize characters' attempts to find or forge a language for male-male love as a redeeming alternative to the banalities, evasions, and violence of the language of the dominant culture.

I write this preface at the beginning of 1995, when lesbians and gay men must fight to maintain the toehold we have gained in American and British society. The hopeful signs of acceptance from large segments of American society are counterbalanced by the hostile noises from the increasingly powerful right wing. The embraces are always countered by the bashings, and the struggle within the body politic between decent, compassionate citizens and mean-spirited radical conservatives is echoed in the gay community in the squabbles between moderate assimilationists and those intent on trying to rekindle the dying embers of 1960s left-wing radicalism. The gay artist and the gay critic must accept the risk of being attacked from both straight Right and gay Left.

There is also the continued specter of AIDS haunting gay life, art, and politics. For all the money and time spent on research in the past decade, there is no sign of sure vaccine or cure. And AIDS is still used by our opponents as a club to beat gays down. Even supposed allies in film and television insist on equating gayness with AIDS and are willing to show gay men suffering and dying but are reluctant to show gay men who, in William Faulkner's words, endure and prevail. Most of the plays in this collection, all written in the age of AIDS, mention or allude to AIDS, but the characters in these plays are not passive victims; they are men finding and asserting themselves in tragic circumstances.

This collection is a sure sign that, despite ravaging disease and hostility from some noisy corners of the body politic, American and British drama is now gay drama. The fine plays in this book demonstrate that gay experience is central to contemporary culture. There is sadness in the portraits of self-hatred and self-destructive behavior—gays still have a lot of fighting to do—and hope in the unabashed, uncompromising pictures of gay pride and love.

◐   ◐   ◐

A word about the order of plays here: I decided against chronological order, always tidy but only of historical interest, in favor of an arrangement that groups plays that seem particularly comparable and that moves the reader through the book in a meaningful, coherent way. The collection begins with the three most "political" plays, the American *The Harvey Milk Show* and *Randy's House* and the British *What's Wrong with Angry?* All three combine political statement with popular theater. Peter Gill's *Mean Tears* and Martin Sherman's *A Madhouse in Goa* are both intense character studies and satiric critiques of a contemporary society devoid of spirit or conscience. Godfrey Hamilton's *Kissing Marianne* presents an imaginative invocation of a lover by a man with AIDS. *Dark Fruit, Porcelain,* and *Men on the Verge of a His-panic Breakdown* all focus on the intersection of race or ethnicity and gayness. Naomi Wallace's *In the Heart of America* is a fitting finale, recapitulating many of the themes and motifs of the preceding works.

I have invited all the playwrights to provide some background of their own to their plays. I am grateful to those who were able to provide personal comments.

❂   ❂   ❂

I have had the pleasure of seeing all these plays and of meeting most of their creators. I am deeply grateful to all the playwrights represented in this book for allowing me to include their work. I am also grateful to their agents, who have been cooperative and generous: To Carl Mulert at Joyce Ketay, George Lane at William Morris, Mel Kenyon at Casarotto Ramsay, and Diana Tyler at MBA, I offer special thanks. Thanks, too, to my editor at Westview, Gordon Massman, for encouraging me to take on this project and for guiding it so expertly. And gratitude to my trusty helpers at Duke, particularly Gregory J. Tomso.

Thanks to the miraculous Tony Kushner for his superb Foreword.

Thanks to the actors who through their fine performances brought these plays to life (sometimes endangering their careers in doing so), particularly Karl Johnson, Rupert Graves, Chris Coleman, Brian Barnett, Mark Pinkosh, Tom Wisdom, Zubin Varla, and Richard Dormer.

And special thanks to my distinguished colleagues in theater Robert West, Robert Patrick, and Jeff Storer; to my companions in theatergoing, particularly Clifford Hindley; and especially, of course, to my collaborator and companion throughout the drama of life, Walter Melion.

John M. Clum

Notes

1. John M. Clum, *Acting Gay: Male Homosexuality in Modern Drama*, rev. ed. (New York: Columbia University Press, 1994).

2. One semantic note: I use the terms *play, drama,* and *theater piece* somewhat loosely and interchangeably here. Some would say that Pomo Afro Homos' work is not exactly drama, but it is scripted and acted and performed in theatrical settings.

3. Tony Kushner, *Angels in America, Part Two: Perestroika* (New York: Theatre Communications Guild, 1994), p. 148.

DAN PRUITT AND PATRICK HUTCHISON

The Harvey Milk Show

EDITOR'S INTRODUCTION

As OPENLY GAY CULTURE has emerged in the past century, it has, like all cultures, developed a history and a mythology codifying centuries of oppression and resistance. As the riots around the Stonewall Inn in Greenwich Village in 1969 have become our Boston Tea Party, so Harvey Milk has become our Martin Luther King, our hero-martyr. Milk's life and murder have been recounted in print in the late Randy Shilts's superb history *The Mayor of Castro Street,* which was turned into a gripping film documentary. Emily Mann's docudrama *The Execution of Justice,* which focuses on the trial of Dan White for the murder of Harvey Milk, has been performed all over America. In 1995 an opera titled *Harvey Milk* was performed by the Houston, New York City, and San Francisco Operas.

Milk's life and death sum up the 1960s and gay liberation. A successful New York stockbroker drops out and moves to San Francisco to live the gay life. He is the first openly gay person to be elected to the San Francisco City Council. He and George Moscone, the mayor of San Francisco, are murdered by disgruntled ex-councilman Dan White. White receives a ridiculous seven-year jail sentence for his double murder, and the gay community of San Francisco, enraged at the injustice and the homophobia underlying the verdict, goes on a rampage. The story remains horribly relevant as verbal and physical gay-bashing is still authorized by the powers that be and the radical Christian Right continues to use homophobia as a way to keep its flock in line and take their minds off more pertinent issues.

As Harvey Milk is in one sense a story of San Francisco and the 1960s and in another, figurative sense, the story of all gay men in America, so *The Harvey Milk Show* is the story of theater in Atlanta and also the story of gay theater in America in the 1990s. Writer-lyricist Dan Pruitt and composer Patrick Hutchison put together a little revue that had some success in Atlanta and then decided to try a book musical on Harvey Milk. Young Chris Coleman, an ambitious actor-director-impressario who had begun a small theater called Actor's Express, decided to mount *The Harvey Milk Show* in his theater, which was tucked away in a group

1

of warehouses near Atlanta's bohemian Little Five Points. The production was a smash hit and put Actor's Express on the map. The next season Actor's Express doubled its seating capacity and revived the production for another successful three-month run. *The Harvey Milk Show* will be remounted in a larger, more elaborate production for the 1996 Olympics in Atlanta, an irony and a bit of a victory after the official gay-bashing in neighboring Cobb County. The story of Actor's Express and *The Harvey Milk Show* demonstrates how hungry gay audiences are for work about them and how a theater can flourish by being adventurous enough to offer new, gay work. The repertoire of Actor's Express ranges from the Greeks to the present. It is not a gay theater, but it now has a devoted gay audience.

One reason for gay mythology and gay theater is to create a sense of solidarity in their audience by recounting a common history, articulating common problems, and galvanizing the audience to continued unification and resistance. Another is to educate nongays so that they understand their complicity in gay problems and cooperate in their solution. Gay theater also shows nongays that gays will not go away. This can be done only by a popular theater that bridges gay and straight audiences. *The Harvey Milk Show* achieves all this. It may not play as well in places more cynical than Atlanta, but there it has served important artistic and political functions. *The Harvey Milk Show* demonstrates another important aspect of contemporary American theater, straight or gay: There is no longer a New York–based American theater. As this collection attests, theater, straight or gay, is everywhere, from San Francisco and Los Angeles to Durham, North Carolina.

The Harvey Milk Show is, as writer Dan Pruitt puts it, "a southern boy's version of the story." Pruitt and Hutchison take liberties with history (so did Shakespeare). Their version of Harvey Milk's life and death is partly a history of the burgeoning gay liberation movement, partly a love story. The central character is Jamey, a young man from East Texas who has been thrown out of his home for being gay and has come to San Francisco, where he ekes out a life as a cowboy hustler. After he has been bashed, he is taken in by Harvey Milk and becomes Sancho Panza to Harvey's Don Quixote. Jamey is motivated by his love for Harvey; Harvey, by his sense of the rightness of his cause. After Harvey is killed, Jamey moves from rage and self-destructive behavior to a dedication to constructive action. Harvey's Christlike postdeath appearance to Jamey reminds the young man that there's "so very, very much left undone."

The relationship of Harvey and Jamey is the spine of the musical, the fictional bridge of historical past and its continuing pertinence. It is one of a number of effective theatrical devices, including Mr. Jones, the nemesis who represents all the people who oppose Harvey (even Anita Bryant), and the Milk Duds, a trio of multiracial gay men who are a combination of Greek chorus and backup singers.

In recounting in unabashedly romantic fashion the history of a gay martyr, *The Harvey Milk Show* offers its audience an almost religious experience, from the angry chorus at the candlelight vigil, to the Christlike reappearance of Harvey to his disciple, Jamey, in the Epilogue. Yet it is this old-time religious quality that made this musical of a 1960s San Francisco politician written by a small town boy

from South Carolina into a smash hit in the gayest and most gay-friendly city in the South.

AUTHORS' INTRODUCTION

"The wolves, Harve—they just keep acomin'."

—Jamey, Epilogue, *The Harvey Milk Show*

We first started writing together in the early 1980s. Ronald Reagan was in office, and some new "gay disease" was a whispered threat on the horizon of the gay community. We wrote songs to keep our spirits up. We wrote to write about our lives, to remind ourselves where we gay people have been, to remind ourselves of the kind of courage it has always taken for us to merely survive. We wrote to remind ourselves that we shall endure.

When our songs turned into a revue that turned into a stage show called *Different,* the battle against AIDS had turned into a raging war. We sang and danced our hearts out, like the USO entertaining at the front. We were all in the trenches together.

When we started writing *Harvey,* Reagan's heir apparent was in office, and like Reagan, George Bush was doing the usual nothing about the *A* word. (There was even a story that on hearing the statistics on the staggering death toll from AIDS, his response had been, "So? What's the problem?") We were a community giving everything to the battle. We had finally come together. We found beds. We delivered food. We held the hands of the sick and wiped the tears of the grieving. We buried lovers and friends and dads and mothers and brothers and sisters and strangers. We marched and sang and cried. We held onto one another. We endured.

We've endured Ronald Reagan, George Bush, Dan Quayle, Jerry Falwell, Pat Robertson, Rush Limbaugh, and Jesse Helms; antigay initiatives in Colorado, antigay initiatives in Cobb County, Georgia, antigay initiatives in the Northwest, the Midwest, the South, the East. We've endured "Don't ask, don't tell," the rise of the Right, our new position as fundamentalism's Enemy Number One now that communism is done. We endure AIDS daily. We endure.

And now it's 1995. Newt Gingrich and his Republican putsch hover like a scourge from Revelation. The country's new House majority leader has referred publicly to Representative Barney Frank as "Barney Fag" and gotten away with it. ACT-UP's bang has become something of a whimper. The community is tired and dispirited. Everyone is keeping a current passport and an eye on the exit.

But my guess is that we're just getting ready again. We'll roll up our sleeves, take a nice deep breath, and move on to the next act. Perhaps we shall make our entrance with a couplet delivered straight out to Mr. Gingrich:

Take your shot; do what you'll do.
We're gonna be here . . . long, long after you.

And what does all this have to do with Harvey and why we wrote about him?
Probably everything.

Patrick Hutchison (left) and Dan Pruitt (right)

PRODUCTION HISTORY AND RIGHTS

The Harvey Milk Show, book and lyrics by Dan Pruitt, music by Patrick Hutchison. Directed by Stephen Petty.

Chris Coleman played Harvey; Brian Barnett played Jamey. The production had its premiere September 1991 at Actor's Express, Atlanta, and ran again in the 1992–1993 season.

DAN PRUITT AND PATRICK HUTCHISON

The Harvey Milk Show

Cast of Characters

JAMEY: Late teens to early 20s. Texan.
DAN WHITE: Late 20s.
PATRICIA: Jamey's younger sister. Late teens.
HEATHER: 20s. Butch.
JOHN: 20s.
MR. AND MRS. MURPHY: Middle aged.
MR. JONES: 40s.
DEE: 20s. Black queen.
HARVEY MILK: Late 30s.

Other parts played by the ensemble.

Setting

Around San Francisco.

Prologue

SCENE: JAMEY (MIDNIGHT COWBOY)

[Storefronts at night. When the door to a bar opens, a flood of light and disco music spills into the street, as does JAMEY. He is dressed in what is later described as "heavy-duty cowboy drag"—boots, worn denims, and a pearl-buttoned, black cowboy shirt. He stumbles slightly, begins moving along the sidewalk. A COP (DAN WHITE) enters. As he approaches, JAMEY attempts to straighten up.]

5

JAMEY: Ev'nin'.
COP: Yeah.
JAMEY: Nice night.

[A disdainful grunt in reply as COP crosses and exits. Music. One or two male passersby enter, exit, reenter, cruising; then JAMEY alone onstage.]

JAMEY: **(Dance with a Cowboy)**
            Doesn't anybody wanna dance with a cowboy?
            Step on up here and meet buckeroo.
            We could kick out the kinks,
            Maybe have us some drinks—
            Doesn't anybody wanna dance with a cowboy?

            Won't somebody come and cut a rug with a cowboy?
            I've been saving one last one for you—
            You can hum some dumb tune—
            Say you come from the moon—
            Doesn't anybody wanna dance with a cowboy?

[Conversation with imaginary deep-voiced stranger]

"Hi."
Hi.
"Been in San Francisco long?"
Nope—a few months. It just feels like longer.
"I'm . . . Ben Cartwright."
Glad to meetcha, Ben. I'm Jamey. [Remembers] No. No, I'm not Jamey. I used to be Jamey.

[Lost in thought a moment, then remembers the "stranger"]

"Would you care to dance?"
Sure. My deepest pleasure.

            Sail-two-three, slide-two-three,
            Glide like the wide blue sea . . .
            Me? . . . Call me Buck.
            Sail-three-four, slide-three-four,
            Glide once more 'round the floor—

[He loses his balance.]

            Whoa! Wish me luck.

            Don't you poets have a deep romance for a cowboy?
            I can make all your fancies come true.

You can show me the ropes—
I'll live up to your hopes. . . .

[Music under. When he realizes a real and slightly shy STRANGER is watching him, JAMEY assumes his cowboy pose.]

STRANGER: Hi.
JAMEY: [Enjoying his own highly exaggerated cowboy parody] Howdy.
STRANGER: You waiting for someone?
JAMEY: Not anybody in particular.
STRANGER: Well, then, maybe we could go over to my place for a drink or something. I mean, that is, if you're free for awhile. . . .
JAMEY: [Still the exaggerated cowboy] Well, now, I ain't exactly free, but then again, I ain't exactly expensive either.

[He laughs loudly at his own joke as they exit.]

VIGNETTE: TYLER, TEXAS

[Isolated in a spot, fifteen-year-old PATRICIA writes a letter to her older brother.]

PATRICIA:

Dear Jamey,
    I got your letter at school today. It like to scared me to death when they called me to the office. I read it in homeroom. Finally hearing from you after all these months—well, I just don't know what.
    But, Jamey, don't worry. I promise I haven't told Daddy and Mama about your letter. But I still don't understand. What happened? Please, Jamey. I'm almost fifteen and everybody's acting like I was a baby. Somebody needs to tell me somethin'. Please, Jamey. . . .
    What happened?

> **(Letter from Home)**
> *You won't tell me—they won't tell me—*
> *What's it all about?*
> *I'm fam'ly—we're all fam'ly, Jamey,*
> *Fam'lies work things out.*
> *Whatever's going through your head,*
> *Please, Jamey, never doubt*
> *I love you.*
> *Jamey . . .*
> *Jamey, come home.*

The two of 'em are acting like
They'd just as soon fergit.
I try to ask them questions—
But they always tell me "Quit."
Sometimes I go into your room and—
Jamey, I just sit
Thinking of you.
I love you.
Jamey?
Please, Jamey.
Jamey, come home.

[Fade]

Act I

[During the slow crossfade from Patricia to street scene, there is a voice-over of radio disc jockeys. Like all deejays, they think they're a riot.]

JERRY: And a great big good morning to everyone in the Bay Area. This is Jerry Grady—

HERB: and Herb "the herb" Gardener—

JERRY: saying it's 7:31 a.m.

HERB: and this is KDJ-FM—

JERRY: on this, the first official day of spring, March the 20th—

HERB: and it's 1973—for those of you who just got in from Pomona,

JERRY: and a glorious spring day it is. Herb, can you believe this weather?

[They begin to fade as HEATHER, LANDLORD, and others enter street scene.]

HERB: The kind of day that makes you want to introduce your wife to your girl-friend . . .

JERRY: *[Driveling banter]* Not likely . . .

HERB: Just kidding, Honeybun . . .

JERRY: Fine for Honeybun, but what about your wife? . . .

[They yuck it up during fade.]

SCENE: STREET SCENE

[Morning, city storefronts. A few passersby, several people wait for bus, etc. HEATHER and JOHN are leaving the Murphys' door, followed by MRS. MURPHY.]

HEATHER/JOHN: Thanks again.

[They exit. MR. MURPHY, not quite ready for work, enters.]

MR. MURPHY: What was that about?

MRS. MURPHY: They just want to put up some posters. It seems Mr. Milk from down the block is running for some kind of office.

MR. MURPHY: Milk—the guy that bought old man Dawson's camera store? The hippie?

MRS. MURPHY: Yes.

MR. MURPHY: Hard to imagine people voting for a hippie for much of anything—except maybe a haircut. But, then, what do I know anymore?

MRS. MURPHY: I know—I gave up on trying to second-guess the world years ago.

MR. MURPHY: Everything's changing so fast. Even here, even old Castro Street. It's not the neighborhood we used to know, lovey.

MRS. MURPHY: No, but I guess it's just life, Jim—new people, new ideas, new blood.

MR. MURPHY: I suppose. I keep trying, but I don't know—I'm just not ready to become part of "the Pepsi generation." Be honest now, Katie. . . . Sometimes . . . don't you sometimes miss the old days?

MRS. MURPHY: Maybe . . . some . . . sometimes . . .

> **(Better Days)**
> *Lovely . . . but long ago,*
> *Lovely . . . but gone.*
> *Makes no diff'rence what we'd wish, we*
> *Won't hold back the dawn.*
> *Lovely, the memories,*
> *Lovely as lullabies,*
> *Sweet refrains that linger still, but*
> *Still another sun must rise.*

MR. MURPHY:

> *Lovely, and where'd they go?*
> *Lovely, the times.*
> *Time to spend some time together,*
> *Time for nurs'ry rhymes.*

BOTH:

> *Lovely, the memories*
> *Lovely, the songs we've sung—*
> *Who knows if it was the times or*
> *Whether simply being young.*

MR. JONES: *[Enters]* Morning, Jim, Mrs. Murphy.

MR. & MRS. MURPHY: Good morning.

MR. JONES: First of the month—just thought I'd stop by and save you a stamp.

MRS. MURPHY: Certainly. I've already made out your check.

MR. JONES: Of course you have. That's what I like—good, solid people. Sometimes I think we're the last of a dying breed.

MRS. MURPHY: Pardon?

MR. JONES: You see what's going on—the riffraff moving in, trying to take things over. First it was the hippies, then this kind and that kind, till now only the good Lord knows what's going to be moving in next door. If it's not Abdul and his tribe of screaming banshees, it's Bruce and Christopher and their potted plants.

MR. MURPHY: Yeah, well—me, I've always believed in taking people one at a time, whoever they are. They treat me right, I treat them right—that simple.

MR. JONES: *[Cynically]* Right.

MRS. MURPHY: And besides, let's face it—the clock keeps ticking, the world keeps turning, and there isn't one thing we can do about it.

MR. JONES: Yeah, and that's the crime of it.

MRS. MURPHY:

> *Times change, as times must do.*

MR. & MRS. MURPHY:

> *Times change. . . . We, too.*
> *Still, sometimes we'd like to cling to*
> *Simpler times we knew.*

ENSEMBLE:

> *Lovely, the memories—*
> *Lovely, but nothing stays—*
> *Nothing but the still and lovely*
> *Solace of the better days . . .*
> *Nothing but the still and lovely*
> *Solace of the better days*
> *Nothing but the still and lovely*
> *Solace of the better days.*

MRS. MURPHY: I'll get your check.

[MR. JONES follows the MURPHYS into the store. Others wander off or resume their newspapers. HEATHER and JOHN (wheeling a bicycle; basket holds posters and flyers) enter.]

HEATHER: Come on, Dee!

DEE: Never shout at a diva, darling—especially this early in the morning.

JOHN: But we've got work to do—light to bring to the wilderness—and it's the early bird that gets the worm.

DEE: Not in my neighborhood.

HEATHER: Hey, you guys, let's get with it.
JOHN: Yeah! Like Harvey says—

[DEE mouths, "Harvey says; Harvey says."]

"We stand at the crossroads of our history." It's time . . .

(Campaign Song)
Time to wake up—
Time to break apart the lessons time has taught us—
Time to take a part in our own play—to have our say—
Make up for what time has brought us.
HEATHER:
Time to shock 'em—
Time to knock 'em on their self-contented asses—
Time to rock the boat—to say, "We're here"—to make it
clear—no longer will we do with last.
ALL:
Some tomorrow we'll be where it's always sunny.
Some tomorrow we will bear the silver spoon.
Some tomorrow we will share the milk and honey.
Some tomorrow we will win our rights—
DEE:
then sleep 'til noon!
ALL:
Tides are turning—
Time to take advantage of a wave that's cresting—
Time to break the ties with yesterday—we make our way—
Mad and gay—and here to stay—
Some tomorrow, comes a better day.

[MR. JONES has reentered, watched the end of this. As the song ends, he rips a poster down. HEATHER notices.]

HEATHER: HEY! What do you think you're doing?
MR. JONES: What does it look like?
JOHN: Wait. That's Harvey—he's local—lives right here in the neighborhood.
MR. JONES: I know who he is—or all I need to know. I won't have these walls cluttered up with homosexual literature.
HEATHER: Hey, man, last time I heard, this was a free country.

[HARVEY enters, stands watching. MURPHYS, JAMEY, and several others randomly enter and eavesdrop.]

MR. JONES: The country may be, but this building is private property—*my* property.

DEE: But the Murphys said it was alright.

MR. JONES: The Murphys don't own the building. I do. And I say it's *not* alright. Got it?

HEATHER: You asshole.

DEE: Down, girl.

MR. JONES: What did you just call me?

[*COP returns.*]

HEATHER: You heard me.

COP: What's the problem?

MR. JONES: This person has defaced my building, and then when I called her on it, she started using abusive language.

HEATHER: WHAT? Defaced your building!? A poster. A poster.

HARVEY: Could I be of some assistance?

COP: Who're you?

HARVEY: The gentleman in question—in a manner of speaking.

COP: Who?

HARVEY: [*Extends hand*] Harvey Milk . . . running for city supervisor. Remember me come election day.

COP: Never mind that. Some of your people seem to be causing trouble.

HARVEY: But didn't I understand them to say that they asked you about putting up the poster, Mrs. Murphy?

MRS. MURPHY: They did ask me, Dan.

MR. JONES: But it's *my* building.

HEATHER: [*Exasperated*] Look, dude, I think we've all gotten that part.

HARVEY: So of course they assumed it was within Mr. Murphy's power to grant permission. I always ask my people to never infringe on the rights of others. We know only too well that personal rights can never be taken for granted.

MR. JONES: Save your speeches for the Kremlin. But if you're the one responsible, do you also teach them to use language that would be more at home in a whorehouse?

HARVEY: Excuse me, sir, but there are ladies present.

MR. JONES: [*Becoming flustered*] What? I didn't—she was the one—Dan, that woman there . . .

HARVEY: Oh, you mean Heather? You, a grown, rather hearty-looking gentleman, felt threatened by the words of this young lady?

MR. JONES: Young lady! Look at her! And she called me an asshole.

[*Crowd laughs. HARVEY begins playing to them.*]

HARVEY: May I ask you something? Are you married?

MR. JONES: Well, of course. But what does that have to do with anything?

HARVEY: I just assume that if you're married, we seem to be taking up a lot of this officer's time over something that I'm sure you've heard a woman call you at least once in your life.

[Crowd likes this, laughs again.]

MR. JONES: My wife would never use language like that.
HARVEY: Then you must be a very, very lucky man.

[Another laugh from crowd. Then, to COP]

Isn't it about time to close this out with an apology and a handshake?
HEATHER: APOLOGY!

[HARVEY puts an arm around her, swings her in a wide arc out of hearing of the group.]

HARVEY: Look. You know he's an asshole, I know he's an asshole, and I'm sure his own sweet mother knows he's an asshole. But we have a campaign to run. We don't have time for these little skirmishes. Now please—Heather, Heather, Sweet Heather in Leather—please just take it back, and let's get on with it.
HEATHER: But I didn't do anything.
HARVEY: Since when does that matter? A small concession for the greater good? Please? For Harvey.
HEATHER: Jesus, shit! Okay, Harvey. I'll do it. But you remember this.
HARVEY: I promise you. *[He escorts her back. Motions to DEE.]* What are you doing? There's a crowd here. The fliers, the fliers.
HEATHER: What I said—I take it back.
MR. JONES: My hearing must be going. I didn't quite catch that.
HEATHER: I SAID I TAKE IT BACK! you mother—
HARVEY: *[Jumping in]* Right! Well. Good. Great! And now, shake hands—*[He joins their hands.]* Everybody! Let's all shake hands. Harvey. Harvey Milk.

[DEE and JOHN start distributing the fliers.]

COP: Okay, I think we can break this up now. Let's move it. And you, you get your people out of here.

[Crowd dispersing]

HEATHER: But what about the posters?

[HARVEY links HEATHER's arm, leads her away.]

HARVEY: Here, you guys get Heather out of here. Get some breakfast. On me. Here. *[He comes up with a few cents.]*
DEE: Never mind. I'll buy—as usual.
HARVEY: Once again, Dee, thanks.

[They exit. HARVEY backs away to return to the shop. JAMEY approaches.]

JAMEY: That little ol' dyke's quite a pistol.

HARVEY: Who, Heather? She's not a dyke.

JAMEY: Oh, excuse me. Les-s-s-bian.

HARVEY: As it happens, she's neither a dyke nor a lesbian.

JAMEY: That guy said something about "homosexual literature."

HARVEY: I'm the homosexual—she just dresses funny.

[JAMEY laughs.]

Harvey.

JAMEY: Uh—Buck.

HARVEY: Buck? *Buck?*

JAMEY: *[Gives in]* Jamey.

HARVEY: Tell you the truth, I'm a lot more comfortable with the name Jamey than with the name Buck. Buck makes me want to start making up limericks. Let's see—Buck, Buck—what rhymes with Buck? So, where're you from, Jamey?

JAMEY: Texas—Tyler, Texas.

HARVEY: Toby Tyler Texas. I think I drove through Tyler once. East Texas, isn't it?

JAMEY: Right.

HARVEY: That's pretty heavy-duty cowboy drag to be from *east* Texas.

JAMEY: It keeps the tourists happy.

HARVEY: *[Understands the euphemism]* Oh. So what's a nice boy like you . . . ?

JAMEY: You ain't really asking, are you?

HARVEY: Not if you don't want me to.

JAMEY: I'd just as soon you didn't, right?

HARVEY: Okay. Fine.

JAMEY: So what are you going to do if people get wind that you're, you know—

HARVEY: Gay?

JAMEY: Yeah.

HARVEY: They'll know. That's the point—or part of it.

JAMEY: Whaddya mean?

HARVEY: I'm running out in the open—as a gay candidate.

JAMEY: You gotta be kiddin'. You wouldn't stand a Chinaman's chance.

HARVEY: I'll take that up with my Asian friends. But I look at it this way—I've got the bases covered: Catholics don't like me because I'm a Jew—Protestants don't like me because I'm a Jew—Protestants, Catholics, *and* Jews don't like me because I'm gay—gayboy politicos don't like me because I'm ill-equipped experiencewise—and lesbians don't like me because I'm ill-equipped biology-wise. Nobody likes me. That makes me the perfect underdog—and somewhere way down deep, everybody pulls for the underdog.

JAMEY: *[Laughs]* Yeah, well, I don't know about out here, but back in Texas, everybody might root for the underdog, but only 'til he loses. Then they take the poor sonofabitch out and shoot him.

HARVEY: Thank God Texas isn't the world.

JAMEY: Don't let *them* hear you say that.

HARVEY: I was just about to make a pot of coffee. How about it?

JAMEY: Well, I was on my way over to the park, but . . . yeah, why not?

HARVEY: And while you're here, maybe you can help me with the mailing that we
have to get out this afternoon.

JAMEY: Wait—never mind the coffee.

HARVEY: Why?

JAMEY: If you're trying to suck me into this Don Quixote thing you're running,
I'll just pass.

HARVEY: Don Quixote? A hustler who makes literary allusions?

JAMEY: *[Goes icy]* Okay, so you met a hustler who's familiar with Don Quixote—
something to tell your grandchildren. I gotta go.

HARVEY: I didn't mean anything. . . . Look, I'm sorry I struck a nerve, okay?

JAMEY: *[Starting to exit]* Don't lose any sleep over it. See ya.

HARVEY: Hey . . . Buck?

JAMEY: What?

HARVEY: Zo vat da hell? Little cuppa coffee's gonna kill ya? Halv a shtale dough-
nudt, maybe?

JAMEY: *[Smiles, glances in the direction of the park]* Maybe next time. Adios.

HARVEY: Yeah. Adios. *[He watches as JAMEY exits; then he turns to exit and passes
MRS. MURPHY in doorway.]* Top of the morning.

MRS. MURPHY: And to you, Mr. Milk.

HARVEY: Harvey! *[He exits.]*

MRS. MURPHY:

> *Lovely, the memories—*
> *Lovely, but nothing stays—*
> *Nothing but the still and lovely*
> *Longing for a better day . . .*

[Fade to night]

VIGNETTE: THE PARTY

*[JAMEY enters, a hustler's pose. Three GAY-BASHERS and MR. JONES enter.
In a sotto voce pantomime, one approaches JAMEY. The others grab him from
behind, taunt and beat him.]*

MR. JONES: Aw; him fall down, go boom.

(The Party)
> *We're havin' ourselves a party tonight,*
> *And you better believe you're all invited—*
> *We'll kick our heels—*
> *Shoot the crap—*

Blow your mind right off the map—
We're havin' ourselves a party tonight.
We're havin' ourselves a cookout tonight—
And the griddle is hot, the gas ignited.
We'll roast some ears—
Tap some kegs—
Rack some ribs—
Crack some legs—
We're havin' ourselves a party tonight.

[MR. JONES *pulls a knife out of his pocket, opens it, then pulls out an apple,*
which he nonchalantly peels.]

BASHERS:

We're gonna make some noise—
It's a night for celebratin'—
And we know you've just been waitin'
To get stoned;
(And, buddy,)
Boys are boys—
And these boys are hale and hearty—
So you just might be the party
That gets thrown.

MR. JONES: [*While* BASHERS *ceremonially finish the job*]
     We're havin' ourselves a barbecue tonight
     And the boys are all lit and so excited—
     We'll cook your goose—
     Fry a friar—
     Throw another faggot on the fire—
     Havin' ourselves a wingding—
     String 'em up and watch 'em swing—

ALL:

     Having ourselves a party tonight.

[BASHERS *run off.*]

MR. JONES: Well, well, well—look at what the cat drug in. [*Laughs, exits*]

SCENE: FIRST AID

[JAMEY *lies all but unconscious.* HARVEY *enters, see the body on the side-*
walk.]

HARVEY: Hey! Hey . . . are you okay?

[A muffled groan. JAMEY tries to move. HARVEY moves a little closer.]

Oh, Jesus!

HARVEY: Be still. I'll go call for an ambulance.

JAMEY: No.

HARVEY: We've got to get you to a doctor.

JAMEY: No.

HARVEY: You're being stupid.

JAMEY: *[He grabs HARVEY, holds him.]* Don't leave me.

HARVEY: Hey, I know you. You're that kid from Texas. . . .

JAMEY: Jamey. Just stay here a little while—please?

HARVEY: I don't know if I can do anything, but let me take a look. *[HARVEY tears sleeve of shirt down.]* Christamighty. Somebody cut you. Who did this?

JAMEY: I don't know. Somebody grabbed me from behind, then I was down on the ground, and there was this knife and—OW!!!

HARVEY: Sorry. Oh . . . *[Becoming slightly nauseated, light-headed]* I don't think it's as bad as it looks. It's a long slash, but barely under the surface . . . oh . . . *[He bends over to keep from fainting.]* I worked as an orderly in the service, but I never did have the stomach for it—I can't stand the sight of blood.

JAMEY: You're not going to pass out on me, are you?

HARVEY: I wouldn't make book on it.

JAMEY: Thanks for doing this,

HARVEY: Harvey.

JAMEY: Oh, yeah—it scared the hell out of me, Harvey.

HARVEY: Well, you should be scared. Jesus Christ! There are people out here who don't like us. What they *do* like is to kick the crap out of us—and just for the hell of it—queer-bashers, maniacs, and, God knows, the cops themselves—or maybe you just haven't heard.

JAMEY: You don't have to get so riled up. I'm okay.

HARVEY: And you could be dead—would be dead except for a little stupid luck.

[JAMEY pulls his pint bottle out.]

What the hell do you think you're doing?

JAMEY: For the pain.

HARVEY: Oh yeah, great. This stuff thins the blood. Do you want to bleed to death?

JAMEY: And do you want to tell me why you're acting like you're my father?

HARVEY: Well, somebody should, goddammit!

JAMEY: So why the fuck should you care?

HARVEY: I really don't know! *[Cools off, moves to help JAMEY up]* Come on, let's get you out of here.

JAMEY: Never mind! I can take care of myself. *[He tries to get up, collapses in agony, verging on tears.]* AHHHH!

HARVEY: Yeah, you're doing one great fucking job of it. Come on. *[Helps him up]*

JAMEY: *[Almost a little boy]* Harvey . . . maybe . . . maybe you could take me home?

HARVEY: That was the plan. Where do you live?

JAMEY: Over in the Mission District. But I meant, maybe you could take me home—with you—to your home . . . just for tonight?

HARVEY: *[Mock coy]* Well, I don't know. Whatever will the neighbors think? Okay—just for tonight. I'm just down the street. You can take the bed. I'll make up the sofa.

JAMEY: Such a gentleman.

HARVEY: Always. Or at least just for tonight.

[They struggle off. Storefronts open into Kmart.]

SCENE: KMART

VOICE-OVER: Mr. Wollensky, price check aisle 3. Mr. Wollensky, aisle 3 please . . .

[One or two shoppers mill about while HEATHER, DEE, and JOHN set up two mikes for "campaigning."]

DEE: Woo, child, we've made it now! Look at me, mama—I'm the Queen of the Shopping Mall.

HEATHER: Okay, dudes, let's hit it. Testing, test, test.

JOHN: Test, test . . .

BOTH: *[To Dee, distracted at other mike]* Dee!

DEE: Oh. Testes, testes. *[Playing]* A . . . B . . . C . . . D . . . Dee. That's mi-mi-mi-mi-mi-me.

JOHN: A, E, I, O . . . U-u-u-u-u-u-you.

DEE: A . . .   JOHN: E . . .   HEATHER: I . . .

ALL: O . . . U . . .

> Bay . . . beee . . . why . . . so . . . blue? . . .
> Baby, baby, why so blue?
> Baby, why so blue?

[ALL move to one mike. HARVEY enters, shakes a hand or two while the group sets up a soft, rhythmic background.]

GROUP: **(There's a Fire)**
> Baby, baby, why so blue—
> Baby, why so blue?
> Baby, baby, why . . . (etc.)

HARVEY: Good morning, Kmart shoppers . . .

> **(There's a Fire)**
> *When you see your life as no more than a token,*
> *When you feel left out, unattended to,*
> *When each vow they make is just another broken,*
> *And you come to doubt that anything is true,*
> *When the wolves you've kept at bay keep getting bolder,*
> *And you're tossed about just trying to make it through—*
> *When you're lost—*
> *When it's cold—*
> *Take my hand—*
> *Here's a shoulder—*
> *Never mind . . . come inside . . . there's a fire.*
>
> *When they get ahead and all you get is older,*
> *When you come to dread the road in front of you—*
> *When you're lost—*
> *When it's cold—*
> *Take my hand—*
> *Here's a shoulder—*
> *Never mind . . . come inside . . . there's a fire.*
>
> *Come inside where it's warm*
> *There's a balm for the soul;*
> *There's a calm from the storm—*
> *When it's out of control—*
> *When you're lost—*
> *Scared to death—*
> *We'll get through it together—*
> *Never mind . . . come inside . . . there's a fire.*

[At end of song, a little mingling; mikes are carried off. HARVEY has been speaking with an older woman with shopping cart.]

HEATHER: *[As ALL exit]* Harve? You coming?
HARVEY: Be there in a minute. This young lady can't find the sink stoppers.

SCENE: COFFEE CONVERSATION

[Harvey's apartment. JAMEY's loud laughter. He and HARVEY are having coffee at a small table.]

HARVEY: It was wild—but you've got to reach the people somehow. Still, they must have wondered what in the hell this crazy bunch of people were doing.

JAMEY: I'll bet. *[More serious]* Harve . . . what *were* you doing?

HARVEY: What do you mean?

JAMEY: What's all this about? You've already said you don't expect to win.

HARVEY: Not tomorrow, no—but who knows, someday maybe . . . So for now I'm doing it for today. And I guess I'm doing it for the wolf.

JAMEY: Wolf?

HARVEY: *[Embarrassed smile]* That's what I call it—something that happened a long time ago, back in New York. I was around about your age, I guess, and I'd "encountered" this lovely man who says he wants to see me again and I should meet him the next day—three o'clock, Bronx Zoo, the penguin cages. So next day here I am, running around madly looking and looking for the penguin cages, absolutely sure he's waiting and wondering where the hell I was. But—no penguin cages. Finally I stop and ask this zookeeper, and he says the Bronx Zoo doesn't have any penguins.

JAMEY: Oh.

HARVEY: Right. And of course, the truth finally hits me—he's never had any intention of meeting me—and I'm a total idiot. So now I'm totally humiliated—I'm fighting back tears and trying to find my way *out* of the goddamned Bronx Zoo when something catches my attention. There's this wolf, stalking back and forth, back and forth in its cage—you know how zoo animals do until they become . . . resigned, I guess. Then, all of a sudden, it stops dead still and looks at me—directly into my eyes—and this like cold shiver runs through me.

JAMEY: Why?

HARVEY: I didn't get it then either. But what I finally figured out, years later, was that back there in the Bronx Zoo, I had been looking directly into my own soul.

JAMEY: What?

HARVEY: Desperation. The feeling that no matter how successful I was or how many friends were there, and no matter how loving the beautiful young man sleeping next to me, the wolf would be there, too, down inside my skin, reminding me that none of it and nothing would ever be enough to make up for the *aloneness,* this like, desperate longing.

JAMEY: Yeah, loneliness I understand. But longing for what?

HARVEY: Not loneliness—at twenty it's loneliness; at forty it's aloneness. A longing for . . . completion maybe. Something you never got early on. You know, sometimes I'd like to get a whole fleet of those great big yellow school buses and drive up into the front yard of every kid in the world who's ever been called "Sissy" or "Tomboy" and say, "Hey, come on, kid, you're going with me. And we're all gonna go to some place we can all be together, where none of us will ever again have to explain anything to anybody."

JAMEY: Somewhere over the rainbow.

HARVEY: Sure. Why not?

JAMEY: You really are out to save the world.

HARVEY: Just alter it a little. After I got out here, I decided. I'm tired of being the wandering Jew. I'm tired of trying to change *me* when, dammit, it's the *world* that needs changing. And when I decided that, something happened—the wolf and I began a sort of truce with each other. *[Dramatically]* So now out here on this western crust of the continent, all the way across the country from New York, we decided to make our stand.

[JAMEY laughs, enjoys the story.]

JAMEY: You know, Harvey, I like you—but I think you just might be crazy as hell.
HARVEY: And wouldn't be the first to say so.
JAMEY: You've really had a bunch of different lovers?
HARVEY: Well, let's just say a few more than several.
JAMEY: Maybe you just didn't meet the right one.
HARVEY: The odds are pretty heavy against that particular theory.
JAMEY: It's nice here.
HARVEY: What? This is nice?
JAMEY: A kitchen. I've just got that rented room over in the Mission District. I haven't sat and talked at a kitchen table since I left Texas.
HARVEY: Haven't you met anybody since you've been here?
JAMEY: I've met people, yeah—lots of people. But nobody seems to be particularly interested in conversation.
HARVEY: Well, I am. So talk—sing me the ballad of Toby Tyler Texas.
JAMEY: Don't call me that.
HARVEY: You certainly get your quills out when the conversation gets around to you. I don't usually get into self-revelation so early on either, but for whatever reason, these last few days I've been spilling my guts out to you. So it's like I used to say to Johnny Whittenauer back in the pup tent, I showed you mine; now show me yours.
JAMEY: I'd just as soon not talk about me.
HARVEY: So far I know you're a fairly bright kid who wants to hide behind some silly cowboy drag and prove something to someone by being real bad and selling himself to any schmuck with a ten dollar bill.
JAMEY: Twenty.
HARVEY: Oh, twenty—that puts you right up there with Madame Pompadour. So what's the story, Jamey? . . . "Buck?"

[Silence, then . . .]

JAMEY: Have you ever had someone you were really close to turn into a stranger on you like that?
HARVEY: Yeah, I'm afraid I have.
JAMEY: *[Struggling]* But I mean someone you knew would always, always . . .
HARVEY: People can disappoint you.
JAMEY: No—you don't understand. *[Starts to open up]* See, Daddy and me—my dad and I were best—closest . . . It was always him and me, you know—no matter what I was in—ball games, little award things, school stuff, you know. He

was always there, right in the front row, cheering for me. See, we were like . . .
heroes . . . to each other. . . .

HARVEY: And . . . ?

JAMEY: *[Shuts down]* And then we weren't.

HARVEY: When he found out . . .

JAMEY: When I told him. When I was dumb enough to think maybe there wasn't
anything I couldn't tell him.

[On another part of the upstairs tier, lights up on PREACHER (MR. JONES).]

PREACHER: You have broken his heart, Jamey.

HARVEY: It's a hard thing to do.

JAMEY: Tell me about it. It was the middle of the summer, but you'd have thought
I was freezing to death the way I was shivering—my teeth were chattering so
hard I could hardly get the words out. But finally everything—the words, the
feelings, all of it—just started coming. . . .

PREACHER: And the father ran rejoicing to meet his son, his prodigal son, so long
gone away, having turned his back on that which was good and right and
blessed. And the father asked, "Are you clean now?" And the son replied, "Yes,
now I am clean and whole."

HARVEY: How did he take it?

JAMEY: He just sat there and started filling his pipe—in total silence, taking out a
pinch of tobacco and tamping it down, then another and another . . .

PREACHER: You have broken his heart, Jamey. You must be clean. You must be
washed in the blood. You must choose, Jamey—just as your father must
choose—between the righteous and the unholy.

JAMEY: Then he lit it and took a few puffs and turned to look out the window for
a few minutes that seemed like forever. . . .

PREACHER: You have broken his heart, Jamey. You must choose—the way of the
unspeakable or the arms of love in the father.

JAMEY: Finally he just stood up and walked out of the room.

PREACHER: He has come to me, Jamey, and together we have gone to the Lord. He
cannot be asked to embrace the unholy. And so you must leave. You no longer
have a home.

JAMEY: And he's never spoken another word to me.

HARVEY: Jesus Christ.

JAMEY: I doubt it. You know, somehow I always would've thought it would've
been *me* that he'd've believed in. So much for heroes, huh?

(Where's the Hero?)
Why were we all taught
Once upon a time,
There are giants, there are heroes—
All the bull we bought—

Every stupid rhyme—
There are giants, there are heroes—
"There's a someone who
Comes to pull you through
When it's gettin' out of hand"—
Where's the giant?
Where is Superman?
Where's the hero?

Where's the rousing cheer
When you're laid out flat?
Where's a hero when you need one?
Where's the friendly ear?
Where's the halftime chat?
Where's a hero when you need one?
When you miss home plate—
When you drop the weight—
Where's your biggest, bestest fan?
Where's the gipper?
Where's the [spoken] "Sure you can"?
Where's the hero?

PREACHER: You have broken his heart, Jamey.

Where's the boy of gold?
Where's the wonder kid?
Where's a hero when you need one?
Doing what he's told,
Being what he's bid—
Where's a hero when you need one?
Where's the winning run?
Where's the shining son?
Where is Papa's pride and joy?
And where's Papa?
Where's his golden boy?
Where's the hero?

JAMEY: Harvey, why have you been so good to me?
HARVEY: I'm trying to get my first aid badge, and I need somebody to practice on. Why do you think? I like you.
JAMEY: Thanks.
HARVEY: You're welcome. Now shut the fuck up and get back to bed—I've gotta get back to work.
HEATHER: *[Offstage]* Harvey, we're out of copy paper.

HARVEY: I'm coming. I'm coming.

JAMEY: Harve, I'm gonna leave today.

HARVEY: Today? So what's the hurry? You're still hurt. Tomorrow maybe—you can leave tomorrow.

JAMEY: You've put up with me for three days already. I feel bad about putting you out of your bed and all. Besides, I'm a lot better.

HARVEY: So if you're a lot better, *you* can sleep on the goddam lumpy sofa.

JAMEY: If I'm a lot better, I can go back to my place.

HARVEY: *[Angry without knowing why]* Fine. Suit yourself—whatever. So I'll be seeing you around, huh?

JAMEY: Right.

[HARVEY starts to leave.]

Or maybe what I could do is . . . just . . . stay just for tonight.

HARVEY: Right. Just for tonight.

JAMEY: Right.

HARVEY: Right.

[Big smiles from both. Blackout. Music: "When it's dark—etc." from "There's a Fire" into PATRICIA's second letter.]

VIGNETTE: LETTER 2

PATRICIA:

Dear Jamey,

I got the locket. It's beautiful. It's my favorite of all my "sweet sixteen" birthday presents. JerriAnn—you remember JerriAnn—that blond-headed, kind of prissy thing that I never could stand? Well, as it turns out, she's become my best friend. So anyway, JerriAnn says to tell you she's pea-green with envy about the locket.

Oh, and Jamey, I hope you don't mind—I talked with JerriAnn about what you wrote me—to try to sort it out. She helped some. I guess neither one of us quite understands, but what we could come up with is this: Love is love, and maybe a lot of the other stuff don't really matter. I know I love you, and nothing anybody could tell me would ever, ever change that.

(Letter from Home [Reprise])
Whatever happens in your life,
Please, Jamey, never doubt—

I love you—
Thinking of you—
Jamey, please, Jamey—
Jamey, come home.

Your loving sister,
Patricia

[Fade]

SCENE: CAMPAIGNING AT THE FACTORY

[A cold early morning. HARVEY and JAMEY, on either side of a factory gate, pass out campaign brochures. A group of WORKERS straggles through.]

HARVEY: Good morning. My name is Harvey Milk, and this Tuesday I'll be in the race for city supervisor. Your vote's important, so make it count. Good morning . . . (etc.)

JAMEY: Morning. Tuesday primary— Harvey Milk—city supervisor— 'preciate it. Tuesday primary— Harvey Milk—city supervisor— 'preciate it. Morning. Tuesday primary—Harvey Milk—city supervisor—'preciate it. Remember—Milk . . . Harvey Milk . . . as in "milk and cookies." . . .

MAN: Or like in "milk the people"—like every other goddammed politician. *[MAN wads up the brochure, throws it down.]*
JAMEY: No, wait, here. Read it—please.

[JAMEY holds out another brochure. MAN ignores it and exits. JAMEY retrieves the wadded brochure, smooths it out.]

HARVEY: Tough house.
JAMEY: I'll say.
HARVEY: *[Shivering]* Those weather people call this an "unseasonal Arctic chill"— "chill"—cold enough to freeze the tits off a termite. *[New York tough, to God]* HEY! Could we get a fucking break down here?
JAMEY: Almost 7:30. I've got to split. I'm driving the early shift; then I have class this afternoon. Do you want a ride?
HARVEY: I'll bus it back. If people see me going around in a taxi, they'll think I'm already taking bribes.
JAMEY: Well, I'll see you at home—around 6:00?
HARVEY: Talk to Heather when you get in. She's going to need you on the plans for Monday.

[A LATECOMER enters hurriedly.]

JAMEY: Morning. Tuesday primary—Harvey Milk—city supervisor—'preciate it.
MAN: Never heard of him.
JAMEY: This is Harvey—a friend of working people.

[HARVEY extends a hand, disdainfully ignored.]

MAN: Right. Like I say—never heard of him.
JAMEY: You will, though. You will. When taxes have gone out of sight—or you
    need something and nobody at City Hall will even talk to you . . .

[LATECOMER is gone]

    or you need a brain implant . . . AAAGH! *[He kicks the fence behind him.]*
HARVEY: Lighten up, peewee.
JAMEY: It's easier talking to this wall than to some of these people.
HARVEY: Might be more interesting, too.

[JAMEY smiles.]

    You know, if I didn't know better, I'd say we've made a believer out of you. Huh?
    . . . Huh?
JAMEY: I guess I'd . . . like to be.
HARVEY: But you're not. Busting your butt, working as hard as me or harder . . .
    and yet you still can't believe things will change—that we're going to make it
    happen.
JAMEY: What I believe in, Harvey, is you. I believe that you believe it, and that's
    enough for me. It comes to the same thing.
HARVEY: No, baby, it's not even close.
JAMEY: *[Nonplussed]* Well . . . see you tonight.

*[JAMEY starts to exit, makes an abrupt U-turn back to HARVEY, who is wait-
ing for him. A light kiss as COP enters; JAMEY sees him, breaks away from
HARVEY. HARVEY turns, sees COP, and gathers JAMEY back to him. An elon-
gated, exaggerated screen kiss. They part. HARVEY passes by COP.]*

HARVEY: Can't live with 'em, can't live without 'em, huh, Officer?

[COP exits. One last WORKER enters.]

HARVEY: My name's Harvey Milk, and I'd appreciate your support in the race for
    city supervisor. . . . *[WORKER ignores him, exits. Then, to himself . . .]* Harvey
    Milk—candidate in the race for . . . Harvey Milk . . . over-the-hill hippie who
    thinks he's gonna change the world . . . *[Smiles at himself]* Harvey—you old
    fool . . .

(Young Man)
When you're young, you believe in stars
That a kindly world has promised and sent you—
Shining there over where you are,
So you'll never lose your way in the dark.
But the morning will spring
Some surprises:
No golden ring—
No golden dawn on a new horizon—
Mornings will bring
Compromises—
Trying to make it from day to day,
Pipers to pay all along the way . . .

Then
When you look, you can count the scars
From the hands the world has promised and lent you—
Little jabs, little jolts and jars,
Little lies and each one making its mark.
And the tear in your eye—
Never show it;
Tears multiply,
Fears multiply, but you find you've survived
As the years hurry by,
Then you'll know it:
Nothing's forever and iron clad;
Nothing's forever, the good . . . or . . . bad. . . .

Young man,
Don't believe, don't believe there is certainty—
Young man,
Nothing's always true.
Young man,
Don't believe, don't believe quite so much in me—
Life has its mean little job to do—
Young man, you've got to believe in you. . . .

But I swear on a guiding star,
For the time that we'll be given together,
While I can, I'll be where you are—
When you look, it's me you'll see by your side—
I'll bring love and respect—
And some laughter,
Vows to protect,
Now I'd protect you by telling you,

We can never expect
Ever after—
Learn to believe in the time we've got—
Something we mightn't have quite a lot of—

Young man,
Don't believe, don't believe there is certainty—
Young man,
Nothing's always true.
Young man,
Don't believe, don't believe quite so much in me—
All I can give you to hold onto:
Young man, you've got to believe in you. . . .
Jamey, learn to believe in you. . . .
For as long as you can . . .
Young man . . .

[*Fade to black*]

SCENE: WE LOST!

[*Lights up in apartment. With paper cups and a half-gallon bottle of wine, HEATHER, DEE, and JOHN sit together like a pile of laundry.*]

HERB: [*Voice-over*] . . . have been officially declared the winners in today's city elections. Jerry.

JERRY: [*Voice-over*] And a related story: In a city in which anything—or anyone—can happen, one of tonight's losers is the admittedly homosexual candidate Harvey Milk. Milk, who had been running behind in the polls, made a much better showing [*starting to break up, laughter in background*] than anticipated—will you stop it?—much better showing than anticipated—[*Background laughter louder*] I'm trying to do the news. Come on, dude, this is serious stuff—

HERB: [*Voice-over*] [*Laughing riotously*] This Milk guy—"behind in the polls" and vice versa, huh?

JERRY: [*Voice-over*] [*Cracks up, tries to compose himself, in vain*] You're going to get us kicked off the air. . . . Ahem—as I was saying—Milk who has been running behind in the p—[*He loses all control.*]

HEATHER: Damn . . . shit . . . hell . . . piss . . . turd . . . screw . . . fuck.

DEE: [*Offering wine*] Mmh?

HEATHER: Eh. ("Why bother?") Mmm. ("I guess.")

DEE: [*Passes bottle to John*] Mh?

JOHN: [*Accepts*] Uhn.

[*Further silence*]

JOHN: *[Bursts into song]* When you see your life as no more than a token . . .

DEE & HEATHER: SHUT UP!!!

JOHN: Well, at least we still have our sense of humor.

HEATHER: Mama said there'd be days like this. Come to think of it, the old broad didn't expect there'd be any other kind.

JOHN: We can't let this get us down.

DEE: Yes, we can.

JOHN: But we knew we were going to lose.

HEATHER: I know we knew we were. But we really did! So I don't know about you guys, but I'm going to sit here and do lots of wine, lots of whining—and absolutely wallow in self-pity.

DEE: I'm with you, tuffmuff. To misery.

HEATHER: Well? Either you're with us or ag'in us.

JOHN: But . . . *[Brightening]* There's always tomorrow.

HEATHER: You know the trouble with you, John? You have a real attitude problem.

   [JAMEY enters.]

JOHN: Did you find him?

   [JAMEY shrugs.]

HEATHER: "Out." That's all he said—just "out"?

JAMEY: Yeah—he's okay.

HEATHER: It's almost 12:30. I'm starting to get worried.

JAMEY: About Harvey? Come on. So what are we doing?

JOHN: Getting shockered.

DEE: That's "schnockered," Chinaboy. You know—"clocked."

JOHN: I know it's schnockered. My tongue's getting thick. *[A beat]* Racist.

DEE: Oh, please . . . *[Pouring a cup for JAMEY]* Here, you have some catching up to do.

JAMEY: You won't tell Harvey? He worries about me—you know—*[Drinking]*

HEATHER: Screw it. You deserve it. We all do. Hell, we lost. We . . . lost . . . the fucking election.

DEE: *[Operatically, "Jolly Good Fellow"]* We lost the fucking election. . . .

JOHN & DEE: We lost the fucking election. . . .

ALL: We lost the fucking election. . . .

HARVEY: *[In doorway]* But not the fucking war.

   [ALL buzz around him. He and JAMEY kiss. "Where have you been?" etc. In a hat and carrying a shopping bag, he bustles into the room, all energy.]

HARVEY: I've been out—walking, shopping, preparing.

   [Together]

JOHN: Shopping this time of night?   DEE: Preparing—for what?

HARVEY: [Answering each] Not exactly shopping—borrowing. Begging actually. Preparing. For the campaign.

ALL: What? What do you mean? Campaign? (Etc.)

HARVEY: The campaign. The real, overall campaign. And we're right on target. Hell, we did even better than we thought we would—tenth place out of thirty-two candidates our first time out of the gate ain't exactly chopped liver. So it's time to pump it up—give them a little light, a little music, a little theater. And [flourish] ... a change of costume ... [Pulls a rumpled suit out of a shopping bag.] How's that for a schmatte? Isn't it awful? Oh, and a change of image. [Dramatically removes his hat, reveals a conservative haircut. Others react in shock.]
   Dear lady. Good gentlemen. It's time. . . .

> Though tomorrow
> They might list my name among the dear departed,
> We'll just let 'em crow—
> We'll seize the reins and start at go—
> Our campaign will let 'em know
> Harvey Milk is gonna give the world a damn good show!

[Blackout]

SCENE: DRESSING OF THE GLADIATOR

[Lights up on COP (DAN WHITE), MR. JONES, now a cigar-chewing politician, enters.]

MR. JONES: Dan?

COP: Yeah?

MR. JONES: Me and the boys have been keeping an eye on you, and I just wanted to come down here and shake your hand.

COP: Why?

MR. JONES: [Holds up a newspaper] You seen this? People are starting to take this Milk guy seriously—skipping along behind the pansy, right down the primrose path.

COP: What's that got to do with me?

MR. JONES: Well, see the way we figure it, you get this crazy trying to get elected over there in District 5; then we need to get somebody else over here from District 8 to sort of balance things out—one of our own—somebody that knows how to be a team player. And I think you're our boy.

COP: Me? I'm no politician.

MR. JONES: Exactly. What you are is what we need—a good man, an honest man, a down-to-earth, real man.

COP: Well, yeah . . .

MR. JONES: A man who's already proven himself. Who was it that was over there in Vietnam defending his country's honor against the threat of foreign domination?

COP: Well—me.

MR. JONES: And who is it who's out here on the streets every day protecting his country's integrity from the blight of internal corruption?

COP: Me.

MR. JONES: Damn right, you. You know what you believe in—that's all you need to know. You do know what you believe in, right?

COP: Well, sure.

MR. JONES: What then?

COP: Well, just what *everybody* believes in.

MR. JONES: Which is—?

COP:

> **(The Seduction)**
> *I believe in my God, who is the One True God,*
> *I believe in my Land, which is the One True Nation*
> *I believe in Duty, in the Lord and the Mission,*
> *In protecting the Glory, Order, Pride, and Tradition—*
> *And as it has been,*
> *It shall be again*
> *Forever,*
> *Amen. . . .*

MR. JONES: I knew you were our man. Like I said, I've had my eye on you, Dan, and I like what I see. Yes, sir, I like what I see—a lot.

[Seductively]

So clean and pure, so clear of eye,	
Take off the tie.	*[Confused protest from COP]*
Convictions sure, so firm and strong—	
Play along—	*[Removing COP's tie]*
You're resolute—and slender-hipped—	
Get this unzipped.	*[His jacket]*
You're quite a beaut—you'll get the vote—	
Now the coat.	
Their pulse will quake, their hearts will melt—	
I'll take the belt.	*[Holster, billy club, etc.]*
There're hands to shake and babes to kiss—	
I'll keep this.	*[The gun]*

Yessirree . . . I like what I see. . . .

[Begins dressing WHITE in a coat and tie]

There's a kind of faith your kind of face engenders—
You'll become the golden boy of City Hall;
You're the cream of crops of possible contenders,
And when cream begins to rise, the milk must fall.

Soon his moment in the spotlight will be ended,
And we'll usher out this faggot folderol,
Common decency and right must be defended—
And Dan White's the man to do it—
Quite the man to do it—
Dan's the man to do it for all.

   [Pins a giant "Dan the Man" button on WHITE's lapel. Crossfade.]

VIGNETTE: CAMPAIGNING

HEATHER, DEE, JOHN, & JAMEY: *[Passing out fliers to audience]* Vote for Harvey.
. . . Vote for Harvey . . . Harvey Milk. . . . Vote for Harvey Milk.

SCENE: TEATIME

   [Four gay politicos (male and female) take tea and watch the campaign vi-
   gnette disdainfully.]

FIRST VOICE: Hmmmmmmm. *[Taps teacup with spoon]* The Artistic and Profes-
   sional Society of Homoerotic Enthusiasts for Positive But Cautious Societal
   Change According to the Tastes and Dictates of Us . . . is hereby in session.
      Milk?
OTHER THREE VOICES: None for me, thenk Yew!

      (That's Not the Way I'd Do It)
FIRST VOICE:
            Seems this street buffoon has lit some kind of fire—
            And the movement seems to burn with new esprit—
SECOND VOICE:
            I'd agree we really need a new messiah,
ALL:
            But I always rather thought it would be me.
THIRD VOICE:
            There's no place for crass publicity and high jinks;
FOURTH VOICE:
            He's devoid of shame or tact or protocol—

FIRST VOICE:
> *And the lady doth protest quite too much, methinks—*

ALL:
> *And that's not the way I'd do it—*
> *Not the way I'd do it—*
> *Not the way I'd do it, at all. . . .*

[Crossfade]

SCENE: THE GAY PRESS

[HARVEY, at table cluttered with work, is reading a community newspaper. He shuffles paper under a stack when JAMEY enters.]

JAMEY: I've seen it.

HARVEY: Oh.

JAMEY: You'd expect to get slammed by the establishment papers, but from other gay people—*[Reading from the paper]* "The aging, sold-out-to-the-establishment Milk, long known to have a certain taste for—in quotation marks—'rescuing' young boys, is now cohabitating with a young 'friend'—the guy likes quotation marks—a young friend with a reported history of alcoholism and prostitution. With the sterling examples you have set in your own life, Mr. Milk, how can we *not* entrust our future to you?"

> Nice.

> The world out there doesn't have to bother keeping us down. All it has to do is sit back and watch us rip each other to shreds. Harvey . . . do you want me to move out?

HARVEY: What?!

JAMEY: I mean, if I'm an embarrassment to you . . . maybe it would look better for you, for the campaign.

HARVEY: What look better for me? Creeps like that make things look any way they want them to look. We live our life. We're working for what *is*—not the way things look. You can't let this stuff get to you. This is just one more radical rag newspaper and one more radical idiot with a pencil and an ax to grind. So this month they say I devour children; next month they'll have me walking on water. C'mere.

[JAMEY sits on HARVEY's lap.]

We're both worn down. We'll get a good night's sleep and wake up tomorrow, and that thing won't seem half so hateful.

[A beat]

TOGETHER: Yes, it will.

[Crossfade]

THREE VOICES FROM TEATIME:
> *And that's not the way I'd do it—*
> *Not the way I'd do it—*
> *Not the way I'd do it, at all.* . . .

HEATHER, DEE, & JOHN JOINED BY ONE FROM TEATIME:
> *Time to mend it—*
> *Time to end the hate and petty fears that cause it—*
> *Time to lend the world a wider scope—*
> *A brighter hope—*
> *Time to open up the closet* . . .

SCENE: ENTRAPMENT

[Lights up on HARVEY, CAMPAIGN ORGANIZER (one of Teatime voices), and MR. JONES (in plaid jacket and sunglasses), who stand around a portable tape recorder on the table. The tape (voice-over) sounds like a crackling porn film, voices barely audible above the static.]

[Voice-over:] You like it, hmmm. . . . You like it, man. . . . You like it? . . . *[Barely audible]* Yesss. You like it. . . . You like it, man. . . . Hmmm? . . . You l—

HARVEY: Cut it off.

ORGANIZER: *[Ecstatic]* In *flagrante* fuckin' *delicto*! And oh, how the mighty have fallen.

HARVEY: Why did you bring this here?

ORGANIZER: Why? Larry Stanton—one of our strongest, most homophobic opponents—turns out to be a closet queen getting it off in tearooms, and you're asking me why? We can use it. We can call the papers or at least threaten to—we'll make the bastard get off our back.

HARVEY: No, I mean why?

ORGANIZER: What?

HARVEY: Why? Say we use it. Say we win the election by becoming just like them—the same old crap. Same tactics, same blackmail, same old gun held to our heads—only now it's us with our finger on the trigger. We've become *them*. And if that happens, what's the point of any of this?

ORGANIZER: But—ends and means, Harve. We have enough ammunition here to blow the son of a bitch right off the planet—get him out of our way—and you refuse to use it? I just don't get it.

HARVEY: *[With finality]* Yes . . . you . . . do.

[Crossfade]

TWO VOICES FROM TEATIME:
> *And that's not the way I'd do it—*
> *Not the way I'd do it—*
> *Not the way I'd do it, at all. . . .*

HEATHER, DEE, JOHN, & TWO FROM TEATIME: [One is ORGANIZER from scene.]
> *Some tomorrow hist'ry's gonna be rewritten,*
> *Some tomorrow we'll demand a brand new page;*
> *Some tomorrow we won't have to try to fit in—*
> *Some tomorrow when we welcome in a grand, new age.*

[Crossfade]

SCENE: THE POTATO EATERS ("TEMPTATION" 3)

[JAMEY, holding several jars, comes to the table at which HARVEY is already sitting. There are two plates, with two or three small potatoes on each.]

JAMEY: We're out of butter. But we have mustard, Worcestershire sauce, this chutney your mother sent, . . . and some pickle relish.
HARVEY: On baked potatoes? No butter?
JAMEY: No.
HARVEY: Why?
JAMEY: Because.
HARVEY: Because?
JAMEY: Because we're broke.
HARVEY: Too broke for a lousy stick of butter?
JAMEY: *[Gets up abruptly]* Yeah, Harve, that broke. Too broke for a lousy stick of butter—too broke for half a lousy stick of butter. What little we take in from the camera store and my fares goes for fliers and posters and campaign photos and whatever else—
  [Becoming frantic] This afternoon I went through our dirty laundry to see if maybe there was a quarter down in the corner of one of our pockets that I'd missed when I checked the first time and—nothing. We're way over our credit with the Murphys, and I'm not going to go back in there and ask for another thing. I know they'd let us stretch our credit, but I just won't do it.
HARVEY: Worcestershire.
JAMEY: What?
HARVEY: I'll try the Worcestershire sauce—at least it's wet. *[Shakes a few drops onto potatoes]* Sit down, baby.
JAMEY: Why do I feel so guilty about this?

HARVEY: *[Eating slowly]* Middle-class morality—poverty as the original sin.

[They eat in silence for a moment.]

HARVEY: You know, when I worked on Wall Street, I'd go out to dinner and barely touch the food—sometimes leave half a steak on the plate and not even ask for a doggie bag. I guess it would just get thrown out.

[More silence]

JAMEY: Would you pass the sour cream, please?

HARVEY: *[Reaches to do so automatically, then realizes the joke]* Oh yeah, and I'll have some when you're finished—and some of those chives—

JAMEY: What about a pinch or two of this nice crisp, crumbled bacon? . . . And I don't know, I think I'll have the T-bone.

HARVEY: I've changed my mind about that asparagus—with lots of hollandaise—

[Lights start to fade slowly, as do their voices.]

JAMEY: And we've got dessert, remember—banana pudding, cherries jubilee, chocolate mousse, Neapolitan ice cream, and Oreo cookies—

HARVEY: Well, I'll try, but after all of this, I couldn't possibly. . . . Well, perhaps just a little bit of the . . .

[Crossfade]

[MR. MURPHY, MRS. MURPHY, and NEIGHBOR form a group on one side of the stage.]

MR. MURPHY:
> *Harvey understands the working needs of labor—*
> *And our boycott woulda flopped except for him—*

MRS. MURPHY:
> *As it turns out he's become a real good neighbor—*
> *And he helped to get the pension checks for me and Jim—*

[SUPPORTERS move into position for the "living billboard" (they hold up lettered cards as at a football game) and HARVEY's climactic entrance.]

SUPPORTERS:
> **(Come Tomorrow)**
> *Some tomorrow human rights will be respected,*
> *Some tomorrow human dignity will win;*
> *Come tomorrow Harvey's gonna be elected,*
> *Come tomorrow we will welcome "some tomorrow" in.*

Come and join us—
Come tomorrow, comes the new emancipation—
Join the celebration—
Raise a cheer and join the fray—
Say, "We're here and here we stay!"
Come tomorrow comes a better day. . . .

[HARVEY enters; cheers and applause as he moves toward mike, down center.]

HARVEY: Hello, San Francisco.

Tomorrow is election day. Tomorrow the people of San Francisco have the opportunity to give the rest of this nation a great gift. That gift is hope.

With your vote tomorrow, you tell the world that there is a place in the world that welcomes and values each and every citizen. A city that says, "You matter. And you. And you. And you."

There are people even today, even in this great land, who are born into exile. They are the exiles who are too poor or too dark or too different for society to care. Those whose eyes are shaped too differently, whose skin is a different hue, whose bodies have different abilities—those whose customs are too different, whose gods and beliefs have different names—those who are told that even *love* is forbidden.

These are the refugees in their own land—the disenfranchised, the disillusioned, the forgotten.

San Francisco has a long history of welcoming in the refugee. And tomorrow San Francisco is going to walk into the voting booth and deliver a resounding message to the rest of the world and particularly to these—these *American* refugees, "Come in. We're glad you're here. Welcome home."

(We, the People)
We, the people, stand united
For the rights of ev'ry one;
Let the slightest not be slighted—
No one's due must go undone.

We, the people, shall proclaim it,
To the least of these, our kin—
These who love might dare to name it
These who dare are welcomed in. . . .

These the smaller, these the younger,
These who crave a gentle breast,
These whose hearts and bellies hunger,
These who strive and find no rest . . .
These the slighted, mocked, and taunted,
These outside the rightful feast,

> These whose doors the wolves have haunted,
> These who daily face the beast . . .
> These the faceless, these unheeded,
> These who taste the bitter blade,
> These the wasted, these unneeded—
> Let no promise be betrayed. . . .
>
> Let the people stand united—
> Let our children stand and sing;
> Let the torch at last be lighted;
> Let the sound of freedom ring. . . .

ALL:

> We, the people, stand united—
> Let the people stand and sing;
> Let the torch at last be lighted;
> Let the sound of freedom ring. . . .

[Shouting above second chorus, then joins them]

HARVEY: Tomorrow is November 16th, 1977. We stand at the crossroads of our history!

> We, the people, stand united—
> Let the people stand and sing;
> Let the torch at last be lighted;
> Let the sound of freedom ring. . . .

[Curtain]

Act II

SCENE: WELCOME TO SAN FRANCISCO

[JAMEY waiting at the train station, eagerly searching the passengers that straggle in]

VOICE-OVER: Passengers arriving through gate 5 from Los Angeles and points east, AMTRAK welcomes you to San Francisco. And on track number 6, track number 6 now boarding for Seattle and points north. All aboard, please, all abooooard!

[PATRICIA enters, festooned with small shoulder bags and carry-on luggage, which she drops when she and JAMEY spot each other.]

PATRICIA: [Rushes, screaming across the stage] AAAIIIIIEEEEEEEEEEEEEEEE!

[He spins her around and around when she jumps into his arms.]

JAMEY: Look at you.

PATRICIA: Jamey.

[More hugs]

JAMEY: *[Blurts without a pause]* I can't believe you're here.
Where are your bags?
Is this everything?
Riding on the train for three days—
Why didn't you fly.
Are you hungry?
Have you had anything to eat?
You must be starving?
Stay a few days with me and Harve before you go over to your dorm, why don't you, so we can get to know each other again—I feel like—

PATRICIA: Me eith—

No, I have to go—

I brought some—

PATRICIA: *[Putting a hand over Jamey's mouth]* Will you slow down. We've got time. I'm going to school here now, remember? We can see each other every day if we want to.

[They hug again.]

JAMEY: Oh God, it's so good to see you. I still don't believe it. So you do have bags, or you don't?

PATRICIA: Do.

JAMEY: And food—I've got dinner started at home, but can you wait—are you hungry?

PATRICIA: No. Just tired, reeeeeal tired—and feeling like I'm still moving.

JAMEY: Do you want to sit down while I go to baggage claim?

PATRICIA: I don't think I ever want to sit down again. Besides, it'll probably take both of us to carry them.

JAMEY: *[Picking up bags]* How much more could you have?

PATRICIA: You know me . . .

JAMEY: I've made all kinds of plans, things to do, places to show you and all. Harvey wanted to come down here with me, but he's so busy since he got elected, I hardly get to see him myself. I thought we could stop by the park on the way in so you can meet him.

PATRICIA: At the park?

JAMEY: *[Laughs]* Yeah. That's where he's called a press conference—Harve loves a press conference—he's announcing this crazy new ordinance he's trying to get passed—but you'll see.

[Start exit]

I still don't understand why you didn't take a plane.
PATRICIA: Planes crash.
JAMEY: So do trains.
PATRICIA: Not from five miles up in the air, they don't.
JAMEY: *[Stops abruptly]* Oh!
PATRICIA: What?
JAMEY: Welcome to San Francisco!

[They exit.]

SCENE: DOG SHIT

[HARVEY and the MILK DUDS are surrounded by several reporters and cameramen in the park.]

HARVEY: My thanks to you all for coming.
REPORTER: Whatcha got for us, Harvey? More gay rights stuff?
HARVEY: You know from my campaign that I believe in public officials being answerable to every public need of every citizen of this good city—every need, no matter how large or seemingly small. People of the media, San Francisco has a problem.

(Pooper Scooper)
And when the
Public's frustration
Becomes indignation,
It's our obligation to act.

People are tired of the nuisance of—how shall I put it?—canine digestional by-products. I'd ask you to take a look around. Our parks and streets are turning into a kennel. And so I've called you here to announce that I'm proposing a new doggy cleanup law.

> *I call my new legislation:*
> *The Elimination*
> *Of Elimination.*

In fact,

> *Just for your evening edition—*
> *This small exhibition*
> *Will make my position*
> *Quite clear;*
> *And while I have your attention*

> *It's time that I mention*
> *This simple invention*
> *Right here—*

The noble pooper-scooper. A dollar forty-nine at any five-and-dime or discount store—a simple solution to the problem that nobody wants to talk about. You got film in that thing, boys?

HARVEY:	DUDS:
Uptown they'd like to whitewash it,	*"Ahh, shhit"*
To quell or kibosh it,	*"Ahh, shhit"*
And otherwise squash it—	*"Ahh, shhit."*
They've tried.	
But we cannot just hush-hush it—	*"Uuuushhit"*
It's time that we flush it—	*"Uuuushhit"*
Stop trying to brush it	*"Uuuushhit"*
Aside—	

Come on, San Francisco! Let's clean up our act.

ALL:

> *That's the simple ordinance—*
> *You heard the song,*
> *Now here's the dance. . . .*

[A soft-shoe. On the last step, the MILK DUDS mime stepping in dog droppings and limp off.]

HARVEY:

> *And as freedom is founded on the rights of its individuals,*
> *Each person's rights are grounded in his own responsibility.*
> *So let every mutt do what he must,*
> *Just be sure you collect his residuals—*
> *You'll be doing your duty*
> *By keeping the beauty*

[Razzmatazz exit]

> *Of our dear old San Francisco dooo-deee freeeeee!*

[REPORTERS exit, laughing (and charmed). Crossfade.]

SCENE: THE OFFICE

[HARVEY's office. HEATHER in front of desk, JOHN, DEE, and JAMEY on floor, are reading and sorting mail into stacks. PATRICIA, behind desk, answers the phone.]

PATRICIA: Supervisor Milk's office. No, I'm sorry—he's not in. May I take a message? *[Can't find pencil]* Oh, just a moment. John! *[Gestures "pencil"]*

JOHN: *[Getting up to return pencil to Patricia, hands two stacks of mail to Heather, who sorts them onto the desk.]* Congratulatory. Eviction problems.

DEE: *[More stacks]* Police harassment . . .

PATRICIA: Okay, all set. Sorry.

JAMEY: Job threats . . .

DEE: Personal help . . .

JAMEY: Lunatic fringe, propositions . . .

DEE: And lunatic fringe, lunatic.

PATRICIA: *[Quiet shock]* What?!

[PATRICIA, stunned; HEATHER fields call, listens a moment, quietly replaces the receiver.]

PATRICIA: That was horrible, just—horrible. . . .

HEATHER: You'll get used to it. Jamey, we gotta see that your little sister gets toughened up. You're a long way from the honeysuckle, kid.

JAMEY: Are you okay?

PATRICIA: I can't believe what he was saying. . . .

HEATHER: They're all pretty much the same. "Tell the queer not to go in no dark alleys." . . .

JOHN: Remember the one about the silver bullets. "There's a golden pistol that holds six silver bullets, and on each is his name inscribed." . . . Spooky.

DEE: My own personal favorite: "Cut that kike faggot's balls off"—I thought the little ethnic slur was a nice touch.

PATRICIA: This isn't funny.

JAMEY: No, I guess it isn't. But like Harve keeps on telling me, "Get used to it, kid. Goes with the territory."

HEATHER: Either you learn to laugh about it, or they break you.

PATRICIA: *[Shudders]* How can you all stand it? How can *he* stand it?

HEATHER: You just go on, honeybunch. Fuck 'em if they can't take a joke.

JAMEY: That Anita Bryant–Miami thing isn't helping things any.

DEE: No-talent old sow.

JOHN: Why does everybody say that? Would this nasty little hate campaign of hers be more justified somehow if she *did* have talent?

DEE: No, but if she did, maybe she'd've kept her tired old ass in show business and wouldn't have to find some other way to grab the spotlight.

HEATHER: Now this local yokel Briggs is trying to jump on her bandwagon.

PATRICIA: Briggs—the Proposition 6 guy? What is it? Why should people want to fire someone for their private lives? I mean, I had this fifth grade teacher—you remember Miss Nettie, Jamey—she lived with her friend for years, and nobody thought anything about it. At least I never thought about it till recently. And I suppose it was like that for Miss Nettie and her friend. She lived her life privately and was one of the best teachers I ever had. So why do people want to make such a big issue out of it?

JAMEY: Because people are afraid of things they don't understand.

HEATHER: And a fear campaign will buy you a hell of a lot more news coverage than a photo of you and your cocker spaniel.

Hey, look alive, dudes—Harve should be here soon. We have to be at the TV station in less than an hour.

JAMEY: Where's the hate-crime report? I told him I'd stay here and look it over.

HEATHER: Bottom drawer.

PATRICIA: *[To Heather]* Do I look alright for the taping?

DEE: Look who she's asking. Come, come, come. Let mama show you a little something about style. Oh and speaking of style, child, you should have been here the night of the election—all of us marching behind Harvey, right down Market Street, just screaming—and me, I looked just like the fourth Supreme.

JOHN: Yeah, the ugly one.

DEE: Will the real Nancy Kwan please shut up?

[HARVEY enters, choking down a sandwich, changing jackets, etc.]

HARVEY: Ready?

JAMEY: You skipped lunch again.

HARVEY: So shoot me. Who has the time?

HEATHER: Another interview with you and Dan White—you two are getting to be a regular Nelson Eddy and Jeanette McDonald.

HARVEY: Yeah—we take turns with the mountie uniform.

DEE: There's something weird about that Dan White guy.

JOHN: I think he's cute.

DEE: You would.

PATRICIA: *[Giggles]* I'm sorry, y'all, but I guess I'm still not quite used to one man calling another one "cute."

HARVEY: If that's the most shocking thing you run into in San Francisco, little sister, it'll surprise the hell out of me.

DEE: Yeah, go touch up, girl—your roots are showing.

HEATHER: It's almost showtime, *muchachos—vámonos!*

[All except HARVEY and JAMEY exit.]

HARVEY: Jamey?

JAMEY: There was another phone threat, Harve.

HARVEY: Come on, babe—you know it just goes with the territory.

JAMEY: —goes with the territory.

HARVEY: So you coming or what?

[JAMEY holds up the report.]

Oh yeah, I forgot. Thanks again for doing that.

JAMEY: No problem—*"whitewash it,* "just goes with the territory."

[HARVEY exits.]

Harve, I'm scared. . . .

(If You're Here)
You always have such faith in what is yet to come—
I don't dare it—
Since you have so much faith—and I could sure use some—
Could you share it? . . .

I fear the game's begun—
The cards are scrambled,
The wheel is being spun,
The die is tossed.
You only see the game
And not the gamble.
I'd like to be the same,
But what's the cost?
But still you have your quest—
Still Don Quixote—
And so I'll do my best
And make it clear:
If there're castles to be built,
I'll be with you to the hilt—
And if windmills need some tilting,
I'll be here.

I'd love to see the world
As you conceive it—
To see our colors swirled
Across the sky.
So show me your belief
And I'll believe it—
And sadly share the grief
If dreams should die. . . .
But let me share your joy
In each new vict'ry
And let it be your voice,
The voice I hear;
If a howling wind should blow—
And if bitter waters flow—
I'll make it—oh, but only
If you're near.

So ask me whatever you choose to
Come hell or high water—it's crossed.
But, Harve, if I ever should lose you,
I'm lost. . . . I'm lost. . . .

If dragons haunt the wood,
We'll just slay 'em,
Then be on our merry way
And never fear;
Let the darkest fate occur—
I'll hold fast and never stir,
But I only have the courage
If you're near—
Though I shouldn't—even so,
In my heart I guess I know
I can only stand to go on
If you're here.

[Fade]

SCENE: THE TAPING

MODERATOR: Thanks for being with us tonight.

HARVEY & WHITE: Thank you.

HARVEY: [Quipping] It's the Milk-White show.

MODERATOR: A lot of people might find it surprising that two supervisors from such diametrically opposed backgrounds seem to be aligned on the major issues that have come before the board thus far.

HARVEY: "Politics makes for strange bedfellows"?

WHITE: [Uncomfortable at "bedfellows"] Both Supervisor Milk and I believe in working for the good of all the citizens of San Francisco.

HARVEY: And as for background, both Supervisor White and I come from middle-class, working people. That makes for a rather strong commonality.

MODERATOR: But wouldn't Supervisor Milk's being the first openly gay elected official indicate some major difference in political viewpoint?

HARVEY: The rights of gay people are just one of the many issues on which the people of this city elected me.

WHITE: And you know, if you think about it, there are nine of us on the Board of City Supervisors. Nine—just the same number that's on a baseball team. So it's just like in baseball, the nine of us have to all learn to put aside our differences and pitch in and work together for the sake of the team.

MODERATOR: Many see what's going on in Dade County, Florida, as the first volley, the Fort Sumter if you will, of a major political backlash in this country.

And now Senator Briggs's recent proposal—the banning of homosexuals from teaching in public schools. Do you see a backlash happening here?

HARVEY: History tells us that the original Spanish fort on which the city of San Francisco was eventually founded was one of the first experiments in the commune, or communal living system between the Spanish settlers and the Native Americans already in the area. Even our very history is that of people working within their differences for the common good.

WHITE: Teamwork.

HARVEY: What today might sound like the war cries of the Anita Bryants and John Briggses of this world are really just the dying gasps of institutionalized bigotry and injustice. The time of superstitious suspicion, ignorance, and hatred is dead and gone.

WHITE: Besides, it doesn't really matter what you might think about the guy next to you. When you're down in the locker room, when you're out there on that field, everybody's got to be pulling in the same direction.

MODERATOR: So neither of you sees Anita Bryant, John Briggs, and their issues as being a divisive element in the political landscape of the city?

[Before they can answer, CONGA DRUMS! and "Los Faggotos Caribes" (flaming chorus boys in Copacabana costumes) enter and take over the stage.]

LOS FAGGOTOS: AnEEta! AnEEta!

(Anita!)
You've seen her in a magazine,
Our runner-up, our almost-queen,
She's peddled cosmetics and real estate,
Orange juice and Avon and pills for losing weight
And when our gal's career seemed to've lost its fizz
It seems she found the Jesus biz. . . .

[MISS ANITA (MR. JONES in drag) makes "her" entrance.]

MISS ANITA: Hallelujah and howdy to ya!
LOS FAGGOTOS: Lalalalala
MISS ANITA: *[Croaks off-key]* La—
LOS FAGGOTOS: Lalalalala
MISS ANITA: *[Croaks same off-key note]* La—
LOS FAGGOTOS: Lalalalala la la
MISS ANITA: *[Hand to ear, trying to find note, gives up]* Oh, fuck it.
   To look at me you never would guess I'm invincible,
   The media and me seem to be in cahoots—
   It seems I have the knack
   Of covering my lack of principles—
   And we don't want our children taught by no fruits,

No, we don't want our children taught by no fruits. . . .

And I believe in God, guts and glory, and safety belts—
And when they raise a flag, ev'ryone should salute—
Remembering The Maine—
You wash the car, it rain—and something else—
Oh, we don't want our children taught by no fruit,
No, we don't want our children taught by no fruit. . . .

LOS FAGGOTOS:

Oh, mango, mango, mango,
Let the melon do a tango,
Let the guava and casaba blow a flute—
Let a litchi do a lemon,
A papaya, a persimmon—
Miss Anita doesn't give a fig or hoot!

MISS ANITA: Ho, noh . . .

LOS FAGGOTOS:

But raisin, raisin, raisin—
Pomegranates can be brazen,
We must learn to pluck out evil by the root.

MISS ANITA:

And don't let some big banana
Who's a plant from New Hanava
Tell you children should be learning from a fruit!

Although my words are dumb, I deliver them heatedly—
Though no one could accuse me of being acute—
It seems I seem to faze
By using the same phrase repeatedly—
Like we don't want our children taught by no fruit,
No, we don't want our children taught by no fruit. . . .

LOS FAGGOTOS:

Oh, mango, mango, mango,
Let the melon do a tango,
Let the guava and casaba blow a flute—
Let a litchi do a lemon,
A papaya, a persimmon—
Miss Anita doesn't give a fig or hoot!

MISS ANITA: No, she dozuuunt. . . .

LOS FAGGOTOS:

But raisin, raisin, raisin—
Pomegranates can be brazen,
We must learn to pluck out evil by the root.

ALL:

And don't let some big banana

Who's a plant from New Havana
Tell you children should be learning from a fruit.

[CONGA! The conga line moves around the stage and picks up more "PAS-
SENGERS" as it resembles more and more a train—the conga movements more
subtle, the kick more violent.]

MISS ANITA: *[Drops cute voices, harsh]*
    And we're going to ride this baby right out of Dade County. . . .
    The world is waiting!
    Bye-bye, Bible Belt. . . .
    Whatcha know, Wichita?

[Each PASSENGER joins conga line.]

NEW PASSENGER: Wichita's gay rights ordinance: REPEALED!
MISS ANITA: Glad to see ya, St. Paul, Minnesota. . . .
ANOTHER PASSENGER: St. Paul's gay rights ordinance: REPEALED!
MISS ANITA: Seattle, Washington . . .
THIRD PASSENGER: Seattle's gay rights ordinance: REPEALED!
MISS ANITA: Eugene, Oregon . . .
FOURTH PASSENGER: Eugene's gay rights ordinance: REPEALED!
MISS ANITA: CALIFORNIA . . . HERE I COME!

[HARVEY enters. HARVEY addresses the audience. As the song begins, he ad-
dresses members of the conga line.]

HARVEY: Proposition 6 suggests that there are some people who—just because
they may be gay—are not fit for public service. We're told it's for the good of the
children. *[Holds up a handful of letters]* Every day letters come into my office
from kids—twelve-, fourteen-, sixteen-year-olds. These are cries for help. These
are cries of hope. They see my election to public office as their own personal
rainbow, a promise the people have made to them.
  So those of you who pretend to worry so much about who's teaching our
children—what are you teaching *these* children?

[WHITE has joined line, behind ANITA.]

    (Save the Children)
    Grinning faces,
    Empty phrases,
    Make sure suspicion endures—
    "Save the fam'ly"
    "Save the children"
    As if they only are yours. . . .

Same as always—
Use the children—
Don't mind the price to be paid.
Hide your hatred—
Use the children—
Back up your selfish crusade.

But what of the kid in Altoona
Who starts to believe he can survive?
And what of the kid from Oklahoma
Who's starting now to see
Some reason she's alive?

Shall we tell them?
Let's explain it—
Sorry, but you've been exempt.
Preach your gospel—
Tell your children—
Teach them to share your contempt.

[*At appropriate moments, a few, then eventually all, PASSENGERS leave the line abashedly.*]

But what of the kid from North Dakota
Who looks for someone to understand?
And what of the kid from South Chicago
Who now thinks the future's in his hand?

What of the kid from West Virginia
Who now turns away from suicide?
And what of the kid from eastern Texas
Who tries to find his place—
The grace he's been denied. . . .

Teach the children—
All the children—
Teach ev'ry one to stand tall.
Save the children—
All the children—
The children belong to us all.
The children belong to us all. . . .

[*HARVEY approaches ANITA.*]

So your hate crusade has played out—
Nothing's quite the way you planned it—
We've been asking for acceptance . . .

Now we demand *it!*

[MISS ANITA rips off the wig and ludicrous hat. There is an instant of direct confrontation. Blackout.]

VOICE-OVER: RESIGNATION ANNOUNCEMENT

JERRY: In a surprising announcement this afternoon, Dan White has resigned as a member of the city's Board of Supervisors. Though there have been rumors of a rift with certain other supervisors concerning Proposition 6, White denies that his resignation has anything to do with the defeat of Senator Briggs's bill, which would have banned homosexuals from the public school system. He has cited personal problems as the reason for what an unnamed supervisor is reported to have called White's quote "public hissy fit" end of quote. And end of the news. . . . Now . . . back to music with Herb "the herb" Gardener!

HERB: And this is not *necessarily* for Dan White, you understand. A little bit of Detroit Station with "If You Can't Take the Heat, Stay Out of the Kitchen" . . .

SCENE: CALLING HOME

[Night. JAMEY and PATRICIA amble along the street.]

JAMEY: I love this city.

PATRICIA: Is it always like this? I've heard that San Francisco's like early autumn all year round.

JAMEY: Pretty much—a few warm and cool snaps, but, yeah, pretty much like this year round.

PATRICIA: If I should stay here after school, I think I'd miss the different seasons.

JAMEY: Like back in Texas? Freezing cold winters and summers so stifling hot you can't breathe. As far as I'm concerned, they can keep it—all of it.

PATRICIA: You don't ever miss home?

JAMEY: This is home. Harvey's my home.

PATRICIA: I like Harvey.

JAMEY: Me, too.

PATRICIA: I noticed. It's a different world out here.

JAMEY: That it is.

PATRICIA: Sometimes I wish . . . I don't know, I see Mama and Daddy in their tiny little shoebox of a life, and I think maybe if they somehow or other had been able to see more—be more out there—maybe they wouldn't feel so afraid of the world, of life. If they could just open up a little, maybe they could climb over that wall they've built around themselves.

JAMEY: They won't.

PATRICIA: Maybe. But I don't want to give up on them.

[A phone booth.]

Jamey! Give me a dime.

JAMEY: Why?

PATRICIA: Let's call them.

JAMEY: Let's *us* call them?

PATRICIA: Yeah—now. Let's try.

JAMEY: I have.

PATRICIA: Well, with both of us working on it, we'll just wear them down. Now come on, a dime. Oh, never mind, I have to have one here someplace.

JAMEY: Oh, here.

[She goes into phone booth.]

No. Wait. *[Depresses the phone cradle]* This is home.

(Home)
Home isn't some little place you were born or
Some people who happened to you,
Home is a place with someone in your corner,
Allowing you might have your own point of view.
And home isn't Tyler or Texas or three-thirty-one,
Seven-o-seven-three;
Home is a place where the each lives for either—
It's people like Harvey and me.

PATRICIA: Yeah, Jamey, but—for better or worse—it's Mama and Daddy, too. And me. And you. There, then.

Home isn't perfect, but, Jamey, they need you—
In spite of the way they may seem—
They're simple people who thought they should lead you
To live out their version of their narrow dream. . . .
And maybe they thought you should be what would show them
They'd won—some award on a shelf—
And making them see might not be what you owe them—
But something you do owe yourself. . . .

This isn't so much for them as it is for you. You've got to try.

JAMEY: Why?

PATRICIA: Because this hurts you so much . . . because even though they're wrong—terribly wrong—you still love them.

BOTH:

> *Home is a place you don't just walk away from*
> *Without leaving something behind—*
> *Home is a place that you don't spend a day from*
> *Without taking pieces—a thought brought to mind—*
> *Just when you think that you've left it behind you,*
> *You suddenly find with a start,*
> *The long-standing longing, the heart strings that bind you,*
> *The yearnings that memories impart—*
> *The things that still cling to your heart. . . .*

PATRICIA: *[Quietly]* Come on.

[JAMEY reluctantly follows her into phone booth. Slow fade.]

SCENE: LATE NIGHT SATURDAY

[HARVEY is working. Phone rings. He answers.]

HARVEY: Dan, will you stop this? . . . Oh, sorry, Carl. . . . Yes, of course you can let him in. Right. *[He hangs up. Phone almost immediately rings again.]* Yes? . . . Now look, I'm not going through anymore of this, Dan. . . . Well, like I said, you should have thought of that before. . . . No, I'm not about to intercede. As far as I'm concerned, it's between you and the mayor. If he wants to let you take back your resignation, then fine. . . . I'm sorry, we must have a bad connection. It sounded for all the world like you just called me a smug little faggot. I've always wondered when you'd finally get around to saying that.

[He slams down the phone, takes it off the hook, goes back to his work. JAMEY enters.]

JAMEY: Thanks for telling the guard to let me in. It's like trying to get into a prison around here.
HARVEY: Sure.
JAMEY: "Sure." You'd think the idiot would have recognized me, as many times as I've been up here.
HARVEY: I guess he just wanted to make sure it was okay.
JAMEY: Why wouldn't it be okay?
HARVEY: Because you smell like a brewery.
JAMEY: So I had a coupla beers. So?
HARVEY: So I'd venture to guess it was more than a couple, and you don't handle even a couple very well.

[JAMEY starts to bristle, tries another tack, moves behind Harvey, reaches around to stroke him seductively.]

JAMEY: I know of a couple I can handle *real* well.

HARVEY: Come on, Jamey.

[JAMEY silently mimics, "Come on, Jamey." HARVEY tries to lighten things.]

So where'd you go tonight? I thought you and Patricia had plans.

JAMEY: We did. We had dinner and then we—and then after she left, I stopped by The Corral for a bit—the place was packed—got on my nerves.

HARVEY: Sorry.

JAMEY: "Sorry."

HARVEY: Look, Jamey, what do you want? I don't like talking to you when you're like this.

JAMEY: When are you going to come home?

HARVEY: I'm not sure. There's a bushel of stuff here I need to take care of.

JAMEY: So what else is new?

HARVEY: Certainly not this conversation.

JAMEY: Come on, Harve—I never see you anymore. We work our asses off forever to get you elected, and then you get elected and I think, "Great, now he's elected—now maybe we can have a little time together," but now you're working harder than before, except now maybe it's worse because at least then I was right beside you the whole time and—*[he starts crying]* and I know I'm acting like a spoiled brat—but I miss you. I just . . . miss . . . you.

HARVEY: *[Goes to JAMEY]* What is this all about?

JAMEY: Is the wolf back, Harve? Are you going to leave me?

HARVEY: What? What are you so upset about?

JAMEY: Nothing. . . . I called home tonight—well, Patricia placed the call, really, but then she gave me the phone. Mama talked to me and everything—like maybe things were better—but then nothing would do but her trying to get Daddy to come to the phone in spite of me begging her not to. But I shouldn't have worried about it. He wouldn't talk to me. He still won't have anything to do with me, Harve. And when he wouldn't come to the phone, Mama and him started arguing and she started crying and told me I should be patient and give him time. *[Almost hysterical bark of laughter]* Hah! "Give him time." After five and a half years I should be patient! Give him time! Why do I give a good goddamn, goddammit?

[HARVEY holds him a minute.]

HARVEY: I goddamn don't goddamn know, goddammit. Here, boy, you know what we're going to do? Right now, you and I are going to go home and get in bed together, and we're going to hold one another and pretend that we're the only two people that have ever, ever existed.

JAMEY:

(Dance with a Cowboy [Reprise])
No, it's getting late,

And I'll be alright—
You have work to do. . . .

HARVEY:

All of this can wait.
All I need tonight
Is to be with you. . . .

Right now, boy,
And how, boy,
My cowboy . . .

I am more than just a little fond of this cowboy—
Though you may sometimes doubt that it's true—
Still, by now you should know
Even though I don't show
How each night I thank my lucky stars for this cowboy. . . .

[Music continues.]

Dance?
JAMEY: What? Here?
HARVEY: Yes.
JAMEY: I'd feel silly.
HARVEY: Good.

[An awkward moment of where to put hands, then left hand on shoulder, right hand on waist, they move into a smooth waltz. A few turns and they waltz off during fade.]

SCENE: INSOMNIA

[WHITE sits in his dark "living room," mutters to the blue glow of his television set. MR. JONES stands behind him.]

WHITE: Bastard wouldn't give me back the job. I told him I was sorry. . . . A mistake, I made a mistake. . . . Wouldn't listen, wouldn't even listen, and that Milk shit thinks it's funny . . . real funny, real fuckin' funny. . . .

[MARY ANN WHITE, in hair curlers and robe, enters, stands in doorway.]

MARY ANN: Danny? *[No response. He is stone still and icy.]* Come to bed, honey. You can't keep doing this. Turn it off, okay? Well, at least turn the sound on. I can't stand this! Danny? *[She exits.]*

WHITE: Nobody plays by the rules anymore. I'm a team player. And I played by the rules. Family—wife, kids, good family man, that's what they say about *me*. Church. Little League. People've always liked me. I'm a likable guy.

MR. JONES: You're right, Dan.

WHITE: I walk down the street, people—good people—say, "Hi, Dan. How's it going, Dan?"

MR. JONES: You're right, Dan.

WHITE: I know I quit—but I didn't mean to. And now Moscone won't let me take it back. And Milk thinks it's funny—he's happy about it. Leave the government to his kind. I deserve a second chance. I paid my dues—I came up the hard way, the right way.

MR. JONES: You're right, Dan.

WHITE: Harvey Milk doesn't even own a car. He doesn't make house payments.

MR. JONES: You're right. You are right. We both know what this is all about. The pestilence, the scum come clawing, chewing away the very fabric of freedom. They want to silence us—put a foot on our backs and crack our spines, to crush the voice of right and reason. Dan . . . Dan . . . listen. . . .

WHITE: But they listen to him; sure, they listen to him.

MR. JONES: Listen. . . . Listen!

(The Swarm)
Hear the pestilence approach,
Calling all into the picnic,
Every pissant, rat, and roach—
They come crawling to the picnic,
And they've got their eyes
On the bigger pies.

They all want the pies we brought—
They've grown discontent with humble—
They disdain what God hath wrought,
So they swarm and march and grumble,
They come wormin' in—
"Let the vermin in!"

We are brothers here at war—
I can level with you, can't I?—
They're all hording to our shore,
And each gook and chink and slant-eye
Has got quite a yen
For what's ours, my friend.

Give it all to Chan and Heimie,
Wags and wogs and wops and guineas,
Let's buy Lulamae and Stymie
And their nineteen pickaninnies
Welfare Cadillacs
With our income tax.

Don't forget the dykes and queers
With their sins and songs of Sodom,
Who proclaim their vice in cheers—
And who'd have us at the bottom—
But then you might swing
With that sort of thing. . . . [WHITE offended]

No, forgive my little jokes—
I can tell a fellow fellow—
One who knows the country chokes
On the black and pink and yellow—
One who feels like me
We must keep it free.

Flies and fleas and gnats and nits,
Lice and chiggers, mice and maggots,
Indonesians, hippy shits,
Spics and niggers, punks and faggots—
You just let in one,
Soon you're overrun.

Rats have stripped the cupboard bare—
Leeches slither 'cross the casement—
Locusts fill the very air—
There are termites in the basement—
Then a rumbling sound,
Is it tumbling down?
Do we let our house collapse?
Do we live with infestation?
Just do nothing—or perhaps
A . . . small ex . . . ter . . . mi . . . na . . . tion. . . .

[MR. JONES produces WHITE's gun from Act I and puts it in WHITE's hand.
He enfolds it with both of his own. Fade.]

SCENE: QUIET AS A TOMB

[Sunday morning, office. HARVEY, on phone.]

HARVEY: Me too, Jamey. Maybe we ought to fight more often. I think I fell in love
with you all over again last night. I didn't realize how long it had been since—

[Four gunshots offstage]

What the hell was that? It sounded like some Republican's ego just exploded.
Hold on. . . .

[DAN WHITE enters.]

Dan, what—

[WHITE raises the gun, fires twice. HARVEY falls. WHITE moves closer and fires two more times into Milk's head. Blackout.]

RADIO ANNOUNCEMENT: *[Montage of voices (repeats to build montage as necessary)]* We interrupt for this bulletin. There has been a shooting at City Hall. In unconfirmed reports Mayor Moscone . . . may be involved. . . . Rumors that one of the supervisors . . . possible suicide . . . take you live to City Hall . . .

[Spotlight on DIANNE FEINSTEIN]

FEINSTEIN: As president of the Board of Supervisors it is my duty to inform you that both Mayor Moscone and Supervisor Harvey Milk have been shot and killed. Supervisor Dan White is the suspect. . . .

[FEINSTEIN exits. A single voice begins "Anthem," is joined by others as one by one the FULL CAST enters the stage. Each carries a candle. (At the appropriate time a backdrop of tiny lights is added to the stage full of candles to recreate the candlelight march on the evening of the assassination.)]

ALL:

(Anthem)
What is left when the dove flies?
Just the song of the wing . . .
What is left when all love dies?
Where's the song left to sing?
Not a sound,
Not a sound,
Not a sound,
Just silence . . .

What will come in the darkness,
When the night chokes the dawn?
What will come in the darkness,
When the day's hope is gone?
What will come?
What will come?
What will come?
Just numbness . . .
What becomes of the mourning
When the heart goes to stone?
What will come with the morning
For the ones left alone?

Just the dew,
Just the dew,
Just the dew,
And muted . . .

What becomes of the hollow
When the vessel has burst?
What will come fill the hollow?
What will come for the thirst?
Just a sigh,
Just a sigh,
Just a sigh,
That's all. . . .

What is left when the dove flies?
Just the song of the wing . . .
What is left when all love dies?
Where's the song left to sing?
Not a sound,
Not a sound,
Not a sound,
Just silence . . .

[Fade]

SCENE: OUTSIDE THE COURTROOM

[HEATHER and DEE wait agitatedly in a courthouse corridor. An ominously silent JAMEY stands off to himself.]

HEATHER: I hate this. Have you been watching that jury?

DEE: Mmm-hmmm. That old stone-faced dude in the corner of the jury box—same clothes every day, brown suit, yellow tie? When they were playing the tape of Dan White's confession, Old Picklepuss had tears in his eyes.

HEATHER: *[Becoming more agitated]* The "Twinkie Defense," for Christsake! The guy walks into City Hall, murders two people in cold blood—his lawyer tells the jury, oh, it's okay, he was just a little upset, just a little sugar high, too much junk food, could happen to anyone, right? And I swear to God, those bastards were lapping up every stupid word of it.

DEE: People believe what they want to believe. And you can believe that if our straight, white mayor was the only one lying dead right now, they'd have Dan White plucked and ready for frying. I guess you get extra points for shooting a faggot.

[JOHN and PATRICIA rush on.]

JOHN: They've come back in with the verdict.

[*Together*]

DEE: What—already?

HEATHER: It's only been three hours.

JAMEY: How long?

PATRICIA: It isn't good.

JAMEY: *How long?*

JOHN: Seven years and eight months.

JAMEY: Seven years and ei—what, no medal?

[*Muttered invectives and reactions*]

DEE: I may be sick.

HEATHER: You know, I've always considered myself a pacifist, but I don't know—right now I just want to beat the shit out of somebody.

JOHN: The trouble is you won't be the only one. When the news gets out, this city's going to be a powder keg.

JAMEY: [*Quietly*] Good.

HEATHER: No. John's right. We're going to have to organize some kind of damage control—keep things from getting out of hand. People are going to be crazy. Things could turn ugly fast.

JAMEY: Good! Let them feel *our* violence for once.

DEE: Come on, Jamey.

JOHN: Wait, think. That's not what Harvey was about.

JAMEY: Harvey's dead! Or am I the only one here who remembers that?

HEATHER: [*Offended, slightly angry*] We all do, Jamey.

JOHN: We didn't get justice here. But vengeance is not a substitute.

JAMEY: Why don't you put that in a fortune cookie?

[*A shocked, awkward silence*]

DEE: We better get moving. There's not much time to get something together.

[*They start to exit. HEATHER stops to extend the last entreaty.*]

HEATHER: Jamey?

[*JAMEY does not budge. HEATHER exits. The silence extends a moment, then quietly . . .*]

PATRICIA: They're right. We have to do something.

JAMEY: No.

PATRICIA: But we should—

JAMEY: No! Go home, Patricia—back to school, back to Tyler, whatever. *You can* go home—you know?

PATRICIA: Please don't do this.

JAMEY: I'm sorry. I love you. I do. And I know you've done your best to understand. But right now all I have is this rage . . . such rage. . . . I thought it began the day Harvey died, but I was wrong. I think it's been there my whole life. The world has always drawn a line between us—those of us like me and those of you like you. And we've never been allowed to cross that line—not really. Now you can't cross over either. Not unless you know what it feels like to be despised for this—the things here—to be despised for your very heart. And you will never know what that feels like, thank God. And, yes, I do love you. But for now, little sister, you don't have a part here. Go home. Please.

[PATRICIA stands futile a moment, then exits. JAMEY stands, moves to center, and screams.]

BURN IT DOWN, GODDAMMIT!!!

[He runs off. All hell breaks loose. A few rioters come on, throwing rocks, bricks, bottles, then more. Jangling music, sirens, patrol car calls, angry chanting mob sounds, radio announcements of the riots at City Hall, newsreel footage of burning cars projected onto the actual smoke that fills the stage. Other violent effects underline the confrontation of an outraged community against a heavily armored riot squad. When the smoke clears, the stage has been left a shambles.]

Epilogue

[JAMEY, in levis and a sports jacket, enters the darkened stage. He extracts a flask from inside his jacket, opens it, brings it to his lips. The cast stands silently behind him against a background of stars. An a cappella voice sings one verse of "Anthem." . . . HARVEY enters.]

HARVEY: Hello, Toby Tyler Texas.

JAMEY: Hey, Harve.

HARVEY: I thought you quit with that crap.

JAMEY: *[Bitterly]* Just celebrating, Harve. Dan White gets out tomorrow—after four and a half years—time off for good behavior, no doubt.

     A toast—Truth, Justice, and the American Way. *[He takes a big slug.]*

HARVEY: Wait for the fat lady, babe. It isn't over yet. In a few months Dan White's going to go out and buy a brand new pistol, put the barrel into his mouth, and pull the trigger. People who hate have to destroy. And if their hatred has no place to go, they end up destroying themselves.

JAMEY: Right . . . and look at the hell created in the meantime.

HARVEY: Yeah. Look at it.

JAMEY: What?

HARVEY: You, that's what. Does anything about us, our work, our life together—
does any of it mean anything to you?

JAMEY: Why do you think I'm still so goddamned . . . MAD?!

HARVEY: Good! Be mad. Mad is energy and energy is the power to say, "This is
not going to do." Then you have to learn to let it go. Let it go, Jamey. You have
your job—do it.

JAMEY: I am. We are. We're working. But the wolves, Harve—they just keep
acomin'.

HARVEY: *[Parody]* So—you just keep agoin'.
Who knows from tomorrow?

(Young Man [Reprise])

HARVEY:

When you're young, you believe in stars,

JAMEY:

Then you find that stars can suddenly tumble;

HARVEY:

So in time you abandon stars—

JAMEY:

Then you find you're overwhelmed by the night;

HARVEY:

And fear conquers trust
Like a cancer,
Hopes turn to dust—

JAMEY:

Idols will rust, given time enough to—

HARVEY:

Somehow you must
Find some answer—
Something to offer, some recompense,

JAMEY:

Something to make it all make some sense. . . .

HARVEY:

But . . . now you know not to trust the stars,

JAMEY:

Looking up, you'll lose your footing and stumble—

HARVEY:

Look inside—learn to use the scars—
Look to each defeat to teach you to fight. . . .
Use the tears that you've shed—
Or they'll blind you—

JAMEY:

Blood that's been shed—

HARVEY:

Use it instead; let the past remind you
Just look ahead—
Not behind you—
What did I promise when we first met?

TOGETHER:

Hold to the dream, and we'll make it better. . . .

HARVEY:

Young man,
Don't believe, don't believe there's a guarantee.
Young man,
Nothing's always true.
Young man,
Don't believe, don't believe in the used-to-be.
Dare and believe in what we've begun—
Still there's so much, Jamey, left undone . . .
So very much, Jamey, left undone. . . .

TOGETHER:

So very, very much left undone . . .
So very, very much left undone . . .

So now . . . lights down on Harvey . . . up on Jamey. . . . Action. *[Softly]* Take care of yourself, baby.

[As HARVEY exits, JAMEY's hand reaches out toward him, then slowly upward, and forms itself into a fist. Slow fade, curtain.]

PATRICK WILDE

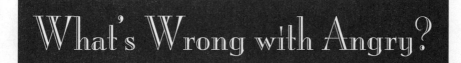

What's Wrong with Angry?

EDITOR'S INTRODUCTION

There is a greater tradition of unabashedly political drama in Great Britain than there is in the United States. Since the 1950s playwrights such as John Osborne, Arnold Wesker, and Howard Brenton have used the stage as a platform for views on the declining state of England, and since the 1960s minorities, women, and gays have developed theatrical groups to argue for their positions. The Gay Sweatshop, founded in 1975, was for years a major voice not only for gay theater but also for gay politics.

Gay political theater was struck a harsh blow in 1988 when the British Parliament passed Section 28 of the Local Government Act, which stated that:

A local authority shall not:
  a. Promote homosexuality or publish material with the intention of promoting homosexuality.
  b. Promote the teaching in any maintained school of the acceptance of homosexuality as a pretended family relationship.

This act achieved its aim of frightening local councils out of funding gay-positive theater, thus threatening the existence of groups such as Gay Sweatshop and theaters that produced progay work. A number of theaters reacted defiantly. The heavily subsidized Royal National Theatre mounted an all-star revival of Martin Sherman's *Bent* as a test case. Though no one cut off the National's funding, smaller groups were still vulnerable and frightened. Patrick Wilde's unabashedly polemical *What's Wrong with Angry* is a healthy challenge to the prevailing antigay government rhetoric and the government-induced timidity of many theaters.

The play is also a challenge to Britain's somewhat contradictory laws regarding homosexuality. On the one hand, private consensual homosexual acts are not a legal offense, provided the parties involved are over eighteen; on the other hand, homosexuality may not be presented in a positive light as it is seen as an affront to "traditional family values." A homosexual household is in the eyes of the law a "pretended family relationship." In the past few years the goal of many gay political groups has been the lowering of the age of consent for gay people from twenty-one to sixteen, the age for heterosexuals. After a heated parliamentary debate a compromise age of eighteen was passed into law. This means that it is illegal for boys of seventeen to have homosexual sex. Americans who live in states with sodomy laws on the books may look at Britain's laws as enlightened, but compared to the rest of the European Community, they are repressive.

It is not surprising that two of the more successful gay dramas of 1993 and 1994 focus on the age-of-consent laws. Jonathan Harvey's *Beautiful Thing* sweetly dramatizes the love of two sixteen-year-old boys on a South London council estate. Harvey's play was a hit on the fringe and a total sellout during a brief run at the Donmar Warehouse in Covent Garden; in the fall of 1994 it transferred to the West End. *What's Wrong with Angry,* written by, directed by, and featuring Patrick Wilde, had an extended sellout run at the Battersea Arts Centre, and a film production has been discussed.

There are two central characters in *What's Wrong with Angry:* sixteen-year-old Steven Carter, a student at an all-boys Catholic high school in out-of-the-way Basingstoke, and Simon Hutton, a thirty-year-old gay teacher at Steven's school (ironically named English Martyrs). Steven is suffering the horrors of being a horny gay adolescent. He would love the sex and romance his heterosexual peers crave but sees no one who is unashamedly out. There are no role models for Steven except anguished, closeted men who depend on furtive sex in public bathrooms. Simon Hutton, the one person who could help Steven, could also lose his job for doing so. The official policy of English Martyrs toward homosexuality is denial. Hutton's reticence has limited his life as well. He has moved from the furtive gropings of the bathrooms to the midnight world of the gay clubs, but he has not found in gay society the love Steven dreams of. That would take more courage than Hutton can muster.

Like all successful political drama, *What's Wrong with Angry* is also good popular entertainment. Wilde has written a play that speaks to central issues for gay men everywhere and has done so in a fast-moving, entertaining way. *What's Wrong with Angry* is a crowd pleaser filled with laughter and music as well as anger. And Wilde does not let his hero succumb to the paralysis of victimhood. We see him at the end dancing, his arm raised in defiance. As director, Wilde gave his script the dynamic direction it needed, and the play was helped enormously by the charismatic performance of nineteen-year-old Tom Wisdom as Steven. His performance made him one of the most sought after young actors in Great Britain.

AUTHOR'S INTRODUCTION

The British are not very good with sex. Sex of any kind. They view it as dirty, funny, embarrassing, a necessary evil—anything but loving or romantic.

Little wonder, then, that homosexuality is still the ultimate taboo. Britain stands alone in the so-called civilized world in having a discriminatory age of consent for gay men. Only a few years ago a new law made it illegal to promote a positive image of homosexuality; that is, to educate people not to hate, attack, despise, or ostracize gay people.

It is against this background that *What's Wrong with Angry* is set. Basingstoke is a large town just thirty miles from London, where, as in most of the country, the experience of coming out is very difficult. As an out gay man for some fifteen years, I was tired of well-meaning friends, even gay friends, telling me it was easier to be gay "nowadays." True, a large and hedonistic gay scene operates in the capital city, and other major cities boast smaller but just as self-perpetuating ghettos. I remained convinced, however, largely because of my relationships with several young men over the years (most notably a man from Basingstoke!), that for a young person coping with homosexuality is still a process that must be undertaken in secret, in dangerous situations, and with no support, least of all from the much-vaunted great British family.

As an actor and director, I had never seriously considered writing my own play, but I really felt a need to express my anger at this heartbreaking system, which condemns thousands of young people to years, perhaps lifetimes, of misery. I was sick of people describing older gay men as getting bitter. We're not bitter; we're angry!

A society that leaves such a high proportion of its young people to their own devices (homosexuality is unlikely to be broached as a serious topic of conversation in British schools), that creates a situation in which 20 percent of gay men admit to attempting suicide in their teenage years, cannot by any stretch of the imagination be called civilized.

I wanted to write a play about an ordinary boy who knew he was gay and had no problem with it. Children are taught by other people to fear sexuality. Just as no one is born racist, no one is born homophobic or frightened of being gay. These things are taught.

In 1994, the day after the second production of *What's Wrong with Angry* closed, Parliament lowered the age of consent for gay men from twenty-one to eighteen. This is still two years higher than for heterosexuals. Effectively this means that thousands of young men, in pursuing the physical and emotional urges God or nature has given them, are criminalized.

PRODUCTION HISTORY AND RIGHTS

What's Wrong with Angry was produced by Riverforest Productions and first performed at The Lost Theatre in Fulham, London, on 8 September 1993 by the Wild Justice Company. The production was directed by Patrick Wilde, with lighting design by Eric Willitts and Liam McDonald.

The following were principals in the large cast:

Steven Carter. . . . . Tom Wisdom
Simon Hutton . . . . Adam Fowler
Linda Rodgers . . . . Joann Condon
John Westhead. . . . . Miles Petit

On 20 January 1994 the play transferred to the Oval House; it later moved to the Battersea Arts Centre, where Patrick Wilde played Simon Hutton.

PATRICK WILDE

What's Wrong with Angry?

For David, Liam, and, in spite of himself, Luke

Cast of Characters

STEVEN CARTER: 16 years old. Just finishing the fifth year at English Martyrs Roman Catholic all-boys school.

PATRICK CARTER: Steven's father. Over 40.

MARY CARTER: Steven's mother. Over 40.

LINDA RODGERS: Steven's best friend. 16. Overweight.

JOHN WESTHEAD: 18. Head Boy at English Martyrs. Good looking, intelligent, athletic.

SIMON HUTTON: Teacher at English Martyrs. 30.

GLEN: 24. Actor. Very attractive.

JENNY KEELEY: Head Girl at Notre Dame girls school. 18. Beautiful.

KEVIN: Sixth former. John's friend.

DAVE: Sixth former. John's friend.

GEORGE CARTER: 23. Steven's cousin. A wheeler-dealer in the city.

KAREN: Attractive. 22.

Various other characters are played by members of the company.

Setting

The action, with the exception of the "wake" scene, takes place in Basingstoke, about thirty miles from London. The action covers the last two weeks of a summer school term.

Lighting and sound are very important. The scenes should flow into each other without blackouts. Lighting should be used to create each environment so that a minimum of furniture is called for.

Act One

SCENE 1

[Music starts. Suggested track: "Rhythm Is a Dancer" by SNAP. A spotlight comes up on a schoolboy centre stage. As lights come up slowly, we see four men. They start to move about the stage in regular patterns, cruising each other in semidarkness. Eventually they freeze as a light comes up on SIMON HUTTON. He is on the phone at home.]

HUTTON: Steve. Steven. Listen to me. You're not making sense. *[Pause]* What? Steven, I am listening; I'm just not hearing you. Move away from the juke box. *[Pause]* I've told you I can't. My position is . . . difficult. Go home and sleep on it. Things'll be better in the morning. They always are. Believe me, Steven. No, don't do that! Steven! Steve! *[STEVE has hung up. Slowly HUTTON replaces his receiver. He continues to talk as if to himself, and throughout the play his solo speeches become more and more to an imaginary audience as he gets drunk.]* Believe me. My position is difficult. So what about your position? What are you going to do, Steven? What are you going to do now?

SCENE 2

[Birdsong. The men start to move. Light slowly down on HUTTON, and as the other lights resolve, we see the outside of a public toilet in a park. The signs "Ladies" and "Gentlemen" are clearly visible. Downstage is a bench. On it is seated STEVEN CARTER in his school uniform. He is reading a book but occasionally glances back at the toilet. The men disappear into the toilet, except for one who hangs around the entrance fixing his gaze on Steve. Eventually the MAN comes and sits on the bench. Continues to stare at STEVE, who ignores him. The MAN opens his legs wide. No reaction from STEVE. The man starts to stroke and grope his own groin.]

MAN: Got anywhere to go? Oi. Got anywhere to go? *[Pause]* We could go to my place. It's not far. I've got a car. How about it? I've got videos. *[Pause]* No. There's always the woods. Shall we go up to the woods? It's pretty safe. I've got poppers. Do you like poppers? You'll love them. *[STEVE resolutely reads his book.]* What do you like? Eh? Bet you like to suck. Or I'll suck you? Go on! You know you want to. *[MAN strokes his groin again.]* I'll pay you. Fiver for a blow job. *[Pause]* Ten?
STEVE: Look, I just want to read my book. Sorry.
MAN: *[Strokes his groin again.]* I've got nine inches. *[Pause. He gets up angrily.]* Little shit! Don't give me that "innocent little boy" crap. I've seen you hanging

round here before. You know what's going on in there. Don't you? Prick-teaser. *[Starts to go into toilet. Stops.]* Join me inside if you want. If your book gets too boring. Little shit! *[Exit to toilet. STEVEN checks to see if the MAN has gone. Gets up and starts to leave. GLEN enters. As they pass each other, they look back simultaneously and stop. Then GLEN continues into the toilet. STEVE stands still and then hurriedly returns to the bench and starts reading again. Eventually GLEN reemerges and sits on the bench. They don't acknowledge each other.]*

GLEN: *[After a pause]* Enjoying it?

STEVE: Sorry?

GLEN: The book.

STEVE: Oh yeah. *Hamlet.* By William Shakespeare.

GLEN: Exams? Bet you'll be glad when they're over.

STEVE: In a way. I quite enjoy it actually. Shakespeare, I mean.

GLEN: He speaks very highly of you too. *[STEVE laughs. They stare at each other briefly. GLEN breaks the moment.]* Cigarette?

STEVE: No. Sorry. I don't. Sorry.

GLEN: Nothing to be sorry for! Wish I could stop. Don't you ever start.

STEVE: Sorry.

GLEN: Stop saying sorry.

STEVE: Sorry. I'm . . . nervous.

GLEN: *[Feigning indifference]* Do you go to the theatre then?

STEVE: Not really. Can't afford it. They think it's . . . poofy. Anyway, there's not much round here.

GLEN: Right! Not exactly a contender for European City of Culture. Basingstoke. God, I miss London.

STEVE: Wow! You moved here from London. Why would anyone move HERE from London? Bloody hell! I can't wait till I'm old enough to get out of this dump.

GLEN: And how old are you?

STEVE: Look, I was just leaving.

GLEN: Don't let me stop you. *[GLEN continues to smoke, looking out front. STEVE looks at him awhile, then opens his legs wide. GLEN ignores this. STEVE begins to caress his own groin. GLEN sees this and suddenly gets up to leave.]*

STEVE: Sorry, I didn't mean . . . I thought . . . oh shit! Sorry.

GLEN: Stop saying sorry. It's just . . . well, I'm nervous, too. *[They stare at each other a few seconds.]*

STEVE: You're . . . lovely.

GLEN: You're not so bad yourself. *[He sits.]*

STEVE: Most of the other guys who come here are old.

GLEN: That's not a crime.

STEVE: Or ugly.

GLEN: I guess that is.

STEVE: You're the best-looking bloke I've ever seen here.

GLEN: Do you come here often? *[They laugh at the cliché.]*

STEVE: Quite often. Well, often!

GLEN: At your age!

STEVE: Why do you keep going on about my age? *[Suddenly panicked]* Fuck! You're not a—oh shit!

GLEN: Don't panic. I'm not a policeman. Played a few in my time, though.

STEVE: Wow! You're an actor. I want to be an actor. Wow! Are you famous? Should I know you?

GLEN: Not if you don't go to the theatre much.

STEVE: But I'm sure I've seen you.

GLEN: Well, you may have seen me persuading the nation that the greatest hardship in life is having to take two bottles into the shower. Or that the very, very best a man can get is a razor blade.

STEVE: Wow! Was that you? I thought you said you weren't famous!

GLEN: *[Laughs]* God! You're so cute! *[They stare again.]*

STEVE: Can we go to your place?

GLEN: Sorry, I live with someone.

STEVE: Oh. Might have known you'd have a boyfriend.

GLEN: What about the woods?

STEVE: Too dangerous.

GLEN: Pity.

STEVE: I live five minutes away.

GLEN: You must be joking. What about your parents?

STEVE: They're out. In London. They won't be back till late. My nan's very sick. About to snuff it.

GLEN: Great! I mean that they're out, not that your nan's . . . Shall we go then?

STEVE: *[As they get up]* Yeah!

GLEN: How old did you say you were?

STEVE: I didn't. Sixteen. You?

GLEN: Not sixteen.

SCENE 3

[The lights begin to change. Music: "You're My Venus" by Bananarama. STEVE and GLEN stand opposite each other and slowly caress each other's face. Round them the set changes to STEVE's bedroom. Bed. Bedside cabinet with phone. Stereo music system. Record collection. As the lights resolve, GLEN exits. The music is now coming from the stereo. STEVE dances. LINDA RODGERS is lying on the bed.]

LINDA: Tart!

STEVE: Jealous! Oh, Linda. He's lovely. And he goes like a train!

LINDA: Tart!

STEVE: And he's got eyes like Tom Cruise. He's so witty and gorgeous and—

LINDA: Dangerous!

STEVE: Don't start that again. He's one of the nicest people I've ever met.

LINDA: Because he fucked you?

STEVE: No, because he was sensitive and funny and said he thinks I'm very mature. And he didn't fuck me. You know I'm always safe.

LINDA: Safe! What's safe about bringing a stranger into your home? And what's safe about picking people up in toilets? You promised me you wouldn't do it anymore.

STEVE: I don't. Well, I don't go in anymore. I just sit outside minding my own business.

LINDA: Steve!

STEVE: Can I help it if people want to talk to me?

LINDA: Talk to you!

STEVE: Yeah. Glen and I had a really interesting chat—about Shakespeare, actually. He's a famous actor, you see, and—

LINDA: Oh, Steve! Babe! This is Linda you're talking to. Don't bullshit me! If some strange bloke start talking to you outside a public bog, he's only interested in one thing, and it's not your opinion of Shakespeare's use of animal imagery in *King Lear*.

STEVE: He's not a strange bloke. His name's Glen, and it was *Hamlet* anyway!

LINDA: But why there? It's so . . . yuk!

STEVE: Maybe it is. But where else? Listen. I know you think it's disgusting—

LINDA: I didn't say that.

STEVE: No. You said yuk. Okay. So you think it's yuk. Well, it could be yukkier. Do you know how many times I get offered money up there? I never take it. Because then I would feel yuk.

LINDA: Don't tell me you're looking for love!

STEVE: Oh, what's the point? You're not hearing me.

LINDA: Of course I'm—*[STEVE has turned the music up very loud and is dancing again.]* Steve. Steven Carter, I really hate you sometimes. *[She gets up and turns music off.]* Now you listen to me! Don't you dare hit me with all that "nobody understands" crap! When you told me you thought you were gay, I wasn't even surprised.

STEVE: Was it the Jason Donovan calendar I asked for at Christmas?

LINDA: It was the "Bananarama Boxed Set" which gave it away.

STEVE: Cow!

LINDA: Oh, babe! I just think you're too young.

STEVE: You're never too young to like Bananarama.

LINDA: It's only because I care. Give yourself a chance. It could be a phase.

STEVE: Well, if it is, it's a phase I've been going through since I was eleven.

LINDA: Eleven!

STEVE: That's how old I was when I discovered masturbation. Mind you, it was another three years before I realised I could do it on my own.

LINDA: Stop trying to shock me. I'm unshockable. Just slow down; you're confused.

STEVE: What on earth makes you think I'm confused? I've never been more certain of anything in my life. Listen, supposing I said to you, "Linda, you're confused; just wait a couple of years before you decide if you really like men or not." What would you say? You'd say, "But I know now!" Well, I know now, and I want to enjoy myself now while I'm young and attractive. Just like you do. Well, while you're young anyway. Besides, what else does a dump like Basingstoke have to offer me?

LINDA: But you're obsessed with sex! Even straight people of your age don't do it as often as you. It's a different bloke every time you call me! I've only done it once, and that was in the Costa Brava with a Spanish waiter who kept saying really romantic things like "Nice beeg Eeenglish girlee." I've never had a boyfriend.

STEVE: Ah! That's the point. You've never had one, but if you did, you could be open about it and show off about it. You could use that word. Boyfriend. I'd love to have a boyfriend. Then maybe I wouldn't need to . . . Someone to go to the pictures with. Do ordinary teenage things with. Introduce my parents to. Someone like Glen.

LINDA: Oh, come on! He's old enough to be your father!

STEVE: He's twenty-four.

LINDA: There you are. He's old enough to be someone's father. Why not hang on for someone your own age?

STEVE: Because as far as I can make out, everyone my own age is straight. I go to an all-boys school, and I feel as if I'm the only one. All my classmates are always going on about this bird and that, how they managed to get three fingers up Sally or Natasha or Sonia. It's so . . . yuk!

LINDA: Do you fancy any of them?

STEVE: God, no! They're all so immature. *[Pause]* Except . . .

LINDA: Who? Oh go on, Steve, tell me.

STEVE: You'll only take the piss.

LINDA: Who, me? Go on, except who?

STEVE: If you laugh, I'll never talk to you again. John. John Westhead.

LINDA: Wow! Why should I laugh? He's gorgeous.

STEVE: Gorgeous! Everytime I see his Head Boy badge, I wish it was an invitation.

LINDA: I sure wouldn't kick him out of bed for eating biscuits!

STEVE: Now who's obsessed with sex? He's different. Special. I love . . . his eyes, his walk, the way he seems so popular while being aloof. He's special. I love him.

LINDA: Oh, babe! How sweet!

STEVE: There! I knew you'd take the piss. Why is it sweet? It hurts.

LINDA: Sure it's not just a crush?

STEVE: For three years?

LINDA: Well, he's a bit of a hero, isn't he? Beautiful, intelligent, good at sports—

STEVE: Okay, okay! There's no need to rub it in. Anyway, there's something else. You see, unlike every other bastard at that place, he doesn't . . . well he doesn't . . .

LINDA: Bully you! He doesn't come to your rescue either.

STEVE: In my dreams he does.

LINDA: Yuk!

STEVE: Sometimes I wish he did bully me. At least then I'd exist for him. It's hopeless.

LINDA: Because he's straight.

STEVE: Supposing he wasn't. Suppose I found anyone my own age. I can just see us walking down the corridor together hand in hand. *[Pause. Seems lost in thought.]* Oh, sod it! Who needs John Westhead when there are people like Glen in the world? *[He starts to examine his face in the mirror in the fourth wall.]* Oh, no. Another spot. *[Starts to squeeze it]*

LINDA: *[Comes up behind him and puts her arms round him]* You seeing him again?

STEVE: Glen? Yeah. I said I'd meet him on Thursday outside the . . .

LINDA: The toilet! Why there?

STEVE: So I can tell him if it's safe to come back here.

LINDA: Ring him.

STEVE: He couldn't give me his number.

LINDA: Please be careful. It's only because I care.

STEVE: Yuk!

LINDA: I just don't want you to get all bitter and twisted.

STEVE: *[Turning to hug her]* Please stop worrying. *[Door slams downstairs.]*

FATHER: *[Offstage]* Steven? We're back.

STEVE: Hi, Dad. Mum. Linda's here.

LINDA: *[As DAD comes up stairs]* They still think we're going out together?

STEVE: Convinced of it. Every time I say I'm going to see you, Dad gives me his "that's my boy" smile and winks.

LINDA: I'm not sure I approve.

STEVE: Why?

LINDA: You're not exactly my type.

STEVE: You're not exactly mine! *[They collapse on the bed "fighting."]*

FATHER: *[Entering]* Oh, sorry, Linda.

LINDA: It's okay, Mr. Carter. We were just . . . I was helping Steven with his homework.

FATHER: *[Smiling]* I can see that.

STEVE: How's Nan?

FATHER: Hanging on. She's seems a bit better. Well, she's old you know.

STEVE: That's not a crime.

FATHER: No. But it happens to all of us. She's had a good innings. She'd love to see you, Steve. We're going again on Thursday.

STEVE: Sorry, Dad. Geography on Friday. Last paper. Maybe at the weekend.

FATHER: I hope she hangs on that long. Don't worry, son. She'll understand. He's a good lad, Linda. Knows how important qualifications are. I've told him, if you really want something in this world, you've got to work for it. Doesn't matter how difficult things seem to be—never give up. Right, Steve.

STEVE: Right, Dad.

FATHER: Well, I'd better go down to your mum. She's a bit upset. Enjoy your . . . homework. *[Smiles and winks at STEVE. Exit.]*

LINDA: Well, we know what homework you'll be doing on Thursday. Tart!

STEVE: I love it when you talk dirty! Thanks for listening, Lins. I don't know what I'd do without you.

LINDA: See! Girls have their uses.

STEVE: Mmmm! Nice beeg Eeeeenglish girleee. Be gentle with me! *[They start to fight on the bed, and LINDA tickles STEVE.]* No! Don't! Stop it! Don't!

SCENE 4

[Sinister music. LINDA exits and the set changes to an empty space. STEVEN stands and four schoolboys surround him, each about ten feet away from him. He speaks continuously from the last scene, but the mood has changed: "Don't! Please don't! Don't hurt me. Please!" Light comes up on HUTTON. STEVE and the boys are in semidarkness.]

STEVE: Please. I'll do anything. Just leave me alone!

HUTTON: Alone. I bet you think you're alone, don't you? You're not, Steven. There are thousands. Millions like you.

STEVE: Please!

HUTTON: I meant what I said, too. About it getting better. I think you understood what I was trying to say. You smiled. I helped. Of course I helped.

STEVE: Help me. Someone!

HUTTON: Didn't I? I wanted to spell it out. . . . I wanted you to know that it was the same for me at school. The name-calling.

BOY 1: Queer bastard!

HUTTON: The beatings. The spitting. Somehow the spitting was worse than the violence. Made me feel . . . dirty. But the graffiti was the worst. It was so . . . permanent. Official. Me and my crime immortalized on desktops. I used to wake up every weekday morning with a knot in my stomach. What new horrors—

STEVE: Don't!

HUTTON: —terrors did the schoolday hold? But I survived. To be proud of what I am. So why couldn't I tell you that? Because . . . Ring again. Ring, Steven, and tell me you're alright. And I'll tell you you're alright. Ring me. Sod my job. Sod the law! *[As the light fades on HUTTON and comes up on the rest of the space, the boys charge at STEVE with a primal, terrifying yell. This becomes a cry of "goal" as STEVE escapes the melee and sits at the side on the floor, reading. Two boys start kicking a ball around. Two others, KEVIN and DAVE, break downstage.]*

KEV: Fancy diving off for a fag, Dave?

DAVE: No chance, Kev. Me and John have got to see old Pubic before assembly to sort the arrangements for the disco.

KEV: I still don't believe it's going to happen.

DAVE: It's going to happen!

KEV: But there's never been so much as a barn dance at this place before. Christ, if ever a school was aptly named—"English Martyrs."

DAVE: True. But there's never been a Head Boy like Johnny Westhead before either. You should have heard him charm Pubic.

KEV: What did he say?

DAVE: Well, he asked him why he was so against the idea of a dance, what he was worried about. Pubic got all red-faced and blustery the way he does and talked in veiled terms about feeling that young men from a single-sex school suddenly confronting the opposite gender in the sinister atmosphere of low lights and a primal beat may lead to undesirable consequences. He then muttered something about unexplored passions waiting to explode.

KEV: Bloody hell! Doesn't he know we've all been exploding for years?

DAVE: John just pointed out that the most wonderful thing about being at English Martyrs was that we had all learnt to behave like "gentlemen."

KEV: I would've pissed myself.

DAVE: I nearly did. Especially when Johnny said we wanted the disco so we could prove we could behave like gentlemen and if Pubic didn't trust us, wasn't he admitting the failure of his teaching philosophy? The old git just caved in under the weight of John's charm and logic!

KEV: *[As JOHN enters]* And here's the man himself. Johnny boy!

JOHN: Kev. Ready to see the old fart, Dave?

DAVE: Let's get it over with.

KEV: Here, he's not likely to change his mind, is he?

JOHN: No chance. Friday's the night! The tickets are printed now, and I've just delivered one hundred to Notre Dame.

KEV: Notre Dame Convent School for Girls. Christ, it gives me a stiffy just saying the words!

DAVE: Now there's some unexplored passion waiting to explode! Did you see Jenny Keeley?

JOHN: Yes, I saw Jenny Keeley.

KEV: Who's Jenny Keeley?

DAVE: Their Head Girl, dickhead. What a woman. Legs, tits, and brains! I had such a dream about her the other night.

JOHN: Did you?

DAVE: No. It was fun trying, though.

JOHN: Hands off! She's mine—or she will be after the disco. *[The school bell. STEVE gets up, and as he walks across the playground, he is jostled by the two other boys.]*

BOY 1: How's your bum, Carter?

BOY 2: Want to see my willy?

BOY 1: Bringing a nice boy to the disco, are you? *[They grab his bag and start throwing it between them. KEVIN joins in.]*

STEVE: Please don't!

DAVE: Leave it, Kevin. We are supposed to look after the younger boys.

KEV: It's only a bit of fun. Anyway, whoever said Steven Carter was a boy? *[KEVIN and DAVE exit.]*

BOY 2: *[Spilling the contents of the bag on the floor and picking up an exercise book]* What have we got here? "SC loves JW."

BOY 1: "SC Loves JW." Steve Carter loves just wanking. *[Laughter]*

BOY 2: *[Hits STEVE in stomach]* Wanker! *[As STEVE doubles over, the boys attempt to take his trousers off, chanting, "Get 'em off; get 'em off."]*

BOY 1: Watch it. Hutton's coming! *[Spits at STEVE, who is lying on the floor in a foetal position]* Queer bastard! *[All exit rapidly except JOHN, who starts to approach STEVE. STEVE kneels up, and they make eye contact. Exit JOHN.]*

HUTTON: *[Entering. He looks in the direction the boys have exited.]* Bastards! You alright? *[STEVE scrambles to his feet, holding his trousers up.]* Now what's going on?

STEVE: My trousers for a start. *[He pulls them up.]*

HUTTON: Don't try to be smart.

STEVE: I thought that's why I was here.

HUTTON: Look, Steve. I only want to help. Who was it?

STEVE: It was . . . just a bit of fun. Look, sir, I'll be late for assembly. I'm alright.

HUTTON: This happens to you a lot, doesn't it? I'm not blind.

STEVE: They don't mean it. . . . It's just a bit—

HUTTON: —of fun. Your idea of fun, is it?

STEVE: *[Near to tears]* I just wish they'd . . . WANKERS! Sorry, sir.

HUTTON: Steven, if there's anything you want to talk about—

STEVE: Yeah! *[Pause]* My fly button's broken.

HUTTON: You don't have to put up with this, you know. No one should. Doesn't it upset you? Being picked on. Being called . . .

STEVE: Called what?

HUTTON: I'm not deaf either. Things like, queer bastard—

STEVE: Yes, sir. Yes, it upsets me. Because you see, sir, I'm not a bastard.

MR. AYRES: *[Entering]* Come along, Carter. You'll be late for assembly.

STEVE: Sorry, Mr. Ayres. *[He staggers off still holding his trousers up.]*

MR. AYRES: *[Calling after him]* And is that any way for a gentleman to walk? Straighten up, lad. Straighten up!

SCENE 5

[Music. A couple of cruising men come on and stare at each other. STEVE and LINDA embrace and hold each other in the middle of the stage. The set reverts to the bench outside the toilet. STEVE and LINDA sit on it as the light comes up on HUTTON.]

HUTTON: Do you want to know about my first time, Steven? I was fourteen. On my way home from school one day I got caught short. There was a toilet behind the bus garage. As I stood at the urinal, somebody came out of a cubicle, started to leave, then changed his mind and went and washed his hands. I remember thinking how his parents must have brought him up properly. And then . . . and then he came over and stood at the urinal and unzipped. I was just giving myself a little shake, ready to leave, when I noticed he was doing the same—only he was giving himself a big shake. And I looked closer and . . . and I ran out of the door and up the stairs and into the light. And I ran half the way home. Out of breath, I stopped. And then . . . and then I ran back. Even faster. He'd gone, of course, and I was . . . disappointed. God knows why. I wasn't even sure what I'd gone back to do. But I was disappointed. And then a cubicle door opened ever so slightly. And I stared at it. And it opened a bit more. And I stared some more. And I saw someone inside. I don't know who was taking the bigger risk, me by staying there or him . . . because he suddenly just opened the door wide and gestured with his . . . free hand . . . for me to come in. *[Pause]* And I did. And he closed the door and put his jacket on the floor at the bottom of it. And in complete silence I "made love" for the first time in my life. To someone I've never seen since. Whose face I cannot remember. And it was exciting and incredibly, indescribably naughty, and . . . and I felt I "belonged." Shocking, eh? I felt I belonged in a toilet. I'm sure that's why grown men still do it. The gay ones, anyway. Nostalgia. I have gay friends who are out and proud, have long-term partners, go to pubs and clubs. But they still cottage. Some of them take a packed lunch and a flask of tea. *[Pause]* Ring me, Steven. You don't belong in a toilet. *[Light slowly down on HUTTON. Lights up on rest of the space. The two men go into the toilet. Birdsong. STEVE has his Walkman on. For a few moments he and LINDA sit in silence. LINDA is restless. STEVE occasionally glances back at the toilet.]*

LINDA: Well, at least you could talk to me! *[Pause. STEVE continues to listen to his Walkman.]* I'm really nervous. *[Pause]* Look, you said the gorgeous Glen was meeting you at 4:30. He's forty-five minutes late. Now I know what you meant when you said he goes like a train. Why you want me to meet him, I don't know. So he's got eyes like Tom Cruise. Lot of good that'll do me. Steve. Steven. He's not coming. Let's go. I'm nervous. *[A third man comes on and slows down to stare at STEVE. LINDA protectively puts her arm round STEVE and sticks her tongue out at the man, who goes into the toilet.]*

STEVE: *[Reacting and talking too loudly because he has his Walkman on]* IS IT HIM? SHIT! HE'LL TURN UP.

LINDA: *[Indicating Walkman]* Shhhhh!

STEVE: *[Taking Walkman off]*

LINDA: Listen, babe, I really think he would have been—*[STEVE puts headphones back on.]* Oooh! Steven Carter, I really hate you sometimes! I could be at home now, locked in my room with my maths revision. But I'm sitting here with you so you can be locked in your room with Tom Cruise. Or at least his eyes. Men! I put up with a lot from you, you know. All your moans. Your problems. Want to hear some of my problems? Want to hear about period pains or fanny farts or feeling as fat as a pig every time you see a supermodel? They're not problems, are they? Oh, no. Don't talk to me about problems.

STEVE: *[Taking off headphones]* Sorry?

LINDA: I said don't talk to me about problems.

STEVE: Okay. *[Pause]* He probably got held up.

LINDA: By his balls, I hope. Look, Steve, I've got to go. If he turns up, I'll only be in the way and embarrassed, and anyway I don't even fancy Tom Cruise—any part of him—so I'll call you later to see how you got on. Pythagoras awaits. *[Kisses him and starts to leave]*

STEVE: Lins? *[She stops.]* What's a fanny fart? *[Exit LINDA.]* Women! *[He looks at his watch, gets up, starts to leave, then steels himself and heads for the toilet.]*

SCENE 6

[The lights change to interior of the toilet. The sound is sinister again, incorporating the noise of dripping water. The scene should be very dark, the only real light coming from the entrance. Three men stand at the urinal. Two are close together, the third some distance away. A fourth smokes. STEVE enters and two of the men at the urinal quickly shuffle apart. STEVE hides in a shadow. The two men shuffle back together. The smoking man looks at STEVE, who moves away. One of the two men leaves. The smoking man goes to the urinal. The third man rejects his advances and he leaves. STEVE goes to the urinal. The other man leaves so that STEVE and the third man remain. They shuffle together and grope each other.]

STRANGER: *[Whispering]* Don't. It's too busy. Dangerous.

STEVE: Got anywhere to go?

STRANGER: No. You?

STEVE: I live round the corner. There's no one there.

STRANGER: I'm not sure.

STEVE: Go on. It's not far.

STRANGER: Okay.

STEVE: I'll see you outside. On the bench. *[He zips up and leaves.]*

SCENE 7

[Sound and lights change to outside the toilet. STEVE sits on the bench.]

STEVE: Come on! Come out! *[Pause]* Come out! Come on! *[He is looking back at the toilet. Eventually the stranger comes out. It is JOHN. STEVE rises slowly and JOHN stops dead in his tracks.]* Jesus! *[He sits down and buries his face in his hands.]* I don't believe it. *[Looks around again]* Please, God! Tell me this isn't happening. *[He faces front again. JOHN unfreezes, starts to leave, then stops and walks slowly to the bench. Sits.]*

JOHN: Alright, mate. *[STEVE is unable to speak.]* Carter, isn't it?

STEVE: Yes.

JOHN: You live round here, then?

STEVE: Yes. Just . . . not far.

JOHN: Fag?

STEVE: Sorry.

JOHN: Ciggy?

STEVE: Oh, I . . . ta! *[He takes one. JOHN lights it and his own.]*

JOHN: We only moved here a few weeks ago. *[Pause]* I was . . . I was just exploring the area. Nice park.

STEVE: Yeah. Nice. *[He coughs because of the cigarette.]*

JOHN: Filthy habit.

STEVE: What is?

JOHN: Smoking. I only started because all my mates did. Peer pressure they call it. Makes you do all sorts of things you don't want to—peer pressure.

STEVE: Oh yeah. Peer pressure, I mean—*[Coughs]*

JOHN: Not very good at that, are you?

STEVE: No, I don't usually. That is . . . I don't.

JOHN: *[Smiling]* Peer pressure?

STEVE: Pressure, anyway. *[STEVE stubs out the cigarette.]* Look, Westhead, I really should be going. Last exam tomorrow.

JOHN: How are they going? And my name's John.

STEVE: Oh, you know. I'll be glad when they're over.

JOHN: Then what?

STEVE: Sixth form next year. Imagine, two more years of that dump.

JOHN: Yeah, can't say I'll miss the old place.

STEVE: What are your plans?

JOHN: Year off. Travel round Europe. Spot the cliché, eh? Then Oxford, I hope.

STEVE: Wow! Great!

JOHN: *[Looking into space]* Yeah. Great. *[Pause]*

STEVE: Listen, Westhead . . . I mean, John. What happened just now. In there. *[JOHN continues to look out front.]* Well, I'm sorry if I . . .

JOHN: Forget it. My mistake.

STEVE: Mistake?

JOHN: Mistake.

STEVE: Why? Did you think I was somebody else?

JOHN: Of course not. I mean . . . I just went in for a piss, okay! I . . . I don't know what came over me.

STEVE: In there it's usually a question of not knowing *who* came over you.

JOHN: Yeerrk!

STEVE: Don't you start. *[Pause]* I didn't know it was you—

JOHN: Well, I certainly didn't know it was you!

STEVE: I mean, I could tell you were young . . . good looking.

JOHN: Does that make a difference, then?

STEVE: Of course it makes a bloody difference.

JOHN: It's true, then? What the other guys say. That you're . . . dodgy.

STEVE: I've been called worse things. Yes, I'm dodgy.

JOHN: Fuck me! *[Realises what he has said]* I don't mean . . . I just mean . . . fuck me! Sorry.

STEVE: I'm not.

JOHN: You mean you like it! You're glad to be . . .

STEVE: Delighted . . . to be dodgy.

JOHN: Fuck me!

STEVE: Can't say I'm keen on being kicked to shit every day, but it has its compensations.

JOHN: Such as?

STEVE: It's fun. *[They stare at each other a few seconds.]*

JOHN: You going to the disco tomorrow?

STEVE: Maybe.

JOHN: Not really your scene, I guess.

STEVE: Yes it is. . . . I mean, I love dancing.

JOHN: Me, too.

STEVE: Bet you're really good.

JOHN: Not bad. When I'm pissed. Anyone can dance when they're pissed.

STEVE: They think they can. *[Nervous laugh from both]* Well, like I said, I've got revision to do.

JOHN: Oh yeah. What is it tonight?

STEVE: Geography. I hate geography!

JOHN: I used to love it.

STEVE: Oxbow lakes, erratic boulders. Boring or what! *[Pause]* John, about what happened. I won't . . . I mean, I couldn't . . . Well, don't worry. I won't tell anyone.

JOHN: Yeah, I used to really get off on geography. *[Pause]* Thanks.

STEVE: *[Getting up]* See you, then.

JOHN: Catch you later.

STEVE: *[After a pause]* Listen, I don't suppose you fancy coming back for a coffee. My parents are out. Not that they'd mind, about the coffee. I mean, what's theirs is mine.

JOHN: Better not. Things to do. Anyway, I don't like coffee.

STEVE: Oh. Right. See you, then. *[He runs off. JOHN waits, then gets up.]*

JOHN: Steve. Steven. I like tea.

SCENE 8

[JOHN freezes. The rest of the set changes to STEVE's bedroom in semidarkness. Music: "Winner Takes It All" by Abba. Light on HUTTON centre stage.]

HUTTON: Sometimes, Steven, nothing makes sense. There are no rules. You see, those of us who cope, who grow up well adjusted, we're still at the mercy of the army of the confused. The legion of the totally fucked up! *[He looks at JOHN as if he is in the same scene.]* They want to have their cake and gobble it! They want the fun without the danger. The thrill without the stigma. I remember Kerry wanting me to meet her new boyfriend. She was a really good mate and had been to clubs with me often. Said she felt safe in gay places. Unthreatened. She was also one of the "why are all the best-looking men gay?" brigade. Anyway, I think she wanted me to meet this guy because he was proof that some straight men can be good looking, too! And boy was he good looking. The three of us spent a really strained evening in a pub. He hardly acknowledged me. No eye contact. Well, eventually he drove us home and dropped Kerry off first, which was odd. When we got to my place, he asked to use the loo, and when he'd finished, he came into my room and started taking his clothes off. In silence. And I watched. And he lay on the bed. And I remember thinking what a good mate Kerry was . . . and then I thought about what a lovely body he had. And I got on top of him and tried to kiss him. And he said . . . he said, "No! I don't want any of that queer stuff. Just fuck me!" Make sense of that. *[Light down on HUTTON and lights up on bedroom. Music is now coming from the stereo. JOHN is looking through STEVE's record collection.]*

JOHN: Fuck me! Abba! Bananarama! *[He finds the Jason Donovan calendar.]*

STEVE: *[Entering with two mugs]* You did say no sugar, didn't you? *[JOHN is embarrassesd at being caught.]* Here.

JOHN: Ta.

STEVE: Sit down. There's only the bed, I'm afraid. *[JOHN sits. Pause]* Is it okay?

JOHN: The bed?

STEVE: The tea.

JOHN: Oh. Yeah, great.

STEVE: Biscuit?

JOHN: No, thanks. Mind if I smoke?

STEVE: Well, I don't, but my parents—

JOHN: Oh yeah. Of course. Stupid of me.

STEVE: It's okay. I'll open a window.

JOHN: No. Don't worry.

STEVE: And I can whizz round with Mr. Sheen after you've gone.

JOHN: What?

STEVE: We haven't got any air freshener. My mum'll think I've been cleaning my room. I always use it after . . . people have been here.

JOHN: It's okay. Honest. As I said—filthy habit. Why don't you sit down?

STEVE: Thanks. I mean, okay. *[He perches uncomfortably on bed.]*

JOHN: *[Takes a biscuit]* Nice room.

STEVE: Thanks. *[They both drink and munch in silence.]*

JOHN: Do you fancy him, then?

STEVE: Who?

JOHN: Jason Donovan?

STEVE: Oh . . . well . . . sorry, I feel a bit embarrassed now.

JOHN: Why?

STEVE: Well, I've never really talked about it to a bloke before.

JOHN: It's alright. I'm just . . . interested. Intrigued. Well, do you fancy him?

STEVE: Jason? Well, I wouldn't kick him out of bed for *[notices JOHN is about to take a bite]* . . . anything.

JOHN: How long have you known . . . that you're . . .

STEVE: Dodgy? Well, I can remember . . . I remember going away with the cubs when I was eight. There was a dirty mag passing around—it was called *Big Ones*—and all the other boys, all the other eight-year-old boys, thought it was great and said things like "Fwoooor!" and decided which girl they most fancied. Then one boy—Tony Hatton—said quite openly to me, "Don't know what all the fuss is about. I'd rather see another boy's willy any day." And I said . . . "So would I." Looking back on it, he was offering me a "show me yours and I'll show you mine" situation. But I didn't realise. We went and flew a kite instead.

JOHN: Fuck me! Eight years old.

STEVE: *[Getting up to change the record]* Any requests?

JOHN: *[Making himself comfortable on the bed by moving up it so he is sitting with his back to the headboard]* Yeah! No more Abba.

STEVE: Jimmy Sommerville.

JOHN: Okay. I like some of their stuff.

STEVE: Ever listen to the lyrics?

JOHN: No. Good stuff, though. To dance to.

STEVE: *[Having put on a record, "There's More to Love," Bronski Beat]* Fancy a dance? Sorry, joke! *[STEVE sits next to JOHN.]*

JOHN: Do your parents know?

STEVE: No one knows officially. Except Linda. And you now. The wankers at school don't beat me up because I'm gay. They do it because I don't play football or smoke. Because I'm different. An easy target. If it wasn't me, it would be someone else.

JOHN: I'm sorry. *[He puts his hand on STEVE's leg.]*

STEVE: Sorry?

JOHN: Yeah. Worse than that, I feel guilty. I see what they do to you, and I want to help, but I can't. Sorry.

STEVE: Don't be. The other day was worse than usual. Because you were there, and they made me look a right tit . . . in front of . . . *[They stare at each other briefly.]*

STEVE: Where was I?

JOHN: Your parents.

STEVE: Oh yeah. I suppose I'll tell them one day. I don't think my dad will understand.

JOHN: Because he's Catholic?

STEVE: That's part of it. It's just that I don't think he'd . . . comprehend. I remember watching a film with him once. It was a western—he loves westerns—but this was a sort of send-up. Anyway, there was this red Indian in it who was as camp as a row of . . . wigwams! He was obviously dodgy, but the penny didn't drop with my dad until he started snogging this cowboy. I was sitting there wondering if this was how the Village People started when my dad said, "He's a gay!" Rather bravely I said, "So?" To which Daddy replied, "But he can't be. He's a red Indian!" You see, he couldn't cope with two stereotypes overlapping. So I guess he wouldn't cope with me being gay. I can't be, you see? I'm his son. That's my stereotype. My role. He would be as shocked as if I said, "Sit down, Dad. I've got something to tell you. I'm a red Indian." *[They laugh. JOHN moves his hand up STEVE's leg to his groin. JOHN puts his hand inside STEVE's trousers. STEVE rolls on top of JOHN, and briefly they fumble and grope. Then STEVE tries to kiss JOHN. JOHN suddenly pushes STEVE off and sits on the foot of the bed.]*

JOHN: Don't!

STEVE: What?

JOHN: I can't handle that.

STEVE: Kissing? Hey, don't panic. Lots of gay blokes don't like kissing.

JOHN: I'M NOT GAY! *[Pause]* Look, I'm sorry. I don't know why I'm here. I only came for a coffee.

STEVE: You don't like coffee.

JOHN: Stop being so fucking clever. *[Pause. JOHN sees STEVE is hurt.]* Look, I'm sorry. I'm really glad we talked, and I think it's great the way you cope, but . . . well, I guess I just made—

STEVE: A mistake. Me, too.

JOHN: I'd better go.

STEVE: I'll see you out.

JOHN: *[Getting up]* It's okay. I can manage. Bye. *[Leaves]*

STEVE: Look—

JOHN: *[Calling from offstage]* Just leave it!

STEVE: *[Calling after him from bedroom door]* John. John! Don't worry. I won't tell *[front door slams.]* . . . anyone. Promise. *[He picks up a can of Mr. Sheen and sprays the room as the music builds to a crescendo.]*

SCENE 9

[The music is cut off by the sound of the school bell, which signals the start of assembly. MR. AYRES stands at the front of the now-empty stage and addresses the audience as if they were the assembled boys. Behind him DAVE, KEV, STEVE, JOHN, and three other boys stand in a semicircle, frozen in half-light. Main light on AYRES only.]

MR. AYRES: Gentlemen. As usual at this last assembly of the year I have much to say to the outgoing sixth form. I would like to highly praise John Westhead and his Sixth Form Council for their sterling work during the last twelve months. I think particularly of the charity swim, which raised eight thousand pounds for those less fortunate than ourselves.

Once again we have high hopes that this year's exam results will be something to be proud of. Three boys have been offered places at Oxford or Cambridge and will carry thence the banner of English Martyrs and then to the world. These fine establishments will continue the work we have begun here, which, as you know, is not just making men of you but making gentlemen. Those of you going to the lesser universities will find that if you use your time wisely, you will find university life still the best preparation for life in the big, wide world. Always remember what you have been taught here. Make the most of any opportunity. *[JOHN looks at STEVE, who continues to look out front.]* When a golden opportunity presents itself and you miss it, you will regret it for the rest of your life. *[STEVE looks at JOHN, who looks away.]* Do not allow your life to become full of these regrets, these missed opportunities for happiness. Remember the school motto. *[Now JOHN and STEVE look at each other.]* "Carpe diem." Seize the day!

Gentlemen of the sixth form, and indeed you little gentlemen of the rest of the school, when you leave the safe and fostering world of these walls, you will become part of the adult world, a world which is becoming increasingly difficult. The values which you have been taught here are becoming more and more eroded by so-called liberals and do-gooders. You may find yourself ridiculed for believing in honest, hard work. As you watch the increasing number of spongers and hangers-on who get handouts from the state, you may wonder why you should work hard to support yourself and your family when the man next door gets free money to buy a video or some such item. Well, gentlemen, remember one word and you will never go wrong—dignity. Dignity is the one thing you must never lose. If you can look yourself in the eye—*[feeble joke]* in the mirror, of course—and say, "I respect you," then others will respect you, too.

You will have to confront people whose attitude I believe is called "right on." In fact, it is no longer right on to say, "Right on." We must now say, "Politically correct"! Politically correct means not opening a door to a lady. Not singing, "Baa! Baa! Black sheep." It's about talking about "spokespersons" and "chairpersons." Worst of all, it seems to be about ridiculing the values of the family.

Ah, boys! The family. God's greatest gift to personkind. Now you all come from good Catholic families. You all know the security and help that only a family can offer. Most of you will know the wonderful feeling of being able to turn to your father or mother and tell them your problems, any problems, and they will listen and help and advise you. Pity, then, those victims of a "liberal" society whose parents are separated or divorced, who do not know the balanced upbringing of a father and a mother.

Pity also those misguided people who insist that unnatural relationships are not only to be tolerated but encouraged. *[JOHN looks away from STEVE.]* In the words of a former prime minister, "We are living in a society where children are being taught that they have an inalienable right to be gay." Well, I am proud that we have never neglected to impart into your young minds those values inspired by the great Holy Family of Our Lord Jesus Christ and of the sanctity of womanhood as epitomised by Our Blessed Virgin Mary.

On the subject of the opposite sex, I have been prevailed upon by John Westhead to allow the first school discotheque to take place on these premises. I make this break from school policy to show my faith in the teaching you have had here. That you will not abuse yourselves in our school hall. That you will show the young ladies who come here how gentlemen behave. I must insist that no alcohol is to be consumed and that the hall is clear by 11:00 p.m.

Finally, may I ask John Westhead to come up on stage and accept the trophy for outgoing school captain. *[Applause. JOHN comes round the front of the stage and takes the trophy. Lights up on rest of stage as AYRES exits. Boys come to JOHN to congratulate him.]*

KEV: Well done, Johnny boy!

DAVE: Let's hold the famous trophy. *[There is general playing around with the trophy and laughter. STEVE watches from a distance.]*

KEV: What are you staring at, Carter.

STEVE: Nothing, I was just—

KEV: *[Approaching him aggressively]* Just what?

JOHN: Er . . . Kev. *[KEVIN stops. All the boys look at JOHN.]* Take this back to Pubic. It's got to go back in the display cabinet. *[He holds out the trophy to KEV, who looks at STEVE, then takes the trophy and exits. The other boys disperse, one of them kicking STEVE in the backside as he does. JOHN and STEVE remain.]*

STEVE: Thanks.

JOHN: What for?

STEVE: You know.

JOHN: Oh. Forget it. *[Pauses]* Catch you later. *[Exit JOHN. STEVE freezes.]*

SCENE 10

[Single light on STEVE. His parents come on and stand upstage of him. They freeze. As STEVE turns to look at them, the set changes to the living room in his home. Sofa. Armchair. Voice-over of AYRES: "Most of you will know the wonderful feeling of being able to turn to your father or mother and tell them your problems, any problems, and they will listen and help and advise you." As the lights come up, exit STEVE and DAD. LINDA enters and sits. MUM goes to the doorway.]

MUM: Steve. Steven! What are you doing up there? Linda's been here half an hour. You'll be late. Steven!

STEVE: *[Calling from offstage]* Coming. I'm coming!

MUM: What he does up there I'll never know. Probably cleaning his room again. He's forever cleaning his room!

LINDA: It's alright, Mrs. Carter. I'm early. Anyway, we don't want to get there too soon. It won't really get going till about 10:00. The girls all arrive on time and cling to the walls in bitchy groups while most of the blokes are at the pub. It's only towards the end that people get brave enough.

MUM: For what?

LINDA: You know . . . getting off.

MUM: Getting off where? *[Pause]* Oh! Getting OFF!

LINDA: It finishes at 11:00 as well! God! That last hour will be desperate.

MUM: Well, you and Steve can avoid the rush hour. You've got each other.

LINDA: Right.

MUM: Linda, love.

LINDA: Yes.

MUM: *[Sitting]* Talking about you and Steve. I hope you don't think I'm prying . . . but I'm worried.

LINDA: Oh?

MUM: You're very close to Steven, aren't you?

LINDA: Very.

MUM: This is so delicate. I really can't bring myself to speak to him about it. You see . . . I know.

LINDA: My God!

MUM: It's alright, love. Steven's father and I have always tried to have an open attitude to these things. Mainly because he's an only child. We want him to have a healthy attitude to sex. But I do worry.

LINDA: Really, Mrs. Carter. I think you should talk to Steven about it.

MUM: But Linda. It's your problem really.

LINDA: It's not a problem.

MUM: Oh, but it could be. And . . . well, call me old-fashioned, but it's your responsibility in the end. Men don't worry about these things.

LINDA: What things?

MUM: Babies, Linda. Babies. As I was saying, it's obvious that Steven and you are very close. That you must . . . "get off" from time to time. You're both at an age where you may want to go further. It's natural. But just be careful, Linda. We'd love a grandchild, but not just yet!

LINDA: *[Relieved]* Thank God! Er . . . thank God you're so open about . . . it!

MUM: Just you be safe.

LINDA: Don't worry. Steven and I are safer than you can possibly imagine.

MUM: Good girl. *[Calling from door]* Steven, will you hurry up? It's supposed to be the girl who keeps the boy waiting. And I've got a train to catch.

LINDA: Where are you going?

MUM: London. Brian's mother really is very low. She probably won't last the weekend. Marvellous old woman. So wise. She usually ends up comforting us when we visit! The other day she said, "Don't worry about me, dear. I've enjoyed my life. I've had good kids, and they've given me wonderful grandchildren. That's what it's all about," she said. "Life. Seeing your grandchildren before you pop off so you know it's all going to continue. That you've done something for the world." She's so right.

LINDA: I suppose that Steven has a great responsibility to you . . . being an only child and that.

MUM: How do you mean?

LINDA: Well, what if he didn't want children?

MUM: Don't be silly, love. Everyone wants children. Just not right now, okay!

STEVE: *[Entering. He should have on a white T-shirt.]* Taraaagh! Will I do?

LINDA: You'll do for me.

MUM: Overdone it with the aftershave, though.

STEVE: Don't you start.

LINDA: It's not as if you need to shave!

STEVE: Bitch!

MUM: Steven! That's no way to talk to a lady!

STEVE: I'm talking to Linda. Anyway, just think of it as my "instead-of shave."

MUM: You know what your father says when you put too much on.

LINDA: What?

MUM: He says, "My God, Steven. You smell like a bloody poof."

LINDA: Really?

STEVE: I've told him, "Dad, it says, 'For Men' on the bottle. 'Savage Instinct, Pour Hommes.'" He says, "Funny sort of *hommes* if you ask me."

MUM: Well, have a nice time the pair of you. I'll ring if there's any news. *[Kisses STEVE]* Bye, Linda, and remember what I said to you. *[Exit]*

STEVE: Oh, yeah. "What is't, Ophelia, she hath said to you?"

LINDA: You'll never believe it. I nearly died. I thought she was going to ask if you were gay. Instead, it seems she's scared shitless you're going to get me pregnant.

STEVE: Blimey. What did you say?

LINDA: I told her we were always safe!

STEVE: "Homosexuality. The ultimate contraceptive."

LINDA: I thought that was your aftershave.

STEVE: Piss off. I'm a real *homme,* I am. It says so on the bottle. Now come on. You're making us late.

LINDA: Steve, do you think you'll ever, well . . . would you like a child?

STEVE: No, thanks. I've eaten already. *[They exit.]*

SCENE 11

[The lights change to the disco. Stage changes to a bare space. Music: "Bring Your Daughter to the Slaughter" by Iron Maiden. STEVE and LINDA exit. A

few girls come on and dance timidly. Some boys, including KEV and DAVE,
prowl around them in a circle. A few seconds of this, then KEV and DAVE break
downstage to a table with soft drinks on it. The lights change again, and the
music becomes quieter as it is now coming from an adjacent room. The lights of
the disco can be seen flashing next door.]

KEV: What a fucking disaster!

DAVE: It's early yet.

KEV: Bollocks it is! It's 10:30. Hardly anyone's dancing.

DAVE: John's dancing. Still, it's alright for him. He's good at it.

KEV: Yeah! I just look like I've got a food mixer stuck up my arse. How am I supposed to pull looking like that?

DAVE: *[Offering him a drink]* Don't panic. Try this.

KEV: Please! No more soft drinks! I'm pissing Coke. I hate the stuff.

DAVE: Not this stuff you won't. Go on; try it.

KEV: *[Takes a swig]* Wow! Now that's what I call the real thing! How did you—

DAVE: Forward planning. I stashed a bottle of whisky in the loo earlier today.
Everytime I feel like a top-up, I go to the bog!

KEV: Clever cunt! *[Goes for another swig]*

DAVE: Hey, go easy! *[Takes back the drink]*

JOHN: *[Entering from disco. He should also wear a white shirt.]* God, I'm pissed!

DAVE: How are you getting on with Jenny?

JOHN: Oh, she's playing the fucking ice maiden as usual. Thawing, though. She
actually danced with me just now. Well, I think it was me. She looked at me a
couple of times.

KEV: Fiver says you don't pull her.

JOHN: Done! Watch this, men. *[Empties his glass quickly. Goes towards disco.*
STEVE and LINDA enter from the disco, where they have been dancing. STEVE
and JOHN bump into each other. They look at each other briefly as LINDA con-
tinues to the table. JOHN continues into the disco. DAVE does, too. STEVE slowly
goes back to the door to the disco, and through it he watches JOHN dance offstage.
LINDA continues to the table, and KEVIN hones in on her.]

KEV: Hi. I'm Kevin. And you are?

LINDA: Thirsty. Steve! *[He ignores her.]*

KEV: Hi. Having a good time?

LINDA: Until five seconds ago. Steve. Coke? Steve. Save me!

KEV: Fancy a real drink?

LINDA: No, thanks.

KEV: Something else. Er . . . Diet Coke? *[She ignores him. Pause.]* You're not a bad-
looking girl, you know. I mean, just because you're a bit . . .

LINDA: Fat.

KEV: Big. I mean, cuddly. I like cuddly girls.

LINDA: *[To herself]* Jesus! Steven. Oh, for God's sake!

KEV: So . . . Kirsty, what are you doing after? Fancy a kebab?

LINDA: I don't think so.

KEV: Well, I could see you home. Where did you say you lived?

LINDA: I didn't. Anyway, Steven's seeing me home.

KEV: Steven? *[Looks at STEVE, who is still looking at the dance floor]* You mean you and Carter . . . fuck me!

LINDA: No, thanks.

KEV: Your loss, darling.

LINDA: I'll live.

KEV: *[Meeting STEVE as he goes towards the disco]* So you're not a bender after all, Carter. Still, not exactly an oil painting, is she?

LINDA: *[Hearing this and going over to him]* No, she's not. She's cuddly, and until a few seconds ago you assumed in your superior, male, egotistical way that because I am a fat girl instead of a slim oil painting, I should be gagging for the delights of a quick shish followed by a quick grope.

STEVE: Linda!

LINDA: Because, mate, there are only fifteen minutes to go and you haven't pulled yet. I can't imagine why! What girl, especially a fat, unattractive girl, could resist you? Fag breath, shit-for-brains, and zits, too! I can just imagine sex with you. The pathetic fumbling to undo a bra strap. The slobbery kisses. Belching into some poor girl's mouth because you've had too much chili sauce. And then the main event, which is either over in seconds or not at all because you're too fucking pissed!

KEV: Shall I take that as a definite no?

STEVE: Take it up your bum!

KEV: I thought that was your boyfriend's department. *[About to go]* Oi, Carter. Why did God make poofs? So that fat women would have someone to go out with. *[Exit to disco]*

STEVE: Calm down, Lins.

LINDA: God! His sort make me sick. Just because he's got a willy, he thinks he's God's gift to womankind.

STEVE: Personkind.

LINDA: What?

STEVE: Nothing. Anyway, he's not that bad. One of the better ones. He's probably pissed. I found a bottle of whisky in the bog earlier today. Guess what I did.

LINDA: Shock me.

STEVE: I poured some of it away.

LINDA: Ooooh! You devil!

STEVE: And pissed in the bottle.

LINDA: I'm shocked.

STEVE: Revenge is mine!

LINDA: You evil little git. *[Pause]* How's the beautiful John doing with Jenny Keeley?

STEVE: How should I know?

LINDA: Well, I assume that's who you were staring at while I was being chatted up by something out of Jurassic Park.

STEVE: God! He's such a good dancer.

LINDA: Babes! Stop torturing yourself. He's straight. And stop staring at him.

STEVE: I can't. Anyway. He stares back.

LINDA: In your wildest dreams!

STEVE: Lins . . . Oh, God. I've got to tell someone. What the fuck! You see, yesterday—

LINDA: *[A dance record begins next door. It should be raunchy, rhythmic, and sexy. Suggested track: "Ride on Time" by Black Box.]* Oh! I love this one. Come on! Let's dance.

STEVE: I don't feel like it.

LINDA: Oh, stop feeling so sorry for yourself! *[Exit to dance floor]*

SCENE 12

[Empty space. We are in the disco. For a few seconds we see JOHN dancing on his own. He dances powerfully and erotically. Lights up on the rest of the disco-goers. Then KEVIN dancing as if he has a food mixer up his arse. He tries to dance with several girls. One of them slaps his face. Light on STEVE just watching. Then JOHN and JENNY dance together erotically. STEVE turns away and begins to move to the music. Eventually we see various pools of light with individuals dancing in them. STEVE begins to dance brilliantly. Eventually he and JOHN are dancing separately but identically, suggestive of sex.]

D.J.: *[Voice only.]* Well, I'm afraid that's all we have time for, boys and girls. Please could you be as quiet as possible as you leave the premises. Now come on, guys. What are you waiting for? Grab the girl of your dreams for the last dance. Don't be shy. Boy meets girl. It's what makes the world go round! *[Slow record. Suggested track: "The First Time Ever I Saw Your Face" by Roberta Flack. JOHN makes an elaborate show of asking JENNY to dance while others watch admiringly. Eventually everyone pairs off. LINDA asks STEVE to dance, but he moves away to watch JOHN and JENNY. KEVIN hones in on LINDA, who slaps his face. JOHN and JENNY kiss, and STEVE turns away, unable to watch. For awhile both LINDA and STEVE are isolated as the others smooch. Eventually STEVE and LINDA dance. The lighting becomes ultraviolet so that only JOHN and STEVE in their white shirts are starkly visible. Although they are dancing with their respective partners, the suggestion is that they are dancing with each other. Just as the music ends and the lights return to normal, JOHN is kissing JENNY and STEVE is trying to kiss LINDA.]*

LINDA: *[Pushing him away]* Hey! Don't you start.

STEVE: Sorry. I thought you were someone else.

LINDA: Charming. I'll get our coats. Alright if I call a cab from your place? *[Exit. STEVE turns round to see JOHN on his own staring at him.]*

STEVE: Hi.

JOHN: Having a good time?

STEVE: Great. You?

JOHN: Great. How's your nan?

STEVE: Just about hanging on. My parents have gone to London to be with her.

JOHN: Oh. Sorry.

STEVE: You're a wonderful dancer.

JOHN: You, too.

JENNY: *[Entering with her jacket.]* Come on, Head Boy. How about that curry, then?

JOHN: Oh . . . sure. Er, Jenny, this is Steve. Steve, Jenny.

JENNY: Hallo.

STEVE: *[Ignoring her]* I'd better go. Linda's waiting. Have a nice . . . curry. *[Exit]*

JENNY: Rude little boy.

JOHN: He's alright.

JENNY: How about it, then. The place by the cinema's good.

JOHN: What? Oh. Listen, Jenny, I wonder if you'd mind if we didn't. . . . I mean, I've got a bit of a headache.

JENNY: That's supposed to be my line.

JOHN: And I really should help clear up here.

KEVIN: *[Overhearing]* That's alright, mate. We can manage. Anyway, got nothing better to do. *[To JENNY]* What's the matter with the girls at your place? Frigid or what?

JENNY: There we are, John. Your charming friend has offered to stand in for you. And I'm sure I can find a way to soothe your poor little head. *[She tries to touch him.]*

JOHN: Back off!

JENNY: I'm sorry. I just thought—

JOHN: Well, you thought wrong! Leave it. Okay! Just leave it! And as for you *[to KEVIN]*, you can stand in for me wherever you like. *[Exit]*

KEVIN: Hey! That's a fiver you owe me. *[Turns to JENNY]* You heard the man. Fancy a kebab? *[She slaps him and exits.]* Shit!

SCENE 13

[Light up on HUTTON. Music: "Everybody Hurts" by R.E.M.]

HUTTON: Shit! Shit! What can I tell you? Seize the day. For fuck's sake, seize the day. Seize it! Grab it! Enjoy it! *[The lights change, and we are in STEVE's bedroom. STEVE and LINDA sit on the end of the bed staring into space.]*

LINDA: Well, I don't see what all the fuss is about. If you ask me, they deserve each other. Two spoilt little rich kids. Superior, arrogant—

STEVE: Don't! Don't talk about him like that. He's not like that.

LINDA: Sorry I spoke! *[Pause]* Just trying to cheer you up.

STEVE: Don't bother. I'm uncheerupable. I want to die.

LINDA: God! It really does get boring sometimes. You don't have a monopoly on rejection, you know. At least you're not me.

STEVE: Cuddly.

LINDA: Sweetheart. I am not cuddly, not a big girl, not well rounded. I am absolutely fucking enormous. The only offers I get are from dickheads like Kevin "Shit-for-brains" and even then only after he's tried every other girl in the place. At the end of the evening. Dancing with the desperate.

[Together after a pause]

LINDA & STEVE: Men!

LINDA: So you see, I've got more to hate Jenny Keeley for than you.

STEVE: That's all you know.

LINDA: So what don't I know.

STEVE: Nothing.

Can't say. I promised. You wouldn't believe me anyway. I'm not sure I believe me!

LINDA: *[Doorbell rings]* Suit yourself. That's my cab. *[Kisses him]* Thanks for tonight, babe. And forget about John Westhead. Plenty more sharks in the sea. *[Pause]* You're a really good dancer, you know?

STEVE: So I'm told.

LINDA: *[Doorbell again]* Okay, okay, I'm coming. Love ya!

STEVE: Me, too! *[Exit LINDA. STEVE gets up and starts getting undressed. The front door slams. Footsteps are heard coming upstairs. STEVE is examining his face in the mirror in the fourth wall.]* Did you forget something? *[He freezes, looking in the mirror as JOHN enters. Slowly he turns, and JOHN moves slowly into the room. They stare at each other.]*

JOHN: Help . . . me. Please. PLEASE HELP ME!

[Music crescendo. Slow blackout.]

Act Two

SCENE 14

[Lights slowly up. Gay disco. Music: "Macho Man" by Sinitta. Several men dance aggressively but very well. The one in the middle should be wearing a leather jacket. The lighting is sporadic, so it is some time before we realise that it is HUTTON. Eventually the music stops very abruptly. The other men freeze in semidarkness, and HUTTON alone is lit.]

HUTTON: Out. Out. What does it mean? In the closet. Out of the closet. Into the ghetto. Simon Hutton, by day mild-mannered teacher of history, by night the dancing queen. I used to love the scene. When I was growing up in the closet-dom of Croydon, I couldn't wait until I was old enough to go to London all on my own. London, with its bars and its clubs. London, where the streets were paved with men. Where I wouldn't have to be afraid anymore. Where I wouldn't have to hide. I was nineteen when I plucked up the courage to go to a gay club. To "Heaven." Christ, I didn't know there were that many gay people in the whole world. I was young then. And that night, for the first time in my life I realised that not only was I young, but I was beautiful. Desirable. Wanted. I realised I didn't have to do it with the first old queen who flashed at me in a cottage. But I was young and vulnerable, and even there I was still afraid. I still wanted to hide. But something kept me there and has kept me going back for years. The beat. *[Music: "Cruising" by Sinitta]* A rhythmic pulse from the dance floor which was exciting and defiant and was . . . sex. I was drawn to the flashing lights, and as I stood by the dance floor, I noticed something else. A smell. A strange, exotic smell. It was a mixture of beer and sweat and amyl nitrate and a million different aftershaves. But most excitingly, most seductively of all, it was the unmistakable, undeniable smell . . . of men. *[The men come forward to join HUTTON.]* This was where I belonged. Here, among others, so many others like me. Open, happy, uninhibited. No more shame. Oh, Steve. It used to be so exciting. In the eighties it was all "high-energy." Gay music. Angry, defiant music. I was young and sexy and no one had ever heard of acquired immune deficiency syndrome. Sex was as easy as dancing. We used to dance to a song called "So Many Men, So Little Time." Jesus. I still go to clubs now. Why? Because that's where I still belong. And, Steven, I expect you will find that's where you belong. *[The dancing men are now still, in couples.]*

MAN 1: I haven't seen you here before.

MAN 2: No. I don't like these places.

MAN 1: Oh, me neither. I hate the scene.

MAN 3: *[Separate group]* You don't look like a Sagittarian.

MAN 4: Well, I'm not typical.

MAN 1: It's all so shallow, don't you think?

MAN 2: Very shallow. People just don't talk to each other.

MAN 1: Oh, I know!

MAN 3: Do you live in London?

MAN 4: Yes. But . . . I live with my boyfriend.

MAN 1: It's very cynical. People only come here for sex. Sex, sex, sex!

MAN 3: I live in London, too.

MAN 4: Good.

MAN 3: On my own.

MAN 4: Good.

MAN 2: Sex, sex, sex. I sometimes think it's all gay men think about.

MAN 1: Oh, I know.

MAN 4: Do you have a car?

MAN 3: No.

MAN 4: Oh.

MAN 1: It's so shallow.

MAN 2: Cynical.

MAN 1: Meaningless. *[Pause]* Would you like to spank me?

MAN 3: You're really cute.

MAN 1: Tie me up?

MAN 3: Lovely eyes.

MAN 1: Cover me in cling-film?

MAN 3: What travel zone are you? *[Lights down on men]*

HUTTON: But that's the choice. In the closet or on the scene. At least on the scene you can pretend you're happy. Even at my age. Even when you're not beautiful anymore. A few pints inside you, turn the music up, stick a bottle of poppers up your nose, and you can conquer the world. And besides . . . everyone looks beautiful in ultraviolet.

SCENE 15

[During the last speech the bedroom set has returned. JOHN and STEVE are standing as they were at the end of Act One.]

JOHN: Please. Help me. I need . . . I need to use your loo.

STEVE: Didn't they have one in the Star of Bengal?

JOHN: What? Oh. I wasn't hungry. *[Shows him a bottle of whisky]* I found this. Have some if you like.

STEVE: Er . . . no thanks. First on the right.

JOHN: *[Exiting]* Thanks.

STEVE: *[When JOHN exits, STEVE picks up his shirt but can't decide if he should put it on. In the end he does. Picks up his aftershave and puts some on. Reads the bottle. Puts more on.]* Carpe diem. Carpe diem. *[Picks up the whisky but quickly puts it down. Leaps on bed in time to look nonchalant as JOHN enters.]*

JOHN: *[Entering]* That girl—Linda?—she gave me such a strange look.

STEVE: She's good at those.

JOHN: And then she said, "Men!" and got into a cab. What did she mean?

STEVE: Oh, she's just being . . . Linda. *[JOHN goes to pick up the whisky.]* Er, I don't think you should drink that.

JOHN: You don't approve?

STEVE: No. I just think you've had enough.

JOHN: I haven't had nearly enough.

STEVE: *[They are both now holding the bottle and struggling for it.]* Please, John. Don't. I—

JOHN: Fuck off.

STEVE: Look, I really think—*[The bottle falls on the floor and spills. Pause.]* Ooops! Another job for Mr. Sheen. *[JOHN sinks to his knees and begins to cry.]* Sorry. Look, it's only a bottle of whisky. I'll buy you another one. With no extra additives.

JOHN: Please. Help me! Please. I'm so scared. So fucking scared.

STEVE: I know.

JOHN: And confused.

STEVE: I know.

JOHN: You don't fucking know. You're not confused. What gives you the right to be not confused?

STEVE: I'm getting there. *[JOHN suddenly kisses him aggressively.]* Coffee?

JOHN: I don't like coffee.

STEVE: You don't like kissing. *[They look at each other and kiss again, this time much more slowly and affectionately.]*

JOHN: The other day in the toilet—you see, when I said it was the first time, I wasn't lying. It was the first time . . . in there. But . . . but it wasn't the first time ever. *[He doesn't look at STEVE as he talks.]* Last summer. Brighton. Amanda. God, I'm so pissed.

STEVE: Take your time.

JOHN: Me and Amanda. My ex-girlfriend. We went to Brighton for a week last summer. It was lovely. Walks along the beach. Kissing in the moonlight. All that romantic crap. Sounds naff, doesn't it?

STEVE: Sounds wonderful.

JOHN: One night Amanda had to go and visit some relatives or something, so I went and had a drink on my own. I was walking back to the hotel along the beach, and I got to the old pier, you know, the derelict one. As I was walking under it, I noticed a couple of blokes in the shadows. I remember clenching my keys in my hand so I could deck them if they tried to mug me. But then . . . then I noticed that there weren't two of them. In the shadows, behind the pillars, everywhere . . . there were men. I stopped. I still don't know why. And then I moved behind a pillar and watched. And . . . and I realised that I was . . . you know . . . aroused. I thought it was just the mystery, the danger. But then this bloke creeps over to me. And I look at him, and even in the dark I can see that his eyes . . . his eyes are beautiful. Beautiful, challenging men's eyes. And he puts his hand on my . . . and I'm scared and drunk, but I'm thinking . . . yes . . . do it . . . do it. And he tries to kiss me and I pull away and he takes his hand away but . . . but I grab it . . . and put it back on my . . . and he starts to undo my fly buttons, but he's clumsy and I do it for him. And he takes it out and starts . . . slowly at first . . . then faster. Suddenly I freaked and ran . . . and ran as fast as I could trying to stick my . . . back in my . . . and I got to the hotel. Amanda was asleep. But I woke her up . . . and I fucked her. And fucked her. I fucked her. But I wasn't seeing her eyes. I was seeing men's eyes. Challenging, mocking men's eyes. *[Pause]* For the rest of the week, every night, I had to keep going back. I found excuses to go out on my own at night—to get cigarettes, clear my head, anything. During the day I told myself I wouldn't, but the thought of what was going on under that haunted, mysterious building drew me back night after night.

STEVE: "Pier" pressure.

JOHN: I usually just watched. But on the last night it happened. With the same bloke as the first night. Those eyes . . . Jesus. They seemed to look into my . . . Anyway, this time I didn't stop. And it was wonderful and dangerous and so, so exciting.

STEVE: Oh, Johnny.

JOHN: But half an hour later I was lying by my girlfriend trying to explain why I didn't want to make love to her . . . and I felt dishonest and frightened and so fucking dirty. And I vowed to myself never, ever to do it again. And I haven't. I really don't know why I . . . with you. And I'm straight. I love sex with girls. But now I can't help thinking . . . Steven, if you ever breathe a word of this, I'll—

STEVE: I won't. I . . . like you too much.

JOHN: I like you, too. It's just . . . oh God. What's wrong with me? *[He cries.]*

STEVE: Shhh! Don't worry. It's alright. Shhh.

JOHN: God. I'm so drunk. *[STEVE lays JOHN down on the bed and goes to put some music on. Suggested track: "The First Time" by Roberta Flack. He turns the light off so the only light is moonlight.]*

STEVE: Listen. You can . . . I mean, don't think I'm . . . but you can . . . if you want . . . you can stay here tonight. You can sleep in here and I'll go into—

JOHN: Don't leave me. Please. Please.

STEVE: Okay. *[They stare at each other and then kiss. STEVE starts to caress JOHN slowly.]*

JOHN: *[Whispering]* Yes. Yes. Do it.

STEVE: *[Whispering]* Johnny. There's nothing wrong with you.

[Lights down on them as they lie down on the bed. Lights up on HUTTON.]

SCENE 16

HUTTON: It can be so beautiful, Steven. I was so in love once. Beautiful. He was. Romance. He kept . . . again and again. I'd be so scared . . . fumbling in the dark . . . silent sex . . . and he'd say . . . no, I can't. And I never used to mind because HE was there, and I really only wanted . . . touch . . . hold him . . . see those eyes. And I'd kiss him on the forehead . . . safe sex . . . and go to sleep. And then I'd wake up because he'd be all over me . . . and then he'd stop and say he couldn't . . . and I felt . . . dirty . . . MY fault. It went on for years. But the confusion, it was made bearable by . . . the love. Love. The beautiful moments. By the sea once. He was standing on a jetty looking out to the ocean. And he turned to face me . . . and behind him the most incredible sunset exploding on the water in a blaze of colour. And there in front of me . . . the most beautiful . . . angel . . . eyes . . . perfection. And I felt a surge inside me which was nothing to do with my . . . Overwhelming. Privileged. Moment in time. And I cried because of the impossibility of that moment. And it happened to me. It HAPPENED. To ME. Fuck the sex. Live the romance, Steve. Live the love.

[Lights up on the bed. JOHN is asleep. Radio alarm goes off.]

RADIO: —report on this beautiful Sunday morning. I've got a request for Julie on her birthday. Julie, Derek says he loves you very much and that the last year and a half have been the happiest of his life. *[Music: "Happy Birthday Sweet Sixteen" Neil Sedaka. JOHN wakes slowly. Turns off the radio.]*

JOHN: Steven.

STEVE: *[Calling from offstage]* I'm getting breakfast. I'm afraid we had all the bacon yesterday.

JOHN: What time are your parents due back?

STEVE: They're back. They're down here with me.

JOHN: Shit!

STEVE: Mum says if you make an honest man of me, she'll help you choose the curtains.

JOHN: You wanker! Wanker. Steve. Can I let my parents know I'll be home soon?

STEVE: How soon?

JOHN: Look, I've been here all weekend. I told them I was at Kevin's. Can I?

STEVE: Be my guest.

JOHN: Ta. *[As he dials and waits for an answer, he picks up and examines a half-empty bottle of baby oil from beside the bed.]* Hi, Mum. Listen, I'm still at Kevin's, but I'll . . . What? When? . . . Oh, er . . . well, we had a bit of a row last night, and I . . . I went and stayed at Dave's. I've . . . I've just come back here this morning. *[Pause]* Who? Oh, Jenny. Yes, she is nice. . . . You did what? No. Sorry. Of course. *[Pause]* Look, apologise to Dad for worrying him. I'm really sorry. I'll be home for lunch. . . . Look, I must go. I'm on someone else's . . . I mean, Kevin's phone. See you later. *[Puts down phone]* Shit. Shit!

STEVE: *[Entering]* Marmalade or honey?

JOHN: Oh . . . I'm not fussed.

STEVE: *[Sitting on edge of bed and pouring tea]* You know, I was thinking about what you said about going away together this summer. What about Brighton? It would be—*[He stops as he notices that JOHN is trying to put his underpants on under the covers.]* What are you doing?

JOHN: Getting dressed.

STEVE: But why—why so shy all of a sudden? We've been making love all weekend, and now you don't want me to see your willy?

JOHN: Just leave it alone, will you?

STEVE: It's you who can't leave it alone. *[Pause. As STEVE returns to the tea, JOHN comes forward on the bed and hugs STEVE from behind.]*

JOHN: Sorry. *[Kisses him on cheek]* It's just . . . this is all so . . . strange.

STEVE: You'll get used to it. *[JOHN continues to dress.]*

JOHN: I won't . . . it's . . . not me.

STEVE: Who is it, then?

JOHN: Even if I got used to the . . . sex, I couldn't get used to the lying. Apparently Kevin rang last night.

STEVE: Shit.

JOHN: I think I managed to squirm out of it with my mum. But I hated lying to her. She and Dad have been worried sick.

STEVE: Sorry.

JOHN: And Jenny rang as well, and Mum gave her Kevin's number. What am I going to say to her? Or Kevin? And then there's that Linda. What if she—

STEVE: She won't say anything.

JOHN: *[Taking STEVE's hand]* Steve. I'm scared. I've never had to cover up about what I do before.

STEVE: What about Brighton pier?

JOHN: That was different.

STEVE: Because you only came once that time?

JOHN: There's no need to rub it in.

STEVE: Yes there is. It's good for the complexion.

JOHN: What? Oh. *[Pause]* Is it?

STEVE: So I'm told.

JOHN: Listen, Steve—

STEVE: No. You listen, Johnny. Sod it. This can't work.

JOHN: Why?

STEVE: Because of all you've just said. Look, since you got here on Friday, you've come on to me, come on me in five seconds flat, told me you enjoyed it but wouldn't like to do it again, then done it again. Every time we make it, you tell me you have too much to lose by being gay, or you have to make some crappy statement about how you prefer girls. Ramming your sexuality down my throat. And then you get horny again. And ram something else down my throat. Basically I don't know if you're coming or going.

JOHN: *[Holding him]* I'm sorry. Please, give me a chance. *[STEVE laughs.]* What's the matter?

STEVE: If you knew how long . . . how many nights . . . and you're asking ME to give YOU a chance.

JOHN: Well?

STEVE: Tomorrow night? If my parents are still away.

JOHN: Great. I'd better go now.

STEVE: Okay. Thank you for . . . coming.

JOHN: Thank you for having me. *[They laugh and embrace. Freeze. Light on HUTTON only.]*

HUTTON: I saw two men . . . once . . . opposite sides of the road. Knew each other. "Oi. Cunt!" said one. "Fucking wanker," said the other. Guess that meant "Nice to see you, my friend." If only men could . . . but . . . still the easiest way one man can prove he's better than another . . . is to stand in an arena and hit him so many times that he draws blood or so hard that he obliterates his brain cells and he falls over. All in the name of sport. And yet me . . . you, Steven . . . us . . . love . . . affection . . . *[Lights up on the two boys still embracing]* An act of gross indecency.

STEVE: You're beautiful. *[Boys kiss as light goes down on them.]*

SCENE 17

[Immediately light up on MR. CARTER in a hospital phone booth]

DAD: Hallo. Steven? Listen, I've got bad news. *[Pause]* Yes. This morning. In her sleep. She was quite peaceful. *[Pause]* What? Sorry, son, I can't hear you properly. Listen, I haven't got much change. I want you to come to London for the funeral. *[Pause]* Tuesday, but I want you to come tomorrow. *[Pause]* What's the problem? Your exams are over now. . . . Anyway, we'll be back on Thursday. *[Pause]* Listen, Steven, I'm not asking you; I'm telling you. She was your bloody grandmother, for Christ's sake. If it wasn't for her . . . anyway, the whole family will be here. *[Pause]* What do you mean "Oh, the family." Yes, the family, your family. Now get the train tomorrow. And ring the school. *[Pause]* What? Yes, bring her if you like. And Steven, bring a tie. *[Pause]* No, not a family tie, just a tie. A black tie. *[He puts down the phone. The light fades on him as the schoolbell rings.]*

SCENE 18

[Lights up on JOHN and KEVIN smoking in the school smoker's corner.]

KEVIN: It's okay, mate. I understand.

JOHN: But I was well out of order.

KEVIN: Yes, you were, you wanker.

JOHN: I just felt so . . . pressured. Like every fucker at the disco was thinking, "Is he going to pull her?" Like it was inevitable. Beautiful-looking bird like Jenny. Beautiful guy like me.

KEVIN: Whoever said you were beautiful?

JOHN: You'd be surprised. Anyway, it just felt like I was going through it to prove something.

KEVIN: But you do fancy her?

JOHN: Of course I do. She's great. I rang her last night, and she's forgiven me.

KEVIN: Really? You're a lucky man. So I owe you a fiver. Typical bloody Johnny Westhead happy ending.

JOHN: I'm not sure. I mean, I'm not sure I want to get involved.

KEVIN: Who said you had to get involved. Just get IN.

JOHN: She's not that kind of girl.

KEVIN: Is it Amanda?

JOHN: What?

KEVIN: Well, ever since you two split up last summer, you don't seem . . . how can I put this . . . well, you don't seem very interested in . . . girls.

JOHN: What are you getting at? I love girls. I do.

KEVIN: Okay, okay. Keep your hair on. I'm just trying to say you're still hung up about Amanda, that's all.

JOHN: Look, I don't want to talk about it. Okay. I'm sorry I behaved the way I did to you at the disco. Now let's drop it. Okay?

KEVIN: Okay.

JOHN: Okay.

KEVIN: I'm sorry, too. For dropping you in it with your parents.

JOHN: Forget it. You weren't to know where I was.

KEVIN: No, I wasn't, was I? *[Pause]* Johnny?

JOHN: Yeah.

KEVIN: Where were you? *[Notices HUTTON approaching]* Shit! *[They quickly get rid of the cigarettes and fan the smoke away.]*

HUTTON: *[Entering]* Ah, John. There you are.

JOHN: Sir. We were just—

HUTTON: Having a fag. Listen, I've got a message for you. Steven Carter rang in to say his grandmother died.

JOHN: So?

HUTTON: Don't be too sympathetic, will you? He's had to go to London for the funeral.

JOHN: Why are you telling me?

HUTTON: He just wanted you to know he can't make tonight, that's all. Just passing on the message, John.

JOHN: Er . . . thank you, sir. *[Exit HUTTON. Awkward pause.]* I . . . er . . . I told Carter I'd let him have my . . . history notes. For next year.

KEVIN: Right.

JOHN: I was going to . . . meet him to . . . history notes.

KEVIN: Right.

JOHN: Well, catch you later.

KEVIN: Right.

JOHN: Right. *[Pause]* You're right about Jenny. I'm a lucky guy.

KEVIN: Yeah. See you. *[JOHN and KEVIN exit to opposite sides of the stage very slowly as a church bell strikes. Lights change to a single shaft of light. Almost "heavenly."]*

SCENE 19

[Bell continues. STEVE, his parents, LINDA, a priest, and various relatives walk on slowly as if following a coffin. Tableau of family round a grave. Bell

stops and lights change to interior of a suburban house. Sofa, table with drinks on it. As the light change happens, STEVE breaks suddenly downstage, followed by LINDA. The rest form small groups having conversations.]

LINDA: You alright, babe?

STEVE: Yeah. Sorry. All that crap the priest came out with got on my tits. He didn't even know her. He got her bloody name wrong twice. God, and all my relatives looking suitably grief stricken. None of them bothered with her while she was ill.

LINDA: Your mum and dad were good to her, though.

STEVE: I know.

LINDA: They looked after her.

STEVE: I know.

LINDA: They're special.

STEVE: I know!

LINDA: *[Pause]* Steve. There's something else, isn't there. Something bugging you. *[Pause]* It's John, isn't it?

STEVE: Yes. Yes. Yes. Oh God, Lins, I'm so in love. I'm so happy. I feel guilty for feeling happy here, but I just want to yell it out—"John Westhead loves me!"

LINDA: How do you know?

STEVE: Because we've done it. Loads. And he loved it. He loved me.

LINDA: Oh, Steve.

STEVE: Look, Linda. Why can't you just be happy for me? I want to share this feeling with everyone, my mum, my dad, but I can't. So why can't you just—*[He notices GEORGE.]* Oh, shit, it's him.

LINDA: Who?

STEVE: Cousin George. He's about to come and talk to us. He's twenty-two and he's got the lot—company car, company girlfriend. And he says irritating things like "*Pas de probleme*" and "I'll give you a bell later in the week." And he calls me—

GEORGE: *[Coming over]* Einstein? How you hanging?

STEVE: Hallo, George.

GEORGE: How are the old exams going?

STEVE: They've gone.

GEORGE: You confident?

STEVE: *Pas de probleme.*

GEORGE: *[To LINDA]* Sorry, you must be?

STEVE: Sorry. George, this is Linda. Linda, this is boring. *[STEVE goes and stands aloof.]*

GEORGE: What's eating him?

LINDA: Oh, he's just thinking about his man. I mean nan.

GEORGE: Yeah. God bless her, wherever she is. *[Pause]* So you're Einstein's girlie. I've heard a lot about you.

LINDA: I've heard a lot about you.

GEORGE: All bad I hope.

LINDA: Yes.

GEORGE: I must say you're a bit of a surprise.

LINDA: Must you?

GEORGE: Yeah. Well, strictly between you and me, we were all a bit worried about Steven. Bit of a late starter. In the girlie department. Still, looks like you've made an honest man of him.

LINDA: No need for that. *[Lights down on rest of the stage. Light only on STEVE. The relatives talk to each other in small groups.]*

MUM: Well, yes, Steven was always a bit shy when it came to the opposite sex.

DAD: Linda's a lovely girl.

RELATIVE 1: It was a lovely service.

RELATIVE 2: We couldn't get a babysitter.

PRIEST: So many flowers.

RELATIVE 4: How many have you got now?

RELATIVE 3: Nice of the priest to say what a close family we are.

RELATIVE 4: And they're getting married in October.

GEORGE: Top up anyone?

MUM: I don't think we've seen you since Tracy's christening.

RELATIVE 5: Well, she took him back, after what he'd done.

GEORGE: Sausage roll?

PRIEST: Well, if you can't turn to the family in a crisis—

RELATIVE 4: The rest of the family are dropping sprogs left, right, and centre.

RELATIVE 5: And we had her first birthday party last week. She looked so cute in her little dress with all her friends round her. *[The remainder of the conversation should happen almost simultaneously, the following words being clearly audible, building to a crescendo.]*

GEORGE: White wedding?

RELATIVE 2: If you can't turn to the family—

RELATIVE 3: What a close family we are—

MUM: Only child.

DAD: Opposite—

GEORGE: Can I get anything for anyone?

DAD: Sex.

RELATIVE 1: Christening.

RELATIVE 4: Wedding.

RELATIVE 5: Babysitter.

RELATIVE 5: Lovely girl.

MUM: Lovely service.

DAD: Lovely—

ALL: FAMILY. *[The lights change immediately to normal. STEVE rushes to join LINDA.]*

STEVE: Lins, I've got to get out of here.

LINDA: Okay, let's go for a walk.

STEVE: No. I mean OUT. I want to go back to Basingstoke.

LINDA: Sweetheart, no one ever WANTS to go back to Basingstoke.

STEVE: I do. Tonight.

LINDA: Oh, Steve. He'll still be there on Thursday.

STEVE: And so will my parents. Tomorrow's the last chance we'll have to—

LINDA: Bonk.

STEVE: Be together, alone, touch, talk, hold each other—for ages.

LINDA: So tell your dad you're going back tonight.

STEVE: He'll freak. He says I belong here. Well, I don't. I don't fucking belong here.

LINDA: Darling, you're cracking up.

STEVE: Don't be melodramatic. *[Pause]* Faint.

LINDA: What?

STEVE: Just do it.

LINDA: "Don't be melodramatic. Just faint."

STEVE: Please.

LINDA: Steven Carter, I really—

STEVE: Hate me, loathe me, detest me, just faint! *[LINDA faints, melodramatically.]* Linda! My God, she's fainted. Lins. Linda. [The family crowds round.]

MUM: Linda. Linda love.

RELATIVE 1: Loosen her blouse.

RELATIVE 2: Make sure she hasn't swallowed her tongue.

DAD: Get her some water.

RELATIVE 3: Give her some air.

RELATIVE 4: Get her on her back.

GEORGE: Sit her up.

RELATIVE 5: She's coming round.

LINDA: *[Very hammily]* Where am I?

STEVE: Are you alright?

LINDA: What happened?

ALL: You fainted.

MUM: Now what's this all about?

LINDA: I don't know.

STEVE: She was fine a minute ago.

LINDA: I was fine a minute ago.

MUM: Do you want to go upstairs and lie down? That's alright, isn't it, Bridie?

RELATIVE 1: Of course it is.

STEVE: No, it isn't. I mean, you've got to be back in Basingstoke tonight.

LINDA: I do? Oh yes, I do.

DAD: Well, you're not going home on the train alone. Steven, you'll have to go with her.

STEVE: Oh. I guess so.

LINDA: It's okay; I can manage.

STEVE: No, you can't.

MUM: Steven's right, love. Let him take you home. I'll get you some tea. *[All relatives have now exited.]*

STEVE: How are you feeling?

LINDA: Stupid.

STEVE: No change there, then.

LINDA: You're such a git.

STEVE: You were brilliant. Drink your tea; then Basingstoke here we come.

LINDA: Git. *[Pause]* He'd better be worth it; that's all I can say. *[The light changes slowly to a small area. All exit except for STEVE. JOHN enters, drying himself with a towel.]*

STEVE: Oh, he's worth it. He's everything. *[Schoolbell]*

SCENE 20

[School changing room, suggested by bench and a locker. STEVE has changed his black jacket and tie for blazer and school tie. JOHN is just finishing changing.]

JOHN: It can't be worth it. Jesus. I was so fucking embarrassed.

STEVE: I've said I'm sorry. How did I know Hutton would give you the message in front of Kevin?

JOHN: No. Not embarrassed. Scared. My life flashed before me. My future life anyway. My parents crying, my friends dumping me. And the police.

STEVE: The police.

JOHN: Yeah, we broke the law, didn't we?

STEVE: The law's bollocks.

JOHN: Is it?

STEVE: Is it!

JOHN: Keep your voice down. Do you want the whole school to hear?

STEVE: Yes! *[Pause]* The law—

JOHN: Is there to protect us.

STEVE: From what? Who are we hurting?

JOHN: Ourselves maybe.

STEVE: Johnny, please—

DAVE: *[Entering]* Hurry up. Kev and I are bunking out for a pint. Bet you could do with one after what you've been doing.

JOHN: What the fuck's that supposed to mean?

DAVE: After two hours of tennis. Did you win?

JOHN: Of course.

DAVE: Stupid question.

JOHN: I'll be with you in a sec. Just doing my hair.

DAVE: Okay. We'll be in the common room. *[Exit]*

STEVE: *[Long pause]* My parents are back tomorrow. *[Pause]* I've no idea when my house will be free again. *[Pause]* John. Please. Please come over. Just to talk. I mean, we don't have to . . . you know . . . if you don't want to.

JOHN: Of course I fucking want to. But don't you see? I don't WANT to want to.

STEVE: But what about all the things you said? About going away together . . . about—

JOHN: Steve, mate—

STEVE: I'm not your mate.

JOHN: What are you, then?

STEVE: I thought I was your . . . It doesn't matter.

JOHN: Look, the others are waiting. Catch you later. *[Pause]* I'm really sorry . . . about your nan. *[Exit]*

STEVE: *[Sits motionless on the bench, then notices JOHN has left his bag. Picks it up and goes to the door.]* John, you left your—*[He comes back into the room. Throws the bag violently and the contents spill out.]* Bastard! Fucking bastard. *[He kicks and throws the contents around. Suddenly he has JOHN's tennis shirt in his hands. Holds it to his face.]* I love you, you bastard.

KEVIN: *[Entering with DAVE]* What the fuck! They're John's things. You little shit. Pick them up.

STEVE: Yes. Sorry. *[He starts putting things back in the bag.]*

KEVIN: You will be. *[Grabs STEVE, pinning him against the locker. Goes to hit him.]*

JOHN: *[Entering]* Kevin! What's going on?

KEVIN: This little queer's been going through your gear.

STEVE: Johnny, I—

JOHN: Let him go, Kev. It's my problem. I'll sort it. I said leave him.

KEVIN: *[Releasing STEVE]* Okay, you sort it. We'll keep watch outside. And since when does he get to call you Johnny? *[Exit]*

STEVE: Johnny. John. I'm sorry. I was . . .

JOHN: Shut it.

STEVE: I was just so—

JOHN: I said shut it. How dare you. You've really asked for it. *[He hits his bag and whispers.]* Scream.

STEVE: Sorry?

JOHN: Just scream, shout, moan. *[He starts hitting the bag often. STEVE responds by screaming. This goes on for awhile. They both find it very funny. JOHN grabs STEVE's lapels and shakes him as they both try to suppress their laughter. Suddenly they look at each other and stop. They are about to kiss as KEVIN enters.]*

KEVIN: Someone's coming. *[He notices what's happening. JOHN looks at KEVIN. He then rams STEVE's face very hard into the locker. As he hits the floor, JOHN kicks him violently.]*

JOHN: Queer bastard. *[Exit JOHN and KEVIN. STEVE eventually staggers to his feet. He is nearly crying as he examines his bleeding face in the mirror in the fourth wall. HUTTON enters.]*

HUTTON: Jesus Christ! *[He tries to examine STEVE's face, but he shrugs away.]* Bastards. Steven, this can't go on. Tell me who did it. I saw Westhead leaving. . . .

STEVE: No. No. It wasn't him. *[He picks up JOHN's shirt and starts cleaning his wound with it. HUTTON notices the shirt.]* He didn't mean it. It was expected.

He didn't . . . had to . . . He . . . loves me. . . . I know he does. . . . I . . . I love . . .
[He breaks down completely.] He's the one who should be crying. He's the one
who's fucked up. I know what I feel.

HUTTON: I know.

STEVE: I'm so fucking lonely.

HUTTON: I know.

STEVE: Angry. I'm so fucking angry.

HUTTON: Be angry. It helps.

STEVE: How do you know?

HUTTON: *[Turning STEVE to face him]* I KNOW! *[Pause]* Look, Steven, I've already said too much. But I will say that it gets better. You have to keep fighting.

STEVE: What about love?

HUTTON: If you want to love, you have to fight. Here's my home number. If you
ever need to talk, well, please ring.

STEVE: Thanks.

HUTTON: And I'm going to talk to Mr. Ayres. Don't panic. I won't name names. I
just think it's time Pubic knew just what kind of "gentlemen" he's creating. Yes,
the staff call him that, too. *[STEVE smiles.]* He needs to know for the sake of all
the others who have the right to . . . you know!

STEVE: *[Smiling]* I know. *[Exit]*

SCENE 21

*[Lights change suddenly. JOHN in single light. During the scene the set changes
to the park.]*

JOHN: I don't want a drink. I've got to . . . see you. Steven. Steve! Please help—

KEVIN: *[From shadows]* You just don't seem very interested in—

JOHN: *[Running about to try answering the voices]* I love girls. I do. Steven.

JENNY: How about that curry you promised me.

JOHN: What's wrong with me?

KEVIN: Since when does he get to call you—

STEVE: Johnny—

DAVE: After what you've been doing.

STEVE: There's nothing wrong with you.

JOHN: Steve! I LOVE—

MR. AYRES: The value of the family.

JOHN: I love—

BOY 1: Queer bastard.

BOY 2: SC loves JW.

JOHN: I love girls. I do.

KEVIN: Where were you?

JOHN: I do!

STEVE: You have too much to lose.

JOHN: I do!

MAN 1: Do you like to suck?

JOHN: I do! I do! I do! I . . . LOVE . . .

SCENE 22

[As he screams "Steven," the lights change to park lighting. All have exited as STEVE walks past the park bench on his way home.]

JOHN: STEVEN! *[STEVE keeps walking.]* Steven! Please stop.

STEVE: *[Stopping]* If you're looking for your shirt, it's in the changing room.

JOHN: Sod the shirt. Please. I just wanted to say . . . sorry. I had to. Don't you see? . . . I'd have lost face.

STEVE: And what about my face?

JOHN: I'm so ashamed. But I just had to. . . . It was—

STEVE: Peer pressure. Forget it. What's a smack in the face between lovers?

JOHN: I'm not your lover.

STEVE: Oh, sorry. Then me and your twin brother recently spent two days making love together.

JOHN: Look, can we sit down? *[They go to the bench.]*

STEVE: Well, we've been here before. How romantic.

JOHN: Stop talking about romance.

STEVE: I was being sarcastic. Not exactly Mills and Boon, was it? The sun was just going down, and the air was heady with the scent of urine.

JOHN: Steven, please. That's just the point. I think you do see this as romantic. That we "made love." I guess I can't ever deny what happened, but I can't relate it to love. You can't make love to a bloke.

STEVE: I can.

JOHN: It's not what I believe in, what—

STEVE: You've been taught.

JOHN: Oh, bollocks. Do you think anyone takes that garbage about "gentlemen" and family values seriously?

STEVE: Yes. Yes, I do. And even if they don't, school's not the only place you're taught. It comes at you from all sides. The family, the telly. Affection is about men and women; romance is "boy meets girl."

JOHN: Don't exaggerate.

STEVE: Listen. Don't you watch the commercials? Beautiful blokes throwing themselves into the arms of beautiful girls. What does that mean? Coca Cola is for straights only. Or how about "Say it with flowers. Let HER know you care." Or the cute little five-year-old boy who kisses the cute little five-year-old girl.

JOHN: What the fuck are you saying? That five-year-olds might be gay!

STEVE: No. No. I'm saying that five-year-olds kiss and hug and hold hands with anyone they love. And why does that stop? Because one day someone says, "Come on, you're a big boy now. Big boys don't hold hands." What a shame! What a fucking shame.

JOHN: Steven, I don't want to hurt you—but you scare me. I don't want to turn out like you.

STEVE: Dodgy?

JOHN: No. Bitter. You're already so bitter.

STEVE: I'm not bitter. I'm fucking angry.

JOHN: Don't be angry with me. I . . . care about you.

STEVE: Sorry. Not allowed. I'm a bloke, remember? Anyway, you're just scared if I get too angry, I'll tell people about us. Well, I won't. I couldn't.

JOHN: You're amazing. I would.

STEVE: Yeah, well, I'm not you, thank God. And anyway, I love you.

JOHN: I . . . thanks. [JOHN goes to touch STEVE, who gets up.] I'd better go. I've got to meet . . .

STEVE: Jenny?

JOHN: Yeah.

STEVE: After the way you treated her?

JOHN: I know, I'm a lucky guy.

STEVE: She's a lucky girl.

JOHN: Yeah . . . well. Glad we talked. No hard feelings, eh?

STEVE: Johnny, I'm sure you'll have plenty more "hard" feelings. And plenty more "mistakes."

JOHN: Yeah, well. Catch ya later.

STEVE: See you, mate. [JOHN goes.]

SCENE 23

[Lights fade on boys. Light only on HUTTON, who is taking something out of his jacket.]

HUTTON: I tried to help Steve. I was braver than I thought I was going to be. Too brave. I blew . . . just got so . . . angry. I tried to make it hypothetical. I read old Pubic a newspaper clipping I've carried with me for years. [The set has changed to AYRES's office. Desk. Two chairs. AYRES is seated. On the other half of the stage STEVE sits in an armchair in darkness. Lights up on whole office.]

HUTTON: "Dear Barbara, There is a problem that is making my life such hell that I am thinking of killing myself, although I am only sixteen. I am homosexual. I am going out with a girl who has no suspicions. We have been having sex for a year now, but she can't turn me on the way the boys at school do."

MR. AYRES: Simon, please—

HUTTON: "I really want to grow up and have children, but I desperately want sex with a man. If I do, I know that being a homosexual will ruin my life."

MR. AYRES: Maybe it will.

HUTTON: And what does Aunty Barbara say to this poor, lonely, frightened child? "This obsession you have with homosexuality is fairly common amongst young people. Fortunately, it usually goes away. You are certainly in a turmoil and need help to understand yourself. If you telephone the Samaritans, they may be able to help. Their number is in the phone book. I don't think you are a true homosexual, or you wouldn't have such a good, loving relationship with your girl."

MR. AYRES: Sound advice.

HUTTON: From a tabloid! Mr. Ayres, all this boy needed, wanted, was for anyone to tell him that it needn't ruin his life. Now maybe he's just one of the 20 percent of gay men who admit to attempting suicide in their teenage years. Now I tell you there's a similar boy here.

MR. AYRES: Enough. I refuse to listen.

HUTTON: That's the fucking problem.

MR. AYRES: Simon. Please, I am trying to help. But my position is difficult. I'm as angry as you about the bullying, but if you won't tell me the names of the boys involved, even the victim, there is nothing I can do. As for this other issue, the boy may indeed be going through a phase most people come out of.

HUTTON: Not everyone.

MR. AYRES: Then it's up to people in our position to encourage them to see the value of resisting temptation. To offer support.

HUTTON: But it's such a frightening thing that none of the homosexuals here would dare talk about it. They're not all as brave as Carter.

MR. AYRES: You make it sound as though we have an epidemic.

HUTTON: It's not a disease. Listen, even if you take the most conservative estimate—

MR. AYRES: No more statistics, please!

HUTTON: —in a school this size there must be fifty boys with homosexual potential.

MR. AYRES: That's a distressingly inappropriate word. And you suggest we should encourage them to achieve this "potential."

HUTTON: I'm suggesting we should do anything to ensure they achieve their potential as loving people. To feel they belong. So they don't grow up bitter and confused. We have to help. It's why we're here.

MR. AYRES: Is it, Simon? I used to believe that once. But now we're here to market the school. My job is about damage limitation.

HUTTON: What about the damage to this boy?

MR. AYRES: Simon, I'm answerable to the government. And I'm scared to upset ANYONE. I'm answerable to the law.

HUTTON: But there are good laws and bad. The age-of-consent law—

MR. AYRES: Is there to protect young people.

HUTTON: From what? Doesn't anyone realise that it does anything but protect them? It actually removes any possible safety net. Supposing, just supposing, there were parents who would accept that their son of sixteen was gay. How can they support and encourage when the law says that that child is a criminal? So where do they go, these criminals?

MR. AYRES: Now I can't talk about this anymore.

HUTTON: Oh, so now it's against the law to talk about it, is it?

MR. AYRES: Since you mention it, Simon, for five years it has been illegal for a local authority to promote a positive image of homosexuality.

HUTTON: Jesus!

MR. AYRES: If the boy wants help, he must talk to his parents. I'll ring them. Carter, you said.

HUTTON: Oh Jesus. Look, Mr. Ayres, at least let me talk to Steven.

MR. AYRES: Mr. Hutton, the matter is out of your hands. Thank you for bringing it to my attention. However, I must say I find your obvious obsession with . . . this subject . . . very alarming. If you value your position at this school, please note that I positively forbid you to talk to Carter about it. And Simon, I have the law on my side.

HUTTON: Steven, what have I done?

SCENE 24

[Lights down on office. Lights up on living room. MR. CARTER is standing.]

STEVE: Dad, it's not your fault.

DAD: No? Then whose fault is it?

STEVE: Nobody's. Fault, blame, guilt . . . it's nothing to do with any of that. It just is.

DAD: What a time for this to happen. I've just lost my mother and now . . .

STEVE: I'm still here, Dad.

DAD: This is my life you're destroying. Your mother's life.

STEVE: And what about my fucking life?

DAD: How dare you use that word to me.

STEVE: Dad. It's only a word. Fuck, gay, straight . . . they're only words.

DAD: You think you're so clever. An answer for everything.

STEVE: I thought you were proud of me.

DAD: Proud? Of . . . Christ, the thought of you in bed with another man makes me feel physically sick.

STEVE: Do you ever imagine me doing it with Linda? That was alright, was it? Reassuring to know your son was a real man. That make you feel okay? Bring a smile to your face, did it? *[DAD goes to hit him.]* GO ON! Hit me. You won't be the first, and you won't be the last. Why? WHY? What are you all so scared of? *[DAD sits and cries.]* Dad. Dad, please. I'm sorry you're hurt. And I'm sorry Mum's . . . but I'm not sorry that I'm . . .

DAD: You selfish sod. Can't you think about the rest of us? What about Linda? She'll be devastated.

STEVE: I doubt it. She's known for months.

DAD: Why tell Linda?

STEVE: I had to tell someone.

DAD: You could have come to . . . *[Breaks down again.]*

STEVE: *[Thinks about holding him but can't]* Dad. Cry. It helps.

DAD: Your mother'll be in soon. She's never seen me like this.

STEVE: She's never seen you cry. My God!

DAD: Listen. It's not too late to spare your mother's feelings. I've tried to tell her that there must be some mistake. That you're confused. I sat here waiting for you to come home, wanting, praying that you would say, "Dad, it's not true." Why didn't you, Steven? Why couldn't you have lied?

STEVE: Because I've been brought up by you. And Mum. The two people who I love more than anyone in the world. Because I want them to love me, the real me and not someone I pretend to be to keep their love. Because I'm sick of lying. *[Front door slams.]*

DAD: Well, for your mother's sake, lie. Tell her you've thought it through and you were just confused.

STEVE: That word again.

DAD: What's wrong with you? Can't you do even that much to help?

MUM: *[Entering]* I'm sure it's going to rain. I got back just in time.

DAD: He said it might rain. Michael Fish. *[Pause]*

MUM: I'd better fix supper.

DAD & STEVE: *[Together]* I'm not hungry.

MUM: Tea then.

DAD: I'll do it. *[Kisses her]* Steven's got something to say to you. *[Exit]*

STEVE: Mum, I . . . I just . . . Oh, Mum! *[He breaks down in his mother's arms.]*

MUM: Oh, baby. My baby.

STEVE: Mum, the last thing I wanted was . . . and I'm so sorry if . . . Dad wants me to tell you that I'm . . . and I AM! Now I AM CONFUSED. Please . . . please don't reject me.

MUM: Steven, we love you.

STEVE: But Dad's so . . . angry.

MUM: He's confused, too. Listen, love. When your father was a young boy, he used to be an altar server at Mass. Well, there was this man who was sort of head altar server. He was a friend of the family and invited your dad round for tea. I can't remember what he said to your dad's parents, but they trusted him. . . . Well, he was an altar server. They were wrong to trust him. Because he . . . tried to . . . and your Dad managed to run away. But he was so scared that he didn't go home for hours. And when he did, he got a terrible hiding for worrying his parents.

STEVE: He should have explained.

MUM: He was ashamed. He thought it was his fault.

STEVE: It wasn't. And now, well, this guy, he must have tried it with others since.

MUM: I don't think so. He became a priest. But you see, since then your dad has had a hatred for people like that.

STEVE: I'm not like that. I'm . . .

MUM: Steven. Son. I know things seem bad now, but give yourself a chance. Things may change. Mr. Ayres suggested you go to the new sixth form college after summer. It's lovely there. They don't wear uniforms, it's more relaxed, and it's . . . well, mixed. Maybe being at an all-boys school . . . I mean, you don't know many girls. Things will sort themselves out.

STEVE: My God. My God. Why is no one hearing me?

SCENE 25

[Lights immediately only on HUTTON's phone. Phone rings and HUTTON enters to answer it. He sits.]

HUTTON: Hallo. Who? Steven . . . Sorry, Steve, I can hardly hear you. Where are you? *[Pause]* Which pub? Have you been drinking? *[Pause]* Oh, Steven, you fool. You're underage. Now just go home and . . . What? Er . . . no, you can't come here. *[Pause]* Because . . . well, it just wouldn't be right. *[Pause]* Speak up. . . . Of course I'm listening. *[Pause]* Yes, yes, I'm sorry. I didn't mean to give him your name. *[Pause]* How did they take it? *[Pause]* Give it time, Steven. He'll come round. Now just go home. *[Pause]* Well, if you don't belong there, where do you belong? *[For the remainder of the speech it is important he moves and speaks identically to his first speech of the play.]* Move away from the juke box. Steve. Steven. Listen to me. You're not making sense. *[Pause]* What? Steven, I am listening; I'm just not hearing you. Move away from the juke box. I've told you I can't. My position is . . . difficult. Go home and sleep on it. Things'll be better in the morning. They always are. Believe me, Steven. No, don't do that. Steven! Steve! *[STEVEN has hung up. Slowly HUTTON replaces the receiver and takes a swift swig from his whisky glass.]* Believe me, my position is difficult. So what about your position? What are you going to do, Steven? What are you going to do now?

SCENE 26

[STEVE in single white light. Holds a bottle of pills up. The other characters emerge gradually from the shadows as they speak.]

STEVE: Dad. Dad. Mum. Please don't reject me.

HUTTON: Well, if you don't belong there—

STEVE: I'm still your son.

DAD: The thought of you in bed with another man—
LINDA: Yuk!
MUM: Big boys don't hold hands.
STEVE: I know you think it—
DAD: Makes me feel—
GLEN: Filthy habit.
DAD: Physically sick.
STEVE: I'm sorry. Please, listen to me. Somebody.
HUTTON: No. You can't come here.
STEVE: I'm so fucking lonely.
LINDA: Would you like a child?
MUM: Only child.
STEVE: I want to die.
LINDA: Stop feeling so sorry for yourself.
JOHN: Help me. Please, help me.
HUTTON: But my position is difficult.
STEVE: Now I'm confused.
GLEN: How old are you?
MAN 1: Innocent little boy.
MR. AYRES: Straighten up, lad; straighten up.
MUM: You're confused.
STEVE: What on earth makes you think I'm—
LINDA: Don't tell me you're looking for love.
MAN 2: Sex sex sex.
HUTTON: Fuck the sex—
MAN 2: Do you like to suck?
HUTTON: Live the romance.
LINDA: It's a different bloke every time you call me.
HUTTON: Live—
STEVE: I want to die.
HUTTON: —the love.
JOHN: You can't make love to a bloke.
STEVE: It's fun.
JOHN: It's true, then . . . that you're—
BOY 1: Queer bastard.
JOHN: Dodgy.
MR. AYRES: Misguided.
DAD: Sick.
LINDA: Confused.
MR. AYRES: Unnatural.
STEVE: What are you all so scared of?
HUTTON: There are millions—
STEVE: Everyone my own age is straight.
DAD: He's a gay.

JOHN: I'm not gay.

MR. AYRES: As you go through life—

STEVE: What about my fucking life? *[He holds up a bottle of pills.]* I love you, Johnny.

JOHN: Queer bastard.

STEVE: I won't tell anyone.

JOHN: Yes. Do it. Do it. *[STEVE unscrews pills.]*

STEVE: I'm so—

JOHN: —scared. So—

STEVE: Fucking.

JOHN: Scared.

STEVE: Angry.

JOHN: I love sex with girls.

LINDA: It could be a phase.

STEVE: Leave me alone.

JOHN: Give me a chance.

STEVE: I love—

JOHN: I don't think I'd like to do it—

STEVE: But you said.

JOHN: Terrible mistake.

STEVE: But—

JOHN: All that romantic crap.

STEVE: Sounds wonderful.

HUTTON: Exciting—

JOHN: Dirty.

HUTTON: Naughty.

JOHN: I couldn't get used to the lying.

STEVE: What do you want?

JOHN: I don't want to want to.

STEVE: I love you.

MUM: We love you.

JOHN: I'm not your lover.

KEVIN: Whoever said—

STEVE: You're beautiful.

DAD: You smell like a bloody poof.

JOHN: Do it. Please do it.

STEVE: Touch—

JOHN: Do it.

STEVE: Talk—

JOHN: Do it.

STEVE: Hold each other.

JOHN: Do it—

STEVE: What do you want?

JOHN: Don't leave me!

HUTTON: What are you going to do now? *[STEVE rushes upstage.]*

MR. AYRES: *[The light is now at the front of the stage. He comes into it so only AYRES, JOHN, and HUTTON are strongly lit. The others face upstage.]* Apparently he got hold of his mother's painkillers and took the lot. Why would he do that?

JOHN: Makes you do a lot of things you don't want to do.

MR. AYRES: Poor boy.

KEVIN: Whoever said Steven Carter was a boy?

JOHN: Peer pressure.

HUTTON: Why—

KEVIN: Did God make poofs?

HUTTON: Why didn't I let you come and see me?

DAD: Steven. Steve.

HUTTON: Because it's against the law. Oh, Steve—

MUM: Oh, baby—

DAD: Open your eyes, Steve. Please, God—

JOHN: Oh my God.

HUTTON: I just thought I'd tell you personally before—

MR. AYRES: I'll announce it at assembly.

HUTTON: I mean, you and Carter seemed to be . . .

JOHN: Lovers. Yes, we were.

KEVIN: Fuck me, Johnny. Poor bastard. He must have been so fucked up. Probably better off dead.

JOHN: No! He was . . . beautiful. You were beautiful, Steven.

MR. AYRES: I'll send the parents some flowers.

KEVIN: Jesus, I know we used to take the piss and that, but it was only a bit of . . . Jesus!

LINDA: Steve. Babe. How can you be . . . you were the most . . .

JOHN: Beautiful.

LINDA: Alive person I ever—

DAD: Steven, of course I'm proud of . . . was proud.

HUTTON: Where do they go, these criminal lovers, these criminal children?

MUM: Come back to us and we'll tell you that.

HUTTON: Into the toilets. Into the woods.

MUM: It doesn't matter what you are. I—

LINDA: I love you.

JOHN: I love you. I love you. I love you.

MR. AYRES: Gentlemen, it is my sad duty to inform you that one of our number has been taken from us.

HUTTON: Oh, Steve. Bravery like yours was the way forward. You were a fighter.

MR. AYRES: Steven Carter took his own life. One can only assume that the pressure of examinations affected him rather badly.

HUTTON: You just wanted them to see that we—

MR. AYRES: This merely emphasises what I have always said.

HUTTON: We are your brothers.

MR. AYRES: Whenever you feel the need to talk about a problem, you can always turn to the staff here.

HUTTON: Your fathers, for Christ's sake—

JOHN: For Christ's sake.

HUTTON: We are your children. And those of us who do make it, who take the risks, who get beaten and murdered in so called motiveless attacks, we huddle together in a self-perpetuating ghetto and turn the music up. Why not fight back?

JOHN: You're already so bitter.

HUTTON: Fight back.

LINDA: I don't want you to get all—

HUTTON: Bitter. Why—

LINDA: Twisted.

DAD: What's wrong with you?

HUTTON: Fight back.

JOHN: What's wrong with me?

LINDA: What's wrong—

HUTTON: Why always bitter?

JOHN: What's wrong—

LINDA: What's wrong—

DAD: What's wrong—

HUTTON: What's wrong with—

STEVEN: *[He suddenly bursts forward, and the other characters scatter offstage.]* NO! *[Blackout. Single light on STEVE. He is breathing heavily. Shakes pill bottle and sees that it is still full.]* Dear Mum and Dad. Dear . . . Everyone. I'm sorry, but I just can't take anymore. It seems that, hard as I try to love in my own way, you are all determined I should be sad and guilty. There would seem to be only one way out of this situation. *[He examines the pill bottle.]* I have decided . . . to live . . . my life as I want to, no matter what it takes. Will just one of you help me? Tell me I'm alright. Not confused. Not going through a phase. Not the only one. Not ill. Not a criminal. Will you? WILL YOU?

SCENE 27

[He collapses backwards. Birdsong. Slow light change to park. STEVE and LINDA are lying on the grass.]

STEVE: You've only known him six weeks.

LINDA: I know. But he's special.

STEVE: Because he fucked you.

LINDA: No. And anyway, he hasn't . . . we've only kissed seven times. I can't believe how lucky I am.

STEVE: Because he's got a Mercedes?

LINDA: No. Because he's kind, intelligent, beautiful. And he's got a Mercedes.

STEVE: You're beautiful.

LINDA: Don't start.

STEVE: What?

LINDA: All that inner beauty crap. What good is inner beauty?

STEVE: You're very pretty, Lins.

LINDA: I've lost half a stone, you know. Only another couple and I'll be normal.

STEVE: Linda! I thought you were happy the way you were. Out and stout.

LINDA: People change.

STEVE: If they want to—

LINDA: Well, I—

STEVE: Or other people want them to. *[Notices a man outside the toilet]* I don't believe it. *[Goes over to man]*

LINDA: What. Oh, Steve, please. Your parents will . . .

STEVE: Hi. Remember me?

GLEN: What. Oh, sure. Hi.

STEVE: How's things?

GLEN: Okay. You?

STEVE: Oh. Settling down. My parents found out.

GLEN: *[Panicked]* About what?

STEVE: Me being gay.

GLEN: How did they take it?

STEVE: I'm seeing a therapist.

GLEN: Really? Look, it's nice to see you, but . . . can you go away?

STEVE: Listen, I really enjoyed it with you.

GLEN: Please just go.

STEVE: And I forgive you for not turning up last time—

GLEN: Look, I'll give you money, anything, just piss off!

KAREN: *[Coming out of the Ladies]* God, there's always a queue in these places. You blokes don't know how lucky you are. Oh, sorry.

GLEN: Oh, yeah. This is . . . sorry I've forgotten—

STEVE: Steve.

GLEN: Oh, yeah. Steve. Steve, this is Karen. My wife.

STEVE: Pleased to meet you.

KAREN: Likewise. *[Pause]*

GLEN: Er . . . Steven came to see me in . . . a show once. We got chatting after.

KAREN: Oh, really? Which one?

STEVE: Er . . .

GLEN: It was that experimental rubbish.

KAREN: It wasn't rubbish. Well, you weren't anyway. Good, wasn't he, Steve?

STEVE: It was one of the most enjoyable performances I've ever experienced.

KAREN: Steady on. You'll make his head swell.

STEVE: Probably. Yes. It was so energetic, so penetrating, so . . . truthful.

KAREN: I think you have a fan.

STEVE: Yes, Karen, I think your husband is one of the best actors I've ever . . . come . . . across.

GLEN: We'd better be off. See you.

KAREN: Bye.

STEVE: Bye. Good luck. *[To KAREN]* You'll need it.

LINDA: Who was that?

STEVE: Glen. Remember Glen?

LINDA: Sort of.

STEVE: His eyes.

LINDA: Oh, yeah. Tom Cruise.

STEVE: No. Not that. Fear. Blind terror. The same as Johnny's eyes before he hit . . . why am I frightening?

LINDA: You don't scare me.

STEVE: Glen offered me money. No one's ever offered me money to go away before.

LINDA: You must be losing your looks. *[Pause]* You alright, babe?

STEVE: What? Oh. Yeah.

LINDA: How's your shrink?

STEVE: He's not a shrink. He's a therapist.

LINDA: Whatever. What's he like?

STEVE: He's . . . absolutely fucking gorgeous. *[They laugh.]* Fancy coming home? We could watch a vid.

LINDA: Sorry, babe. I'm meeting Rikki.

STEVE: Oh.

LINDA: Some other time.

STEVE: Sure.

LINDA: See you soon. Love ya.

STEVE: Me, too. *[Exit LINDA. The lights change. The forestage is lit, as is the toilet. HUTTON downstage.]*

HUTTON: It'll be hard, Steven. No matter how brave you are. I thought I was brave. Live and learn. *[As he does this speech, music. Suggested track: "What Is Love?" by Haddaway. STEVE tries to approach the other characters in the shadows in turns, but they all couple off, male and female.]* If we were all brave, all equally brave, the world would be surprised by our numbers. Remember, if you want to love, you have to fight. Maybe if gay people talked more about love and less about sex, we might start getting somewhere. Smash through the fear. *[STEVE is now isolated.]*

STEVE: What are you all so frightened of?

HUTTON: On the other hand . . . turn the music up. *[STEVE dances defiantly and aggressively with two beautiful gay men while all the other characters shuffle from foot to foot in a ritual of mediocrity. Towards the end of the music all leave except JOHN and STEVE. JOHN walks slowly towards STEVE, who is still dancing unaware of him, nearly joins STEVE but exits. As the music climaxes, STEVE stands alone, defiant. Arms in the air. Freeze. All lights down except a single spot on the sign saying, "Gentlemen." Fade to black.]*

JOHN M. CLUM

Randy's House

AUTHOR'S INTRODUCTION

FOR MUCH OF MY CAREER I was a director as well as a scholar-critic, but in the late 1980s playwriting became much more of a lively interest than directing. After seeing Peter Gill's *Mean Tears* in London in 1987, I felt that I, too, had to write plays. The first, an opus entitled *Zinka's Boys,* was too derivative and too autobiographical. Eventually I found my own voice(s), and my plays are now being produced and published.

For two years my partner was on the Emory faculty, and I commuted from Durham to Atlanta. In August 1993 we returned from sane London to très gay Atlanta to find a civil war in progress in neighboring Cobb County, stirred up by a local production of Terrence McNally's play *Lips Together, Teeth Apart.* While sinful Atlanta passed domestic partnership benefits for city employees (later rescinded by the state legislature), the Cobb County Council passed a resolution cutting all arts funding to zero and another resolution condemning the "gay lifestyle." At one of the many heated meetings and rallies, a gay man wisely suggested that if people got to know each other, the demonization might stop. As a

Duke Photo Department/Les Todd

first step, he dared anyone to visit his home. Out of that quixotic proposal—and
the sadness I feel in seeing that my students in the 1990s have as much trouble
coming out as students did twenty-five years ago—came *Randy's House,* which I
consider a play about real "family values." My aim was not only to write interesting
gay characters but also to try getting inside those on the other side of the battle.

PRODUCTION HISTORY AND RIGHTS

Randy's House was given a staged reading by Washington's Theater Conspiracy at
the D.C. Arts Center on April 30, 1995, directed by Jason Palmquist. The cast included Rosemary Knower and Nick Olcott as Marian Tucker and Rick Martinez.
Marcus Lane played Tom. The play was produced as part of the Manbites Dog
Theater's (Durham, N.C.) second "Don't Ask, Don't Tell Theater Festival," in May
1995, directed by Enoch Scott. Beth Bacon and Stephen Schilling played Marian
and Hunter Tucker. Mario Griego played Rick Martinez.

JOHN M. CLUM

Randy's House

For Joey Zacharias, the dearest and the best

Cast of Characters

RICK MARTINEZ: Late 30s. Handsome Hispanic. A doctor. Bright. Fiercely committed to what he believes and protective of the people he loves.

SAM CHAMBERS: Late 30s. A professor. Nice to a fault. Believes the best of everyone. Gentle.

TAYLOR CHAMBERS: 17. Sam's son.

HUNTER TUCKER: A heterosexual version of Sam. Almost like something out of Frank Capra. A small-town newspaperman who married the owner's daughter. Truly believes he can do some good.

MARIAN TUCKER: Late 30s. A survivor, but an angry conservative. Wants the world to be the way she imagines it. Has little respect for her husband's liberalism. Is trying desperately to ignore what is happening to her only son. Teaches school because she's too driven to stay home, but teaches at a private school.

BAILEY BOONE: 60 to mid-70s. Marian's father. Tough southern patriarch. Has been a powerful figure in what was once a small town but is becoming a suburb. Not one of those Tennessee Williams monsters. This one rules by his total self-assurance and sense that whatever he does is right. And he's charming.

TOM TUCKER: 17 and deeply troubled. Haunted since he witnessed his lover's rape and death.

RANDY: 17.

RANDY'S FATHER: Can be played by Bailey.

Setting

A town in Cobb County, Georgia, 1993.

[The setting of the play should be very fluid. Simple set pieces that can be moved on and off by the actors. Or all the areas set up in various areas of the stage: a kitchen, a living room, a bedroom that can serve as Tom's or Taylor's. When the audience enters, a group of chairs is set up for the County Council meeting. A table in the center. Two chairs on either side of the table.]

---

1. GEORGIA. COBB COUNTY COUNCIL
MEETING, AUGUST 1993.

[When the lights come up on the action of the play, SAM and RICK are in two chairs, HUNTER and MARIAN in the other two, and BAILEY at the table.]

SAM: *[Addresses imaginary audience around him and County Council facing him]* My name is Sam Chambers. I teach at Emory and live in this town with my partner, Dr. Richard Martinez, and my son, Taylor. I should be angry at what is happening here tonight. But I'm only sad. You think that we—my family is bringing something alien and evil into your community. We saw a house that we loved, that we wanted to fix up and make our home. Like many of you, we commute to the city, work long hours, and want to come home to someplace nice. We raise a kid and send him to a school we're happy he's in. We lead the same kind of ordinary, some would say dull, lives you do. Quiet nights, work on the house on weekends. You say you don't want people like us in your community. You don't know us!

I would like to invite—dare—any of you to come spend an evening in our home. It sure would put an end to your worries that awful things are going on. In the meantime, don't damn us without any evidence. Thanks for your time.

[SAM sits down. RICK looks daggers at SAM.]

HUNTER: *[Rises]* I'm Hunter Tucker. As you know, I've lived here most of my life. As editor of the *Ledger,* I know most of you and most of what happens in this community. And I know we're better than we are looking tonight. As a reporter, I'm trained not to speak without solid evidence. We're all judging people before any offense has been committed. Sam, I'm going to take you up on your invitation. Furthermore, I invite you and your family to spend an evening in our home. I'm sure more joins us than separates us.

[HUNTER sits down. MARIAN looks daggers at him. RICK steps forward as the other characters leave the stage with the chairs.]

RICK: A real Frank Capra moment. The newspaper editor and my lover doing their liberal schtick. I would have preferred a grenade myself. But then Sam and I are the gay version of *CNN Crossfire.*

[SAM comes forward, stands next to RICK.]

SAM: It's not that simple.

RICK: That's Sam's favorite phrase. Find the complexity. He's an English professor. Find the niceness in people. He's a liberal. He should have lived with Hunter, and I belong with Hunter's wife—the one mentally shooting daggers at her husband.

SAM: Then you'd have to deal with her father. *[To audience]* That's him at the table running the show.

RICK: Like father, like daughter. She wants us in her house about as much as I want her in ours.

SAM: Believe me, this is the only way we can make progress.

RICK: Bullshit!

SAM: You're right. *Crossfire.*

RICK: *[To audience]* I'm a doctor. I spend my days prolonging the lives of people who have a disease I can't cure. I can't cure families either.

SAM: There's nothing wrong with our family.

RICK: The good folks around here don't agree with you.

SAM: *[To audience]* Here is Cobb County, Georgia.

RICK: The conservative side of the Atlanta suburbs. Atlanta is as gay a city as you'll ever see. Rainbow flags proudly flying in all the best neighborhoods. On the east are suburbs with more gays. On the west are crosses and what's left of the Ku Klux Klan. So we, of course, moved west.

SAM: We weren't the only ones.

RICK: No. We saw a great old house.

SAM: Not one of those Atlanta bungalows, but a real old Southern Gothic house. Right out of Faulkner.

RICK: Unfortunately, so were the neighbors.

SAM: So that's where we are. And this meeting? Well, a local theater put on a play suggesting that gay people weren't so bad and that straight people might learn to like us.

RICK: The righteous folk went into a feeding frenzy. Banned funding for the arts and tonight are having this meeting to vote on a resolution condemning the "gay lifestyle."

SAM: I've always forbidden my students to use the word *lifestyle.*

RICK: There are worse words than lifestyle, darlin'. Anyway, surprise, surprise!! The resolution passed.

BAILEY: *[Stands]* I am pleased to announce that the County Council has passed the following: Resolved that the gay and lesbian lifestyle is incompatible with the traditional family values to which the people of Cobb County subscribe.

SAM: It's just a resolution, not law.

RICK: Right! Hasn't the last fight made you a bit more cynical?

SAM: *[To audience]* We just fought for custody of my son.

[TAYLOR enters.]

This is Taylor.

TAYLOR: Hi.

SAM: After Taylor's mother and I separated—

RICK: Sam loved the closet.

SAM: No, I didn't. Or I would have stayed married.

RICK: Married right after college. Stayed married till he was thirty.

SAM: So?

RICK: Sam was the only English professor in the p.c. eighties to think homosexuality was unfashionable.

TAYLOR: Come on, guys.

SAM: I'm sorry to say he's right. But I came around and came out. And we've been together for seven years. My ex-wife died last spring in a car crash. Awful California drivers. Her parents fought like hell to keep Taylor.

RICK: The lawyers really played dirty.

SAM: Too dirty. They lost, thank God. And whatever they say, we're a family.

RICK: This story is about the making and unmaking and collision of families— families into which you're born and families you make yourself. It's about us and the Tuckers—those folks at the meeting? Well, as you'll see, we made visits to each other's houses, but not quite the way Sam and Hunter envisioned.

SAM: The big variable in all this is our sons. Our Taylor and Hunter and Marian's son, Tom. Seventeen and not controllable quantities in any social experiment. While Hunter and Marian and Rick and I were at the meeting, Taylor was over at their house with their son.

[SAM, TAYLOR, and RICK exit.]

2. TOM TUCKER'S BEDROOM.

[Bedroom area. Now Tom's room. Tom and Taylor on the floor playing a video game.]

TAYLOR: I give up. You're too good.

TOM: I play all the time. By myself.

TAYLOR: That's not much fun.

TOM: It's okay.

TAYLOR: Don't you know anybody at school?

TOM: Everybody. But they don't want to know me.

TAYLOR: I thought you were new here.

TOM: We've lived here forever. I went to a private school. I had to leave.

TAYLOR: Oh.

TOM: Don't you want to know why? Everybody around here does.

TAYLOR: It's up to you.

[TOM holds up scarred wrists.]

I'm sorry.

TOM: You didn't do it.

TAYLOR: I know, but. Shit, I don't know what to say.

TOM: My best friend shot himself. Last summer. So . . .

TAYLOR: I'm glad you didn't succeed.

TOM: Are you?

TAYLOR: Yeah. I need a friend around here.

TOM: So do I.

TAYLOR: I'm treated like a fucking leper. And it's going to be worse after tonight.

TOM: Why?

TAYLOR: Don't you know what's going on?

TOM: You mean about the homosexuals moving in?

TAYLOR: The homosexuals? That's my father and his partner.

[*Silence from TOM who gets up and looks at TAYLOR. There's a sense that TOM has made a strong decision.*]

Does that bother you?

TOM: No. Really.

[*Sound of a car pulling into the driveway.*]

My folks are back.

TAYLOR: The meeting must be over. I'd better get home.

TOM: Taylor, are we friends?

TAYLOR: I said so, didn't I?

TOM: We've got to be.

3. THE TUCKERS' KITCHEN.

[*Lights down on bedroom and up on kitchen area. HUNTER, MARIAN, and MARIAN's father, BAILEY, enter kitchen area.*]

BAILEY: That was the most damn fool thing I ever saw you do. What got into you?

MARIAN: I'll make some decaf.

BAILEY: Decaf, hell. I need a stiff drink.

HUNTER: I could use one myself.

[*HUNTER goes and pours two drinks. Gives one to BAILEY and keeps one for himself.*]

BAILEY: Really? I thought you must have had a few already.

HUNTER: I don't think talking about this is going to do any good.

BAILEY: God knows you put your foot in it already.

MARIAN: We've got to talk about it. You've got us in a real mess. How are we going to get out of this?

HUNTER: I don't plan to get out of anything.

BAILEY: This town is about to blow to pieces, and we can't afford to take the wrong side.

HUNTER: I'm trying to bring people together.

BAILEY: Not those people.

HUNTER: They seem perfectly decent folks to me.

BAILEY: I don't call sexual perversion decent. They don't even have the decency to keep quiet about it. I'd keep your fondness for those queers to yourself.

MARIAN: Please. I'm not in the mood to move.

HUNTER: No one's going to have to move.

[TOM and TAYLOR come in.]

TOM: I want you to meet my friend, Taylor. This is my mom and dad and my granddad. *[Handshakes, etc.]* Taylor just moved down the street.

MARIAN: Oh yes? Which house?

TAYLOR: It's not actually down the street. We're over on Wisteria.

TOM: Randy's house.

HUNTER: We just met your father at the town meeting.

TAYLOR: Oh yeah? What happened?

HUNTER: I'm sure your father will tell you.

TAYLOR: Bad news, huh?

BAILEY: Most people don't think so.

TAYLOR: I'd better be going. It's past my curfew. Nice to meet all of you.

HUNTER: Nice to meet you, Taylor.

[No response from BAILEY and MARIAN]

TOM: See you tomorrow?

TAYLOR: Sure.

[TAYLOR and TOM exit.]

BAILEY: That's all we need.

HUNTER: He seems like a nice kid.

MARIAN: You think everyone is nice.

HUNTER: Maybe. I try to.

BAILEY: *[To MARIAN]* You'd better nip this in the bud.

HUNTER: Nip what?

MARIAN: Let me handle this.

HUNTER: He's our son. Yours and mine. Not yours and Bailey's.

BAILEY: We know.

HUNTER: What's that supposed to mean?

[TOM returns.]

MARIAN: From now on, no visitors without my permission.

HUNTER: Marian, this is the first visitor in . . .

MARIAN: What do you know about this boy?

TOM: He lived in California with his mother. She died. He just moved here to live with his father.

MARIAN: That's all?

TOM: What's the . . .

MARIAN: *[Before he can finish]* . . . You cannot be friendly with that boy.

HUNTER: I see no reason why they shouldn't. . . .

BAILEY: I sure as hell do.

HUNTER: KEEP OUT OF THIS! Tom will find out what he needs to know about his friend in good time.

BAILEY: Son, were you listening at all tonight?

HUNTER: I didn't feel very good about what I heard tonight. And I don't feel too good about what I'm hearing in here.

BAILEY: You're opening one hell of a can of worms, Hunter. And there may be no one around you can call a friend.

HUNTER: If that happens, I reckon you'll have something to do with it.

BAILEY: I certainly won't protect you. We're businessmen, remember. And we're dependent on the goodwill of the people around here if we're going to keep in business.

HUNTER: We run a newspaper. That's not just a business.

BAILEY: Don't preach to me about the high calling of journalism. Nobody has to read a newspaper anymore. We reflect the values out here, or we're out of business.

HUNTER: Values?

MARIAN: Dad is right and you know it.

BAILEY: You're getting yourself into a no-win situation. Sleep on it. You can still get out of this gracefully.

MARIAN: I'll see Dad out. You had better have a talk with your son.

TOM: I'm right here, Mom. Don't talk as if I'm not here.

MARIAN: *[Laced with irony]* I know you're here, Tom.

BAILEY: Tom, son, would you go up to your room for just a minute or two?

TOM: Gladly, sir. *[He exits.]*

BAILEY: That resolution tonight is serious business. A lot of important people are behind it.

HUNTER: And some aren't.

BAILEY: The point is, I'm behind it, and I don't care about those who aren't.

HUNTER: I see.

BAILEY: Marian and I don't want any more trouble with that house on Wisteria.

HUNTER: What do you two have to do with that house?

BAILEY: If I find out he's with that boy, I'll have him out of here and into military school before he knows what hit him.

HUNTER: I think I have some say in that. I'm his father.

BAILEY: Then act like it, for God Almighty's sake! Lay down the law!

HUNTER: Whose law? Yours?
BAILEY: I'm going home.
MARIAN: I'll see you to your car.

[MARIAN and BAILEY exit.]

HUNTER: *[Calls]* Tom!

[While HUNTER waits for TOM, he tries to control his anger and think through what he is going to do. After a pause, TOM enters.]

TOM: What happened? What's wrong with Taylor?
HUNTER: Your friend's visit couldn't have been timed worse.
TOM: Why are they always mad at you?
HUNTER: Let's talk about Taylor now. Okay?
TOM: Sure.

[MARIAN reenters, sits by the door.]

HUNTER: I want to handle this, Marian.
MARIAN: And I want to hear how you handle it.
HUNTER: Fine.
TOM: What did Taylor do?
HUNTER: He didn't do anything. Look, Taylor lives with his father and his fa-
   ther's—friend—
MARIAN: Lover. Male lover. They're homosexuals.
TOM: I know.
MARIAN: You know. And do you know about Taylor?
TOM: What?
MARIAN: What! That he's homosexual, too?
TOM: He didn't say that.
HUNTER: There's no reason to assume that.
MARIAN: I'd bet on it.
HUNTER: LET ME HANDLE THIS! Sam, Taylor's father I'm sure is a decent man
   who is trying to raise his son decently. But there are a lot of people who don't
   want people like Taylor's father and his friend living out here.
TOM: That's crazy!
HUNTER: His father's friend is a doctor who treats AIDS patients. That scares
   people, too.
TOM: So what?
MARIAN: So we'd rather you not be too close to Taylor.
TOM: He's my friend!
MARIAN: I don't want that boy in this house. And you are forbidden to go to that
   . house.
TOM: This isn't going to happen again!! I belong there!!!

[TOM runs out of the room. HUNTER runs after him. MARIAN sits stock-still at the table. After a pause, HUNTER returns.]

HUNTER: What the hell did that mean?

MARIAN: I'd like to burn that house to the ground.

HUNTER: That's a bit extreme.

MARIAN: Is it? First Randy's death. Then Tom breaks down and tries to kill himself.

HUNTER: Shock and grief.

MARIAN: You know as well as I that people didn't think it was normal.

HUNTER: Your father didn't think it was normal.

MARIAN: Now we have that gay couple and their boy in that house. All Tom needs is to latch onto that boy and be seen all over with him.

HUNTER: Are you worried about Tom or what people will say?

MARIAN: You know the two are connected. Randy's parents were smart to leave.

HUNTER: Probably in disgust, given the monumental lack of compassion they received.

MARIAN: It wasn't something people here wanted to deal with.

HUNTER: People! Who the hell are these almighty people? I wish you'd worry less about people and more about what's right for us.

MARIAN: Like inviting those men to dinner?

HUNTER: It won't kill us.

MARIAN: If they stay, more will come.

HUNTER: You sound like old Lester Maddox trying to keep blacks from eating his fried chicken. Seeing old Lester out at the meeting tonight was the perfect touch.

MARIAN: Old Lester became governor after that.

HUNTER: Let's hope times have changed.

MARIAN: Not that much.

HUNTER: They seem like nice men. I don't want anything bad to happen to them.

MARIAN: They're asking for it.

[Phone rings.]

I'll check on Tom.

[HUNTER answers phone.]

HUNTER: Hello. Yes, Dale. . . . Well, I'm just trying to keep an open mind. . . . The paper has taken no stand on the issue. . . . I take it that's an ultimatum. . . . Well, I'll take that under advisement. . . . You've been good loyal clients, Dale. . . . I'll let you know. . . . Good night.

[HUNTER hangs up. MARIAN enters.]

That was Dale Wilson. The threats begin. Support the resolution in my editorials, keep away from those people, or his store will pull their advertising.

MARIAN: Really. Tom's gone again.

[MARIAN moves forward as lights dim on kitchen.]

I know you think I'm the monster in this story. I don't care. Yes, I'm a fighter. Every household needs a fighter, and God knows, Hunter doesn't want the job.

I've lived all my life here. I teach at the Christian school. I like the fact that the people here are united by their beliefs, their values—yes, values—We want things to stay the same. For us and for our children. Change isn't always progress. Look at the news!

It looks like I don't love my son. He doesn't love me! Tom was always a stranger to me. He acted like he knew he had come to the wrong house but didn't want to be rude about it. After Randy's death he became a living accusation.

But what can I be accused of? Everything I did was to protect him, to make him see that this is the good life. It is. He'll see it some day.

He's gone to that house. Well, I'll be the bitch and drag him out of there. *[She exits.]*

4. SAM AND RICK'S HOUSE

[Lights up on SAM and RICK's living room. RICK and SAM enter.]

RICK: Just for the record, it's you I'm pissed at. Their venom was to be expected. But to suck up to those redneck bastards!

SAM: I just want to see if we can live here in peace.

RICK: Maybe you and that Tucker character can move in together.

[TAYLOR enters.]

SAM: Where were you tonight?

TAYLOR: Up the street. Tom Tucker's.

RICK: Son of *the* Tuckers?

TAYLOR: I guess. What happened at the meeting?

RICK: Didn't the Tuckers tell you?

TAYLOR: They told me to ask my father. So what happened?

SAM: Our kind are officially unwelcome in this county.

RICK: The County Council has given everyone a hunting license. Beat up faggots. Burn down dykes' houses.

TAYLOR: Great. Did anybody fight back?

SAM: Oh yeah, a few brave souls. A lesbian couple spoke up. One guy. They said they had lived here for years and were hurt at the welcome mat being pulled out from under them.

RICK: Hurt? They should be outraged. Spit in their fucking faces. What the hell are we doing here?

TAYLOR: Rick's got a point. What the hell *are* we doing here?

SAM: We liked the house, remember? And we're sending you to the best public high school in the area.

TAYLOR: So this is for me! Great!! So I can go to a school where I'm treated like a leper.

SAM: You didn't tell me there was trouble at school.

TAYLOR: You didn't ask. I haven't been attacked—yet—but they make it clear I'm not welcome.

RICK: Shit! Nothing changes!

TAYLOR: Did you go through this?

RICK: Oh yeah! People get real excited about cultural purification. And they pass their hatred on to their kids.

TAYLOR: What am I supposed to do?

SAM: We'll see about getting you into a private school.

RICK: Or we move.

TAYLOR: Maybe I should go back to California.

SAM: Back to your grandparents?

TAYLOR: I had a life there.

[SAM, clearly hurt, starts out of the room.]

I'm sorry, Dad. I want to be with you guys, but I hate this. I lose Mom. I lose my friends. You guys have been great, but I want a life.

RICK: The joys of suburban living.

SAM: You wanted this, too.

RICK: I had misgivings. I'm the only dark-skinned person out here who's not mowing people's lawns. That's a little bit unsettling. Then there's the matter of hating fags. But maybe if you invite them all to dinner, they'll come to love us.

SAM: Let's just drop that.

TAYLOR: What's this dinner thing?

RICK: Oh, this is the best part. Old Sam invited anyone who wanted to see how normal we are to drop by. We'll have to put metal detectors by the front door.

SAM: I have to begin from the premise that these are decent people.

RICK: Who want to run you out of the county. Christ, inviting them over! They want to burn this place down, not visit it!

TAYLOR: Don't worry. No one will take you up on your invitation.

RICK: Your friend's father did.

TAYLOR: That's why she and her father were so pissed off!

RICK: Dish, child.

SAM: Can I get a beer first?

RICK: One for me, too.

TAYLOR: And me.

SAM: Forget it. *[He goes to kitchen.]*

RICK: *[To TOM]* Okay. The inside story on the Tucker household.

SAM: *[Offstage]* Talk loudly so I can hear.

TAYLOR: For a beer.

SAM: *[Off]*: Alright. One. If the information's worth it.

TAYLOR: Tom is in my class. He called me up and asked me over. We studied math and played video games. He's a nice guy. Sad, though.

RICK: I'm not surprised. So there's one kid who's friendly.

TAYLOR: Yeah, but he doesn't have any friends either. He just stays in his room all the time. Like Rapunzel.

RICK: Don't go camp on us, Taylor. Your grandparents will repossess.

TAYLOR: His parents gave me the cold shoulder. His mother did. And his grandfather. His father's all right.

SAM: *[Offstage]* So. Details. What happened tonight?

TAYLOR: His parents and grandfather came home from the meeting. Mrs. Tucker looked like she was about to go ballistic. And the old man was harrumphing all over the place.

RICK: They were probably as pissed about her hubby's niceness as I was about my hubby's performance. It was like watching the death throes of liberalism.

SAM: *[Returning with drinks]* Then, to top it all off, they discover their son has been playing with the son of the house of sin.

TAYLOR: You got it!

SAM: You've earned your beer.

RICK: I'd love to have been a fly on the wall.

TAYLOR: There was a real family feud. Him against her and Daddy.

RICK: But Daddy owns the paper. Hubby only edits it. And I bet she's old family who married beneath her. Mr. Liberal will lose.

TAYLOR: Anyway, Tom and I walked in, and the temperature dropped to zero.

SAM: I'm sorry.

TAYLOR: Tom really needs a friend. So do I.

RICK: I have a feeling his mother won't be keen on you two being buddies.

TAYLOR: Yeah. I'm sure of that. Too bad. We're the two outcasts at school.

RICK: It is too bad.

TAYLOR: It gets worse.

SAM: Oh God!

TAYLOR: I shouldn't tell you this. . . .

RICK: Dish, child!

TAYLOR: Tom tried to slash his wrists last year—after his best friend shot himself.

RICK: Jesus! It doesn't take Sherlock Holmes to figure this one out!

TAYLOR: What do you mean?

SAM: Yeah. What do you mean?

RICK: And you're trained to analyze stories? Later.

TAYLOR: Randy—the friend—lived here.

RICK: Oh shit! We are in for it.

[Sound of a brick crashing through a window. Alarm system goes off. SAM runs out.]

Brick or grenade?

SAM: Brick.

TAYLOR: That's a relief.

RICK: Let the games begin.

RICK: I'll turn on the outside lighting. What was it?

TAYLOR: *[Has brought in brick from other room]* A brick. With a note. *[He unwraps note and reads it.]* "Get AIDS and die, faggots." People really say that? "Get AIDS and die!"

RICK: Oh yeah. All the time.

TAYLOR: It's so unbelievably cruel!

SAM: That hate! It doesn't scare me. It infuriates me. And the most infuriating thing is that it makes *me* hate. I don't want to feel like this.

RICK: It's a hell of a lot better than swallowing their bullshit and hating yourself.

TAYLOR: Can we please turn off the alarm?

[SAM does so.]

SAM: Now what?

TAYLOR: I'm going out and take a look around.

[TAYLOR goes to the front door. RICK stops him.]

RICK: Are you out of your fucking mind? Didn't you see *Deliverance?*

TAYLOR: No.

RICK: We all should have seen it before we decided to move here.

SAM: I'm worried about arms escalation. Today a brick, tomorrow a burning cross, Sunday guns.

RICK: I'm getting our gun.

SAM: You know I don't approve.

RICK: Tough! *[He gets gun from kitchen. Returns.]*

TAYLOR: Should we call the police?

RICK: You must be kidding!

TAYLOR: Yeah. Right. Maybe we ought to put up a for sale sign before they burn the place down.

RICK: Our version of the white flag? No fucking way! We stay!

SAM: Whoa! A minute ago you were screaming, "What am I doing here?"

RICK: That was before the brick. There are lots of reasons to leave this godforsaken place. . . .

SAM: This is God's country, lover. . . .

RICK: But this is still America, isn't it? Land of the free? Home of the brave? Well, we're free to live here, and I hope we're brave enough to hold our ground.

SAM: You're sure on your soapbox tonight.

TAYLOR: Rick's right. We really shouldn't run from this.

SAM: Not so fast! Your mother was terrified that if she died and you had to live with us, you'd get beaten up, ostracized, by other kids. Your grandparents sued for custody to avoid that.

RICK: They also didn't want you living with fags.

SAM: There was that, too.

TAYLOR: I took self-defense in San Diego. I'll just have to get back in practice.

RICK: Quick.

TAYLOR: I know.

SAM: So we stay.

RICK: We stay. And no more pretending these are nice people who want to get along with us. This is war. Sam?

SAM: This goes against my nature. . . .

RICK: Sam!

SAM: I will keep my mouth shut in public places.

RICK: Good boy. Batten down the hatches.

SAM: What do we do about the vigilantes?

RICK: You and I probably should sleep in shifts. One of us should stay downstairs and keep watch.

SAM: What are we going to do if they come back?

RICK: Sound the alarm. Make a shitload of noise. And keep the gun where we can get at it.

SAM: I'll take the first shift. *[To TAYLOR]* And you've got school. Don't try to sneak Letterman on either. Sleep.

TAYLOR: Spoil sport. Goodnight guys. *[He kisses RICK and SAM. Exits.]*

RICK: That's the first time he's done that.

SAM: Sometimes I think he's your son more than mine anyway.

RICK: Ours now.

SAM: I don't want the kid to have any more traumas. He's lived through a lot this year. His mother dying, the custody battle with her folks.

RICK: Taylor will be alright. But those other boys. Poor Randy. Sad, sad, sad.

[TAYLOR runs in. Stops in middle of room. Listens.]

TAYLOR: Somebody's outside.

RICK: I heard them.

SAM: Front or back?

TAYLOR: Back.

SAM: What if the bastard's armed?

RICK: Bullets would be coming through the window the way the brick did. They're out to scare us, not to kill us. So far.

TAYLOR: I heard only one guy.

RICK: *[Grabs gun]* You two stay here. I want to catch this asshole. It may be the one who threw the brick.

SAM: You're crazy.

[RICK goes out front door. SAM and TAYLOR watch from inside room.]

SAM: He's going to get himself killed.
TAYLOR: Worry about the other guy.

[RICK returns with TOM held at gunpoint.]

TOM: Please. Put the gun down.
TAYLOR: *[In unison with TOM]* Put the gun down. It's Tom Tucker.
RICK: Of course.

[RICK puts gun away. TOM goes over to TAYLOR.]

TAYLOR: Tom, what were you doing out there?
TOM: I had to talk to you.
SAM: Don't you think introductions are in order?
TAYLOR: This is my father, Sam.
SAM: Glad to meet you . . .
RICK: . . . at this ungodly hour.
TOM: *[To RICK]* You're . . .
RICK: An alien, actually. Sam and Taylor are earthlings I hold in thrall.
TAYLOR: That's Rick Martinez, my father's partner.
RICK: Lover. Why are you here, Tom?
TOM: My mother said I couldn't see Taylor anymore.
RICK: Surprise, surprise!
TOM: They're going to make trouble.
TAYLOR: Who?
TOM: My mother. My grandfather.
RICK: We've figured that out. They've got help. We've already lost a window.
TOM: I'm on your side.
RICK: Against your family?
TOM: My father's okay.
SAM: Your father is outnumbered. So are we.
RICK: Why did you have to run over to tell us this tonight?
TOM: I had to be here. He lived here. Randy. I loved him.
SAM: *[To RICK]* That's what—???
RICK: Exactly.
TOM: Randy was my best friend since we were little kids. We started playing with
   each other, you know. Having sex. That summer it got serious. He was every-
   thing to me.
RICK: Did anybody know?
TOM: We didn't think so. We thought it was our secret.
RICK: And you were mistaken.
TOM: We used to go to this graveyard by an old church a couple of miles out of
   town.

5. THE GRAVEYARD.

[RANDY enters the graveyard area downstage with sleeping bag. TOM joins him. They strip to their boxers and climb into sleeping bag together. Then they take off boxers and throw them by their clothes.]

TOM: I love it here.
RANDY: It's okay.
TOM: Just okay?
RANDY: It's sort of creepy.
TOM: But it's ours.
RANDY: We're the only ones who think so.
TOM: That's alright. Nothing of this belongs to anyone else. Us. Here. We own this.
RANDY: That's bullshit, Tommy. We own squat.

[TOM gets out of sleeping bag. Sits hugging his knees.]

Come back in here, Tommy.

[RANDY sits up, puts his hand on TOM's shoulder. TOM recoils.]

TOM: Summer's over. I wanted tonight to be special.
RANDY: I know. It's just that I can't keep up with you.
TOM: You like it as much as I do.
RANDY: I mean feelings. I just don't feel as much as you do.
TOM: That's okay. I love you, Randy. It's okay.
RANDY: No, it isn't. School starts tomorrow.
TOM: So what? Nothing has to change.
RANDY: Bullshit!
TOM: We can still get together on weekends.
RANDY: I don't know, Tommy.
TOM: Why not?
RANDY: My father says I've got to date more.
TOM: That's stupid. You don't have to.
RANDY: Yes, I do. You'd better, too.
TOM: Why?
RANDY: Why do you think? They're suspicious.
TOM: Your parents?
RANDY: My dad. Your mom, too. Did you see how she ignored me tonight?
TOM: She's that way with everybody. The Ice Goddess. She ignores me!
RANDY: I saw your granddad downtown today. I said hello. He turned and crossed the street. He used to take us fishing!
TOM: He was thinking about something else. You know how he is.
RANDY: They know, Tommy. I know they know. Will they tell my father? He'll kill me!

TOM: We've been careful.

RANDY: No, we haven't. We're on the phone every night.

TOM: Lots of guys are.

RANDY: Tommy, we don't have girlfriends. Everybody knows we haven't screwed anyone.

TOM: Yes, we have.

RANDY: Listen, Tommy! We can't fuck up our lives. I want a decent life with a job and a home.

TOM: And a wife and kids?

RANDY: Maybe. That's what's expected if you're going to live around here.

TOM: That's not a good reason.

RANDY: I know. I don't know.

TOM: You want to stop?

RANDY: No, but . . .

TOM: Then what choice do we have?

RANDY: None. It's just . . .

TOM: Maybe we should just go home now.

RANDY: Tommy, come back in here. Please!

[*TOM gets back in sleeping bag. They snuggle together.*]

See? Isn't that better?

TOM: I love you, Randy. I can't give you up.

RANDY: I don't want to give you up either. But they're going to catch us, Tommy.

TOM: I don't give a shit anymore.

RANDY: Don't be stupid.

TOM: I don't.

RANDY: [*Sits up quickly*] Someone's coming.

TOM: Nobody ever comes out here.

RANDY: Somebody's coming now. I swear. Listen.

TOM: Shut up and they won't find us.

[*A flashlight beam hits the two of them from downstage.*]

VOICE (RANDY'S FATHER): Get out of that bag, both of you.

RANDY: Daddy . . .

FATHER: Now! I've got a gun.

RANDY: Daddy? How did you . . .

[*RANDY's FATHER enters from down right. We see only his back throughout the scene.*]

FATHER: Shut up. Just get out of that bag.

[*TOM and RANDY get out of the bag, trying to keep themselves covered.*]

Tom. You get on your clothes and go home.

TOM: What are you going to do?

FATHER: To you? Nothing. This never happened. None of this with you two ever happened. And don't you tell anyone otherwise.

TOM: Thank you.

FATHER: It's no favor to you. I don't want anyone knowing about this. Now get your clothes, and get the hell out of here.

[TOM grabs his clothes and hurriedly puts them on. RANDY starts toward his clothes.]

[To RANDY] You stay put.

TOM: *[Putting on his clothes]* What are you going to do? You can't hurt him.

FATHER: I said get out of here! Now!! And if you try to get in touch with this piece of shit, I will call your parents. Hell, I'll put an ad in their fucking newspaper. Then I'll come after you with this.

[RANDY's father cocks his rifle. TOM runs out. RANDY is still frozen in the light. FATHER moves menacingly toward RANDY.]

RANDY: How did you know we were here?

FATHER: Shut up, faggot. I'm going to teach you a lesson.

[RANDY backs away from his father, falls on sleeping bag. Father kneels in front of him, pins him down. Lights down on RANDY and FATHER as RANDY screams, "NO!!!"

Blackout, during which FATHER exits.

Lights up. RANDY is huddled up on sleeping bag. The rifle is lying on the ground. RANDY sees the rifle. He places the butt end on the ground and kneels with the barrel in his mouth. Blackout. Gunshot echoes through theater.

When lights come up on living room area, TOM is back with TAYLOR, SAM, and RICK.]

6. SAM AND RICK'S LIVING ROOM.

TAYLOR: Did Randy's father know you saw what happened?

TOM: I don't think so. They moved away right after Randy killed himself.

RICK: And your folks?

TOM: No one is supposed to talk about anything ugly around here. Randy killed himself. I lost my best friend. Period.

SAM: Holding all this in must have been awful.

TOM: I've spent a year feeling like I was going to puke. I dream of Randy's father's face behind that light. And the gun. And Randy's face.

[TAYLOR puts his arm around him to comfort him.]

TAYLOR: It's okay.

TOM: I had to get it out. It's my fault. He'd be alive if we hadn't . . .

RICK: How could you blame yourself? You didn't kill him. Blame his father. Don't blame yourself. Or Randy.

SAM: Taylor, take Tom into the kitchen and get him something to drink.

[TAYLOR and TOM exit to kitchen.]

Well, this story isn't going to win on *America's Funniest Home Videos*.

RICK: Fishy, though.

SAM: You don't believe him?

RICK: Sure. But how did Randy's father know where they were?

SAM: Now we've clicked over to *Murder She Wrote*.

RICK: The kid looks absolutely haunted.

SAM: If we decide to make a cause of this kid, we're really declaring war.

RICK: War has already been declared. A father raped and beat the shit out of his son for loving someone. A brick came through our window. You want everything to be nice, Sam. It isn't. It's not a nice world.

SAM: So what do you propose? That we sue the kid's parents for custody?

RICK: I'm not sure yet. But we've got to help him. People fall into your lap. Tom has fallen into ours. We have a responsibility.

SAM: To do what?

RICK: We let the kid know he's got friends. That's all.

SAM: Around here that's called recruiting.

RICK: Who's side are you on?

SAM: I'm simply stating facts.

RICK: That's not a fact. It's a prejudice. We're not closeted priests fondling our charges. We're out, remember? And doing the honorable thing.

SAM: Sometimes your righteousness is truly nauseating.

RICK: Ditto to your wimpy pragmatism. You want to fold? Escape? Leave this kid to be a basket case?

SAM: I'm worried about Taylor.

RICK: I'll bet the ranch that Taylor will not want to fold on this.

SAM: It's not his fight.

RICK: Maybe it is his fight. Ever think of that?

SAM: What does that mean?

RICK: Maybe he's gay. Ever talk about it with him?

SAM: No. He just got here a couple of months ago.

RICK: Never? Never told him the facts of life? Never warned him about safe sex?

SAM: No. I guess I assumed his mother did.

RICK: You must be kidding! She didn't want to believe he had eyes for anyone but her.

SAM: That's . . .

RICK: Beside the point. Sorry. Talk to Taylor.

SAM: I just can't broach that subject yet.

RICK: Yet? He's almost seventeen.

SAM: I know. But . . .

RICK: Are you afraid the spirits of his grandparents and the ghost of his mother will steal him away? Afraid you'll corrupt him?

SAM: Yes, damn it! I am afraid of being blamed if . . .

RICK: You don't want him to be gay!

SAM: Would you?

RICK: I made my peace with that subject a long time ago. I thought you had, too.

SAM: I have.

RICK: Bullshit! This explains your need to have those shitheads approve of you.

SAM: I want their respect. Don't you?

RICK: I only want them to leave us alone. Jesus! You're still ashamed!

SAM: That's not true.

RICK: I've had enough of this discussion for one night. *[He starts off. Stops.]* One final word. It doesn't take tea leaves to see what's going to happen between Tom and Taylor.

SAM: What?

RICK: Tom needs to love someone. And be loved. We'll soon know if Taylor's— perish the thought!!—one of us. Goodnight, asshole! *[He starts off again. Door-bell rings.]* Gosh, I wonder who that might be? You answer. You're his pal.

SAM: What do we do about Tom?

RICK: We're not going to start hiding people in closets. We tell the truth.

SAM: You're such a fucking boy scout.

RICK: *I'm* the boy scout????

SAM: Now behave.

RICK: I promise not to fire the first shot.

[SAM goes to the door. HUNTER and MARIAN are there.]

SAM: Come in.

[HUNTER shakes RICK's hand. MARIAN stands in silent disapproval.]

RICK: *[To MARIAN]* So you just couldn't wait to take us up on our invitation.

MARIAN: It's a bit late for irony. Is our son here?

SAM: He's in the kitchen with my son. I understand you met Taylor earlier.

HUNTER: Yes. We did.

MARIAN: I'm surprised you didn't send him right home. It's almost midnight on a school night.

RICK: He wasn't in any condition to go right home.

MARIAN: What does that mean?

SAM: He was rather upset. He was worried about Taylor's safety, I think.

MARIAN: We told him he was not to be friends with Taylor.

SAM: So we heard. May we ask why?

MARIAN: Do I really have to spell it out?

RICK: Yes.

MARIAN: I don't believe you're his father.

HUNTER: This isn't the time for a battle. We just came for our son.

SAM: Taylor is a good kid. He'd be a good friend for Tom.

MARIAN: I don't think so. I think he'd cause Tom to be ostracized.

RICK: From what I understand, Tom doesn't have any friends.

MARIAN: He'll never have any if he hangs around with your son.

SAM: Taylor has always been very popular.

MARIAN: He won't be here. People aren't going to let your son in their house. Or their children in yours.

RICK: I can imagine who will stir up "the people."

MARIAN: They're already stirred up.

SAM: We know. We just had a brick sail through the dining room window.

HUNTER: I'm sorry.

MARIAN: Maybe you'll take the hint.

RICK: I respect your honesty, Mrs. Tucker. I really do. Your values reek, but you don't beat around the bush.

SAM: Your son came here of his own free will tonight. He was distraught. We thought he should cool down a bit before he went home.

MARIAN: What did he tell you?

RICK: Ask him. I'll get him. *[He exits to kitchen.]*

SAM: Rick is very angry about what happened at the meeting.

HUNTER: I can understand that.

MARIAN: May I ask what you intend to do?

SAM: We intend to stay.

[TOM and TAYLOR enter with RICK.]

MARIAN: I see. Tom, we're going home. Now.

TOM: These people are my friends. I'm not going to turn my back on them because you want me to.

MARIAN: This isn't the place to discuss this.

RICK: What better place?

MARIAN: I can't imagine a worse place.

RICK: Not enough Ethan Allen?

MARIAN: I hate this house. I hate your being here. I hate your poisoning this town.

TOM: Maybe you'd like them all to do what Randy did!

MARIAN: Keep Randy out of this.

TOM: Randy and I loved each other.

MARIAN: We're going home. I am not having this discussion.

HUNTER: It is late. . . .

MARIAN: EVER!! I knew this house would poison everything.

SAM: Tom and Randy happened before we came on the scene.

MARIAN: So this has already been discussed tonight? Has it, Tom?

TOM: I told them. I had to tell someone.

RICK: Wait a minute! You knew about Tom and Randy?

MARIAN: Of course I knew.

TOM: Randy thought you and he knew. And you never said anything!

[*TOM fights to control his rage. All that he has pent up the past year is getting ready to blow. TAYLOR stays near him.*]

HUNTER: I'm sorry, but I'm a bit lost here.

MARIAN: As usual, you're a bit naive. Tom and Randy were having—what would you gentlemen say?—an affair?

HUNTER: Were you, Tom?

TOM: Yes. All that summer. It seemed natural.

MARIAN: Natural!

HUNTER: Oh my Lord. Why didn't I see it?

MARIAN: Because you didn't want to see it.

TOM: How did you know?

MARIAN: You changed so much.

TOM: I was happy!

HUNTER: Why wasn't I told?

MARIAN: And what would you have done? Been wonderfully warm and support-ive? That was the last thing we wanted.

HUNTER: We? Of course. You told your father, but not me.

MARIAN: I knew he'd know what to do.

HUNTER: It's none of his business! But, of course, everything is his business. The paper, the county, our life.

MARIAN: This conversation is finished.

TOM: Why didn't you tell me?

MARIAN: What did you want me to tell you? That it was disgusting? That I get sick thinking about it? That I was mortified? That sometimes I think Randy did the right thing?

TOM: Then why didn't you give *me* a gun?

[*TOM, crying, runs out into kitchen. TAYLOR runs after him.*]

HUNTER: I'm going to my son. [*He exits into kitchen.*]

RICK: [*To SAM*] You might check on yours.

SAM: Yes. I'll be right back.

[SAM exits. MARIAN sits stone-still.]

RICK: *[After a silence]* I'm going to have a brandy. Want some?
MARIAN: Yes. Please.

[RICK gets brandies.]

None of this had to be talked about. With anyone. It was over.
RICK: I see. If the faggots hadn't moved down the street into Randy's house, you could have pretended that nothing ever happened.
MARIAN: They were boys experimenting with something dangerous. Who could have known Randy was so mixed up?
RICK: What about Tom? He's been grief-stricken for a year?
MARIAN: He'll get over it.
RICK: And the suicide attempt?
MARIAN: That's none of your business.
RICK: It is now.
MARIAN: Questionable. And I refuse to be made the bitch in your woman-hating homosexual fantasy.
RICK: Lady, I don't hate women. I like them a lot. I just hate bigots.
MARIAN: I'm not a bigot. I believe in certain things—absolutes. There is right and wrong. I still believe that.
RICK: And Hunter.
MARIAN: Hunter thinks he lives in Mister Roger's neighborhood.
RICK: You and Hunter sound like me and Sam.
MARIAN: Don't try to equate your life with mine.
RICK: Too bad, darlin'. You might have had a friend.
MARIAN: Please. I'm tired.
RICK: I'm tired, too. And I'm not interested in your problem with gay people. I just don't want it to be our problem. Like you, I'm perfectly willing to be as much a monster as I need to be to protect my turf and my loved ones. And, lady, I can outbitch you any day. Because there is one big difference between us. I enjoy being a bitch!

[A pause. MARIAN looks at RICK. He looks back.]

MARIAN: Noted.
RICK: Good.
MARIAN: This is—was—Randy's house. Did Tom tell you that?
RICK: We—knew.
MARIAN: Well, your friend . . .
RICK: Lover.
MARIAN: Lover. Got this house under false pretenses.
RICK: How's that?

MARIAN: He came with a woman friend to see it. Then with two women and you. Never just the two of you.

RICK: You think Sam and I should have come hand in hand?

MARIAN: You two had separate phone listings in Atlanta.

RICK: I didn't want calls from his students, and he didn't want calls from my patients. You thought we did that to put one over on the citizens of this fair town?

MARIAN: Some people assumed that.

RICK: How do you know all this?

MARIAN: My father is chairman of the bank that sold you the house. Where your mortgage is.

RICK: And somebody didn't do their homework.

MARIAN: That somebody is out of a job.

RICK: Daddy's merciless.

MARIAN: That's one way to look at it.

RICK: What's another?

MARIAN: My father holds the line.

RICK: One thing puzzles me about you people. You're crystal clear on what you're against, but I can never figure out what you're for.

MARIAN: What are you for?

RICK: My family. The people I love. I'll fight to the death for us. You can't make us ashamed of our life together.

MARIAN: A lot of people think you should be.

RICK: Sam's a fine man. I didn't trust anyone when I met him. I had been disowned by my parents, thrown out of my fraternity in college, and fallen in love with a few guys who hated themselves too much to love. Sam showed me that love is possible.

MARIAN: Obviously he didn't show that to his wife and son.

RICK: Leaving them was very hard for him. But he was gay and deserved a real marriage.

MARIAN: So he left his wife and child for you.

RICK: Yes. And I'm not about to be judged for that.

MARIAN: I didn't say a word.

RICK: You didn't have to. A look is worth a thousand words. Jesus! It never ceases to amaze me how you righteous people get your kicks being horrified.

MARIAN: Don't stereotype me.

RICK: Excuse me! What have you been doing to us? Sam and I are as committed a couple as there is in Cobb County. That's our choice. We both love Taylor. We don't have sex with him. We leave incest to you family values people. And Tom is safe from me. I'm not into teenage boys.

MARIAN: And Taylor?

RICK: What? Is he into teenage boys? I don't know. Ask Tom.

MARIAN: How would Tom know?

RICK: I'm sure Tom has asked Taylor. Or will.

MARIAN: That's hitting below the belt.

RICK: Like you, I believe in putting all my cards on the table. Were Randy's parents encouraged to leave? Were there financial rewards?

MARIAN: This is really none of your business.

RICK: Our two lady friends? They run the gay newspaper in Atlanta. This would make wonderful investigative journalism.

MARIAN: They could get sued.

RICK: Not if they did their job right.

MARIAN: And if I tell you?

RICK: And we're left alone?

MARIAN: I can't guarantee that.

RICK: I think Daddy could. My guess is the pot was sweetened to get Randy's folks and all other traces of Randy out of here. *[Pause]* I'll take silence as assent. And after all that money and effort, a bunch of faggots move in and gussy the place up. And your son is back over here. Delicious!

MARIAN: I'm glad you're enjoying this.

RICK: Oh, I am! How did Randy's father know where Randy and Tom were that night? Was your Daddy involved in that, too?

MARIAN: I think you've asked enough questions.

RICK: Shucks! I've just begun.

MARIAN: I'd appreciate it if you would get my husband and son. We should be going home.

RICK: Just one final question. Did you know Randy's father raped him that night after he chased Tom off? And left the gun for Randy to use?

MARIAN: Did Tom tell you that?

RICK: Tom was there.

MARIAN: *[Stunned, but trying not to show it]* I hadn't heard that. And I doubt it.

RICK: Do you really? Well, I guess we're all caught up now. I'll get Hunter and Tom.

> *[RICK exits. MARIAN gets some more brandy. She starts to cry but stops herself. HUNTER enters.]*

HUNTER: Tom's pretty shaken up. Almost hysterical. Rick's giving him a tranquilizer. He's staying here tonight.

MARIAN: I beg your pardon. He isn't staying here.

HUNTER: He's in good hands. Rick's a doctor, remember?

MARIAN: If Tom needs a doctor, he can go where he's always gone.

HUNTER: To your old family doctor? Are you sure you want him to have a report on what transpired here tonight?

MARIAN: Since when do you worry about that?

HUNTER: *I* don't.

MARIAN: What do expect me to say, Hunter? Touché? You win?

HUNTER: Never that, Marian. Never that.

MARIAN: Being around the boys has certainly steeled your nerve.

HUNTER: I don't consider a physician and a professor to be boys. At any rate, they didn't steel my nerve, as you put it. That meeting your father engineered did that. And your merciless behavior toward Tom.

MARIAN: You know no one here would accept what was going on with Randy.

HUNTER: It was no one's business but ours.

MARIAN: Don't be naive.

HUNTER: You would sacrifice your son for the sake of appearances? It's disgusting!

MARIAN: Oh, shut up, Hunter!

HUNTER: I've said my piece.

MARIAN: Are you staying here, too? Is the bed big enough for all of you?

HUNTER: Oh, Marian, you're off form tonight. Surely you can do better than that.

MARIAN: But you think my son is staying here despite any protest or objection. There are laws, Hunter.

HUNTER: Call your father, as I'm sure you will. He'll find one or two or bend a dozen. Meanwhile Tom either stays here—under a doctor's care I might add—or I take him to an emergency room. There's no law against his being here.

MARIAN: I don't want him here.

HUNTER: I do. An impasse.

MARIAN: I want to go home.

HUNTER: I'll drop you off.

MARIAN: Where are you going?

HUNTER: I don't know. To think.

MARIAN: About what?

HUNTER: I hate what I've seen and heard tonight. I have to think about what that means for me.

MARIAN: Are you thinking about leaving me?

HUNTER: I'm sure Daddy will stop that, too.

MARIAN: He damn well might.

HUNTER: Marian, I need to figure out what's left for us.

MARIAN: *You* need to figure that out? I figured it out a long time ago. We do what we have to.

HUNTER: Have to? By whose law?

MARIAN: If we separate, you may just lose everything. The paper, your son. Everything.

HUNTER: You and Daddy would see to that, wouldn't you? Why do you want to keep me?

MARIAN: Because I refuse to face the mockery of having you leave me. I refuse to have people think I failed at this marriage.

HUNTER: You haven't failed. You've worked very hard at it. It's just that it shouldn't have been such work.

MARIAN: What should it have been, Hunter? Pleasure?

HUNTER: There are couples who enjoy each other.

MARIAN: Like Sam and Rick? Or Tom and Randy?

HUNTER: I don't know about Sam and Rick. Or Tom and Randy. Though I should have known.

MARIAN: What would you have done about it?

HUNTER: I don't know. Maybe nothing. Tom was happy for the first time in his life the year before Randy died. Finally we had a happy kid. Then Randy's death and he was worse than ever. A time bomb.

MARIAN: He thinks I'm partly responsible for Randy's death.

HUNTER: Aren't you? You told "Daddy."

MARIAN: He had a man-to-man talk with Randy's father.

HUNTER: Who raped his son and left the gun for him to kill himself. My God!

MARIAN: So they got that news to you?

HUNTER: Sam told me.

MARIAN: I don't believe it happened.

HUNTER: You'd have made a great Nazi. It did happen. And you're responsible for that brutality. You and your father. Randy was as good as murdered.

MARIAN: That's a bit strong.

HUNTER: Is it? Did you feel any sorrow for that boy? He just about lived with us since he was five.

MARIAN: Not after what he did.

HUNTER: He didn't do it alone, Marian. Do you feel as little for Tom? Would you care as little if Tom had succeeded in killing himself last fall?

[MARIAN doesn't answer.]

All this time I've worried that you were holding in your feelings about last fall. You weren't feeling anything, were you?

MARIAN: Oh, I was feeling something. Such anger I thought I would burst.

HUNTER: You're merciless, Marian. Like your father. Like so many of the good folk whose opinion means so much to you. I hate that southern hardness.

MARIAN: As much as I hate softness?

HUNTER: Humanity is not softness, Marian. This is a nightmare. I've got to get out of here.

MARIAN: So do I.

HUNTER: I'll drop you off home.

MARIAN: I'll walk.

HUNTER: As you wish.

MARIAN: You will not leave me.

HUNTER: That will be my decision, Marian. Not yours or your father's.

[MARIAN exits.]

Sam, Rick.

[SAM enters.]

SAM: Rick's upstairs with Tom. He'll be okay.

HUNTER: We're leaving. Thanks.

SAM: Are you going to be okay?

HUNTER: Don't worry about me. Worry about Tom. And yourself.

SAM: We'll get Tom to school.

HUNTER: Thanks. I'd like to look in on Tom before I go.

SAM: Sure. Go ahead.

[HUNTER exits. SAM flops on couch. RICK enters.]

RICK: Hunter's checking on Tom.

SAM: I know. Everything alright up there?

RICK: Tom's out like a light. For a few hours, at least.

SAM: And Taylor?

RICK: He's pretty tired. He'll sleep.

SAM: And you?

RICK: I'll live. I can deal with the Marians of this world. I admire her will, however misguided. I can deal with the bigotry. If it gets out of hand, there's always the city to hide in. What I can't deal with is your ambivalence about being gay. If you aren't clear on that, where are we?

SAM: I'm clear on us. But Taylor? I don't know if I want him to go through what we went through.

RICK: You fought it for so long, Sam. Through two years with a shrink and ten with a wife.

SAM: I fought it because I didn't think what we had was possible. Now that I have it, I'll fight with all I have to keep it.

RICK: Are you sure?

SAM: Yes, I'm sure. I'm sorry about what I said before. Taylor should be so lucky as to find a Rick Martinez.

RICK: I'm spoken for. Though there are moments I regret it.

SAM: I can be an idiot. And you're right. I love you.

RICK: Likewise.

[RICK's beeper goes off.]

Shit. That's all I need. I'll take it in the study.

[RICK exits. HUNTER enters.]

HUNTER: The boys are asleep.

SAM: Rick just got paged. He may have to go to the hospital.

HUNTER: I'd better go, too.

SAM: Where are you going?

HUNTER: For a drive, I guess. To think.

SAM: You're welcome to crash here. Join the crowd.

HUNTER: I really need to get out and think.
SAM: I understand.

[*RICK enters during following speech.*]

HUNTER: I can't stay with her. How could she know all that and not tell me? She and her father put the gun to that boy's head.
SAM: Marian and her father are just products of this place.
HUNTER: They're more responsible than that, Sam. They don't get off that easily.
RICK: I've got to go to the hospital. One of my patients is in crisis. One more piece of information—Marian's father got Randy's parents out of here—money and threats.
HUNTER: If anything nasty happens around here, it will get in the paper, despite him.
RICK: That's nice, but will any of your readers give a shit? Gotta go.

[*RICK kisses SAM. Exits.*]

HUNTER: I'm truly sorry about all this.
SAM: So far it's only words and a broken window. Worry about your son.
HUNTER: Thanks, Sam. Good night.

[*HUNTER shakes SAM'S hand. SAM hugs HUNTER. HUNTER awkwardly returns the embrace, then exits. SAM sits on sofa, eyes wide open. During next scene, SAM dozes off.*]

7. TAYLOR'S BEDROOM.

[*Lights out on SAM, up on bedroom. TAYLOR is asleep on the floor; TOM is on the bed. TOM wakes up. He looks at TAYLOR on the floor.*]

TOM: Taylor, are you awake?
TAYLOR: Yeah.
TOM: What was your mother like?
TAYLOR: She was pretty tough, but devoted.
TOM: Did she talk to you?
TAYLOR: Sure. Too much sometimes.
TOM: Do you miss her?
TAYLOR: Yeah. But Dad and Rick are being great.
TOM: They're incredible.
TAYLOR: We should get some sleep.
TOM: She knew all the time, Taylor. She never said a word to me.
TAYLOR: You never said anything to her either.
TOM: You know why I didn't! She'd have sent me away.

TAYLOR: But you want to get away.

TOM: Not to where she'd send me. She'd send me off to a military school or something.

TAYLOR: She just wants you to fit in.

TOM: Her way. I don't want to fit in here. *[After a pause]* You'll stick with me?

TAYLOR: Yeah. We'd better stick together. It's two against just about everybody. You ever take self-defense?

TOM: No. I don't think—

TAYLOR: You're going. We'll start this weekend. Now let's get some sleep.

> *[Pause. Then TOM gets out of bed and cuddles up next to TAYLOR on the floor.]*

Tom? Either you get back in the bed, or I'll sleep in it.

TOM: I just need to hold you.

TAYLOR: I'm not Randy.

TOM: I know.

TAYLOR: I like you. As a friend. That's all now.

TOM: Are you—

TAYLOR: Gay? I don't know. I don't think it matters much.

TOM: What do you mean?

TAYLOR: Just that. It doesn't matter if it's a guy or a girl as long as you feel something more than just a hard on. I'm waiting for that.

TOM: I did for Randy.

TAYLOR: I know. I know it doesn't seem that way, but you're lucky. I'd like to feel something like that. But I don't now.

TOM: Has anyone ever given you a hard-on?

TAYLOR: Sure. Too many people.

TOM: Guys?

TAYLOR: Some. Some girls.

TOM: I've only been turned on by guys.

TAYLOR: Maybe that makes things easier. Less confusing.

TOM: Have you ever had sex?

TAYLOR: No.

TOM: *[Puts his arm around TAYLOR's waist]* Would it be such a big deal if we—

TAYLOR: *[Sits up]* Now? It would screw things up big time. And things are pretty screwed up now.

TOM: I know. What's going to happen tomorrow?

TAYLOR: How?

TOM: When I have to go home. And face her.

TAYLOR: I don't know. You're going to have to do it sometime.

TOM: I could disappear.

TAYLOR: How far could you get with no money?

TOM: People have done it.

TAYLOR: The best thing you could do tonight is get some sleep. You'll have a clearer head tomorrow.

TOM: Can't we sleep together? Just sleep. I promise.

TAYLOR: Just sleep. Sure. But we might as well use the bed.

[TOM and TAYLOR curl up on the bed.]

TOM: Have you ever been like this?

TAYLOR: No.

TOM: Do you mind?

TAYLOR: I guess not. Go to sleep.

[TOM puts his hand on TAYLOR's crotch.]

Don't.

TOM: You have a hard-on.

TAYLOR: So do you. Go to sleep.

TOM: I hope you'll feel more someday.

TAYLOR: So do I.

TOM: For me.

TAYLOR: I want us to be friends.

TOM: So do I. That, too.

TAYLOR: You go too fast.

TOM: Randy said that too.

TAYLOR: I believe it. Shhh! Sleep.

8. TAYLOR'S BEDROOM.

[The lights dim to suggest a passage of time. Lights come up on bedroom. RANDY is by the bed.]

RANDY: Tommy.

TOM: *[Sees RANDY. Jumps up.]* Randy? My God! What are you . . .

RANDY: I live here.

TOM: You mean?

RANDY: Just like Patrick Swayze in *Ghost*.

TOM: And I'm Whoopi Goldberg, right?

RANDY: You could do worse. *[Looking at TAYLOR. Pulls covers back for a better look.]* You could do worse than him, too.

TOM: You've changed.

RANDY: Death will do that to a girl.

TOM: You never used to talk like that.

RANDY: We all camp out here. It's a riot. Queer paradise.

TOM: Don't leave me again.

RANDY: I'm not coming back, Tommy. I just wanted to say a proper good-bye. And to warn you. This house is about to blow. If you smell any smoke, scream bloody murder. Get your friends out of here. Particularly him. You don't want to lose him.

TOM: He's not interested. . . .

RANDY: Bullshit! Be patient. He'll take care of you, Tommy. I wouldn't have. Gotta go. Love ya.

[RANDY bends down and kisses TOM. RANDY exits.]

TOM: Me, too.

[TOM watches him go, then looks at TAYLOR. Pulls covers around them both and lies with his eyes open. The sound of broken glass. The whoosh of a gasoline-created fire.]

TOM: [At the top of his lungs] FIRE!!! FIRE!!!

[Blackout. TOM comes forward.]

Did I dream Randy? No. I've dreamt him every night for a year. This was different. He was different. And he was right. There was the broken glass and that whoosh—like in a movie. Bright flash. I could hear Sam screaming. And me screaming. Taylor jumped up. We ran downstairs and got Sam out of that room. It was all heat and fire.

Was Randy right about Taylor? I hope so.

[When the scene is set, it will be in the Tuckers' kitchen. MARIAN is on the phone to her father.]

9. THE TUCKERS' KITCHEN.

MARIAN: No, Daddy, don't come over. . . . Please. DON'T! I've got to go through this one alone. . . . No, there's nothing you can do. . . . NO MORE, DADDY. HAVEN'T YOU DONE ENOUGH? . . . I'm sorry. . . . I know. I agreed on all of it. But not this! . . . But that was words! . . . No, I'm not talking out of both sides of my mouth. . . . Tommy was there, Daddy. He's in the hospital. . . . Don't say that. Tommy could have been killed. . . . I know, but he was hysterical. Rick is a doctor. . . . Hunter is in with him. With them. . . . They didn't want me in there, Daddy. . . . Tommy hates me. Hunter despises me. Those men think I'm the wicked witch of the west. . . . No, I don't care. Yes, I do care. Am I . . . silly? What's silly? . . . I don't know. We'll have to talk about that. . . . No. I mean Hunter and I will. And Tom . . . I don't know what I feel for him. For either of them. . . .

Don't, Daddy. I love you. You know that. But my home is a mess, and I've got to put it in order.... I AM NOT CRACKING UP!!!

[HUNTER enters. He is exhausted and covered in soot.]

Hunter's here. I've got to go.... Do you want to tell him that? ... I'll tell him. Goodnight, Daddy. Sorry I woke you.

[MARIAN hangs up phone. She sits. She puts her head down on the table and cries. HUNTER looks at her. He does not move to her.]

HUNTER: The Molotov cocktail went through the living room window. Sam was asleep on the couch. He's pretty badly burned. Tom and Taylor got him out.
MARIAN: The house?
HUNTER: The fire department took its own sweet time getting there. The house is gutted. The police are making a report. They won't do anything.
MARIAN: Can Tom come home tonight?
HUNTER: Rick's finding out if they can be released. He'll bring the boys home.
MARIAN: One big happy family.
HUNTER: Not very happy right now. Tom wants Taylor to stay here if they get out tonight.
MARIAN: And Rick?
HUNTER: I don't know. I offered.
MARIAN: And you?
HUNTER: I'll sleep here. Somewhere. Perhaps you want to go to your father's.
MARIAN: I'm staying here.
HUNTER: With all these horrible people in your house?
MARIAN: I've been thinking all night. I believed everything that happened was because of what those boys did.
HUNTER: Sin and retribution.
MARIAN: Yes.
HUNTER: It was Randy's fault he was raped and led to kill himself? It's Sam's fault he was almost killed tonight?
MARIAN: It makes less sense now.
HUNTER: Tonight I saw two men kiss. I've never seen that. My system went cold—like it didn't know how to take in that data. It was a loving kiss. I can't imagine feeling that for a man. But it is love, Marian. I don't understand it, but it is love. I want to understand. I want to feel more for Tom than I do. I didn't see anything bad.
MARIAN: Every fiber of my being tells me it's wrong.
HUNTER: Can you love Tom?
MARIAN: I don't know.
HUNTER: Do you want to?
MARIAN: Yes.
HUNTER: That's something. What was the message from "Daddy"?

MARIAN: He wants you to help cool things down.

HUNTER: That's what he's thinking about now? Jesus! Doesn't he care at all about Tom?

MARIAN: He thinks that Tom shouldn't have been there.

HUNTER: I see. Blame the victim.

MARIAN: He says he had nothing to do with the fire.

HUNTER: He led the campaign against those people.

MARIAN: He said he thought words would do it.

HUNTER: Words! Some people take his words rather literally.

MARIAN: You're to play it down in the paper. There was a fire. That's all.

HUNTER: And a man was almost burned to death. Our son could have been killed!

MARIAN: He wants you to keep out of this.

HUNTER: Or?

MARIAN: He didn't say.

HUNTER: There are other papers.

MARIAN: Are you going to quit?

HUNTER: No. I might shop the story.

MARIAN: There's no story.

HUNTER: I'm sure there is one. And Daddy's involved.

MARIAN: He said he thought you'd try to be a hero.

HUNTER: Better to try to be a hero than to settle for being a rottweiler.

MARIAN: You'll lose. You're not ruthless enough.

HUNTER: Did he say that?

MARIAN: No. I did.

HUNTER: Maybe I should say, "Thank you." But I know you can no longer play fair and win. The viciousness that is unleashed in the name of values! It's sickening!

MARIAN: Please, for God's sake, get off your high horse!

HUNTER: Self-righteousness is in fashion right now.

MARIAN: Well, I'm sick of it all. Daddy's constant rage at the evils of the world. Your goodness. Tommy's wounded look. I just want it all to be over.

HUNTER: It isn't going to be. They're going to stand their ground.

MARIAN: And Tommy's going to stand it with them.

HUNTER: I think so. More power to him.

MARIAN: And you?

HUNTER: I'll cheer them on. Help them when I can. But I'm an outsider.

MARIAN: And Tom isn't an outsider?

HUNTER: With them? You know he isn't.

MARIAN: But he's an outsider with us?

HUNTER: He has been for quite awhile, I'm afraid. Hasn't he?

MARIAN: Yes. He has. So there's a war going on, and our son is on the other side.

HUNTER: There needn't be a war.

MARIAN: My father disagrees.

HUNTER: Do you have to agree with him on this?

MARIAN: I don't know!

HUNTER: That's a start. But do you really have the guts to fight him?

MARIAN: I don't know. I don't know if I want to.

HUNTER: Exactly. The irony is that Sam and Rick want the same things we do.

MARIAN: I doubt that.

HUNTER: You don't know them.

MARIAN: Neither do you.

HUNTER: I saw a lot tonight.

[TOM enters with TAYLOR and RICK. They are all in scrub suits. TAYLOR and TOM have bandages on their arms where they were burned. HUNTER hugs TOM, who tries to break out of the hug.]

Tom, are you feeling alright?

TOM: No I'm not feeling alright. Taylor is spending the night here.

RICK: I wouldn't agree to this, but I really have nowhere for him to go now.

HUNTER: It's fine. Isn't it, Marian?

MARIAN: Sure. This is Freedom Hall.

HUNTER: Why don't you boys go on to bed? You must be exhausted.

[TOM and TAYLOR exit.]

RICK: I rustled up some scrub suits for the boys. I'll do something about clothes for Taylor tomorrow.

HUNTER: Don't worry about it. He can borrow some of Tom's. Do you need a place to stay?

RICK: I'll go back to the hospital. To be near Sam. [To MARIAN] Don't worry.

MARIAN: You are the least of my worries right now.

RICK: Likewise, I'm sure.

HUNTER: Do you want anything?

RICK: Got any coffee?

MARIAN: I'll get it.

HUNTER: I'll check on the boys.

[HUNTER exits. MARIAN gets up and pours coffee. RICK looks at MARIAN.]

RICK: Are you alright?

MARIAN: What do you think? My home has fallen apart.

RICK: Really? Mine has burned down. With my lover in it.

MARIAN: How is he?

RICK: Do you really care?

MARIAN: I don't know.

RICK: That's honest. He's badly burned. Smoke inhalation. And shock.

MARIAN: I'm sorry.

RICK: Are you? You might be interested to know that Tom was the real hero. He got Taylor up and went right through the fire to get Sam. I'll always be grateful to him.

MARIAN: How bad are his burns?

RICK: Tom's? He'll be okay. Some scar tissue, maybe, but they can fix that. Tom's pretty used to scar tissue.

MARIAN: Oh, really? I've done that to him, I suppose.

RICK: This place has done that to him.

MARIAN: You people love to be martyrs. You're totally innocent, and we bigots are out to crucify you. Right? We're supposed to think it's all just great. Come on in everybody with your rainbow flags and pink triangles and leather and earrings, promiscuity and disease. You're welcome.

RICK: God, I'm tired of this. We, you might have noticed, do not wear earrings or leather. And it would be none of your business if we did. I watched one brave young man die tonight alone. Yes, of AIDS. His parents wouldn't come to the hospital. They thought his illness and death were his own fault. Merciless bastards. Then I got the news about my home and family. A fine man was almost burned to death. Our home was firebombed by hateful bastards who think like you. Strange as it may seem, I think that's a hell of a lot worse than earrings and consensual sex. Fuck you, lady. Fuck you all.

[RICK finally breaks down. He throws his coffee against the wall. He sinks down onto the floor sobbing. MARIAN looks at him a moment. She gets up and moves toward him, not knowing quite what she is feeling or what to do. She pulls a tissue out of her pocket and awkwardly offers it to him.]

Thanks.

MARIAN: I don't know what I believe anymore. I don't know what I feel anymore. I hate this ambiguity, this confusion.

RICK: Your son could have been killed in there! That would have simplified your life.

MARIAN: Don't think I didn't think that. And hate myself for thinking it.

RICK: At least you hated yourself for a change.

MARIAN: I don't like the things I've felt. They're part of me. And not so easily gotten rid of.

RICK: I know. You breathe them in the air around here.

MARIAN: I'm sorry about your—Sam—and the house. It's wrong.

RICK: It sure as hell is.

MARIAN: Earlier tonight I said I hoped your place would burn down. I'm sorry for that, too.

RICK: You think you gave someone the idea?

MARIAN: I think a lot of people had the idea.

RICK: I'm sure of that.

MARIAN: Do you still plan to stay?

RICK: I swore at age twenty that I'd never be run out of anyplace again.

MARIAN: You're an ornery cuss, aren't you?

RICK: Some people have to be.

MARIAN: Exactly.

[MARIAN gets sponge and starts cleaning up coffee and mug. RICK helps.]

We're probably going to have to move.

RICK: Why?

MARIAN: Hunter wants the world to know about what happened tonight. He wants to discover who's responsible. Daddy will fire him.

RICK: Even if that hurts you and Tom?

MARIAN: He's given up on Tom. And I'm supposed to keep Hunter in line.

RICK: Jesus! And if you don't?

MARIAN: We've got my teacher's salary.

RICK: He really would disown you, too?

MARIAN: What were you saying about unconditional love?

RICK: It's not one of the traditional family values?

MARIAN: It's not at the top of my father's list.

RICK: I've always believed if you're dumped on by the family you were born into, make another one.

MARIAN: That's not so easy around here.

RICK: I know. I see what my patients go through. Don't you ever get pissed off at your father? Haven't you ever told him to bug off?

MARIAN: I thought lightning would strike.

RICK: It struck us.

MARIAN: It will strike again. It could strike us. He's the voice of the people around here, Rick. They don't do things for him because of his money or power. They do things because they agree with him.

RICK: Do you know the Ku Klux Klan's active again in Florida? They're not after blacks anymore. Or Jews. They've got us now. And the Pat Robertsons of this world are on TV every day revving them up—and making millions doing it. Hitler missed out. There's big bucks in hate these days. And somebody's got to draw the line against these people.

MARIAN: That's just what they say.

RICK: I know. I've heard them.

MARIAN: *[After a thoughtful pause]* I want Taylor to stay here as long as you need.

RICK: Why the turnaround?

MARIAN: For Tom. I'd like Tom to think we're family. He hasn't for a long time. I was frightened for so long that he'd be . . .

RICK: Gay? The suspense is over. He is.

MARIAN: I know. I've got to stand up for him.

[RICK puts his arm around MARIAN. They hug a moment.]

RICK: You're terrific.

MARIAN: You were right before. I do need a friend.

RICK: Done.

MARIAN: I don't want Tom to get sick.

RICK: AIDS? He shouldn't. If he's careful. I could explain. Or you and Hunter could.

MARIAN: About sex?

RICK: About safe sex, yes.

MARIAN: I can't even think about him doing that.

RICK: He will anyway. He has.

MARIAN: Then explain. Please. Thanks.

[HUNTER enters.]

HUNTER *[To RICK]* Are you okay?

RICK: Yeah. We were just having a heart to heart.

HUNTER: Really?

MARIAN: We haven't scratched each other's eyes out.

HUNTER: So I see.

[Phone rings. HUNTER answers it.]

Hello. . . . Yes it is. . . . Oh yes, Dennis. . . . Yes, it's been quite a night. . . . I see. . . . Does he know? . . . That's miraculous. . . . Thanks. I'll put Rick on. . . .

[HUNTER hands phone to RICK.]

RICK: Yes, Dennis. . . . No shit. . . . Alright. . . . Thanks. We'll see you soon. *[He hangs up.]* Marian, you'd better sit down.

MARIAN: I'm alright. Who was that?

RICK: A new young assistant D.A. was called over to the prison. Dennis Pugh. Sam was his favorite prof at Emory. He's kept in touch with Sam and me.

HUNTER: It's purely an accident that Dennis was called into this. Wiley's out of town for a week. He'd have seen to it that this didn't happen.

MARIAN: What?

RICK: Hunter?

HUNTER: The license number belonged to Jimmy Foster's pickup. He works at the print shop. The fire was set with a solvent they use there.

MARIAN: And?

HUNTER: He's not a good soldier. He doesn't want to go down for this by himself. He's willing to testify against the person who paid him to do it.

MARIAN: Oh my God.

HUNTER: Marian, your father will get around it. A jury will never convict him in this town. Too many people don't think what he did was wrong.

MARIAN: Does he know?

HUNTER: Yes.

MARIAN: No matter what happens, he'll never believe he's wrong.

RICK: *[To MARIAN]* Are you alright?

MARIAN: I need a drink.

RICK: I'd better get back to the hospital. Hunter has the number where I can be reached. Good night. *[He starts to leave.]*

MARIAN: Rick?

RICK: Yes.

MARIAN: I'll bring the boys to the hospital after school.

RICK: Thanks.

MARIAN: And you and Sam can use the guest room.

RICK: Let's not get carried away.

MARIAN: I'm serious. We owe you that much. And you are our neighbors.

RICK: We sure are. Thanks. We might take you up on that.

[RICK exits. Bedroom area down right.]

10. TOM'S BEDROOM.

[MARIAN moves from kitchen across stage to bedroom area. TOM and TAY-LOR are snuggled together asleep in the bed. MARIAN sees them and gasps audibly but quietly. She watches for a long moment, then goes and maternally pulls the covers up, tucking the sleeping boys in. TOM wakes up.]

TOM: Oh my God! What are you doing?

MARIAN: I was just tucking you in.

TOM: You haven't done that in years.

MARIAN: I felt like doing it tonight. Okay?

TOM: He was really upset. He cried himself to sleep.

MARIAN: In your arms.

TOM: Yes. I—

MARIAN: We need to talk.

TOM: You can't stop my feelings.

MARIAN: I know. Nor can I stop mine all at once. Didn't you read *The Merchant of Venice* in school?

TOM: What's that got to do with—

MARIAN: Oh, everything! Somehow it came to mind tonight as I was thinking about things. I've taught it for years and never really thought about it. "The quality of mercy . . ." I've been . . . merciless. I was raised to be merciless. I want to change that.

TOM: Good!

MARIAN: But you have to be merciful, too. It's not so easy, believe me!

TOM: Oh, I know!

MARIAN: When I figured out what was going on with you and Randy, I told my father. And he told Randy's father.

[TOM pushes MARIAN away.]

TOM: Do you really expect me ever to feel anything good for you?

MARIAN: The quality of mercy, Tom. Please hear me out. I was wrong. I'm sorry. I'm almost forty and I've never stopped being Daddy's daughter. I don't know how your father has put up with it, but he has. In a way I was angry at him for putting up with it. Now, before it's too late, I want to be your mother. We both have to want that. You haven't always been easy on me either, you know.

TOM: I know.

MARIAN: So? Truce?

TOM: Not this fast.

MARIAN: Fair enough. Can we talk again?

TOM: Tomorrow.

MARIAN: Yes, tomorrow. *[She gets up, starts to leave. Looks back at the two boys. Quietly, really to herself]* I think I envy you.

TOM: What?

MARIAN: Just foolishness. Good night.

TOM: Good night.

> *[MARIAN tucks TOM's blanket around him and leaves. She returns to the kitchen. HUNTER is now sitting at the kitchen table with a drink.]*

11. THE TUCKERS' KITCHEN.

MARIAN: I could use one of those.

HUNTER: Coming right up.

> *[HUNTER fixes drink for MARIAN. They sit at table.]*

MARIAN: I looked in on the boys.

HUNTER: And?

MARIAN: As you saw them. All tangled together. More like bear cubs than lovers, but maybe that's wishful thinking.

HUNTER: I know that's going to take some getting used to.

MARIAN: It helps to know it's not easy for you either.

HUNTER: I'd like to think it's our problem, not theirs.

MARIAN: Problem? Caught you!

HUNTER: I was raised here, too.

MARIAN: I know. We've got other problems. Like living on my salary.

HUNTER: I don't plan to be unemployed.

MARIAN: I'm glad to hear it. What are you going to say to him tomorrow?

HUNTER: I'm not going to say anything. I'm going to write the story and run it. If he wants to fire me after that, fine.

MARIAN: He will. But that's alright?

HUNTER: You're joining me on my liberal high horse?

MARIAN: Only if it's going somewhere.

HUNTER: A lot of fighters have been mobilized tonight.

MARIAN: More on the other side.

HUNTER: I've always liked the story of David and Goliath. What about you?

MARIAN: I've always been a fighter.

HUNTER: I noticed. Gird your loins. Your father's car just pulled into the driveway.

   [BAILEY enters.]

BAILEY: I imagine Dennis Pugh has talked to you.

HUNTER: Yes. And to Rick Martinez.

BAILEY: Wiley's flying right back to take over the case. There have been some procedural irregularities.

HUNTER: We assumed there would be.

BAILEY: Nothing will happen.

HUNTER: There's always the high calling of journalism.

BAILEY: You don't think your exposé will appear in my paper?

HUNTER: It will appear somewhere.

BAILEY: You're going to risk your livelihood for those two? You're crazy. Marian?

   [MARIAN doesn't answer for a moment.]

Marian?

MARIAN: Daddy, I've spent most of my life accepting without question everything you believed and said. Like you were Jehovah. I don't anymore. And, frankly, I've come to dislike Jehovah. I don't know what I believe about a lot of things, but I know that what happened was wrong. Very wrong. And that I want to get to know my son. His friend Taylor will be staying here for awhile. As will his father and Rick.

BAILEY: That boy is here now?

MARIAN: Yes. He's in with Tom.

BAILEY: Then Tom's coming with me.

   [Before he can be stopped, BAILEY storms out of the kitchen, through the house, and into TOM's room. HUNTER and MARIAN follow.]

12. TOM'S BEDROOM.

[He sees TOM and TAYLOR in the bed and flies into an even greater rage.]

BAILEY: Get the hell out of that bed!

[He starts pummeling TOM. TAYLOR pulls TOM out of the other side of the bed as HUNTER holds BAILEY. MARIAN slaps BAILEY's face.]

MARIAN: You keep away from our son.

HUNTER: There will be none of that in our house. Understand?

MARIAN: Are you alright, Tom?

TOM: I'll be alright.

BAILEY: You are not family to me.

MARIAN: That's up to you, Daddy. We're not going anywhere.

BAILEY: That's what you think.

[BAILEY exits. He's hurt, but he exits through the house like a wounded general. HUNTER puts his arm around MARIAN, she around him.]

HUNTER: Let's check your wounds, Tom.

TAYLOR: It's just bruises.

TOM: I'm okay.

MARIAN: Are you sure?

TOM: Yeah. He's not finished with us.

MARIAN: Doesn't look like it.

HUNTER: Let's all get to a hotel in Atlanta. I can phone the hospital and tell Rick where we are.

TOM: We've got to stay. We've got to fight them.

MARIAN: I'm afraid we do.

TOM: Boy, you've changed tonight.

MARIAN: Some. I want us to be a family.

TAYLOR: He wouldn't burn this place down.

HUNTER: I wouldn't put it past him. It's the saddest thing about human history— that you've often got to protect yourself from the good people. Can you sleep?

TOM: No. You, Taylor?

TAYLOR: No.

MARIAN: Well, come on down to the kitchen. Let's see what we've got to eat.

[They all exit to the kitchen and sit around kitchen table. HUNTER comes forward. As he talks, RICK and SAM join group at the table. They sit silently laughing and talking.]

HUNTER: The war isn't over by any means. But we're not going to retreat. You've just got to believe that the haters will lose—eventually. Most people really don't enjoy hating.

This, at least, is a happy scene. After all, what wishy-washy old Sam and me believed came true. That things only change by people getting to know each other. And Marian and Rick, the fighters, are right that you've got to make a stand for what you believe in. But be willing to change if you're wrong.

After all, we've got to teach our children family values.

[HUNTER joins the group at the table. Everyone at the table joins hands as the lights fade out.]

PETER GILL

Mean Tears

EDITOR'S INTRODUCTION

PETER GILL, OBE, HAS been a major figure in British theatrical life for three decades. As a young director at the Royal Court Theatre, he directed some of Joe Orton's early work. Later Gill founded Riverside Studios in Hammersmith, one of the major fringe artistic venues in London. Peter Hall hired him to be associate director of the National Theatre of Great Britain and to direct the National Theatre Studio, which became a major breeding ground for new playwrights. Gill has directed theater and opera all over the United Kingdom, most recently with the Royal Shakespeare Company.

Playwriting has been a second career for Gill, but over the years he has written a series of powerful, highly personal works for the theater. His early works are about displaced young men in his native Wales. There is a sense in *Small Change* and *Kick for Touch* of an unrealized possibility of happiness through homosexual love, but the young men in Gill's plays cannot act on that desire.

Mean Tears was developed at the National Theatre Studio and produced under Gill's direction at the National Theatre in 1987. Set in contemporary London, the play is both a depiction of a man's addiction to an unworthy love object and a dark satire of a group of people incapable of real human commitment or even loyalty. The play begins with the feckless, bisexual Julian reading from Shelley's "Epipsychidion" the passage in which Shelley justifies his rejection of the "code of modern morals" and its adherence to monogamy. In a sense the rest of the play shows the price of living according to Shelley's doctrine. The men and women in Gill's world seem to want and need love but run from the possibility of a committed relationship. The narcissistic Julian uses the people who love him as mirrors. "What would you say about me behind my back?" he asks Stephen in the first scene, but Julian has little interest in what people say to his face. Why do people love the empty, feckless Julian? Specifically, why does the highly articulate writer Stephen love Julian? Stephen is the one character in the play capable of making a commitment, but he chooses to commit to a totally unworthy love object. And

163

Stephen is intelligent and perceptive enough to know what he is doing. "I seem inevitably to be caught up in a passionate and romantic attachment for someone who needs you but doesn't want you," Stephen tells his friend Paul, but Stephen can't cure himself of his addiction to Julian. Stephen is like a character in a nineteenth-century opera, hopelessly, passionately obsessed but living in an era of self-absorption. Stephen calls Julian "the pure filament of self-obsession," but is Stephen's obsession for Julian also an avoidance of real human commitment and connection? Julian leaves a copy of Beethoven's opera *Fidelio* with Stephen. Stephen comments that the opera is about "freedom and constancy." It is about exactly the kind of loyalty, devotion, and love Gill's characters can't envision, much less experience. Stephen can quote the Marschalin's lines in Strauss's opera *Der Rosenkavalier,* but the Marschalin knew how and when to nobly give up her young lover.

Mean Tears is daring in its severe critique and its depiction of emotions so extreme they are barely contained. The desperation here is far from quiet. The play is as emotionally naked as anything John Osborne ever wrote and less mean-spirited.

Gill's script has few stage directions because he directed it himself. The play was written to be performed on a bare, raked stage: no doors, no walls, no furniture, and only a few necessary props. This sparseness allows for a fluidity of action but also reflects the characters' indifference to their surroundings. It also places the focus where it belongs—on Gill's brilliant, whirling language.

A personal note: It was seeing *Mean Tears* in 1987 that made me realize that I had to write on gay drama and that I had to try my hand at playwriting. The nakedness of this extraordinary play moved me greatly. I might add that no one was more encouraging to this fledgling playwright than Peter Gill. I am delighted to be able to share this play with more readers.

Casarotto Ramsay Ltd.

PRODUCTION HISTORY AND RIGHTS

Mean Tears was first performed at the Cottesloe Theatre of the Royal National Theatre of Great Britain on 22 July 1987. The production was directed by the playwright and designed by Alison Chitty.

Stephen . . . . .Karl Johnson
Julian . . . . .Bill Nighy
Paul . . . . .Garry Cooper
Celia . . . . .Hilary Dawson
Nell . . . . .Emma Piper

Mean Tears from *Mean Tears/In the Blue—Two Plays by Peter Gill*. Copyright 1987. Peter Gill. Reprinted by permission of Oberon Books Limited.

All rights whatsoever in this play are strictly reserved, and application for performances should be made in advance, before the beginning of rehearsals, to Casarotto Ramsay, Ltd., National House, 60-66 Wardour Street, London W1V 3HP ENGLAND.

Editor's Note: Since Julian reads Shelley's "Epipsychidion" throughout the play, let me point out that the passage he reads to Nell at the beginning of Act Two picks up where he left off reading to Celia at the beginning of Scene II.

PETER GILL

Mean Tears

Cast of Characters

JULIAN
STEPHEN
PAUL
CELIA
NELL

Stephen is in his late 30s. The others are in their late 20s.

Setting

London. An indication of Stephen's room able to include other locations as indicated. Scene divisions are not intended to stem the flow of action.

One

I

[JULIAN and STEPHEN]

[JULIAN reading and smoking. STEPHEN working at some papers.]

JULIAN: Listen.

[STEPHEN opens a letter with a knife.]

STEPHEN: Go on.

JULIAN:

> *I never was attached to that great sect,*
> *Whose doctrine is, that each one should select*
> *Out of the crowd a mistress or a friend,*
> *And all the rest, though fair and wise, command*
> *To cold oblivion, though it is in the code*
> *Of modern morals, and the beaten road*
> *Which those poor slaves with weary footsteps tread,*
> *Who travel to their home among the dead*
> *By the broad highway of the world, and so*
> *With one chained friend, perhaps a jealous foe,*
> *The dreariest and the longest journey go.*

Isn't that great?

[*Pause*]

What would you say about me behind my back?
STEPHEN: I wouldn't say anything behind your back.
JULIAN: You wouldn't?
STEPHEN: No, I wouldn't. Anything I'd say I'd say to your face.
JULIAN: Oh yeah? Look at the bags under my eyes. Like what would you say? Is this shirt okay?
STEPHEN: Yeah.
JULIAN: It's not.
STEPHEN: It is.
JULIAN: But what would you say behind my back?
STEPHEN: Stop it.
JULIAN: My hair . . .
STEPHEN: I'd say.
JULIAN: What would you say?
STEPHEN: I'd say, "He's got nothing and he is everything."
JULIAN: Fuck off, Stephen.
STEPHEN: What?
JULIAN: Fuck off.
STEPHEN: What?
JULIAN: Just fuck off.

[*Pause*]

I wish I could change.
STEPHEN: Why should you change? You're alright as you are.
JULIAN: But I want to change, so how can you think I'm alright as I am? I should change.
STEPHEN: I don't want you to change.
JULIAN: You do.

STEPHEN: No, fuck it. Give yourself . . .
JULIAN: You wish me to change.
STEPHEN: No.
JULIAN: And I should change.

   [Pause]

   I shall end up an old man in a hotel room.
STEPHEN: For fuck's sake, you're young, young. Be young. Or you'll *always* just be
   young.

   [Pause]

JULIAN: Stephen, why do you bother with me?
STEPHEN: Julian.
JULIAN: No, why?
STEPHEN: You're my representative in the world of ball games.

   [Pause]

JULIAN: Stephen. Are you making fun of me? Just tell me.
STEPHEN: No.
JULIAN: Are you laughing at me?
STEPHEN: No.
JULIAN: Really?
STEPHEN: Look. You know I'm not. Why should I be?
JULIAN: I just thought you might be.
STEPHEN: Well, I'm not.

   [Pause]

JULIAN: Stephen, I'm fond of you, you know. You're . . .
STEPHEN: Last of the good guys, me.
JULIAN: It's just, can't you . . . ? No, forget it.
STEPHEN: What?
JULIAN: It's alright. Do you want a cup of tea?
STEPHEN: Oh. Christ. Julian!

   [Pause]

JULIAN: I'm a horrible person. Do you think I've got glandular fever?
STEPHEN: Yes. No.

   [Pause]

JULIAN: Fuck it. No cigarettes.
STEPHEN: You're a terrible boy, you are.

JULIAN: Am I? I'm not. Am I?
STEPHEN: You're terrible! Here.

   [He gives JULIAN two cigarettes.]

JULIAN: Two? Where'd you get them? You're great.
STEPHEN: You're a bloody terrible boy.
JULIAN: You really think I am, don't you?

   [Long pause]

   Stephen, do you think I shall ever get married?
STEPHEN: Of course you will.
JULIAN: I don't think I shall ever get married. I shall end up an old man in a hotel
   room.

   [Pause]

STEPHEN: Did you phone home?
JULIAN: No. Yes.
STEPHEN: What did you say?
JULIAN: I said I was sorry.
STEPHEN: What about?
JULIAN: There was a row.
STEPHEN: What about? When?
JULIAN: Oh. Nothing, everything, the usual. Him. And them sending us away to
   school.
STEPHEN: Yes, we're all victims of the class struggle.
JULIAN: We fucking are.
STEPHEN: Are we?
JULIAN: Were you sent away to school?
STEPHEN: No.
JULIAN: At five? Halfway across the world?
STEPHEN: No.
JULIAN: No.
STEPHEN: That I *was* spared.
JULIAN: Oh fuck off, you.
STEPHEN: I *mean* it. Come on.

   [Pause]

JULIAN: Stephen.
STEPHEN: What?
JULIAN: It's . . . nothing.
STEPHEN: What?
JULIAN: Was it my fault?

STEPHEN: How could it be your fault? It happened to you.

JULIAN: I thought it was my fault. I thought he'd blame me. Dad. Not locking my front door.

STEPHEN: But you locked the front door.

JULIAN: I know. That's what started the row. I threw the table over. I'm fucking glad. Was it my fault?

STEPHEN: How could it be your fault? It was you it happened to.

JULIAN: I'm sorry.

STEPHEN: Don't be sorry about it. There was a burglary. You were burgled. *You. You* were.

JULIAN: Do you mind? Are you angry?

STEPHEN: I'm not.

JULIAN: You are.

STEPHEN: Why should I be angry?

JULIAN: It's the insurance.

STEPHEN: Are you insured?

JULIAN: Yes.

STEPHEN: I'm not.

JULIAN: My father insured me. I fucking hate him.

STEPHEN: Come on, Julian.

JULIAN: He gave me a briefcase with a combination lock for Christmas.

STEPHEN: You're such a snob.

JULIAN: Am I? I'm not. Am I?

STEPHEN: Which of those alternative comedians were at university with you, Julian?

JULIAN: None of them. I've told you those kind of people hated me.

STEPHEN: Oh, aye?

JULIAN: They did.

STEPHEN: Yes.

JULIAN: They did, Stephen. You're such a bastard. Am I a snob?

STEPHEN: Didn't you bonk or knob any of those girls who tell jokes about how they got thrush?

JULIAN: Stephen. *[Laughs]*

STEPHEN: No, of course most of them went to Manchester, didn't they, or Sussex, or Bangor? The thing about your mob when they do comedy is they make you realise how funny Jimmy Tarbuck is.

JULIAN: Well, I don't know of any Welsh humour of any sort.

STEPHEN: No, and there are no fucking folk songs in the Welsh coalfields either.

JULIAN: Yeah, and according to some sources there's no fucking coal either.

STEPHEN: Ohowoho. You're the only uneconomic pit round here. Were you up with Manfred M. . . . ? No, before your time. Julian. Did you go to school with Mike D'Abo? No, no, no, no, no, no.

JULIAN: You're so intolerant.

STEPHEN: I don't know. I was very understanding when you said you liked Don't
Look Now.

> [*Pause*]

JULIAN: Stephen. Do you like the Velvet Underground?
STEPHEN: Some of the Velvet Underground.
JULIAN: So you know that song "I'm Waiting for the Man"?
STEPHEN: I know that song "I'm Waiting for the Man."
JULIAN: That's a song about heroin.
STEPHEN: Is it?

> [*JULIAN sings "I'm Waiting for the Man."*]

JULIAN:

> *I'm waiting for the man*
> *Twenty-six dollars in my hand*
> *Up to Lexington 125*
> *This trick is dirty, more dead than alive.*

STEPHEN: Hey, you.
JULIAN: What? Alright. So I do heroin now and again. I can handle it. I just got a
touch of flu today. That's all.
STEPHEN: Listen, Lord Althorp. I mean it.
JULIAN: Would you?
STEPHEN: Yes.
JULIAN: Don't be stupid.

> [*STEPHEN sings "I'm Waiting for the Man," laughing.*]

No. You sound like Dylan. Do you like Dylan?
STEPHEN: Bob, yes. [*Pause*] Don't roll another joint.
JULIAN: One more. Can I? Can I? Can I?
STEPHEN: What do you mean *can* you? You've already rolled one.

> [*Pause*]

What are you doing? What? You're going to veg out in front of the telly and
watch one of your Bilko tapes? As long as it's not Hancock.
JULIAN: "I'd be walking with an empty arm."
STEPHEN: God, please, no, anything. Bruce Springsteen.

> [*JULIAN begins to sing "Born in the USA"; another agonised noise from*
> *STEPHEN.*]

JULIAN: Don't you even like Bowie?

STEPHEN: He's about as lasting as Nelson Eddy, David Bowie.

JULIAN: Who's Nelson Eddy? Don't you like anything at all?

STEPHEN: Look, I like the Band. I like the Kinks, Joe Cocker, Merle Haggard, Billie Holliday, Bessie Smith. George O'Dowd has a perfectly good voice. Cliff Richard has a perfectly good voice.

JULIAN: Oh! Really!

STEPHEN: Julian, I am not the rock critic for *Isis*. I am not interested in the irony of the Velvet Underground as perceived by . . . Terry Jones. Cliff Richard has a perfectly good voice.

JULIAN: So has David Bowie.

STEPHEN: Yes! I know. So has Nelson fucking Eddy.

JULIAN: You're the most restrictive person I've ever met.

[Slight pause]

Who's Nelson Eddy?

STEPHEN: Ask your fucking father when next you have a row. "This one's for Brian."

JULIAN: Don't.

STEPHEN: "Life like a dome of many coloured glass stains the white radiance of the Universe."

[Pause]

Come on, Julian.

[Pause]

JULIAN: The worst time was having to go to bed at 7:00 in the summer evenings with the light through the curtains. That was the worst time. The naughtiest boy was called Roebuck. I always think you're like Roebuck. He kept lizards in his pockets. And he hatched a bird from an egg he'd taken in the woods. They were always beating him for something or scrubbing him up to look angelic. And he never gave in.

[Pause]

I don't know what I'd ever do without you. I think I'd just fall apart.

[Pause]

Stephen, listen, do you think I've got a sense of humour?

STEPHEN: Of course you have.

JULIAN: No, honestly.

STEPHEN: Yes. Tell me that joke.

JULIAN: Shall I? I'm tired.

STEPHEN: Come on.

JULIAN: Do you mean when Roebuck said, "Sir, what's the Latin for hinge?"

[Laughter]

STEPHEN: No.

JULIAN: Well, when we were out, Roebuck and I, we used to find a telephone box, dial O, and when the operator answered, we used to say, "Is that you, operator?" And she'd say, "Yes," and we'd say, "Well, get off the line; there's a train coming."

[Laughter]

Oh, I hate it here.

STEPHEN: What?

JULIAN: England. I don't understand it. Let's go to Venice and Florence and Pisa, La Spezia and Viareggio and Leghorn and Rome.

STEPHEN: Hang on, we haven't been to Lords yet. You said you'd take me to Lords.

JULIAN: Would you like to go to Lords? It's great at Lords. We could spend the whole day there.

STEPHEN: Alright. I've been to Rome.

JULIAN: I've been to Florence. What does that matter? Did you go to the Baths of Caracalla? He wrote "Prometheus Unbound" in the Baths of Caracalla. Are they beautiful? Listen. *[Reads]* "This poem was chiefly written upon the mountainous ruins of the Baths of Caracalla, among the flowery glades, and thickets of odiferous blossoming trees, which are extended in ever winding labyrinths upon its immense platforms and dizzy arches suspended in the air. The bright blue sky of Rome, and the effect of the vigorous awakening spring in that divinest climate, and the new life with which it drenches the spirits even to intoxication, were the inspiration of this drama."

STEPHEN: Come on then.

JULIAN: What?

STEPHEN: Let's go.

JULIAN: Stephen.

STEPHEN: Where did he write "Epipsychidion"?

JULIAN: I don't know. Lerici, I suppose.

STEPHEN: Let's go there then.

JULIAN: I haven't got any money.

STEPHEN: I've got money.

JULIAN: No. I can't take your money.

[Long pause]

STEPHEN: You look at me as if I was fucking black magic, you know.

[JULIAN sleeps, joint in hand. PAUL enters.]

STEPHEN: Hello.
PAUL: You okay?

[Tokes on JULIAN's joint. Picks up book.]

Who's reading this?
STEPHEN: Fuck off.
PAUL: [Laughs] Are you reading this?
STEPHEN: Don't.
PAUL: Have you been sailing paper boats in the park?
STEPHEN: Fuck off, Paul.

[PAUL gives the joint back to JULIAN. JULIAN wakes.]

JULIAN: Paul . . . is this shirt okay?
PAUL: Great. Where'd you get it?
JULIAN: Do you like it?
PAUL: Great. See you later.

[Points towards book, laughing]

STEPHEN: Fuck off, Paul.
PAUL: So long.

[Leaving]

STEPHEN: Paul.
PAUL: What?
STEPHEN: Fuck off.
PAUL: [Laughing] Oh, Celia's downstairs.

[CELIA enters.]

CELIA: Hello.

II

[JULIAN and CELIA]

JULIAN: [Reading to CELIA]
        Meanwhile, we two will rise, and sit, and walk together,
        Under the roof of blue Ionian weather,
        And wander in the meadows or ascend
        The mossy mountains where the blue heavens bend
        With lightest winds, to touch their paramour

> *Or linger, where the pebble paven shore,*
> *Under the quick, faint kisses of the sea*
> *Trembles and sparkles as with ecstasy . . .*
> *And we will talk, until thought's melody*
> *Becomes too sweet for utterance, and it die*
> *In words, to live again in looks, which dart*
> *With thrilling tone into the voiceless heart,*
> *Harmonising silence without a sound . . .*

Isn't that great?

CELIA: *[Looking at volume]* I wrote an essay on "Epipsychidion" when I was at university, but I never read it. There was a book out at the time. I cribbed it from that.

JULIAN: *The Pursuit.*

CELIA: I think so.

[Pause]

JULIAN: Are you having lunch?

CELIA: I suppose so.

JULIAN: Shall we have lunch together? Would you like that?

CELIA: Shouldn't we wait?

JULIAN: I suppose we should.

[Enter PAUL and NELL. They all greet one another.]

PAUL: Where's Stephen?

JULIAN: Out I should think.

PAUL: Where?

JULIAN: He should be on his way back from the library.

PAUL: Shall we go and meet him?

NELL: Yes, is it far?

PAUL: No.

NELL: Shall we bicycle?

PAUL: No.

NELL: Shall we see you?

JULIAN: I expect so.

NELL: See you then.

[PAUL and NELL go.]

JULIAN: I don't think Paul likes me.

CELIA: Paul!

JULIAN: Fuck him.

CELIA: Is Nell a friend of Paul's?

JULIAN: I don't know. Look. Come on. Let's go to lunch. I hate crowds, don't you?
CELIA: Alright. Where shall we go?
JULIAN: I know a very nice place. Well, I think it's nice. Do you want to try it?
CELIA: Of course. Where is it?
JULIAN: Holland Park.
CELIA: That'll be nice. Where? Oh! That . . . girl's name.
JULIAN: Yes.
CELIA: Where are my keys? [JULIAN finds them.] What about Stephen?
JULIAN: Fuck Stephen.

[They start to leave.]

Look, do you mind if I go and collect some blow first? You don't mind, do you?
CELIA: No.
JULIAN: Do you?
CELIA: No.

[Slight pause]

JULIAN: Celia. Listen, is this shirt okay?
CELIA: Yes.

[PAUL and NELL return.]

NELL: We gave up at the front door.
PAUL: Nell did. You off somewhere?
JULIAN: Yes. Is that okay?
PAUL: What?
JULIAN: Is it?
CELIA: Come along. Bye-bye, Paul.

[They say good-bye. CELIA and JULIAN exit.]

PAUL: Here, take this. If I'm seen with Private Eye, I'm in trouble.
NELL: With whom?
PAUL: With myself. How long before you've got to go?
NELL: Fairly soon.
PAUL: You always say that.
NELL: Do I?
PAUL: You do. What is it?
NELL: I've never been here before.
PAUL: Yes, you have.
NELL: Not here.
PAUL: How's Keith?
NELL: He's fine, fine. He's fine.

PAUL: Is he in town? *[Listening, calling]* Stephen!

   [STEPHEN enters, carrying books and papers.]

STEPHEN: Hello. Hello, Nell. Here. *[Gives PAUL some magazines]*

PAUL: Thanks.

STEPHEN: They didn't have the *London Review of Books,* so I got *Newsline.* He loves print. Newsprint. He's the only person I know who says he reads *City Limits* for the sport. Where's Julian?

NELL: They've . . .

PAUL: Haven't seen him.

III

[JULIAN and STEPHEN]

JULIAN: Say.

STEPHEN: No, I'm not saying. You work it out. Why should I come out with a lot of recriminations? You're happy. Off you go—have a drink—meet whoever—if you didn't want to meet me tonight, you just had to say—now—go and meet whoever for whatever reason—you see now I'm doing it. What I didn't want to. I hate you for this. I do. If you apologise once more and don't even follow the apology through with something and then go on apologising, I'll . . . I don't mind. I don't want you to change. I'll—I'll just wait for the time when I can say—why did I ever feel this about you? I look and watch and wait for you like a kid outside a pub sitting on the kerb or a step. Tired and waiting and still I wait. And I still wait. And I wait still. Look at the clock on the wall. But I haven't a time to expect you by. But twenty minutes have passed. I go back to my book to read something that makes me look up to see if you've come yet. The noise I've blocked out reestablishes. Glasses. Getting ready for the last haul before time is called. Phone at the other end. Singing has stopped. Clock. Don't look at faces—as I return one redheaded woman gesticulating imposes herself. Crisp packets crackle. Glasses again. The noice is not unpleasant. Bit loud. I look up. I shall go. Leave you a note saying I've gone. Had you something more interesting. Wasn't there a half promise? See you in the. I'll go. Not angry. Or shall I stay? Oh, come on. Is it? No. I know you're not coming. I leave a polite note saying, "You bastard."

JULIAN: Look, I've got to go.

STEPHEN: Where are you going? I'm sorry. I don't think anyone has ever been so cruel to me ever. So gratuitously. No. Yes. Cruel. They have been, I suppose. Ever. Not casually, culpably. Don't apologise. I can't think about it anymore. I've managed to survive months of this; I've managed even to survive the redhead with the short stories. But I can't go on unprotected any longer.

JULIAN: Stephen. Lindy! Stephen.

STEPHEN: You told me you thought she was very nice. You told me you thought she was very talented.

JULIAN: Did I? Oh God.

STEPHEN: And then she sent *me* the manuscripts.

JULIAN: I'm not worthy of you. Why don't you just give me up? I'm not worthy of you.

STEPHEN: You've got some light. Some glow. I find myself crying and you know—I don't even know what it is I'm feeling. I don't know if I'm unhappy or not. I don't even fucking like you. I've located a part of myself in you. And I dread the feeling in the future of my sense of worthlessness now at having been so shallow all the time.

JULIAN: But you can't let it be like this. Me!

STEPHEN: Because there has to be a reason to get up in the morning. I have to have some defence.

JULIAN: Against what?

STEPHEN: That place.

JULIAN: Where? Work? Against what?

STEPHEN: The mendacity. The envy. The fear. The lack of principle. The mismanagement, the lack of vision, the self-interest. One's self-interest. The atmosphere of witch-hunt, the wish to make things worse. The mishandling, the pusillanimity. The unkindness. The lack of any care, the lack of guts to even stab Caesar when he's dead. "Speak hands for me." The trivial nature, the residue of complacency and dissatisfaction and graft. The exhausted ideals, the lack of perspective, the dead wood, the mediocrity, the vacillation, the meanness of spirit, the gutless, not even opportunism. The terminal air.

JULIAN: I can't go on with this. I can't go on talking because you . . . such . . . You mustn't. I can't stand it. I can't have it. Do you understand? I'd like to bang my head against a wall. If this is about Celia. If you're quizzing me about Celia. There's nothing I can do about it. Do you understand? Do you understand? Do you understand? You just want me to be infinitely flexible and you resent my life. You do, Stephen. And you're so very clever at making me feel obscurely guilty and I *resent* it. I *resent* it. I'm tired. I haven't got the same emotional stamina as you!

STEPHEN: You selfish little bastard. It's not emotional stamina. You're a coward. You're tired because you're doped out and you're a coward.

JULIAN: Leave me alone. I'm wrecked. I've got a headache.

STEPHEN: You have no strength; you're a fucking coward. It's weakness. You're just weak. "Just give me some space for a minute—space—give me space. I need space. You don't allow me my space. I have to have space, okay." Sixties doped-out nonsense like that. Don't apologise—you're like a drunk. And if you're going to get as stoned as you were last night. There comes a point when one can't have anymore to say to you.

JULIAN: Do you think you were sent by God to change me? You make me feel guilty. Why do you look with such reproach?

STEPHEN: Don't you dare use the word *reproachful* to me as a reproach. What you're saying is if I look reproachful, you don't like it. I'll punish you. I'll hold it against you, you say. I want something—you really can't give it. You make me feel hopeless, hopeless, hopeless, hopeless, hopeless, hopeless. What you're saying is I'm tired mummy. I'm tired. You perceive a look as a reproach. You don't like reproach and you say I'm tired. I'm going fucking mad. I hear something on the radio and I laugh because it's going to be something I like and I think, got you, you bastard. Then I feel the pain of wanting to share it with you—pain that you wouldn't really want to . . . and then I feel I can't sustain the hate—the feeling current in me is too weak and the tears start and then, to cap it all, before our next programme they play Schubert's "Seligkeit." Do you remember when I was a character witness over your driving offence? And I thought in that awful court if I was in jail, you'd forget to come or come late. I'd look at the clock and five, ten, fifteen minutes late you'd be. Then awkward. It will be time to go. I used to like love songs. Now they have no meaning. Sentimental songs have to be pretty good now.

JULIAN: We don't ever have any fun anymore. You're depressed anyway. That's okay. Don't worry.

STEPHEN: Well, then, let's say good-bye. No. Come on. In that case don't let's fuck about. Just tell me to fuck off.

JULIAN: No. Come on, Stephen. Don't be stupid.

STEPHEN: Shake hands with me. Come on.

JULIAN: No.

STEPHEN: We both seem to be determined to be ourselves to our mutual disadvantage. And let no one think they are protecting me by any hole-in-the-corner affair, when what they are protecting is something quite else.

JULIAN: It's not you; it's . . .

STEPHEN: The man Celia's going out with? That aging television man who irons his jeans?

JULIAN: I feel I'm locked in a tennis court and people keep serving balls to me and I have to play and I can't compete.

STEPHEN: But you do compete. You've put me in this tennis court.

JULIAN: Look, this isn't flippant; she's captured my heart.

STEPHEN: I think you only exist by hurting. Being hurt . . . I can talk.

JULIAN: Look, I've got to go. Don't despair.

STEPHEN: Despair? Despair! Despair's okay. It's anxious despair I don't like.

JULIAN: I don't exist for you, Stephen, really. You'd like to blow me out.

STEPHEN: Do you know, we don't know who the other is.

JULIAN: I do. I know who you are.

STEPHEN: But if what you say is true, and I expect it is, you're forgetting I *do* care! I honestly *do!*

JULIAN: And me.

STEPHEN: You're forgetting. Try as I can, I'm not as immoral as you are.

JULIAN: Oh, don't moralise, Stephen.

STEPHEN: Sorry. Sorry.

JULIAN: Look, I've got to go. I'm really tired. And I've got to be up. I really have. . . . I've got to get myself into shape. I've got to go for a run. Is is okay?

STEPHEN: Don't give Celia my love.

IV

[CELIA with flowers in a pretty china jug]

CELIA: [Calling] Are you alright, Julian?

[Pause]

These are lovely. Look how they've lasted.

[Pause]

Julian, have you seen Florence?

[Listening]

Fine. Happy. Happy

[Calls to her cats]

Chloë . . . baby, baby . . . Florence . . .

V

[STEPHEN and PAUL]

[STEPHEN drinking. PAUL enters.]

PAUL: What's this, then?

STEPHEN: I'm alright.

PAUL: What's this, then? [Picking up a bottle of pills] What are these? Where did you get these? Okay?

STEPHEN: Terrible.

PAUL: Is it?

STEPHEN: It's terrible. Can I come into your bed?

PAUL: I expect so.

STEPHEN: I'm going to kill him. I'm going to fucking kill him. I'll knife him. Please can I come in with you? Where can I get a shooter?

PAUL: What do you want a shooter for?

STEPHEN: I'm going to shoot him.

PAUL: Oh. Okay. But I don't know where you can get a shooter.

STEPHEN: Someone must know.

PAUL: Nobody I know.

STEPHEN: I'm going to kill him.

PAUL: What is it?

STEPHEN: It's the anger. And the—anger. It's *terrible.*

PAUL: He takes up with a dislocated Liverpudlian who hit the hippie trail and who talks about Tibet and anarchy. He goes down to West Indian clubs, which he calls shebeens; plays pool in the George Canning. He can play two chords of "The Wild Rover" on his guitar. He has the street wisdom of his mother's housekeeper. Why do you want to kill a figure of fun? He loves black music. Reggae. Ska. Scratch. Hip-hop. He really thinks, somehow, it brings black and white together. It's no different. Jazz. Rhythm 'n blues. Tamla Motown. People have always liked a black man with a banjo.

STEPHEN: Don't be vulgar, Paul.

PAUL: Look. You can't . . . He may genuinely like the music, right? But these street acquaintances . . . The only reparation being made is to himself. And it does no good for him, with his nervous off-accent in a minicab to West Indian drivers who want honky out of the car as soon as possible. They still fucking hate in the same way I do. Look at the drugs. Look at the hypocrisy surrounding drugs. They say they're after the pushers. They only get the middlemen who depend on the Julians. The poor fucking . . . But they won't jail Julian.

STEPHEN: You smoke dope, Paul.

PAUL: Yeah, I know.

STEPHEN: Why are you so angry with him?

PAUL: I think perhaps because I'm jealous.

STEPHEN: Why?

PAUL: I think I must hate something he stands for in you. Have you ever seen him spray his yucca? The yucca . . . And Shelley . . . ? Whatever happened to Blake? They used to arrogate poor Blake in my day. Oh, I don't know. . . .

STEPHEN: It's because in the beginning there was no one else in the frame. He knew no one. Because all this street acquaintanceship is so very touching. And because he was alone. Or rather he felt abandoned. He can't tell the difference between being alone and being abandoned.

PAUL: You mean you can't, Stephen.

STEPHEN: It's the pure filament of self-obsession.

PAUL: Come on. He's not worth it.

STEPHEN: What do you mean, he's not worth it? Of course he's not worth it. Who is worth it? Worth it. I know he's not worth it. He knows he's not worth it. And it's dawned on you he's not worth it. Worth it!

He really doesn't have a life—he really is still only a string of appetites. Some of which he can satisfy. Oh, he's weaker than I am. He has no, no, no, understanding of other people. When he says he doesn't gossip, it's because he doesn't have any interest in anyone. When he is interested, it's because someone has been kind to him. He's like a light bulb. Lights up no matter who pulls the switch. Stick with it, I say. Don't see him. Don't protect your future loss. But what am I going to do for the rest of the evening?

He can't reciprocate even a desire for a friendship. Although he seems to want to and to an extent needs to define himself by me. I even dislike him. He is callow and yet sweet natured—or, at least, what is charming about him indicates sweetness and warmth. We went to the Bacon exhibition. He can't bear human images. Bare figures against a plain background. Couldn't understand. What is it in Keats? He can't live without an irritable reaching after fact and reason. Some of the figures he understood, but he saw them as businessmen. Politicians. Things to hate. Oh!

What's the opposite of negative capability? Positive incapacity. I lack almost entirely that objectivity which is supposed, by some, to be the prerequisite of being an artist.

PAUL: Look, Steve . . .

STEPHEN: I don't want a suitable love object. I just want revenge on a couple of people, frankly. He's fucking Celia. He's in love with Celia.

PAUL: Everyone's in love with Celia.

STEPHEN: Are you in love with Celia?

PAUL: No.

STEPHEN: You fucked her.

PAUL: I have not.

STEPHEN: What's wrong with Celia? Ring this number. If Celia answers, put the phone down.

PAUL: It's an ansaphone. What does that mean?

STEPHEN: Nothing. He sent her fucking flowers. Ring this number.

PAUL: Christ! Steve . . . No answer.

STEPHEN: Oh . . . God. Roses. I think I was a very loving child and never grew out of it.

PAUL: Come on. Let's go down.

STEPHEN: No, I'm okay.

VI

[NELL drying her hair]

NELL: Darling!

[Pause]

What time's your train?

[*Pause*]

Keith, damn!

[*Her hair tangles*]

Keith. What time's your train? Want a lift?

[*Pause*]

Okay.

VII

[*CELIA and PAUL*]

PAUL: Do you know what he's doing to himself?
CELIA: No. What do you mean?
PAUL: What do you think I mean?

[*Emptying pills violently onto the floor*]

You live four streets away, Celia. He won't do anything but sleep.
CELIA: You know Stephen!
PAUL: Stephen? I know Stephen.
CELIA: Look, Paul, I'm sorry; he'll have to put up with it. I didn't mean that. Oh! He's alright, isn't he?
PAUL: Celia. I never thought you were stupid. What is it? You look as if this was the love of your life. Is it? I hope it is.
CELIA: Why?
PAUL: This smug radiance had better be worth it.
CELIA: Why?
PAUL: It's on the cards, I think. It really is. He's going to do something, Celia, only not, apparently, intentionally.
CELIA: But you're keeping an eye on him, aren't you?
PAUL: I never took you for a hard girl either. How is Golden Boy? Have you taught him to play bridge? I hope he's a better partner than you are.
CELIA: Paul. Stephen's, I owe . . .
PAUL: Your fucking job to Stephen.
CELIA: But Stephen's. Well, *you* know Stephen.
PAUL: Look, Celia. What are you saying? What? What? I do know Stephen. What's Golden Boy think he's doing? He's a real beauty, he is. A real fucking sleeping beauty. He's like a dumdum bullet, and what do you mean? . . . Oh, I'm going.

CELIA: Paul, I'm sorry, Paul. What about these, Paul?
PAUL: I'm leaving them for Golden Boy.

VIII

[STEPHEN alone]
[JULIAN enters carrying a record set.]

STEPHEN: Hello.
JULIAN: I've come to see you. Is it okay?
STEPHEN: Yeah, yeah. How are you?
JULIAN: I'm alright.
STEPHEN: What's that—*FIDELIO!* Julian! Where'd you get it?
JULIAN: Fuck off.
STEPHEN: Sorry. Where'd you get it? Is this for me?
JULIAN: No. Yes, it is for you.
STEPHEN: Where did you get it? Did Celia give you this?
JULIAN: Yes.
STEPHEN: Yes. Her last boyfriend was a musician. I suppose the next one will get a copy of the *Oxford Book of Romantic Verse.* I'm sorry. . . . I'm sorry.
JULIAN: No, no, no, it's okay.
STEPHEN: Are you staying?
JULIAN: Can I?
STEPHEN: Of course.
JULIAN: For a bit, I'll have to go later. Is it alright?
STEPHEN: Of course.
JULIAN: Stephen, why haven't I seen you?
STEPHEN: Julian!
JULIAN: Why are you laughing? What did I say? What is it?
STEPHEN: It's alright; it's alright.
JULIAN: You know I don't care for her half as much as I care for you.
STEPHEN: This is really fucking awful.
JULIAN: What is?
STEPHEN: It's just I can't bear the thought of someone knowing more about you than me.
JULIAN: She doesn't know more about me than you; nobody knows more about me than you. I don't know more about me than you.
STEPHEN: Why are you doing this?
JULIAN: I don't know.
STEPHEN: There's a pullover of yours in there.
JULIAN: Is there?
STEPHEN: I've been wearing it. Do you mind?

JULIAN: No.

STEPHEN: Because it smells of you. Pathetic, isn't it? Have you seen *Fidelio?*

JULIAN: No.

STEPHEN: Have you listened to it?

JULIAN: No.

STEPHEN: Have you been to the opera?

JULIAN: Yes.

STEPHEN: What did you see?

JULIAN: *Der Rosenkavalier.*

STEPHEN: Did you like it?

JULIAN: No.

STEPHEN: Quite right. *[Whistles]* "Hab mir's gelobt, ihn lieb zu haben auf der richtigen Weis, Daß ich selbst seine Lieb zu einer andern Noch lieb hab! Hab mir freilich nicht gedacht, daß es so bald mir auferlegt sollt werden!"

[JULIAN sleeps.]

JULIAN: What's that?

STEPHEN: *Rosenkavalier.*

JULIAN: What's *Fidelio* about?

STEPHEN: Well, there's . . .

JULIAN: No. No, no. What's it about?

STEPHEN: It's about freedom and constancy. You should know about that.

JULIAN: What's *Der Rosenkavalier* about?

STEPHEN: Julian! You've seen it.

JULIAN: I know.

STEPHEN: It's about nothing.

JULIAN: Is it good?

STEPHEN: Very good.

JULIAN: Which is the best? Is *Fidelio very* good?

STEPHEN: *Very, very* good.

JULIAN: Yes, I thought it might be. I didn't like *Der Rosenkavalier.* I don't like the fucking opera. Do you?

STEPHEN: Yes. No. I dunno. I don't go. No.

JULIAN: Is *Der Rosenkavalier* good?

STEPHEN: Very good.

JULIAN: I don't understand anything.

STEPHEN: Come on.

JULIAN: Stephen.

STEPHEN: You'd better go.

JULIAN: Stephen.

STEPHEN: Shall I call you a cab?

JULIAN: Yes, I'd better go.

STEPHEN: You're such . . . There's a towel of yours in there as well, and half a bottle of JoJoba, and the Eucryl smoker's, and a pair of swimming trunks, and a tube of Daktarin, and the African fucking honey, and the Eau du Portugal.

JULIAN: That's okay.

STEPHEN: And a packet of three with one to go.

[JULIAN has left the recording of Fidelio.*]*

IX

[CELIA and JULIAN]

CELIA: Are you alright?

JULIAN: Fine.

CELIA: What is it?

JULIAN: I'm alright, honestly. You?

CELIA: Not very. Are we going?

JULIAN: Don't you want to?

CELIA: Not really.

JULIAN: Don't let's go then.

[Pause]

What is it, Cels? You've been like this for hours. What've I done?

CELIA: Nothing. Honestly. Let's stop. Let's stop it.

JULIAN: Something . . .

CELIA: You can't accommodate to anybody, can you?

JULIAN: What?

CELIA: Everybody must accommodate to you.

JULIAN: What? Christ! Christ! What? To me? Who's been doing the accommodating if I haven't been doing the accommodating?

CELIA: Alright.

JULIAN: It isn't alright. Oh no, it isn't alright. It isn't alright. Oh no. Everything you want to do, I do. I meet your friends. I go to restaurants with people you like. I go to concerts because you like them. I spend my time here. You haven't even visited my flat.

CELIA: I have.

JULIAN: *Once.* My friends. All I did was not go to your parents for the weekend. That's all, Celia. It isn't alright.

CELIA: I didn't mind you not coming for the weekend.

JULIAN: You minded.

CELIA: I didn't. I'm perfectly satisfied with *my* parents. I can't help it if my father's a school inspector and my mother's a teacher. I can't help it if you don't like them.

JULIAN: I don't know if I like them or if I dislike them, anyway. There's no reason for me to like them.

CELIA: Or dislike them.

JULIAN: I don't. I don't know them. I don't want to know them. All this cosiness. I don't want to see them or visit them or walk the dogs. Any of that nonsense. I don't want to know mummy or daddy. This is enough. Quite enough.

CELIA: Julian!

JULIAN: Quite enough. Quite enough. Quite enough.

X

[STEPHEN and JULIAN]

STEPHEN: Will I see you later? Oh no.

JULIAN: Why not?

STEPHEN: You've got to have dinner with Celia, haven't you?

JULIAN: That's tomorrow night.

STEPHEN: It isn't.

JULIAN: Isn't it? Where's her note? Christ, it is tonight. Oh God, I'm so tired. I think it's glandular fever. Stephen. Do you think? Listen, do you think I've got glandular fever? She says, can we meet where no one can gawp? Really, who's interested in people gawping? Anyway, I'll have to go, won't I? Perhaps I'll just go for a drink. I'll ring her; we'll just go for a drink. What do you think? I'll have to have a shower.

STEPHEN: Listen. I can't say anything. You go for a drink. I think there's something grotesque about this, anyway.

JULIAN: Isn't this how you do these things?

STEPHEN: I don't know.

JULIAN: Oh Christ, I haven't got any money, and I haven't got my cheque book. Do you think it matters?

STEPHEN: No. Look, you'll have to pay. I've got thirty quid. Do you want it?

JULIAN: Can I have twenty-five?

XI

[STEPHEN and JULIAN]

STEPHEN: What is it?

JULIAN: Nothing.

STEPHEN: What's the matter?

JULIAN: Leave me alone.

STEPHEN: What is it?

JULIAN: I'm in trouble.

STEPHEN: What trouble? Oh God.

JULIAN: What? No.

STEPHEN: What then?

JULIAN: She gave me a lift home, and when we got there, she started crying.

STEPHEN: Why?

JULIAN: I asked her how the cats were.

STEPHEN: How were they? Didn't one of them bite you once?

JULIAN: Yes. Florence.

STEPHEN: Christ.

JULIAN: I made her come in, and we talked for hours and hours and hours and hours till two in the morning. She went home. Then I felt sorry for her and myself and went over there. What am I going to do now?

STEPHEN: I don't know, Julian.

JULIAN: She says she fought hard for her independence. Fuck her. I dreamt I was in a desert in America and you deserted me. I suppose you will. Won't you . . . ?

XII

[CELIA and PAUL]

CELIA: It's when you can't change anything. I've tried. I've not been able to. I've only made it worse. Will you tell him for me that he must or I'll die? How stupid. Will you speak to him? Oh . . . will you please?

PAUL: Celia . . .

CELIA: No. He's . . .

PAUL: Yes. He's not much use to you, is he? Is he?

CELIA: He's left nothing. This for a little love. This for that. And yes . . . no. Oh, I hope I never have to see him again. I do. I do. I do. I won't come out. Do you mind?

PAUL: Celia.

CELIA: I must go to work on Monday. I haven't been to work for two weeks. But I can't stay off any longer. I haven't seen anyone. Please, you won't tell him I've spoken to you, will you?

PAUL: Of course I won't. Come on, Celia.

CELIA: No. I'll stay in. Thanks. Thanks.

XIII

[JULIAN and STEPHEN]

JULIAN: You know that girl? That tall girl? I think she was flirting with me.

STEPHEN: Don't. Please don't. Don't. By every bloody thing, don't.

JULIAN: Why not? Why not? Can't I?

STEPHEN: Look, she lives with a very nice bloke. Just don't.

JULIAN: What's his name?

STEPHEN: Keith. I've never met him.

JULIAN: She asked me if I was having an affair with you.

STEPHEN: Aye, she would. Are you? That's why she was flirting with you.

JULIAN: Is it? Really, is it? Do you like her?

STEPHEN: I don't really know her.

JULIAN: It's alright. She won't like me; those kind of girls never do. What's she like?

STEPHEN: She's a hockey field Venus. Half good looking, like you. Grew too tall to be a dancer, I shouldn't wonder. They live in Cambridge in one of those big houses on the Chesterton Road, and her aunt was Wittgenstein's doctor's receptionist, or north Oxford and their mother was an actress but gave it up to have nine brutally concerned children. Or she lopes along Chiswick Mall, the daughter of a judge. And gives you pebbles or driftwood for Christmas. Trouble. Take a very long spoon. I bet she was at the Band Aid concert.

JULIAN: She told me there's a very good double bill at the Rio in Dalston. And that restaurant on Newington Green.

STEPHEN: Yes. I suppose the return match'll be at the Ritzy in Brixton.

JULIAN: No. She's . . . Keith? She's a terrible flirt.

[Pause]

Am I only half good looking?

Two

I

[JULIAN and NELL drinking white wine]

JULIAN: [Reading]
> Our breath shall intermix, our bosoms bound,
> And our veins beat together; and our lips
> With other eloquence than words, eclipse
> The soul that burns between them, and the wells
> Which boil under our being's inmost cells,
> The fountains of our deepest life, shall be
> Confused in Passion's golden purity . . .

We shall become the same, we shall be one
Spirit within two frames . . .
One hope within two wills, one will beneath
Two overshadowing minds, one life, one death,
One Heaven, one Hell, one immortality,
And one annihilation . . .

Isn't it great?

NELL: It's like making love.

JULIAN: Is it?

NELL: Do you want some of this?

JULIAN: Thanks.

NELL: What is it?

JULIAN: I'm restless.

NELL: Oh.

JULIAN: Not with you. I don't know what I'm doing. Work. Everything. I'm a sort of displaced person. I feel like some sort of refugee here.

NELL: How? Come on. Because you were born abroad? Really?

JULIAN: That I suppose. A result of feeling that school was where they called home and home was in Malaya and now I don't know where I am.

NELL: Why don't you go back?

JULIAN: I'd like to. I'd love to.

NELL: I've never been very far . . . Elba.

JULIAN: Oh, Malaya . . . oh, you should.

NELL: What are you laughing at?

JULIAN: Thinking of here and there.

NELL: Where were you born?

JULIAN: Kuala Lumpur. But mainly I think of the Cameron Highlands house.

NELL: Not a plantation? Really?

JULIAN: Really.

NELL: How very glamorous. I can see how you feel as you do. Though I like where we live. Where I was born, in fact.

JULIAN: Where?

NELL: North. On the borders. There is something utterly strange and beautiful and compelling about border country, I think. . . . I went to Wales once and we got to somewhere out of Shakespeare . . . Mortimer's Cross. And I got this feeling, scary. Beautiful. I expected Red Indians. But our borders . . .

JULIAN: Do you go home?

NELL: I love going home. In spite of . . . mainly for the place. The village. The town. Our house and when we're all together, I suppose.

JULIAN: In spite of what? What does your father do?

NELL: He's a doctor. He's a consultant, in fact. Mainly in Newcastle. But sometimes in Edinburgh and even London. But he won't move here. He likes the north and the Scots, though he's very English. We all went to boarding schools in the south, and my brother went to public school here. You must come. My mother likes visitors and us all there. Though I don't like her very much.

JULIAN: Why?

NELL: Well, of course I do. But. What is it about Malaya? Is it like India? How they write about it. Is it like that?

JULIAN: Yes. Longing. But it's everything, the people.

NELL: Did you have an ayah? No, that's India.

JULIAN: Yes, we had an amah. She was called an amah. My favourite had to leave—to go back to her village. It's just everything. The green. England! The green in Malay. I'm sure where you live is beautiful. We used to go to Scotland. But there. Everything. The rain. I stood in the rain once and my parents were rowing inside. I ran off the verandah and into the rain. The rain was just soaking me. English rain is so hateful, somehow. Mean. Untrustworthy. Cold.

NELL: What did your father do before he retired?

JULIAN: Not as romantic as you think but yes, tea. After the war he worked for a company in Penang and then Kuala Lumpur. He met my mother there. They aren't grand, you know. My mother comes from Southampton.

NELL: I'm sure there must be grand people even in Southampton.

JULIAN: He was commissioned in the war. And then after was very hard working and enterprising and clever and competitive.

NELL: Was it his plantation?

JULIAN: No. *[Laughs]* He worked for a company. Later a huge American multinational company. He ended up chairman of one of their subsidiaries back in Kuala Lumpur. He's loaded. I know he hates it here. More than me. He won't say. He was very big in the emergency. Not back in the army. But I don't know ... being important ... holding civilians together. Of course he thinks things have gone from bad to worse, which of course they have. Do you play mahjong?

NELL: What? No.

JULIAN: My father and mother and their Sussex friends actually play mahjong. He's, oh Christ, it's impossible. He's bright; I know he is. But he's so competitive. He knows the truth. I think he's lost his soul. My parents don't deserve a better chronicler than Somerset Maugham. They really don't.

NELL: Are you like him?

JULIAN: No, I'm not!

NELL: Alright, angel, come on.

JULIAN: I look like my mother. She's pretty despicable, I'm afraid. She's vain and weak and spoiled. Is that bad of me? His temper I have, I suppose. No, I don't. You?

NELL: I can cope with my father, but I hate him for putting up with my mother. I hate her quite passionately, really. Maybe because she'd had this man for years and my father knows. And her daunting competence I hate. I like my sisters and especially my brother, of course.

JULIAN: What's he called?

NELL: Giles.

JULIAN: Do you want a smoke?

NELL: Look, I should go.

JULIAN: Don't go.

NELL: Look, this isn't supposed to be on. I've got to see Keith before he leaves, though I'm fed up with him at the moment, actually.

JULIAN: That's between you and Keith.

NELL: Are you having an affair with Stephen?

JULIAN: You keep asking that. Does it look like I am?

NELL: Look, my brother's gay.

JULIAN: So is mine. Or at least that's what he just told his wife.

NELL: Giles, when he was at public school, I was always jealous of his romances.

JULIAN: Really.

NELL: He was once in love with someone called John Graham, and he, John Graham, threw Giles over for someone called Philip Richards, and Giles was so angry. So angry, he made himself ill, and he took two aspirins and was in the sanitorium for three days. He said it was my mother, and I think it even was my mother. But it wasn't; it was John Graham. And that's how he got John Graham back. And when he, John Graham, left school, he came back during the term and took Giles out in his motorcar. I thought it was incredible. I still do. Exciting.

JULIAN: Not for Philip Richards, I should think. Do you want a smoke? Do you smoke?

NELL: Sometimes.

JULIAN: Have a smoke.

NELL: Okay. I'll ring Keith. Then I'll read something to you.

II

[STEPHEN, JULIAN, and PAUL]

JULIAN: I'm going out.

STEPHEN: Don't go out. Come on. Sit down. What's the thing about one of your friends that you most like to remember?

PAUL: I don't know.

STEPHEN: I know what it is about you.

PAUL: What?

STEPHEN: In the other house I was sitting on the sofa by the fire, reading *Great Expectations,* and there was a soft tread on the step and a light tap on the door, and in you came and you said, "Miss Barrett, Miss Barrett, I've come to take you away."

JULIAN: Look, I've got to go out.

STEPHEN: Don't go out.

JULIAN: I'm fucking going out to get some stuff, okay? Okay, Paul?

STEPHEN: Don't. Come on.

[JULIAN exits.]

Oh, Christ.

PAUL: A thing to hate. The public school as an image of England. They can take the slipper, these boys, but they don't know how to put their dukes up. And instead of going in the army where they belong, they persecute the rest of us.

STEPHEN: Oh, don't, Paul.

PAUL: I was in college with someone who went home at the end of the winter term, and his parents had moved without leaving an address. There are families and families, Stephen.

STEPHEN: Young people are like unborn babies. It's the fate of each generation to have the young express themselves in different ways. Flappers. Teddy Boys. Flower children. Skinheads. And the old must put up with it. To me they look like unborn babies. Spoiled. I spoiled it. Seeking more. Not accepting the unfinished edge of things. Not letting it drift as it will. And put the effort in when it's needed. But why can't he say . . . ? Why can't he show . . . ?

PAUL: He can't because he's like that. And you'll have to put up with it or ship out.

STEPHEN: What am I to do? I can't just drop him. I don't want to. Shall I give him up?

PAUL: Yes. And what will you do then? You're addicted to him. It's an addiction.

STEPHEN: What do you know about Nell?

PAUL: When she left school, she did something first. She didn't go to Cambridge straightaway, I know. She wouldn't, I think. What was it? I don't think it was the VSO.

STEPHEN: I bet it was VSO.

PAUL: Nor the National Youth Theatre.

STEPHEN: It must have been one or the other. It must have been. I bet she played Helena. God, Vanessa Redgrave's got a lot to answer for, except perhaps her politics. Have you ever seen her? She's like a less subtly violent Nell. I bet Nell's shadowly concerned.

PAUL: I think she's fantastic. She burns me.

STEPHEN: Who, Nell?

PAUL: No. Nell . . . Well . . . She has, Stephen, in her time.

STEPHEN: But she isn't twenty-four anymore.

PAUL: I'd give her one.

STEPHEN: You've given her one.

[PAUL laughs.]

PAUL: How was it at the weekend?

STEPHEN: Home?

PAUL: Yeah. Your mother okay?

STEPHEN: No. I think I'm too much bother for her now. I think my concern makes her even more agitated.

PAUL: Is she in for long this time?

STEPHEN: I don't know. She just sits there and suddenly her eyes light up. I seem inevitably to be caught up in a passionate and romantic attachment for someone who needs you but doesn't want you. It's like an article in one of your magazines down there. The children on YOP schemes. Young boys joining the army. Brothers and brothers-in-law in and out of work. We went over to Cardiff for a meal. My younger sister, Kath, she's like a sansculotte. We had to wait for a taxi for hours because she wouldn't go with the firm that took the blacklegs to Merthyr Vale. She says they're killers by implication.

PAUL: Aren't they?

STEPHEN: My father says—"I tell you, Stephen, I'm glad I'm not a young man. It's worse than the thirties. I tell you, Stephen, in 1926 when I was a shop steward." I never knew he was a shop steward; he never told me he was a shop steward. "We couldn't get two fellers to come out on strike, and we warned them, and when we went back, the manager sacked them." He could have only been twenty-four in '26. "You in work, Stephen? How's work? When you going back?"

PAUL: Yeah. Neurotic symptoms in the upper working class. Routledge Kegan Paul. It comes to something when your happiest times were when your mother went to put flowers on her father's grave. Playing in the long grass. Playing and watching. Pleasant like another child would watch its mother knitting. No tears. Sunny day. Come here. There we are. Beautiful grasses. Secretly I think my father would be relieved if I voted Tory. I think it would be proof that I'd done something. But we seemed to have moved class without breaking faith with chaos.

STEPHEN: I don't know about my father—if I voted Tory, it would be the only thing that would bring my mother out of the mental hospital. There was this play and a man on a park bench and he said, "I feel I haven't been part of life." Just like *The Cherry Orchard*. Something like that. Have you been part of life?

PAUL: I don't know what that means.

STEPHEN: It goes through one, I suppose, in its own way. If we will let life live us instead of being afraid or thinking other lives should be our lives. It's our own life we must live.

The new cruelties are the old ones, you know. The new respectability is just the grasping for individual freedom by a safe majority so they destroy individuals weaker than themselves.

The loneliness of all those people lonely. They'd be less unhappy if they knew they were just lonely. Loneliness of the summer evenings of family life. The winter evening of after football. That rancourous mean-spirited arguing about sport. De-dum de-dum de-dum de-dum. Partick Thistle. Heart of Midlothian. Queen of the South. The loneliness not knowing it. The chocolate swiss roll. My brother's football gear. My sisters arguing. Alone. Among them. Chewing gum under the table stuck to my trousers. Iron it out. The loneliness. Dusk, 4:30, winter. That sigh from her. That sigh. That snore from him.

[JULIAN enters.]

JULIAN: Hello.
STEPHEN: Alright?
JULIAN: Yeah. Do you want some of this, Paul?
PAUL: Aye.

III

[JULIAN and STEPHEN]

STEPHEN: What is it?
JULIAN: Nothing.
STEPHEN: Fuck it, Julian. You were all over me half an hour ago. What is it?
JULIAN: You're the last person I should tell.
STEPHEN: Then if I'm the last person you should tell, why are you pulling this? When you look like this, you're either dying or angry or frightened.
JULIAN: Well, if I look like this, why don't you take the hint and leave me alone?
STEPHEN: Alright.
JULIAN: I'm fucking furious.
STEPHEN: Why?
JULIAN: I can't, Stephen.
STEPHEN: Oh Christ, why am I putting myself through this? I don't know what to do—is it a test? What is it? You make me feel nothing. I'm nothing. I'm so ashamed of this. Half an hour ago . . . This is wrong. Being with you makes me feel like a woman with none of the compensations, and I don't like it. This being controlled by a boy. Nobody can win with you, can they?
JULIAN: I'm not competing.
STEPHEN: You say I'm in competition with you. That's because if somebody puts an experience of theirs up against yours, then you think it somehow robs you. I'm not trying to. At least I don't think I am. Oh God.

[Pause]

Come on, Julian.
JULIAN: I asked her out and at the last minute she changed her mind.
STEPHEN: Who? Oh God.
JULIAN: She said she had to see Keith. Why did she do that?
STEPHEN: Well, mm. Hang on. *[Moves away, hand to his mouth]* It's alright. Oh, Julian. They do live together.
JULIAN: Sometimes.
STEPHEN: Well, I don't know. This is like being under the guillotine.

JULIAN: Ah. Fuck it. I'm fed up with this. Nothing gonna come of this. It's alright, you're alright, we're alright. I'm going to ring her and tell her to fuck off. Oh, she won't be there.

STEPHEN: Leave a message on her ansaphone.

JULIAN: She hasn't got an ansaphone.

STEPHEN: Of course she's got an ansaphone. All your girlfriends have ansaphones. They're like iron lungs to them. What colour are her eyes?

JULIAN: Er . . .

STEPHEN: What colour are my eyes? Don't look.

JULIAN: Grey. I can talk about her mouth if you like.

STEPHEN: I always knew you thought a woman's place was on her knees with a mouthful of cock.

JULIAN: Stephen.

STEPHEN: Julian.

JULIAN: I wish I'd never met her. But I like her. She likes you.

STEPHEN: Thanks.

JULIAN: Do you like her?

STEPHEN: I don't really know her. I can see why you like her.

JULIAN: She's kind.

STEPHEN: You mean she's classier than Celia. She won't make you feel so parvenu.

JULIAN: Is she better than me?

STEPHEN: Oh! No.

JULIAN: Ah, fuck her.

STEPHEN: It's alright.

    [STEPHEN exits.]

JULIAN: Stephen, is she better looking than me?

STEPHEN: What?

    [STEPHEN returns.]

JULIAN: It's alright.

STEPHEN: It's alright. Sick. Here, this must be Nell's brooch. She left it in the bathroom.

                  IV

    [NELL chasing JULIAN]

JULIAN: No no no. Here. *[Giving her some flowers]* Don't.

NELL: Thanks! Oh . . . they're beautiful.

JULIAN: Do you love me?

NELL: What?

JULIAN: I do.

[NELL laughs.]

No!

NELL: They're beautiful! Do you love me?

JULIAN: With all my heart. You?

NELL: "I love you with so much of my heart that I have nothing left to give."

JULIAN: Where's that from?

NELL: Aha! Got you! These really are beautiful. You have one.

JULIAN: I can't carry a rose.

NELL: Come on.

JULIAN: No.

NELL: Come on.

JULIAN: No.

NELL: Oh.

JULIAN: Oh. What is it?

NELL: I suppose we shouldn't. . . .

[Pause]

Stephen's in this, isn't he? Isn't he?

JULIAN: No. Well, people are in everything, aren't they? Have you had a holiday?

NELL: Yes.

JULIAN: I haven't.

NELL: Oh, poor boy.

JULIAN: Don't.

NELL: Come on. Oh!

JULIAN: What? What is it?

[NELL begins to cry.]

Don't.

[Goes to her]

NELL: Don't. Keith's coming back. And then he's coming to town to live properly.

JULIAN: That isn't a proper thing to discuss.

NELL: Isn't it? Must we only discuss what you want to discuss?

JULIAN: No. Don't be angry.

NELL: Anyway, things will have to take their course.

JULIAN: I'll wait, you know, for as long as it takes.

NELL: Are we going to lunch?

JULIAN: Yes. What . . . what are you doing this afternoon?

NELL: Work.

JULIAN: I'm damn well taking the afternoon off.

NELL: That's rather irresponsible.

JULIAN: Can you take the afternoon off?

NELL: I *can* . . . but I won't.

JULIAN: Come on. Come on.

NELL: Haven't you had a holiday, really?

JULIAN: No. Where did you go?

NELL: We went to Spain. Fantastic. What is it? Well, *we did* go. Where . . . where are you going?

JULIAN: Oh. The Maldives or . . . I want to go to Italy. I was going with Stephen. He won't come.

NELL: When?

JULIAN: In a couple of weeks. I'm not going alone. I'm not going without you. Will you come?

NELL: Alright.

JULIAN: Will you? *Will* you? I'll get the tickets. I'll do the hotel. I know, I'll hire a car.

NELL: Where?

JULIAN: We'll fly to Pisa and drive to the bay of Viareggio. It'll be great. . . . *[Pause]* What about . . . ?

NELL: I'll handle that. And Stephen?

JULIAN: I've told you. *Will* you take the afternoon off?

NELL: Wear this and I might.

   [Gives him a rose]

v

   [PAUL and STEPHEN]

PAUL: Coming for a drink?

STEPHEN: Aye. Okay.

PAUL: Do you want to wait for Boy Blue?

STEPHEN: No.

PAUL: We'll wait.

STEPHEN: No.

PAUL: We'll wait.

STEPHEN: No.

   [JULIAN enters carrying a Paul Smith carrier bag.]

PAUL: We don't have to wait.

STEPHEN: We're going for a drink.

JULIAN: No, I've got to pack.

STEPHEN: Come for a pint.

JULIAN: No. A pint. Oh no. Fuck it.

STEPHEN: What is it?

JULIAN: I've lost my driving licence. *[Violently]* I've got an international bloody driver's licence, and I don't know where it is!

PAUL: I'm going for a drink then, okay?

STEPHEN: Hang on. Well, where can it be?

JULIAN: I don't know.

PAUL: See you in the pub.

STEPHEN: Hang on, Paul.

JULIAN: I'll ring home; it may be there.

PAUL: So long.

STEPHEN: Hang on. It'll be there.

PAUL: I'm going. *[Exits]*

STEPHEN: Paul!

JULIAN: I don't want to go.

STEPHEN: It'll be great. You'll meet people.

JULIAN: Here. *[Gives him the bag]*

STEPHEN: What's . . . !

JULIAN: You wanted it. *[Takes out a shirt]*

STEPHEN: What? Julian, the money.

JULIAN: Do you like it? Do you? Do you really like it?

STEPHEN: It's the most expensive shirt I've ever had.

JULIAN: Do you really like it? Do you? Is it okay?

STEPHEN: Great. I'll put it on.

JULIAN: Oh Christ. I've got to go. I've got to go home for the weekend and then Gatwick on Monday. Oh God.

STEPHEN: It'll be alright. Take them something.

JULIAN: I've got something.

STEPHEN: And keep your mouth shut.

JULIAN: Okay.

STEPHEN: Hear me.

JULIAN: Yeah.

STEPHEN: Do you hear me?

JULIAN: Alright. I'll ring you from the airport before the flight takes off.

STEPHEN: You won't, Julian.

JULIAN: I will.

STEPHEN: How can you?

JULIAN: I'll ring you.

STEPHEN: Will you?

JULIAN: I promise. I've got to go, okay?

STEPHEN: Have a nice time.

JULIAN: Shouldn't think so.

STEPHEN: You will.

JULIAN: Do you really like the shirt?

VI

[CELIA and STEPHEN]

STEPHEN: [Offstage] He won't be long.
CELIA: Fine.
STEPHEN: [Offstage] He shouldn't be long.

[Pause]

[STEPHEN enters with a tea tray.]

Only teabags.
CELIA: That's fine.

[STEPHEN pours tea.]

STEPHEN: He's usually in by now. Is that him? [Calling] Paul! No.

[Pause]

Work okay?
CELIA: Great. I've been promoted.
STEPHEN: Really?
CELIA: Yes.
STEPHEN: Paul didn't say.
CELIA: Paul doesn't know. That's partly why I came round.

[Pause]

You look well, Stephen.
STEPHEN: I am well. More?
CELIA: No. Thanks. No. Haven't finished this.
STEPHEN: This is terrible tea.

[She picks up a copy of The Face.]

CELIA: Do you read The Face?

[The Face is covering the recording of Fidelio.]

STEPHEN: No, I don't read The Face. This tea is really awful. Don't finish it. I'll make some more.
CELIA: No. Who's that?
STEPHEN: [Listening] Paul.
PAUL: Yeah.

[PAUL enters.]

STEPHEN: Where have you been?

PAUL: What do you mean, where have I been? To work is where I have been. Hello stranger. Okay?

CELIA: Hello.

STEPHEN: She's been promoted.

PAUL: Have you? I'll get a cup.

STEPHEN: No. Put the kettle on. This is awful. The water didn't boil.

PAUL: Okay.

STEPHEN: No, I'll do it.

   [STEPHEN exits.]

CELIA: Thank God you've come. I'll have to go.

PAUL: Why?

CELIA: Well.

PAUL: Julian? He's in Italy.

CELIA: Oh. With whom?

PAUL: Himself. Do you care?

CELIA: I don't. I don't, Paul. Honestly I don't.

PAUL: Anyone new? Going out with anyone?

CELIA: Paul. Yes, I am actually.

PAUL: Really, Celia. Your public secrecy. I'm glad about the job.

CELIA: Yes.

STEPHEN: *[Offstage]* I won't be long.

CELIA: Look. I'll have to go. I just wanted to tell you.

   [STEPHEN enters.]

STEPHEN: I made proper tea.

PAUL: This domesticity's a bit of a change.

STEPHEN: Guests.

CELIA: None for me. I'm off.

STEPHEN: Oh. Sure?

   [She kisses him. He returns the kiss. She starts to go. He stops her.]

You look pretty today, Celia. Well, you always look pretty. But today especially. Must be the job.

CELIA: Yes. Bye. I'll let myself out.

PAUL: No.

CELIA: Really. Bye.

   [CELIA exits.]

STEPHEN: Do you want some tea?

PAUL: Yeah.

STEPHEN: Pour it then, will you? I don't want any.

VII

[JULIAN and STEPHEN]

JULIAN: Don't let's go on. It was awful really.

STEPHEN: Come on. You look great. Was it really awful? No girls? No girls, Julian? What about the grove of Catullus?

JULIAN: Look, Stephen. Look, I can't. It just makes me nervous.

STEPHEN: Okay. You know you said you'd ring from the airport.

JULIAN: Oh my God. When I got back? I didn't.

STEPHEN: When you left.

JULIAN: Did I? Oh . . .

STEPHEN: Have you rung home?

JULIAN: No. I haven't rung home.

STEPHEN: Have you rung anyone?

JULIAN: Do you mean Nell? Why should I ring Nell? Why shouldn't I ring Nell?

STEPHEN: I don't know. Tell us about Italy, Julian.

JULIAN: You know I'm not good with women. She's a friend. Just a friend. Can't I have a friend?

STEPHEN: Why not? I've got a friend. Thank God for a friend. Thank God for Paul!

JULIAN: Is he your best friend? Aren't I your best friend? I thought I was your best friend. Nell. I can't act normally as far as she's concerned. She's afraid she's going to hurt you. Celia said you have to get on with it.

STEPHEN: Infatuation.

JULIAN: What?

STEPHEN: Look it up. Go on; look it up. You don't need to look it up. I looked it up. It doesn't help. "Nativity once in the main of light crawls to maturity." You're like the main of light. Angel. Isn't that what she calls you? Christ, Nell. "While you've a Lucifer to light your fag, smile boys that's the style."

JULIAN: You're the most restrictive person I've ever met. She calls me that. Yes. Why not?

STEPHEN: Because, Golden Boy, it's so obvious.

JULIAN: I've enough crowding inside my head. I've enough criticising myself. I don't need you crowding and criticising me. Don't say, look at that, look at that, listen to this. You're like, you're like . . . You're endlessly trying to describe me.

STEPHEN: This is going to end up with one of us dead.

JULIAN: You'll have friends if anything bad happens.

STEPHEN: If you had a bit more character, you'd have ended up a born-again Christian. I used to love you more than I hated you. Now I hate you. I hate you.

Do you know I hate you? I've got to go through with this to learn never to do it again. Never. Never to let it happen to me again. I don't know what to do. You'll have to do something. I'm tired after work and I don't know what to do and it's all my fault; it's so humiliating. Why do I seem to be just letting this humiliation happen? I could kill you. Better than being dead. *[Pause]* You really didn't like anything but the swimming and the food at all. Didn't you go into a church?

JULIAN: Yes, we went into a church. . . .

STEPHEN: What is it? What's the matter, Julian?

JULIAN: Nothing.

STEPHEN: Was she Italian?

JULIAN: I'll kill you if you go on about that holiday.

STEPHEN: You'd be doing me the greatest of favours.

JULIAN: Oh, come on. You can't say that. Oh Christ. Don't say that.

STEPHEN: Well. Where's the postcard?

JULIAN: Would you like it? I didn't post it.

   [Gives postcard to STEPHEN]

STEPHEN: But there's nothing on it.

JULIAN: I was lying.

STEPHEN: I don't care. Write on it now.

   [JULIAN writes on the card.]

STEPHEN: There we are. Now I've got it.

JULIAN: There was your card waiting. When I got in. Welcome home.

STEPHEN: Look, don't make me feel bad for sending you a postcard! Because you didn't send me a postcard.

VIII

   [STEPHEN and PAUL]

STEPHEN: I wonder if he's taken her to lunch in Holland Park.

PAUL: Where in Holland Park?

STEPHEN: A bar. Sounds like one of his girlfriends.

PAUL: I know.

STEPHEN: Have you been there?

PAUL: No. What's it like?

STEPHEN: It's like Bluebeard's castle.

PAUL: What?

STEPHEN: I mean, he takes all his serious attempts there. I spent a whole day there once.

PAUL: What's it like?

STEPHEN: It's like a cross between a detoxicated opium den and the copper kettle. Moorish screens. Brass tables. Sofas. Dying palms. A dozing cat. Bits of church furniture. Ecclesiastical bric-a-brac. Bentwood chairs. Jacobean beams. Mock Persian carpets stapled to the back of pews. Full of boys like him and girls like Nell.

PAUL: How do you know he's taken her there?

STEPHEN: I know. The book matches'll turn up. You see I know what things are going to be like. He didn't ring me. So I rang him at 2:30.

PAUL: In the morning?

STEPHEN: Yeah. I'm sorry. I'm sorry, he said. I put the phone down. Then later I made a transfer charge call. So he'd think I was in a phone box. I heard him put the phone down. Then I got dressed and went out. It had been raining. I was cold. I went out to make a call from a phone box. So he could hear that sound, that infuriating sound before the money is inserted. And then let him know it was me and then put the phone down. But I didn't believe that the phone box *would* be out of order as I had imagined. *Would* be broken, and the next, and the next street. And that I would be walking the streets in the wet until 5:00 in the morning and it would be exactly as I had imagined. I went into the casualty department at St. Stephen's. "I'm confused," I said. "Could you ring this number?" And they did. "Are you alright? Would you like to see a doctor?" "No. I don't exactly know where I am. . . . Could you just . . . here's my phone book . . . ring this . . . no, *not* . . . *not* at that number but at—oh, where is it? Here we are—at *this* number—he'll be there and ask him to come and get me." "Sit down. Have some tea." "No, I'm alright. Actually, don't make that call. I'm in the driving seat again. I just wanted to know if such help was available. Thank you. Thank you. In case of emergency . . . such as has just occurred." And then I walked some more and then another broken phone box somewhere behind Olympia. And this young man was walking down the street and he waited for me. What do you do? Do you want a drink? I've just got off the bus. Where are you going? Battersea. You're going the wrong way. He was Scots. I thought I was hallucinating. The revenge was too much. What do you do? Oh . . . You? I write stories and poems. Bleak stories and poems I write. He was thin. And I suppose drunk. I suppose. I couldn't tell. He was soaked through. I didn't want it to happen. What's the matter? I've had a row with someone. Oh, I've just got off a bus. Where are we? Are you alright? Do you know where you are? Aye. We were at home. Do you want a drink? A scotch? It's Irish. Aye. Shall we go to bed? Aye. Do you want this drink? No. And then of course. Suddenly. I don't like this. Where's the light gone? I said, shall I put it out? It went out. I don't like this. Are you alright? Yes, of course I'm alright. I don't like this. What's the time it says? Five o'-clock. I don't like this. I'm married. What's the time. Five o'clock. No, it's not. Yes, it is. It's my birthday. I'm twenty-six. I'll have to go. I don't know what this is. Don't worry about this. I'm not. Do you feel bad? Not at all. Not at all. Where am I? Tell me where to go. You're miles away. I've got to go. I so wanted him to go. But I tried to persuade him to stay. His clothes were wet through. I wasn't very convincing. It was a cashmere overcoat. I got this in Brick Lane. Ten pounds it cost. I haven't any money. You'd better stay. I'm depressed. The answer to depression is suicide. Why are you depressed? The row. I've got to go. What's going on? Will I get a bus? It's quarter past five! Give me directions. We kissed. "A fond kiss." He came from Glasgow. Why didn't I give him any money? I had money. Why didn't I give it to him? He was thin and poor. Tell me.

PAUL: I don't know.

IX

[STEPHEN and JULIAN]

STEPHEN: Hello.
JULIAN: Can I walk down with you?
STEPHEN: Yeah. Yeah.
JULIAN: It's nice to see you.
STEPHEN: Mmm . . .
JULIAN: It is. You don't know how nice it is.
STEPHEN: Don't, please. I can't. Please.
JULIAN: You haven't seen me for four weeks. It's nice to see you.
STEPHEN: Don't, Julian.

[JULIAN is crying.]

STEPHEN: What's the matter?
JULIAN: I can't bear it.
STEPHEN: What?
JULIAN: She won't see me now. I can't bear it, Stephen. Don't, someone'll see.
STEPHEN: What does that matter?
JULIAN: She won't see me.
STEPHEN: Has she gone back to Dobbin?
JULIAN: Mm . . . Keith. I think so. We did go to Italy together.
STEPHEN: Ha! What? Ha!
JULIAN: You knew.
STEPHEN: I didn't know.
JULIAN: You did know.
STEPHEN: I really didn't know.
JULIAN: You did know.
STEPHEN: I really didn't know. I know now, though. It doesn't matter. *[Pause]* That was a dirty bloody trick, you know.
JULIAN: What could I do?
STEPHEN: Not go.

JULIAN: How could I not?

STEPHEN: I bet the first coat you ever wore was reversible.

JULIAN: Don't. I don't think I can bear it, Stephen.

STEPHEN: Yes. It must be unbearable. Come on. Come on.

JULIAN: No.

STEPHEN: Why do I want this abasement?

JULIAN: I don't know. You tell me. I don't want it.

STEPHEN: What?

JULIAN: What you said.

STEPHEN: It's the thought of your prostituting intimacies. "With all my heart." I can hear you say it. Rerunning conversations you've had with me. Do you know what it feels like to know a year of your life is being spunked over someone else on the beach at Lerici?

JULIAN: Have I done this to punish myself?

STEPHEN: You mean, like a copycat murder? I dunno. I should think so. . . . I still can't help loving the idea of you. The idea of something real in you. That was recently there in you. That is in you. Come on.

X

[STEPHEN and JULIAN]

STEPHEN: *[Offering JULIAN a drink]* Here.

JULIAN: No.

STEPHEN: Go on.

JULIAN: No.

STEPHEN: Well, why did you come round?

JULIAN: I don't know. Is it late?

STEPHEN: Must be.

JULIAN: How late?

STEPHEN: Three . . .

JULIAN: This is just a bundle of misery. Why is she doing it? Is she confused? Is she wicked? Fucking me over—like I've fucked you over. You can feel satisfied now.

STEPHEN: No. I don't feel satisfied. I'm apprehensive. Yes. Of you. Again. But if you start anything—I warn you—I'll join straight in. You've taken all my sexuality and wasted it in . . . Nell. She's had me through you.

JULIAN: I can't bear it.

STEPHEN: Drink this, then. Let's go to sleep.

JULIAN: No. No.

STEPHEN: You just reject everything I have to offer. The drink. The blanket. I don't do for you. And you have to reject even these comforts. You don't give anything. I only take by giving and you can't even take this. I can't get her for

you. I can't go on being punished for this. Ring *her*. Punish *her*. Ring bloody
Keith. Give *him* a basinful. Drink this.

JULIAN: No. I'm going home. Thanks. I'm going to blow myself away. Perhaps
that will satisfy everyone.

XI

[*NELL and JULIAN*]

NELL: Angel.

JULIAN: I came hoping to see Keith, actually. Actually.

NELL: Did you? Why should you want to see Keith?

JULIAN: Because I did. Alright?

NELL: If you try to see Keith, I'll never see you or speak to you again. Ever. *Do you
understand?*

JULIAN: Why are you doing this?

NELL: What, doing what?

JULIAN: Why did you ring me?

NELL: Because I wanted to see you. I missed you.

JULIAN: Did you?

NELL: I'm sorry. I shouldn't have then.

JULIAN: No. No. No. Listen, Nell. Listen.

NELL: Yes.

JULIAN: Listen, Nell. If you weren't with Keith, who would you be with?

NELL: Oh dear. Don't be silly. You know.

JULIAN: I don't know.

NELL: You do.

JULIAN: Honestly. Really. Really? . . . Please.

NELL: You know I can't.

JULIAN: But it's over between you and Keith.

NELL: Is it?

JULIAN: I know it is. It can't be going to go on forever. Now now.

NELL: No. I can't see it lasting forever. But you know . . . I love Keith.

JULIAN: Stop it. Stop it.

NELL: But you must know that I do.

JULIAN: I don't want to hear.

NELL: Well, don't.

[*Pause*]

JULIAN: And what about me?

NELL: And you. And you.

JULIAN: Please. I'll do anything. I'll wait.

JULIAN: And what . . .

NELL: Angel.

JULIAN: I will. I'll wait.

NELL: Would you?

JULIAN: I will. I've said I will. I'll wait until it's finished. You told me it was finished between you and Keith.

NELL: When did I say that?

JULIAN: In Italy, virtually . . . I'd just . . .

NELL: What?

JULIAN: I'd like to . . . again. I'd like to see your face change because of me. I saw
it light up because of me. At the door. I just want to have that effect on you
again. That's all. I just want to fuck you to see you change. Your eyes hollow and
your skin and your mouth. Please, Nell.

NELL: Look, Keith's coming back tomorrow.

JULIAN: I don't care. Let me stay the night. Please.

NELL: No.

JULIAN: Then why did you ring? Are you mad or what?

NELL: And if things are different between him and me, it's because of . . . this.

JULIAN: What?

NELL: Look, you'll have to go.

JULIAN: No.

NELL: Julian.

JULIAN: No.

NELL: Julian.

JULIAN: No.

NELL: Alright. Alright.

XII

[NELL and PAUL]

NELL: They call it an abortion. It's an abortion. My mother calls it an infection. A
miscarriage is what it is usually known by. But it's a spontaneous abortion. I
would have had a termination anyway. I don't want a baby. Anyway, I think
probably I've got a slim chance, so they say. I suffer from cervical incompetence.
I've got to have it done. I'm bleeding.

PAUL: Nell.

NELL: I'm strong, you know.

PAUL: Are you? Where's Keith?

NELL: He's coming down. He's been very kind. He's coming with me.

PAUL: Julian?

NELL: He doesn't know. . . . Yes, I suppose it could be. What about Julian?

XIII

[STEPHEN and PAUL]

STEPHEN: Tell me what to do, he said. Speak to her. I'll write. Don't write, speak. I rang her girlfriend.

PAUL: Who?

STEPHEN: She says she never gave him any reason to hope. I can't understand what's going on in her mind. But I suppose third parties don't count in these matters. He spoke to her. Then rang asking me for a drink. When I arrived. He was . . . they were at the other end of the bar with that look of relief on his face that is his main reason for relating to people at all. I, de trop clearly. I went knowing he'd ring at 11:00. He did. I didn't answer. He rang back at 12:15. I answer. He says, can I ring you back in a quarter of an hour? He had to go and see the man. He does dutifully. Ring. Christ. And doesn't want to speak. He's doped out and tired and full of hope. What on earth is she doing? I'm not sophisticated, you know.

PAUL: She wants the best of both worlds. Isn't that what we all want?

STEPHEN: Really.

PAUL: Stephen, don't be such a kid. For Nell it's like the 2:30 at Newmarket. It's either Dobbin or Boy Blue. I think she's afraid of being thrown by Boy Blue. I give you six to four on Dobbin. Always excluding the possibility of a suitable outsider.

STEPHEN: I think she says things—so he says—like "If we're fated to be together, we will be. No matter what happens, I'll always love you." Ghastly things like that.

PAUL: She's trying to draw it to a close.

STEPHEN: Why?

PAUL: Well, she does owe Keith. And she does love him. And it must be faced, Stephen, that Keith must reach those parts of Nell that Julian doesn't get to.

STEPHEN: They're getting a joint mortgage. Nell and Keith.

PAUL: No, they're not. A joint mortgage is the fashionable way of saying, I do.

XIV

[PAUL and JULIAN]

[PAUL reading a letter]

PAUL: "Angel, the time has come. . . ." I don't want to read this.

JULIAN: Go on. Please. I don't know what to do, Paul. When I opened it and read "The time has come" I thought.

PAUL: I could see you might. I really don't want to read it, Julian.

JULIAN: I've told her I'll wait. Is she a bitch? Is she? Look, Paul, you know her. Tell me. Read it.

PAUL: "I've never hurt so much . . . ! No one has made me hurt so much!" Does she accept all the blame?

JULIAN: Yes.

PAUL: [*Laughs*] Yes. "I'm sorry. My fault. No blame." She certainly has a flowing pen. . . . Ah . . .

JULIAN: What?

PAUL: "I only hope I have the strength of will not to see you again."

[*Reads more*]

Did you know she'd been in hospital before this?

JULIAN: Yes. But not . . . it was mine. I know it.

PAUL: How do you know?

JULIAN: Paul. You know. Because one knows.

PAUL: Does one?

JULIAN: Yes.

PAUL: Have you shown this to anyone else? Have you shown this to Stephen?

JULIAN: Yes.

PAUL: You've shown this to Stephen! Did he know about . . . before this?

JULIAN: Yes. What am I going to do, Paul?

PAUL: What's the point of saying things like if you don't watch out, you're going to get into trouble one day. Nell I know about. There's nothing to be said for Nell. Nell's what used to be called a free spirit. She's like Gwendolyn Harleth as seen by Rebecca West in a book which Virago found too dull to republish, "Was she beautiful, or not beautiful?" It's Nell spelt with a K.

JULIAN: What do you know about Nell?

PAUL: You know there isn't any ownership involved. I know a lot about Nell. I even like Nell. I can still say I like her. I do. I have, and I do, and Stephen doesn't know, and we have since you met, and we have since you got back from Italy. But that's between me and Nell. Why didn't you keep this between you and Nell? What's Stephen done to *you*? He *isn't* your father, you know. You're going to get yourself into trouble. You are sometime. It's no good saying anything to Nell. She's degenerate as far as personal feelings go.

XV

[*JULIAN*]

JULIAN: I'm in purgatory. It lifts momentarily, and then I wonder, why doesn't she ring? Then I think about Stephen. . . . I know it was mine. I know. Dad. I hate

Stephen. I'll ring him; he'll understand. Why doesn't he leave me alone? How could she do it? I'm going to ring her. I rang her. Ansaphone, ansaphone. She encompasses me. Why? She loves me. Why? Stephen. Why? Stephen. I rang him. I've got to go to bed, I say. Why? He rings back. I can't take him. I don't say anything. Why has she done this? I hate her. Dad. I hate him so much. I asked Stephen, should I buy her flowers. I'm wrecked. Oh please, where is she? She's *fucked* me. And I'm in trouble with Stephen. Stephen. Why doesn't he leave me alone? I need to talk to him. He pisses me off. I'm not ringing Dad. I do hate him. Stephen's so fucking selfish. The rubbish he talks. I'm not seeing him. Fuck him. If he's angry, good. I'm fucking angry. Really fucking angry. Where is she? Why has she done this? Shall I ring her? I really hate her. Fuck them. I'm in torment. Where is she? I'm not ringing Stephen. What'll he do? Fuck him. Dad. I've put a message on her machine. I can't cope. I can't live without her. I hate her. I hate Stephen. Dad. I really *do hate.*

XVI

[STEPHEN and JULIAN]

STEPHEN: No.

JULIAN: What?

STEPHEN: She isn't better. She isn't more beautiful. She isn't cleverer. She isn't—than you. You're fighting her for possession of yourself.

JULIAN: Yeah? I saw two people in the street just now kissing, flirting, laughing. An ugly young man and a young woman looking much older than their age. She without teeth—he with bad teeth. Unkempt, dirty, drunk. Like children. Oblivious to everyone else. Why them? I've got nobody. Look, everyone is married. I'm losing her and you. Why do people tell you things and then not help you? I know she wants me really. I know.

STEPHEN: Oh, my dear, shall we never be able to . . . Shall you always be the thing you're . . . Shall you not want me? Shall we always be? Oh, my dear, what a god-awful pity, eh? That people suited and yet not suited. In rebellion. Struggling. You're like one's child. I can't desert you. This amidst all the welter of hate, envy, nerves, frustration. People will say you're very silly and spoilt—but they won't have seen the glimpses, will they? They won't. They'll perceive the charm. The looks. But they won't have seen you look ugly or have seen you when you've squeezed a few tears out. Or how bright you are or how painful your self-knowledge is. We colluded in a fantasy. We are colluding in a fantasy.

JULIAN: She wants me. I know she does, really. But she's too scared to leave him.

STEPHEN: I'm like a dog scratching at the door.

JULIAN: She is. She's . . .

STEPHEN: I know she hasn't finished with you yet. I'm not certain you can honestly say you're finished with her. What if she arrives with her suitcases?

JULIAN: I'd be glad of the opportunity to shut the door.

STEPHEN: You wouldn't.

JULIAN: What do you know what I'll do? Why do you think you know everything about me? What do you want?

STEPHEN: Ownership of you is what I want, alright? Okay? Does that suit you? You want to say it, too—say it to someone as mediocre as you are. Someone you think of as *really* mediocre, really. "Is she better than me?"—You don't mean it. You think she's mediocre, which I don't think of you really, you fucking, fucking bastard. I don't think you even think that about her. Nell. Do you? Yours is not as unhinged an obsession, is it? It's much more acceptable. But you still want to say it—so you can say, I've suffered, too. I've been fucked over; she's fucked me over. You're storing up things she's never imagined, aren't you? To say to her eventually. But you want her to fuck you over so you can say, I've paid. I deserve worse in most instances, but in this one I've paid for the others. And when and if she says it's over *again,* I'll be there. You've got right on your side, haven't you, really? With all your pretence and free thinking, you're right, you're right. The legacy of romanticism . . . What Lady Caroline Lamb said about Byron has lent glamour to all the cheap irresponsibilities of people like you and Nell ever since, without acknowledgement that Byron actually produced something at least as substantial as all the misery he must have caused. But you're so right. So right. But even mad, red, rich, dead, not very cred Shelley wasn't right on about everything. The avoidances in "The Symposium"—what about them? Atheism, freedom, feminism, free love—up to a point. But there was something left to answer, and there was no one living whose ideas he could colonise in *that* respect. What about the boy at Syon House? The master at Eton? Although even after having written the coldest-hearted poem any man could have written to his wife, he at least saved her from dying from a miscarriage. Something you would be too doped out or preoccupied to cope with. What about Hogg and Trewlawney and Williams? I think it was a drowning of convenience. I think there was something irreconcilable. You know there's nothing intrinsically special about you. You haven't earned this attitude by anything you've done—except swim the mile. Your attitude is a result of money spent on your quite inadequate education and your inability to jump class with any grace. In spite of the dope and the street credibility, your mind is essentially suburban. Nuclear fallout. I love it. It's the only classless thing there is. Do you know I don't know whether or not anything of what I've been saying has any basis in truth at all? They were true words when I spoke them. Or the feelings underpinning them were true. There was feeling. But what I was saying. The opinions, the rationalisations, I think they were just ways of trying to say something else really. I don't think what I'm saying now is . . . I think it's genuine enough information. But lies. I think. Not deliberate—don't have the words—or am forbidden them. How can one just keep saying, I love you or I need you or I love you? Over and over. You'd be bored. One has to say other things when one wants not to speak at all, but to say please or help or come or love or please or cry. Over and over and over.

JULIAN: Stephen. Do you remember once inviting me to tell you to fuck off? Fuck off. Just fuck off.

[STEPHEN picks up the knife that he used to open a letter in the first scene.]

JULIAN: Christ. Stephen. Stephen.
STEPHEN: Don't move. Paul! Paul! Don't move.

[PAUL enters.]

PAUL: Stephen.
STEPHEN: He's okay; it's okay. Don't you move. It's okay. Now see this. If I wanted to, I could scar you in the only way that would matter to you. Look at me. I'm your mirror for the moment. Look at yourself. I could. It's alright. I'm not going to. Here, Paul.

[Gives the knife to PAUL]

PAUL: Stephen.
STEPHEN: He can't be loved. He won't be loved. Will you? You see, he won't be loved. You won't.
PAUL: Stephen.
STEPHEN: No. *[To JULIAN]* Listen.

> *Little Boy Blue come blow up your horn*
> *The sheep's in the meadow, the cow's in the corn*
> *But where's the boy who looks after the sheep?*
> *He's under the haystack fast asleep.*

[Pause]

> *Will I wake him? No, not I*
> *For if I do, he is sure to cry.*

Isn't that great?

MARTIN SHERMAN

A Madhouse in Goa

EDITOR'S INTRODUCTION

MARTIN SHERMAN is best known in the United States for his play *Bent*, which has become a central work of resistance and liberation in the gay literary and theatrical canon. The popular use of the pink triangle, the badge of gayness in Nazi concentration camps, as a symbol for gay liberation came from the success of *Bent*. A tenth anniversary London production of *Bent* in 1989, featuring its original star, Ian McKellan, became a battle cry of resistance against the new Clause 28, which forbids government-supported organizations from disseminating any materials or presenting any work that offers a positive image of homosexuality.

Yet *Bent* is only one of a number of major dramatic works Martin Sherman has written over the past twenty years. *When She Danced,* his touching, funny depiction of the later days of Isadora Duncan as seen through the eyes of a young, gay pianist, has been revived a number of times in London, most recently on the West End in 1991 with Vanessa Redgrave. *Messiah, Passing By,* and *Cracks* have all been successfully produced and published in England. American critics have inexplicably been less kind to Sherman.

Although Sherman lives and works in London, he is American born and educated. He was resident playwright at New York's Playwrights Horizons in the mid-1970s but realized that London was the place where playwrights were appreciated and where he could find a relatively stable, supportive theater community to nurture and produce his work. He also realized that he would be more likely to get his plays produced in America if they had had successful productions in London. (It was Frank Rich's *New York Times* review of the London production of Part One of Tony Kushner's *Angels in America* that led to its Broadway production. The success of Sherman's *Bent* in London led to its Broadway production.)

A Madhouse in Goa has never been produced in New York. It opened at the Lyric Hammersmith, in West London, one of the most important centers of new and experimental theater, with a fine cast led by Vanessa Redgrave and Rupert Graves (the beautiful Scudder in the Merchant Ivory film of E. M. Forster's *Maurice*). Its success

there led to a successful West End transfer. *Goa* is Sherman's most original and virtuosic piece.

A *Madhouse in Goa* is really two related one-act plays about personal and artistic betrayal. In the first play, "A Table for a King," set on the outside dining area of
an inn in Corfu in 1966, David, a neurotic, closeted, young, would-be writer,
meets Mrs. Honey, a grand, wealthy dowager right out of Tennessee Williams.
Mrs. Honey urges the extremely uptight young man to "unbutton," which he does
with a beautiful young Greek waiter whose only English comes from the lyrics to
pop songs. This "unbuttoning" leads to the blackmail of David and Mrs. Honey.
"A Table for a King" is a humorous tour de force centering on two grand charac-
terizations: A bizarre Neil Simon meets an uncloseted Tennessee Williams affair,
but with a bittersweet aftertaste. For at the heart of the piece is David's betrayal of
Mrs. Honey, enacted to maintain his closeted position.

In the second play, "Keeps Rainin' All the Time," we discover that "A Table for a
King" was a best-selling semiautobiographical novel written by Daniel Hosani. It
is 1990 and Daniel lives in a home on the edge of a cliff on Santorini. Years of
drugs compounded by shock treatments and a stroke have left Daniel without the
gift of coherent language. This hilarious, yet apocalyptic second play depicts a
world being destroyed by freaks of nature and human invention: Volcanic erup-
tions, tropical storms, AIDS, cancer, nuclear fallout, and terrorist murders
threaten and destroy the characters. Wonderfully, Sherman is not solemn in the
face of all these disasters; they are the background for a comedy of personal and
artistic betrayal. As Daniel diluted the political dimensions of his own experience
to turn it into a best-selling novel—a betrayal of his life, his friends, his politics,
and the truth—so his closest friend sells the rights to the novel to a born-again-
Christian Hollywood producer with "the brain of a lemon" who wants to turn the
book into a heterosexualized Hollywood musical with a happy ending. But what
harm can be done when the world is about to come to an end, a result of political
chaos and nuclear "accidents"?

Sherman's double bill is both economical and grand. We can only be amazed at
how much action and resonance are packed into both short plays and how deftly
the plays build on each other. A *Madhouse in Goa* represents Sherman's best work
thus far.

AUTHOR'S INTRODUCTION

A *Madhouse in Goa* was an attempt to deal with many aspects of life on our planet
as I saw it in the late 1980s, filtered through a gay sensibility. I was fascinated to
observe that not a single critic viewed it as a gay play when it opened in London
in 1989, an attitude not of enlightenment but of curious denial, as if there are certain prisms that cannot reflect a worldview. The play went on from its London
success to productions throughout Europe but as of this writing has never been

produced in America because, quite simply, no one has asked. Ever. As my grandmother would say, "Go know!" I'm sure, however, that she would offer an apple strudel and a cup of lemon tea to John Clum for finally bringing this play to my native shore.

© Crickmay/Camera Press/Retna

PRODUCTION HISTORY AND RIGHTS

A Madhouse in Goa was first performed at the Lyric Hammersmith, London, on 28 April 1989. It later moved to the Apollo Theater with the same cast. The production was directed by Robert Allan Ackerman and designed by Ultz. Lighting design was by Gerry Jenkinson and "Mabel's Song," by Richard Sissons.

A Table for a King

David . . . . Rupert Graves
Mrs. Honey . . . . Vanessa Redgrave
Costos . . . . Ian Sears
Nikos . . . . Larry Lamb

Keeps Rainin' All the Time

Daniel Hosani . . . . Arthur Dignam
Oliver . . . . Larry Lamb
Heather . . . . Vanessa Redgrave
Dylan . . . . Ian Sears
Aliki . . . . Francesca Folan
Barnaby Grace . . . . Rupert Graves

MARTIN SHERMAN

A Madhouse in Goa

For Sue Fleming and Philip Magdaleny

Cast of Characters

Part One: *A Table for a King*
DAVID: Early 20s. American.
MRS. HONEY: Early 60s. American.
COSTOS: 18. Greek.
NIKOS: 30s. Greek.

Part Two: *Keeps Rainin' All the Time*
DANIEL HOSANI: Late 40s. American.
OLIVER: Late 40s. British.
HEATHER: Late 40s. American.
DYLAN: Heather's son. 19. American.
ALIKI: Mid-20s.
BARNABY GRACE: Late 20s. American.

Part One: *A Table for a King*

[*Darkness. DAVID's voice is heard.*]

DAVID: [*Voice only*] A star fell on Albania. I saw it. Just a few minutes ago. And across the dark Ionian Sea, riding a cool breeze from the Levant, the heavens dance. The moon, burnt orange, shines like an illuminated teardrop. [*Pause*]

Oh shit! What's an illuminated teardrop? What a dreadful sentence. Why do I sit here writing about the Levant? I don't know what the Levant is. Or where. It sounds so romantic, though. If only I wasn't alone. Why do I keep this idiot journal? I have to get out of here. Away from this island. Why did I come to Corfu? Will 1966 go down in history as the summer I chased my melancholy across Europe? Oh! Pretentious! Cross it out! Why can't I write a decent sentence? Do people look at me and laugh? What am I doing here?

[*The lights rise on the veranda of the Kistos Inn. A tiny village in Corfu. Summer. 1966. The inn—small, very white, and comfortable—stretches out behind the veranda. The veranda itself is occupied by a number of tables, some of them set for breakfast. A door on one side leads to the kitchen. There are steps on the other side that lead to rocks, which descend, in turn, to the sea that stretches out before the veranda. A group of beach chairs is piled on top of each other near the steps. It is a blazing hot morning.*

MRS. HONEY sits at the centre table—the largest table and one with a commanding view. She is in her early sixties, American. DAVID, also American, sits at a nearby table. He is in his early twenties. He wears slacks and a long-sleeved shirt, buttoned to the top. His movements are awkward and insecure.]

MRS. HONEY: Waiting! I'm waiting. Hello. I'm waiting!

[*COSTOS walks in from the kitchen, carrying a tray. He is Greek, eighteen, handsome, wearing shorts and a T-shirt. He is humming "Yesterday" by the Beatles.*]

Where is Yannis Kistos? Yannis Kistos or his brother Nikos Kistos? The proprietors of the Kistos Inn? I demand to see the Kistos Brothers! Tell them I'm waiting. For my tea.

[*COSTOS puts the contents of his tray—breakfast—on DAVID's table. He is still humming.*]

And my toast. For my breakfast.

[*COSTOS walks off with the tray.*]

[*To DAVID*] Glory Hallelujah! I declare . . . this is not a well-run establishment. I'm sure you've noticed. I saw you arrive yesterday morning. Time enough for you to observe how poorly run this establishment is. Sweet Jesus! And yet the Kistos Brothers own a popular inn. Oh, yes. Difficult to believe, isn't it? It does supply the most luxurious accommodations on this part of Corfu, but what does this part of Corfu have to offer, I ask you? A few goats, a dirty taverna, a puny village, and that dreadful view of the Albanian coast. Have you seen anything *move* on the Albanian coast? I have never even been to Albania. Yes, it is a popular inn, Chez Kistos Frères. Do you know who ate here Friday night?

Lawrence Durrell! They wanted me to give up my table for him. This table. Quite the best table. I always insist upon it when I make my reservations. I have been here three times. I suppose it is a very special place, the Casa Kistos, don't you think? Serene. Well—what has he done, I ask you? Lawrence Durrell? Write a quartet. I'm not impressed. You're supposed to compose quartets, I believe, not write them. Have you read it? There's a wonderful hotel in Alexandria, and I don't believe he mentions it at all. Of course, by wonderful I mean quite inexpensive but clean. I suppose nobody in his quartet does anything inexpensive. Or clean. Well, well, well, I don't know, I don't know. I did give up my table. Yes, I did. So I do think I deserve breakfast. Lordy—I do. *[She takes a bell out of her pocket and rings it.]* Waiting! Call Nikos. Call Yannis. Waiting! I'm waiting! I carry my own bell. It's indispensable. Service is appalling everywhere, don't you think? *[Pause]* We have a great deal in common—you and I—a great deal, well perhaps not a great deal, but one thing. We are both travelling alone. Now I will say this for the Kistos Inn. They have single rooms. Solitary travellers are the most despised race on earth; of course you realize that. It is usually impossible to obtain a single room. I always advised my children to marry at an early age so they would qualify for double rooms. Unfortunately, they listened to me. Unlike this waiter. *[She rings the bell again.]* He understands English perfectly. He's just insolent. So—you're a photographer? I saw your camera. It must be very heavy. I suppose that's why you stoop. I noticed your posture at once. What's your name? *[Pause]*

DAVID: David.

MRS. HONEY: Now *that* is a fine hotel. The King David. In Jerusalem. Are you Jewish?

DAVID: Yes.

MRS. HONEY: Lordy. An artist *and* a Jew. I do hope you're homosexual as well; they all three seem to complement each other, don't they? I, of course, didn't grow up with any Jews, not in Mississippi. I met them later, a few, on my travels. Where are those siblings? Nikos? Yannis! Will you take my photograph? I long to have my photograph taken. At *my* dinner table. Perhaps L. Durrell has left his spirit at the table. Perhaps it will materialize on film. Oh—please—will you?

DAVID: Well . . . I'm not very . . .

MRS. HONEY: It will be an adventure, won't it? I did have my photograph taken in Calcutta once. I had just purchased a camera. I thought my children should have a record of my travels. I asked a sweet little beggar to take my picture. I paid him, of course—he must have been terribly hungry, and he had a stoop, just like yours, and only two fingers, one on each hand, which made it difficult to hold the camera, but marvel of marvels, he focused the thing and clicked it, too, and then smiled the most wonderful smile and ran off with the camera. I tried chasing him, but I think his two fingers gave him extra speed. It always helps to travel light. That, of course, was before I realized my children were not interested in seeing photographs. I wonder if he still has the camera? I have wondered, in the clear light of retrospect, you understand, if he was a leper. I've always had a morbid fear of lepers. Now where would a leper get a roll of film developed? I won't say that question has haunted me, but I *have* wondered. . . . I think it's fair to say his stoop was a permanent stance. So you will—won't you—take my photograph? Please say yes.

DAVID: Well . . . [*Smiles*] Yes.

MRS. HONEY: Thank you. Now, if only I can get breakfast. You seem to have yours. [*She rings the bell again.*] I must confess, the bell is hopeless. Never gets me anything. Still . . . [*She rings it again, vigorously.*] Waiting! I'm waiting. Sweet Jesus, I'm waiting!

[*The lights fade. DAVID's voice is heard.*]

DAVID: [*Voice only*] I met an amazing woman this morning. On the veranda, waiting for breakfast. Her name is Mrs. Honey and she is from Mississippi and she travels all over the world and she never stops talking and I promised to take her photograph. Now why did I do that? I'm so stupid. I *am* stupid. And lonely. And sad. And confused and ugly and desperate. Why am I here? [*His voice fades off.*]

[*The lights rise on the veranda. Afternoon. It is very hot. DAVID is fidgeting with his camera. The camera is very old and a classic of its kind, resting on a tripod and using plates to record its images. It has a hood to cover the photographer when he wants to check the light. DAVID also has a small portable light meter in his hand. MRS. HONEY is sitting at her table, wearing a very light cotton dress, her eyes closed, absorbing the sun.*]

MRS. HONEY: I feel like I'm under water. Floating. Not real. In a different time. [*She opens her eyes.*] That camera—my husband, the dentist, had one just like it. Many years ago. Is it an antique?

DAVID: I don't know. It takes the best . . .

MRS. HONEY: I can't hear you. [*She closes her eyes again.*]

[*COSTOS enters, carrying a tray. He grins at DAVID. DAVID, embarrassed, ducks underneath the hood. COSTOS walks through the veranda humming "Homeward Bound" by Paul Simon. He walks off. DAVID comes out of the hood.*]

DAVID: It takes the best . . .

[*NIKOS enters. He is Greek, in his thirties, and wears shorts and a T-shirt. His English is only lightly accented. He carries a deck of cards. He sits at a table near MRS. HONEY and starts to play solitaire.*]

NIKOS: A photographic session?

[*MRS. HONEY opens her eyes.*]

MRS. HONEY: Nikos! Yes—indeed. You have a distinguished guest. A famous photographer.

DAVID: *[Embarrassed]* No, I'm just . . .

NIKOS: We have many distinguished guests here. This *is* the finest inn on this part of the island. It was very kind of you to give up your table for Mr. Durrell.

MRS. HONEY: Well—he is an artist. Artists make things grow.

NIKOS: *[Losing at solitaire]* Son-of-a-bitch!

[*DAVID is circling them with the light meter.*]

MRS. HONEY: Nikos, you're in the light. Surely he's in the light.

DAVID: No. It's fine.

NIKOS: I am in the way?

DAVID: No.

MRS. HONEY: Of course you're in the way. Nikos went to Oxford.

DAVID: Really?

MRS. HONEY: I find, in general, that if you've been to Oxford, you're in the way. Of course, I can't imagine why he and his invisible brother run a hotel in such an insignificant village. Can you? Speak up, child.

DAVID: Well, I don't . . .

NIKOS: Now, my dear Mrs. Honey—I must ask you for another favour. *[He hits his cards.]* Bloody hell.

MRS. HONEY: You play solitaire with such passion.

NIKOS: It is not a sad game, not a lonely game, Mrs. Honey. Not for a Greek.

[*DAVID stands next to the camera, holding a small switch connected by wire to the camera.*]

DAVID: Now!

MRS. HONEY: What?

[*DAVID presses the button.*]

DAVID: There.

MRS. HONEY: Oh. I had my picture took.

DAVID: *[Removing the frame]* I liked the look on your . . .

MRS. HONEY: Imperious?

DAVID: Yes.

NIKOS: Another favour. *[To his cards]* There. That's better.

MRS. HONEY: What did you study at Oxford?

NIKOS: Political science.

MRS. HONEY: But that's meaningless. Especially in Greece.

NIKOS: That's why I run a hotel. *[To his cards]* Beautiful.

MRS. HONEY: *[To DAVID]* Take another photograph. With Nikos.

DAVID: Yes?

MRS. HONEY: The two of us.

NIKOS: No.

MRS. HONEY: Yes. Please. You would like that?

DAVID: I would.

MRS. HONEY: Speak up, child.

DAVID: I mumble. I'm sorry.

MRS. HONEY: You what?

DAVID: Mumble. *[He circles them again with his light meter.]*

MRS. HONEY: Well, yes, you swallow your words. So did the dentist. Too much saliva, he said. I'd say a miserable childhood. Which would explain your clothing. You're so overdressed. It's blazing hot, isn't it? My, my, you're buttoned. What is the temperature, Nikos?

NIKOS: I must ask you . . .

MRS. HONEY: Oh, Nikos, ask not, ask not. Come—have your picture took, too. Leave those silly cards. It is a lonely game, no matter what you say. I used to play it endlessly. While the dentist was dying. It's a game for *that*. Stand here. Put your arm around me. Host and guest. Milk and honey.

NIKOS: If it pleases you. *[Rises]* Where?

MRS. HONEY: Right here. *[Motions by her side]* Do you like this, dear?

DAVID: Closer.

MRS. HONEY: Pardon?

DAVID: *Closer.*

MRS. HONEY: Swallow all the saliva and then speak. Closer, Nikos. Just stand still. He has to run around with that silly little thing and focus. You're a handsome man, Nikos. Nice legs. The dentist's legs were appalling.

NIKOS: Tomorrow evening, my dear Mrs. Honey . . .

MRS. HONEY: Oh, Nikos, you're so single-minded. Don't you ever ramble?

NIKOS: There is a special guest coming for dinner.

MRS. HONEY: When?

NIKOS: Tomorrow evening.

MRS. HONEY: Oh. You said that.

NIKOS: Yes.

MRS. HONEY: Well, that's nice. I hope he enjoys it. Will you be serving something with lamb?

NIKOS: I must ask you . . .

MRS. HONEY: You mustn't, you mustn't. Don't talk. He doesn't want your mouth to move.

DAVID: It's alright. I'm not ready. *[He ducks under the hood.]*

MRS. HONEY: I think he said he's not ready. The child mumbles. He's also very slow. But I'm sure he wants to get your legs into the shot. Actually—in truth—I rarely saw the dentist's legs.

NIKOS: I must ask you to give up your table once again.

MRS. HONEY: I always had excellent diction. Never mumbled. You ask too much.

NIKOS: For one evening only.

MRS. HONEY: One evening too many.

NIKOS: It is a special favour.

MRS. HONEY: It is *my* table. Mine. It has the best view. Of the olive trees. Of the beach. Of the sea. Of that empty little rowboat in the water. Of Albania. I come to this hotel because of the view of Albania.

NIKOS: I am serious.

MRS. HONEY: I am, too. About the table. I do reserve this table, as well as my room, four months in advance. Do any of your other clients do that? I seriously doubt it.

NIKOS: This guest is very special.

[*DAVID comes out from under the hood.*]

MRS. HONEY: [*To DAVID*] Aren't you ready yet?

DAVID: Almost.

MRS. HONEY: I'm sorry.

DAVID: *Almost.*

MRS. HONEY: Almost. More special than Mr. Durrell?

NIKOS: Yes.

MRS. HONEY: Has he written a quintet, then? Lordy, this insignificant village is crawling with great artists.

DAVID: *Almost ready.*

MRS. HONEY: You needn't shout. The dentist was the same way; if he wasn't mumbling, he was shouting. Smile, Nikos. Tell me, who is this very special guest? Is it Mr. Auden or Mr. Stravinsky or, gracious me, Mr. Picasso? Are they all rushing to Corfu? Do they think the view of Albania might inspire them?

NIKOS: I could choke you. Mrs. Honey.

[*MRS. HONEY laughs. DAVID stands next to the camera, holding the switch.*]

DAVID: Now.

MRS. HONEY: What?

DAVID: I said now.

MRS. HONEY: Oh. Now. Now, Nikos. Smile. Just imagine your hands around my neck, and smile.

[*NIKOS breaks into a broad smile.*]

NIKOS: He is not an artist.

MRS. HONEY: Then he doesn't deserve a table.

NIKOS: He is a king.

DAVID: [*Presses the switch*] Got it.

MRS. HONEY: A king!

[*DAVID quickly turns the plate over and replaces it in the camera.*]

DAVID: One more.

MRS. HONEY: Goodness—dime a dozen.

DAVID: This one will be faster.

MRS. HONEY: You meet kings and princes and dukes everywhere these days. Running around without their countries, looking for a free meal. Where is this one from?

DAVID: Can you smile again?

NIKOS: From here.

MRS. HONEY: Here?

DAVID: Please?

NIKOS: Yes. Here.

MRS. HONEY: Greece?

NIKOS: Greece.

DAVID: Please!

MRS. HONEY: Sorry?

DAVID: Say cheese.

MRS. HONEY: Why?

DAVID: [Presses the switch] Thank you.

MRS. HONEY: Oh, Nikos. Well, well, well. So it's that king. Your king. This king. *The* king. Dining at the Kistos Inn?

NIKOS: He has a home nearby.

MRS. HONEY: With Mr. Durrell? Are they lovers? Oh, you Greeks are so sly. Does the king come here for your legs?

NIKOS: Choke.

MRS. HONEY: [To DAVID] Take one of Nikos—by himself.

NIKOS: No—no—no. [He moves away and sits at his table again and resumes his game of solitaire.]

MRS. HONEY: Nikos is obviously more important than he seems. Oh, Nikos, Nikos. [Pause] No. I won't give up the table.

NIKOS: You can sit at my table.

MRS. HONEY: It's too far away. It's near the kitchen. It attracts Greek mosquitoes.

NIKOS: You can sit with the honeymoon couple.

MRS. HONEY: *With* them?

NIKOS: I'll put them with the Germans.

MRS. HONEY: That would destroy their marriage. So would I. I have a wicked tongue. No, no.

NIKOS: You can sit with the French scientist.

MRS. HONEY: He'll talk to me. In *French*. No, no.

NIKOS: You can sit with your friend here. [He points to DAVID, who is dismantling the camera.]

MRS. HONEY: The child likes his solitude.

DAVID: I don't really mind. . . .

MRS. HONEY: He wants to be alone with his thoughts. He's happy that way. Alone. No, no, no. The king will have to sit with the Germans or the French scientist or even with you, although if you did study political science, I don't think you would have anything to say to him. No, Nikos, I won't give up my table. If he were an artist, like Mr. Durrell . . . then I'd grumble and I'd protest, but in the end, I'd graciously give in. But a king! A politician! He has blood on his hands, Nikos. Quite simply that. On some level—even if he's a nice young chap—he's a killer. You must know that. You studied that. A murderer. Oh, let him go to the local taverna. Let him dine with his deeply distressed subjects. But this table—is mine. *[Pause]*

NIKOS: I must have it.

MRS. HONEY: Mine.

NIKOS: I *will* have it. *[He throws the cards off the table and stands up.]*

MRS. HONEY: I've paid for it.

NIKOS: *[Smiles]* We've just killed each other not too long ago, Mrs. Honey. My people. Brother against brother. As they say. We watched each other die. *[Pause]* A Greek isn't a Greek if he tells the truth. Pardon my lapse. For this is the truth. I will have the table. *[He kisses MRS. HONEY on her forehead.]* Dear lady, I always enjoy your visits here. *[NIKOS leaves.]*

[Silence]

MRS. HONEY: Smooth. Don't you think?

DAVID: I don't know.

MRS. HONEY: Too smooth. There's a story there. How does a Greek boy from Corfu get to Oxford? Where did he learn perfect English? Why does he run a hotel? And where on earth is the other one, his brother? Oh, there is a story there. And we will never know it, you and I; we will never know it. When we travel, we pick up impressions, that's all. Never the truth. We're never invited inside. *[Pause]* You and I. *[Pause]* Will they be pretty photographs?

DAVID: I hope.

MRS. HONEY: Are you pleased?

DAVID: I think so.

MRS. HONEY: Aren't you hot? All those buttons.

DAVID: No.

MRS. HONEY: I have very little in life, you see. The dentist is dead. The children don't need or want me. I see deceit everywhere. I have very little. Occasionally, in some insignificant village, in some country I barely know, I have a table. Do you understand? Why are you so quiet? Look at your hair. It just sits there. You must give it some *style*. *[She runs her finger through his hair, messing it up, trying to give it some body.]* Someday, you will understand. *[The lights fade. DAVID's voice is heard.]*

DAVID: *[Voice only]* Why did I bring this awful camera? No one travels with a camera like this. It's so heavy. The plates weigh a ton. Why do I think I can take photographs? When I try to carry the camera *and* the suitcase together, it's a living hell. I keep throwing clothing away to make the suitcase lighter. It never gets lighter. It's a nightmare. The suitcase keeps brushing against my leg. And now the skin is falling off my leg. I have a rash on my arm as well. And my stomach hurts all the time. Maybe I'm dying. I think that I'm dying. What am I doing here? *[His voice trails away.]*

[The lights rise. The veranda. Evening. DAVID is sitting at the table, writing in his journal. MRS. HONEY enters, wearing a nightgown. She is carrying a bottle of wine and two small glasses.]

MRS. HONEY: Sweet Jesus! What an evening. Do you hear a cow out there? I have some wine. And glasses. I couldn't sleep. I saw you on the veranda. I had waking dreams. Do you know them? Amazing landscapes, but one eye is open. Cows are much too noisy. Nikos Kistos has invaded my dreams. Manically chopping my table up with an axe. Here. *[She sits at her table.]*
Move over here, to the table in question.

[DAVID joins her at her table.]

They've waxed it. See? Have some retsina. It tastes like nail polish. I don't drink too often. But this evening . . . well . . . it just isn't right, some evenings aren't, out there—in the world—not right. . . . *[She pours him a glass of wine.]*
DAVID: *[Takes the glass]* Thank you.
MRS. HONEY: Drink it down very fast. Nikos Kistos is an evil man, mind my words; he's planning something. I smell enemies. I do, I do. Mind my words.
DAVID: *[Drinks his wine]* Oh, my God.
MRS. HONEY: A bit like lava, isn't it? Have another. *[She pours him another glass.]*
Glory be, child, don't you want to unbutton something?
DAVID: *[Drinks the wine]* Ohh!
MRS. HONEY: *[Drinks the wine]* It's good for you. Go on. Another.
DAVID: I can't.
MRS. HONEY: I insist.
DAVID: Well . . .

[She pours him another glass.]

Okay. *[Giggles]* It tastes awful. *[Drinks the wine]* Do you, do you, do you . . . ?
MRS. HONEY: What?
DAVID: Do you . . . ? *[He pauses for breath.]*
MRS. HONEY: Speak up, child.
DAVID: Do you know where the Levant is?
MRS. HONEY: Oh. Somewhere, dear. Definitely somewhere. Somewhere out there. *[Drinks her wine]* We're not savouring this, are we? *[She pours DAVID another glass.]* Something to do with the Mediterranean. Places like Cyprus . . . Syria . . . Lebanon . . .
DAVID: *[Drinks his wine]* Jesus!

MRS. HONEY: Do you know Beirut? That's probably part of the Levant. You must go there someday. It's an absolute jewel. I travel, you know—place to place to place. . . . *[She pours herself another glass.]*

My, this stuff grows on you. I'm never anywhere for too long. They know my name at every American Express office in Europe and Asia. Not Australia. Doesn't interest me. I have this table reserved for another ten days. Damn Nikos Kistos! I don't want to move. *[Drinks the wine]* A tiny bit more? *[She pours another glass.]*

Well. Beirut. Now, I'm not partial to nightclubs, but in Beirut nightclubs are as natural as the sea. There's one that is, in fact, by the sea; it has a spectacular, if rather grotesque, stage show, and, for a finale, a long, giant, life-sized train winds its way across the nightclub floor, weaving around the tables, with chorus girls standing on top of the railway cars, and cages coming down from the ceiling, those too with chorus girls, and flowers raining down on the tables, and gold coins as well, falling past the chorus girls in the cages onto the chorus girls on the train.

[DAVID looks at her, dumbfounded.]

Lordy! What a silly thing to remember. Well. Beirut. *[She holds her glass up in a toast.]*

DAVID: *[Holds his glass up]* Beirut.

MRS. HONEY: The glass is empty. I do get fond of certain places. Usually much later. After I've left. I'll give you the address of a lovely hotel there. And that nightclub. You will go there some day. On your travels. Nikos Kistos worries me, boy.

DAVID: I'm sick of my travels.

MRS. HONEY: He wants this table, he does. It's only a piece of wood. Such a fuss.

DAVID: I'm sick of my travels.

MRS. HONEY: And he's devious. And it's a king. Spells trouble.

DAVID: I'm sick of my travels.

MRS. HONEY: What? Oh. Which travels?

DAVID: These. Here. There. This summer. My summer in Europe.

[Pause]

MRS. HONEY: Where have you been?

DAVID: Everywhere.

MRS. HONEY: For instance?

DAVID: Paris.

MRS. HONEY: *[Smiles]* Ah!

DAVID: It was horrible.

MRS. HONEY: Oh.

DAVID: London.

MRS. HONEY: Ummm.

DAVID: A nightmare.

MRS. HONEY: I see.

DAVID: Rome.

MRS. HONEY: Roma!

DAVID: I hated it.

MRS. HONEY: Hated it?

DAVID: Venice.

MRS. HONEY: Miserable?

DAVID: Miserable.

MRS. HONEY: *[Laughs]* I think you need these last few drops. . . . *[She empties the dregs of the wine bottle into his glass.]*

DAVID: Why is it so funny?

MRS. HONEY: Did you not find Venice a little, a bit, a tiny bit—itsy-bitsy bit— beautiful? *[She laughs again.]*

DAVID: Yes.

MRS. HONEY: Then why was it miserable?

DAVID: I don't know. Yes, I do. You see, it was me. I was . . .

MRS. HONEY: What?

DAVID: Nothing.

MRS. HONEY: Go on.

DAVID: No.

MRS. HONEY: Spit it out. *[Laughs]* I used to say that to the dentist—spit it out. Of course, he said the same thing to his patients. I wonder who picked it up from whom.

[Pause]

DAVID: I was lonely.

MRS. HONEY: *[Laughs]* Oh. I'm sorry. I have a laughing fit. I don't mean it. Glory be! Lonely? Dear, dear.

DAVID: No one has talked to me. You're the first person on this entire trip who has talked to me.

MRS. HONEY: It's all those buttons. You're so covered up. You do not invite conversation. I'm amazed you're not wearing a necktie. Are your parents the very religious type? Do they abhor the human body? I have heard that Orthodox Jews make love through a hole in the sheet—is that true of your parents?—and if so, do they tear a hole, or is it meticulously cut? Well, well, well—you are not a happy specimen, are you? Still in school?

DAVID: Just out. Out. Into the darkness . . . *[He stands up—can't handle it—sits down again.]*

MRS. HONEY: And child, your hair. It's so homeless. Did you notice, in London, during your nightmare stay there, that some of the young men are now wearing their hair long and wild and quite beautiful? Let your hair grow, boy. And muss

it a bit. And treat yourself to sideburns. And slash away your trousers. Yes—
show us your legs. Do you have a shape to you? Let's see it, child.

DAVID: I'm drowning.

MRS. HONEY: Oh dear.

DAVID: I'm tottering . . .

MRS. HONEY: You're drunk.

DAVID: On the edge . . .

MRS. HONEY: Very drunk.

DAVID: Of an abyss!

[*MRS. HONEY stares at him and starts to laugh again.*]

MRS. HONEY: I'm sorry.

DAVID: I don't have nice legs. [*He starts to cry.*] I'm drunk. Michael! Do you have
more wine? My legs are scrawny. My kneecaps stick out. He doesn't love me at
all. He lied to me.

MRS. HONEY: Shh! You will wake the hotel up. Nikos Kistos will have us arrested
for drinking. He's planning something, Nikos Kistos. The king could order a fir-
ing squad.

DAVID: I'm burning!

MRS. HONEY: It's the sun. It was extremely strong this afternoon.

DAVID: I'm on fire.

MRS. HONEY: Or then again, he could try to poison me.

DAVID: I'm lost in an inferno!

[*MRS. HONEY looks up.*]

MRS. HONEY: [*Sharply*] Inferno? Dear, dear. Retsina, you old dog. Now, let's pull
ourselves together.

DAVID: I'm so unhappy. I want to die! I want to join a kibbutz!

MRS. HONEY: Well, at least you have a sense of priority.

DAVID: I'm twenty-three. . . .

MRS. HONEY: *That* old!

DAVID: So much of me has been washed away. . . .

MRS. HONEY: You tend to overdramatize. Did you know that? Is that why you
take photographs? Are you attracted to the theatre? Do you have any friends?

DAVID: I'm falling . . . falling. . . .

MRS. HONEY: Oh, I'm no good at this. Mothering.

DAVID: Into the abyss . . .

MRS. HONEY: Never suited me. Ask my children. They loathe me for good reason.

DAVID: The abyss . . .

MRS. HONEY: No, child. It's not an inferno. It's not even a brushfire. It's not an
abyss. Do you know what an abyss is?

DAVID: What?

MRS. HONEY: Watching the dentist disappear before your eyes. Cancer. That's an abyss. Watching his flesh melt away from his face. Watching a truck drive through his body every night. That's an abyss. Now dry your eyes and go to bed. We mustn't wake the evil Kistos up. The Kisti. Where is his brother? *[She stands up and looks at the sea.]*

Not being loved is nothing. Easy. Fact of life. The dentist didn't love me, certainly not after the first year, but then, I never stopped jabbering, so who can blame him? And I didn't love the dentist; he was a fairly tedious man, although that is no reason to die such a cruel death. No, I married him to get away from my parents' home, and I did, God knows, I did. He took me to Utah, to the desert, the clean, quiet, empty desert, which, believe it or not, I much preferred to Mississippi. And I liked his last name. To be called Honey in perpetuity. Who could resist? And when he finally met his humourless maker, I found I had nothing to do but stare at the desert. The dentist was a companion, you see. He rarely spoke, and when he did, it was usually about bleeding gums, but still, he was there, sitting next to me, boring me, but not with malice, and we took comfort in being bored together. But left alone, I was useless. All I was trained to do in Mississippi was to read magazines and chatter. My children fled from my endless chatter. My daughter married a man every bit as dull as the dentist. Isn't that always the way? And my son, who has some spunk and brains, moved as far away as he could. They were both petrified I'd visit them, so they suggested I take a trip. I packed a suitcase. It's been four years and I'll never return. They send me money every few months. To American Express. And now I chatter in different locations for a few weeks at a time. And move on. And that, too, is an abyss.

DAVID: I'm embarrassed. I didn't mean to . . .

MRS. HONEY: My son sent a letter with his last cheque. He's left his job. He's heading for San Francisco with his wife. He says the world is changing. There's a new kind of life. He says he has *hope*. Well. Glory Hallelujah, bless his soul. *And*—his hair is very long. He sent a photograph. I think he looks quite stunning. He's not much older than you. *[She brushes DAVID's hair.]* Please. Let it grow. *[Pause]*

Well, well, well. Time to return Nikos Kistos to my dreams. Time to close my eyes and see him pulling at my table, like a demented puppy. Down, Nikos, down! *[She brushes her hand across his face.]*

Breathe a little. Let some fresh air in. Throw away your camera. Forget your hurt. Forget your family. Buy some shorts. Have adventures. But first—go to sleep. Sleep is good for growing hair. *[She kisses him. He stares at her.]*

DAVID: Mrs. Honey?

MRS. HONEY: What?

DAVID: Your nightgown—is on upside down.

MRS. HONEY: Well, so it is. Fancy that. *[She leaves.]*

[DAVID sits alone at the table. He runs his hand through his hair and starts to pull on it, as if to make it grow. Silence.]

COSTOS enters from the beach. He is wearing a bathing suit. A beach blanket hangs over his shoulder. He sees DAVID. He smiles. He starts to hum "Strangers in the Night." DAVID looks up at COSTOS, startled. He sees COSTOS smile and smiles back tentatively, then turns away. COSTOS walks into the kitchen.

DAVID gathers his notebook, the two glasses, and the empty wine bottle and starts to leave. He is a bit unsteady on his feet. He looks for some place to throw the bottle.

COSTOS reenters, carrying a large glass of water. DAVID stops, transfixed by COSTOS's body.]

COSTOS: Water.

DAVID: What?

COSTOS: You wanted water?

DAVID: No.

COSTOS: Glass of water.

DAVID: No.

COSTOS: I make mistake?

DAVID: Yes.

COSTOS: Think you want water.

DAVID: No. *[Pause. DAVID starts to leave again.]*

COSTOS: I bring it to your room.

DAVID: Bring what?

COSTOS: Water.

DAVID: No.

COSTOS: Room number six?

DAVID: Yes.

COSTOS: I bring it.

DAVID: I don't want water.

COSTOS: I was going to bring at any rate.

DAVID: You were?

COSTOS: After I swim. Tonight. To room six. To you.

DAVID: You were?

COSTOS: Yes.

DAVID: Why?

COSTOS: But now you here. Better. So drink it here. *[He holds out the glass.]*

DAVID: But I don't want . . .

[COSTOS stares at him.]

Well . . . I suppose . . . *[He takes the glass.]* Thank you.

COSTOS: You see. I know what you want.

DAVID: It's only water.

COSTOS: Drink it.

[Pause]

DAVID: Alright. *[He drinks the water.]*
COSTOS: Is good?
DAVID: Yes.
COSTOS: Greek water is good?
DAVID: Excellent.
COSTOS: You know Barbara Ann?
DAVID: Who?
COSTOS: Barbara Ann.
DAVID: No.
COSTOS: Song. By Beach Boys.
DAVID: Oh. Oh! I see. Beach Boys. No. I don't listen to . . .
COSTOS: I'm still wet. From sea. Dry under stars. Here. Take chairs. *[He goes to the side of the veranda where the beach chairs are piled up and drags two to the centre of the veranda.]* You help me.

[DAVID helps him with the chairs.]

Good. We lie down.

[COSTOS throws his blanket on one of the chairs and lies on it, stretching out, provocatively. DAVID stares at him.]

Go on. You, too.

[DAVID doesn't move. COSTOS—impatient—taps the chair next to him.]

Here. Here. Under stars.

[Pause]

DAVID: Why not? *[He lies down on the other chair.]* My God! *[Staring at the sky]* Look at them.
COSTOS: Tomorrow big day.
DAVID: Is it?
COSTOS: King is here.
DAVID: I know.
COSTOS: We have good king.
DAVID: Yes.
COSTOS: No king in America.
DAVID: No. So many stars. I feel almost . . .
COSTOS: Greece happy with king . . .
DAVID: Almost . . .
COSTOS: King is like father.
DAVID: Almost someplace else.

COSTOS: You know Sergeant Barry Sadler?

DAVID: Who?

COSTOS: "Ballad of Green Berets." War song. Big hit. Vietnam. You like it?

DAVID: I don't know it.

COSTOS: No wars in Greece anymore. You know this—? *[Sings]* "Under the board-walk, we'll be fallin' in love. Under the boardwalk, boardwalk."

DAVID: No.

COSTOS: Drifters.

DAVID: Oh. I see.

COSTOS: Move chairs closer. *[He reaches out and pulls DAVID's chair directly next to his, then puts his arm on DAVID's shoulder.]* I know what you want. I have many brains. I go to university next year. You go to university?

DAVID: I did.

COSTOS: You leave.

DAVID: Graduate.

COSTOS: You smart person, too. You study with the camera?

DAVID: A little. Yes.

COSTOS: I can tell. Smart person. Take pictures for money?

DAVID: Not yet. Someday.

COSTOS: *[Sings]* "Cool cat, lookin' for a kitty. Gonna look in every corner of the city." Know that?

DAVID: No.

COSTOS: Lovin' Spoonful.

DAVID: I never listen to contemporary . . .

COSTOS: *[Sings]* "And baby, if the music is right, I'll meet you tomorrow, sort of late at night." *[Pause]* How I learn my English. Sonny. Cher. Mamas. Papas. Simon. Garfunkel. Good teachers. My English good?

DAVID: Very.

[COSTOS moves his arm past DAVID's shoulder and lays it on DAVID's chest.]

COSTOS: You have girlfriend?

DAVID: No.

COSTOS: I have many.

DAVID: Oh.

COSTOS: Boyfriends, too.

[Pause]

DAVID: Oh.

[COSTOS starts to caress DAVID's chest.]

COSTOS: You have boyfriends?

DAVID: No.

COSTOS: Not even one?

[Pause]

DAVID: No.

COSTOS: You not serious.

DAVID: I am. Serious. No. *[Sits up]* I think I am going to sleep now. *[Rises]* I'm just a little drunk.

[COSTOS grabs DAVID's legs.]

COSTOS: You stay.

DAVID: I can't.

COSTOS: What make you drunk?

DAVID: Retsina.

COSTOS: It is good, retsina?

DAVID: Yes. But bitter.

COSTOS: Bitter—good?

DAVID: Yes. Bitter very good. But too much. I feel strange.

COSTOS: You feel happy?

DAVID: Happy? No! No happy. *[Pause]* Strange.

COSTOS: Strange—good?

DAVID: I don't know. I can't answer.

[COSTOS pulls DAVID down to his chair.]

What are you doing?

COSTOS: Look at stars. Beautiful. Greek night. Sound of waves. Magic. I know what you want. I have many brains. I will go to university. I'll be smart person, too. *[Sings]* "We'll sing in the sunshine. We'll laugh everyday." Know that?

DAVID: No.

COSTOS: Gale Garnett. Big hit. No sunshine now. Stars. *[He brushes his hand across DAVID's mouth.]*

DAVID: Stars.

COSTOS: It is very hot, no?

DAVID: Yes.

[COSTOS takes DAVID's hand and places it on his chest, then sings.]

COSTOS: "Then I'll be on my way." *[Pause]* I am very hot. You also?

DAVID: Yes.

COSTOS: Why you never unbutton? *[He moves DAVID's hand across his chest.]* Greece very hot. You like Greece? *[He puts DAVID's hand on his nipple.]*

DAVID: Very much.

COSTOS: You think Greece beautiful?

DAVID: Very.

COSTOS: Unbutton. *[He starts to unbutton DAVID's shirt.]*

DAVID: No. *[He sits up.]*

COSTOS: What is wrong?

DAVID: Nothing.

COSTOS: I want to look at you.

DAVID: You do? Really?

COSTOS: Yes. Sure. *[Sings]* "And it's magic, if the music is groovy."

DAVID: Everybody wants me to unbutton. But I don't. . . . Oh. What the hell. *[He pulls his shirt open.]* Unbuttoned! Oh God, I think I tore it. I tore my shirt. This is a catastrophe.

COSTOS: Leave open.

DAVID: I only have a few shirts with me. And this one drip-dries and . . .

COSTOS: Like shirt torn. Sexy.

DAVID: Sexy?

COSTOS: Yes.

DAVID: Really?

COSTOS: Really.

DAVID: Me? No. . . .

COSTOS: Your skin so white. No beach?

DAVID: No beach, no. Can't swim. I visit ruins. No beach. My family . . . they think modern bathing suits are . . . Oh, that's silly. . . . I don't listen to them anyway. . . . I . . . can't swim, though. . . .

COSTOS: *[Sings]* "Hey, Mr. Tambourine Man, sing a song for me." I know what you want. I have many brains. *[He pulls DAVID's shirt completely open.]*

DAVID: It's cold. There's a draught.

COSTOS: It's hot. *[Sings]* "Hot town, summer in the city." *[Pause]* Put hand here. . . . *[He places DAVID's hand on his crotch.]* *[Sings]* "I'm not sleepy and there's no place I'm going to." *[He pulls DAVID down.]* Lips here. *[He kisses DAVID.]*

> *[DAVID pulls himself up. COSTOS pulls him down again and as he does so takes the beach blanket out from under his body and drapes it over them, covering both of their bodies.]*

Here. I make you relax. You like blanket? Pretty Greek blanket. There. Now you do not have to look. Just feel. Better. I have many brains. I know what you want.

> *[There is now much mutual activity underneath the blanket.]*

You like?

DAVID: Yes. I like.

COSTOS: Very much?

DAVID: Very much.

COSTOS: *[Sings]* "In the jingle-jangle morning, I'll come following you." *[He speaks in a murmur as he explores DAVID's body.]* Do you feel the jingle-jangle? You come following through under the boardwalks? What a day for a daydream. All my thoughts are far away. Do you believe in magic? Homeward bound, I'm homeward bound. . . .

DAVID: Oh . . .

COSTOS: These boots are made for walking. . . .

DAVID: Ohh . . .

COSTOS: Walk all over you.

DAVID: Yes.

COSTOS: I make you happy?

DAVID: Yes.

COSTOS: Very happy?

DAVID: Yes.

COSTOS: Sputnik. You go up like Sputnik. All the leaves are brown and the sky is grey. . . .

DAVID: Yes.

COSTOS: I've been for a walk on a winter's day.

DAVID: Yes.

COSTOS: Sputnik. Into space.

DAVID: Ohh . . .

COSTOS: I'm not sleepy and there is no place I'm going to. . . .

DAVID: Ohh . . .

COSTOS: If I didn't tell her, I could leave today. . . .

DAVID: Ohhh.

COSTOS: California dreamin' on a winter's day. . . .

DAVID: Ohhh! *[DAVID has an orgasm.]*

[Pause. COSTOS sits up, startled.]

COSTOS: So soon? Sputnik land so soon?

DAVID: I think so.

COSTOS: Too soon.

DAVID: I'm sorry.

COSTOS: I do not give pleasure?

DAVID: Yes. I'm sorry.

COSTOS: You do not like me?

DAVID: But I do.

COSTOS: Not very much.

DAVID: I do. Honestly. Very much. You give pleasure.

COSTOS: You make joke.

DAVID: No.

COSTOS: This truth?

DAVID: Yes. Truth.

COSTOS: Promise.

DAVID: Yes.

COSTOS: Great pleasure?

DAVID: Yes. *[Pause]* Great.
COSTOS: I make you happy?
DAVID: Yes. *[Pause]* Thank you.
COSTOS: Kiss me thank you.

[DAVID kisses him.]

Now I believe.
DAVID: Good.
COSTOS: Now give present. *[He sits up.]*
DAVID: Oh. Really?
COSTOS: Yes.
DAVID: I must be dreaming.
COSTOS: No dream. Give present.
DAVID: You don't have to.

[Pause]

COSTOS: Have to what?
DAVID: Give me a present. *[Smiles]* You already did.
COSTOS: You make joke?
DAVID: No.
COSTOS: *You* give present.
DAVID: What?
COSTOS: You give present. To me.

[Pause]

DAVID: Oh.
COSTOS: I close eyes.

[COSTOS closes his eyes and holds out his hand. DAVID stares at him in silence. COSTOS opens his eyes.]

Little present.

[Pause]

DAVID: Why?
COSTOS: For pleasure.
DAVID: But I thought . . .
COSTOS: Because I give pleasure.
DAVID: I thought . . .
COSTOS: To say you like me.
DAVID: I thought . . . You found me. . . .
COSTOS: To show I make you happy.

DAVID: I thought you thought I was . . . I thought you wanted to . . . I thought . . .
     [Pause] I am stupid.
COSTOS: *[Sings]* "Cool down, evenin' in the city, dressed so fine and a lookin' so
     pretty."
DAVID: I was almost . . . someplace else. I am very stupid.
COSTOS: Watch.
DAVID: What?
COSTOS: Your watch.
DAVID: Yes?
COSTOS: Give me your watch.
DAVID: No.
COSTOS: Little present.
DAVID: Not my watch.
COSTOS: I like watch.
DAVID: It's *mine.*
COSTOS: I wear watch and think of you . . . underneath stars.
DAVID: No.
COSTOS: You buy another.
DAVID: Absolutely not.
COSTOS: Radio.
DAVID: I don't have one.
COSTOS: You must.
DAVID: I don't.
COSTOS: Americans have radios.
DAVID: I don't.
COSTOS: Listen to music.
DAVID: I don't.
COSTOS: Beatles.
DAVID: No radio.
COSTOS: Ring.
DAVID: No.

     [COSTOS points to the ring on DAVID's finger.]

COSTOS: This ring. Very nice.
DAVID: No.
COSTOS: Fit my finger. *[He pulls at the ring.]*
DAVID: No.
COSTOS: Same size.
DAVID: No.
COSTOS: Pretty ring . . .
DAVID: No. My grandmother gave it to me.
COSTOS: Grandmother?
DAVID: Yes. Old lady.

COSTOS: Oh. *[Pause]* Very good. Very good. Grandmother. You keep.

DAVID: Thank you.

COSTOS: Camera.

DAVID: Certainly not.

COSTOS: Not big one. You have small one, too.

DAVID: No. No cameras.

COSTOS: I go to room number six; I take camera. Small one.

DAVID: No.

COSTOS: Not big one.

DAVID: Neither one.

COSTOS: You don't like me.

DAVID: I do.

COSTOS: I do not give pleasure.

DAVID: You did.

COSTOS: You make fun of me.

DAVID: I don't.

COSTOS: You insult me.

DAVID: I'm not.

COSTOS: Then give me camera.

DAVID: I won't.

COSTOS: I lie on floor.

DAVID: No camera.

[COSTOS *lies down on the ground.*]

COSTOS: I lie on floor. I scream. I say you hurt me.

DAVID: Hurt you?

COSTOS: *[Holds his groin]* Here. In the sex. You do bad things to me. I cannot move. I cry. You hurt me. I call the police.

DAVID: Police?

COSTOS: They come to room. Number six. They put you in prison. I am young. Seventeen. Against the law. I scream.

DAVID: No.

COSTOS: You hurt me. I cannot move. I am screaming. *[Shouts]* Police!

DAVID: Stop it.

COSTOS: You give me camera?

DAVID: No.

COSTOS: Police!

DAVID: You'll wake everybody up.

COSTOS: Police!

[DAVID *puts his hand over COSTOS's mouth. COSTOS bites it.*]

DAVID: Ouch!

COSTOS: You touch me. You hurt me. You hurt my sex. Tomorrow king come. King find me. Under table. Almost dead. King take me in arms. King cry out— "My people, my people!" I screaming now. Police!

DAVID: You will wake the entire hotel.

COSTOS: I scream louder. Police!

DAVID: Alright! The watch! Take it! [DAVID takes the watch off his wrist and holds it out.]

[Pause. COSTOS sits up.]

COSTOS: For me?

DAVID: Yes.

COSTOS: A present?

DAVID: Yes.

COSTOS: Your watch?

DAVID: Yes.

COSTOS: You sure?

DAVID: Yes.

COSTOS: You like me?

DAVID: Yes.

COSTOS: I make you happy?

DAVID: Yes.

[Pause]

COSTOS: Very happy?

DAVID: Very happy.

COSTOS: Then I take it. [He grabs the watch.] What a surprise. A present! [He puts the watch on.] I am beautiful, no?

DAVID: No.

COSTOS: Thank you. I am beautiful. I have watch. I make you happy. You make me happy. I give you great pleasure. Now I go to sleep. You are nice. Pretty present. Pretty stars. Pretty night. [Sings] "We'll sing in the sunshine. We'll laugh every-day." [He picks up his blanket.] [Sings] "We'll sing in the sunshine." [He drops the blanket on his shoulders.] [Sings] "And I'll be on my way." [COSTOS leaves.]

[DAVID sits at a table. He leans back on his chair, closes his eyes, and begins to sing in Hebrew.]

DAVID: "Ma nishtanah, halilah hazeh, mikahl halalos . . . "

[The lights fade.]

[DAVID's voice is heard.]

DAVID: *[Voice only]* When I was a child, I sang it at Passover. "Ma nishtanah . . ." Why is this night different than any other? Why did that come racing into my head? Am I losing my mind? Michael! *[Pause]*

One thing washes over another. How long will it take for my hair to grow? Why do I sleep in my underwear? Cross this out. Don't write in this journal when you're drunk. Why is this night different? Because they talk to me now. Touch me. But it's still the same! *[Pause]*

If only my hair were long . . . if only something would change . . . *[His voice fades away.]*

[The lights rise. The veranda. The next morning. MRS. HONEY is sitting at her table.]

MRS. HONEY: Waiting! I'm waiting. Hello! I'm waiting. *[She rings her bell.]* I demand my breakfast. *[She rings the bell again.]*

[DAVID enters. He goes to his table.]

This is war, child. Good morning.

DAVID: Good morning.

MRS. HONEY: They have instituted a blockade of my table. They have imposed sanctions. They are attempting to terrorize my stomach. This inn offers room and famine. Did you sleep well?

DAVID: No.

MRS. HONEY: Nor I. I anticipated trouble. *[She rings the bell.]*

[Shouts] I shall protest to the ambassador! *[Pause]*

They shall not succeed. Mr. Gandhi, decent as politicians go, often went without food, and *he* became a country. I myself was such an atrocious cook that I would spend days not touching a morsel. The dentist, poor thing, and the children *had* to eat my disastrous offerings—but I possessed the wisdom to abstain. I believe your own religion has a day of ritual starvation.

DAVID: Yom Kippur.

MRS. HONEY: Indeed. Then I hereby declare Yom Kippur at this table.

DAVID: On Yom Kippur you atone for your sins.

MRS. HONEY: Fair enough—that will help me pass the time. My primary sin was to book the wrong inn. But book I did, and stay I shall. Nikos Kistos has joined battle with the wrong pain in the neck. *[Pause]* Did you hear noise last night? Screaming?

DAVID: No.

MRS. HONEY: In my mind, then. There was screaming in my mind. *[She looks at DAVID.]* Do I spy a top button undone? And what is this late hour?

DAVID: I overslept.

MRS. HONEY: Did you?

DAVID: Yes.

MRS. HONEY: Glory be! Has retsina had a salutory effect? A little vice is not to be sneezed at.

DAVID: What?

MRS. HONEY: Too much wine is an excellent thing sometimes. After all, you need something to atone for on what is it called?

DAVID: Yom Kippur.

MRS. HONEY: "Dear God, I undid my button; forgive me." You're well on your way, boy, well on your way.

DAVID: I'm hungry. I want my breakfast.

MRS. HONEY: It is a pity you were not up slightly earlier, however. You might have witnessed a stupendous argument. The honeymoon couple. It seems she has misplaced her wedding ring, and he is none too pleased about it. I had an enormous temptation to offer some solicitous advice and thus make things worse, but it's difficult to cause trouble on an empty stomach. And they did manage to wolf down their tea and toast, no matter how fierce their disagreement. I am not beyond stealing scraps. *[She rings the bell.]*

If only this were louder. If it were not so heavy, I would travel with a gong.

[COSTOS enters, humming "What a Day for a Daydream." He winks at DAVID. DAVID turns away. MRS. HONEY takes it in. COSTOS clears the dishes from a nearby table. He totally ignores MRS. HONEY.]

I'm not going to say a word. I know he's going to ignore me. I have been sitting here for exactly one hour, screaming for service and ringing my bell, and he has paid me no mind. Do you like the way he looks? What do you think of his legs? Do you think he's ready to grow a beard yet?

[DAVID shifts uneasily in his chair.]

Have you noticed that he always hums? The dentist hummed, of course, but dentists are supposed to, so they can drive their patients mad. In anyone else it is most unattractive.

[NIKOS enters, with his deck of cards.]

NIKOS: Good morning, dear lady.

[Pause]

MRS. HONEY: Well, well, well.

[NIKOS sits at a table and starts to play solitaire.]

NIKOS: Beautiful day.

MRS. HONEY: I suppose.

NIKOS: Not a cloud in the sky.

MRS. HONEY: No.

NIKOS: Good for the suntan.

MRS. HONEY: Excellent.

NIKOS: Have you enjoyed breakfast?

MRS. HONEY: Oh dear—how foolish of me. I forgot all about breakfast. I've been enjoying the view. Do you see that rock jutting out into the sea? There's an old woman dressed in black sitting on it. She has one eye. Most interesting. I could watch her all day.

NIKOS: Would you like breakfast?

MRS. HONEY: Oh. I don't know.

NIKOS: We would be happy to serve you.

MRS. HONEY: Well, if it makes *you* happy, Nikos.

NIKOS: *[To COSTOS]* Ferte ris to ithico p roime.

COSTOS: Malista, kirie. *[He goes into the kitchen.]*

MRS. HONEY: Well, well, well.

NIKOS: She has the evil eye.

MRS. HONEY: Who?

NIKOS: The woman on the rock.

MRS. HONEY: And it's her only one. What a pity. *[Pause]* Is it aimed at you or me?

NIKOS: You look very pretty this morning, Mrs. Honey.

    [Pause]

MRS. HONEY: I loathe small talk. I practise it all the time, but I loathe it in others. I smell deceit. I can taste it. You won't get the table, Nikos.

NIKOS: I'm winning.

MRS. HONEY: What?

NIKOS: At cards.

    [COSTOS returns with a large tray containing two breakfasts. He lays a break-fast for DAVID—orange juice, toast, and tea. MRS. HONEY watches him with hungry eyes. COSTOS is humming "Mr. Tambourine Man," making DAVID even more uncomfortable. COSTOS then brings his tray to MRS. HONEY's table and gives her juice, tea, and toast—and an extra plate, covered with a lid, which he lays down with a great flourish.]

MRS. HONEY: Ah. This is sumptuous.

NIKOS: Of course.

MRS. HONEY: You seem to have given me something special.

NIKOS: Have we?

MRS. HONEY: Something not required. Something not on the menu. Something beyond orange juice, tea, and toast.

NIKOS: A surprise, then.

MRS. HONEY: Indeed. *[She stares at NIKOS, sizing up the situation.]* Take it away.

NIKOS: Lift the lid.

MRS. HONEY: I don't want it. Take it away.

NIKOS: Lift the lid.

MRS. HONEY: I'm not hungry. Take it away.

NIKOS: Lift the lid.

MRS. HONEY: I think not. The specialty of the house is trouble. I smell deceit. Take it away.

[NIKOS rises and goes to her table. He lifts the lid off of the plate. A jewel box lies underneath.]

How on earth?

NIKOS: What is it?

MRS. HONEY: My jewel box.

NIKOS: Your jewel box, dear lady?

[MRS. HONEY stares at him.]

MRS. HONEY: Yes.

NIKOS: Astonishing.

MRS. HONEY: Where did you get my jewel box? Have you been rummaging through my room? I shall issue a complaint. I shall go to the police. This was packed away in a suitcase.

NIKOS: It is most attractive.

MRS. HONEY: Yes.

NIKOS: An antique.

MRS. HONEY: The dentist gave it to me. A long time ago. *What is it doing here?*

NIKOS: It is yours, though?

MRS. HONEY: You know it is.

NIKOS: Why don't you open it?

[Pause]

MRS. HONEY: Ah. *[Pause]* I think not.

NIKOS: Don't you want to make sure . . . ?

MRS. HONEY: Make sure?

NIKOS: That nothing is missing.

MRS. HONEY: No.

NIKOS: I think you must open it.

MRS. HONEY: I think I must not.

[NIKOS flings the jewel box open. MRS. HONEY does not look at it.]

Nothing is missing.

NIKOS: You haven't looked.

MRS. HONEY: No. I haven't.

[She closes the box. NIKOS opens the box again.]

NIKOS: Beautiful things.
MRS. HONEY: Yes.
NIKOS: Won't you look?
MRS. HONEY: No.

[NIKOS removes a necklace from the box and holds it up.]

NIKOS: This is lovely.
MRS. HONEY: My mother's.

[NIKOS removes a bracelet and holds it up.]

NIKOS: Exquisite.
MRS. HONEY: My mother's as well.

[NIKOS holds up an earring.]

NIKOS: And this?
MRS. HONEY: I bought it in New Delhi.

[NIKOS holds up a ring.]

NIKOS: And this?
MRS. HONEY: I don't know.
NIKOS: You don't know.
MRS. HONEY: I've never seen it before.
NIKOS: You've never seen it before?
MRS. HONEY: It's not mine.
NIKOS: It must be.
MRS. HONEY: It isn't. It's too vulgar. It's not mine.
NIKOS: Then whose is it?
MRS. HONEY: I have no idea.
NIKOS: And what is it doing in your jewel box?
MRS. HONEY: I have no idea.
NIKOS: Ah, but it could be . . . it looks remarkably like . . .
MRS. HONEY: Oh. I see. I see. Oh, yes. I see.
NIKOS: The ring that until this morning adorned the finger of that sweet young
    girl on her honeymoon. She mislaid it.
MRS. HONEY: Indeed.
NIKOS: Is it hers?
MRS. HONEY: I would not know.
NIKOS: I think it is.
MRS. HONEY: It would not surprise me.

[NIKOS holds up a watch.]

NIKOS: And what is this?
MRS. HONEY: A watch.
NIKOS: Yours?
MRS. HONEY: No.
NIKOS: Whose?
MRS. HONEY: I have no idea. I think this game is over.
NIKOS: Whose watch?
MRS. HONEY: I don't know. Nikos, leave it be.

[NIKOS turns to DAVID.]

NIKOS: Is this your watch?
DAVID: Mine?
NIKOS: It looks like yours.
DAVID: No, it doesn't.
NIKOS: It looks like the watch I have noticed on your wrist.
DAVID: No.
NIKOS: Let me see your wrist.

[Silence. DAVID doesn't move.]

Please.

[DAVID holds out his wrist.]

No watch.
MRS. HONEY: Is it yours, child? Tell the truth.
DAVID: Yes. I think it is.
MRS. HONEY: How did it get here?
DAVID: I don't know.

[MRS. HONEY goes to DAVID.]

Listen to me, child, this is very important; this is crucial. Relatively few moments are crucial in life. This one is. Do you have any idea what happened to your watch? Do you have any idea how your watch has come to be in my jewel box?

[DAVID is silent.]

Do you, child?

[Silence]

DAVID: No.

MRS. HONEY: Then I'm lost. *[She returns to her table.]* Lost. *[To NIKOS]* And I suppose your cousin is the police chief?

NIKOS: No.

MRS. HONEY: Oh?

NIKOS: My uncle.

MRS. HONEY: *[Smiles]* Of course.

NIKOS: I'd hate to disturb him.

[Pause]

MRS. HONEY: You needn't. An Oxford education has served you well. You are clever, you and your brother. What have you done with him? Have you murdered him? There is, of course, no one to help me. I am totally unattached. The king must have his dinner. I believe there is a bus at noon. A local bus filled with livestock. Before I reclaim my jewel box, please tell me if it contains any other surprises. Has the French scientist misplaced an ankle bracelet? And the Germans? Have they suffered a loss?

NIKOS: No. Just a ring and a watch.

MRS. HONEY: Well then . . . *[She closes the jewel box.]* Take the breakfast away, Nikos. I've lost my appetite. *[Rises]* It *is* stupid. For a table! Good Lord. *[MRS. HONEY leaves her table. She walks past DAVID.]*

DAVID: I'm sorry.

MRS. HONEY: It's not your fault. Don't worry. Others will talk to you. You'll see. *[She starts to leave, then turns back.]* I would like the photograph. Send it to me?

DAVID: Yes.

MRS. HONEY: Thank you.

DAVID: Where?

MRS. HONEY: Care of American Express.

DAVID: Which city?

MRS. HONEY: Choose one. *[MRS. HONEY leaves.]*

[COSTOS clears her table, humming. He looks over at DAVID. DAVID looks away. NIKOS is at his table again, playing solitaire. DAVID looks out to sea. The lights hold on them as we hear DAVID's voice.]

DAVID: *[Voice only]* There is a cool breeze tonight. From the Levant. And clouds. You cannot see the stars. You cannot see Albania. And it is raining. The afternoon was glorious, however. Very hot. I wasn't here when she took the bus. I was on the beach. The rain started around 5:00. It's very light rain, more of a drizzle. The king cancelled his dinner. He didn't want to get wet.

[COSTOS continues to clean the table. NIKOS continues to play solitaire. DAVID continues to stare at the sea.]

Part Two: *Keeps Rainin' All the Time*

[Santorini. Summer. 1990. An enclosed veranda. There are beach chairs on the veranda as well as a wicker rocking chair. There is a door leading into the house and doors to a kitchen and a bathroom.

Behind this house, in the distance, a vista of Fira, the main village of Santorini: tiny whitewashed houses on tiny whitewashed streets, crisscrossing each other, built higher and higher on steep cliffs overlooking the sea.

It is raining but still very warm. Early morning.

DANIEL HOSANI stands on the veranda, watching the rain. He is in his late forties. He is American, wasted looking but oddly handsome. He wears shorts and an open shirt. OLIVER enters. He is British, in his late forties.]

OLIVER: There you are, luv. It's five in the morning. I didn't hear you get up. What are you looking at? Rain. Nothing out there but rain. You can barely see the volcano. Silly life we lead, isn't it? Wake up every morning and stare at a dead crater in the middle of the sea. Still, we like it, don't we? Come on now, Mr. Hosani, let's sit down. *[He takes DANIEL's hand and leads him very gently to a chair.]* That's a good boy. Aren't we a good boy? Down we go. . . . *[He carefully places DANIEL in the chair.]*

You have some colour in your face. Yes, I like that, I like that. It's the sleep. You slept thirty hours. Means you're depressed, don't it, luv? Let's see. . . . *[He places his hand on DANIEL's wrist and takes an acu-pulse.]*

Not bad, not bad. . . . *[He takes another pulse.]*

Ummm . . . *[He takes another pulse.]*

Plenty to be depressed about. Another accident. While you slept. A plant in France. Fire. Reactor still burning. The air's filled with it. Coming this way. The rain will bring it. What a way to start the nineties. *[He takes another pulse.]*

Hmmm . . . liver's a little low. Hasn't stopped raining. Used to freshen things, rain. Don't blame you sleeping, luv. Your back's not too good—it's alright; we'll fix it. . . . Let's see—what else happened while you've been asleep? Heather's come from New York. Dylan's with her. And a Hollywood producer arrived last night with a girlfriend. He wants to film your book. As a *musical*. Oh, that's got the pulses racing!

DANIEL: Cream cheese.

OLIVER: Exactly.

[DANIEL pulls away from OLIVER.]

DANIEL: Beautiful.

OLIVER: What?

DANIEL: The apricot is beautiful.

OLIVER: Well, yes, always has been.

DANIEL: Don't discover me.

OLIVER: I don't think I can.

DANIEL: Please.

OLIVER: Don't worry.

DANIEL: Tangerine.

OLIVER: Don't know tangerine.

DANIEL: Tangerine! *[He sits on the edge of the chair.]*

OLIVER: Why are you getting so excited? Come on . . . let's be a good boy. . . . Let's calm down. . . .

DANIEL: I want to gallop.

OLIVER: It's better if you don't talk, Mr. Hosani. You know that.

DANIEL: Do you adagio?

OLIVER: No.

[DANIEL stands up.]

DANIEL: It's a nomad. Over there. Nomad! Splendour! Steal it. Mama! *[He walks forward.]*

OLIVER: You can't walk outside. It's raining.

DANIEL: Tangerine.

OLIVER: I don't know tangerine. Come on, down we go. . . . *[He places him back into the chair.]* That's right. . . . That's a good boy. . . . There's nothing outside. . . .

DANIEL: If . . . if . . .

OLIVER: Yes, yes. . . .

DANIEL: If I could lamb chop.

OLIVER: If only we could all lamb chop.

DANIEL: I want to . . .

OLIVER: Well, you can't, not today. . . . Let's just lie back. . . . That's better, isn't it? . . . Don't we feel better now? . . . Nice and quiet . . . let's be very calm. . . . *[He goes to the table and removes a tray filled with needles.]*

DANIEL: Starlight.

OLIVER: There. Calm. *[He takes an acupuncture needle and sticks it into DANIEL's forehead.]* Like a good boy.

DANIEL: Starlight.

[OLIVER puts a needle into DANIEL's hand.]

OLIVER: Yes, luv, starlight. *[Pause]* Whatever that is.

[Blackout]

[Church bells ring—many kinds of church bells. The lights rise. Three hours later.
HEATHER is in the rocking chair. She is in her late forties, American, and wears a light caftan. She is smoking a cigarette. A map lies on her lap. DANIEL is on the beach chair next to her, staring straight ahead. The needles have been removed.]

HEATHER: I guess volcanoes are classic manic-depressives. Don't you think? Danny? It's so calm, it's been calm for thousands of years, but once that piece of rock out there was the life of the party. *[Pause]*

Oh shit, Danny. *[Pause]*

It's not supposed to rain like this. The weather has altered, you know. Summer is no longer summer; dry is no longer dry. The planet's distressed. I couldn't see the stars last night. Do you realize they are exactly the same stars that you and I stared at in Corfu? It doesn't seem that long ago. We were so young. Now look at us, eh? But *they* haven't changed. Danny? *[Pause]*

Oh shit, Danny. *[Pause]*

You know, you've grown handsome. There's some kind of irony in that. Your looks have improved with age. You were so awkward then. At least that part of the book is true. Danny? *[Pause]*

My son is going to kill himself, and he doesn't even know it. What am I going to do? *[Pause]*

You used to have so much to say. *[Pause]*

I have no pity for you. *[Pause]*

Oh shit, Danny. *[Pause]*

[Calls into the kitchen] Oliver—what are you doing?

OLIVER: *[Offstage]* Be right there.

HEATHER: I'll bet the tourists have fled. What's a Greek island without sun? Don't the church bells ever stop ringing? We're on the edge of a cliff. This whole town is on the edge of a cliff. That's not reassuring. *[Pause]* Is it?

[OLIVER enters with a tray.]

OLIVER: Coffee?

HEATHER: No thanks.

OLIVER: Wake you up.

HEATHER: He won't talk.

[OLIVER gives DANIEL a cup of coffee.]

OLIVER: Sometimes he does. Sometimes he doesn't.

HEATHER: Where's Dylan?

OLIVER: Still sleeping.

HEATHER: Why isn't he up?

OLIVER: Drink some coffee.

HEATHER: Take it away. Caffeine's dangerous. I can show him this map. I have a plan. He'll think I'm crazy, though. He always does. Where's what's-his-name from Hollywood—Barnaby Grace?

OLIVER: Sleeping.

HEATHER: Everyone's sleeping. *[She starts to cough, then wheeze, then can't catch her breath.]*

OLIVER: Are you alright?

[*HEATHER's breath comes back, she stops coughing. OLIVER places his hand on her wrists and takes her pulse.*]

HEATHER: No. Don't. [*She pulls her wrist away.*] You'll be alarmed. I don't want your needles. I'm in remission, anyway. Everything's alright.

OLIVER: Why are you smoking?

HEATHER: I can't stop. I tried. You put needles in my ear once, remember? Ha! Didn't help. Well—we all have at least one passion that's killing us. The joke is my lungs are fine. It's everything else that's shot. [*Pause*]

Hey, Danny, I'm dying. Did you know that? [*Pause*]

You could address that point at least, you bastard. [*Pause*]

What is he thinking of? When he dreams, does he hear the right words? Does he ever make himself laugh? [*Pause*]

This house was a good idea. At least he's someplace beautiful—and reasonably bizarre. That's important for him. Did you know they call Santorini the island of vampires? Is that it, Danny? Is that what you've become? Then if only you'd *bite*. [*Pause*]

Hey, Danny, remember—[*Sings*] "We'll sing in the sunshine. We'll laugh everyday." [*Pause*]

The voice is gone, eh? I thought the part of the brain that receives music is self-contained. Is it, Oliver?

OLIVER: Seems to be.

HEATHER: Guess my singing no longer qualifies as music. No more two-bit career. Well, folk songs are out of date anyhow, aren't they? [*Pause*] Will you play tapes for him?

OLIVER: Soon.

HEATHER: You're so wise. Where the hell is Dylan? Do you know he's leaving for Paris in the morning?

OLIVER: Yes.

HEATHER: He's killing himself.

OLIVER: Do you want some tea?

HEATHER: Can't you sneak a needle into Dylan and knock him out for a week?

OLIVER: Do you want some orange juice?

HEATHER: Maybe. Where are the oranges from? What kind of soil do they grow in?

OLIVER: Oranges grow on trees.

HEATHER: [*Laughs*] Oh, Oliver, thank God you're here.

OLIVER: I get paid well.

HEATHER: I know. I sign the cheques. Do you ever give yourself needles?

OLIVER: Have done.

HEATHER: Could you kill yourself?

OLIVER: With a needle?

HEATHER: Yes.

OLIVER: I suppose.

HEATHER: Painless?
OLIVER: Quite.
HEATHER: Lucky you.

[DYLAN enters. He is nineteen. He is wearing a bathing suit and has a Walkman plugged into his ear.]

DYLAN: Morning, guys.
HEATHER: Where are you going?

[DYLAN doesn't hear.]

Dylan!
DYLAN: Huh?

[HEATHER motions towards the tape machine.]

HEATHER: Turn it down.

[DYLAN turns the volume down.]

DYLAN: What?
HEATHER: Where are you going?
DYLAN: Swimming.
HEATHER: In the rain?
DYLAN: Yup.
HEATHER: You'll catch cold.
DYLAN: I'm going to, like, get wet either way. Wet's wet. [He starts for the door.]
HEATHER: Dylan?
DYLAN: Now what?
HEATHER: Have you reconsidered your plans?
DYLAN: Nope.
HEATHER: Don't go to Paris.
DYLAN: Oh, Mom, give it a rest, will you?
HEATHER: There's a cloud heading for Paris. . . .

[DYLAN turns the volume up.]

DYLAN: Can't hear you?

[HEATHER rises.]

HEATHER: Filled with radioactive fallout. [She pulls the plug out of his ear.]
DYLAN: Ouch! You're being, like, very sixties.
HEATHER: This is real.
DYLAN: Mom, everything is real. If I dealt with real, I wouldn't deal.
HEATHER: What?

DYLAN: Your radioactive cloud is hoppin' around. It's, like, on a jag. It's a regular tourist bus. If it's Tuesday, like, it must be Venice, you know? It's coming to Greece, too. And Tokyo, New York, Moscow, all them places . . . Like, where do you want me to go, Mars?

HEATHER: Sumba.

DYLAN: What?

HEATHER: It was just a thought.

DYLAN: Is this one of those days when you're out to lunch?

HEATHER: I was just thinking about Sumba.

DYLAN: I'm, like, afraid to ask—but—what's Sumba?

HEATHER: An island. Near Sumbawa.

DYLAN: Oh, of course. I should have known. *[He pats her on the head.]* I'm goin' swimming.

[HEATHER sits on the floor and spreads out her map.]

HEATHER: Look—I'll show you.

DYLAN: I don't believe this. Maps!

HEATHER: *[Tracing a path on the map]* Here . . . this is Java. . . .

DYLAN: Who would believe this?

HEATHER: And Java is not far from Sumbawa. . . .

DYLAN: I'm, like, not telling this to my friends, no way—they think you're weird enough. . . .

HEATHER: You're not looking!

[DYLAN sits next to her.]

DYLAN: Mom, this ain't good for you.

HEATHER: Alright, it is a bit unusual, but don't reject it without some thought. I do have my own logic. I phoned Fred last night, in New York. Remember Fred, the television weatherman?

DYLAN: No. Did you ask him when the rain's gonna stop?

HEATHER: He knows about prevailing winds.

DYLAN: Oliver, please, give her a needle.

HEATHER: He says no place is totally safe. . . .

DYLAN: This is loony tunes.

HEATHER: But as far as he can tell, the *safest* spot is just about here. . . . *[She points to a place on the map.]*

DYLAN: Where?

HEATHER: Here.

DYLAN: Sumba?

HEATHER: Yes.

DYLAN: It's in the middle of nowhere.

HEATHER: Exactly.

DYLAN: A couple of banana trees and some sand.

HEATHER: Probably.

DYLAN: I'll bet you're serious about this.

HEATHER: I'll give you the money. I'll even go with you.

DYLAN: To Sumba?

HEATHER: Yes.

DYLAN: Do they have daily flights from Santorini?

HEATHER: This is *serious.*

DYLAN: Mom, you're goin' round the bend. This kind of obsession with nuclear disaster has made you positively ga-ga. You, like, really want me to parachute into the South Pacific?

HEATHER: It's a bit fanciful, I suppose. Alright—let's compromise. Forget Sumba. Stay here.

DYLAN: I'm goin' to Paris. And I'm goin' for a swim. And they both ain't gonna kill me.

HEATHER: Dylan, the accident was yesterday. The cloud is at its fiercest now. Paris will get the worst of it.

DYLAN: So I'll glow slightly more than usual. Mom, this is, like, the third accident in two years. We've all fried our insides already, you know? It doesn't matter if I go to Paris. And if I do go to Paris, I can sell my language computer, and if I sell my language computer, I can make, like, maybe half a million bucks, and then possibly I can, like, be free to radiate on a slightly more mellow plane. You know what I mean, huh?

HEATHER: You're just a kid. What do you care about half a million dollars?

DYLAN: Oh, play that back—just play that one back. You know, you should be proud of me. I ain't a junkie, like everyone else. I am, technically, like, a genius.

HEATHER: You have no passion.

DYLAN: Passion sucks. *[He points to DANIEL.]*
Look at him. That's passion. Look at you, eating yourself up all your life because the world is wrong. So, hey, Mom, it *is* wrong, it *is* unfair, it *is* galloping down the drain—so what else is new? What the hell can you do about it? You're killing yourself, like, quicker than any bomb would. You've got major fallout inside of you. You're supposed to take it easy. You're all tensed up. Why don't you exercise?

HEATHER: I'll be tranquil—absolutely tranquil—if you stay away from Paris.

DYLAN: Fuck off, okay?—just fuck off—I won't take the blame for your insides. I don't take the blame for nothin'.

> *[ALIKI enters. She is in her midtwenties and very beautiful. She wears a bikini and has a Walkman plugged into her ear.]*

ALIKI: Good morning.

OLIVER: Morning.

> *[ALIKI walks outside. DYLAN stares after her.]*

DYLAN: Who is *she?*

OLIVER: The producer's companion. Name's Aliki. Greek. A student. She picked him up in an Athens bar.

[HEATHER and DYLAN look at OLIVER, amazed.]

I asked.

DYLAN: Shit. *[He goes to the door.]* I don't totally lack passion. *[He follows ALIKI outside, turning the volume up on his Walkman.]*

HEATHER: *[Shouts after him]* That's not passion. *[She starts to cough and gasp.]* Damn it. . . .

[OLIVER goes to her.]

No, Oliver, I'm okay.

OLIVER: You're not, luv.

HEATHER: I am. I can't catch my breath. I'm okay. Leave me alone. *[She stops gasping—breathes easier.]*

Where the hell is Barnaby Grace? We have to discuss that film. See? I'm alright now. Maybe I should phone someone. But who? Fred, the weatherman? Dylan won't believe him. His father's dead. There's only me.

[OLIVER seats her in a chair and massages her neck.]

Alright, you can do that. . . . He's invented a computer that stores twenty thousand words in twelve languages. Isn't it amazing? And the kid can't even speak *English.* Oh, Oliver, your hands, your hands . . . Did you know that Danny's parents tore their clothing into shreds and fasted for twenty-four hours when his book came out? They disowned him. Their son was dead. I thought it totally inhuman then. Now I envy their skill. What kind of mother am I if I don't know how to make my son feel guilty? Ohh . . . your hands . . .

OLIVER: I want you to relax.

[HEATHER pulls away from him.]

HEATHER: No—no. I don't have time. Why don't you put on his tapes? Go. Go!

[OLIVER stares at her, then walks away. He picks up a Walkman on the table and places a cassette in it. He goes to DANIEL and gently helps him to rise and move to another chair on the other side of the veranda.]

Come on, luv, time for some music. Your guardian doesn't want to relax. She's not smart, not like you.

HEATHER: The world is burning—how the hell can I *relax? [She sits on the floor next to the map.]* What does it take to make a wind shift?

OLIVER: These are all Greek folk melodies. We like them, don't we? That's my boy.

[OLIVER places the earphones on DANIEL and turns the Walkman on. DANIEL smiles. OLIVER moves away.]

The music sounds slightly Hebraic. That's why he responds.

HEATHER: Remember the days when people listened to music *together*?

[BARNABY GRACE enters. He is American, in his late twenties.]

BARNABY: Morning.

HEATHER: Ah. Mr. Grace.

BARNABY: *[Looking over at DANIEL.]* Is that really him?

HEATHER: More or less.

BARNABY: Daniel Hosani. It's hard to take in.

HEATHER: Take it in.

BARNABY: It's a real believe-it-or-noter, isn't it?

HEATHER: Pardon?

BARNABY: I thought he was dead.

HEATHER: Not quite.

BARNABY: I can't believe it's him.

HEATHER: It's him.

BARNABY: He's in a living-sad situation, eh?

HEATHER: Pardon?

BARNABY: Had some kind of stroke?

HEATHER: Oh. Yes.

BARNABY: When?

HEATHER: Three years ago.

BARNABY: Wow. He must be slow-timing it now. *[Pause]* I can't believe it's him.

HEATHER: You said that.

BARNABY: Daniel Hosani.

OLIVER: Would you like some coffee, Mr. Grace?

BARNABY: Yes—please—if it's a sugarless situation.

[OLIVER goes into the kitchen.]

HEATHER: Coffee isn't healthy.

BARNABY: I'm sorry if I was strange when we arrived last evening.

HEATHER: Strange?

BARNABY: Incoherent.

HEATHER: Oh. It's alright. Don't worry. You're incoherent this morning as well.

BARNABY: I was exhausted. All those steps.

HEATHER: From the harbour?

BARNABY: Yes. We climbed up eight hundred of them to get here. I counted. A real grow-tired experience. Is this island really made of lava?

HEATHER: Some of it.

BARNABY: No wonder it's such a look-strange place. *[Pause]* Daniel Hosani.

HEATHER: Yes—that's very good—that's his name. Now why don't we discuss the film you plan to make?

BARNABY: I can't believe it's him. I admire him so much. What a feel-good writer. I was only fifteen when I read the book. But I understood every word.

HEATHER: Ah.

BARNABY: It made me glad to be alive, even though it had its depressing moments.

HEATHER: Ah.

[*OLIVER arrives with some coffee.*]

It had a real smile-on-face tang with a slight seem-sad taste.

[*HEATHER pulls OLIVER aside.*]

HEATHER: Oliver—I've just had a blinding flash. My species is extinct.

BARNABY: It's still a favourite of mine.

[*OLIVER hands him the coffee.*]

Thank you. I listen to it often.

HEATHER: Listen?

BARNABY: Books-on-tape.

HEATHER: Oh yes.

BARNABY: You can listen while you work.

HEATHER: Yes.

BARNABY: I haven't *read* a book in years.

HEATHER: Well, well, well.

BARNABY: She says that all the time.

HEATHER: Who?

BARNABY: Mrs. Honey.

HEATHER: Oh. *[Pause]* He picked it up from me.

[*DANIEL begins to hum a tune, a Greek melody.*]

Listen!

OLIVER: He remembers melodies.

HEATHER: I used to know this song. . . . *[She begins to hum.]*

OLIVER: Sometimes he'll sing a word or two in Greek.

BARNABY: *[To OLIVER]* Am I correct in assuming he is now a thinking-impaired citizen?

OLIVER: Excuse me?

BARNABY: His mind is disabled.

OLIVER: His mind is fine.

HEATHER: You don't know anything about air currents, do you, Mr. Grace?

BARNABY: I've come here to make a pitch.

HEATHER: Yes, yes.

BARNABY: But how can I throw my concepts to a brain-scramble?

HEATHER: You throw them to *me*. I'm his legal guardian, God help me. Well, there was no one else. His parents no longer acknowledged him. His book was too openly gay. I'm his oldest friend, maybe his only friend. I was even with him that summer.

BARNABY: You were *there?*

HEATHER: Yes.

BARNABY: But you're not in the book.

HEATHER: Who says the book is true?

BARNABY: It has to be.

HEATHER: It's writing.

BARNABY: It's filled with truth.

HEATHER: That's different.

BARNABY: I can't believe it. . . . I can't believe you were actually there. . . . I can't believe he's actually Daniel Hosani. . . . I can't believe what's happened to him.

HEATHER: Why not? What's happened to him is completely unoriginal. I have no pity for him. None. Damn him! You can't imagine that's Daniel Hosani? Big fucking deal, who was Daniel Hosani anyhow? A yo-yo, an American yo-yo. Do you know what I mean? Up and down. Famous too soon, thrown aside too quick. It's too boring. It happens to almost everyone. Do you understand? He was dispensable. Disposable. He was waste. You've probably produced four bad movies with his story in it. A kid writes a book. The critics say he's the new Fitzgerald. It sells a million copies. He's all over television. Magazine covers. Fashion layouts. . . . He's happy. He drinks, he snorts, he fucks. He has a wonderful time. He's famous. But he can't write any more. So he gets depressed. He goes away. He becomes a Buddhist. Then he does write again. About being famous. His second book. The critics say he's lost his innocence. The public isn't interested anymore. He's depressed again. He travels again. He becomes a Catholic. Lovers come and go. He is not really very nice. And then the royal mile—Alcohol. Cocaine. Heroin. Car crashes. Hospitals. Shock treatment. Stroke. It's the same old story. Now he can't find the right words. It's a form of aphasia. What did it: the stroke, the shock treatment, the drugs? Who knows? His mind substitutes. He will, for instance, say olive tree instead of automobile. Sometimes he says the right word. There's no pattern. He makes sense and he doesn't. His brain's gone and it's not. He's alive and he's dead. What more do you have to know?

[DANIEL stops humming.]

Look—time is running out fast. I wanted to lay eyes on you. I have. Good. Now I want to hear your ideas. I even want Danny to hear them. Your offer is financially not unattractive. So talk to us. How do you plan to make this movie? How can you turn Danny's book into a *musical?*

BARNABY: I have a vision about this. Daniel Hosani wrote a people-story and we should return to people-stories in Hollywood and people-stories should sing. I have the studios with me in this, and much of the industry, and most importantly, Jesus.

HEATHER: Pardon?

BARNABY: Jesus.

HEATHER: Oh.

BARNABY: You see, I was lost myself, very lost, and then I found Him. A light-blinder, alright. Now I think of Jesus as my coproducer. We're incorporated, if you know what I mean. He turned me away from gadgets and back to humanity. You see, we've spent years making look-smart films about—say—a boy and his pet monkey and his spaceship, and we got carried away with that spaceship and all the special effects it entailed. Jesus has taken me away from space. He hit me with a down-to-earther. Now I want to concentrate on the boy and the monkey. And I want to know, I really want to know, what makes that monkey tick. *[Pause]*

HEATHER: Ah.

BARNABY: Look, I have things with me—notes, charts, tapes, outlines—let me show you. . . .

HEATHER: I really want Danny to hear this.

BARNABY: Good. I'll get them. *[BARNABY leaves.]*

HEATHER: Oh my God, Oliver, he's twelve years old, he has the brain of a lemon, he talks in tongues, and he thinks the book is about some fucking monkey!

OLIVER: Won't this upset Mr. Hosani?

HEATHER: I hope so.

OLIVER: You're up to something.

HEATHER: Maybe.

OLIVER: You're totally unfocused.

HEATHER: I know.

OLIVER: Let me help.

HEATHER: No. Leave me alone. Don't help me. There is no time.

[DYLAN and ALIKI run in from the pool. They are both wet. ALIKI still has her Walkman plugged in.]

DYLAN: Towels! Help! Oliver! Towels!

OLIVER: He thinks I'm the maid. *[He goes into the bathroom.]*

[ALIKI is dancing to the beat of her music. DYLAN puts his wet hands on her back.]

ALIKI: Don't.

DYLAN: Why not?

ALIKI: Hands—freezing.

[DYLAN goes to HEATHER.]

DYLAN: She's, like, bored to death with that producer. Maybe I can lure her to Paris. What do you think, Mom?

HEATHER: I think you should stay here.

DYLAN: Listen, drop the red alert for a sec, okay? Forget nuclear and think sex— do you like her?

HEATHER: Does my opinion matter?

DYLAN: Of course not.

> [OLIVER returns from the bathroom with two large bath towels. He gives one to ALIKI and throws one to DYLAN.]

OLIVER: You're welcome.

DYLAN: [To ALIKI] Can I, like, dry you?

ALIKI: What?

DYLAN: [Shouts] Can I, like, dry you?

ALIKI: No.

DYLAN: You can dry me.

ALIKI: What?

DYLAN: Dry me.

ALIKI: Dry yourself.

DYLAN: Do you wanna go to Paris?

ALIKI: No.

DYLAN: Do you wanna kiss?

ALIKI: No.

DYLAN: Do you wanna see my computer?

ALIKI: [Laughs] No.

DYLAN: Ah, shit, come to Paris. Fly with me to Athens, like, this afternoon and then Paris tomorrow.

> [ALIKI removes her earphones.]

ALIKI: This afternoon? Athens?

DYLAN: Yes.

ALIKI: Three o'clock flight?

DYLAN: Yes.

ALIKI: We were supposed to take this plane. But this Jesus Man change plans. Now we take boat to Crete.

DYLAN: Like, forget him. Come with me.

ALIKI: You very sure? Three o'clock?

DYLAN: Yes.

HEATHER: Dylan? Are you going to shower?

DYLAN: Mom—not now. I'm seducing.

HEATHER: Take a shower.

DYLAN: I'm already wet.

HEATHER: From the rain. You don't know what's coming down in the rain. There's still some fallout around from this winter's accident.

DYLAN: Oh, put a lid on it.
ALIKI: She is very right. Take shower.
DYLAN: Yes?
ALIKI: I think so.
DYLAN: You do?
ALIKI: Listen to your mother.

> *[DYLAN looks at ALIKI, then HEATHER.]*

DYLAN: Beats me. *[He goes to the bathroom door.]* Okay. I take shower. *[He enters the bathroom.]*

> *[Pause]*

ALIKI: I take shower, too. *[She goes into the bathroom.]*

> *[Pause]*

DYLAN: *[Offstage]* Jesus!
HEATHER: Jesus seems to be on everyone's lips today. *[Pause]* Oliver?
OLIVER: What?
HEATHER: Did that just happen?
OLIVER: Suppose so.
HEATHER: She's in the shower with my son?
OLIVER: Suppose so.
HEATHER: Oh. *[Pause]*
  Have they been introduced? *[Pause]*
  Well. *[Pause]*
  Well . . . *[Pause]*
  What do you think they're doing?

> *[OLIVER removes the headphones from DANIEL.]*

OLIVER: Here, let's have that now, Mr. Hosani. No more music. That's right; that's a good boy. Do we want to take a walk around the house?

> *[DANIEL shakes his head "no."]*

Alright, let's just sit here then.

> *[DANIEL brushes OLIVER aside with his hands.]*

Alright, luv, I'll leave you alone.
HEATHER: Do you think they're washing each other?
OLIVER: Probably.
HEATHER: That's nice. *[Pause]*
  That's very clean. *[Pause]*
  Did they lock the door?

OLIVER: Didn't hear the latch.
HEATHER: Ah. *[Pause]*
   It's unlocked, then?
OLIVER: Yes. *[Pause]*
HEATHER: Still raining outside?
OLIVER: Yes.
HEATHER: Shame.
OLIVER: Yes.
HEATHER: Rain.

   [A long pause. Suddenly both HEATHER and OLIVER sprint to the door of the bathroom. They stand at the door, listening.]

   This is awful.
OLIVER: I know.
HEATHER: Completely immature.
OLIVER: I know.
HEATHER: We shouldn't be doing this.
OLIVER: I know.
HEATHER: What do you hear?
OLIVER: Water.
HEATHER: What else?
OLIVER: Just water.
HEATHER: Look through the keyhole.
OLIVER: Absolutely not.
HEATHER: Go on.
OLIVER: I've never done anything like that in my life.
HEATHER: Just a peek.
OLIVER: No.

   [HEATHER laughs and tickles him.]

HEATHER: A tiny peek.
OLIVER: It's good to see you smile.
HEATHER: Go on.
OLIVER: Alright. *[He gets down on his knees and peeks through the keyhole.]*
HEATHER: Well?
OLIVER: Steam. I see steam.
HEATHER: And?
OLIVER: More steam. *[He rises from his knees.]*
HEATHER: Then open the door.
OLIVER: *What?*
HEATHER: Just a crack.
OLIVER: You open the door.
HEATHER: Don't you fancy him?

OLIVER: Of course not.

HEATHER: Really?

OLIVER: Well. A little.

HEATHER: So open the door.

OLIVER: You open it. Do *you* fancy him?

HEATHER: He's my son!

OLIVER: So?

HEATHER: Well—I fancy him the way mothers do. *[Pause]*
Which is probably more than you think. *[Pause]*
   But not quite enough for alarm. I do like the way he looks naked. Like his father. Open the door. It has to be you. I've always given him independence. I mustn't intrude. But you can. Go on, go on. . . .

OLIVER: It's against everything I believe in.

HEATHER: I know. Go on. *[Pause]*

OLIVER: This is awful. *[Pause. OLIVER quietly opens the door, just a crack. He looks in.]*

HEATHER: Well?

OLIVER: Umm . . .

HEATHER: Yes?

OLIVER: Ummm . . .

HEATHER: What's ummmm?

OLIVER: Nice.

HEATHER: Nice?

OLIVER: Very nice.

HEATHER: What are they doing?

OLIVER: Umm . . .

HEATHER: Oliver!

OLIVER: Ummm . . . ummm . . .

HEATHER: Oh shit. *[She pushes OLIVER aside and looks through the crack.]*
Oh. Ah. *[Pause]*
Ummm . . . *[Pause]*
Nice. *[She closes the door.]*
   It's sweet. It's so sweet. Isn't it sweet?

OLIVER: Yes.

HEATHER: Rubbing soap over each other.

OLIVER: Yes.

HEATHER: Feeling each other.

OLIVER: Yes.

HEATHER: That's very sweet.

OLIVER: Yes. *[OLIVER opens the door again and looks, then closes the door.]*

HEATHER: What are they doing now?

OLIVER: Soap—still.

HEATHER: Oh, Oliver—remember pleasure?

OLIVER: Barely.

HEATHER: Losing yourself.

OLIVER: Not really.

HEATHER: There *were* times, weren't there?

OLIVER: Few.

HEATHER: Do you have lovers?

OLIVER: People find me comforting and wise, two qualities that totally negate sex appeal. That's the truth, luv. I know how to make people feel better, genuinely feel better, and it has nothing to do with stroking a nipple. If I say I want that, they think I've betrayed their trust. The last time was five years ago.

HEATHER: My God!

OLIVER: And he didn't speak English. He had no idea I could soothe.

HEATHER: Don't you miss it?

OLIVER: All the time.

HEATHER: That's what I hated most about the hospital. My luck—the doctors were all young and handsome. They would lean over me and breathe on me and smile and touch me, and I felt so humiliated—all those tubes up my nose and scars down my body. I wanted to feel something or even to think something sexual, and I couldn't.

OLIVER: Just as well, luv. Sex is too dangerous now.

HEATHER: That's not true. You can do it—but safely. *[Pause]* My God, do you think they're being cautious? What are they doing?

OLIVER: *[Peeking through the door]* Soap.

HEATHER: That's a lot of soap. Dylan isn't cautious. If he was, he wouldn't go to Paris. For Christ's sake, Oliver, we have to get them out of there.

OLIVER: You're off again.

HEATHER: Do you have a condom?

OLIVER: What?

HEATHER: Slip a condom under the door!

OLIVER: *[Laughs]* Heather . . .

HEATHER: It isn't funny. I'm deadly serious. Slip a fucking condom under the door. Stop laughing. I don't want him to die. The world is burning, Oliver.

OLIVER: Stop it. *[He grabs her by the neck and steadies her.]*

[BARNABY enters carrying a pile of notes.]

BARNABY: I'm ready. I have everything. Except my companion. A real look-pretty, but I've misplaced her. She attached herself to me in Athens, you know. I don't want you to think . . .

HEATHER: You needn't explain. She's swimming.

BARNABY: In the rain?

HEATHER: Yes. I am curious, I must admit—how do you square her with Jesus?

BARNABY: He's very flexible about my personal life.

HEATHER: Ah.

BARNABY: You know, I still can't believe that you were there.

HEATHER: Where?
BARNABY: Corfu.
HEATHER: Oh. Oh yes.

[OLIVER takes HEATHER aside and whispers to her.]

OLIVER: Shower's stopped.
HEATHER: Good.
OLIVER: Not good. Coming out.
HEATHER: Oh shit. What do we do?
OLIVER: Divert.

[OLIVER returns to the bathroom door. HEATHER takes BARNABY's arm
and leads him away.]

HEATHER: Yes—I was with him all summer.
OLIVER: And Mrs. Honey?
HEATHER: Yes.

[The bathroom door starts to open. OLIVER leans against it and closes it. The
door pushes him foward; he pushes it back.]

BARNABY: What was her actuality factor?
HEATHER: Pardon?
BARNABY: Was she real?
HEATHER: Sure. By and large. Basically. There was a woman named Foster. [She
manoeuvres BARNABY into a chair facing the sea.]
BARNABY: And the table?
HEATHER: Yes. I suppose. Fairly true.
BARNABY: And they made her leave?
HEATHER: In a way.

[OLIVER lets the bathroom door open. He motions ALIKI out onto the veranda. She sees BARNABY and slips quietly off.]

BARNABY: They found the watch on her?
HEATHER: Oh yes.
BARNABY: Amazing.
HEATHER: But then she was a kleptomaniac.
BARNABY: Oh. And David?
HEATHER: Well, Daniel was there. But then so was I. He certainly wasn't travelling
alone.
BARNABY: And the waiter seduced him?
HEATHER: Probably the other way round.

[OLIVER motions DYLAN onto the veranda. DYLAN quietly sneaks off.]

BARNABY: Oh. And poor Mrs. Honey just kept on travelling?

HEATHER: Yes. But he left the reason out.

BARNABY: The reason?

HEATHER: Actually, the reason for the dentist's death.

BARNABY: The dentist?

HEATHER: Her husband, remember?

BARNABY: Oh, of course, but he's offscreen.

HEATHER: Indeed. Danny failed to say that the dentist's cancer was caused by radiation. That little desert place in Utah was known as a downwind town. Do you know what that is?

BARNABY: No.

HEATHER: Downwind from Nevada, from the atomic testing site. They had been exposed to radiation for years. No one ever told them to take precautions. Out of fifty families in that desert town only three escaped cancer. Mrs. Foster was too bright by half—she figured it out by the time the dentist died, but no one would listen to her, certainly not the government, who actively denied it until a few years ago, and not her children, who were in great danger themselves. They told her to shut up the way Dylan tells me to shut up. She was consumed by blinding sanity. Which made her rather a leper. She was never good company. So she took off—for everyplace else. He left all of that out.

[Pause]

BARNABY: That isn't something we can use.

HEATHER: Use?

BARNABY: In the movie.

HEATHER: Guess not.

BARNABY: Jesus doesn't disapprove of nuking, you know.

HEATHER: Oh?

BARNABY: In its place.

[Pause]

HEATHER: Oh—that Jesus! I'm sorry—I thought you meant the other one.

BARNABY: Are you making fun of me?

HEATHER: Yes.

BARNABY: We get used to that in Hollywood. But you have disappointed me.

HEATHER: How?

BARNABY: I did think the book was only pretend-fiction. I thought it all actually happened.

HEATHER: You're like me, Grace; you take things too seriously.

[OLIVER walks onto the veranda.]

OLIVER: All clear.

BARNABY: Shall I pitch the film now?

OLIVER: Mr. Hosani needs a rest.

HEATHER: From what?

OLIVER: I know him, luv. He needs a bit of time. He's in a mood.

BARNABY: You seemed in a hurry.

HEATHER: I am. Desperately. Have you written songs? Is there a score? Do you have a tape?

BARNABY: Yes. *[He holds a tape up.]* Here.

HEATHER: There's a cassette player in the kitchen.

OLIVER: We'll set it up. *[He takes BARNABY's arm and leads him towards the kitchen.]*

BARNABY: I feel very odd. This island is odd.

HEATHER: Are you frightened?

BARNABY: Not since Jesus.

[OLIVER and BARNABY go into the kitchen.]

HEATHER: How can anybody not be frightened? *[She sits on the floor next to DANIEL's chair and takes DANIEL's hand.]*

I wish you could tell me something. Anything. It's not even that I think you're wise, or ever were. I just need you. I can't focus. I don't know what to worry about first. Dylan going to Paris. Dylan upstairs with that girl. Dylan getting nuked. Dylan getting AIDS. Dylan getting religion. The remains of my own system. The world cracking in half. Dylan doesn't think I'm playing with a full deck. When I told him that I worried about the destruction of the rain forests because someday *he* might wake up without oxygen, he was about to have me committed. I've gotten to the point where I can't even have a meal without panic. I had lunch at an outdoor restaurant last week. I looked at the menu. I could not order eggs because they cause heart attacks. I could not order chicken because they are injected with dangerous antibiotics. I could not order meat because livestock have eaten contaminated grass. I could not order fruit because they have been sprayed with deadly chemicals. I could not order vegetables because the produce in that town looked extra large as though it had mutated from the fallout. I could not order bread because yeast is now thought to damage the immune system. I could not order fish because the waters they swim in are contaminated. I sat there clawing at the menu, crying, laughing, and screaming at the same time, aware that there was one indisputable fact—I was *hungry* and I didn't know what to do about it. Then I realized I was having this minibreakdown outside, in the afternoon sun, and now that the ozone layer has been destroyed, the afternoon sun is slowly killing us. So I calmed down and had a banana split. What the hell. It's immaterial for me, anyway—I'm here courtesy of chemotherapy. I have only seconds left. But the kids, the kids . . . What can they eat? What can they breathe? Who can they sleep with? Sometimes I feel so guilty for bringing Dylan into this mess. Oh shit, Danny, can't you tell me something? You don't care anyhow. Look what you've done to yourself. You know who had the right idea? Mrs. Honey. Mrs. Foster, that is. Crusty old dame. Do you remember her letter? What *do* you remember? She wrote to us both from India. From Goa. Did you ever read it? I've saved mine. She said her travels finally took her to Goa, and by then she found the entire world was off its rocker, not just America. Someone told her that if you lost your passport in Goa, the police put you into the local madhouse until you could prove who you were. Well, that appealed to her. Amused her. She thought it was the first intelligent thing she had heard in years. So she tore up her passport and retired gracefully—into Bedlam. She's still there. Both her children have died. But she has never been ill, a fact that must seem quite logical in a madhouse. She sends me a postcard every summer. She must send one to you, too. Does Oliver read them to you? She loved being Mrs. Honey. Even though you left out the important stuff. *[Pause]*

I wish you could tell me something, something to make me feel less afraid. *[Pause]*

Anything. *[Pause]*

DANIEL: Applesauce. *[Pause]*

HEATHER: Thanks, kiddo. Thanks a lot. I was losing my nerve. I have something to do and I was losing my nerve. But applesauce really helps. I needed that. *[HEATHER rises and walks into the kitchen.]*

[Blackout]

[The Greek melody that DANIEL was humming plays in the distance. The lights rise. One hour later.

DANIEL is sitting in another chair on the veranda. Voices are heard in the kitchen. ALIKI walks out of the kitchen. She sees the map on the floor. She picks it up and looks at it.]

ALIKI: Maps. Ah so. Ah yes. Interesting. *[She traces her finger on the map.]*

Here we are. Little island. Funny little island. Looks like no place else. Like moon. *[She goes to DANIEL.]*

You do not eat? Jesus Man in kitchen talking and talking and talking. Makes me very not interested. Jesus Man serve purpose. Now Jesus Man kaput. You understand? Later you understand. I read your book. Why you not say the king no good, why you not say the colonels come in the next year, why you not say Greece in pain? You understand country in pain? I think maybe not.

[DYLAN enters.]

DYLAN: Hey. *[He kisses ALIKI—she moves away.]* Come here. . . .

ALIKI: Yes?

DYLAN: I leave, like, for the airport in a few hours.

ALIKI: So bye-bye.

DYLAN: Come with me.

ALIKI: I promise to go to Crete.

DYLAN: That creep, like, doesn't even notice you. Why do you want to be with him?

ALIKI: I make promise.

DYLAN: Break promise.

ALIKI: No. I have reason. So I go to Crete. But I leave Crete tomorrow and fly to Athens. I meet you tomorrow in Athens.

DYLAN: Meet me tomorrow in Paris.

ALIKI: No. Athens. Make Paris day later.

DYLAN: I can't. It's business.

ALIKI: Make Paris day later.

DYLAN: Has my mom, like, put you up to this?

ALIKI: No. Your body. [*She runs her hand across his chest.*]

DYLAN: Jeez!

ALIKI: This is true. You know what we do in Athens?

DYLAN: I think so.

ALIKI: You so sure?

DYLAN: Tell me.

[*ALIKI, aware that DANIEL is listening, whispers into DYLAN's ear. DYLAN's eyes widen.*]

Sweet Aunt Lizzie!

ALIKI: And then . . . [*She whispers into his ear again.*]

DYLAN: What's that?

ALIKI: Greek words.

DYLAN: What do they mean?

ALIKI: You make computer. With languages. Look it up.

[*DYLAN takes a tiny computer out of his pocket.*]

DYLAN: This is it. This is my baby.

ALIKI: Look words up.

DYLAN: Say them again.

[*ALIKI whispers into his ear.*]

Okay. Now—press Greek. Press letters. Press English. Then . . . [*He stares at the computer.*]

Holy shit!

ALIKI: You make Paris one day later? [*Pause*] Well?

DYLAN: I'll change the appointment. One day.

ALIKI: We meet at Cafe Homer in Plaka. Six o'clock.

DYLAN: How do I, like, know you'll be there?

ALIKI: I be there.

DYLAN: Yeah, but how do I know?

ALIKI: I prove it to you. Wait.

[ALIKI runs off. DYLAN walks over to DANIEL.]

DYLAN: Hey—Danny . . . there's this thing in your book—I never read it, but that's only because I don't read books, but Mom told me the story and there's this guy who's supposed to be you but he's not really you, although he sort of is, you know, and Mom says he has, like, fears about sex and, like, I thought, hey, that's crazy, nobody's got that no more, but I tell you something—this girl is wild, this girl scares me—I'm over my head, like. You know what I mean?

DANIEL: Don't sneeze.

DYLAN: What?

DANIEL: Don't sneeze.

DYLAN: What's that mean?

DANIEL: Don't sneeze.

DYLAN: What the fuck does that mean?

DANIEL: Don't sneeze.

DYLAN: Maybe I can invent a computer that can translate your mind, huh?

[HEATHER and BARNABY walk in from the kitchen.]

Don't tell Mom we had this talk.

BARNABY: I'm very nerves-orientated.

HEATHER: Pardon?

BARNABY: Scared shitless.

HEATHER: Don't be.

[OLIVER enters from the kitchen with a glass of orange juice and brings it to DANIEL.]

BARNABY: Do you think he'll like my presentations? Will we effect a compatibility relationship? Will he even understand what I'm saying?

HEATHER: Don't worry about it.

OLIVER: *[To DANIEL]* Here's some fresh orange juice.

HEATHER: Just come with me.

OLIVER: I want you to drink it. You're not getting enough nourishment. Don't give me that glum face.

[HEATHER leads BARNABY to DANIEL.]

HEATHER: Danny—this is Barnaby Grace.

OLIVER: Drink the orange juice, luv; don't be difficult.

HEATHER: Mr. Grace is a very important film producer from California.

[DANIEL stares straight ahead.]

BARNABY: He's not looking at me.

HEATHER: Doesn't matter. Mr. Grace wants to make a film of "A Table for a King." I've asked him here to speak to you. . . .

BARNABY: I can't tell you what an important moment this is for me, Mr. Hosani. . . .

OLIVER: Will you please drink the juice?

BARNABY: I've wanted to meet you since I was fifteen.

[DANIEL drinks the orange juice.]

OLIVER: That's a good boy. All down.

BARNABY: I have a deep empathy syndrome with your work.

OLIVER: I think he wants to nap.

HEATHER: He can nap later.

[OLIVER takes DANIEL's pulse.]

OLIVER: He's tired.

HEATHER: He's not tired.

OLIVER: I don't like his pulses.

HEATHER: I adore his pulses.

OLIVER: He needs a nap.

HEATHER: There's no time.

DYLAN: Mom, maybe he does, like, need to rest.

HEATHER: Shouldn't you be packing for Paris?

[DYLAN holds his hands up in the air.]

DYLAN: Hey! Hey! Hey!

HEATHER: Barnaby is leaving in a few hours as well. It has to be now.

OLIVER: Just a short nap.

HEATHER: No dice.

[OLIVER pulls her away from DANIEL.]

Ouch!

OLIVER: What's got into you?

HEATHER: Stop protecting him.

OLIVER: I'm paid to protect him. He mustn't hear about this film. It will distress him.

HEATHER: Can't be helped.

OLIVER: What the hell are you doing?

[HEATHER returns to DANIEL.]

HEATHER: Barnaby is going to tell us about the film.

BARNABY: Well, Mr. Hosani, as I see this project, and I consider it from the very start, a go project . . . *[To HEATHER]* He's not looking at me.

HEATHER: He can hear.

BARNABY: My strong point is eye contact.

HEATHER: Trust in Jesus.

BARNABY: Oh. Yes. Well—okay . . .

HEATHER: But condense.

BARNABY: Yes. Yes.

> *[ALIKI enters. She is carrying a bag. She stops, then sits down and watches BARNABY.]*

Mr. Hosani, I truly respect your book and I want to treat it with love because Jesus says love is the answer. . . .

HEATHER: *Condense.*

BARNABY: Oh. Yes. I see your book in a positive light. As a life-affirmer rather than a down-in-the-dumpser. And music can help because it's difficult for an audience to focus on a story anymore without a strong soundtrack and a lot of quick images, a lot of fast brain messages, and, of course, you will have a very generous financial cut of the album. . . .

HEATHER: Tell him about Mabel.

BARNABY: Oh. Mabel. Mabel is one of those roles that comes along once in a lifetime.

DYLAN: You never told me about a Mabel, Mom.

BARNABY: Mabel is Mrs. Honey. She needs a first name, and, of course, I've made her younger, about thirty. You see, there have to be a few slight alterations. I've conducted several market surveys on aspects of the plot. Mabel, for instance, will have a very tender romance with David—I have to cut the gay stuff, the market won't hold that post-AIDS—and Jesus is wary of it, anyway—and David's not Jewish anymore, even though Judaism was an initial interest of Jesus, we find there's low audience concern for the subject, so then the waiter who seduces David becomes, of course, a waitress, and that scene is a blessing in terms of soundtrack, all those old sixties hits—but the *essence* of your story remains exactly the same, even though now it's a young boy who falls in love with a slightly older woman, played by a major star, who he betrays ultimately—and yes, that is the down side—but wait!—the think-positive aspect is that she never gives up her position about the table, which is a lesson to all of us about holding onto our beliefs, this is, in fact, a movie about holding onto our beliefs, and thus a modern parable for the Crucifixion, which was the ultimate hold-on, wasn't it?—and it climaxes in the film in a song that I know will be not just a song but a megasong and, most important, a megasong with a message—which ends with—here . . . *[He reaches for the tape recorder.]*

This is the music. . . . *[He switches the tape recorder on—a piano is playing.]*

And you'll have to excuse my voice, but I want to give you some idea—*[He sings to the music.]*

> *They can woe me.*
> *They can charm me.*
> *They can hurt me.*
> *They can harm me.*
> *They can send in*
> *An army.*
> *But as long as I am able*
> *I won't give up my table*
> *Or my name's not Mabel*
> *No—*
> *I won't give up*
> *I won't give up*
> *I won't give up*
> *Not even for*
> *A king.*

[He turns the tape recorder off.]

Now I know you're probably asking how can we hold the interest of a modern audience for so long with just one woman singing plot—well, let me throw this to you, bit by bit—I promise you we will not lose the concentration factor—we're going to have a series of quick images. Here, I'll break it down. "They can woe me. They can charm me"—short shots of Mabel being courted by about a hundred waiters—it's a hotel now, not an inn—okay? "They can hurt me, They can harm me"—Mabel being tortured. "They can send in an army"—a shot of an *entire* army—we'll film it in some country with lots of cheap labour, so don't worry. "But as long as I am able, I won't give up my table"—a fantasy sequence of Mabel at her table and aging, growing older and older—which has appeal for citizens-in-retirement. "Or my name's not Mabel"—this is beautiful, we bring in the animators to draw the name Mabel, surrounded by stars and moons and little birds and squirrels. "No—I won't give up, I won't give up, I won't give up, not even for a king"—a long pan of Mabel holding onto the table through a gale-force wind, surrounded by the army and the waiters and the king and the entire royal household! So you see, for those who are not listening-orientated, there's plenty of visual dividends, and the essence of your message, that a little wooden table can be worth fighting for against all the big boys, will be given a new strength and power and will resound, not unlike the Gospels, through the ages, forever and ever.

[Silence]

DYLAN: Holy shit.

[DANIEL stands up.]

HEATHER: Danny!
BARNABY: Mr. Hosani—is it a go?
DANIEL: Oysters!

[DANIEL starts to choke BARNABY. OLIVER tries to pull DANIEL away.]

OLIVER: Come on, luv, let's stop this now. . . .
DANIEL: Oysters! I park you. I park you.
OLIVER: It's alright, luv, it's alright. . . .
DANIEL: He is bluesing me; he is bluesing me. . . .
OLIVER: It's alright. . . . Let's take our hands away. . . . Let's calm down. . . . *[He pulls DANIEL away from BARNABY.]*
    That's right. . . . That's a good boy. . . . Come on, now . . . no tears . . . *[He leads DANIEL to a chair.]*
DANIEL: Canasta. Canasta.
BARNABY: There's a tension-factor here I wasn't prepared for.
HEATHER: Don't worry.
BARNABY: Stop telling me not to worry.
HEATHER: You have a deal.
BARNABY: What?
HEATHER: You have a deal. Phone my lawyer when you get back to the States. The book is yours.
BARNABY: Blessed Jesus!
HEATHER: Indeed. But I think you better pack. Get to your boat early.
BARNABY: The Lord's been with me, he's my shepherd, he's clinched my deal. . . .
HEATHER: Please go. Just go.
BARNABY: Okay. Thank you. *[He runs off, patting ALIKI on the head as he does so.]* Come on, sunshine, we're leaving.
HEATHER: He restoreth my soul. Ha! *[She starts to shake—lights a cigarette.]*
OLIVER: *[To DANIEL]* Now you mustn't weep—it's all going to be alright. *[He brings over a needle.]* I'm just giving you a needle.
DYLAN: Mom, what's wrong with you?
HEATHER: Nothing.
DYLAN: You shouldn't smoke.
HEATHER: You shouldn't go to Paris.
DYLAN: Lay off.

[ALIKI goes to DYLAN. She removes a jewel box from her bag and holds it out towards him.]

What's that?
ALIKI: A box for jewels. Mine.
DYLAN: Oh?

[ALIKI removes a bracelet from her arm.]

ALIKI: I take my bracelet. . . . *[She puts the bracelet into the box.]* I put it inside. *[She removes a ring from her finger.]* And my ring. *[She places the ring in the box.]* Inside.

DYLAN: Yeah?

[ALIKI hands him the box.]

ALIKI: And I give to you.

DYLAN: Why?

ALIKI: So you return it to me in Athens. So you know I keep my promise.

DYLAN: I can't, like, take this.

ALIKI: The problem, I think, is not if I meet you in Athens. The problem, I think, is if you meet me. Now you have to. Yes? *[ALIKI kisses DYLAN and exits.]*

[OLIVER has put a needle into DANIEL's forehead.]

OLIVER: There, that's better, isn't it? That's much better.

[HEATHER looks over at DANIEL.]

HEATHER: Shit, Oliver, did you give him a needle?

OLIVER: Yes.

HEATHER: Will it put him to sleep?

OLIVER: Soon.

HEATHER: But he needs to feel *something,* even if it's anger. . . . *[She goes to DANIEL.]* Danny, I've sold your book.

OLIVER: Leave it alone now, luv.

HEATHER: It's going to sing and dance, kiddo. You've invented a Mabel.

OLIVER: Just leave it alone.

HEATHER: That idiot will make hash out of it.

DYLAN: Hey, Mom, maybe he shouldn't hear this.

HEATHER: Danny, the book is bullshit.

DYLAN: Mom . . . *[He grabs her hand.]*

OLIVER: Take her away, Dylan.

HEATHER: Hands off! The book is bullshit. You didn't tell the truth. About the dentist. About the waiter. About you. Too contentious, too political, too blatant, too unpopular. You said an artist has to select. Well, your selections took you right into the pages of *Vogue.* And no doubt you're right. If Mrs. Honey babbled on about atomic bombs, it would have seemed far too obvious, and she wouldn't have been in the least endearing. And if the waiter had whispered sweet nothings about Marx and Lenin into your ear while you were making love, as he did, instead of singing sixties pop songs, it would have lost its universal touch, I suppose, and the readers would have had to deal with the fact that by the time the book was published that kid was probably in prison being tortured, and that ain't Book of the Month Club, is it? And I know, I know your lies look more like truth than the truth itself, and I know that my way it would actually have been diminished, but Danny, maybe if you had just tried it, Dylan wouldn't be going to Paris today.

DYLAN: Leave me out of this, you hear?

HEATHER: We tell such lies, Danny. Now that idiot is going to take your artful lies and make them artless, that's all.

DANIEL: Ocean.

HEATHER: Yes—ocean—you understand, don't you? I had to do it. For both of us.

DANIEL: Ocean.

HEATHER: For the money.

DANIEL: Ocean.

HEATHER: You forgive me, don't you?

DANIEL: Ocean . . . [He closes his eyes.]

HEATHER: Danny, forgive me.

OLIVER: He's asleep, luv.

HEATHER: [Shouts] Why did you give him that goddamn needle? [She starts to cough and gasp—cannot catch her breath.]

DYLAN: Hey—Mom . . .

OLIVER: Let it out, luv. . . .

HEATHER: I'm alright, I'm alright, don't crowd me, leave me alone. . . . I just can't catch my breath. . . .

   [OLIVER signals to DYLAN to give her air. She calms down.]

There . . . it's alright. . . .

DYLAN: Hey, Oliver, I think maybe . . . [He signals towards the needles.]

OLIVER: Yes. Good idea.

DYLAN: Come on, Mom, sit down. [He takes her to a chair.]

HEATHER: I've left word with the lawyers. The film will bring in a fortune. It's all going to the right organizations, all of it. It will be written in the contract. The money will go to fight against nuclear energy, against political oppression, against AIDS, against religious extremism—I've spread it over nineteen important groups. . . .

DYLAN: Right, Mom.

HEATHER: I had to do something good with our lives. Everything seems so wasted.

OLIVER: Here, luv, just one . . . [He places a needle in her forehead.]

HEATHER: If only I knew how to get to Goa.

DYLAN: It's alright, Mom. . . .

HEATHER: If only I could stop smoking.

DYLAN: It's alright. . . .

HEATHER: Shit . . . Dylan . . . I've done it wrong, haven't I? I've given the money to too many groups. I'm still unfocused. Maybe just two or three. I've done it wrong. . . .

DYLAN: It's alright.

HEATHER: There's just so much to worry about, so much. . . . *[She closes her eyes.]*

DYLAN: Sure, Mom.

HEATHER: Ocean.

DYLAN: What?

HEATHER: Ocean . . . *[She falls asleep.]*

DYLAN: Boy, this stuff really works.

OLIVER: It causes a deep sleep for one hour. A very restful sleep. Just one hour. It's cleansing.

DYLAN: Yeah? Hey—do you think? . . . Well, I don't have to go to the airport for another two hours. And I'm very tense. *[He sits on the floor.]*

I mean, I don't, like, get tense a lot. I don't worry like my mom. Or my dad. She don't see too much of my dad in me and that, like, upsets her. He was this poet from Chile. I don't remember him much; they weren't together too long. There was some sort of revolution there, in Chile, and he went back, and then there was this takeover, like, and they arrested him because of his poetry, and they put him in a stadium and they threw kerosene on him and set him on fire. Mom thinks I should get into politics because of that, but that isn't, like, a positive example, you know what I mean, and actually, in its way, that's what turned me towards computers. I mean, I didn't know the guy and that was his scene, not mine; it don't have nothin' to do with me. Who needs kerosene, huh? I guess I should read a printout of his poems someday. See, I've got this IQ for technical things that's really incredible, and I can make, like, a lot of money by the end of this week, and I have this unbelievable girl meeting me tomorrow, and all that's enough for me to handle; in fact, I think she's, like, too much to handle, so one hour of, like, sleep, Ollie. . . .

[OLIVER places a needle into his forehead.]

Ouch. I thought you didn't feel it.

OLIVER: Only when it goes into the head of a genius.

DYLAN: I mean, what do you think of Aliki?

OLIVER: Don't know.

DYLAN: Danny kept saying something about her.

OLIVER: What?

DYLAN: "Don't sneeze." I wonder what that meant?

OLIVER: Don't know.

DYLAN: I'm tired. Do you think I'll, like, say ocean, too? *[He closes his eyes.]*

OLIVER: I doubt it, Dylan.

[OLIVER touches him. DYLAN is asleep. OLIVER looks at DYLAN, then at HEATHER and DANIEL. They are all asleep, with needles in their foreheads.]

Rest, my little chicks. Rest. *[OLIVER takes a cassette player from the table. He sits in the rocking chair. He puts the headphones on and turns the machine on. He rocks gently, listening to music and closes his eyes.]*

[BARNABY and ALIKI enter, with their suitcases. They look at the others. BARNABY is about to try to speak to them, but ALIKI shakes her head no and points him to the door. They walk to the front door. BARNABY leaves. ALIKI starts to follow him, then stops and walks back into the room. She stares at DANIEL, HEATHER, DYLAN, and OLIVER. The lights fade on the room, except for one bright light on ALIKI, a look of utter contempt on her face. Blackout.]

[Church bells. The lights rise. Four days later.
OLIVER is sitting in the rocking chair. He is not listening to music. DANIEL walks in, slowly, with difficulty. He walks onto the veranda. OLIVER doesn't look up. There is a low, rumbling noise off in the distance.]

OLIVER: Well, look who's up and about. Feeling better, are we? That's a good boy. Slept well, eh? Four whole days. That's a record for you. Eyes open to take a little nourishment, then back shut into never-never land. Four days.

[DANIEL sits down.]

Sitting down, are we, luv? That's good. Do you hear that noise? Like thunder. In the distance. Spoils the peaceful drone of the rainfall. Hasn't stopped raining. You didn't miss any sun. *[He looks at DANIEL.]*
I guess we were depressed, weren't we? Does your face have more colour in it? Probably. We like our sleep. *[Pause—he looks away.]*
Well—what have you missed? A lot. You've missed a lot. *[Pause]*
Heather's in the hospital. She had a choking fit as soon as Dylan left. That's when you went to sleep, wasn't it? Yes. *[Pause]*
The cancer has crawled up through her system and is surrounding her windpipe. Leaning on it, actually. Do you want to hear this? Do you want to go back to sleep? They think they can reduce it a bit. They figure she has a few weeks. But you know Heather; she'll turn weeks into months if she can. I have a lot of time for Heather. I'm just afraid the fight may leave her when she hears about Dylan. *[Pause]*
Are you sure you don't want to go back to sleep? I'm not giving you a needle. Not now. *[Pause]*
Dylan's plane exploded. Everyone dead. A bomb. Hardly got into the air. Just over the crater. They found some wreckage. On the cliffs. The explosive device had been placed in a little jewel box. Pretty clever, eh? *[Pause]*
Are you tired again? What is that sound? I liked Dylan. Did you? It was Aliki, of course. Except her name's not Aliki. It's Maria something-or-other and she's not Greek; she's Lebanese. Did you suspect something, you little devil? "Don't sneeze"? What did that mean? A Palestinian courier had been booked on that flight; that's supposedly who she was after. He cancelled at the last moment. They're not sure if she belonged to a Muslim extremist group or another Palestinian faction or the Israeli secret service. Or the CIA. Or the KGB. My guess is

all of the above. Well, doesn't matter really, does it? Another gesture for free-dom, no matter how you squeeze it. *[Pause]*

They traced Aliki-or-Maria to Crete. Well, I could have told them that's where she was. She and Barnaby had taken a hotel room. They found Barnaby. His throat was cut. Aliki-Maria has disappeared. *[Pause]*

Thin air. *[Pause]*

Well, you can take some comfort in the knowledge that your book will never be a musical now. Assuming it upsets you at all. *[Pause]*

I know the world at large would consider you a total mess, but I rather think you lead a charmed life. I'm not giving you a needle. What is that noise? *[Pause]*

I'm leaving you. I've placed an advertisement in the *Herald-Tribune* for a re-placement. I'll find you someone very convivial. It seems that I myself am on a sinking ship. I'm waving good-bye as well. Do you understand? I found a lesion on my arm. I had the necessary tests. I have AIDS. I suppose it can be classified as ironic. The last time I was with someone was five years ago. And only for a minute. Well—so it goes. *[Pause]*

It hasn't registered yet, really. I'm numb. I'm not even angry or sad. Just numb. Funny, that. *[Pause]*

But I am quite sure of one thing, and that's that I'm not ending my days with you. *[Pause]*

I used to work in a clinic. Didn't get paid well. But it meant something. It helped. I have healing gifts. Don't I, luv? I think I've been wasting them on you. But right now, with this odd numbness, everything seems wasted. *[Pause]*

I don't hate you. Don't think that. But if you have gifts, you should use them, shouldn't you? It's a way of facing the madness and shouting "stop." You, of course, can't even say, "stop." If you tried, it would come out as "ice cream." *[Pause]*

So you've missed a lot. It pays to stay awake these days. *[Pause]*

What stories are you writing in your head? What faces do you see? Do the heavens dance? Does a star fall on Albania? Do you feel the cool breeze from the Levant? Does the breeze comfort you? Do you know at last what it means? *[Pause]*

What is that noise?

[The sound grows louder. DANIEL rises. He walks to the edge of the veranda. He stares out at the sea.]

DANIEL: Apricot.
OLIVER: What?
DANIEL: The apricot is erupting.

[The noise grows very loud. DANIEL starts to laugh.]

GODFREY HAMILTON

Kissing Marianne

EDITOR'S INTRODUCTION

F OR YEARS ONE OF THE major inspirations of gay artists has been the creative and personal partnership of composer Benjamin Britten and tenor Peter Pears, for whom Britten wrote much of his work. What more ideal relationship: creator and performer, artist and muse, collaborator and lover. Britten and Pears were a gay couple for their time, living a loving coupled life but reluctant to open themselves to hostility by talking about it. Their collaborations—often musical-dramatic depictions of thwarted homosexual desire—were also of their time, made timeless by the greatness of Britten's music.

Godfrey Hamilton and Mark Pinkosh, who make up the Starving Artists Theater Company, are a Britten and Pears for the 1990s. English-born Hamilton, who worked in various jobs in the London theater, met and fell in love with Hawaiian-born actor Mark Pinkosh. In Pinkosh, Hamilton found his muse and a uniquely expressive actor to write for. In Hamilton, Pinkosh found a writer who could create material tailor-made to show off his gifts as an actor. Together they could create gay theater that mixed the poetic and the political. Unlike the work of Britten and Pears, Pinkosh and Hamilton's theater pieces, like their lives, celebrate uncloseted gay love. Hamilton and Pinkosh settled in Santa Cruz, California, where, despite earthquakes and conservative rumblings in the distance, the spirit of the 1960s still prevails. This idyllic place becomes the setting for *Kissing Marianne*.

In just a few years Starving Artists has secured a solid reputation, particularly in the United Kingdom. Its 1993 solo piece *Sleeping with You* was praised by London critics when it appeared at the Drill Hall, London's principal gay theatrical venue, and was a hit at the Traverse Theatre during the Edinburgh Festival. *Kissing Marianne* played in London during a seemingly endless heat wave in 1994, but audiences flocked to the decidedly un-air-conditioned Drill Hall to see this powerful play, which went on to the Traverse during the Edinburgh Festival for more critical adulation and sellout houses. *Kissing Marianne* was so successful that Starving Artists is one of the few companies to be invited back to the Traverse Theatre for a third consecutive festival season.

Kissing Marianne looks deceptively simple. Only two chairs are required on stage (plus some lighting and sound cues). Words and acting paint the various locales around Santa Cruz. The focus is on the intense relationship between Josh and Will. Josh lives in his feelings. Like his dog, Tyler, Josh is a creature of flesh, instinct, and devotion. Will, a writer, may be politically correct in the mode of the writers named and satirized in the play, but however sexually liberated he seems, he is intellectual, analytical, cut off from his feelings. The play brings these brothers together after a thirteen-year separation. Or does it? Has Josh imagined this meeting? Does the play really take place in Josh's imagination?

Kissing Marianne raises a number of questions about gay sexuality and spirituality in the age of AIDS. One of the first volumes of gay literary criticism was entitled *Like a Brother, Like a Lover*. Hamilton's play asks how the metaphor of brotherhood, or, more specifically, incest, defines the emotional and spiritual intensity of gay relationships. It also has the courage to ask whether gay men were sold a bill of damaged goods by some of their intellectual leaders, particularly the celebration of promiscuity and the equation of anonymous sexual encounters with love.

Hamilton is a real poet for the stage. His language is daring, powerful, yet playful. He can touch on the dark, frightening aspects of human experience and still exalt. Behind Josh's lyrical cries for love and Will's rational self-justifications is the wail of rocker Marianne Faithfull, a British pop icon less known in the United States but clearly central to Hamilton's memories.

AUTHOR'S INTRODUCTION

My work is invariably inspired by my honey, Mark Pinkosh. I met Mark in London (my hometown) ten days before his return to Honolulu, where he ran his own theater company—Starving Artists—which he created when he was just twenty. I was a parochial Londoner. I thought visas were needed to go south of the Thames. Mark and I fell in love instantly in April 1988. After ringing up a $4,000 transoceanic phone bill, we reasoned it would be cheaper for me to go to Hawaii in person. After a twenty-three-hour journey the plane descended through the Polynesian night. Mark greeted me with fragrant leis of pikake (jasmine), royal ilima flowers, and white ginger. We lived together in paradise for four years, making plays and running Starving Artists, before we moved to California.

About *Kissing Marianne:* It was written in the eye of a domestic hurricane. There was a stream of houseguests and constant visitors at our tiny house in Santa Cruz, on the central California coast. The landlady announced she was dying and that we had to move at once so she could sell the house in a hurry to cover medical bills. Our houseguests rallied, we found a new home with more room, and we moved in my desk, notebooks, journals, pen, ink, PC, and printer. Then, as I sat writing, the rest of the house was moved in around me. The play had been commissioned by Julie Parker at London's Drill Hall Arts Centre. A deadline approached. I was in a kind of heaven, banging away on a keyboard while my stuff was eased in around me. The last cherished items to arrive were Mark and the various dogs and cats. The play opened in time, ran through a London heat wave, moved up to the Edinburgh Festival, where it ran at the Traverse Theatre, then returned to California.

I love the landscapes of America. Mark and I still live in Santa Cruz. As I write, a white heron struts at the bottom of the garden and a deer is nibbling Mark's flowers. Ten minutes away the redwoods continue to amaze—the oldest living beings on the planet in a cathedral of a forest. The ocean is ten minutes' drive. *Kissing Marianne* is set in this landscape. In the big, wide space of the Drill Hall, in the intimate Traverse Theatre, our director David Prescott's simple staging and Mark's edgy, passionate performance brought the landscape to life.

This need I have to write—it's about family and tribe. Lesbians and gay men have been creating plays since the first anthropoids gathered at the first fireside. We were there, and ever will be, and it's time for all of us to remove from our guts that toxic little insect called *shame*. Being gay is about *falling in love*. We know who we really are when we fall in love. How could I not be OUT? I love Mark so much—to hide in a closet would be to lie about the most beautiful man in the world and how I feel about him.

PRODUCTION HISTORY AND RIGHTS

Kissing Marianne is a production of Starving Artists Theater Company. It was directed by David Prescott. Lighting design was by Douglas Kuhrt.

Josh . . . . Mark Pinkosh
Will . . . . Bruce Tegart

Kissing Marianne was commissioned by London's Drill Hall Arts Centre, where it received its premiere on 12 July 1994.

GODFREY HAMILTON

Kissing Marianne

Cast of Characters

JOSHUA: Early 30s.
WILL: Early 30s.

Setting

Santa Cruz, California.

Music is crucial. The original production drew on Counting Crows' album *August and Everything After* and, obviously, lots of Marianne Faithfull, particularly her *Dangerous Acquaintances* album.

---

1. REDWOOD FOREST. DUSK. DRIFTING MISTS.

JOSHUA: Tyler! Tyler!
  C'mere boy! *[Whistles]*

  C'mon!!! Over here!

  I could live at night, simply at night / the clear deep dark.
  The trees, the creek splashing over rocks.
  So still and hot / earthquake weather.
  Come find me, please come home . . . c'mon . . . fly to San Franscisco
  dropping down through the fogs, the city in peaks of light below . . .
  drive down the coast highway / I need to be with you.

I'm standing over my small town watching the coast highway in the dusk,
watching for your headlights. Come through my safe little town,
past the spikey white church . . .
past the wooden Victorian houses / so delicately painted / sunset colors
and storm sky colors / the long twisting road
up to here

and the whispering in the trees . . .

the sky pale mauve / perfectly lilac going to indigo
and the moon rising over the trees
and the dog in the creek
splashing and tumbling / and the moon so huge—

Tyler! Drop it! Don't eat it! Drop it!
Tyler! C'mere!

Come home to me. The trees so high, they hide us from the night,
it's safe and soft,
the footfalls muffled. Leaves, woodchip, ferns, brittle
and breaking underfoot / we'll watch the moon playing catch me / you can,
glimpsed through the tall redwoods. Aw, man, I need you here. Come ON.
I need you so.
Hear me howl / remember your touch /
again and again / this longing, this longing
but you feel so far away . . .
A sense of—
who is—
who is that watching / what is that in the trees

a darkness following me
and where is my dog?

O my god, where is my dog

a deer staring at me.
Perfect round eyes
and the light falling through the leaves—

Tyler!

You know something? Why folks put leashes on their dogs?
It's not—it's not in case the dogs . . . I mean
it's not so the dogs won't get lost, it's so . . . so they—
I mean the folks, so they can keep up with the dogs.
So I can keep up with my dog

O my god, the moon / thank god for the moon

Tyler!

And when the moon hits high in the night
downtown / the raccoons will be out
roaming the streets
toppling trash cans / skunks and neighborhood cats
running circles round each other / possums
diving outta the trees . . .
what are they feeling in the air and the earth, man oh man . . .

these trees have been here since forever
these trees are the oldest living things . . .

the silence suddenly. And the darkness making shapes

Tyler! OVER HERE! C'mon c'mon quick!

[Lights shift; a figure moves towards JOSHUA.]

2. JOSHUA'S PLACE. EVENING.

WILL: Hi. Can I come in?

JOSHUA: Oh. Oh no. Oh man.

WILL: Happy birthday.

JOSHUA: Nonono. Yes. This is . . . you're kidding me man . . . I—

WILL: Hi Joshua. Can I stay with you? Please? Joshua? It's me. It's really me, yes. I came to wish you happy birthday.

JOSHUA: I—

WILL: Thirty is a dangerous age, yes? I came with a gift. Honest. Can I come in?

JOSHUA: It worked! O man. What do I say? O man.

WILL: It's a very nice gift. I came a long way to bring it. Can I come in? Please?

JOSHUA: Yes. Yes you can. O yes, please.

WILL: And I've brought my toothbrush.

JOSHUA: Oh. That's . . . right. That's . . . good.

WILL: Is that—hey . . . Joshua! You've finally got a dog! How long have you had a dog?

JOSHUA: Thirteen years.

WILL: What?

JOSHUA: I've had a dog for thirteen years Will.

3. WILL ALONE. DEEP NIGHT.

WILL: I believed we all could connect in the most rhythmic way . . .
I thought two strangers could meet in a bar
connect

and go fuck in a corner.
Fear ran rings around me.
I felt I was unravelling under my skin
the connecting tissue seemed to disengage, my mind drifting away my
heart losing its beat, slowing to a standstill in my chest.
My muscles like lizards / crawling across my bones
salamanders packed against marrow.
I waited in bars afraid to make the first move
afraid every move would make me look foolish
and as the nights wore on
the men in the dark corners seemed more and more
attractive.
I'm always the last to leave,
trailing home with another lonely man like me,
terrified / the end of another lost night.

And when you ask me how I'm feeling or "are you okay"
I can't say I'm scared
although it would be so sweet and simple to say.
I ran away.
See me run.
Staring at ceilings.
Waking next to people I don't love / and once I've sprayed them
inside and out / like a frightened tomcat / see
how little I care / let alone like or love.

Easy in the city / Times Square
I follow a man with pale green eyes / into the Hotel Edison.
The elevator / we smile / he leaves open the door to his room.
I awake beside him at three / my belly
crusted and sore / I slide from the bed / softly
at the window / watch the steam rise
from the drains grates and gutter.
My very own life and I don't know how to take part in it.
I want to be strong for everyone
but myself.
And I end up invisible,
seeing nothing when I stare into mirrors.

4. WALKING THROUGH TOWN. EVENING.

JOSHUA: You like my little town?
WILL: This little town. Yes. I like it. There's not much to see.

JOSHUA: In the fall, it is heaven. I mean it Will. It is . . . heaven. The colors. The trees are red, the light is gold and molten and—yes. Heaven.

WILL: The drive over the mountain.

JOSHUA: Over the hill. Yes. In the dark.

WILL: I didn't like the patch fog.

JOSHUA: It's the cool nights after the hot days.

WILL: It collected in the gulleys. I slowed right down. I couldn't see a yard in front of me and something scared me in the mist it ran across the road in the fog. It was silver.

JOSHUA: A skunk. A raccoon.

WILL: I was scared.

JOSHUA: Then you saw the lights of the town—

WILL: And the lights of the bay.

JOSHUA: —across the water?

WILL: I saw more lights glinting.

JOSHUA: You saw good. Yes. Shimmering. Monterey across the bay— deep and wide / deep blue, dolphins and sea lions. So. How did you find me?

WILL: I tracked you down.

JOSHUA: Why did you find me?

WILL: It took a while and I had to.

JOSHUA: The years have made me that irresistible?

WILL: The years have been difficult and kind. I have so much to tell you. Are you ever—

JOSHUA: No. Never.

WILL: Where are you taking me?

JOSHUA: We'll eat. Somewhere Mexican, chile rellenos. Okay?

WILL: I can't tell you how many nights I craved a—

JOSHUA: Good. I'm glad. We'll have chile rellenos and then we can . . .

WILL: Yes, we can, can't we? Talk. Buy some birthday booze—

JOSHUA: Talk. Oh, we'll talk. I've got some things to show you. You could have called.

WILL: I should have. Some whisky? On the way back?

JOSHUA: I said you *could* have. Don't say should. I hate *should*.

WILL: It didn't seem urgent.

JOSHUA: Exactly. Don't give me your imperatives, young sir.

WILL: But it was important. Whisky it is. What's that smell?

JOSHUA: Skunk.

WILL: Skunk? No. Sniff.

JOSHUA: What smell? Be precise Will.

WILL: Rich. Tickles the back of your skull.

JOSHUA: Maple. When the sap drips out it smells like the town is one big waffle on a big BIG plate. I have clean sheets for you.

WILL: Will the others mind?

JOSHUA: Others? There are no others Will.

WILL: A dog.

JOSHUA: What did you expect? Really Will, what did you expect?

5. JOSHUA AND WILL STARING AT THE STARS.

JOSHUA:
    And once I came home from a movie with my folks
    and the movie was *The Absent-minded Professor*
    and I wanted to grow up to be Dean Jones and I wanted
    my dad to grow up to be Fred MacMurray
    and it was late. After-movies late.
    And my dad had carried me home from the movie
    sleepy over his shoulder
    and I dreamed that my toys were all made outta Flubber
    and we could bounce away together.
    And in the night / before bed / I sipped milk
    and I snuck out into the backyard / in my pajamas
    and I looked up and there were many many stars
    when I was a kid when I was so small / as tiny as the stars
    and I was a spit of light whirling
    and the whole black bucket of space tipped sideways and
    spilled me / I said yes
    and I said yes
    and the galaxy burped. And I was standing in the yard

    and I never felt so happy
    in all the years since
    when I was a kid.
WILL: When I was little so little
    everything had life everything had breath
    the rocks had breath the fields the trees
    the snake knew my name and the dogs prowling in packs were barking
    at me / join us join us!
    The oil in the gutter
    the wet street in winter
    and light was coiling in the slicker.
    When I was a kid everything had a mind everything had a heart of its own
    and I could see the warm veins pulsing thump thump and the arteries
    in the moon
    and after it rained the air was full of stuff that flickered
    and I knew
    it was the angels of the air
    when I was a kid.

6. JOSHUA'S ROOM. NIGHT.

JOSHUA: So whaddya think?

WILL: O man this is—nothing's changed—you've added to it—couldn't you charge admission!? Are these the original posters? *She Creature / Invasion of the Saucermen / Creature from the Black Lagoon*—heh heh! Far out! You could start your own business—

JOSHUA: I wanted to.

WILL: What stopped you? Wow. Are those, like, complete sets of *Famous Monsters* magazine?

JOSHUA: And *Castle of Frankenstein* and *Midi-Minuit Fantastic*—

WILL: —*Fantastique.*

JOSHUA: Yeah. What you said. Complete! More'n you could afford!

WILL: You're morbid.

JOSHUA: No more than you, listening to that smack-voiced drama queen you sang along with—

WILL: Leave Ms. Faithfull out of this. Remember when your haunted house press-book got trashed?

JOSHUA: *House on Haunted Hill.* And it was the lobby card.

WILL: "You'll fry your brains on that stuff Joshua" "Comic books won't pay the rent"

JOSHUA: Maybe not. They kept me sane tho'. Like you and Marianne. I have videos. *Forbidden Planet / The Hills Have Eyes—Blood Feast.* Didja ever see *Lost Boys?*

WILL: Yes! Keifer and Corey. Edward Herrmann—

JOSHUA: —Herrmann! Right! This little town of mine was the location for that movie. That opening . . . opening helicopter shot, that's our very own . . . my very own boardwalk—

WILL: Let's go see the boardwalk! Let's ride the roller-coaster—

JOSHUA: —log flume, carousel, ferris wheel—

WILL: —salted pretzels—

JOSHUA: —you're interrupting—the powers that be insisted that the movie use a . . . fictionalized name . . . for the town. It became Santa Carla. Because at that time . . . this little town of mine was the bizarre murders capital of the United States and—

WILL: —vampires are bad for business.

JOSHUA: Well exactly. Very bad for business. Because they never mind their own . . . they want a slice of yours . . . your business, see? They see something they like—

WILL: —two boys, for example. Boys crazy for each other.

JOSHUA: —for example. And they want some of that—

WILL: Gimme some of that!

JOSHUA: Gimme some of that!

WILL: So how do they go about getting what they want?

JOSHUA: Suck it / drain it / slurp it out.

WILL: How . . . exactly?

JOSHUA: Provoke. Feast on anger. You forget to keep the drawbridge up, and before you know it, they're inside, hacking away, after your liver your pancreas your *gallbladder* / that's a very tasty morsel.

WILL: Still angry, huh?

JOSHUA: Aren't you? How can you not be? Ya gotta use it . . . as stealthily as possible. Then ram a wooden spike through their hearts.

WILL: Does that really do the trick?

JOSHUA: When you stake one, perhaps there's some other organ you have to get at. Some secret vampire organ. Pineal. Pituitary. Of course, they only seem to be going for the throat. It's the sex they want. Where the fuck have you been for thirteen years? What the goddamn fuck did you think you were DOING? What the—the—how COULD YOU? I thought you were dead.

WILL: No you didn't.

JOSHUA: Don't tell me what I'm thinking! Stop telling me what I'm supposed to be feeling! I was afraid, I was scared to death, and you left me. There was an estate, there were lawyers, and we couldn't find you. I felt it in here / I'm feeling it now, this ring of hurt in here. Goddamn you, Will.

WILL: What did you do with my comic books?

JOSHUA: What?

WILL: Do you have my comics? My collector's editions? *The Man with X-ray Eyes?*

JOSHUA: I traded them. You didn't leave me much else.

WILL: Ouch. You need something more to drink—

JOSHUA: Where were you when I was trying to graduate? Why didn't you hear me? And no thank you / no more / no, *Will,* I'm loaded enough. My frontal lobes are dissolving like snails in sea salt. I hate booze. Why are you doing this?

WILL: I thought you liked getting drunk and getting stoned.

JOSHUA: I nearly died. Fuck. What do you want from me?

WILL: In New York City. I had a professional lunch. With Quentin Crisp. In a diner on East 3rd Street. He ordered two eggs over easy, a side of fries, a side of toast, and jam. Sounds very American. But think about it. A solitary Englishman in retirement, ordering his egg and chips and tea at 5:00. We don't change. Not really. We just change our tactics.

7. JOSHUA ALONE. STARS AND NIGHT.

JOSHUA:
They've all announced
my dad already dead, unless (they said) he concedes
to those pains—o, the state of his heart.

Dad stands bandy-legged
not yet dead
but sad and hurt
his face sags within circles of family demand.

My father on my right,
we cower—we two
before my mother's sudden startled corpse
and my brother has gone.

I think: we're cowed by her body. I refuse this.
Her body: its death pulses, blood settling in deep places, her
skin draining, eyes turning
to yellow parchment, and her piss drenching the cold sheet.

And at long last I give my dad a hand to hold
and he grips as a baby grips a finger.
I wait for him to cry.

For months thereafter:
Dad throws parties
takes women to dinner
his pockets stuffed full of rubbers.

He lives to lust after my friends
like Karen
"She never refuses a little snug cuddle"—
and Sandra who is tiny
"Her bosoms are huge"
and swing when she bops to Otis Redding.
"Any man would go for this Josh / a real man / a man
wants plenty of this"
Then there is Doug whom I adore,
the way the sun takes to him
and fills his skin with tan, though Dad doesn't notice.

Dad and I, we have them all in, open house
on a Friday night—
Sandra helps with the chips, dips, and bites, Dad of course fetches
whisky and gin,
the neighbors complain
so we ask them all in.

Eighteen months on:
Dad's heart snaps
he dies in terror and pain
I hear his heart make a great crack.
He looks as if, inside his skin, many fingers
grip his bones.

Is this the heart I inherit?
After the last shout in the dark—
telling ourselves that life goes on, theirs and ours, and listening
for a whimper in the night, a clue that he's survived the closing
of the dark gate?

Do you suppose when his heart broke
that something escaped,
cracked open, and finally let Dad out?

8. JOSHUA'S PORCH. NIGHT. CICADAS.
ANOTHER BOTTLE OF WHISKY.

JOSHUA: What are you doing out here? It's a beautiful night, isn't it?

WILL: A little better. I want to take my shirt off—

JOSHUA: —are you hot?

WILL: I'm warm. Help me.

JOSHUA: What will people think, I wonder. Me here half loaded with a half-naked man—

WILL: They'll think, why does he do things by halves?

JOSHUA: What's that?

WILL: What's that what?

JOSHUA: That.

WILL: Someone put a knife through it.

JOSHUA: Fighting again.

WILL: Feel it.

JOSHUA: Bumpy.

WILL: It still hurts. It never healed properly. I held the skin together.

JOSHUA: Like that li'l bird we had? That held its broken leg together till it healed?

WILL: Yep. See? I'm learning to be a good animal.

JOSHUA: I nearly died. While you were away.

WILL: While I was out?

JOSHUA: Yeah. Did you feel it?

WILL: No. Should I?

JOSHUA: I called for you. As hard as I could. Guess my heart wasn't in it.

WILL: Maybe you should've used the phone.

JOSHUA: Yeah right / you were so easy to locate—

WILL: Why have you made your bedroom the same as the one in Omaha?

JOSHUA: My room. My room was the safest place I ever had, Will. So safe. Me and the movies inside my head, rescuing myself. Then you joined me. In here. We've been to some places, haven't we?

WILL: Better 'n any I've been to. The best places are in there. Here.

JOSHUA: You could have made a new home with me.

WILL: No. This is like every small town anywhere in the world. They're all the same. And the folks who move to the cities, the same, they turn the city into another small town, treading the same paths every day, taking their address books and transferring names and taking people out of their lives, the world made smaller by two, and three, and fifty, till there's nobody left but the walls and the empty mirrors and the TV and and—you've moved from Omaha to here and nothing's changed. It's the same room.

JOSHUA: One fucking postcard Will. One. What possessed you? I had to graduate on my own, I—

WILL: I missed you—

JOSHUA: I lied. I just lied. I didn't graduate. O, you got to graduate like a good boy. Daddy's best boy. Then you got the hell out. Mom and Dad dying on us and you fuck off to tell the world what a wonderful place it is / tell us all how happy joyous and free we all are since the sixties made it okay to fuck ourselves to death. After Mom died I had eighteen months of Dad and me / and then I had twelve years of me and my dog / and the two of us coped. And I got laid about once a year. And I nearly died.

WILL: Happy birthday Joshua. You're thirty. Happy happy birthday. It's important.

JOSHUA: Why is it?

WILL: Saturn return. Hell, who knows? It just is. You can't sweep your side of the street without me. Because. What's your dog called?

JOSHUA: Tyler. Hey boy. Woof. Hey hey / who's this: "Why can't you be more like other kids? Why don'tcha—"

WILL: —"help your mother with the chores!"

JOSHUA: "What's wrong with you!"

WILL & JOSHUA: "Look what you're doing to your mother!"

WILL: —"you never smile."

JOSHUA: —"so goddamn serious."

WILL: Hey HEY . . . Josh . . . "TAKE IT BACK WHERE YOU FOUND IT!"

JOSHUA: —right back where you found it.
  He needs me
  he wants me
  see his tail wag when I touch him
  see his tongue kiss my cheek / can I keep him
  please
  he needs me see he loves
  o he loves me

WILL: "Get that damn mutt outta here
  get it outta my house
  this is my house goddamnit not a fucking hotel"

JOSHUA: "Can't you see what you're doing
  to your mother!"
  Fuck Will / I hated him I hated her.

WILL: She did her best.

JOSHUA: IT WASN'T GOOD ENOUGH.

Hey hey try this: "Get ready for church!"

Get ready for church.

WILL & JOSHUA: "You're going to church whether you like it or not."

JOSHUA: I said no and he hit me.

Look. He hit me / see it? / Still.

WILL: Let me keep him please so small so scared

he wags his tail when he sees me

he needs me / he needs me

he's so smart he's so cool

he wags his tail when he sees me—

JOSHUA: Bastard. Bastard. Goddamn you, you fuck . . . you fuck!

My head it hurts and my heart I cannot feel my heart

he wagged his tail when I stroked him

his tongue was wet and he licked me

his nose was wet and he kissed me

O Will. Touch me. Touch me.

WILL: Joshua?

JOSHUA: Okay. Okay. Tyler. It's okay. I'm okay.

WILL: Joshua? Do you want your gift now? I brought you a copy of my book.

JOSHUA: It's okay Tyler. I'm okay.

WILL: I dedicated it to you.

JOSHUA: I know Will. I read it.

WILL: Oh.

JOSHUA: I bought it. Here. In town. I actually paid good money for it.

WILL: Didja like it?

JOSHUA: Um . . . I liked the piece on Marianne Faithfull. I quite liked the stuff about Quentin Crisp, even if I didn't get your point. But—okay—what's with all the spiritual shit? You're deluded man. The bathhouses were a religious experience? Will, you've gotta get your head out from between your legs. The tip of your little dick is not God Almighty! Okay, okay . . . lemme see . . . okay listen . . . "—in the deep abysmal dark—"

WILL: —Abyssal.

JOSHUA: —abyssal!? Oy. "Deep abyssal dark of the backrooms, there is no class no caste no social structure, no masks, no suits and ties to remind us of our professional contracts, there's just the sheer animal ecstasy, the dissolving of walls and boundaries until it seems the orgasms we share are spilling across the night— sex has freed us to find our way home—"

WILL: And?

JOSHUA: Oh please.

WILL: I'm not judging. I'm an observer.

JOSHUA: Bullshit upon bullshit. Anyone can sit on the sidelines passing judgment, Will. Anyone!

WILL: Okay. Isn't that what you're doing to me?

JOSHUA: No Will, I'm not. This is passion. This is heart. John Preston, Edmund White, Paul Monette, and you. Completely enslaved to your dicks but nononono, what's really happening, brothers and sisters, is that I'm a master of kundalini yoga and I have freed myself from all physical laws! Yeah right! You couldn't deal with all the passion in our bedroom, our own safe place in the dark . . . o fuck you man! I have more ecstasy running on the beach with my dog than you ever had with a throatful of dick. You wouldn't know ecstasy if it came up and bit you on the fucking ass, *man*!

WILL: It has. And I do. Come here.

JOSHUA: Vampire. I'm amazed you haven't shacked up with Madonna yet.

WILL: What's wrong with you?

JOSHUA: Barely two T cells to rub together.

WILL: Aw . . . Joshua.

JOSHUA: Aw me no aws, big brother.

WILL: How?

JOSHUA: How? How?

WILL: I mean—

JOSHUA: Blood to blood / juice to—o, read the pamphlets. There's one drawback. Just one. Horror movies aren't fun anymore. Apparently they're all metaphors for who I am. Or I'm a walking metaphor. I have a bullet with Susan Sontag's name engraved on it.

WILL: I'm . . . fine.

JOSHUA: So am I.

WILL: I mean I . . .

JOSHUA: Well of course. Here's Joshua the homebody at the hearthside with his dog and his slippers, and big bro Will is out cruising the planet banging everything that moves, and you'll live until they have to take you out and shoot you. And I'll be dead.

WILL: I didn't—I don't—

JOSHUA: You'd fuck a woodpile on the chance there was a snake in it.

WILL: That's a good one. Yours?

JOSHUA: No. I stole it. *Night Moves*. Arthur Penn.

WILL: 's good. Crap. But clever. Are you okay?

JOSHUA: Oh yeah! I bounce back. I'm made out of Flubber. Boing boing boing.

WILL: You nearly died.

JOSHUA: Nearly. Life has been quite wonderful since. This friend in my blood is the best thing that ever happened to me. There's no point minuetting around anymore. If I love someone, I'm gonna make sure they know it. That's why I called you here.

WILL: Gonna tell me to get lost or that you love me?

JOSHUA: I adore you.

WILL: O.

JOSHUA: O. Wanna run? Uh-oh. The wabbit wants to wun. Doesn't it. Mom. Dad. Me. Uhoh another one's dropping off the perch. Another night howling at the

moon grieving grieving nuhuh—Well. I'm gonna die. You're gonna die. I have
the edge on you tho'. And it's really quite . . . cool.

WILL: I don't believe in God Joshua.

JOSHUA: What's the rottweiler got to do with it? Oh, stop being so fucking Christian, Will. Didn't do Mom much good either.

WILL: I'm not.

JOSHUA: But y'are Blanche Y'ARE. Put your shirt on Will. Please. Is she nice?

WILL: Who?

JOSHUA: Marianne Faithfull.

WILL: Yes.

JOSHUA: I thought she must be.

WILL: Why?

JOSHUA: People who've nearly died. You either turn crazy with fear, or you become unbelievably cool.

WILL: Like you.

JOSHUA: Like me.

9. DINER. DAYLIGHT STREAMS THROUGH WINDOWS.

JOSHUA: So, what're ya gonna do now?

WILL: Hair of the dog?

JOSHUA: No, I feel really cramped and poisoned. I mean do next.

WILL: I'll work something out. Use my imagination.

JOSHUA: That's a given.

WILL: What's wrong with what I've been doing?

JOSHUA: What have you been doing?

WILL: Enough.

JOSHUA: So why're you here, Mr. Enigma?

WILL: I told you.

JOSHUA: I think we have a li'l communication problem here, I'm not asking
how're you gonna make a living. Or how are you intending to live your life. I
mean: just how long are you planning on staying? I need to know. So I can work
out if you're welcome or not.

WILL: What's your threshold?

JOSHUA: I need you. All the time. It's no fun without you.

WILL: What do you do next?

JOSHUA: You. I want you. Like the old days, like the new days.

WILL: Are you out of a job?

JOSHUA: I don't want money, Will. I have money. This is the coolest town in California, and that's saying something. They look after people here. Now that's
community. I have my medical insurance paid for and I have cool doctors, and

you can't move for acupuncture needles and rolfers and aura masseurs, this town is the home of woowoo out there stuff.

WILL: Not exactly vampire city.

JOSHUA: I didn't say that. This is one place they haven't colonized. They can't. Unless you invite them in. And I don't.

WILL: What would you have done—if I hadn't shown up? For your birthday?

JOSHUA: Ah, now that's a very interesting question, see, the situation—

WILL: —You want more coffee?

JOSHUA: Yeah. The situation would not have arisen. I willed you here, Will. And my head's sure paying the price. Will, booze makes me very ill. Please don't bring it into the house again.

WILL: How many happy returns do you have left?

[Cups extended to waitress.]

JOSHUA: —Hi! How're you today? Yeah, sure was a rough night . . . thanks . . . thanks. I love her hair. Big hair! You know, you haveta have big hair if you want to sling hash in a diner—

WILL: Big hair?

JOSHUA: Yeah! You know what they say—the higher the hair, the closer to god! And you know, you know . . . it's so important to smile at the waitresses in the diner. Any diner.

WILL: You figure?

JOSHUA: I know so. Look. I'm driving through town. And there's a kid, with his mom, at the crosswalk—I wait for them to cross. He's about four. And he's draggin' behind and I wave at him. He just can't take his eyes off me and his mom is pullin' him along, she's . . . oblivious. And he . . . his eyes are pleading . . . not to his mom . . . to me . . . "Wait! Wait for me! I'll catch you up! Wait? Please."

WILL: That's why we have to smile at servers in diners?

JOSHUA: He recognized himself. Don't you get it? It's so simple. It's—it's—okay okay, I've got it . . . remember the guy at the gas station? When we were kids. In the back of the car, Sunday drive with Mom and Dad, uuugh! The guy filling his car, watching the counter on the gas pump . . . blue jeans, no shirt and you and I . . . both did that—oh—OH . . . inside?

WILL: I didn't think you saw. I thought you weren't looking—

JOSHUA: Everyone was looking, Will. Straight guys were looking.

WILL: I mean looking at me—

JOSHUA: I wasn't. I just knew. And that feeling wasn't . . . down here . . . it was . . . heart. Reaching out to . . . fold him in . . .

WILL: Smiling at waitresses?

JOSHUA: A woman sees me on the street, I hardly notice her . . . but I remind her of her son who went off to Vietnam and never came home.

WILL: What's. Your. Point?

JOSHUA: The boy who bags my groceries at Safeway, the woman at the checkout, oh Will, don't you get it don't you see, we're all connected, we're family. Whether you like it or not.

WILL: Joshua, I don't think people are very nice.

JOSHUA: But we have our moments. Will, you're an observer, you watch the patterns moving around so you can go write a thesis on the great kaleidoscope of life, and maybe you can sneer a little if that corner of the pattern is a teeny tiny bit off-color. Just a bit . . . mawkish. A bit too heavy on the underscoring, so . . . overemotional. Will, that's not good enough. Too easy. We can't just watch the parade, taking notes so we can tell everyone how they could do it better. We have to get up and march. You've got to PARTICIPATE.

10. WILL ALONE. DEEP NIGHT.

WILL:
I ran away. Look at me running.
San Francisco, the Embarcadero, the dykes in green body paint
shimmying down the avenue. Then an hour at the street party
staring at the street drummer, the sweat drips from his chest,
soaked leather loincloth: some city Tarzan
and I want him and I want him
and I remember videos with Joshua / *It Came from Beneath the Sea—*
cheering the giant octopus / it slurped down the Embarcadero.
Joshua says "You count carefully. See? It's only got 5 tentacles.
That's because Ray Harryhausen charges by the tentacle. It
was a low budget picture."
And the evening on Polk Street, sad boys in dark doorways,
lost and lonely boys / and the cold men cruise up and down in Hyundais
and Mercs / a cortege / this is one of those places
death likes to hang out, hitching rides.
And I ran away / look at me running.
In London, I see her by chance in the street, by Notting Hill Station,
I follow her down Westbourne Grove, wondering if she knows what she's
meant to me / she's in black leather / of course.
In my wallet, I carry an old photograph of her / years ago—Ophelia / her
face reminds me of her song and her song reminds me / her song . . .
and the night closes around in the back streets of Notting Hill, and
she disappears into the dark that seems to follow her. And I want
to sleep and dream, so I trail an American
(I can tell he's American. The profile, plaid shirt, Timberlands.)
"Take me home."
He takes me home,

he shows me the blood on the walls where his boyfriend used to shoot up.
"He nearly died," he says "but he's better now."
And I fall asleep on his chest, dreaming of her,
she's singing "Sister Morphine," and she's only streets away from me
not knowing I'm asleep here
dreaming
that we are at special poetry reading, there's
William Burroughs there's Ginsberg
and she . . . she is guest of honor. I lean into her hair.
I'm kissing her.
In the morning
I wake to the blood on the walls.

11. WEST CLIFF DRIVE / LIGHTHOUSE PARK. AFTERNOON.

JOSHUA: Look Will, when the waves pull back, the sand looks green as jade. Each footprint holds light / like walking on a mirror / can you hear the sea lions under the wharf, barking all day and night, desperate to be fed?

WILL: Whaddya think Josh?

JOSHUA: About?

WILL: Are you scared you're gonna die?

JOSHUA: Not at all.

WILL: You get angry when you're scared.

JOSHUA: I'm not scared. I'm frustrated. I have so much to do.

WILL: I want to—I want . . . I want to be in love with you again. I think / I—I missed you so much.

JOSHUA: A call would have been nice. A letter. Something to tell me who you were . . . being. Becoming. I had to imagine. I hoped you were turning into someone I'd want to go on loving. What if you'd become someone I wouldn't want to look in the eye? You never replied to a single card.

WILL: You read what I've been thinking. And you don't approve.

JOSHUA: I had to get very New Age about it. Try and vibe you at a distance. Ask my angel to go talk to your angel. Let's go down there—

WILL: Down where?

JOSHUA: The steps down the cliff there. To the beach.

WILL: Can we take the dog there? Is it allowed?

JOSHUA: Where is the dog? Tyler? O fuckit now what's he eatin'? Hey! Tyler! Drop it! Drop it! O wait here a second Will—

WILL: Where was he?

JOSHUA: In the bushes. Here boy! Good boy! O . . . very interesting activities in the bushes today. . . . See that guy in the grass? Over there, the long grass like wheat? Under the burned trees . . . the cypresses . . . that guy! Whoops! There he goes again, going under!

WILL: What's he doing?

JOSHUA: Buck naked, in the grass, with a hard-on? Figure it out! Look! There he is again! Say hi! HI!

WILL: Is this a cruising spot?

JOSHUA: Uh . . . It sure seems like it. Look at the scenery today, o mymymy o my. I once . . . come on Will, this way . . . Tyler, Tyler, come! I once . . . back in the country, I was on a farm one summer, about two years after you left and I took a real vacation in the country and . . . this way . . .

WILL: That guy up there on the lookout . . . man. Will you look at that—

JOSHUA: Hey—listen. I went out into the fields one day, and the dog was such a bundle of puppy energy, we wandered into big fields of wheat, it was honey-colored, waving, like thick animal fur in a strong breeze, and the dog just blended into all that limitless. . . .

WILL: Is he looking at us? I think he's checking you out—

JOSHUA: Naw . . . he's here every day. Probably goes home to a wife and kids. . . . O Will for god's sake he *smokes.*

WILL: So?

JOSHUA: Like, how totally *uncool* guy—listen, I went into the field and . . . and I wanted to . . . get to know . . .

WILL: —that guy on the beach. Gray shorts. A young Robert de Niro, with muscles . . . Joshua? Go on. . . . I'm listening, what were—

JOSHUA: —Forget it / it's not important—

WILL: I want to hear what you've been—

JOSHUA: Okay it is important. Not here. Not now—

WILL: —there are some beautiful bodies on these beaches. Omilord look at the surfers. O my just lookit—

JOSHUA: *Aaaaaahhhh!* I'm glad you came. Answered my call.

WILL: I hate to disappoint you. I was speaking at UC Berkeley. And I never had the slightest doubt about your location—

JOSHUA: —and you, the traveller who never changed his address—

WILL: I bet you were in the auditorium somewhere—

JOSHUA: —No. I had a couple of spies there. You're still at it. Same old dangerous superannuated pederast crap.

WILL: —and you're in the phone book. So it was very easy to find you / you made it very easy—and the endless calls from lawyers of course.

JOSHUA: —trying to find out where to send your college fees, your interest checks, your—

WILL: Do you need help? Let me help. Are you sure you have health insurance—

JOSHUA: —I don't want your money, Will. I gave it over to you in the first place. Isn't that what Dad would've wanted?

WILL: He didn't want you to be on welfare and wanting for a good doctor's—

JOSHUA: I'm not on welfare. And I am cared for. By the community.

WILL: Pederast crap?

JOSHUA: You and your writer friends.

WILL: Ah. The Ivy League literary boys. I wouldn't call them friends. I might say professional colleagues—

JOSHUA: Edmund White and Paul Monette and—

WILL: What? Hardly—

JOSHUA: If there were a sex politics crime tribunal, Edmund White would be first up in the dock.

WILL: Where'd you pull that one from?

JOSHUA: I want to talk to you. Make sure you GET IT.

WILL: What has Edmund White to do with it?

JOSHUA: Right! And what has Quentin Crisp done to deserve it? Haven't Marianne Faithfull and Patti Smith and kd lang been through enough without your . . . iconographing . . .

WILL: Is that like pornographing?

JOSHUA: See? See? You're doing it—

WILL: What's Edmund White got—

JOSHUA: That's why I called you.

WILL: You didn't *call* me / you didn't summon me by incantation.

JOSHUA: Yes I did!

WILL: I'm selling my book, turning up on the campus circuit, hoping my agent can swing me a slot on *Larry King Live* in the same segment as Joan Collins and I have to be charming because I want my book to sell . . . and while I'm in the Golden State I think, "I know—I'll look up my little brother whom I miss and—" and there was no mystical summons.

JOSHUA: I ASKED YOU TO COME AND YOU HEARD ME! PLEASE!

WILL: Okay. If that makes you happy. But I'm glad you moved here. I won't be making personal appearances in Omaha.

JOSHUA: That's why I moved here.

WILL: Eh?

JOSHUA: Nothing. Tyler. Come on.

12. EUCALYPTUS WOODS. BUTTERFLY MIGRATION TRAIL.

EARLY DUSK.

JOSHUA: The trail is marked by a wooden track—

WILL: Rough boards roughly joined—

JOSHUA: —zigzagging thru the ironwoods and eucalyptus and the trees drip sap / at the end of the trail there's a platform surrounded by trees—

WILL: I can hear tree frogs croaking. And butterflies hanging in . . . vast bunches, thousands—

JOSHUA: —hundreds of thousands of butterflies resting on their migration south, monarchs, red ripe wings—

WILL: —the woods are shimmering—

JOSHUA: —millions of butterfly wings fluttering—

WILL: —the tops of the trees are scarlet—

JOSHUA: —bleeding

WILL: —wow.

JOSHUA: Cool, huh? Would you want to leave? When heaven is right here?

WILL: What?

JOSHUA: Are you in love?

WILL: No.

JOSHUA: Do you have a lot of sex with a lot of men?

WILL: . . . Yes.

JOSHUA: That hurts.

WILL: Why don't you like my books . . . really?

JOSHUA: You never write about me. Us.

WILL: How do I do that?

JOSHUA: Simple. You just get honest. Get real. Tell the story.

WILL: I do.

JOSHUA: Yeah, I listen to your *Reports from the Frontline* on Public Radio. In the trenches with HIV. You don't understand the first thing about it.

WILL: I'm an observer after all, eh? Okay?

JOSHUA: The politics of rationalization—

WILL: I'm apolitical Josh—

JOSHUA: Send for the debating team, the great moderator's here—You are a queer who is in love with his own brother and you are apolitical! Every word you write is politics! When you stand in front of an auditorium full of gold-Master-Card-carrying dreadlock-wearing rasta-wanna-be middle-class white kids, you are being political!

WILL: You could have had it too.

JOSHUA: I don't want it—I never wanted it.

WILL: You can still . . . let me help—

JOSHUA: I don't want your money. I make out on my own.

WILL: —in fact, once you find a subject you want to study, your attitude will change, you'll become more involved—start meeting a whole new set of people—

JOSHUA: —I am involved—with it ALL—

WILL: —and your T cells will start responding and—

JOSHUA: I don't want to go back to school. University has made you so STU-PID!!!!

WILL: Then what do you want?

JOSHUA: I want to open a rescue center.

WILL: That takes money. Do you want a hospice or is it just for street kids? Let's do some preliminary budgeting—

JOSHUA: You don't get it you don't get it you—

WILL: Don't look wounded. I love you. You'll always be my brother. But I'm not in love with—

JOSHUA: William. I want to open a rescue center for dogs. A no-kill no-turnaway rescue farm. And find homes for them.

WILL: O like for greyhounds. There's plenty of those places already. Why don't you volunteer—what's that?

JOSHUA: Ah, the great American tradition of volunteerism! So, am I to be a thousand and one points of canine light all by myself? Did you vote for George Bush?

WILL: I don't vote. Is this dead?

JOSHUA: It got too cold. They can't get airborne if they don't warm up.

WILL: A frog will get it. A bird.

JOSHUA: You are a predator.

WILL: Like the movie? Of course. Silly me.

JOSHUA: Exactly like the movie. Camouflaged in the trees. Hiding out in the ivy-covered walls of cheap shit Euro-imitation universities. You're American, Will, stop trying to be high European.

WILL: Do you even have a passport?

JOSHUA: Just what we need! Another well-heeled queer roaming around Paris and Rome, bleeding all over the Acropolis, shacked up in Barcelona to write out the great grief-struck sunsets on the Golden Horn—

WILL: Cape Sounion actually. You should get your facts right. Before you start—

JOSHUA: You and Paul Monette. You and Edmund White. Platinum-card-carrying globetrotters.

WILL: I couldn't be keeping better company. Excuse me that these guys aren't working for Roger Corman. Not scripting *Chopper Chicks in Zombie Town*. How out of touch can I be, forgive me—

JOSHUA: Those guys you interviewed for your book, you slept with? Those guys in the bars? Ohhh . . . but that's okay. It's okay . . . it's all research! Isn't it?

WILL: Scared of dying. Don't be. I'm here for you—

JOSHUA: Ivy Leaguers lusting after blue-collar boys and working-class lads. . . . You'll be writing about noble savages next—

WILL: Those blue-collar boys get plenty out of it. They get to say they fucked a celebrity—

JOSHUA: How very *Geraldo!*

WILL: I've heard a whole posse of men brag how they slept with Tennessee Williams—

JOSHUA: But they're not writing books about it claiming it was a PEAK SPIRITUAL EXPERIENCE! Tantra! Sex and fucking Zen! Christ! Let's all blow the factory boys and claim we're tickling God's right testicle!

WILL: So. Am I on the shelf marked fraud, with all the best, the most accomplished gay writers, all of us grade *f* for fake—

JOSHUA: Best? "One proposal that sounds reasonable to me would be to lower the age of consent to twelve, regardless of the age of the older partner"—

WILL: I never wrote that.

JOSHUA: It's there in your book. In your interview with Edmund White. Why are you giving him a platform?

WILL: I don't censor. I observe. And I'm not about to pass moral judgment on perfectly intelligent and creative human beings just because you want me to—

JOSHUA: You could take a stand. Either way, I don't care! At least have an opinion—

[Butterflies take flight: millions of wings whirring.]

WILL: Omigod! Look at 'em go! Why are they all freaking out like that?

JOSHUA: BUTTERFLY PANIC!

WILL: Isn't nature amazing—

JOSHUA: It's all we've got.

13. JOSHUA ALONE. NIGHT. INDIGO AND ROSE.

JOSHUA:
Dad never wanted to be the self-made man.
Never wanted to own the biggest emporium on Main Street.
Our dad wanted to prowl
the Valley of the Kings
coming across a moment in the sands
a perfect infinite moment
that he alone had uncovered / could give back to the world.
Dad longing
to prise lapis lazuli from the gods
offer his heart / to the god with the head of the wild night dog.

Dad among the camel spit and jackals.

But we're too scared to give ourselves what we need.

Mom giving cash to tent-show preachers
speaking in tongues
raging
mainlining Jesus Christ
when all she's ever wanted is to sing.
Around the house at night
humming to herself / breaking into little arias
when she thinks no one can hear

"What if we all did
just what we wanted?
That would never do"

and he blames her / he blames her

"Why can't your mother
be there for me?
Other men's wives do.
Other men's wives are there
for them."

and I feel like I'm his dad / fathering him.

While you're hiding in the dark
I run to their room / it smells like an open wound
he's cradling her
she's breathing like her lungs are rusty wire
and dad, desperate / terrified—

no wonder you left, no wonder. But how could you?

When life without his true, one love
hurts too much / when Dad dies
my dog and me, we watch, alone.
Silence. And his lips pale blue
as if he's under a blue veil
covered in soft dust.

Do you suppose he knew he was loved?

I'm scared. I see what you're putting out there,
and *you're doing it too.*
Staying apart. Watching. Spying on life.
Sneering a little,
bitching a little.

Do you know you are loved?

14. JOSHUA'S PLACE. EVENING.

WILL: Where'd you go? Where've you been?

JOSHUA: The boardwalk.

WILL: O. I was worried. Busy?

JOSHUA: Nope. Alpine chair ride dangling empty, skeletal roller-coaster. Weirdest
thing, carnivals without people. Ocean like steel. And fog on the water. Like the
movie. The movie? John Carpenter? Think Adrienne Barbeau! "I oughta warn
someone! The fog is comin'! Aiee! The fog is comin'!" Flee! Flee! Ow! Then that
ankle thing happens . . . why do they do that? I've never seen a real woman do

that, have you? Imagine growing up thinking that's all you can do—run for your lives!—Then that ankle thing happens . . . the fog is comin'! So I'm talking to myself, the way you do . . . okay okay, to be honest with you, I was talking to Oprah Winfrey. Do you ever do that? She's so easy to confide in, isn't she? You wouldn't think tens of millions of television viewers were watching. Oprah and me, we're real close. Like that, me an' Oprah. Oh yes. I call her 'Prah. Oh, we're very very close, but I do wish she'd settle. She's big she's small she's big she's small, honey, just pick on a size and settle! You'll be beautiful whatever you choose honey. And oh, oh, don't even get me started on Steadman. So where was I? 'Prah and me, we're discussing this and that and the thing is, 'Prah is so straight-friendly. Oh yes. She has so much time for straight people. And I say, "Well now 'Prah. The thing is, I have nothing against straight people. Oh no! Some of my best friends are straight! I think the man who does my hair is. I mean, shake any family tree, a couple of straights are gonna tumble out. But 'Prah honey . . . well, would you want your daughter marrying one? I mean . . . they move in next door, then another couple move in, soon the whole neighborhood's going straight and then what happens? They go and build a Kmart! It's true! They do! But I have nothing against them . . . in their place. The thing is 'Prah, the thing is . . . I just don't . . . I don't . . . look, I just don't think straight people should be teaching in our schools. There! I've said it! And I don't care!" And then Will, this is amazing, then it was as if . . . well suddenly I was talking to god. Just like . . . snap, there she was!

WILL: What did she look like?

JOSHUA: A rottweiler. With big hair . . . so I asked "Why doesn't it work when I piss in the yard to keep out the raccoons at night?"

WILL: Different acid-alkaline balance.

JOSHUA: God speaks. Hey.

WILL: Oh, get serious.

JOSHUA: "I won't grow up I won't grow up"—call me Peter Pan. Be my Wendy Darling.

WILL: No.

JOSHUA: Nana dog?

WILL: No!

JOSHUA: Wow. Sorry Mom. C'mon be a kid with me.

WILL: You have to grow up. Your resentments are childish.

JOSHUA: No, not if it means being a predator.

WILL: We didn't know what we were doing.

JOSHUA: Of course we didn't. Wasn't it great! Thank god I fucked you and not some over-the-hill novelist.

WILL: Everything's changing for a lot of people, very suddenly, they're coming to terms with something frightening. Tragic. Making contexts—

JOSHUA: I'm your brother.

WILL: The stories need telling.

JOSHUA: What about our story?

WILL: So much loss and sadness and—and bargaining with god—

JOSHUA: You're rattling around the world with your tape recorder and your notebook, a Victorian explorer banging in where he isn't wanted—

WILL: I do, I do love you, don't be so sad, don't be so needy—

JOSHUA: The philosophy you're dredging up has nothing to do with being queer! It's just a pack of selfish old men justifying themselves before they die!

WILL: Bitterness and anger are a waste of time. Poisonous emotions, they'll make you sick—

JOSHUA: DON'T you fucking patronize me, you overeducated condescending asshole—

WILL: I really want to help you. Don't get overwrought, calm now. There are medics in the city—

JOSHUA: I never felt better in my life.

WILL: Great! That's great! Fine. That's good. Okay . . . okay. See, see . . . I'm trying to get . . . look . . . history's being made. I don't want another kid to go through this—what you're going through—

JOSHUA: Oh puh-*leez!* Where are you in your books? These people you talk to . . . what do you feel about Mister Burroughs? Do you ever dream about them? What're your secret dreams about Marianne? Could you? Hmmmm? Would you? Hmmmm . . . ? Bet you could!

WILL: You're turning into a Kmart Walt Whitman knockoff.

JOSHUA: At least I read what you're writing! You should try it sometime. You took the money and ran and left me here in the real world mopping up the mess. You weren't scared of Mom trying to make sense of it all, snorting lines of holy writ, Dad with his pain his his his terror you, you privileged—

WILL: Privilege! I see a soup kitchen on your Main Street Joshua, handing out clothes and food for people with no place else to go, and in the middle of the line there's a bunch of white kids smoking dope, you just know they can call Daddy collect anytime, get another line of credit when they want it—

JOSHUA: Whereas you just waited for him to die.

WILL: See! You want the money, admit it! You want what I have!

JOSHUA: I want you. I just want you to come home.

WILL: Home to what? We didn't have anything.

JOSHUA: Excuse me? We were in love!

WILL: Two brothers diddling with each other in the dark—

JOSHUA: The hell we were! We were two brilliant kids in love—I'd have died rather than give you up and you got scared. Run off to your redbrick university for a course in cerebral detachment, spout Greek love and high culture, blaze off on those vacations in Bangkok and Mykonos, fuck all the natives and head back to the East Coast and write hip essays on high art and low boys—

WILL: Why do you hate me?

JOSHUA: Awww, fuck you, I'm not biting.

WILL: I wanted to see you so bad.

JOSHUA: Gone quick hasn't it?

WILL: What has?

JOSHUA: All these years. See? How quick they go?

WILL: You vomited all over me and my work. Start thinking, brains are for thinking Joshua. Designed for it. Maybe you'd be better off looking after your dogs,
this kind of feeling is toxic, you should get help—

JOSHUA: You're terrified, you're terrified of feelings, you can pull the blinds,
smoke up a fog and huddle over a bottle of whisky thinking great shivery
thoughts. But you'll still be afraid of feeling!

WILL: I feel more passion in one night than you've felt in ten years. I've shared my
heart with men in the most beautiful places on earth—

JOSHUA: Oh yeah, clambering around in the bushes playing Heidi the goat girl!
Oh, my sexual adventurer. You fuck because you're afraid of feeling and you're
afraid of feeling because *you love me! It is having no boundaries that is killing us.*

WILL: Killing you. With envy.

JOSHUA: I'm very much alive thank you. You're the one who sounds dead to me.

> [JOSHUA pushes WILL. Pushes again. WILL lashes out. Slams JOSHUA
> against the wall. Again and again. They fight. Vicious, furious, final. JOSHUA
> falls; WILL pins him to the ground. An exhausted surrender.]

WILL: So. What now?

JOSHUA: I love you and I wanted you to live with me and be my best friend.

WILL: I'm your brother.

JOSHUA: And I want you to sleep with me every night like we used to and pick up
our dream where we left off.

WILL: I don't think I can.

JOSHUA: Maybe not.

> [JOSHUA painfully gets to his feet.]

I'm going to walk my dog. Because I love him. So. Are you coming, or what?

15. THE REDWOODS. LATE AFTERNOON.

JOSHUA: Ty-lerrr! Ty-lerrr! C'mere boy! C'mon! Over here! so old, Will, so old—
Will. First time I walked this path, a deer came across me. A doe. And so silent.
Staring right into me, huge eyes, poised, completely poised and still. Staring. As
close as this. And then and then—Will, this is the odd . . . the strangest . . .
thing, this is weird . . . she teleported.

WILL: No.

JOSHUA: She's staring and and and—then she's not there! Slid into silence so
completely . . . merged.

WILL: It's a backdrop, isn't it?

JOSHUA: This?

WILL: The fallen trees, this this . . . is this moss? This thick? Ferns, the the . . . what is that stuff?

JOSHUA: Sorrel.

WILL: It looks fake. A Disney backdrop.

JOSHUA: A glass painting from *King Kong*.

WILL: Yeah. I want hot popcorn and cold soda. Lookit that! Looks like sea dragons. And what's that?

JOSHUA: Chipmunk.

WILL: Really? It's a little devil.

JOSHUA: And there are horse trails, Will. It's wonderful. Suddenly a beautiful white horse, ridden by the most beautiful man in the world . . . just appears . . . it's a fantasy come true he's come to rescue me at last! "Hi! Where have you been all these years! What kept you!" Come to carry me away . . . scoop me up in his arms . . . carry me away . . . over the hill . . . This is a magic place Will. Some wishes come true before you know you've wished them. Have you noticed . . . your breath has changed? Your breathing, Will. Calm and deep. Because of the trees. Two-thousand-year-old lungs.

WILL: So fucking high. The redwoods. So high.

JOSHUA: You can walk inside them.

WILL: No shit!

JOSHUA: I'll take you inside a tree. Round the next corner. Where a lieutenant made his home when he was making maps for the railroad. He lived inside a tree. In 1846.

WILL: No time at all.

JOSHUA: No time at all.

WILL: I need to talk to you.

JOSHUA: So talk.

WILL: I need you to hear me.

JOSHUA: I'm hearing.

WILL: Really hear. I love you Joshua. I love you so much. I missed you. I dreamed you. I had to find you.

JOSHUA: Tyler. Come here, boy.

WILL: I woke up clutching pillows and cried because it wasn't your face I was holding. I ran next to you in the big fields like we used to. In the old days. It was so real. And I woke and it hurt so much I begged god to send me back into my dream. I stared at strange city skylines and I heard your voice. And I turned I saw you yes YES! I smelled you in the evening and in the middle of the night and and and—

JOSHUA: I nearly died.

WILL: I know. Of course I heard you. I hear you all the time. How do you tell anyone this Josh? . . . How do I . . . you mean everything. I hung around bars and clubs looking for Mister Perfect to show up. The bars close, I'm one of the guys left when the lights are going out. All of us left without partners in the dark, we're looking at one another thinking, he doesn't look so bad. Suddenly he looks . . . okay. And none of them were you. I thought I didn't deserve to fall in love.

JOSHUA: I called you. I closed my eyes. Will I want you Will I need you I need you—

WILL: Josh—

JOSHUA: Will. Where the fuck have you been?

WILL: I'm here.

[Slowly they come together, take one another's hands, embrace, touch, brushing lips and fingers and kiss, deeper and stronger, kissing and licking and. . . . As they make love . . . they begin to howl and bark, the moon rising as they begin to run, padding, lolloping, and . . .]

JOSHUA & WILL: So my four feet pad the long miles under moonlight. The sidewalk the dirt road the dry field, so.

And so my four legs lollop,
great hound that I am!
Among my many names, so—
watcher and wanderer I know myself to be
and WOOF! and WOOF! Now what's this taste this big full earth
between my teeth this taste, maggoty and game
seeking the roots of my tongue?

I trust my tongue
I love this nose / my special nose / wet and black
staring back at me from moonlight pools
sniffing rats and dirt and grass
this gorgeous stink floods my head
splashes the stones I call my skull
the smell is so
very so / its smell is radiance

I dream I dream
my dog dreams of dogness.
I pound past dark warehouses and docks
skimming in dreams of devotion
the days of sticks in full fields
and fish drifting in a lake

and this longing this longing that keeps me running
hounding him down the nights
deep in the roots of my tongue and taste

my man my man
so / my nose to the damp ground
my man my man
stay where you are—I'll find you.

Dirt grass and rats
I'll find you—
the moon so huge
and my heart is squirming

and my man so far away.

[The light finds them huddled in the grass like sleeping puppies.]

JOSHUA: I wanted a cuddle more than anything.

WILL: So did I. Do I. Why's it so quiet?

JOSHUA: Earthquake weather. Hot and still. I want to be cuddled. It comes from nearly dying—it's all gravy. It is all a fucking miracle, every moment, and most of what we do to fill the silence isn't really important. You have to smile at the server in the diner. Make small talk with the boy at the checkout.

WILL: And that's your final word on it all?

JOSHUA: That's what it all comes down to . . . Paul Monette is a wonderful writer, I think.

WILL: So why do you hate him so much?

JOSHUA: Where's the dog? Where's—Tyler? Tyler!—Oh. There. I wonder what he thought we were doing. I remember once . . . you were about sixteen, seventeen, and you came running home from the record store and your eyes were shining and you said "Josh, hey Josh you gotta listen, listen to this!" and you played me "Sister Morphine." Marianne Faithfull. And you said "Listen—not exactly Maria Callas! But listen to the feeling! The feeling!" You were so alive—

WILL: You still haven't answered my question.

JOSHUA: Why do I hate the sultry groves of academe? Because . . . I can't compete. With them. For you. If you were a baseball legend or a prizefighter I'd hate the team, the coach, the referee, the stadium the ring the ropes in which you were magnificent. If you were a salesman I'd hate the vacuums and the microwaves. But, but you see, I don't hate them, I . . .

WILL: Yes. You need to understand something. I'm not sure I can tell it right—

JOSHUA: Are you going to start crooning "The Wind Beneath My Wings"?

WILL: And why not?

JOSHUA: Because I'll slap you if you do.

WILL: I envied you then what I envy you now . . . your . . . wholeheartedness. You still love horror movies, the best people like horror pictures, the best people carry toys in their luggage.

JOSHUA: Oh yeah! My bear's gonna be buried with me.

WILL: You know how to take a walk in the woods. You get the wow-ness of things. I lost it. I don't think I ever found it. And I always believed that if you were in love with me, then you didn't have very good taste.

JOSHUA: Mm. Okay. I became ill quite rapidly. As if I'd been running with open arms to meet . . . whatever comes next. Then I got well again, up and down . . . have you any idea how much effort I put into keeping Dad's business going, as if I had to . . . so you could always depend on me if you needed to? . . . Then suddenly it was all too much. Bankrupt. And I walked away from the chaos and lo! I haven't been ill . . . not since.

WILL: What will you—what should I do when you—

JOSHUA: Miss me like crazy. You have to go.

WILL: No.

JOSHUA: You have to. We're part of the same problem. I need rescuing. You can't rescue me. You're part of the problem I need rescuing from—

WILL: From which I need rescuing.

JOSHUA: From. Which. I. Need. Rescuing. See? We keep making the same mistakes, over and over, expecting a different result every time . . . and that's insanity. You can't be Mister Blue Jeans at the gas station—I'm not going to die without you.

WILL: I know.

JOSHUA: It'll be so lonely.

WILL: You and your needy dogs. Wagging their tails when they see you.

JOSHUA: Write about me. Please. You must write about you and me. We don't have long lives, and people matter. Tell them. Put it down in your book.

WILL: I'll tell the world how angry you are.

JOSHUA: I'm not angry. I'm frustrated. It's so simple. You gotta get real, big brother. And it'll take that pain away—and you'll live long and happily. I promise.

WILL: I'll be okay.

JOSHUA: Get real. Can't live by codes and passwords. It'll be wonderful. It'll feel like you feel when you stroke a dog.

WILL: That good?

JOSHUA: It'll feel like you feel when you stroke a dog!

[*They tumble and play. Like kids. Like puppies. And gradually WILL fades, merges into the shadows of the forest. JOSHUA stands alone in the radiant dusk and . . .*]

16. JOSHUA ALONE.

JOSHUA: When Will and me, when we're eight nine ten years old, in the car on Sundays—rides in the country. Looking for forests and lakes . . . Well, here we are being a family.

One day riding through the suburbs
headed for the green places in the country / white fences
and gardens, nectarine and walnut trees
and lakes where kids play sailboats
splash their brothers in creeks
and boys run with their dogs
one house stays in my mind / I know it will always stay
in my mind—

I see this thing I will never forget.
A white wooden house. A one-story wood frame
with sky blue trim at the windows.
And a young man leaning in the doorway.

A Sunday moment: his family have been visiting
Mom and Dad right there getting in their car,
a beat-up old Buick, waving g'bye g'bye
and a dog running round the yard
a dog!
And the young man is perfect. He is a perfect moment.
A frayed old shirt / worn old jeans.
And I want to yell: hey mister
rescue me
from the small space between these people
who say they're my mom and dad / the space
between the candy and the seltzer water
the apples in bags for the ride.
I wanna stay with you and your dog
and the door and the yard
please.

And he doesn't see me / the guy in the door / but I've
seen him. And I'll never know who he is
or who he may become and is he happy in his life,
and he doesn't know and never will
that I was close and whispered please / yes please
a dog a yard a home
and we all have been seen
all of us
by sad young kids in passing cars and buses
and each one of us
sometime somewhere
has made someone who is sad and small

look twice and say yes please
that's someone I could want and love
and be.
Yes.

Please.

We've all meant something wonderful
to someone we have never ever met.

Dark Fruit

EDITOR'S INTRODUCTION

THE NEXT THREE WORKS in this collection—*Dark Fruit, Porcelain,* and *Men on the Verge of a His-panic Breakdown*—focus on the relationship of race and ethnicity to gayness from the point of view of three multitalented African-American writer-performers, a Singapore-born playwright-filmmaker, and a Chilean-born playwright, all based on the West Coast. The work of Pomo Afro Homos, Chay Yew, and Guillermo Reyes dramatizes and challenges the fragmentation contemporary society—gay and straight—suffers. These works also show the ways in which those who experience rejection and hostility repress, misdirect, and express their anger.

Dark Fruit, Porcelain, and *Men on the Verge of a His-panic Breakdown* raise crucial questions for gay people everywhere. How do racism and homophobia intersect and conflict? How are they internalized? How can they be fought? Is the old American dream of assimilation possible?

Pomo Afro Homos is an abbreviation of Postmodern African-American Homosexuals, a performance group that in a matter of a few years has established itself as the most eloquent theatrical voice for the gay African-American male. Pomo Afro Homos has performed in clubs, at gay conferences, in theaters and university auditoriums, in London, and—the ultimate high, I am sure—on *Oprah.* Since the group's audiences are primarily gay and often predominantly white, their performances speak to the racism in the gay community as strongly as they speak to the homophobia in the African-American community.

Dark Fruit is the second major collaboration of Pomo Afro Homos. The multitalented Brian Freeman and Djola Bernard Branner were involved with the production of Marlon Riggs's powerful video *Tongues United* (Freeman as executive producer, Branner as a performer). The film inspired the formation of Pomo Afro Homos, which made its debut at Josie's Cabaret and Juice Joint in the Castro District of San Francisco in January 1991. Their first show, *Fierce Love,* was performed all over the United States and at the Drill Hall, the center for queer performance in London. *Dark Fruit* has played Lincoln Center as well as smaller venues all over the United States.

The eight skits that make up *Dark Fruit* offer a strong sample of the team's writing. "Aunties in America: Epiphanies 'n Roaches" satirizes the place of the black man in contemporary gay drama. The sketch is not only hilariously on target but also vividly demonstrates the need for the kind of theater Pomo Afro Homos offers—theater that does not stereotype or objectify, that presents the gay African-American male from inside. "Aunties in America" is one of a number of skits that target the racism within even the most articulate and politically correct spokespersons for the gay community. In subsequent sketches the team shows us a lecture by a white psychologist who asserts that "the cause of homosexual justice is doing more for the advancement of the Negro cause than any other social movement" but unwittingly presents as evidence a dramatization of the racism that cripples the possibility of black-white relationships. Another sketch describes a supposedly integrated gay bar where blacks gather together in a symbolic back of the bus near the ice machine and the bathrooms.

The group also sets its sights on the internalized racism and homophobia among African-American gay men. "Tasty" gives us a successful black man who tells a sex partner, "I could never *be* with a Black man, you know. But every once in awhile I need a little taste." The group attacks black men for being closeted, for not marching together or sleeping together, but it also shows the virulent homophobia that makes African-American men hide. In the letters that end *Dark Fruit*, the group asserts, "We need the love and support of our own community / We need *our* voices to be heard."

Community could read "communities." Brian Freeman has said, "It's very difficult to be out within the black community exclusively, and it's very difficult to be black within the larger white gay community. We are only just beginning to sense ourselves as our own community, one that intersects with both the black community and the larger white gay community. The idea that you have to choose between being black and being gay is ludicrous."[1] As black gay men, the members of Pomo Afro Homos call for the love and support of fellow African Americans and fellow gays. Both communities need to heed their voices, which are too often ignored or silenced. In "Doin' Alright," Brian Freeman tells of the minister's eulogy at the funeral of a black drag queen who was the victim of a gay-bashing: "Minister said he died from being in the wrong place at the wrong time, but when you're poor, black, effeminate, and gay, life is wrong place, wrong time." There are a myriad of social ills contained in this sentence, but the most poignant is the indifference of our narrator as a young man: "Between black-boy bonding and dark diva disco dancing I never did catch Miss Thing's last name." Eventually he will engage in an activism that embraces the Miss Things of this world, the impoverished drag queens who are doubly marginal even in the gay community.

Dark Fruit is justifiably an angry script, but, as in all good theater, the anger is controlled and leavened by moments of humor and pathos. The scenes progress gradually from hilarious satire to anger and a call for activism. Even the music moves effectively from Liza Minnelli singing the old blackface hit "Mammy" in the first sketch to Tina Turner wailing, "We Don't Need Another Hero" at the final curtain. Last but far from least, the writing of the three team members is intensely personal even while functioning as social commentary.

Notes

1. Quoted in Stephen Holden, "In the Margins of 2 Minorities: A Double Fringe," *New York Times,* July 23, 1993, p. C15.

Clockwise from left: Eric Gupton, Brian Freeman, Djola B. Branner

Jill Posener Photographs

PRODUCTION HISTORY AND RIGHTS

Dark Fruit was written and performed by Pomo Afro Homos. The production was directed by Susan Finque, with costumes by Eugene "Yo" Rodriguez.

"Aunties in America: Epiphanies 'n Roaches" was written by Brian Freeman and performed by Brian Freeman, Djola B. Branner, and Marvin K. White.

"Last Rights" was written and performed by Marvin K. White.

"Black & Gay: A Psycho-Sex Study" was written by Brian Freeman and performed by the group.

"Sweet Sadie" was written and performed by Djola B. Branner.

"Doin' Alright" was written and performed by Brian Freeman.

"Tasty" was written by Eric Gupton and Brian Freeman and performed by Marvin K. White.

"Chocolate City, USA" was written by Brian Freeman ("Non, Je Ne Regrette Rien" by Dave Frechette, from *Brother to Brother: New Writings by Black Gay Men*) and performed by the group.

Dark Fruit

Aunties in America:
Epiphanies 'n Roaches!

[The theme from Jaws *plays in the background. Two characters are seated at a small table stage right on which there are a cake and a tea set. They watch the third character, BELIZE, as he acts out the finale of* Angels in America: Millennium Approaches *stage left. Lighting at this point is silhouette, with heavenly beams, much smoke. The VOICE is performed by the other two characters on a mike at the table, with a disembodied quality.]*

VOICE: *[Heavenly]* Prior Walter!

BELIZE: *[He rolls around as if in torment.]* Leave me alone! Just let me sleep!

VOICE: *[Dreamily]* Prior Walter!

BELIZE: Don't come in here!

VOICE: *["Black Girl"]* Prior Walter!

BELIZE: That sound, that sound, it . . . What is that? I'm frightened. Something's coming in here; something's approaching! What is it?

[He screams, then breaks character. Smoke clears, music out, lights bump to a general wash. JACOB and PAUL applaud.]

JACOB: Serve, Belize, serve.

BELIZE: She gives you much drama.

PAUL: So when does this angel get to America?

BELIZE: Right then, honeybabychiles. The *last* Miss Ann Angel: white dress, white wings, white halo, white attitude, white everything—look like a flying igloo— Miss Thing comes crashing through the ceiling.

PAUL: Through the ceiling?

BELIZE: If I'm lying, I'm dying.

JACOB: She can't use the front door?

BELIZE: You know white folks. Then everywhere you look feathers, plaster, epiphanies, and roaches.

PAUL: Now who's got to clean all that up?

[BELIZE just looks at PAUL.]

ALL: Well . . .

JACOB: Paul, Belize, try this cake Miss Raj sent over. She just *peed* in the frosting.

[They start to take a bite, then defer.]

BELIZE: Jacob, I heard Miss Raj hasn't been feeling well lately. I know she's fed up being on the high school circuit.

JACOB: She's fine. The tea is who she was feeling at Keller's last night.

PAUL: Was she out with George?

JACOB: George out? Girl, you know that tea.

[All three mime doors closing and locking. Then they throw away the key.]

PAUL: Belize, I know what you mean about them trying to find their epiphanies thru us. You see, Missy Guare has me up there with all these Upper East Side most worrisome white folks, processing all their yap-de-yap get-a-clue-already angst. Then I have to feed 'em. Then I have to fuck 'em.

JACOB & BELIZE: Yuk.

PAUL: Like some kind of Hattie MacDaniels meets Mandingo biotech fruit. Where is *my* epiphany in that?

JACOB: Six degrees of segregation!

PAUL: Do I look like an anecdote to dine out on to you?

BELIZE: At Denny's. I know girl, 'cause Missy Kushner has me up there every night reading these white kids' asses or wiping their butts. It's all the same to me. In part two I get to wipe Roy Cohn's butt. Find an epiphany in that! Mo' tea?

PAUL: If you don't mind. Jacob, how's *La Cage* treating you?

JACOB: At least they pretend there's epiphanies in there for you. I'm so over Missy Fierstein putting me through Butterfly French Maid McQueen eight times a week. I can live with the eye bugging and noble caretaker nonsense. But, children, it hurts my pride so bad, night after night, to put on heels and have to walk like the last Steppin' Jungle Bunny Fetchit! *[She has a fit of hysteria.]*

PAUL: *[Calming JACOB down]* We know, girl. We know 'cause it ain't even a question that a black drag queen in her first pair of heels can out sashay/chante Naomi, Cindy, and Claudia—

PAUL & BELIZE: No training wheels required!

JACOB: Well, at least we have each other.

PAUL: Which you would never know—out there.

[They all glare straight out.]

BELIZE: But what we gonna do? Quit?

[They all laugh an over-the-top laugh.]

JACOB: Children, it's half hour.

[They start packing up and tie their napkins on their heads mammie style.]

PAUL: It's been real. Where you at these days?
BELIZE: Forty-eighth and Broadway. Like *Cats* girl. Now and forever. Yourself?
PAUL: Home video. And Will Smith don't even kiss.
BELIZE: Pitiful.
PAUL: Child?
JACOB: Dinner theater.
BELIZE AND PAUL: Scared of that!

[Their napkins become headrags. Liza Minnelli's "Mammy" plays, a short dance. They smile at the audience, and the smiles become a minstrel grimace. They pull the rags off their heads, drop them in defiance. Blackout.]

Last Rights

[MARVIN enters solemnly as a slow gospel piano hymn plays. He strikes three high-grief poses. Then music fades.]

MARVIN:
    When I learned of Gregory's death
    I cried silently
    But at the funeral
    Giiiirl, I'm telling you
    I rocked Miss Church
    Hell, I fell to my knees twice
    Before I reached my seat
    Three people had to carry me
    To my pew
    I swayed and swooned
    Blew my nose
    On any and every available sleeve
    The snot was flying everywhere
    Then when I finally saw his body
    My body jerked itself
    Right inside that casket
    And when I placed my lips on his
    Honey, the place was shaking

I returned to my seat
But not before passing by his mother
Who I'm sure at this point
Was through with me
I threw myself on her knees
Shouting, "Help me
Help me, Jesus"
When someone in the choir
Sang out, "Work it, girl
Wooooork it"
All hell broke loose
I was carried out
Kicking and screaming
Ushered into the waiting limo
Which sped me to his family's house
Where I feasted
On fried chicken
Hot-water cornbread
Macaroni and cheese
Johnny Walker Black
Finally in my rightful place

[We hear Sylvester wail as lights fade.]

Black & Gay: A Psycho-sex Study

[A SCIENTIST in a lab coat and glasses enters.]

SCIENTIST: Good evening. I'm Victor Dodson, certified psycho-sexologist, and author of *Black & Gay: A Psycho-sex Study,* available in fine bookstores everywhere. The following blunt response came from one of many Negro males interviewed for the purposes of this study.

[Special up on STREET DUDE in early 1960s attire. He speaks directly to the audience and is extremely combative.]

STREET DUDE: I like to suck cock. What's wrong with that? I don't want nobody trying to "psych" me either 'cause I just don't dig that mind-probin' stuff. I'm black. I'm queer as a three dollar bill. I like to suck guys and get sucked by them. And, incidentally, I like white guys, not black ones. I don't dig dark meat. I'm just partial to white. I guess you might call me a nigger who don't like niggers. *[He laughs.]*

SCIENTIST: Thank you.

[STREET DUDE exits after getting a dollar tip from SCIENTIST. He continues with his slide/talk.]

Our research indicates that the majority of Negro homosexual males seem to prefer sexual relations with Caucasians rather than members of their own race. Furthermore, many white homosexual males very often prefer their sex partners to be Negroid. Naturally, this was not applicable to 100 percent of the cases interviewed. Like any society, it was found that racism exists in the world of homosexuality. Shocking, I know. In view of the fact that society frowns upon homosexuality and discriminates against the Negro, one might assume that the Negro homosexual labors under a double handicap. This has been found *not* to be the case. The Negro homosexual seems to adjust comfortably to homosexual society. He does not feel tied to the ghetto or bound by the generations of ancestral masochism which have played such an important part in his history. He finds a warm and welcome place in the various homosexual haunts. He has no fears of being refused service in a homosexual bar; he is not classified as an inferior when socializing with the Caucasian homosexual. Even a Caucasian heterosexual like myself will accept the Negro on more or less of an even plane if the Negro is homosexual and works at one of the "categorized" homosexual trades: hairdresser, ballet dancer, or interior decorator. When the Negro is occupied by one of these professions, he is generally discriminated against because he is homosexual and, paradoxically, not because he is Negro.

Negro homosexual males have been in evidence since the beginning of history. Accounts of African rituals explicitly describe homosexual relationships as part of the social makeup of many of the tribes. The phony humanism and morality characteristic of Western civilization are alien and obscene to the African mind. The unvarnished Negro, whose ancestors patterned their erotic customs after those observed in the animal kingdom, sees nothing controversial in the sexual act, either heterosexual or homosexual.

The homosexual, both white and black, lives his life outside the perimeter of polite society. This "twilight" society is dawning more brightly with each passing year, and with its dawning is coming the acceptance of the Negro as an equal. The cause of homosexual justice is doing more for the advancement of the Negro cause than any other social movement. Tolerance seems to be the key that creates the common denominator between the white and black homosexual. Tolerance can be taught and it is easily learned. Integration of schools has been a giant step of progress. For if it is not through intelligence and education, then it will be through sex that equality of the races is achieved.

To illustrate this point, we present the following dramatization of an actual case history. The names have been fictionalized for the protection of all concerned.

[The SCIENTIST exits. Scene shifts to a high school classroom. A sex education class is in progress. Slide of male sex anatomy is on the screen. A young black

teenager, CLIFF, sits in a chair watching the presentation. A teacher, MISS EMORY, continues her lecture, as if in progress.]

MISS EMORY: In men who are uncircumcised there is an unpleasant substance which forms between the penis and the foreskin if it is not washed every day. It is called "smegma" and has an objectionable odor. In men with an unusually long penis who have not been circumcised this warm, moist area under the foreskin can become a breeding ground for germs.

[In the middle of class a young white student, PAUL, enters and sits behind the black student, teasing him relentlessly throughout the lecture.]

MISS EMORY: Lights!

[The lights come on. Slide goes out.]

Students, please find the time to discuss what you have just seen with your parents in the privacy of your own home. We'll have a quiz next week. Class dismissed.

[PAUL bolts from the room. CLIFF gathers his books to go but is stopped by MISS EMORY.]

MISS EMORY: Cliff, I'd like to have a word with you.
CLIFF: Yes, Miss Emory.
MISS EMORY: Cliff, I'm concerned about you. Last semester you were such a good little student. Attentive. Diligent. Always ready with an answer and a smile.
CLIFF: Yes, Miss Emory. . . .
MISS EMORY: A real role model to all that riffraff they bused in here. The entire faculty hopes you'll be the first one of your people this high school sends to college. And if your grades hold up, I plan to recommend you for the state's Booker T. Washington Scholarship. But this term, Cliff, you seem distant. Distracted. Are there problems at home?
CLIFF: Everything is fine, ma'am, fine.
MISS EMORY: Cliff, a white woman like myself has never been to Shantytown, of course, but I watch television, and I have a good idea what it's like. All those single-parent households. Your mother, does she drink too much? Do you get a balanced diet? All those fried foods can't be good for you! Tell me, Cliff. You can trust me.
CLIFF: My family is okay, Miss Emory. I'm just a little tired lately. Guess I stay up too late hitting the books.
MISS EMORY: *[Rubbing his head]* Cliff, it's boys like you who will overcome, someday. I want you to know, if you ever need someone to share with—I'm here for you. *[She exits.]*

[PAUL returns. Very all American.]

PAUL: Cliff? Cliff. You and Sharnelle going to the big game tonight?

CLIFF: You're putting me on, Paul. We're lucky to be sitting in the same classroom with you.

PAUL: Who's going to stop you?

CLIFF: This school hasn't been integrated long enough to get folks used to the idea of black boys and girls together with white boys and girls. We're not safe out of our own neighborhood at night, and you know it!

PAUL: Come to the game with me and Muffy. They wouldn't dare lay a finger on you. You know who my old man is.

CLIFF: I don't want to talk about fathers.

PAUL: You know, Cliff, you've never said much about your family—

CLIFF: I hate my father! I hate him! He was no damn good. He spent all his money and all Mama's, too, on drinkin' and other women. Then he went off to Chicago. Mama just about killed herself after he left. That was five years ago. That's why I've got to be a doctor, to make my mama proud. I want to help people when they need help. Mama needed help and there wasn't no one.

PAUL: I'm sorry, Cliff. I know it's hard, but give yourself a break. We'll pick you up at 7:00.

CLIFF: You drive into Shantytown in that new convertible of yours and you'll get ripped off! My people aren't welcome on your side of town, and Uncle Charlie's not welcome on our side. That's the way it is, and that's the way it's going to stay for a long time yet.

PAUL: I was just trying to be friendly.

CLIFF: It ain't much use to be friends with someone who ain't the same color. It just don't pay in the end.

PAUL: But how can we change the world, Cliff, if we don't start right here at Walt Whitman High? Let's skip the game and leave the girls at home. I think you and me should take a walk along the river and just talk. Man to man. How's that for a night on the town?

CLIFF: I'd like that, Paul. I'd like it very much.

PAUL: Good. See you at 7:00.

[Another student, black, enters in time to see PAUL slap CLIFF on the butt, then exit. The other student stares at CLIFF, then smirks as CLIFF exits. He makes faggot gesture after CLIFF is gone, then falls to floor laughing. SCIENTIST enters.]

SCIENTIST: Thank you.

[The student leaves, and the SCIENTIST continues his slide/talk.]

Sometimes we are aware in advance that certain acts will take place through some premonition or perhaps because we desire them and are actively seeking to make them occur. If an individual decides in advance that he wants to have sexual relations with a member of another race, and sets out to find such a member, the overt actions are reasonably explicable, but we must always bear in mind the subconscious motives.

THE WOODS

[CLIFF enters in a long coat, scarf, winter hat, gloves. Sounds of crickets. Lighting looks like a forest. It is cold out. He looks around for PAUL, checks his watch, etc. PAUL enters breathless, running late, very anxious.]

PAUL: Hey.

CLIFF: Hey.

PAUL: Glad you made it.

CLIFF: I should be home studying. Mama's gonna get worried.

PAUL: She'll be alright.

CLIFF: So what did you want to talk about?

PAUL: I dunno. What did you want to talk about?

CLIFF: I dunno.

[Silence]

CLIFF: I should get back.

PAUL: Have you and Sharnelle ever done it?

CLIFF: Sharnelle's no tramp! Sharnelle wants to be a nurse. Sharnelle wants to make her mama proud. I want to be a doctor!

PAUL: I've never done it with a girl either.

CLIFF: But you and Muffy are all over each other like white on rice.

PAUL: It's just a show to keep our parents happy. I don't know how to say this, Cliff, but ever since that first day when I saw you step off the bus from Shantytown, I've felt a special closeness to you. The other white kids called you names that day, but not me, Cliff, not me! The only name I've ever wanted to call you is . . . friend.

CLIFF: Paul . . . I don't know what to say.

[PAUL takes off his glove and extends his hand to CLIFF. CLIFF takes off his glove and slowly goes to offer his hand. They shake, then they laugh, then they embrace. They laugh again with their arms around each other. PAUL's hands fall to CLIFF's butt.]

CLIFF: No, Paul, please don't!

PAUL: Why?

CLIFF: It's all wrong.

PAUL: Look, I don't understand too much about this, but I jack off every night thinking about you.

[CLIFF runs away. PAUL runs after him.]

PAUL: When Miss Emory rearranged the seating and assigned you next to me, I thought I'd blow my nuts. I've always known I was a budding queer, but I never knew I'd get so hung up on a dark boy. But that's what happened, and I decided to do something about it. I'm a real greenhorn when it comes to having sex with anyone, except myself, of course, but at least I know what I want. Maybe afterwards I won't like myself very much . . . or even like you, but that's a chance we have to take. How about it?

[*PAUL tries to undress CLIFF. CLIFF tries to stop him.*]

CLIFF: This is so fast, Paul. Guys shouldn't be doing these kinds of things.
PAUL: I hear it's healthy—
CLIFF: We're from opposite sides of the tracks.
PAUL: I have a car—
CLIFF: What if your father found out?
PAUL: He's a Methodist—
CLIFF: Or my mother?
PAUL: She's a Democrat—
CLIFF: I want to go to med school, Paul. I want to be a doctor!
PAUL: Shut up!

[*He kisses CLIFF full on the mouth. The two of them pull apart in shock, then start throwing off their clothes.*]

PAUL: Yeah, baby, you want it. Let me see that licorice stick. I've got some white lightning for you here. Come on!

[*Just when their pants fall around their ankles, MISS EMORY enters in a winter coat. She is birdwatching. She sees the two entangled like dogs and is shocked.*]

MISS EMORY: Oh, my god! What are you boys doing there? Stop that! Stop it at once! Pull your pants up. Put those things away.

[*They pull their pants up and run in opposite directions.*]

PAUL: Miss Emory, I can explain.
CLIFF: Please, Miss Emory, don't tell my mama; it would kill her.
MISS EMORY: [*To CLIFF*] Be quiet! [*To PAUL*] Paul, Paul, Paul, Paul, Paul. You are from a good white family, and I realize that you, like many of us, have often been confused by this integration madness. You be in my office tomorrow morning at 8 A.M., and I won't say a word to your father.
PAUL: Yes, Miss Emory.
MISS EMORY: Go!

[*She waits for him to leave. He runs by CLIFF, grabs his own clothes, and hides upstage. When MISS EMORY thinks he is gone, she continues.*]

MISS EMORY: But you, Cliff. You are such a disappointment to me. They can take you out of Shantytown, but they can't take Shantytown out of you. Trying to corrupt a good white boy like Paul with your perverted ways. I thought you were different, Cliff. I don't see how I could recommend you for the Booker T. Washington Scholarship after this. It will break my heart to tell your mother.

CLIFF: No! *[He falls to his knees crying.]*

MISS EMORY: A mind is a terrible thing to waste. *[She exits.]*

[CLIFF lies on the floor, crying. PAUL runs to comfort him.]

PAUL: Don't, Cliff, please. We'll figure something out.

CLIFF: I guess I've just been an experiment to you, haven't I?

PAUL: An experiment? What do you mean?

CLIFF: You just wanted to see what it was like with a black boy, didn't you?

PAUL: It's late, Cliff. We'll talk it over tomorrow.

CLIFF: No. We won't! We won't talk it over tomorrow, or the next day, or the day after that! How can I ride the bus with the other kids? Who'd sit next to the high school homo?

PAUL: Cliff, let me drive you home.

CLIFF: Get away from me! Uncle Charlie and his children never change. I trusted you and you used me. I'm leaving town tonight if I have to hitchhike out of here.

PAUL: Don't, Cliff! I love you. Cliff. I love you.

CLIFF: Love? You can't fall in love with a guy. Get away from me. Go away! Just leave me alone!

[He chases PAUL away. CLIFF assembles his clothes and starts to cry.]

Oh, Mama. I'm sorry, Mama. I just wanted to be a doctor!!

[SCIENTIST enters.]

SCIENTIST: Thank you.

[CLIFF bows and exits.]

Despite the sad, yet logical outcome of this story, here we have a fine example of the seeds of tolerance being planted. Some questions, though. Did Paul's warm, generous, unselfish overtures of friendship bring out Cliff's hidden feelings of distrust for white people? Was Cliff actually using Paul to explore these feelings? I think so.

That small town never saw Cliff Wood again. His mother searched, but she never found a trace of him. Rumors spread that he made his way north and quickly lost himself in the homosexual jungle they call New York City. I'm Victor Dodson, certified psycho-sexologist. Good evening.

[Lights fade. Final slide appears on the screen. Michael Jackson's "Black & White" plays.]

Sweet Sadie

[Lights come up as DJOLA pats his lap. Sound of hospital. He is sitting on a step unit.]

DJOLA: *[As Mother]* What? I don't know about that. That child put that red wig on his head. Ha. Ha. What? I don't know about that. Dropped dead. Yes, she did. Stroke, they told me. Just dropped dead. What? Ha, ha. *[She takes off one shoe and sings "Amazing Grace."]*

[As DJOLA] Mother, put you shoes on your feet.

It amazes me that she can no longer distinguish between a soup spoon and a soap dish but can sing a gospel at the drop of a hat. I mean, throw her head back, eyes lifted to Jesus and sing the entire song. And then just smile.

People say I have inherited my mother's smile. See the resemblance? And this makes perfect sense since I've inherited her inability to cry. Well, I'm sure she *can* cry. I've just never seen her do it. The lyrics to that old Spinners song come to mind. *[Singing]* "Sweeter than cotton candy/stronger than Papa's old brandy/once in awhile she would break down and cry/Oh, Sadie/don't you know we love you, Sweet Sadie?"

The closest I came to seeing her cry was that hot afternoon in August right after the Watts riots broke.

[Sound of riot.]

We lived only one mile from Will Rogers Park, where everything was on fire. The air was thick with the smell of burning markets, liquor stores, and Mama's homemade enchiladas. It was hot, hot, hot, and we were all just sitting around watching the news and waiting. That was when the phone rang. We just knew someone we loved had been caught in the crossfire. Mama picked up the receiver, and the rest of us watched the quiet sigh in her shoulders as she listened. She hung up the phone, said quite matter of factly that *her* mother had died of a stroke, and excused herself to the bathroom.

It was years later that I discovered that Mama had not been relieving her bladder, as I suspected, but that she had been crying, actually crying.

[Sound of playground]

[As Child] You must be crazy! Hopscotch ain't no girls' game. Big old watermelon head. My head! Your head got more knots in it than a russet potato. Head look like a big old lopsided bean bag chair somebody sat in watching the late, late, late show. My head? My head? Yo . . . your mama!

[As DJOLA] I have seen lips turned to pulp and eyes popped from sockets over somebody's mama. There is one thing you learn quickly growing up in South-Central L.A. Don't let your mouth write no checks your ass can't cover, especially when it comes to somebody's mama.

[*Scrubbing floor and wiping brow*] You see it was Mama who wrapped her head each and every morning and drove ten miles in the cold to labor forty, no fifty, hours a week on that assembly line. Mama who went without a new winter coat, a new dress, a new headrag to put clothes on your back, food on the table, and the roof above you. It was Mama. Always Mama . . .

Some twenty years before I was born, she birthed and raised three children. Two boys and a girl. So that by the age of forty she figured that childrearing was pretty much behind her. Then at forty-two she had me. "The accident."

[*As Mother*] What? You got an *A* on your spelling test. That's nice, baby. What? What?! Why don't you go outside and play, boy! Cooped up in this house all day with that TV. What you doing? Drawing? Always drawing something. Sitting up in here like some old man. Ha, ha. Poor thing. Ain't got no friends. Why don't you go play on the freeway?

[*As DJOLA*] We changed apartments like most people changed drawers, which meant I attended nine elementary schools in the L.A. City School District. I made friends fast and didn't expect to know them long. Besides, solitude wasn't a bad companion. I locked the door behind me each morning and unlocked it every afternoon. And since I wasn't allowed out of the house until she came in, my best friend was really the TV.

[*Sound of BEWITCHED*]

[*Eating potato chips as a child*] As fat as I am, she hardly knows I'm here. I fry my own eggs in the morning, wash my own dishes, iron my own clothes, shine my own shoes. Can dust, mop, wax floors, windows, and tile. Can even on a good day forge her signature on a progress report. I have my books, my crayons, and, when she's not looking, her fingernail polish. Eventually I won't have to ask her for anything.

[*As Mother*] If you didn't eat so damned much, I wouldn't be so hard-pressed to find you pants. Always got to traipse all over the department store to the husky section, bring the pants home, hem them up or tailor them down. Never can catch a sale at J.C. Penney like other people. Always thinking of yourself. Drive me fucking crazy!

[*As DJOLA*] Born and raised on a farm in Oklahoma, she was from the old school. And like all the adults who surrounded me as a child, Mama was addressed in a certain way. A certain tone of voice was tolerated. It amazes me to this day that a former white lover of mine referred even jokingly to his mother as a bitch, to her face, and lived to tell about it. I shudder to think what might have become of my . . . adulthood had I ever pranced into my mother's house and said, "Hey, Bitch!"

My parents divorced when I was five, and though I saw my father on weekends and holidays, Mama was the primary parent. The relationship between a single mom and a son is often precarious. Still, I had no reason to suspect that ours was unusual.

[*Sound of "The Thrill Is Gone"*]

[As Mother] Hand me a towel, would you, baby? What you think? The black dress or the blue one? What? The green one? Well, you do have an eye for color. My, my, my. Hand Mommie that black bra, would you? What would I do without you? You daddy didn't do much right, but at least I got you in the bargain. You are Mama's little man. Yes, you are. Is my strap showing? Tuck it in for me, baby. Now. My other man will be here in a minute. How do I look? Come on and dance with Mama. *[She dances.]*

[As DJOLA] Don't all little boys zip their mommies up? Fold their mommies' panties? Hand them a towel as they step out of the tub?

We talked only once about sex. The summer after college graduation when I told Mama that I was gay. And I must say, she received the news as graciously as the throat receives a cup of scalding water.

[As Mother] What in the world possessed you to become gay? Don't you know a woman is soft and tender? You're gonna miss having a wife and child. Haven't you ever done it with a girl?

[As DJOLA] I've heard that mothers generally suspect that a child is gay. A tilt in the head, a lilt in the stride, a twinkle in the eye. *Something* gives it away. Mama claimed there had been no signs along the way. Perhaps. The Alzheimer's had washed so many memories out to sea. Still, I remember fixing one of her tacky wigs on my head, rolling her ruby red lipstick over my lips in preparation for a Halloween party, and hearing as clear as the sound of silver striking crystal the voices of my mother and her younger boyfriend.

[As Boyfriend] What's wrong with that boy dressing up like a girl?

[As Mother] Oh, he's gonna be a punk when he grows up. *[She exits the stage and walks into the audience, laughing.]*

[Ranting and raving as the *universal black mother]* You are one selfish and un-grateful man. How could you even think of saying those things about your mama? If I wasn't a Christian woman, I would say things that I would regret in the morning. Have mercy! Blasphemy! That's what it is! She is the one who pushed you from her womb, and you know she did the very best she could. You even changed the name she gave you. What the hell is a Djola?

[As DJOLA] Make no mistake. I have wrestled with these voices, too. Black mothers of the world are guarding the pedestal, and the first step down is long and hard.

I believed for some time that I didn't love her. This woman who tossed me onto the earth to fend for myself. Who never said, "I love you."

I'm sure you would be terribly surprised to find that I have overcome my shy-ness and have lots of friends. Or that I'm shaped like a willow tree. That I have in fact strutted across the stage of an off-Broadway theater wearing a wig as tacky as the ones you used to wear. You've never heard me sing. You've never seen me dance. We've never talked about Baldwin or shared a sunset. You were forty-two; then you were seventy-six. Living in a nursing home with Alzheimer's. What happened?

[Sound of hospital]

You make nonsense phrases. I nod and remember trying to speak to you on Saturdays when you wanted only to pick the daily double. I hold your hand and recall how you stared at my penis upon bursting unannounced into my bedroom. I put food in your mouth and am reminded of the maternal kiss that invariably left saliva on my lips.

Would you doubt upon witnessing this loving interaction that I love my mother? Well, I do. I'm also struck with the fact that I can see her, speak to her, touch her, just as I could as a child, and have absolutely no sense that she cares about anything that I cherish. The fact that she's gone all over again.

The bitch.

[Lights fade. Music "Sweet Sadie" comes up.]

Doin' Alright

Back when I was a very young Miss Thing—back in Boston, Mass.—we lived for awhile in the part of Boston where black families lived that were "doin' alright"— in Dorchester, with the cops, factory workers, city employees, and schoolteachers. We lived on Harlem Street, appropriately enough, where I had a best friend named Dennis. Dennis and I were very big on doing black-boy-bonding things. Like riding our bikes to Houghton's Pond, the local swim hole, swimming out, and knocking the white kids off the raft—yeah! Or better yet, waiting till they bought a box of fried clams, then starting a sand fight. Black-boy-bonding things. But after awhile Dennis's family moved to the suburb of Framingham—they were more than doing alright; they were "doing pretty good"—and I moved onto bonding with other boys, black, white, and otherwise in other ways. Ways which I suspect some of you are quite familiar with. I suspect.

[A mirror ball lights the stage.]

I'm out one night, about fifteen years later, at the 1270, the working-class club for Boston Miss Things. The 1270—about as integrated a place as Boston gets. That is, we each had our corner. Irish by the bar. Italians by the coat check. Puerto Ricans by the DJ booth, and blacks—you know—in the back by the ice machine and bathrooms. Hey, I'm back in the black corner holding court with my fellow dark disco divas. "Yeah, girl, yeah, girl . . . uh huh, I heard . . . I *said* I heard!"— when this fabulous person giving much Donna Summer wig, Donna Summer makeup, and Donna Summer drag makes a beeline towards me screaming my name. "Briiiiaan!" Donna Summer is from Boston, and my brother did once date her sister (a little "Summer" madness?), but this wasn't Donna—this was Dennis! Now Denise. Still technically a boy, but with a few shots of silicone and quite a bit of makeup Denise could pass. Denise was quite real. Real enough to get herself promoted to the head of housekeeping at the Framingham Howard Johnson's Motor Inn. Denise was doin' alright. And during my infrequent visits to Boston over the next ten years, I would occasionally bump into Denise back in the black corner of whatever club we had all moved onto—Miss Thing liked to party—and I'd say, "Denise, how you doin'" and she'd say, "Baby, I'm [*neckroll*] doin' alright!"

[Mirror ball out]

A year or so ago my cousin, one of the few black women in management at a Boston software company, told me about a funeral she had attended for the son of one of her coworkers. Now my cousin didn't know the son, but she went because a woman she worked with, a mother, had lost a child. Period. The mother was not glad to see my cousin. The mother could not look my cousin in the eye. You see, the undertaker had laid her son out as he lived. As a she. This young black male, my age, who his coworkers called "Denise," who was as we say "in the life," lost his to one of the leading killers of black males: another black male. Minister said he died from being in the wrong place at the wrong time, but when you're poor, black, effeminate, and gay, life is wrong place, wrong time.

There's a lot of Michael/Michelles, Stephanie/Steves, Charlie/Charlenes, and Dennis/Denises in this world and somewhere between black-boy bonding and dark diva disco dancing I never did catch Miss Thing's last name. So I can't say for sure this Dennis/Denise is the same Dennis/Denise that I knew. But then again—isn't she?

[Mirror ball spins as Donna Summer plays. Fadeout.]

Tasty

It was one of the better temp assignments I found. Good pay. Nice office. French roast coffee. Now usually when I go out on these assignments, me and the cleaning crew are the only people of color. But this place was different. There was a Latina secretary, an Asian manager, and—how shall I describe him? Well. Let's just say he was a "structural" engineer.

He didn't notice me right away. Partly because I was a temp and partly because he just didn't notice me. But I put on my good Negro best during this special assignment, and he comes up to me and says, "You're a pro. Perhaps we can find a place for you in the company." And I think, "Oh, this is good. Six one, broad shoulders, dark dark skin, low top fade, and these eyelashes that just swept out at you. And these tailored pants that emphasized his bubble butt."

Now I think that he picked up that I was "that way" right away. I don't know how. But this being my first job in a long time, I didn't want to ruffle any feathers.

And I didn't really know if he was gay. And I hadn't dated many black men. Just, you know. None. And I really wanted to keep this job.

So one Friday night I stayed late to work on this direct mail campaign. I spread my stuff out on the conference room table, and I start pulling and pushing and licking and stamping. Pulling and pushing and licking and stamping, when he walks by the conference room door and says, "What are you still doing here? I'd suspect a guy like you would have places to go on Friday night."

I was trying to be cool, so I kept pulling and pushing and licking and stamping, and he says, "Why don't you finish up and I'll give you a ride home?"

"Sure."

Fabulous car. Volvo. Leather seats. On the way he says, "Let's go to my apartment."

Fierce apartment. High drama artwork. Exposed brick. And the *last* home entertainment system.

[Soft soul music swells.]

I sat myself down and he leans over with those Wesley Snipes eyes and says, "Why don't you stay a little longer?"

I said, "What for?"

Child, the next thing I knew there I was on his black leather sofa in my white BVDs and him in his red Calvins. We made our way to the bedroom as best we could. He laid me down. Kissed me on the back of my neck. Nibbled on my butt. I can't tell you exactly what we did. Let's just say it was the most powerful experience of my life. Three times.

When it was over, I just laid there, my head on his chest, and I thought, my God, how perfect. This act of love. Me and this black man together in this room. The first black man in my life. Then I heard the keys in the door.

[Music out]

The door opened. The footsteps approached the bedroom, the bedroom door opens, and in walks this white guy in a three-piece suit who says, "What the hell is going on?"

My friend looks at his friend, laughs, and says, "Sorry, honey. I didn't know you were coming home. Why don't you join us?"

I picked up my BVDs and my face and stormed out of the apartment. The following Monday he doesn't show up for work, but I get a phone call. I ask him why, if he had a boyfriend, he wanted to be with me?

"Why did you sleep with me?"

"Sorry. I *do* have a boyfriend. But when he saw you, you being a brother and all, he just freaked out. I could never *be* with a black man, you know. But every once in awhile I need a little taste. You know what I'm talking about. A taste. Why don't you keep my number? Be my taste. Keep the number."

I got your number.

Chocolate City, USA

[The PERFORMER reads from a book of black gay men's poetry in the rant style of the "Last Poets."]

> *Four years of loving you*
> *You Black masculine multitude*
> *You chocolate sailors*
> *Infinite and numberless*
> *Long have we come*
> *and gone*
> *and being victims*
> *of many an unexpected reunion . . .*

PERFORMER: I've really been getting into black gay men's poetry lately. Do you ever have the feeling that there is a conversation you keep meaning to have with—the world?

I go to a lot of black gay men's poetry readings. Incredibly interesting. The poetry's usually pretty good, the readings challenging. It's the men that are interesting. There are two things you can assume if you go to a black gay men's poetry reading. One, that there will be black gay men there and two, that they can read. Which is much more than you can safely assume at Keller's, the Pendulum, the Monster, or wherever you hang out at.

So I go to this black gay men's poetry reading at a bookstore that happens to be run by a black gay man, and it is great. After the reading another black gay man comes over and gives me his phone number, and two weeks later I call him—I'm not easy. We have a date. It's nice. A week later we have another, and another, and another, and he's black and I'm black and he's gay and I'm gay and in San Francisco that's a lot. Trust me on this point.

Three months later we are still dating, so we decide we are going to take a trip together and we decide we are going to *the* black gay men's ultimate fantasy vacation destination. Not Seattle. Nowheres near Minneapolis. We are going to Chocolate City, USA, Washington, D.C., for the National March on Washington for Lesbian and Gay Rights: For Love and For Life We Are Not Going Back! It's our first trip together! We are not getting along.

The morning of the March I want to march with the people of color contingent. He wants to march with San Francisco/Bay Area. "Why do you want to march with them? I'm sick of them in the Castro. . . ." I storm off to the people of color contingent. It's only 7 people. "Wait. There were 2,000 brothers up in the club last night? Where are you?" I race back to San Francisco/Bay Area—but he's not there. Suddenly the crowd surges, and all 650,000 of us, we are marching, marching down Pennsylvania Avenue. I fall in with the first few black faces I see. It's BWMT: Black and White Men Together. You know what? They are nice, really nice. Do a lot of good work in the community. But on today, of all days, in Chocolate City, USA, my soul is hungry and I do not want Raisin Bran. I do not want Fruit and Fiber. I just want the fruit!

I fall out of Black and White Men Together and stand on the sidelines for an hour. Waiting. Hoping. Finally, up Pennsylvania Avenue I see a wave of shining sepia skin. I think, "Okay, it's Washington, D.C.; things here run on C.P. time— that's Colored People's time for the rest of you. Uh uh. New Alliance Party Storm Troopers. They are scary, very scary. Where is he? Where are we?"

Suddenly, the crowd surges again. We go pouring into the rally area, where up on that stage Holly Near is singing that same old girl-you-need-to-hang-it-up song she has been singing at every rally for the past fifteen years. Aaaah! I push my way through the crowd. I make my way to the front. Finally, I see one black face that I know. That I love. She says she's not gay. Spike Lee says she's not black. I don't care because today Whoopi Goldberg is beautiful because she has pushed Jimmy Maness, a person with AIDS, the entire length of this March in a wheelchair. The clouds part, the sun comes out, Whoopi takes the stage and challenges all 650,000 of us with [mimicking Whoopi]: "How long is it going to take before people get smart, huh? I'm not talking about illiterate people. I'm talking about educated people. Like senators. And congressmen. And the fucking president? Can you do something for me, please? All 650,000 of you, can you do something for me, please? I want to hear what it's going to sound like when you scream, 'How long?' at Mr. Reagan on Tuesday. Can you do that for me please? On three, please? One, two, three—"

[The gospel song "How Long?" plays.]

How long? As Whoopi's words swept us off the mall, past the quilt, and home. To fight. To die. To mourn and to fight again. I wondered. How long? What would it take?

[Two other performers enter dressed as urban youths.]

B-BOY 1: How long before you go back to where you came from?
B-BOY 2: And die?

[Slide flashes: 1991. The B-BOYS play a game of one on one as they chant. The other performer circles them.]

B-BOYS:

> *How'd you get it, huh?*
> *How'd you get it?*
> *You get it from a needle?*
> *You get it from a needle?*
> *You get it from a girl?*
> *Did you get it from a girl?*

> *You got it up the ass, huh?*
> *Up the ass, huh?*
> *You got it up the ass!*

I hate your guts. You deserve what you get! Go fuck yourself, faggot Johnson!

[A scream cuts the chant. A slide flashes: Right Now. Two performers take opposite downstage corners, and each picks up a set of letters, which they alternate reading, then drop the letters to the floor like leaves, covering the stage. The third performer dribbles upstage center and uses the basketball like a drum after each letter.]

Dear Magic,

Heroes are like fast food; they always disappoint. You write a book that nobody reads. You make a video that nobody watches. You start another celebrity AIDS Foundation that nobody needs. You were the cure, Magic. Right? You were. Now you're a sportscaster. What happened?

Dear Media,

Why do you always leave out the voices of black gay men, who have been fighting this as long as anybody? Who built those few organizations that serve black communities? Are we not black? Are we not gay? What is this shit?

Dear GMHC (Gay Men's Health Crisis) New York, Amfar (American Foundation for AIDS Research), Los Angeles, San Francisco AIDS Foundation, ACT-UP Chapters (AIDS Coalition to Unleash Power) that are still here, and Larry Kramer,

Fuck you! We are not here to teach you shit! You don't speak for us!

Dear Black Gay Men,

I am fed up with going to demonstrations without you, then listening to you complain about the white boys that did. Isn't that closet getting kinda cramped?

Dear Shanti Project and All Buddy Programs,

Please don't send some white queen over my house to hold my hand and process my pain. What I need is someone to weave my hair, work some greens, and whip a peach cobbler!

Dear Dr. Leonard Jeffries, Dr. Molefi Kete Asante, Dear Minister Farrakhan, Dear CIA Conspiracy Theorists, Dear FBI Conspiracy Theorists, Dear CDC (Centers for Disease Control) Conspiracy Theorists, and all Afro-centrics,

Kinte cloth makes fabulous drag but lousy bandages. There is no immunity in ignorance, but hey, wear all the crowns you like; it won't raise your T cell counts.

Dear Mount Zion, New Bethel, First Baptist, Second Baptist, Third Baptist, Last Baptist, and All Black Churches,

How many organists will you go through before you do more than light a candle? Choir director seems to be a hazardous occupation. The Reverend James Cleveland's death was not a fluke. Claim him!

Dear America,
  "Renounce your sins and return to Jesus!"
  Shouts one of the zealous flock.
  "The truth is I never left Him,"
  I reply with a finger snap.
  "Don't you wish you'd chosen a *normal* lifestyle?"
  "Sister, for *me,* I'm *sure* I did."

Let the congregation work overtime
For my eleventh-hour conversion.
Their futile efforts fortify
My unrepentant resolve.

Though my body be racked by
Capricious pains and fevers,
I'm not *about* to yield to
Fashionable gay black temptation.

Mother Piaf's second greatest hit title
Is taped to the inside of my brain
And silently repeated like a mantra:
"Non, je ne regrette rien."

I don't regret the hot Latino boxer
I made love to on Riverside Drive
Prior to a Washington march.
I don't regret wild Jersey nights
Spent in the arms of conflicted satyrs;
I don't regret late night and early A.M.
Encounters with world-class insatiables.

My only regrets are being ill,
Bedridden, and having no boyfriend
To pray over me.
Or that now I'll never see Europe
Or my African homeland except
In photos in a book or magazine.

Engrave on my tombstone:
"Here sleeps a *happy* black faggot
Who lived to love and died

With no guilt."

No, I regret nothing
Of the gay life I've led and
There's no way in Heaven or Hell
I'll let anyone make me.

                    Sincerely,
                    Dave Frechette

Dear Dave,
   We miss your fat, greasy, obnoxious black ass and wish you could be here for
this show.

Dear Magic, Dear Black Gay Men, Dear Black America, Dear Hillary and Bill,
Dear America,
   We need equal access to drugs and treatments
   We need the love and support of our own community
   We need *our* voices to be heard
   But—
   What we don't need—
   What we really don't need—is another motherfucking hero!
   Sing girl

*[Tina Turner's "We Don't Need Another Hero" plays. Letters go everywhere in a
cascade. The basketball pounds the floor like a hammer. Fade to black.]*

CHAY YEW

Porcelain

EDITOR'S INTRODUCTION

C HAY YEW BEGAN his playwriting career in his native Singapore. His earliest play, *As If He Hears*, was first banned by the Singapore government and then, after some revision, produced in 1989. Yew then moved to Boston, where he worked in television production and writing, including the New England cult success *Nightshift*. *Porcelain*, the first play in Chay Yew's trilogy of chamber plays about the gay Asian experience, was commissioned by the Mu-Lan Theatre Company in London in 1992 and was successful enough to be transferred to the Royal Court Theatre. It earned its playwright the London Fringe Award for Best Playwright in 1993. Since then it has been produced all over the United States. The second play in the trilogy, *A Language of Their Own*, received its premiere at the New York Public Theater in April 1995. *Half Lives*, the third play, has been commissioned by East West Players in Los Angeles, which plans to mount the entire trilogy. Yew now resides in Los Angeles.

It is ironic that the best-known play about a gay Asian male, David Henry Hwang's *M. Butterfly*, was written by a heterosexual and used a male-male relationship to comment on white men's attitude toward Asians in general and Asian women in particular. Like *M. Butterfly*, *Porcelain* focuses on a romantic obsession that is passionate and destructive enough to be equated with opera. But this is only the beginning of the daring of Chay Yew's daring, deceptively simple play, which looks at the dilemma of being gay and Asian in contemporary London.

Porcelain challenges its audience to understand what made nineteen-year-old, Cambridge University–bound John Lee seek sex and, more surprisingly, companionship in an East London public men's room and what drove him to shoot William Hope (an equally apt name) six times in that same "cottage." Yew starts from a issue that is as controversial for many gay men as it is for heterosexuals— sex in public toilets. Recently on one of the gay networks on E-mail there was a lengthy, emotional "string" on toilet sex. The passionate expressions of the young men on the "net" for the most part echoed the revulsion of conservative, "straight" society. Why would an out, proud man need to have sex with strangers in a men's room—behavior that seems to be a vestige of the closet? One answer, which Yew's play suggests, is that such a man would if there were no other out, proud men showing any interest. John Lee's feelings are more complex than that, however:

> To be honest with you, I hate the toilets. I really do—but there's this trembling in me when I'm there—I don't know what it is, but I like it—I enjoy it. And—there's people there who want me. Even for a moment. And the idiot that I am—thinking I really belong—thinking perhaps all these moments will amount to something—someone who will—like me, love me—isn't that the silliest thing you've heard?

Born, appropriately, with the name of Lone, which he anglicized to John, Lee feels he will never fit in. As a gay man, he is alienated from the culture and family into which he was born. As an Asian in London, he feels ignored, rejected. In the gay bars and clubs he is invisible. Occasionally, for a moment, sex in the toilet gives him a sense of belonging, even love. For a few weeks William Hope offers Lee what he has always wanted, but for Hope the toilets are a place to get sex without having to admit to himself or anyone else that he is gay. Yet, uncharacteristically, after their encounter, Hope invites John Lee out for a drink, to his home and bed, and, briefly, into a relationship. When the relationship starts to become more than physical, to move toward the love John Lee seeks, Hope panics, tries brutally to move the relationship back to a merely physical one, and, when that isn't possible, leaves John and returns to furtive, safe encounters in the toilet. John's anger and desperation at Hope's rejection take him beyond rational behavior into the realm of operatic passion. In his desperation, Lee moves from identification with Puccini's Madama Butterfly, the feminine Asian martyr, to identification with Bizet's Don José, the obsessed, rejected, European, masculine avenger. Like Don José, Lee is discovered cradling the body of the lover he killed.

We might ask why John Lee does not find other Asian gay men. We might wonder if his isolation is not self-induced. But Yew has caught that sense many young gay men have of being alone, of being singular freaks, and Yew evokes the self-destructive behavior that can ensue from those feelings of isolation and self-hatred. What is most tragic about the play is not John's plight but the sense that things haven't changed much for some people since gay liberation. The closet is still a potent force, and many young gay men still feel despair.

Yew chronicles the brief, tragic intersection of Lee and Hope and its aftermath in what he calls "a voice play." On a bare stage, decorated only by the red origami cranes John Lee folds during his imprisonment, Porcelain takes place totally through language. Four actors surrounding John Lee create all the sounds and voices of his world: William Hope, John's cynical court-appointed psychologist, John's father, and the racist, homophobic voices that isolate John. The voices also tell the story John learned from his father, of the crow who tried to become a sparrow, which becomes a parable of John's isolation. Although the audience sees only four seated actors, the fascination of John Lee's character and the power of Chay Yew's writing make Porcelain an intense dramatic experience. Like a beautiful piece of Chinese porcelain, Yew's play is an effective, paradoxical combination of economy and complexity.

AUTHOR'S INTRODUCTION

I wrote *Porcelain* as a student film for my graduate thesis at Boston University in 1991. At the time frequent arrests were being made of men having sex in public restrooms at Boston University and Harvard University. The scandals were titillating fodder for student newspapers. They were also a topic of constant discussion among my circle of college friends: Some were piqued, some were disgusted, and some, like me, wondered what kind of person would indulge in "tearoom trade." With that in mind, I wrote *Porcelain*.

When the actors read the more-risqué-than-usual student script, they quickly turned down the roles. Feeling an urgency to finish my degree, I settled for a different project, shelving *Porcelain* in the process. When I was made resident playwright for the Mu-Lan Theatre Company in London, I decided to resurrect the story and turn it into a play. Mu-Lan, the first Asian-British theater company in London, said it had zero budget, and I asked if the company could at least spare me five chairs for a set. So that was how *Porcelain* came about—just five chairs and five men talking and enacting the crime of passion.

Porcelain, the first play of my trilogy dealing with issues of gay Asians, is based largely on my teenage experiences of loneliness, identity, anger, and sexuality as a member of a racial minority in a Caucasian society. The gay Asian journey continues with *A Language of Their Own*, which centers on emotional relationships between men, and *Half Lives*, about the impact of family on the gay individual.

Photo by José Pombo

PRODUCTION HISTORY AND RIGHTS

Porcelain received its premiere at the Et Cetera Theatre in London on 12 May 1992. The production reopened at the Royal Court Upstairs Theatre on 4 August 1992. Produced by the Mu-Lan Theatre Company. Directed and designed by Glen Goei and Stephen Knight.

John Lee............................ Daniel York
Voices
1. (Psychologist) .... David Tysall
2. .... Adam Matalon
3. .... Julien Ball
4. (William Hope).................... Mark Aiken

It has since been performed by the Burbage Theater, Los Angeles; Dallas Theater Center; Theater Rhinoceros, San Francisco; Consenting Adults Theater, Washington; Eclipse Theater, Chicago, and Diversionary Theater, San Diego.

CHAY YEW

Porcelain

Cast of Characters

JOHN LEE: 19. Asian English.
VOICE 1 (Psychologist and others): 30s.
VOICE 2
VOICE 3
VOICE 4 (William Hope and others): 20s.

Setting

London. The present.

[*On a bare stage are five chairs that face the audience; they are lined in a straight row.*

There are many red origami paper cranes littered about the stage floor and around the chairs. When the play begins, the four characters, VOICE ONE, VOICE TWO, VOICE THREE, and VOICE FOUR, will enter from the wings and sit on the chairs. All VOICES are played by Caucasian men of various ages and are dressed uniformly in black.

Dressed in white, JOHN, an Asian male in his late teens, sits in the middle chair. Deep in concentration, he relentlessly folds paper cranes as the audience enters the house.

It is important that all characters, particularly JOHN and VOICE ONE, do not look at each other throughout the play unless otherwise indicated. No music and sound effects should be employed during the play.]

SCENE 1

[The VOICES come in from offstage and create London street sounds as they take their seats. They may overlap each other's lines.]

VOICE THREE: *[Sound of Big Ben striking 4:00]*

VOICE TWO: *[Sounds of cars honking]*

VOICE ONE: Watch where you're walking, you fucking sod—

VOICE FOUR: *[Sounds of an underground train screeching to a halt at a station]*

VOICE TWO: Mind the gap—mind the gap—

VOICE ONE: No. This is not Piccadilly Circus. This is Trafalgar Square. No, not Piccadilly. Fucking tourists—

VOICE TWO: Say, can you spare some change for a cuppa? Fifty p? Anything? Please—

VOICE ONE: Would you be a love and fetch us a pint of lager from the pub? Bitter lager. No lime. And a pack of Rothmans—

VOICE THREE: So the bloody Paki taxi driver drove me all the way to Primrose Hill instead. You'd think that the lot of them should at least speak English or carry an *A to Z* around with them—

VOICE FOUR: Where's the fucking number fifteen? I'll miss *EastEnders* at this rate—

VOICE ONE: Top news this hour: A man was found dead in a public lavatory in Bethnal Green in East London today—

VOICE TWO: Police suspect murder—

VOICE FOUR: Motive has not been established—

VOICE ONE: The alleged murderer is said to be a nineteen-year-old Oriental male from nearby Whitechapel—

VOICE THREE: London Metropolitan Police is still investigating the brutal murder. Now, more Kylie Minogue on Capital FM—

VOICE TWO: Eyewitnesses to the crime claimed the suspect was cradling the victim after the cold-blooded shooting—

VOICE THREE: The victim, William Hope, a twenty-six-year-old male from South Hackney, was shot six times—

VOICE ONE: Sources believe that he was shot by an acquaintance—

VOICE FOUR: *[Overlapping, gradually louder and more urgent]* The police found the suspect at the site of the violent murder—

VOICE THREE: *[Overlapping, gradually louder and more urgent]* The White House has no further comment on the recent civil rights rally held outside the Lincoln Memorial. In London, there's been a fatal shooting in a public toilet in Bethnal Green this afternoon—

VOICE ONE: *[Overlapping, gradually louder and more urgent]* Two days ago, the Bethnal Green community of East London witnessed a tragic killing. Should handguns be made available to the public? We'll answer these questions on *Good Morning, London* after the break—

VOICE TWO: *[Overlapping, gradually louder and more urgent]* I don't think this would have happened if the police were doing their usual rounds of the public lavs, you know. Now with what's happened, don't think I'd let my eight-year-old son into any public loo—

VOICE FOUR: *[Overlapping, gradually louder and more urgent]* We have clinical psychologist Dr. James Christian here this evening. Dr. Christian, what do you suppose the young man was thinking when he pulled the deadly trigger last week in the public lavatory in Bethnal Green?—

VOICE TWO: *[Overlapping, gradually louder and more urgent]* Well, that's a very interesting point of view. Thanks for calling. The number once again is 071-449-4000, and today's topic is the recent toilet sex murder in—

VOICE FOUR: Bang!

VOICE ONE: Bang!

VOICE THREE: Bang!

VOICE TWO: Bang!

VOICE FOUR: Bang!

VOICE ONE: Bang!

VOICE THREE: Six shots.

VOICE TWO: At close range.

VOICE FOUR: A body falls.

VOICE ONE: Slumped against the urinals.

VOICE THREE: White walls with peeling paint.

VOICE TWO: Cold mosaic floors.

VOICE FOUR: A pool of red.

VOICE ONE: Everywhere splattered with blood.

VOICE THREE: Warm blood.

VOICE TWO: Red patterns.

VOICE FOUR: Flowerlike.

VOICE ONE: Patterns.

VOICE THREE: Slow, moving.

VOICE TWO: Patterns.

VOICE FOUR: Sounds.

VOICE ONE: Tiny, annoying.

VOICE THREE: Sounds.

VOICE TWO: Drips.

VOICE FOUR: From leaky water taps.

VOICE ONE: The dull hum.

VOICE THREE: From the blinding.

VOICE TWO: Fluorescent lights above.

VOICE FOUR: And a boy standing.

VOICE ONE: Breathing hard.

VOICE THREE: Weeping.

VOICE TWO: Outside.

VOICE FOUR: Traffic sounds.

VOICE ONE: Wailing sirens.

VOICE THREE: The disjointed chorus.

VOICE TWO: Of staccato footsteps.

VOICE FOUR: From street pedestrians.

VOICE ONE: Hurrying home from work.

VOICE THREE: Seems distant.

VOICE TWO: Lingering smells.

VOICE FOUR: Hanging still in the air.

VOICE ONE: Gunpowder.

VOICE THREE: Antiseptic.

VOICE TWO: Urine.

VOICE FOUR: Semen.

VOICE ONE: Six shots.

VOICE THREE: A body falls.

VOICE TWO: Bang!

VOICE FOUR: Bang!

VOICE ONE: Bang!

VOICE THREE: Bang!

VOICE TWO: Bang!

VOICE FOUR: Bang!

SCENE 2

*[In the following scene, all VOICES, with the exception of VOICE THREE, take
on an array of men-on-the-street characters, a different character for each line.]*

VOICE THREE: Do you know what cottaging is?

VOICE FOUR: Cottaging?

VOICE THREE: Having sex in lavatories.

VOICE FOUR: Sex in the toilets? Eh—no—never heard of it.

VOICE ONE: Cottaging. Why, yes, I believe that the term came from the fact that
public conveniences were once designed in the style of Swiss cottages. You
know, the little white brick cottages with black wooden frames. Very *Sound of
Music.*

VOICE FOUR: Is this *Candid Camera?*

VOICE THREE: Excuse me, sir. We're doing a documentary on—

VOICE TWO: You're that chap on—

VOICE THREE: Alan White.

VOICE TWO: BBC?

VOICE THREE: Channel Four.

VOICE TWO: Yes, that's it. My, you look a lot smarter in real life. A bit short, perhaps.

VOICE THREE: As I was saying, we're doing a—

VOICE TWO: Well, you've been doing a brilliant job, my lad. The missus and I simply love to watch your juicy news stories at ten.

VOICE THREE: Yes.

VOICE TWO: Sally, the missus, simply raves about your butch travestite curb-crawlers story—top notch—

VOICE THREE: Eh—thank you, sir—

VOICE TWO: And the recent story? On the impact of holiday prices on Fergie? Got me tongue-tied, it did. We stay up for you, Alan.

VOICE THREE: Yes. We're here to conduct interviews for a television documentary—

VOICE TWO: And you want my opinion.

VOICE THREE: Yes and—

VOICE TWO: My, I'm going to be on telly. Wait till Sally hears about this. Me on BBC.

VOICE THREE: Channel Four.

VOICE TWO: It's still telly, isn't it? What's the topic this week, Alan?

VOICE THREE: Toilet sex and we're wondering if—

VOICE TWO: I beg your pardon.

VOICE FOUR: Oh blimey, sure I've heard of it. Seen it even. In Notting Hill—at some of the private clubs, even at parties. There're blokes who'll have a quick shag with girls in the toilets. Yeah—I've seen it. It's really kinky—sexy.

VOICE ONE: Yeah, but I'm not sure. Once I went to the loo in Clapham Common. Yeah—it was in the afternoon; maybe it was evening. I went in to take a quick piss—

VOICE TWO: Cottaging? No, never heard of it.

VOICE ONE: Well, there was this geezer standing there. He's just standing there. Like he's taking a piss or something. For a long time. And all the time he was looking in my direction. Looking at me.

VOICE FOUR: I don't think it's true. The graffiti you read on the toilet walls like "This bloke gives good head—meet at this place—this time." And the phone numbers. I think it's all—you know. It couldn't be—I don't know.

VOICE ONE: He kept pulling on—his—you know—looking at me. Then all of a sudden, another geezer came into the loo, and he started staring at this new geezer.

VOICE TWO: Sure, I know what it is. Saw *Prick Up Your Ears*.

VOICE ONE: He's still doing the business like—and this new chap looked back at him and walked into a cubicle. And the geezer who was clocking me just walked right in after him, wallop.

VOICE THREE: Have you ever participated in toilet sex?

VOICE FOUR: Piss off! What the fuck do you think I am? Fucking queer?

VOICE TWO: Yeah, I got my cock sucked off a couple times before.

SCENE 3

VOICE ONE: It's a bit fucking bright, isn't it?

VOICE THREE: That's TV for you, sorry. Right. Dr. Worthing, can you sign this release before we tape?

VOICE ONE: This is exactly the way we discussed.

VOICE THREE: As I said to you a few days ago, I would like the Channel Four news team to be first in London to broadcast the Lee murder documentary.

VOICE ONE: I don't give a fuck whether you're the first or last. I want to know if this is exactly what we spoke.

VOICE THREE: We will say we got this interview from you after the trial.

VOICE ONE: That's all I want to know. And to protect myself—

VOICE THREE: We agreed that if you feel there's anything unethical about disclosing certain privileged information, you needn't answer the questions.

VOICE ONE: And you want me to—

VOICE THREE: Recount your daily dealings with your client since we don't have access to him.

VOICE ONE: And the money?

VOICE THREE: One thousand pounds will be sent to you after the broadcast.

VOICE ONE: Before.

VOICE THREE: I beg your pardon.

VOICE ONE: I want the dosh before you air the piece.

VOICE THREE: This is not what we discussed.

VOICE ONE: Then I'll walk. I'm sure there are other news shows which will want first dibs on this story.

   [Pause]

VOICE THREE: Before the piece, then.

   [VOICE THREE hands VOICE ONE a piece of paper; VOICE ONE signs it. All this is mimed.]

VOICE ONE: Hey, why are you looking so bloody forlorn? You'll finally get the ratings your show needs and get yourself some fucking credibility.

VOICE THREE: Can we start, Dr. Worthing?

VOICE ONE: It's your money.

VOICE THREE: Do you—I'm sorry, I'm afraid we've got you in a medium shot and if you won't fidget so. Let's start again. Dr. Worthing, tell us about the case you've been working on.

VOICE ONE: The case I've been working on—

VOICE THREE: The Lee case.

VOICE ONE: Oh, right. John Lee, the murder in Bethnal Green. Right, of course, yes—uh—I believe I was asked by the court—

VOICE THREE: You're a—

VOICE ONE: Criminal psychologist. I'm on the case to determine—

VOICE THREE: To determine whether he was sane or insane at the time of the—

VOICE ONE: The murder—yes. The defendant wasn't able to afford counsel and—

VOICE THREE: Yes, we know that.

VOICE ONE: Listen, if you know so fucking much, why are you interviewing me?

VOICE THREE: I'm sorry, Dr. Worthing. I'm just fishing for particular sound bites.

VOICE ONE: Wouldn't it be simpler for everyone here if you gave me a bloody script instead?

VOICE THREE: Tell me about him.

VOICE ONE: Well, he's just finished his *A* levels—waiting to go into university in Cambridge. He's nineteen—that's all I can say on the record.

VOICE THREE: Dr. Worthing, this is a rather personal question. I have some contacts in the public prosecution sector, and they tell me that you are one of the least liked criminal psychologists in the business. Some of them claim that this is possibly your last assignment given your poor track record in the recent year.

VOICE ONE: I beg your pardon?

VOICE THREE: Let me also add that they also said you are unprofessional, rude, and inconsiderate towards your clients. Some even go so far as to say you drink excessively, arriving late to sessions and not even showing up at all.

VOICE ONE: I don't think this is relevant—

VOICE THREE: There are also rumors about the sexual harassment of your female colleagues and coworkers.

VOICE ONE: I have no—

VOICE THREE: According to your peers, you constantly use profanities during counselling sessions? Isn't it unorthodox?

VOICE ONE: Yes, but—

VOICE THREE: Unprofessional, irregular, and rude are the adjectives I have received from—

VOICE ONE: Oh, for fuck sake—

VOICE THREE: Exactly what I mean. Dr. Worthing, am I safe enough to presume that all these allegations are true?

VOICE ONE: No.

VOICE THREE: I'm sorry, Dr. Worthing; we didn't get that.

VOICE ONE: No. It's not true.

VOICE THREE: Once again, Dr. Worthing, audio—

VOICE ONE: It's not true.

VOICE THREE: Thank you, Dr. Worthing. I just want to clear the air before we ask further questions about the Lee case. I have no more questions at this time. Stop tape.

SCENE 4

VOICE TWO: John standing.

VOICE THREE: In the toilet stall.

VOICE FOUR: Nervously.

VOICE ONE: Looking.

VOICE FOUR: Waiting.

VOICE THREE: A man walks slowly.

VOICE TWO: Into the stall.

VOICE THREE: Cramped.

VOICE ONE: In his late thirties.

VOICE THREE: Balding.

VOICE TWO: A trim beard.

VOICE THREE: Wears glasses.

VOICE ONE: Clonish.

VOICE THREE: They seem to be talking.

VOICE TWO: A little.

VOICE FOUR: "Hi."

VOICE ONE: John nods.

VOICE TWO: The clone wets his lips.

VOICE THREE: Slowly.

VOICE FOUR: Knowingly.

VOICE TWO: John's eyes make a quick study.

VOICE ONE: Of the man's body.

VOICE FOUR: His eyes.

VOICE TWO: Transfixed.

VOICE THREE: Touching his body.

VOICE TWO: His trembling hands.

VOICE ONE: Run down the stranger's body.

VOICE FOUR: Unevenly.

VOICE TWO: Nervously.

VOICE THREE: The man holds John's head.

VOICE FOUR: And leads John down.

VOICE TWO: To his swelling crotch.

VOICE ONE: His face against the soft denim.

VOICE THREE: A faint, familiar smell.

VOICE TWO: Smells of soap and sweat.

VOICE ONE: The man's head arches slowly.

VOICE FOUR: Leans on the toilet wall.

VOICE THREE: Pressing against the wall.

VOICE TWO: The man looks at the ceiling.

VOICE THREE: Blinking hard.

VOICE FOUR: Breathing heavily.

VOICE TWO: Through his nose.

VOICE THREE: His body spasms.

VOICE ONE: Long breaths.

VOICE FOUR: Deep breaths.

VOICE TWO: Uneven breaths.

SCENE 5

VOICE ONE: Thanks for letting me smoke. I'll just fucking die if I don't—do you want a fag? Eh—I mean—cigarette.

JOHN: I don't really care for lung cancer.

VOICE ONE: Good for you. It's habit forming. I don't really have all your stuff with me. Your name?

JOHN: John—

VOICE ONE: Yes, that's it. John—John Lee. Eh—my name's Jack Worthing. Doctor—

JOHN: *Importance of Being Earnest.*

VOICE ONE: What?

JOHN: Oscar Wilde.

VOICE ONE: I don't—

JOHN: Jack Worthing is the name of a character—

VOICE ONE: Oh, that's right. The play about people pretending to be other people just to get laid—something like that.

JOHN: I auditioned for the role a few years ago in school.

VOICE ONE: Really? How nice.

JOHN: Didn't get it.

VOICE ONE: Uh-huh. Why?

JOHN: They said I didn't look the part.

VOICE ONE: Oh, I see. I'm sorry.

JOHN: I'm not. You're American?

VOICE ONE: British.

JOHN: You have an accent.

VOICE ONE: I spent many years in America. Studying. Working.

JOHN: Ah, the crow and the sparrow.

VOICE ONE: What are you talking about?

JOHN: Nothing. A stupid story my father told me when I was young.

VOICE ONE: What story?

JOHN: You and I are the same.

VOICE ONE: I don't understand.

JOHN: You'll never understand.

VOICE ONE: Right. Off to work then, shall we? You probably know what these are. Rorschach blot test cards. Pretty, aren't they?

JOHN: Very pretty.

VOICE ONE: So, tell me what you—

JOHN: See?

VOICE ONE: Well?

JOHN: I don't know.

VOICE ONE: Try. Tell me—

JOHN: Patterns—dots.

VOICE ONE: Yes—yes. But what do you see?

JOHN: I don't see anything.

VOICE ONE: Eh—let me rephrase that—what does this remind you of?

JOHN: Patterns—dots.

VOICE ONE: Well, aside from patterns and dots. The shapes. Do the shapes resemble anything to you? Anything in particular?

JOHN: Nothing.

VOICE ONE: Alright, let's try another. How about this one?

JOHN: Patterns and dots.

VOICE ONE: Look here, you're not making any of this—

JOHN: Easy?

VOICE ONE: Why?

JOHN: Why not?

VOICE ONE: Can we put our eyes on this card and tell us the first thought?—

JOHN: That comes into my pretty head?

VOICE ONE: Don't put words in my mouth.

JOHN: What shall I put in?

VOICE ONE: God, my fucking headache.

JOHN: Listen, Dr. Worthing, I know you are here to—

VOICE ONE: Help you.

JOHN: I appreciate your concern, but I don't need your help. Please go away.

VOICE ONE: Listen, I'm only here to do a job, not to make friends. I'm here to find out why you—

JOHN: Killed him.

VOICE ONE: In so many words.

JOHN: I'm guilty.

VOICE ONE: Let the jury be the judge of this.

JOHN: But I am.

VOICE ONE: Look—

JOHN: I am guilty of each and every shot.

VOICE ONE: Listen, John, I'm tired. I'll be honest with you since I feel we should have an honest working relationship. I'm fucking tired. I've got a fucking headache. I'd rather be in bed—

JOHN: Fucking.

VOICE ONE: Right. And you're in here for murder. It's big time, not some small petty—

JOHN: I know.

VOICE ONE: We're talking about life here. Behind the bars, never to see the light of day, with lots of men—

JOHN: Fucking?

VOICE ONE: Men who'll slice you up for fun. Now, let's start again. So what do we see?

JOHN: I don't know. Dots—patterns.

SCENE 6

VOICE THREE: Dr. Worthing, what information did you expect to get out of John Lee through the blot tests?

VOICE ONE: Perhaps an idea of who he is and what he is. Why he did what he did. It's a kind of Tarot cards psychologists use.

VOICE THREE: Was it effective?

VOICE ONE: Not in the beginning. Perhaps he didn't trust me. Perhaps he was just being difficult. Perhaps he still hasn't recovered from the shock—

VOICE THREE: And?

VOICE ONE: Then he gradually opened up and told me things.

VOICE THREE: What kind of things?

VOICE ONE: Things. All kind of things.

VOICE THREE: Like?

VOICE ONE: I thought you're an investigative reporter.

VOICE THREE: I am. So what did John Lee tell you?

VOICE ONE: I can't disclose that special client-counselor information to you, Mr. White. That would be quite unprofessional, don't you think?

VOICE THREE: Then how do you look at this case, Dr. Worthing?

VOICE ONE: What do you mean?

VOICE THREE: You're heterosexual, I presume.

VOICE ONE: Very.

VOICE THREE: You've never cottaged. You're definitely not Oriental. So how do you look at this case as a heterosexual white male?

VOICE ONE: It's a job.

VOICE THREE: No bias?

VOICE ONE: None.

VOICE THREE: Psychologists are, by definition, neutral and impartial to their cases. But you must have some personal opinions.

VOICE ONE: Of course, but—

VOICE THREE: And?

VOICE ONE: Look, this is getting rather—

VOICE THREE: Okay, we'll stop there. Look, just between you and me.

VOICE ONE: This is off the record, right?

VOICE THREE: Oh, definitely. It'd be unethical if we—

VOICE ONE: I think—personally between you and me, I think this whole case is— sick. Public sex is an offence. Murder is an offence. Well, let me put it in simple words—a queer chink who indulges in public sex kills a white man. Where would your fucking sympathies lie? Quite open and shut, isn't it?

VOICE THREE: Quite.

VOICE ONE: But I am keeping an open mind. Have to protect my client's bloody interest.

VOICE THREE: Of course.

VOICE ONE: It's just that I have nothing in common with those types, you know.

VOICE THREE: What types?

VOICE ONE: Those types.

VOICE THREE: I see. It must be very difficult for you as a psychologist to meet such a variety of types every day.

VOICE ONE: It's work.

VOICE THREE: Thank you.

VOICE ONE: Not at all. Anything for you boys at the BBC.

VOICE THREE: Channel Four.

VOICE ONE: Same thing. Say, you don't happen to have a cigarette on you, do you?

VOICE THREE: Sorry, you had the last one. *[Pause, loud whisper]* Did we get that sound bite?

SCENE 7

VOICE FOUR: There were two big trees on a field.

VOICE TWO: One at each end.

VOICE THREE: In one particular tree.

VOICE ONE: Lived a large family of black crows.

VOICE FOUR: The crows were noisy.

VOICE TWO: Loud.

VOICE THREE: Greedy.

VOICE ONE: Clumsy.

VOICE FOUR: Unwieldy.

VOICE TWO: Across the field was another tree.

VOICE THREE: A family of sparrows.

VOICE ONE: Chirpy.

VOICE FOUR: Merrymaking.

VOICE TWO: Graceful.

VOICE THREE: Happy.

VOICE ONE: Beautiful sparrows.

VOICE FOUR: One particular crow always saw them.

VOICE TWO: Always studied and observed them.

VOICE THREE: The lonely crow looked at them.

VOICE ONE: With such longing.

VOICE FOUR: Longing to sing happy, chirpy, little songs with them.

VOICE TWO: Longing to fly in fanciful formations.

VOICE THREE: Climbing up, combing down, bursting free.

VOICE ONE: Soaring heavenwards like a magnificent paper kite.

VOICE FOUR: Swooping earthbound like thunderous ocean waves in a Japanese watercolor picture.

VOICE TWO: The crow made up its mind.

VOICE THREE: Packed its bags.

VOICE ONE: Bade a tearful farewell to its surprised family.

VOICE FOUR: Flew clear across the field.

VOICE TWO: To the tree of singing, happy, chirpy, beautiful sparrows.

SCENE 8

VOICE ONE: What are you doing? You're folding something.

JOHN: Very observant.

VOICE ONE: Paper birds.

JOHN: Origami.

VOICE ONE: Pigeons?

JOHN: Do they look like pigeons?

VOICE ONE: Sparrows, then.

JOHN: No.

VOICE ONE: Crows? I don't know.

JOHN: Cranes.

VOICE ONE: They're—interesting. Why are you folding so many of them?

JOHN: For fun.

VOICE ONE: Come on, why are you folding them?

JOHN: It's something you won't understand.

VOICE ONE: I might.

JOHN: You won't.

VOICE ONE: How would you know I won't?

JOHN: Tradition.

VOICE ONE: What tradition?

JOHN: Japanese tradition.

VOICE ONE: But you're Chinese.

JOHN: So?

VOICE ONE: What's the tradition?

JOHN: Dr. Worthing.

VOICE ONE: Jack, please.

JOHN: Dr. Worthing, let's not get too chummy and pretend you're interested in my life because you aren't.

VOICE ONE: I am interested. The Oriental culture has always—

JOHN: Fascinated you?

VOICE ONE: Yes.

JOHN: How nice. What part of our Oriental culture so fascinates you, Dr. Worthing?

VOICE ONE: I like Chinese food.

JOHN: Is it our obedient and subservient geisha girls? Maybe our suntanned go-go girls who'll fuck you for less than five pounds in Bangkok? Or is it our ancient Oriental erotic acts? Maybe *The King and I? Miss Saigon? Suzie Wong?* Which is it, Dr. Worthing?

VOICE ONE: All those actually, but five pounds a shag sounds reasonable to me.

JOHN: Dr. Worthing, did it ever occur to you that your fascination is rooted in ignorance? Like everyone else—

VOICE ONE: Who's everyone else?

JOHN: Like everyone else, you sit comfortably on the other side of the wall. Perched. Watching us. Studying us. Looking at us. And you never once leave the other side to join us or understand us. You don't want to. We are mythicised by you. We are your interesting geisha girls, bespectacled accountants and dentists, your local Chinese takeaway. Your fascination. And why should you want to climb over and join us? Are you afraid of finding out that we're just the same as you? Have the same feelings and the same fears as you? How we are so much alike? You and I?

VOICE ONE: You must think you're very clever.

JOHN: Enough to detect a stiffening in your voice.

VOICE ONE: It's a very good guess.

JOHN: Nevertheless, a very accurate one, Dr. Worthing.

VOICE ONE: You're full of shit—

JOHN: And you're pathetic—

VOICE ONE: No lousy little queer is going to tell me—

JOHN: My, my. Such unattractive and unprofessional language. Enough to get you dismissed from my case and perhaps from a rosy future in the criminal psychology profession. Who'll have to pay for your excessive cigarettes and lager habits then?

VOICE ONE: Listen, you lousy homo chink—

JOHN: I think we've already established the fact that I'm a homo chink, Dr. Worthing. I presume your silence indicates that this session is over. Do drive safely. Clear skies can be deceiving.

SCENE 9

VOICE THREE: Inspector McLaughlin, what can you tell me about the murder that took place here about a month ago?

VOICE FOUR: There was some commotion in the public convenience by the Bethnal Green tube station. I was dispatched to the area to investigate the case.

VOICE THREE: What did you see when you got there?

VOICE FOUR: There was a crowd of people milling outside the toilets. Some of them were hysterical. They claimed they heard gunshots inside. The victim and the accused were lying in a pool of blood. Mr. Lee seemed to be holding Mr. Hope in his arms, rocking him like a baby. Mr. Hope had blood all over his head and chest, and Mr. Lee was just holding him.

VOICE THREE: What did you know about this toilet in Bethnal Green?

VOICE FOUR: Nothing much.

VOICE THREE: Let me put it this way: Have you heard anything peculiar about this particular toilet before?

VOICE FOUR: No. Should I?

VOICE THREE: Do you feel John Lee is the killer?

VOICE FOUR: Mr. White, I don't know all the facts surrounding the—

VOICE THREE: You don't need facts. Given what you saw, do you think John Lee is guilty?

VOICE FOUR: I don't know.

VOICE THREE: You are a police inspector. You walk into the public lavatory; you see two men—one dead, and the other living with a gun by his side. What was your first instinct?

VOICE FOUR: From what I saw, the accused was mourning, like he was a friend.

SCENE 10

VOICE ONE: So how are you today?

JOHN: In prison. And you?

VOICE ONE: Are they treating you well here?

JOHN: I am tired.

VOICE ONE: How well?

JOHN: It's not exactly Buckingham Palace.

VOICE ONE: You have everything you need, I presume.

JOHN: My own cell. My own shower.

VOICE ONE: Good. Anything else?

JOHN: All the prisoners here look at me very strangely.

VOICE ONE: What do you mean by "strangely"?

JOHN: In the valley of the blind, I'm the one-eyed man.

VOICE ONE: Meaning?

JOHN: They know I'm getting special treatment.

VOICE ONE: How?

JOHN: For a psychologist you ask a lot of stupid questions. Dr. Worthing, you should learn to open your eyes. Because I am different from the rest.

VOICE ONE: You're an alleged murderer.

JOHN: And?

VOICE ONE: And you're gay.

JOHN: Always been the case, hasn't it? Separate from the rest of the world. Even in prison. I'm not sure if I should be grateful in this instance.

VOICE ONE: What else have you been doing?

JOHN: Giving the warden intense blow jobs.

VOICE ONE: What else?

JOHN: Reading.

VOICE ONE: Reading what?

JOHN: A book.

VOICE ONE: What is the book about?

JOHN: The history of Chinese art.

VOICE ONE: Oh.

JOHN: It's either that or cowboy novels with half the pages missing.

VOICE ONE: I can bring you another book the next time.

JOHN: No. Thanks.

VOICE ONE: Good book, is it?

JOHN: Why are you so interested in making small talk?

VOICE ONE: Can't I be friendly?

JOHN: You have ulterior motives.

VOICE ONE: Why are you so defensive?

JOHN: Am I? I thought I was offensive.

VOICE ONE: How far have you gotten? In the book, I mean.

JOHN: You'll find me under Chinese porcelain.

VOICE ONE: First made by the Chinese.

JOHN: Very impressive, Dr. Worthing.

VOICE ONE: I do have that fascination, you know.

JOHN: The fascinating thing about porcelains is the process. Coarse stone pow-
ders and clay fused by intense temperatures to create something so delicate,
fragile, and beautiful: Two extremes, two opposites thrown together only to
produce beauty. Like the fairy tale *Beauty and the Beast*.

VOICE ONE: That's a fascinating—eh, interesting—analogy. Let's take this a little
further. Who do you see yourself as? Beauty or the Beast?

JOHN: What do you mean?

VOICE ONE: In the context of the whole incident. In Bethnal Green. Do you see
yourself as Beauty or the Beast?

JOHN: What do you see me as?

SCENE 11

*[JOHN covers his face with his hands. All the VOICES are looking at JOHN,
taunting him, at first softly, then gradually louder, like a shout. As the scene
progresses, the VOICES get up and surround JOHN in a claustrophobic semicircle and yell at him.]*

VOICE ONE: Queer.

VOICE THREE: Chink.

VOICE FOUR: Poof.

VOICE TWO: Slit eyes.

VOICE ONE: Queer.
VOICE THREE: Chink.
VOICE FOUR: Cocksucker.
VOICE TWO: Slit eyes.
VOICE ONE: Queer.
VOICE THREE: Chink.
VOICE FOUR: Ugly.
VOICE TWO: Homo.
VOICE ONE: Queer.
VOICE THREE: Chink.
VOICE FOUR: Go away!
VOICE TWO: Chink.
VOICE ONE: Queer!
JOHN: No.
VOICE THREE: Chink!
VOICE FOUR: Go back to China!
VOICE TWO: Slit eyes!
VOICE ONE: Queer!
VOICE THREE: Homo!
JOHN: No.

[*VOICES begin to overlap and yell.*]

VOICE FOUR: Go back to Hong Kong!
VOICE TWO: Six shots.
VOICE ONE: Slit eyes!
VOICE THREE: Queer!
VOICE FOUR: A body falls.
VOICE TWO: You don't belong here!
VOICE ONE: Homo!
VOICE THREE: Chink!
VOICE FOUR: Bang!
JOHN: No.
VOICE TWO: Bang!
VOICE ONE: Queer!
JOHN: No.
VOICE THREE: Bang!
VOICE FOUR: Slit eyes!
JOHN: [*Louder*] No.
VOICE TWO: Bang!
VOICE ONE: Chink!
VOICE THREE: Bang!
JOHN: [*Louder*] No!
VOICE FOUR: Homo!

VOICE TWO: Bang!
JOHN: *[Screams]* No!

SCENE 12

VOICE ONE: How about this one?
JOHN: Well, it—it does look like a flower.
VOICE ONE: Orchids? Daisies? Daffodils?
JOHN: A poppy. A red poppy.
VOICE ONE: Where did you see this red poppy?
JOHN: I don't remember.
VOICE ONE: What do you feel when you see this card?
JOHN: Sadness. A certain sadness.
VOICE ONE: I see.
JOHN: Yet, warmth.
VOICE ONE: Who do you see in it?
JOHN: Will.
VOICE ONE: William Hope?
JOHN: Yes.
VOICE ONE: What about him?
JOHN: Don't know. Just him and the red poppy.
VOICE ONE: We haven't spoken about William Hope.
JOHN: There's nothing to speak of.
VOICE ONE: Tell me something about him.
JOHN: He's dead.
VOICE ONE: What else?
JOHN: Surely you must have a folder on him.
VOICE ONE: Yes, but I want to hear it from you.
JOHN: I don't want to talk about him.
VOICE ONE: Do you miss him?
JOHN: Why should I?
VOICE ONE: Shouldn't you?
JOHN: I don't miss him.
VOICE ONE: Really? It says in my folder that both of you were involved in some
    capacity.
JOHN: That's correct.
VOICE ONE: Sexually?
JOHN: Yes.
VOICE ONE: And you?
JOHN: No.
VOICE ONE: I see.
JOHN: Tell me what you see, Dr. Worthing.

VOICE ONE: Only what you want me to see.

JOHN: So we're playing little mind games, aren't we?

VOICE ONE: You are. I'm not.

JOHN: This is all a trick, isn't it? Reverse psychology.

VOICE ONE: Whatever you say.

JOHN: Surely a leopard cannot change its spots.

VOICE ONE: As I said before, I have a job to do. I am here to help, if you want me to. If you don't, I'll try and do my job all the same.

JOHN: You're no fun.

VOICE ONE: Murder isn't fun.

JOHN: It can be.

VOICE ONE: Do you regret killing William Hope?

JOHN: No.

VOICE ONE: Why?

JOHN: Because he deserved it.

VOICE ONE: Do you miss him?

JOHN: You're repeating yourself, Dr. Worthing.

VOICE ONE: Well, do you?

JOHN: I don't—that's why I killed him.

VOICE ONE: Why did you do it?

JOHN: Because I hated him.

VOICE ONE: You hate him.

JOHN: Yes.

VOICE ONE: Really hate him.

JOHN: Yes.

VOICE ONE: How much do you hate him?

JOHN: Why are you asking me this question over and over again?

VOICE ONE: Just wanted to make sure. How much do you hate him?

JOHN: I don't know.

VOICE ONE: Hated him so much you murdered him in cold blood?

JOHN: Yes.

VOICE ONE: Hated him so much that you shot him six times?

JOHN: Yes.

VOICE ONE: Not one shot but six.

JOHN: Yes. Six.

VOICE ONE: Six shots. Two in the face. One in the throat. Two in the chest and one in the groin.

JOHN: Yes.

VOICE ONE: Six shots.

JOHN: I'm tired.

VOICE ONE: Six shots.

JOHN: Yes! What do you want from me?

VOICE ONE: Just the truth.

JOHN: I miss him.

SCENE 13

VOICE THREE: You said you had toilet sex before.

VOICE TWO: Yes. With a lot of men. A lot of men.

VOICE THREE: How many men?

VOICE FOUR: Can't say for sure.

VOICE TWO: Lost count after thirty.

VOICE THREE: Tell me about your experiences.

VOICE TWO: Ohhh, wouldn't you like to know, honey?

VOICE ONE: Are you sure no one will recognise me on television?

VOICE THREE: Why did you do it?

VOICE TWO: You know, that's a question I keep asking myself. I don't know. There's a strange kind of attraction to it. Kind of excitement.

VOICE THREE: What kind of excitement?

VOICE TWO: Sexual excitement. A certain kind of anonymity. It's like an exclusive ritual, a gentlemen's sex club.

VOICE ONE: I wouldn't go, but my wife doesn't like to kiss it.

VOICE FOUR: My girlfriend sucks like she's—she just doesn't do it the way I like it.

VOICE TWO: It's convenient. Like a supermarket. It's there. You walk in, get it, and go home. You don't even have to make small talk, buy him a lager, or exchange phone numbers you know they'll never call.

VOICE FOUR: Those queers there like to suck cock—and they do it good. So I'm just obliging them. Could say I'm doing my bit for gay rights, you know what I mean? *[Laughs raunchily]*

VOICE ONE: I think there's an element of danger to it, too—an element of being discovered. And that's why people like to fuck in parks, back alleys, toilets, offices, and planes. Don't you?

VOICE FOUR: No, I'm not being unfaithful to my girlfriend. I mean, I think being unfaithful to my girlfriend is having sex with another woman.

VOICE ONE: I'm not bisexual, no.

VOICE FOUR: My lover and I have a very open relationship.

VOICE ONE: I don't think there's much cottaging going on anymore, especially when most of the public lavs are shut down and there's always an attendant there. Not anymore. Cottaging went out with disco.

VOICE FOUR: I don't know why there's cottaging. Maybe it has to do with the boarding school system or something.

VOICE TWO: You'll simply have to die when you hear this. I got sucked off by an Anglican priest. Swear to God. See, he preaches in my parish. Didn't recognise me. What a lark! Never thought they'd take the get-down-on-your-knees thing quite so seriously.

VOICE THREE: How old were you when you first had this experience?

VOICE FOUR: About seventeen and it happened in a shopping centre in North London. Brent Cross.

VOICE TWO: Yeah, once I got fucked in the toilet by this blond Adonis. It was a good fuck. Safe sex, of course. My arse just tingles when I think about it. Oh, can I say that on television?

VOICE ONE: It's really unsafe nowadays to be doing toilets. This thing with AIDS is quite frightening. Who knows what type of people are in there?

VOICE FOUR: I know you can't get it from sucking, but who knows?

VOICE THREE: If there weren't AIDS, would you do the toilets?

VOICE FOUR: If the coppers weren't snooping about, maybe.

VOICE ONE: Yeah, why not?

VOICE TWO: *[Airily and in a camp voice]* Not anymore. This girl needs a spring mattress, a down pillow, and the West End soundtrack of *Camelot* before she can do the wild thing. *[He snaps his fingers in a dramatic way.]*

SCENE 14

VOICE ONE: I know what you're feeling.

JOHN: You don't know what I am feeling. Stop trying to say something you don't mean. How can you possibly know what I'm feeling?

VOICE ONE: Because I've lost someone, too. She didn't die, but a loss is a loss.

JOHN: We're not in the same situation.

VOICE ONE: Let's get back to the cards. This reminds you of a red poppy. Somehow you're reminded of William Hope. When did you first meet him?

JOHN: Two—no, three—months ago. January.

VOICE ONE: Where?

JOHN: I don't want to talk about him.

VOICE ONE: Why not?

JOHN: I just don't want to.

VOICE ONE: There must be a reason.

JOHN: I don't have a reason, just a feeling.

VOICE ONE: Of?

JOHN: Pain.

VOICE ONE: You can get rid of this pain by talking about it.

JOHN: I know. But somehow—I like this pain—I need it.

VOICE ONE: Where did you meet William Hope?

JOHN: In a public toilet.

VOICE ONE: Which one?

JOHN: That one.

VOICE ONE: Bethnal Green?

[JOHN nods.]

VOICE ONE: And?

JOHN: I was sitting in the cubicle.

VOICE ONE: Cubicle doing what?

JOHN: Waiting.

VOICE ONE: Waiting for what?

JOHN: Waiting.

VOICE ONE: I see.

JOHN: It was late afternoon—cold—

[VOICE FOUR playing William Hope character]

VOICE FOUR: About 4:30, 5:00. Since work was quiet that day, I decided to knock off early and thought I'd make a quick trip to the loo—you know—before going home.

JOHN: Things were quiet that Thursday—

VOICE FOUR: I don't know why, but I went into the lav at Bethnal Green—Guess I live close by and I've been there before and some chappies got me off.

JOHN: And Will came in—

VOICE FOUR: I went in—thinking, you know, that someone might be there. There's always someone there—if there isn't, you wait. Things do happen, you know. They usually do.

JOHN: At first I thought he was just going to take a piss. Then he started to walk around the toilet. I just kept still in my cubicle—hearing his footsteps.

VOICE FOUR: At first I thought there wasn't anybody there. It was pretty quiet. So I started to check out—

JOHN: He started to walk by the cubicles—really slowly—deliberately. I don't know why but I was anxious—my heart is beating away—I mean, I've done this before but I always get—anxious. And—then he passed mine—my cubicle and—he stopped. He wasn't handsome, but he was—attractive. Dark hair, dark eyes. Something magnetic about his features—almost rough yet—gentle. Though he stood in front of my cubicle for a few seconds, it seemed like an eternity.

VOICE: There was an Oriental bloke—Chinese, Japanese, or something looking at me. He's—not bad looking—looks like any other chink, I guess—

JOHN: He smiled.

VOICE FOUR: He just kept looking—just sitting there—and I wasn't in the mood to play the usual cat-and-mouse games, so I nodded to him.

JOHN: And I nodded. He came into the stall, and we started looking at each other. He shut the door gently behind him—all the while he kept staring at me. It was arresting.

VOICE FOUR: I've never got it off with an Oriental before, you know. They're not my type generally. But there wasn't anyone else around and a mouth is a mouth. And it looks as if he has never done it before. Could be an act for all I know—the innocent puppy dog look. He looked so—what's the word? Fragile? Yeah, fragile. I touched his face.

JOHN: His rough, warm hands touched my face, my head—and he pulled me close—to his crotch—

VOICE FOUR: And rubbed his face around it. I was about to burst in my jeans. My hands cradling his soft black hair. Then he—

JOHN: Unzipped his jeans and took it out. Hard.

VOICE FOUR: It was a warm feeling. Nice.

JOHN: It was—

VOICE FOUR: Good. Good.

JOHN: Yes. Good.

VOICE FOUR: Yes. Yes. Yes. Yes. Slow. Slow.

JOHN: Hmm. Slow.

VOICE FOUR: Hmm. Yeah. Oh God. Oh God.

JOHN: He came over my shirt.

VOICE FOUR: In powerful spurts.

JOHN: Warm and sticky.

VOICE FOUR: *[Breathing heavily]* That felt good. Felt really nice. It was—

JOHN: Beautiful.

VOICE FOUR: A great blow job.

JOHN: It was—beautiful.

VOICE FOUR: I mean, don't get me wrong. I'm not a queer or anything, but, like the other boys, I like to—get off. It's just a physical thing, you know. It's just sex.

VOICE ONE: There, wasn't that simple?

JOHN: I feel so—

VOICE ONE: Vulnerable?

JOHN: I don't like to be—

VOICE ONE: I know. All of us usually don't.

JOHN: I know where I remember seeing the picture of the red poppies. Will has this print that quite looks like that. He hangs it by his bed.

SCENE 15

VOICE THREE: Mr. Lee? You're Mr. Lee, aren't you? Excuse me, Mr. Lee?

VOICE TWO: I am no Mr. Lee. Wrong person.

VOICE THREE: But I spoke to—

VOICE TWO: I no Mr. Lee. I no Mr. Lee.

VOICE THREE: Mr. Lee, I'm Allan White from Channel Four; perhaps you've seen me on—

VOICE TWO: Go away.

VOICE THREE: Mr. Lee, we're doing a special documentary about your son's—

VOICE TWO: Please. Please go away.

VOICE THREE: Mr. Lee, have you anything to say about your son's arrest last week?

VOICE TWO: Don't know what you say.

VOICE THREE: Your son who was—

VOICE TWO: No son.

VOICE THREE: There was a fatal shooting in Bethnal Green—

VOICE TWO: No son.

VOICE THREE: Aren't you the father of John Lee?

VOICE TWO: I have no son.

VOICE THREE: But my—

VOICE TWO: No son.

VOICE THREE: Are you—

VOICE TWO: I have no son! I have no son!

VOICE THREE: Mr. Lee?

VOICE TWO: No son! No son! My son is dead.

SCENE 16

JOHN: Then what happened?

VOICE ONE: She had to go back to the States.

JOHN: She's probably waiting for your call.

VOICE ONE: You think so?

JOHN: I know. Do you love her?

VOICE ONE: I think so. Back to work.

JOHN: Let's talk some more about—

VOICE ONE: Later. Why cottaging?

JOHN: Why do you go the pubs every night?

VOICE ONE: That's not the same thing.

JOHN: It is.

VOICE ONE: Let's start again. Why cottaging?

JOHN: I don't know.

VOICE ONE: Do you find it exciting—having sex in toilets?

JOHN: No. Yes, but that's not the reason why I—

VOICE ONE: You have difficulty meeting men for sex.

JOHN: No, not really.

VOICE ONE: Difficulty in meeting men?

JOHN: Yes.

VOICE ONE: What about the clubs? Don't you go—

JOHN: Sure, I go. Sometimes. And sometimes I wonder why I even bother.

VOICE ONE: Why?

JOHN: Because everyone there looks intimidating, dressed to the nines. Most of them talk among themselves, have a good time, laughing and drinking with their perfect smiles and perfect hair. And I spend the whole night standing alone in a dark corner. Pretending I'm having a barrel of laughs, pretending I'm having a good time. Pretending I'm enjoying the music. Tapping my feet and nodding my head to the rhythm. And waiting for someone to say something to me. Something nice. Say anything to me. Perhaps it's just that I'm Oriental.

VOICE ONE: Why do you say that?

JOHN: White guys aren't into Orientals.

VOICE ONE: There must be some.

JOHN: Old ones maybe. Looking for a houseboy. Trying to relive the old colonial days. Or they are just fascinated by our culture. Like you. I know I'm not being fair, but that's the way I feel. Sometimes I wish I was— *[He laughs]*

VOICE ONE: What's so funny?

JOHN: Nothing.

VOICE ONE: Tell me.

JOHN: I wanted to say—sometimes I wish I was—

VOICE ONE: What?

JOHN: White.

VOICE ONE: Why?

JOHN: I don't know. I see pictures of handsome white guys hugging, kissing, holding hands in magazines like they were meant for each other. Always white guys. But always happy. Always together. Even in pornography. I see good-looking white guys fuck each other, make love to each other. I don't know. I see myself in those pictures, those magazines, videos. Suddenly I'm that beautiful white guy everybody wants to make love to. I don't know. Maybe it's just I've always found it difficult to—

VOICE ONE: Blend in?

JOHN: No. To belong.

VOICE ONE: What would you like to say to these people in the gay clubs?

JOHN: Nothing.

VOICE ONE: There must be something. Let's pretend I'm one of these people in the clubs.

JOHN: This is stupid.

VOICE ONE: It's not. Come on.

JOHN: I don't know what to say.

VOICE ONE: Say whatever's on your mind. Tell me how you feel. I am one of those people you see in a club every weekend. I am standing here with my friends.

JOHN: I can't.

VOICE ONE: Try, John. Tell me how and what you've been feeling.

JOHN: I don't know what to say.

VOICE ONE: Try saying hello.

JOHN: Hi.

VOICE ONE: Hi. *[Pause]* Yes?

JOHN: I want to let you know that I wish you were a little more receptive, more hospitable, welcoming.

VOICE ONE: Carry on.

JOHN: It's not too much to ask, is it? After all, aren't we the same? Can you perhaps smile in my direction? Perhaps speak to me.

VOICE ONE: And?

JOHN: We—we don't have to sleep together. We don't have to—fuck. Maybe we can be friends. Maybe we can dance a little. Maybe see a movie, have dinner together. Maybe laugh a little. Maybe something. I can't anymore; let's stop this.

VOICE ONE: That's good.

JOHN: What's good? I may think all these thoughts, but then I'm back where I started. I find myself standing in that dark corner again. People passing me by. Not smiling. Not saying a word. And I go home alone. It's not so bad going home alone—except sometimes I wish—

VOICE ONE: Yes.

JOHN: To be honest with you, I hate the toilets. I really do—but there's this trembling in me when I'm there—I don't know what it is, but I like it—I enjoy it. And—there's people there who want me. Even for a moment. And the idiot that I am—thinking I really belong—thinking perhaps all these moments will amount to something—someone who will—like me, love me—isn't that the silliest thing you've heard?

VOICE ONE: No.

JOHN: It's sick.

VOICE ONE: No.

JOHN: I just want to be held by these men. For a moment, they do. Hold me. And almost all the time, I treasure that moment. The moment they smile. Then I go back and take a long hot shower. Washing every memory, every touch, and every smell. Only it never quite leaves me. No matter how hard or how long I wash. The dirt, filth penetrates deep into your skin. And for a time I'd try to stay away from the toilet until that familiar loneliness—the need to be held. It's strange. This feeling. This marriage of dirt and desire. The beauty and the beast. It's pathetic. Sometimes I hate myself. *[JOHN crushes a paper crane.]*

SCENE 17

VOICE ONE: The door of the toilet stall.

VOICE FOUR: Open.

VOICE TWO: John is leaning.

VOICE THREE: Against the wall.

VOICE ONE: Looking spent.

VOICE FOUR: Eyes shut.

VOICE TWO: Tight.

VOICE THREE: A young man.

VOICE ONE: Kneeling on the floor.

VOICE FOUR: Gets up.

VOICE TWO: Pulls up his jeans.

VOICE THREE: Zips himself up.

VOICE ONE: Buckles his belt.

VOICE FOUR: The young man.

VOICE TWO: Throws a ball of toilet paper.

VOICE THREE: Into the bowl.

VOICE ONE: Spits twice.

VOICE FOUR: Gently pats John.

VOICE TWO: On the butt.

VOICE THREE: Walks away quickly from the stall.

VOICE ONE: Quickly as if he has something to hide.

VOICE FOUR: John watches him leave.

VOICE TWO: Sits down.

VOICE THREE: Closes the door.

VOICE ONE: He looks up.

VOICE FOUR: At the toilet ceiling.

VOICE TWO: Paint peeling.

VOICE THREE: Interesting shapes.

VOICE ONE: Patterns.

VOICE FOUR: Like the clouds in the sky.

VOICE TWO: Like the blot test cards.

VOICE THREE: It can be anything you want it to be.

VOICE ONE: Depending on how you see it.

VOICE FOUR: And where.

VOICE TWO: In the meanwhile, John sits.

VOICE THREE: Waiting.

VOICE ONE: Waiting.

VOICE FOUR: Waiting.

VOICE TWO: And waiting.

SCENE 18

VOICE THREE: Tell me, Officer, in what capacity were you involved with the recent arrest in the toilets at Holland Park?

VOICE TWO: I arrested a suspect who was exposing himself to me.

VOICE THREE: Can you be more specific, please?

VOICE TWO: I was using the public conveniences in Holland Park a few weeks ago.

VOICE THREE: Were you in uniform?

VOICE TWO: No.

VOICE THREE: Why?

VOICE TWO: I was off duty.

VOICE THREE: Really?

VOICE TWO: Yes.

VOICE THREE: Undercover?

VOICE TWO: Uh—no.

VOICE THREE: Go on.

VOICE TWO: A man in his thirties beckoned to me.

VOICE THREE: What do you mean "beckoned"? Did he call you? Whisper to you? Signalled?

VOICE TWO: He nodded to me.

VOICE THREE: You've never seen this man before?

VOICE TWO: No.

VOICE THREE: I see. Please go on.

VOICE TWO: As I said, the gentleman beckoned to me. Saying he had something to show me. He went into the toilet stall and I followed. Then he took off his trousers and started to play with—I arrested him for public indecency.

VOICE THREE: Let me see. He beckoned to you. Nodded, I mean.

VOICE TWO: Yes.

VOICE THREE: He said he had something—

VOICE TWO: Something to show me. Yes.

VOICE THREE: You actually believed that he had something to—

VOICE TWO: Yes. I was curious.

VOICE THREE: I see, curious. And you followed him.

VOICE TWO: Yes.

VOICE THREE: Into the cubicle.

VOICE TWO: Yes.

VOICE THREE: Alone.

VOICE TWO: Yes.

VOICE THREE: And he took off his trousers.

VOICE TWO: Yes.

VOICE THREE: And you were standing there—still watching him.

VOICE TWO: That's right.

VOICE THREE: Then he started to fondle himself—and you were still standing there watching.

VOICE TWO: Yes.

VOICE THREE: And after awhile, you arrested him.

VOICE TWO: Yes.

VOICE THREE: How long was this? Fifteen minutes? Ten minutes? Half an hour?

VOICE TWO: A minute. Thereabouts.

VOICE THREE: That long.

VOICE TWO: I had to be sure—

VOICE THREE: Sure that he was actually fondling his penis?

VOICE TWO: Right.

VOICE THREE: Stroking it?

VOICE TWO: Yes.

VOICE THREE: Sounds like police entrapment.

VOICE TWO: Does it? It wasn't.

VOICE THREE: Thank you. I'll take your word for it.

SCENE 19

VOICE ONE: Then what happened?

JOHN: After we did what we did in the toilet, I thought Will was going to leave—
you know like the others—without a word—just walk away—but then—he
asked me if I wanted to have a drink with him in a nearby pub.

VOICE FOUR: I don't know why I asked him after we got off at the loo. Listen, this
isn't what I usually do. Make friends at the public loos. Guess I was thirsty and
since there wasn't anyone else around in the loo that evening. And I had no
plans. I thought after a few drinks at the corner pub I could ask him back to my
place so that we could get off again. *[To JOHN]* Hiya.

JOHN: Hi.

VOICE FOUR: What's your name?

JOHN: John.

VOICE FOUR: Will. Say, do you fancy a drink?

JOHN: Sure. Yes. *[A beat]* Of course I went. I mean, there was this guy who I
wanted—fancied very much and he's asking me out. He had a lager and I had a
coke. We talked about what music we liked.

VOICE FOUR: Opera. Puccini.

JOHN: Pet Shop Boys.

VOICE FOUR: Oh.

JOHN: Books.

VOICE FOUR: Brontë.

JOHN: All of them?

VOICE FOUR: Yes.

JOHN: I don't read much, except for schoolbooks.

VOICE FOUR: Hmm.

JOHN: What do you do?

VOICE FOUR: I'm a builder.

JOHN: Really?

VOICE FOUR: Uh-huh.

JOHN: I'm going to Cambridge in a few months. But right now I'm working at my
father's restaurant—as a waiter.

VOICE FOUR: Really.

JOHN: Yes.

VOICE FOUR: It's getting late.

JOHN: Yes.

VOICE FOUR: Listen, do you want to come over? To my flat?

JOHN: Sure.

VOICE FOUR: Good.

JOHN: And I spent the night there.

VOICE ONE: How did you feel?

JOHN: High like a kite. Like the whole world was under my feet. Like nothing could go wrong. Nothing. I couldn't believe this was happening. To me, especially. We made love again and again. It was tender and urgent. That night was very special for me. Later in bed we talked a little more about what we liked, what we didn't. Less awkwardly than we did in the pub. He put on some music, hummed to it around the small flat, and made some coffee. Then he talked about football. Suddenly his eyes lit up with a fiery blue intensity. Going on about the F.A. Cup, which teams were his favourite and which teams were bound to make it to the finals. Don't know why. Don't know why all of the sudden I liked football. I never did before.

VOICE ONE: So William was very special to you then?

JOHN: I suppose so.

VOICE ONE: Then why did it happen?

JOHN: It just did.

SCENE 20

VOICE TWO: The crow flew across the field.

VOICE THREE: The tree where the sparrows lived.

VOICE ONE: At first the sparrows looked at the crow.

VOICE FOUR: With much suspicion and curiosity.

VOICE TWO: The others with fear, contempt, and hatred.

VOICE THREE: Time went by.

VOICE ONE: The crow couldn't be happier.

VOICE FOUR: It often flew with the sparrows.

VOICE TWO: Braving new heights.

VOICE THREE: A soul lost in love.

VOICE ONE: For the very first time, the crow felt free.

VOICE FOUR: Happy.

VOICE TWO: However, the crow flew haphazardly.

VOICE THREE: Ungracefully.

VOICE ONE: Clumsily.

VOICE FOUR: Often colliding into the other sparrows.

VOICE TWO: The sparrows were far too genteel.

VOICE THREE: Polite.

VOICE ONE: Embarrassed to say anything.

VOICE FOUR: Refused to confront the crow about its eating habits.

VOICE TWO: Slurping slimy worms in a vulgar fashion.

VOICE THREE: Eating ferociously.

VOICE ONE: Gorging greedily.

VOICE FOUR: Eating much more than the petite appetites the sparrows possessed.

VOICE TWO: Another topic of private discussion.

VOICE THREE: The crow's enthusiastic singing.

VOICE ONE: The sparrows chirped ever so heavenly.

VOICE FOUR: Mellifluously.

VOICE TWO: Superfluously.

VOICE THREE: The crow cawed hysterically.

VOICE ONE: An unbearable pitch.

VOICE FOUR: Out of tune.

VOICE TWO: Out of rhythm.

VOICE THREE: Loudly.

VOICE ONE: The sparrows winced painfully.

VOICE FOUR: Turned a deaf ear.

VOICE TWO: Smiled forcefully.

VOICE THREE: In time the sparrows accepted the crow.

VOICE ONE: Despite the way it ate.

VOICE FOUR: Flew.

VOICE TWO: And sang.

VOICE THREE: A part of their family.

VOICE ONE: The crow was happy.

SCENE 21

VOICE FOUR: Do you want to hear some music?

JOHN: Sure.

VOICE FOUR: What do you want to hear?

JOHN: Anything. What's that?

VOICE FOUR: *Madame Butterfly*. It's my favourite.

JOHN: It's nice.

VOICE FOUR: Beautiful.

JOHN: What are they saying?

VOICE FOUR: "I'm happy now, so happy. Love me with a little love, a childlike love."

JOHN: Will, did you know it's been two weeks since we first met?

VOICE FOUR: Really?

JOHN: Yes. Can you believe it?

VOICE FOUR: What time is it?

JOHN: About 11:30.

VOICE FOUR: I have to get up early tomorrow.

JOHN: Me, too.

VOICE FOUR: I'm dead tired.

JOHN: I should go soon.

VOICE FOUR: Lie beside me.

JOHN: Hmm, I can hear your heart beating.

VOICE FOUR: You feel nice and smooth.

[They kiss tenderly.]

JOHN: You know something?

VOICE FOUR: What?

JOHN: I'm happy.

VOICE FOUR: Good.

JOHN: Really happy.

VOICE FOUR: Good.

JOHN: Will, we should go out the next time.

VOICE FOUR: The pictures?

JOHN: No.

VOICE FOUR: You mean to the pubs?

JOHN: Yeah, we always seem to stay in; not that I mind, of course.

VOICE FOUR: I'm not comfortable with those types of people.

JOHN: What do you mean?

VOICE FOUR: Well, I don't want to risk being recognised by anyone I know in those places.

JOHN: Sure, okay, I understand. Going to the pubs isn't that important anyway. Besides I like being here. Being with you.

SCENE 22

VOICE TWO: Public sex has always been a part of the gay culture. Parks and health club saunas and shower rooms and YMCAs.

VOICE THREE: Isn't it illegal in the U.K.?

VOICE TWO: Yes.

VOICE THREE: Why sex in public places?

VOICE TWO: I'm not sure I'm qualified to answer why gay people are involved in such activities.

VOICE THREE: Do you think cottaging is a kind of perversion?

VOICE TWO: No, I don't think it's a perversion. Perhaps a better word is "choice." After all, it's among consenting adults. The cause of cottaging is directly related to the society's discrimination against homosexuals. Instead of providing a healthy and acceptable environment for gay men to come out to the public, they are often forced to meet other gay men in less than conventional surroundings.

VOICE THREE: So you're saying that toilet sex is the fault of the society?

VOICE TWO: No, I'm trying to say that it is the result of public inacceptance and intolerance of gays, which have led them to seek—

VOICE THREE: You have your clubs and pubs.

VOICE TWO: We also have job discrimination, police harassment, gay-bashing, poor AIDS health care—

VOICE THREE: What about AIDS? Don't you think—

VOICE TWO: AIDS should be a paramount concern for all those who have sex in public places.

VOICE THREE: Do you think toilet sex spreads homosexuality?

VOICE TWO: One does not spread homosexuality, and besides, not only are gay men involved but bisexual and straight men like yourself as well.

VOICE THREE: That doesn't answer—

VOICE TWO: If you'd excuse me, I feel that this interview must come to an end. Does the word *homophobia* mean anything to you?

SCENE 23

VOICE ONE: Has Will treated you unkindly at all?

JOHN: No.

VOICE ONE: Not once?

JOHN: No.

VOICE ONE: Every couple must have their ups and downs.

JOHN: We have our differences.

VOICE ONE: What differences?

JOHN: Will can be—excitable.

VOICE ONE: Excitable?

JOHN: Aggressive.

VOICE ONE: Did you mind?

JOHN: I suppose not in the beginning, but later it started to—

VOICE ONE: To what?

JOHN: To hurt.

VOICE ONE: Uh-huh.

JOHN: He cares for me. I know he does. In his own way. There were times after we made love, he'd stroke my head, breathing softly. Soft brown hair. And skin like porcelain. Smooth. White. Pure. But there were times—

[VOICE ONE reaches for his lighter and cigarettes and is about to smoke.]

You know, Jack, smoking isn't good for you. Cancer.

VOICE ONE: Yeah, I know.

JOHN: Hope I'm not being too—

VOICE ONE: You're not. Thanks.

JOHN: Sure. By the way, what's her name?

VOICE ONE: Whose name?

JOHN: The woman you were seeing.

VOICE ONE: Eh—Sue—Suzanne.

JOHN: Did you ring her?

VOICE ONE: Yes.

JOHN: And?

VOICE ONE: We're going to work it out.

JOHN: You know, we were happy. Will and I. Really happy together.

SCENE 24

[The stage is pitch black. VOICE FOUR is drunk and is walking heavily onstage.]

VOICE FOUR: Can't see a fucking thing in here.

JOHN: Do you want me to turn on the lights?

VOICE FOUR: No, no.

JOHN: Said you'd be here at 8:00. It's 12:00 now.

VOICE FOUR: Nag, nag, nag. Put on some music.

JOHN: What do you want to hear?

VOICE FOUR: Whatever's on the turntable.

JOHN: Not *Madame Butterfly* again.

VOICE FOUR: I like it.

JOHN: We always hear it.

VOICE FOUR: I thought you liked it.

JOHN: I did.

VOICE FOUR: Then put on something you like.

JOHN: What's this?

VOICE FOUR: *Carmen. [VOICE FOUR hums to the music. Sounds of VOICE FOUR knocking against furniture]* Fuck. Where are you?

JOHN: Here.

VOICE FOUR: Where's here?

JOHN: By the bed.

VOICE FOUR: How convenient.

JOHN: I'm not in the mood.

VOICE FOUR: You'll be.

JOHN: Ouch. Stop it. You're hurting me.

VOICE FOUR: You like it.

JOHN: I don't. *[Pause]* Ouch. Will!

VOICE FOUR: Come here.

JOHN: You are late.

VOICE FOUR: So?

JOHN: You kept me waiting for hours.

VOICE FOUR: It's only a few hours.

JOHN: Where were you?

VOICE FOUR: At the pub.

JOHN: Again?

VOICE FOUR: Why are you so possessive?

JOHN: You kept me waiting.

VOICE FOUR: You had the bloody telly.

JOHN: I came over to see you, not watch telly.

VOICE FOUR: Come here and touch it.

JOHN: Stop it.

VOICE FOUR: You want it. Come on.

JOHN: No.

VOICE FOUR: I'm horny.

JOHN: You're drunk.

VOICE FOUR: I'm not.

JOHN: You smell of lager.

VOICE FOUR: You smell of talcum.

JOHN: I hate it when you're like that.

VOICE FOUR: I'm hard.

JOHN: Get off me now!

VOICE FOUR: You want it.

   [*Sound of JOHN's chair falling on the floor. There are sounds of a violent struggle.*]

JOHN: You're hurting me.

VOICE FOUR: You like that.

JOHN: I don't.

VOICE FOUR: Suck it.

JOHN: No.

VOICE FOUR: Suck it.

JOHN: Fuck you.

   [*Sounds of a slap*]

JOHN: [*Whimpering*] That hurts.

VOICE FOUR: That'll teach you, you fucking tease.

   [*Sounds of a struggle*]

JOHN: Will, stop it. Stop it.

VOICE FOUR: Suck this.

[Sounds of gagging]

VOICE FOUR: You like it, don't you? Come on, tell me you like it.

[JOHN responds inaudibly, still gagging]

That's it. Take it all in, you cocksucker.

[JOHN again responds gaggingly and in deep breaths.]

VOICE FOUR: Yeah, yeah. That's good. Lick my balls. Lick it. Now, suck it. Hard. Yeah. *[He breathes hard.]* Stop. I don't want to come yet. Turn over. I want to fuck you.
JOHN: No.

[Sound of a vicious slap]

VOICE FOUR: Shut the fuck up.
JOHN: Will.

[Another slap]

VOICE FOUR: You want it. My big cock up your arse.
JOHN: Condom.
VOICE FOUR: Fuck condoms.
JOHN: You promised you'd use—
VOICE FOUR: Shut up.
JOHN: Condoms. *[Suddenly JOHN screams in agony.]*
VOICE FOUR: Yes. Nice and tight, the way I like it.
JOHN: *[Moaning]* Will. Take it out. Now.
VOICE FOUR: It feels good.
JOHN: Will. Condom. Please.
VOICE FOUR: Tight.
JOHN: Put it on.
VOICE FOUR: Yes.
JOHN: Will.
VOICE FOUR: You like my tongue in your ear?
JOHN: Don't. *[Pause]* Mmm.
VOICE FOUR: Feels good.
JOHN: Yes.
VOICE FOUR: Do I feel good?
JOHN: You feel good.
VOICE FOUR: Do you like it?
JOHN: Yes.
VOICE FOUR: You wanted it, didn't you?
JOHN: Yes.

VOICE FOUR: Tell me you want it.

JOHN: I want it. Yes.

VOICE FOUR: Say it again.

JOHN: I want it.

VOICE FOUR: I can't hear you.

JOHN: I want it!

VOICE FOUR: Louder.

JOHN: [*Loudly*] I want it!

VOICE FOUR: Want what?

JOHN: You! I want you! I want you! I want you! I love you.

VOICE FOUR: I'm coming!

[*VOICE FOUR groans. Both he and JOHN breathe hard and slowly. Then silence.*]

SCENE 25

VOICE TWO: I have only one son. Lone. I don't know why he change his name to John—English. Maybe he want to be like English friends in school—not be different. Be like them. I remember one day—when he was in primary school—he come home from school—clothes all dirty—got mud all over—school tie torn—books in schoolbag all tear up—small pieces—his hands, legs, nose, all got blood—but he never say one word. Nothing. But this is life. Life here. Have to accept. Have to learn. Even change name cannot do anything. He don't like much Chinese way of life. Always question the way Chinese live, Chinese speak. He once criticise way I speak English—I angry, hit him across face till red. Again he never say one word. I come from Hong Kong long time—in sixties—sacrifice everything I have so children can have good life in England. Think children will be able to be better than other children in Hong Kong. But think I make mistake. Big mistake. I have daughter who shame my family. Go about with a lot of white man. Stay at their house at night. I know. I know. Times not the same. Different. Have to accept but—she also never finish school. Now I have son who no respect me. But he intelligent and go to university very soon. Now no more university. No more son. Neighbour all talk behind my back—of murder. In toilet. Bethnal Green. I so ashamed. So angry. Every morning open restaurant in Gerard Street selling noodle bowls, rice plates. People polite, but I know their minds, their hearts. I see it in eyes. Those silent eyes very loud. My wife pretend nothing happen. Pretend everything okay. Everyone all pretending around me. All pretending. My son no commit crime. No commit murder. My son no homo. No homo! He cannot be—I—I have no son. Son is dead. Dead to me. Dead. Perhaps better he change his name to English. Be someone else.

SCENE 26

JOHN: You look like shit.

VOICE ONE: Late night.

JOHN: Again?

VOICE ONE: I'm predictable.

JOHN: Why do you do that so often?

VOICE ONE: Do what often?

JOHN: Go out to the pubs and drink.

VOICE ONE: Because I can't think of anything better to do.

JOHN: Really?

VOICE ONE: I need to—

JOHN: Get laid.

VOICE ONE: Let's get back to the session. Tell me what happened that afternoon at Bethnal Green.

JOHN: Nothing.

VOICE ONE: Stop fucking about! I thought we have an honest relationship.

JOHN: We do.

VOICE ONE: Then?

JOHN: I don't want to talk about it.

VOICE ONE: You'll have to. Sooner or later.

JOHN: I don't.

VOICE ONE: Listen, you've got to bloody confront it once and for all.

JOHN: You're only here to finish a report.

VOICE ONE: Yes. But I'm also here to help—

JOHN: I don't want your help, I've told you.

VOICE ONE: You need my help.

JOHN: No, I don't.

VOICE ONE: Well, fuck you! Yes. Fuck you. Fuck all of this.

JOHN: You'll never understand. You can't—

VOICE ONE: How do you know I won't understand if you don't tell me the story? We've been playing this pissy merry-go-round question-and-answer session all week, and I've gotten nowhere. I want to fucking know what happened.

JOHN: No.

VOICE ONE: You're always so fucking high and mighty about how people don't understand where you're coming from. So you're Oriental—a chink. So you're gay, poof, queer. So what? Now's your chance to tell me. To make me understand why you fucking did what you did.

JOHN: You'll never understand.

VOICE ONE: Maybe not. But tell me.

JOHN: No.

VOICE ONE: Come on, John. Try.

JOHN: I don't know where to begin.

VOICE ONE: Where did you get the gun?

JOHN: It belonged to my father. Kept it in the restaurant. Just in case of robbers, he said. Said everyone had one, why shouldn't he? Don't know where he got the gun from. It's illegal, probably, just like Pa to do something like that. I took the gun from him.

VOICE ONE: Why?

JOHN: Maybe I just wanted to. Take the gun.

VOICE ONE: To shoot someone?

JOHN: Maybe.

VOICE ONE: Willliam Hope?

JOHN: Maybe.

VOICE ONE: Why?

JOHN: Because.

VOICE ONE: Because?

JOHN: Because. *[Pause]* He didn't speak to me for several days—days turned into weeks—I don't know—I tried ringing him—leaving messages—on his answering machine, but he didn't ring back. So that Saturday afternoon, I decided to go over to his flat. I wanted to see him. Just to talk or something. But when I arrived at his place, I didn't ring the doorbell. I didn't even use the key he gave me. All I did was to stand outside a bus stop across the street. Looking at his flat with the gun in my jacket. Then two—three hours later, he stepped outside. Probably taking a walk. I followed him, and all the time I was following him, I had an uncomfortable but certain feeling I knew where he was going.

VOICE THREE: To the lav in Bethnal Green.

JOHN: I said, maybe not.

VOICE TWO: Maybe he's going to the tube station.

JOHN: Shopping.

VOICE THREE: Maybe a walk in the park.

JOHN: Maybe.

VOICE TWO: Maybe some groceries at Sainsbury's.

JOHN: Maybe a drink at the pub.

VOICE THREE: Maybe he's meeting some friends.

JOHN: What friends?

VOICE TWO: And?

JOHN: And he walked into the lav.

VOICE THREE: I was crushed.

VOICE TWO: Destroyed.

VOICE THREE: But I knew it.

JOHN: Maybe that's why I followed him.

VOICE TWO: To confirm my suspicions.

VOICE THREE: Maybe that's why I took the gun.

JOHN: Maybe.

VOICE TWO: The cheating bastard.

JOHN: I stopped outside. Didn't want to go in. Didn't dare.

VOICE THREE: Dare what?

JOHN: Dare to confront him.

VOICE TWO: Dare to hear the truth?

VOICE THREE: See the truth?

VOICE TWO: Dare to use the gun?

JOHN: I don't know.

VOICE THREE: Maybe he's really taking a piss.

VOICE TWO: Maybe.

VOICE THREE: Yeah. Right.

JOHN: I don't know. Then I saw people, men, going into the lav. But no one came out. For the longest time. I kept fingering my gun.

VOICE TWO: That son of a bitch.

VOICE THREE: You are an idiot.

VOICE TWO: I knew it.

VOICE THREE: All the time.

VOICE TWO: Why? Why are you doing this?

VOICE THREE: Kill him.

JOHN: Feeling the cold steel in my pocket. I started making mental notes of who went in and who went out.

VOICE TWO: Young black guy with an Adidas sportsbag.

VOICE FOUR: White guy in his thirties carrying *The Independent*.

VOICE THREE: Old man in a brown blazer.

VOICE FOUR: White boy with a baseball cap.

VOICE TWO: Still he didn't come out.

JOHN: Then when I thought no one was in there anymore, I walked into the lav.

VOICE THREE: The gun.

VOICE TWO: The loo was empty.

VOICE THREE: Deathly quiet.

VOICE TWO: Deathly still.

VOICE THREE: The gun pressed against his jacket.

VOICE TWO: Pressed against his beating heart.

JOHN: Then I saw Will in the cubicle. Pretending to take a piss.

VOICE THREE: He was pulling his cock.

VOICE TWO: Deliberately.

JOHN: He seemed surprised to see me.

VOICE THREE: Almost frightened.

VOICE TWO: Shocked.

JOHN: Hi.

VOICE FOUR: Hi. Fancy bumping into you, here of all places.

JOHN: Yes. Fancy that.

VOICE THREE: Awkward silence.

VOICE TWO: The gun.

VOICE THREE: Outside traffic noises.

VOICE FOUR: Eh—everyone's gone.

JOHN: Really.

VOICE FOUR: So how have you been?

JOHN: Good.

VOICE FOUR: You alright? You look kinda—

JOHN: You didn't call.

VOICE FOUR: I was busy. Work, you know.

JOHN: I rang. Left messages.

VOICE FOUR: I know.

JOHN: You could have called.

VOICE FOUR: I know, but I was busy—

JOHN: I must have left you a thousand messages.

VOICE FOUR: Yeah.

JOHN: I didn't hear from you at all.

VOICE FOUR: Listen, do you want to go outside so we can talk?

JOHN: No. Let's talk here. It's quieter.

VOICE FOUR: Outside.

JOHN: Here. I want to talk—

VOICE FOUR: Alright, here. *[Pause]* Well?

JOHN: You look—

VOICE TWO: John reached out to touch his face.

VOICE FOUR: I'm okay. Really.

VOICE THREE: Brushing me away.

VOICE TWO: The gun.

VOICE THREE: Against my heart.

JOHN: I—

VOICE TWO: Helpless.

VOICE THREE: Awkward.

VOICE TWO: Stupid.

VOICE FOUR: Look, I'm sorry I didn't ring back.

JOHN: You said you were busy.

VOICE FOUR: I wasn't busy.

JOHN: I see. It's okay.

VOICE FOUR: No, it's not.

JOHN: It is. Really.

VOICE FOUR: I don't think you understand. Johnny, I like you—I really do—but—I think—

JOHN: We should stop seeing each other.

VOICE FOUR: Yes. In that way anyway.

JOHN: Why?

VOICE FOUR: I don't like this situation, that's all.

JOHN: What situation?

VOICE FOUR: Us. Us meeting. Us doing things together.

JOHN: Us fucking each other.

VOICE FOUR: Yes.

JOHN: Why?

VOICE FOUR: I don't know why. I just don't want it.

JOHN: Then why are you here? *[Pause]* I'm sorry.

VOICE FOUR: That's not the point.

JOHN: Forget it.

VOICE FOUR: Let me get to the point: It's over, okay?

JOHN: He said it very evenly—calm.

VOICE FOUR: We are history. Okay? I'm not what you think I am. I'm not that way. I enjoyed doing what we do. But I'm not—queer.

JOHN: Like me.

VOICE FOUR: Told you from the start that I date women and I like to fool around with guys—you know, just to get off—but I'm not like that—like you. And I don't want to play games, the idea of hiding every time—hide and seek. People may start getting strange ideas about me and you—might start thinking we're queer—that I'm queer—something I'm not. Don't misunderstand, whatever we had—was great. I enjoyed it—had a great time—I know you did, too—I don't know, but maybe I just didn't like the idea of turning—perhaps we could be friends.

JOHN: But I wasn't listening. Not a word. All I heard was—

VOICE FOUR: It's over.

VOICE TWO: It's over.

VOICE THREE: It's over.

JOHN: Like some strange, hypnotic melody dancing in my mind.

VOICE TWO: Intoxicating me.

VOICE THREE: Suffocating me.

JOHN: Somehow I anticipated this. I knew this was going to happen.

VOICE TWO: Him leaving.

JOHN: Him saying just that.

VOICE THREE: But he doesn't know better.

JOHN: Maybe that's why I took the gun.

VOICE TWO: Maybe.

JOHN: Maybe I was expecting he'd say this.

VOICE THREE: Maybe.

JOHN: He belonged to me. Only to me.

VOICE TWO: And you took the gun.

JOHN: To make him stay.

VOICE THREE: Force him to stay.

JOHN: No matter what. I was pleading—pleading with him.

VOICE TWO: Begging.

JOHN: Raising my voice. Anything to make him stay.

VOICE THREE: Please don't—

JOHN: Don't say—

VOICE TWO: Please, I'm sorry—

JOHN: I won't anymore.

VOICE FOUR: Listen, this has nothing to—

JOHN: Will, please, you can't—

VOICE FOUR: I'm not queer, Johnny! I'm not one of your kind. I—I've got nothing against—you—your kind—at all. This whole thing was all in your head. Shouldn't have allowed it to happen the way it did—it went too far.

JOHN: I felt so helpless.

VOICE TWO: Desperate.

VOICE FOUR: It's over.

VOICE THREE: Angry.

VOICE TWO: Hurt.

VOICE FOUR: It's over.

VOICE THREE: Pained.

VOICE TWO: The gun.

VOICE THREE: In your jacket.

VOICE TWO: Waiting.

VOICE FOUR: Hey, Johnny, I'm sorry. Really am.

VOICE ONE: Final scene in Bizet's *Carmen*.

VOICE TWO: No.

JOHN: Don't go.

VOICE THREE: Not yet.

VOICE TWO: Please.

VOICE ONE: The Death Scene.

JOHN: Will smiled that smile, that familiar smile I always see in my mind whenever he's away from me.

VOICE THREE: He shrugged his shoulders.

VOICE ONE: Don José arrives at the bullring.

VOICE TWO: Will put his hands in his pockets.

VOICE THREE: And started to walk out of the toilet.

VOICE ONE: Don José begs for Carmen's love.

JOHN: I wanted to shout, but no sound came out. No words.

VOICE TWO: You have a gun.

VOICE ONE: Carmen declares it's over between them.

VOICE THREE: You can make him stay.

VOICE TWO: Force him to stay.

VOICE ONE: Don José implores Carmen to return to him.

VOICE THREE: Then maybe he'll change his mind.

VOICE TWO: He'll see things your way.

VOICE ONE: A triumphant shout from the bullring!

VOICE THREE: Understand what you're trying to say.

VOICE TWO: What you feel.

VOICE ONE: The matador has plunged his sword into the bull.

VOICE THREE: Stay.

VOICE ONE: Plunge!

VOICE TWO: Stay.

VOICE ONE: Plunge!

VOICE THREE: Please stay.

VOICE ONE: Plunge!

VOICE TWO: Your gun.

VOICE ONE: Carmen admits the matador is her new lover.

JOHN: Then I remembered the gun.

VOICE THREE: Take it out.

VOICE TWO: Now!

VOICE ONE: The matador stabs the bull with his glistening blade.

JOHN: Took it out of my jacket.

VOICE ONE: Stab!

VOICE THREE: Aim.

VOICE ONE: Stab!

VOICE TWO: Shoot!

VOICE ONE: Stab!

VOICE THREE: He's walking away.

VOICE ONE: Don José realizes Carmen doesn't love him anymore.

VOICE THREE: He used you.

VOICE TWO: Like everyone else.

JOHN: I—I pointed it at his back.

VOICE THREE: I won't be used again.

VOICE TWO: Stay.

VOICE THREE: I want you.

VOICE TWO: Don't go.

VOICE ONE: Rage and despair overwhelm Don José.

VOICE THREE: Fuck you.

VOICE TWO: You're like the fucking rest.

VOICE THREE: A quick feel.

VOICE TWO: A willing mouth.

VOICE THREE: And a willing arse.

VOICE ONE: Don José pulls out his knife.

VOICE TWO: Love me.

VOICE THREE: Please stay.

JOHN: Stay!

VOICE ONE: The lusty knife glistening in the afternoon light.

VOICE FOUR: What the fuck?

VOICE TWO: Gun pointing to Will.

VOICE FOUR: You're bloody crazy.

VOICE ONE: The crowd cheers, "Viva, viva."

VOICE TWO: Queer!

VOICES ONE, TWO, and THREE: Viva! Viva!

VOICE THREE: Chink!

VOICES ONE, TWO, and THREE: Viva! Viva!

VOICE TWO: Pouf!

VOICES ONE, TWO, and THREE: Viva! Viva!

VOICE THREE: Homo!

VOICES ONE, TWO, and THREE: Kill it!

JOHN: It is loaded.

VOICE THREE: Will looked at him.

VOICE TWO: Disbelief.

VOICE THREE: Snarled.

VOICE TWO: As if daring him to shoot.

VOICE ONE: Carmen laughs.

VOICE TWO: Will continued to go.

VOICE THREE: Stay.

VOICE TWO: What else can I do?

VOICE THREE: You're not walking out.

VOICE ONE: Don José raises the knife to his blood-red eyes.

JOHN: Will?

VOICE TWO: The gun trembled.

VOICE ONE: The matador thrusts his sword into the bull.

VOICE THREE: Don't go.

VOICE TWO: The gun swayed.

VOICE THREE: You're not going anywhere.

VOICE ONE: The bull collapses.

VOICE TWO: Under his sweaty fingers.

VOICE THREE: Stay!

VOICE ONE: The bullring is swimming in the sea of blood.

VOICE TWO: Wrapping around the trigger.

VOICE THREE: Stay!

VOICE ONE: The crowd is cheering and tossing roses.

VOICE TWO: Cock the pistol.

JOHN: Then I started to squeeze the trigger.

VOICE TWO: Bullet in the chamber.

VOICE ONE: Ready to fire.

JOHN: Will?

VOICE TWO: He continues walking.

VOICE ONE: Don José plunges the knife into Carmen.

JOHN: I love you.

VOICE THREE: Bang!

VOICE TWO: His body crumpled.

VOICE THREE: Like a paper crane against a flame.

VOICE TWO: And he fell against the white urinals.

VOICE THREE: His right hand clutching a side of the urinal.

VOICE TWO: Holding tight.

VOICE THREE: He was in shock.

VOICE TWO: You're not going.

JOHN: My hands shaking.

VOICE TWO: Bang!

VOICE THREE: Another shot.

VOICE TWO: You're staying.

VOICE THREE: You need me!

VOICE TWO: You love me.

VOICE THREE: We'll be together.

VOICE ONE: Don José lifts the blood-stained knife.

VOICE TWO: We'll be happy.

VOICE THREE: Bang!

VOICE ONE: The knife plunges again!

JOHN: My eyes were closed tight. When I opened them, I found him on the floor.

VOICE TWO: Spread-eagled.

VOICE THREE: He was still moving.

VOICE TWO: Tough son of a bitch.

VOICE THREE: Gagging sounds.

VOICE TWO: Struggling towards the door of the toilet.

VOICE ONE: He was determined to walk out.

JOHN: Determined to leave me.

VOICE TWO: Motherfucker.

VOICE THREE: You cannot leave.

VOICE TWO: You'll stay.

VOICE TWO: Bang!

VOICE THREE: Bang!

VOICE TWO: Bang!

VOICE THREE: Six shots.

VOICE TWO: Then he was still.

VOICE ONE: No more cheering.

VOICE THREE: His body lay limp on the cold mosaic floor.

VOICE TWO: I've never seen so much red in my life.

VOICE THREE: Except when I was a child.

VOICE TWO: In Hong Kong.

VOICE THREE: Chinese New Year.

VOICE TWO: Red firecrackers littered the narrow streets.

VOICE THREE: Like withered leaves in autumn.

VOICE TWO: The whole toilet was red.

VOICE THREE: The white porcelain turned red.

JOHN: Suddenly I felt drained of all energy, and I dropped the gun. I limped slowly towards his lifeless body and started to hold him. Tight. Called him. Will? Will? But he didn't respond. Didn't move. Hot tears suddenly filled my eyes. I started to rock him slowly like a baby, my baby, and then I kissed him. On his still-bloody lips. Oh God, what have I done? What have I—I wanted to scream. Wanted to die. I kept staring at the toilet. The pretty mosaic tiles—with patterns—flower patterns. Pretty flower patterns. They looked like they were dancing. Flower patterns covered with blood—all over the tiles—and the walls. And the urinals were all red. Red. Oh my God, I shot him. I shot him. I shot him. *[An awkward silence. Suddenly JOHN screams at the top of his voice. It's an animal cry, a cry of aguish and pain that he has been harbouring all this time. He screams repeatedly.]*

SCENE 27

VOICE TWO: The crow was happy.

VOICE FOUR: Content.

VOICE ONE: A part of this feathered family.

VOICE THREE: It sang merrily.

VOICE TWO: Ate and flew.

VOICE FOUR: Slept.

VOICE ONE: Played with the sparrows.

VOICE THREE: The days passed.

VOICE TWO: The crow felt homesick.

VOICE FOUR: It dawned upon the crow.

VOICE ONE: It will never truly belong with them.

VOICE THREE: The beautiful, chirpy, graceful, little sparrows.

VOICE TWO: The black crow may sing, eat, or fly with them.

VOICE FOUR: It will never feel like one of them.

VOICE ONE: Never be one of them.

VOICE THREE: A sparrow.

VOICE TWO: The crow was disheartened.

VOICE FOUR: Once again.

VOICE ONE: The crow bade its farewells.

VOICE THREE: Flew across the green field.

VOICE TWO: Back to the tree.

VOICE FOUR: Back to its family of crows.

VOICE ONE: Where it belonged.

VOICE THREE: Where it truly belonged.

VOICE TWO: Or so the crow thought.

VOICE FOUR: The other crows welcomed it back.

VOICE ONE: They flew and ate with their old friend.

VOICE THREE: Something wasn't quite the same.

VOICE TWO: The crow flew in fanciful circles.

VOICE FOUR: In the air, soaring up and down.

VOICE ONE: The crow ate little.

VOICE THREE: A genteel fashion.

VOICE TWO: The crow burst into song.

VOICE FOUR: Songs it had once sung in the company of sparrows.

VOICE ONE: The other crows found the crow distant.

VOICE THREE: Different.

VOICE TWO: Strange.

VOICE FOUR: Peculiar.

VOICE ONE: Queer.

VOICE THREE: They began avoiding the crow.

VOICE TWO: The crow was never more alone.

VOICE FOUR: It didn't belong to the sparrows or the crows.

VOICE ONE: Again the black crow packed its belongings.

VOICE THREE: It flew away.

VOICE TWO: From the tree of crows.

VOICE FOUR: From the tree of sparrows.

VOICE ONE: In search of another tree.

VOICE THREE: Another field.

VOICE TWO: Another family.

VOICE FOUR: Another life.

SCENE 28

VOICE ONE: How are you doing today?

JOHN: Fine.

VOICE ONE: That's good.

JOHN: You're through with the analysis, aren't you?

VOICE ONE: Yes. I'm going to submit my findings this—

JOHN: And you'll be too busy to come by.

VOICE ONE: Well, there isn't really a need for me to—

JOHN: I see.

VOICE ONE: But—I will. Once I finish the report.

JOHN: We can talk—

VOICE ONE: Sure.

JOHN: I'd like that very much.

VOICE ONE: Yeah.

JOHN: Good.

VOICE ONE: I'll come by. *[Pause]* Has anyone come by to see you at all?

JOHN: No one.

VOICE ONE: Your parents?

JOHN: They're too embarrassed to come.

VOICE ONE: Sorry.

JOHN: I'm not. Are there any questions you have that I haven't answered?

VOICE ONE: No, not really.

JOHN: You know, he means the world to me.

VOICE ONE: I know.

JOHN: I think you should put that down in your report.

VOICE ONE: I will.

JOHN: I had so many plans for the both of us.

VOICE ONE: Uh-huh.

JOHN: Dreams. Things we'd do together. I read in the papers that there'll be a performance of *Carmen* next week in London. Will, he'll like that. Imagine, with all his opera records, he's never once been to a performance. He'll like that. He'll like *Carmen.*

VOICE ONE: But he's gone.

JOHN: Who's gone?

VOICE ONE: William Hope.

JOHN: Oh no he's not.

VOICE ONE: What do you mean?

JOHN: He'll never be gone. Now I have him where I want him.

VOICE ONE: I don't understand.

JOHN: I've finally got Will all to myself now.

SCENE 29

VOICE THREE: So, Suzanne, the woman you said you were romantically involved with, doesn't exist?

VOICE ONE: No, I invented her.

VOICE THREE: Why?

VOICE ONE: To gain someone's trust, you have to blemish the truth.

VOICE THREE: You told John Lee a personal story, and he told you his.

VOICE ONE: Old trade secret.

VOICE THREE: You lied to him.

VOICE ONE: I got what I wanted.

VOICE THREE: Isn't that unethical?

VOICE ONE: Isn't this whole interview?

VOICE THREE: So you found John Lee sane during the time of the murder?

VOICE ONE: Yes, I found him sane.

VOICE THREE: Why?

VOICE ONE: He was sane, like most of us. It was more a crime of passion. He did truly love William Hope, but the relationship was not reciprocal.

VOICE THREE: Taking someone's life is a sane act?

VOICE ONE: No, but the circumstances surrounding the death were. You see, not all of us have the intense passion that John possessed—a passion enough to kill the person he loved.

VOICE THREE: Aren't you making this case a little more romantic than you should?

VOICE ONE: Perhaps. But I think you'd probably find the same answers I did by going through the case.

VOICE THREE: This is certainly quite a change from what you told me before.

VOICE ONE: Yes, I know.

VOICE THREE: What was the verdict?

VOICE ONE: Life without parole.

VOICE THREE: Thank you, Dr. Worthing. We'll leave it there. Have you been back to see John Lee since the trial?

VOICE ONE: Eh—no. But I will. I did promise him I would—when my work's a little lighter. Listen, I've got to go.

VOICE THREE: One last question, Dr. Worthing. You never told me why he folded those paper cranes.

VOICE ONE: A Japanese tradition that if you folded the paper cranes—a thousand of them—your wish would come true.

VOICE THREE: And what wish did John Lee have? For folding the thousand paper cranes?

VOICE ONE: You mean you can't guess?

SCENE 30

VOICE FOUR: Bang.

VOICE TWO: Bang.

VOICE ONE: Bang.

VOICE THREE: Bang.

VOICE TWO: Bang.

VOICE FOUR: Bang.

VOICE TWO: Six shots.

VOICE THREE: A body falls.

VOICE FOUR: Hot blood splatters.

VOICE TWO: On the peeling walls.

VOICE THREE: On the cold hard floors.

VOICE ONE: Red flower.

VOICE TWO: Patterns.

VOICE THREE: On white.

VOICE FOUR: Mosaic tiles.

VOICE TWO: On cool.

VOICE THREE: White porcelain.

VOICE ONE: Smells of.

VOICE FOUR: Gun smoke.

VOICE THREE: Antiseptic.
VOICE TWO: Urine.
VOICE THREE: Semen.
VOICE ONE: A boy.
VOICE FOUR: Holding a man.
VOICE THREE: Two of them.
VOICE FOUR: Alone.
VOICE TWO: In a public toilet.
VOICE ONE: At Bethnal Green.
VOICE TWO: Outside the tube station.
VOICE FOUR: Beside a small park.
VOICE THREE: With flowers.
VOICE ONE: And some trees.
VOICE FOUR: And in one particular tree.
VOICE TWO: A lone black crow.
VOICE ONE: Sits comfortably.
VOICE THREE: On a branch.
VOICE FOUR: Cawing.
VOICE THREE: Cawing.
VOICE ONE: Watching painfully.
VOICE TWO: Watching longingly.
VOICE ONE: The sparrows.
VOICE FOUR: In a nearby tree.
VOICE THREE: Singing.
VOICE FOUR: Sweetly.
VOICE TWO: Without a care in the world.
VOICE THREE: Bang!
VOICE ONE: Bang!
VOICE TWO: Bang!
VOICE FOUR: Bang!
VOICE ONE: Bang!
VOICE THREE: Bang!
VOICE TWO: Six shots.
JOHN: Two bodies fall.

[Short pause and then gradually louder, the overlapping cacophony of London street sounds once again fills the air.]

VOICE THREE: Tara, love. See you at 4:00 for tea. Don't forget the MacVitties biscuits at the midnight shop. Chocolate ones, mind you—
VOICE ONE: Come on, then, off to the pub. The F.A. Cup's about to start in a few minutes—
VOICE FOUR: Sorry, I can't come to the phone. Leave a message and I'll ring back. Bye—

VOICE TWO: Say, would you like to come in for a show? We've got topless girls—

VOICE THREE: Fucking terrorists. They've got the bleeding tubes all shut off because of a bomb scare. Now, how the fuck can I get to Camden?

VOICE FOUR: Do you want tickets to *Phantom?* I've got good seats for—sorry, no speak Japanese. *Phantom.* Only one hundred quid for a ticket. Very little yen. Yes?—

VOICE ONE: More crisis at Buckingham Palace. Now next on the turntable is another member of the British royal family, Boy George—

VOICE THREE: *[Sound of cars honking]*

VOICE TWO: *[Sound of an underground train leaving the platform]*

VOICE FOUR: *[Sound of Big Ben striking 4:00]*

> *[JOHN finishes folding a paper crane and looks at it incredulously. He holds it in the palm of his hand and offers it to the audience. JOHN smiles.]*

GUILLERMO REYES

Men on the Verge of a His-panic Breakdown

EDITOR'S INTRODUCTION

I BECAME AWARE OF New York theater during the last, waning years of the great monologists in the 1950s. Ruth Draper would put in an occasional appearance, Joyce Grenfell would sail over from London to put on one of her zany one-woman shows, and Anna Russell would fill Carnegie Hall. The monologue in the hands of these women was grand entertainment. Now, some forty years later, it is back, but in a more politicized form. Indeed, the monologue has become the major vehicle for political theater. It is inexpensive (one actor!), and it emphasizes the most important aspects of theater—writing and virtuosic acting—in a time in which scenery seems to have become the priority in commercial theater. Anna DeVeare Smith's *Fires in the Mirror*, a one-woman panorama of life during the Los Angeles riots, was nominated for a Tony in 1994. The monologue has also become a staple of contemporary lesbian and gay theater. After all, the one-person show is the ideal form for the age of identity politics. Holly Hughes and Tim Miller have gained the eternal wrath of Jesse Helms for their queer performance art pieces, and David Drake's evening of monologues, *The Night Larry Kramer Kissed Me*, was a hit in cities across America with or without Drake. Unlike earlier monologists, Guillermo Reyes does not perform the eight monologues that make up *Men on the Verge of a His-panic Breakdown*, thus creating a more traditional separation between playwright and virtuosic actor.

Men on the Verge of a His-panic Breakdown was a hit at the Celebration Theater in Los Angeles and won two Ovation Awards (Los Angeles's version of the Tony and Obie Awards): Best Writing of a World Premiere and Best Play Production in a Smaller Theater. Another successful production was mounted at Theater Rhinoceros in San Francisco.

In *Men on the Verge of a His-panic Breakdown* Chilean-born Reyes gives us a gallery of gay Hispanic men. All of them are "out" as gay men but have trouble living as Hispanics in the American West. In some cases the character sees his gayness as his entrée into American society and the good life. The evening is framed by the letters of Federico, "the gay little immigrant that could," who comes to Los Angeles in the midst of the riots with an address book of Anglo men who have slept with him on their visits to his native land. Federico is a survivor who can endure constant rejection and can adapt to the roller-coaster life on American streets. If Federico gets doors shut in his face, Vinnie had a ten-year career as live-in lover to an aged "sugar daddy." But he, like Federico, can be thrown back onto the street.

All of Reyes's characters are survivors. All have tried to assimilate to America from pasts of poverty or political exile and must survive in a capitalist system that sees them as dispensable. Vinnie is replaced by a fresh eighteen-year-old just as he replaced his predecessor. Attempts at total assimilation only lead to chaos. Edward Thornhill III has bleached his skin, changed his name, and pretended to be straight to become a Hollywood actor, only to find himself cast as an Hispanic character, but he can't hide his poor parents, and the producers don't think his real name is Hispanic enough. Paco was placed in a concentration camp by Fidel Castro for being gay. He was one of the Cuban gays sent to Florida by Castro in the Mariel boat lift. Once here, the only way he knew to bridge Cuban and American culture was to follow in his father's footsteps and open an authentic Cuban restaurant. So Paco takes his father's money, with its proviso that he be as far away from his macho father as possible, opens a Cuban restaurant—in Phoenix, Arizona!—and gains the ultimate sign of assimilation: presidency of the Arizona Gay Republicans. But the survival of Paco's Cuban restaurant is threatened by a chain of Cuban restaurants owned by a representative of the next generation, a sleek, totally assimilated young Cuban-American gay man who doesn't even speak Spanish. Paco, the older Cuban queen, now looking like a caricature of a macho Cuban, cannot compete with the younger, assimilated gay man. The sad aspect of Paco's story is that two men, both gay, both of Cuban descent, become not allies but business enemies: "There's only room for one Cuban faggot restaurateur in all of Phoenix!" We see the same divisiveness in the Latino who teaches English to Spanish-speaking immigrants, who sees his acquired language as his hold on an American identity, and despises the nonassimilated students he faces. Self-hatred leads to hatred of those who represent his origins.

Reyes's characters are at the end of their ropes, on the verge of a His-panic breakdown, which Reyes defines as "the extreme of transcultural shock." They are inhabitants of what the rabbi in Tony Kushner's *Angels in America* calls "the melting pot where nothing melted." The most heroic among them are the ones who have refused to assimilate: Federico, who proclaims, "I'm here to stay. . . . Get used to it!" and La Gitana, the Flamenco-dancing drag queen who proudly, bravely dances to her AIDS-caused death. La Gitana reminds us that California was Hispanic before it was Anglo and that she is the spirit of that California past: "I am the Spanish pearl of Fuentevaqueros. I am the treasure that washed unto these shores. A blast from the past. The Spanish jewel blazing deep in the soul of old California."

Reyes's monologues are simultaneously funny and sad, but they offer a catalog of fighters. As Federico tells the audience at the end, "So, you see, I survive whether or not you help me, whether you like it or not, and whether I'm legal or not." Unfortunately, some of the fighters are fighting their own ethnic origins, a crucial part of who they are.

AUTHOR'S INTRODUCTION

Guillermo Reyes is a native of Santiago, Chile, but has lived in the United States since 1971, when he came with his mother to the Washington, D.C., area at nine years of age, and has since become a U.S. citizen. His plays deal primarily with the struggles, loves, conquests, defeats, and comic neuroses of the immigrant in the United States. He has been writing monologues since he was a graduate student at the University of California, San Diego, where he performed some of them for the Theater Department's Cabaret Series.

After receiving his MFA in theater, he moved back to his adopted hometown of Los Angeles in 1991 and only a few months later experienced the traumatizing event of the Los Angeles riots. He was teaching English as a second language to Koreans in Koreatown, significant parts of which were burned during those days of madness. But on 29 April 1992, the same day that the riots erupted, he met a young man recently arrived from Chile and eager to stay in the United States (illegally, if necessary) and lead an openly gay lifestyle. Though surprised by the riots, he wasn't too fazed. "In Chile we've gone through twenty years of this," he said, "and we're still here." A wimpy little riot wasn't going to stop him.

He became "The Gay Little Immigrant That Could," and from there the monologues took on a new focus. They became predominantly gay, dealing primarily with a crisis in the lives of gay Latino immigrants. What became clear as well was

that these themes worked well in the context of both comedy and pathos. Not much of a tragedian, the author chose to give the pieces a stylistically comic flair even when dealing with serious social issues.

PRODUCTION HISTORY AND RIGHTS

Men on the Verge of a His-panic Breakdown received its premiere on 6 June 1994 at the Celebration Theater in Los Angeles. It was directed by Joseph Megel. Felix A. Pire played all the characters.

The text printed here includes two monologues added for the San Francisco production, which opened at Theater Rhinoceros on 10 September 1994 and which was performed by George Castillo (Carlo d'Amore was understudy and played several performances).

Some of the monologues have been published previously in the following publications: "The Gay Little Immigrant That Could" in *The Evergreen Chronicles,* "Hispanically Correct" in *Caffeine,* "Good-bye to Sugar Daddy" in *Viva Arts Quarterly,* "ESL: English as a Stressful Language" in *Alchemy.*

GUILLERMO REYES

Men on the Verge of a His-panic Breakdown

Special thanks to Maria Caceres, Joseph Megel, and Felix A. Pires

The Gay Little Immigrant That Could

[FEDERICO: A young man, early 20s, thick accent]

April 29, 1992

Querida Madre,
Dear Mother,

My first day in Los Angeles and I already have everything I want.

I arrived with the address book in my hand full of possibilities and phone numbers of potential wealthy backers. . . . So I go, "Knock, knock, knock. Hello, I'm Federico. Remember me? You come to my country to help fight for social justice and help pick, ah native bananas? You are courageous American student of native ways who say to me if ever I come to the United States of America, and experience openly gay lifestyle, you help me settle down, find a job, and introduce me to atmosphere rife with sexual openings." *[BLAST!]* The door come shut on my face on my first attempt to fit into openly gay lifestyle.

But not to worry, Mamacita, I try again. Because I believe when you try and try again, doors open. That is the American way of life! You keep trying for that one door to open! I walk the streets of Los Angeles, Mamacita, and I already for myself see the excitement of the American lifestyle. I see fires and smoke in the horizon, and I say, "Oh, that must be those Hollywood folk making another *Lethal Weapon* sequel!" People running, firetrucks rushing back and forth, policemen hiding behind doughnut shops. And I see for myself that America lives up to its image in the movies. I hear a blast! I look around me, a drugstore is on fire, people rush into a shoe store and pick out whatever they want! That is America, Mamacita, such enthusiastic consumer appetite!

I go to my next address: "Knock, knock, it's me, Federico. Remember me? You and I experienced compromising positions while you got away from your country to study fertility rituals among same-sex indigenous couples. Well, I come to experience openly gay lifestyle in your homeland." *[BLAST!]*

The door comes shut on my face again, Mamacita. And one by one, doors shut on my face and my potential wealthy backers forget all the promises they make when they come to my country to deflower native bottom like myself. . . .

Well, I had one more address to go to. So I go . . . "Knock, knock, knock. I'm Federico. I am your pen pal. You write to me for the last five years, and you say if ever I come to America, you help me settle down. You are financially stable man eager to meet men from my country willing to submit themselves to socioeconomic dependency. Well, here I am, *gringuito,* make me your love slave!"

Of course, now I am standing on the entrance to his building, and I notice things very different from what he say in his letter. He is supposed to be handsome young man who work as a model, live in a neighborhood worthy of American prosperous lifestyle, so that we spend weekends together in Palm Springs sprinkling our seed through the desert. But here I am standing on the doorstep of his building—and there is a human body lying on the mat. And it might be dead. Little naked children with swollen bellies run around in the yard and I say, "Oh, perhaps these are his many adopted orphans from the Third World living off his generosity, like I myself would like to be."

But I am knocking on his door now, and the knocker falls off on my hand. I am beginning to suspect he is going through a recession. . . . "Knock, knock, knock. Remember me? I'm Federico. . . ." Then the door open, and a wheelchair pop out, a blanket covering his feet, and a large pink toupee sticks out almost covering his face . . . and I tell him, "You are not the man I correspond with all these years. You don't live in prosperous economic indulgence. You are not model with tight chest, rippling biceps, and solid wardrobe." And then he say—and this is where his voice turn deep and spooky, and the wind stirs the palm trees, which are now on fire—he say, "Young man, curfew begins at sundown!" And I stand, oh, mesmerized. "Go home or the LAPD is gonna get ya!"

The LAPD—what deep meaning was held in such words? But people are running inside, shutting their doors, as the palm trees burn. . . . I begin to understand. There I stand in the hallway of my cockroach-infested American Dream.

I really have no more addresses or phone numbers to go to this time. . . . Night begin to fall. People drive fast home, passing me by. "Curfew!" they shout, "Go home! Curfew!" . . . And I say, *"Ay, que curfew ni que na!* In my country curfew last fifteen years, curfew!" . . . And I am walking. And then I see them again—it's the mob of Hollywood extras! They are taking furnitures from the store. And I tell myself, "I will need a bed to sleep in tonight." So I go get myself one. . . .

I run inside and choose from a wide selection of merchandise. There is a sign: "CLEARANCE! EVERYTHING MUST GO!" Okay. I pick out my little mattress with tiny heavenly angels drawn on them to remind me of my Catholic upbringing, and I set it up in the parking lot. But then I tell myself, "This is not enough for prosperous American lifestyle. I must have some more!" So I run in again, and again until I have my couch, my sofa chair, my bean bag, my love seat for the series of lovers I will meet in the United States once I start to lead openly gay lifestyle full of economic indulgence. . . . Soon enough, I have an entire American living room! It is comfortable, Mamá. It is the most comfortable living room in the world. And America—my America—is one large living room, where anyone can steal his own couch! And to think, I already have it all in my first day in the United States of America.

But something is missing, Mamá; something else is missing in my new prosperous lifestyle, now that I have everything. And that is a man. Can I go looting for a man? . . . Well, that is exactly what I do! I break into the Porno Pleasure House on Santa Monica and find myself ten inches worth of a man, and I bring him into my living room, all ten inches of him staring me in the face—and I hold him in my arms—you always said I liked to play with dolls, Mamá. . . . I have it all then, Mamá. I have a living room with a couch and a coffee table and a rug and a ten-inch man in my hand. I am an American success. But all it takes is some *pendejo* with a cigarette lighter to set the couch on fire. And there it goes, Mamá, the couch first, then the lamp table, the lamp, the bed, the rug, and then finally even the dildo is on fire! And there I stand, watching my American Dream go up in flames, and the looters gather around me and applaud and tell me, "Welcome! Welcome to Los Angeles!" As the ten-inch dildo melts away into the night. . . .

So, you see, Mamacita, I write you this letter from the fire zone. With a piece of pen and paper I took from Thrifty's. I write to you as the National Guard moves into my street—and I say, "Hello! Remember me? I'm Federico! You invaded my country a couple of years ago. I slept with a few of you. . . ." Men, how quickly they forget. . . . So there they are again, bringing order back to the city. And we all return again to the life we had before . . . with twenty dollars in my pocket, a phone book full of wrong numbers, and the hope that the fires will die out and that I will find a place of my own to stay. A place to start again. And buy my first bed, my first couch, and my first man. . . .

Goodnight, Mamacita.
Your son,
Federico

Good-bye to Sugar Daddy

[VINNIE: an anal-retentive-looking man, 30. He was once a very pretty younger man.]

He's 18? . . . No, no bother.

The point is well taken, Sugar Daddy. Don't worry, it doesn't take me that long to pack. I can be out of here in a matter of minutes.

Now, if you could just sign here, and here, and down here. . . . This form will help me seek compensation from the Society of West Hollywood Kept Boys over 30. . . . Please, say no more. You'll be late for the Gay Republican fund-raiser.

I am *not* upset. Please. Let's be businesslike about this. And I'll leave a receipt for your taxes, yes. . . . Don't worry about me. I've been meaning to visit the folks back in Colombia, the ones who survived the last volcano eruption. I've got all the bases covered. Self-reliant, independent, one-man show—that's me. Oh, I'll leave written instructions for the new eighteen-year-old from Wichita, Kansas, so he can deal with your prostate gland medicine.

You'll be late. . . . Good-bye, Sugar Daddy.

*[He watches SUGAR DADDY go. A halfhearted wave good-bye . . . He's left
alone. He looks around the room. He lights a cigarette. He makes a phone call.]*

Hello, is this Lenny? Lenny, darling, how are you? Nice to hear your voice again after all these years. Why it's Vinnie. Vinnie Contreras. Oh, come now. . . . I was twenty; you were twenty-nine. Ten years or so ago, remember?

I came in clutching Sugar Daddy's arm, and we kindly asked you to depart from our presence. Yes, I helped you pack. But no, I don't remember throwing your bags out the window. Let memory be more selective, Lenny! Lenny?!? . . . So what have you been doing with your life? What? Oh, no particular reason, just wanted to keep in touch. No, no, it's not that at all—alright, Lenny, he's eighteen; he's blond, fresh from Kansas. What am I to do, Lenny? Oh, oh, Lenny. . . .

But please let me ask you, and I hope it's not too personal. What did you do after you voluntarily departed from Sugar Daddy's presence? . . . How many years at the shelter? I can't stand poor lighting, you know. But okay, afterwards, what did you do afterwards? Dry cleaning? . . . Oh, I love dry cleaning, you know. I love the hangers and the plastic wrap that makes the clothes look so, you know, pressed! So how much do they pay? . . . Oh, well, that's just slightly below the minimum wage. . . . And no health care—well, that would be too Hillary, wouldn't it?

Listen, Lenny, do you think there might be an opening at the dry cleaners anytime soon? No, I just figured at this time in my life I could use some . . . some flexibility. I'm exploring different venues for making a living. I'd like to be open to career alternatives. . . . So, when do you think there might be an opening? Soon, you said? Oh, you didn't say.

Well, you'll keep me in mind, won't you, Lenny? Oh, no, no, Colombia is not for me these days, you know. I'm not sure if I belong at home at all, you know. No, I couldn't. I couldn't go back. I burned too many bridges. Literally . . . Too many people tend to die when I burn bridges. . . .

Lenny, wait! One more thing—

How did you ever feel about Sugar Daddy? You know, feelings. As in emotion? I know that about a half century separates me from him, but it can happen, right? Can it happen that after so many years, you begin to feel a certain attachment to the creature? Oh, Lenny, there comes a time when even people like us develop feelings, don't you think? . . . No, I'm *not*—I'm *not* crazy, Lenny. After awhile, you begin to develop feelings for those who pay your rent, feelings as noble and complex as any others. Feelings for his loose skin against your thighs, his dentures stuck in your pubic hair, his cancer-ridden lungs breathing sweet warm air against your face.

Yes, Lenny, I love Sugar Daddy. I love Sugar Daddy! Only now do I realize it. Only now have I come to that conclusion. Please don't. Don't hang up! . . . *[Desperate to keep him on the phone]* We must get together for cappuccino in West Hollywood. Tea at Trumps? Attitude at the Studio? You no longer "do" attitude? Lenny!

[He hangs up the phone. He grabs his suitcase and holds it in his arms as a barrier against the world before him.]

Well, I suppose I understand why you had to hang up. I am alone now, ready to hit the streets. So here I go. . . . I am one of the few, one of the brave, one of the Aging Kept Boys of West Hollywood.

I am not afraid. You hear that, world? *[As he "clicks his heels" three times]*
I am not afraid. I am not afraid. I AM NOT AFRAID!

[Lights fade out.]

Hispanically Correct

[EDWARD: A glamorous young man, mid-20s, California San Fernando Valley accent]

Hello. . . . Is this, like, the Hispanic Hotline?

Okay, this is my first time, you know. So, like, I'm supposed to give you the dirt and you're, like, supposed to tell me if it's like Hispanically Correct. Is that right?

Okay, so I'm, like, young and I'm glamorous, okay? And when I first came to Hollywood a couple of years ago, I, like, changed my name, I bleached my skin, and I started frequenting the trendiest straight bars in town. My name now is, like, Edward Thornhill the Third. Well, never mind my real name. I can barely pronounce it, okay?

Okay, so, like, recently this famous American movie actress whose name I couldn't possibly reveal—she like bought the movie rights to a well-known Mexican novel. And suddenly there was this wonderful part for, like, a Hispanic actor, okay? But my agent doesn't even know I'm, like, ethnic. And I have to sneak away to the audition all by myself and I'm really nervous, okay? But once I get there, I'm like really good, okay?

I have a degree from Trish School of the Arts. No, not Tisch School of the Arts—but my friend Trish Lopez from East L.A. has this little studio, where we learn our basic stereotypes, okay? . . . So Rodge, the casting director for the movie, like, he comes up to me and he says, "Wow, we've never seen an Anglo do a Hispanic so good. How do you do it, kid?" And I tell him it comes naturally, okay?

So I come home, and I'm feeling really good, okay? I'm gonna sit by that phone, I'm gonna get that part, become a star and, like, I'm finally gonna have some friends, okay? So I come home, but who should be waiting at my doorstep?—

It's, like, Jesse. She's this really gorgeous Greek-goddess type and all the agents love her because she's got the right name for the nineties: Jesse Dolenewt.* That's her name, Jesse Dolenewt. So there she is, looking gorgeous in this lovely chiffon outfit that, you know, I'd love to borrow sometime.

And I make her come in, and I make her some tea. But she's not feeling too good. Her career isn't going anywhere—she can't act worth shit. So she goes on and on talking about her problems when all I want to do is, you know, talk about myself. . . . So finally I lose my temper and I tell her, "Well, just tell me the story of your life, why don't you, Jesse?" Not a good idea. She turns around and spits on the rug like a construction worker and she says she's really sick of me. She never meant to become my girlfriend. Nooo, her agent recommended it. And she says she isn't even an Anglo-Saxon Protestant from Omaha, Nebraska, like her press release says. No, instead, she's this bleached Latina, and is the chairwoman of the Closeted Minority Lesbian Union. And I'm like freaking out, okay?

And she says she knows everything about me and will expose me to the press unless I, Edward Thornhill the Third, give her, like, a baby! Cause she and her lesbian lover have been trying for years to conceive, but they can't, you know, because they're, like, members of the same sex and you need an egg and a sperm—oh, you know about that? . . . Good.

So I tell her, "Hold on, Jesse! You can go to a real good Nobel Prize–winning sperm bank and get a good deal on an economist, okay?" And she says she doesn't want a genius; she wants a Hollywood actor. Because one day I, Edward Thornhill the Third, might get to become a star.

STAR! *Star.* There's something about that word that gets me really horny, you know? . . . So I tell her, "Let's go for it, Jesse!"

So our bodies collide against each other like meteors and we land on the kitchen tile—and I feel like it's coming, this biblical act, this Genesis in the making, it's coming, IT'S COMING! When who should come walking into my apartment—

It's, like, my parents! They show up looking like real immigrants, you know? They were evicted from their East L.A. apartment because they're, like, poor and can't afford the rent—what a lame excuse! And they, like, come in and make themselves at home, drink up my fine Chablis, and put on the Spanish channel. And, like, Jesse wants to know when I'm going to get rid of these immigrants. And they

---

*Author's note: Update name according to latest events and fashions.

want to know when I'm going to marry this bountiful Christian. They don't speak English. She doesn't speak Spanish. And I'm not about to translate, okay? When who should come walking into all of this—

It's, like, my agent! He's all excited because he got me a gig to play a clown at the annual Nancy and Ronnie Special Athletics for Retards. It's my agent's first 15 percent commission. That's how pathetic he is. And he starts calling up his friends on my cordless phone. And soon all these people start showing up at my doorstep. I don't know who they are, I don't know their names, and they don't even bring a résumé. And who should come walking into all of this, but Oh-My-God, it's like—

Rodge! The casting director of the movie that I tried out for. He stands there for the longest time and then he says, "Congratulations, kid! You're going to become a star!" But then he says, "And all you have to do is change your name to Hispanic."

"But why?" I ask.

"Because," he says, "all these Hispanic activists will be upset if they found out an Anglo got a top Hispanic part. The only one for the year!"

And I have to think on my feet. Think, think, think. Then I finally tell him, "Okay, I'll change my name to Eduardo Troncos." And he says it doesn't sound Hispanic *enough,* and I can't even tell the asshole it's my real name. *[Begins to become frantic]*

So he goes around the room asking people for better-sounding Hispanic names. And my agent wants to know what's going on, and Jesse wants me to go into the bedroom to, like, fertilize her egg, and my parents are all upset because I made them wear these quaint little butler and maid uniforms—well, somebody had to pass out the hors d'oeuvres, okay? And they're all calling, "Eddie, Eddie, Eduardo, Eddie, Eduardo, Eddie, Eduardo!" And I finally snap and start shouting at all these people in this horrible high school Spanish—"*¡Va fuera, va fuera, fuera!*" And I start throwing things at the guests in what's turned into this sick little soirée! Dishes, lamps, copies of my résumé, and eight by ten glossies (it's always a good time to network), and my face snaps and all my plastic is hanging out, making me look more my age.

"*¡Va fuera; va fuera!*" I keep shouting, and the neighbor upstairs complains that I'm using, like, the imperative interchangeably with the indicative! "This is no time for a grammar lesson, asshole! *Fuera! Fuera!*" And I chase everybody out the door, foaming at the mouth, and bang the door shut behind them all! *[Beat]*

So there they are now, trying to tear down the door like zombies from hell, breaking the windows, slipping down the chimney like the uncool dudes they are. The police are on their way. . . .

And what I'd really like to know is, Hispanic Hotline, is it, like, Hispanically Correct to, like, shut out the world and deny it all? Could I return to my real roots, my preformation as egg and sperm? *[He gets progressively more nervous as they come to get him.]*

I don't want to be connected to all this mess, all these rivalries between people like Mexican versus Anglo, English versus Spanish, woman versus man, gay versus straight, Armani versus Polo. Could I, like, become neutral to history itself and, like, make believe the Treaty of Guadalupe Hidalgo was just another crazy zoning law? Tell me it can be done, Hispanic Hotline! Give me a sign!

Oh my God! They're breaking down the door! They're coming to get me, the foreigners, the Anglos, the lesbians, the Hollywood agents and producers! They're coming armed with nets and straightjackets, to take me away! Answer me, Hispanic Hotline! Don't cut me off now! *[Pantomimes being dragged away as he screams]* HEEEEEEEEELP!

[Lights out]

Demon Roommate from Hell

Well, here it is. It's spacious, two bedroom, quaint, airy, close to all the major freeways, and yes, A LITTLE TOO CLOSE TO THE AIRPORT! BUT IT'S NOT always this loud. You'll get used to it, and you can move in now, no deposit, no hidden fees, no problem! No, no catch. Just move in when you'd like and don't be shy about it. Do it now! No pressure, of course.

Look, I'll be perfectly honest with you. I like you! Your sincerity, your apprehension, your inability to grab a deal when you see one! It shows there's a lot about you that needs to be nurtured and reshaped if necessary. I really like that in a roommate! I can see you're out here from—what is it?—Tuscaloosa, Alabama! Southern, bubbly, and blond. And an actor, too, ready to conquer Burbank and its many pleasant environments! Why, I do declare! I'd like to be of help in your new surroundings.

Now before you make any decision, I'll put it all out on the table, just so that it's out there—what else? The house rules! First . . . no unwashed dishes, no dirty socks on the dining table, and no African bees! That's right, African bees! The last roommate used to leave the swing door open, and you never know what can come in. And the African bees, you know they're coming, don't you? They're probably already here living in our midst without us even realizing it, but sooner or later, they'll strike, hundreds of them darkening the Burbank skies, buzzing, and stinging, as hard as piranhas into your neck! So please, a simple rule, watch the swing door and be on the lookout always! They're out there!

The other thing . . . no genitals. The roommate before the last one used to walk around exposing himself in these tight underwear that he bought through the International Male catalog, pure pornography, that catalog, pure pornography! You pay twenty dollars for a teeny piece of cloth that shows off your basket, and that thing is bound to pop out, so I say—what? Smoking? Smoke all you like, just cover your damn genitals!

Which leads to the subject of guests, overnight or otherwise. I'm not that concerned with girlfriends—or boyfriends or whatever—I don't care about that, and honestly I am looking for someone like myself who is sort of openly asexual, which is very acceptable out here in Burbank, and my friends say I'm suffering from sexual repression, but I don't believe that's the case, some of us just don't have relationships, and that's okay, it's part of what it means to grow up and accept your limitations. So sex or no, you're welcome here, but I'm more concerned with . . . RELATIVES!

I don't know about you, but relatives, my relatives, I wouldn't wish them upon any roommate, and I hope you're considerate about that. You know, parents, relatives, distant cousins, especially Dad, my dad, you know, after his experiences with the Chilean dictatorship, oh, that's all he ever talks about and he won't shut up, the dictatorship this, the dictatorship that, we're such victims, he says, such victims, and I say, get over it already—but I won't get into it, it's rather painful, but in other words if you have relatives in need of execution, please don't bring them here because for them I will leave the swing door open and the African bees will take care of the rest! The last roommate could tell you stories about relatives but—

What? What about the last roommate? Why did he leave? It's a very sensitive subject. Please don't force me to—it's a very *doleful* memory. You have a right not to know! But . . . alright. I suppose you can't make a decision without the facts. You do have a right to know how the last roommate and I got along, why our relationship failed, and how he died!

But it wasn't my fault; the police even said it wasn't my fault. No, please don't leave! Hear me out! Nobody ever hears me out! See what happens when people don't communicate! Surely back in Alabama people sit down on the porch and talk over a glass of lemonade and a piece of sweet potato pahh. OUT HERE IN BURBANK IT'S HARD TO TALK OVER THE PLANES. But it's not always this way. . . .

Yes, the previous roommate is no longer with us. I didn't realize his condition, didn't realize his abnormalities—of course, Dad had to come by that day to make things worse. It happened very quickly that night when the roommate brought over a friend, a friend! Keep in mind the roommate was quiet, studious, bookish, all eager to sell that first screenplay over to Disney down the block, wanted so badly to make it in Hollywood, but I noticed he always wore this tight black turtleneck, corduroy pants, a scarf around his neck—this is southern California! No shorts, no short sleeves for him. He was warm alright, but not to others, not to me. He barely greeted me when he came in, and once for breakfast, he just reached over with half his grapefruit and smashed it against my face. He'd seen it in a James Cagney movie, he said. Oh, that's another rule, I prefer cold cereal—if I'm going to be trampled upon and abused by breakfast items, I prefer grains, no citrus fruits, please.

Anyway, he had never brought a friend over and I must admit this friend was a beautiful young man—I don't use such words lightly, not for an asexual person, but I do recognize beauty when I see it, a tall young athlete, in Olympic training no less. What he was doing here with Mr. Grapefruit Man, I'll never know! Part of me resented it deeply. Part of me sought the friendship of such an athletic person, to inspire me to such Olympian heights.

So that's when Dad shows up to complicate things, and the roommate and company leave because they don't want to hear about the Chilean dictatorship, and Dad is going on and on how unhappy he is, how grand his life used to be all because he once was big shit down there in Santiago, as the head torturer of political dissidents, he invented electric pliers and other methods of systematic pain—and now he just hates his new job as the head of the Burbank Dental Clinic. Nothing will ever be the same—but I'm barely listening to Dad, the roommate and the Olympian are in there and I hear noises, is it the bed springs busting? I can't really tell, but my imagination works tremendously and vividly . . . and deep in my heart, I felt something alien to me: jealousy. And Dad is going on and on about how our lives will never be the same, how we used to be part of the ruling elite, and now we're here living under the shadow of Walt Disney! We were respectable once—or at least people were scared shitless when we walked down the block, and I could steal ice cream from little kid's hands, and what the heck! Dad was Secret Policeman! I got away with it! But the dictatorship ended, and suddenly there was talk, talk, of putting the torturers behind bars, and thank God, the great military heroes said no, you don't touch the ex-torturers or we'll stage another coup. So we go free, which doesn't stop the neighborhood people from picketing outside our home. *Torturadores, torturadores!* They shouted. *Torturadores de mierda!* We had to leave; we had to go! Imagine being accused for doing your duty to the nation, for being patriotic, family-oriented people! Only Disney would have understood!

But Dad won't shut up about it now, and so that day I finally tell him I don't care anymore, I don't care if I'm eternally unemployed and incapable of holding down a job, I don't care if he'll get stuck paying my bills until I'm an old man. . . . All I do is collect old newspaper headlines and feed the teddy bears. I don't care if we're no longer the leading torture family of Santiago! And Dad finally slaps me, hard, on the face, as he used to when I was little, as he did to Mom and to Grandma! . . . Satisfied, he leaves it at that and returns to his dental clinic, where he'll do the most damage with people's nerves.

And I'm left here with the roommate and the Olympian inside . . . and I'm scared, I'm scared of what I might do, so I go pour myself my wondrous mineral water. I buy it by the gallons, I keep it fresh, fresh in the refrigerator, and I feel the glaze of a fresh gallon bottle against my skin, and that's when I finally realized—the boys need this more than I do!

So that's when I break through the door and I see them both on the bed, one of them with his shirt off, and I pour the entire gallon of fresh, iced water on their bodies. Time to cool it! Cool it! Cool it!

And that's how the roommate died. . . . Death by Mineral Water! Pneumonia actually! The police were rather gentle with me, figuring how was I supposed to know that the young man suffered from an unusual condition that kept his body temperature low, that's why he always wore turtlenecks and scarves . . . and the young Olympian was one of his trainers, or so he said, who helped him, you know, warm up. I was not charged with anything, it was all an honest-to-goodness little prank, they figured, just an attempt on my part to make him laugh, to crack a smile on that dour little face of his. Well, another screenwriter is dead in Burbank and nobody asks the hard questions! The Olympian beauty is gone to train in Atlanta; Dad is a prominent member of the community thanks to his contributions to the Family Values Trust Fund. I am here eager to start again. I desperately need a roommate!

So . . . the first three months are free.

Hi . . . where did you go? Mr. Alabama? Mr. Ala— *[The phone rings.]*

Hello. Yes, the room is still available. Full of charm, ambience, airy! Would you like to come by tomorrow! Yes, it's near the studios AND THE AIRPORT, BUT IT'S NOT ALWAYS THIS LOUD! *[Ominous tone of voice]* You'll get used to it!

[Lights down]

Federico Writes Again

[In the shadow, we see FEDERICO wearing a Streisand wig and doing a sign language interpretation of "People" while the music plays. He takes off wig, approaches a block or a chair, where he begins his second letter.]

Querida Madre,
Dear Mother,

The excitement of the California lifestyle continues.

I got my first exciting job catering the homes of Topanga Canyon, and in my first day of work, all the houses burn down! I rescue a labrador, and the policemen declare me a hero. They take my picture and give me a five-dollar reward—and then they call the INS, so I have to go running. But they give me five minutes to run because I'm a hero.

And I finally meet somebody who likes me, Mamá. You know what I mean, in the romantic department. He's a deaf impersonator who does Barbra Streisand in sign language. Joey's a blond boy from Kentucky, and he knows some Spanish sign language, too, but I know no sign in any language, and he has to teach me from scratch, and that way he doesn't have to listen to my accent, but I feel I have an accent in sign language, too. My hands mispronounce everything—ay, *qué* clumsy!

He take me to live with him in his Northridge apartment, and we move there on 16 January 1994. We stay up all night just signing away and talking about our lives, and we go to bed snuggled up against each other, and at 4:31 A.M. the building shakes and all the Streisand wigs go flying out the window. And he's all shook up, and in the dark a deaf person can't exactly sign for help, can he? But he's bleeding, so I take him to the nearest hospital—and with my bad English and his sign language, nobody understood what we had to say. Until some nasty nurse tells him he has no health insurance and that he should go back to his own country, and she thinks he's an illegal alien just because he speak sign language!

Until finally, a doctor come to help us. He take out pieces of broken glass from Joey's toes and then stitch him up. But then he take a good look at me, and I feel the piercing wounds of arrows! He's a handsome tall Irishman who take one good look at me—and his eyes reveal the sadness of someone who is successful in everything else except, you know, in the romantic department. He feel sorry for us, true, but more than anything else he feel sorry for himself. He has no lover, so he take us both to stay with him.

And for several months, we both become the doctor's assistants, and we live in Bel Air! Our job was to feed the Abyssinian cats and keep our bodies tanned. We do the dishes by day, and by night we clear the cobwebs of the doctor's private life—if you know what I mean, Mamacita. No more details—I'm blushing! But one day the doctor decides to run for Congress, and with tears in his eyes, he ask us to go because the press is asking too many questions about his houseguests, and he want to declare his opposition to illegal aliens and deaf people.

So Joey and me walk the streets of Los Angeles again, and we wonder where our next job will come from. . . . Who need another sign language Streisand impersonator? . . . Who need another immigrant? I write this letter from the park overlooking the shelter with stationery I take from the doctor.

Isn't that the American way of life, Mamá? Los Angeles is the one place where nature forces you to start again and again—and so the excitement continues! Only in America, Mamá! Only in America!

Castro's Queen

[PACO: A middle-aged man wearing a guayabera and smoking a cigar]

You'll ruin me, you immigrants! I'm not gone for three days and the place looks like the aftermath of *unos quinces*—you know, a debutante ball turned into an orgy! Not even a good one!

Last night on my way home from the airport, I drove by just to check things out from a distance, and what do I find? That my marquee is off, at nine o'clock at night, my marquee is off! How are people going to be enticed into Paco's Cuban Restaurant—an Oasis in the Phoenix Culinary Desert? I drove home with tears clouding my vision. I drove into a cactus. My body is still prickled all over. I am a martyr to the cause of Cuban cuisine. *[Picks off a needle from his arm]* Ouch!

And talk about cacti! I'll have you know my friend Butch Lupe dropped by last night to check things out and guess what she found in my *Pollo à la Cienfueguesa*—a slice of nopal! Mamá's favorite recipe for chicken in yucca sauce cannot be substituted with nopal! Yucca has its own integrity! One does not mess with yucca. What would I do without my lesbian friends to spy for me?! I'm gone for three days to my Palm Springs Workshop for Entrepreneurial Homosexuals

Abandoned by Their Loved Ones Bearing the Full Weight of the Universe, and *this* is what I find?

You're out to destroy me! You Mexicans are all on Castro's payroll. From the busboys down to the chef, what we have here is one giant communist conspiracy of incompetence!

I know we're understaffed, but I provide a decent work environment once the Prozac kicks in, don't I?

I'll tell you right now: Bankruptcy is in the air, and I won't have us lose our jobs on account of one missing piece of yucca. We must not betray the cause of Caribbean cuisine! Where is your work ethic? At your age, I was serving up a storm of *ropa vieja* and *arroz con pollo* at my father's restaurant, La Habana de Noche! I was the owner's son, yet I was not above cleaning tables and emptying trash cans. Even when the revolution came and Dad insisted on leaving, I said, "You do that, but I will serve the revolution. I will bring fine food to the masses!" I believed in the revolution then; I was a convert.

But then Castro decided to round all of us queers up and put us in concentration camps. *Los campamentos UMAP.* We were undesirables. And did I give up *then?* No, I found a way to serve my fellow inmates with a sense of decorum. Tin plates, mushy beans and rice, our hands used as napkins? NO! I developed *concentration camp etiquette.* Castro tried to make us act and eat like the straight man— with our hands; they wanted us to belch out loud—but I made sure my boys burped quietly and cleaned the tip of their lips on cloth napkins that I myself embroidered out of rags, with little palm tree figures and everything. I sneaked in candles from the pink underground, namely, a guard who took a liking to me, to lend our dinners ambiance. I made sure the slop with the stale Russian bread was dashed with *comino* and *oregano* that grew in the fields. *Todo, muy sabroso, eh?*

I was determined to keep alive the flame that El Viejo, Papi, had proudly set up at the Habana. See what I mean? . . . It's true that I shout and curse, but this is no concentration camp. I just demand a work ethic. It'll be good for you, if you people want to make it in America.

Survival in America! That's the motto of the immigrant. Those of us who come here with nothing! You Mexicans have been here longer, learn from me. Even we queers are better off here. Discrimination? Social injustice? In this country? This is nothing compared to Cuba. In the end, we, the Cuban queers, were just dropped on these shores like refuse. The revolution decided we were hopeless. That they could never turn etiquette-minded queers like me into straight revolutionary communists. They put us on a boat to Florida during the Mariel boat lift, and we thought our troubles were over.

I thought El Viejo would welcome me and put me to work in his Miami diner, El Criollo Loco. But it turns out Papi would have preferred for me to be put away for something more normal, such as raping young women; isn't that what straight men do? . . . Papi was ashamed that I was in "those camps," not just your average concentration camps for political dissidents, but "those camps" for undesirables like me. I was the only point on which my father agreed with the revolution.

But now up even my own father turned against me. He said I'd become too obvious. That I'd been much more discreet before. Papi said he'd invest in some business elsewhere, a booming business town, somewhere far away, perhaps I could go away and colonize the desert.

He put up the downpayment for Paco's Cuban Restaurant, and the rest was up to me. There wasn't enough of a downpayment for West Hollywood, or the Village, or the Castro District—somebody should change that name—but anyway, the investment was good enough for Phoenix. El Viejo doesn't want me back. I'm not invited to family get-togethers. And it doesn't matter that I've had a few years of prosperity, and it doesn't matter that I'm the president of Arizona Gay Republicans. El Viejo does not call or write.

And then, here we are facing bankruptcy—there's that Carlos's Havana Room opening by City Hall. Carlos owns *chains* of Havana Rooms! He's a Cuban-American princess, *y casi no habla Español,* Americanized piece of shit that he is! ¡*Come mierda!* He's young, has a well-toned body, and I hear he's even in a long-term relationship!

But there's only room for one Cuban faggot restaurateur in all of Phoenix! That's me, Paco. . . . So, you see, our jobs depend on battling this enemy, which is no longer communism, but the indifference of the universe, the indifference of the desert.

So . . . it's up to you to share my dream. It's up to you to get your shit together and push this dream forward. One day you'll be in my shoes, prospering and aging just as gracefully as I'm doing, and leaving the marquee on, and making sure *Pollo à la Cienfueguesa* is not polluted by nopal!

So, shall we? I mean, you need the job, and I might be able to afford a raise when we pull through. . . . You *will* stay with me, won't you? After all, I *need* you. . . . I meant to say that a long time ago. . . . You will stay? : . . Of course you will. Who else would listen to me like this?

Oh . . . Oh my God! Here they come! Put on the sash, Miguel. Busboys, man your stations and hold the water jugs up high with the pride of a true *Cubano.* Chef, back to the kitchen, and please, don't ignore the yucca!

Here they are, with their ominous-looking briefcases. Is it the lunch crowd, or is it an army of debt collectors? [*He laughs feebly at his attempt at a joke.*] We'll find out soon, won't we? As we push forward in this risky world of freedom, in this wondrous enterprise known as Paco's Cuban Restaurant—an Oasis in the Phoenix Culinary Desert.

Welcome! So glad you could make it! We like you! . . .

[*Blackout*]

ESL: English as a Stressful Language

[*Young Latino male, early 30s—but looks older. A prime candidate for a transcultural shock, otherwise known as a His-panic breakdown. His tone is too happy, as if talking down to children. He's nervous and totes a handkerchief, which he uses to continually wipe his brow.]*

Good morning, my little immigrants. We are here to learn the English language. *[Beat]*

I SAID . . . *[enunciating]* . . . we are here to learn the English language brought to you by the Pilgrims. English . . . don't leave home without it.

Now it's not a simple language. None of that romance language kid stuff—none of that one sound per every vowel. No, in this language you are allowed to make dozens of sounds per each vowel. There's no point in worrying about it—you'll never get it right. Because when it comes to pronunciation, English is a mind-fuck. Repeat after me: English is a mind-fuck.

Feel free to practice. . . . Practice makes *perfecto!* Ooops! *[Spanish slipped out. He looks a bit self-conscious.]*

While you do that, I'll tell you a little bit about myself. I was born in a house "my father built with his own hands," to quote my hero, the late Richard Nixon. *[Wipes a tear]* Dad was a farmer. Yes, we were poor . . . except, of course, when the coca leaves flourished in the spring. We came to America to evade the U.S. Army, if you get my drift, *compadre*—oops. Excuse me.

It's true, then. English is my second language, but it rolled me into its bosom like the mother tongue. It became my predominant language, you might say, overnight. It wooed me into its winning ways and winnowed me out, separating the wheat from the weaker chaff among wou—you.

And that's how I became an ESL instructor. Well, I didn't get accepted into art school, but that's alright. Neither did Hitler. No, instead I ended up sharing my wisdom with a bunch of foreigners who remind me too much of my parents and who'll never learn the language of Princess Di.

So, what's *your* excuse, Maria? Cat got your tongue? You've been sitting there for the past five years. I've seen you grow into an old woman. Along the way, you've given birth to six, seven welfare children. For five years, you have failed to memorize the past participle, let alone the present perfect, the past perfect, and the present perfect continuous. And you can forget the future perfect or the future perfect continuous, as in "Tomorrow I will have *learned*," but the future never quite arrives, does it? Although tomorrow, you probably "will have *conceived*" yet again. . . . Oh, you say the job at the sewing factory wears you down, seventy hours a week and only a few hours left at night for the study of this foreign, so very foreign language—I've heard all the excuses, and the truth is, the truth is . . . your Spanish stinks just as badly. . . . I would fail you in your own language, but I can't; I'm only the English teacher. If I were the Spanish teacher, there'd be blood on the table. *[He breaks!]* SANGRE!—oops.

Now you, you, Julio. The one with the tight jeans. Yes, I've noticed how much tighter they've gotten through the years. I bet you're in love with the teacher, too. One day, we will communicate, you and I. We will break the silence. I will leave my marriage of convenience to that assembly senator's daughter from Orange County. And you, you, Julio, will be there as my receptacle of desire. . . . Yes, I've seen you with Lucita, that Salvadoran girl you picked up at La Taverna Manusiosa. I've seen her waiting for you after class, holding a tray of *tortitas* and *pupusitas*, and all that Salvadoran fast-food stuff. I've seen you devour her food out there by the picnic table—Will you ever devour my homemade *Paella à la Sevillana?* Why not? Hey, I hang out with women myself. I married one. I am very comfortable with my sexual repression. . . . But I am fortunate, at least, in that I can sodomize you with my words and bend you over without lubricants—and you don't understand a word I'm saying!

One day, we will communicate. See things eye to eye. . . . We will rise from the earth, and, ah . . .

What? Hunh? Who interrupted the teacher in his lustful soliloquy? Was it you, Mr. Campos? Another one of your runs to the bathroom? Seventy-five years old and pretending to learn English as a second language, when the truth is, the dirty truth is . . . you come here for company! Company! As in human touch, consideration, to get away from all those monolingual grandchildren who refuse to speak Spanish with you. But how am I supposed to help you? That last stroke wiped out all the past tense, including my favorite, the past perfect continuous.

Here in my classroom you grunt, you aahh, you oohh, you grumble, as your head bobs up and down, up and down. Now is *this* learning, Mr. Campos? At your age, I would have given up. But you, Mr. Campos, you *insist;* you will fight to the bitter end. I disdain heroism, Mr. Campos; that's why I teach grammar! So to answer your question: "No, you may not go to the bathroom until you learn to raise your hand and ask in perfect Chaucerian English." SO HOLD IT!

And you, Mrs. Rosales, sweet little Mrs. Rosales, who came out of nowhere one night and has sat there ever since. We can't tell if you're Mexican or Salvadoran or Guatemalan. The combination of Spanish and English has blown a fuse in your wee little brain, and you can no longer speak any language whatsoever. You sit, you wickedly smile, and you point—what are you pointing at? I wish you wouldn't. Are you pointing at me, by any chance? Please, don't point at me. I didn't do it. Or I didn't *mean* to do it. Whatever I'm guilty of, I'm not guilty of it. I'm only doing my job. . . .

What? For some odd reason, Mrs. Rosales has chosen today to point at the Statue of Liberty. . . . Oohhh, I'm very proud of you, Mrs. Rosales. We welcome your downtrodden sentimentality. *[Wipes a tear.]*

As you know, I care about you all. I care about you, you, you, and *[To JULIO]* I definitely care about you, sugar buns. You are all my future fellow citizens, and I must have a job to survive in these recessionary times. For better or for worse, I am one of you, and we are stuck with one another, aren't we? We may succeed, or most probably fail, but we'll do it together!

Like good family members, we'll go at it, until one day we'll simply eat each other up alive!

The past tense of "eat shit"? Look it up in the dictionary.

Alright, let's get to work! Mr. Campos, empty out your piss-pot in the cacti. Maria, wake up or you'll conceive in your sleep. You, hot buns, smile at me from the *other* end.

One day, we *will* make sense to one another. One day, the horizon will open, the clouds will roll away, and we will communicate. We will stand as one, and we shall all speak English!

And by then, we'll all have to learn Japanese.

Drag Flamenco

[LA GITANA: A young man dying of AIDS. He is sitting on a hospital bed. As the monologue progresses, he dons a flamenco dress, a wig, and some drag makeup.]

How grand? How fabulous can one be in one's own deathbed?

La Gitana, they call me. Oh, I've been called by many names before—the obvious ones: faggot, queer, *puta, maricona,* trash, tramp, *loca, mariposa,* fairy, *mamona, sinvergüenza, perdida, asquerosa, bella y muy tramposa.* But only one of them stuck.

La Gitana, they call me . . . after the gypsy blood in me mixed with the Moorish Andalucian strains in my precious, delicate veins that have sustained generations of my kind. And we have survived and thrived and grown to be grand and *espléndida! . . .* And now La Gitana is back . . . not the roundish little *gordita* that she used to be, a little wan perhaps, a little faint and delicate. If you'd been abandoned by both your lover and your T cells, you'd look a little weary yourself—*¿no crees, mi reina?*

She is ready now to take her place among the immortals. "Bring me the castanets," she insists. "They'll cover some of the lesions on the hands!"

She prepares to stand again in the spotlight among her fans—men who paid for her flamenco fire on their chests. Men who once used her and abused her, maybe even loved her. They're here now and she demands respect—*¡¿más respeto, chico, eh?!* And then there's rumors that *he'll* be here tonight to witness the act. You know, *he.*

He who brought her to the U.S. from Fuentevaqueros, Spain. Desolate land of poets. *Ay, mi Fuentevaqueros. . . .* He lured her away from her magic homeland of dance and poetry. She lisped her way across the continent like a good Spanish girl until the two made a home in Los Angeles, part of the old kingdom once. She felt right at home!

At first she was a stripper, they say. Her man—the one with the slicked back "do" and the open shirt and chains around his chest—learned early the marketing of she. Her. La Gitana. He understood that her talents, her passion, unraveled themselves in her wrists, in the movements of castanets like little tremors of southern California earth, and then in her heels, the blood sent from the fists down to the little delicate toes, creating a forceful collision with the earth until sparks flew and the old kingdom of España was on fire in her veins. . . . It came naturally to her, she was—*[She coughs, unable to finish the sentence.]*

And yes, she loved him. Rather, she felt drawn to him as some are to a drug all too powerful to resist, a habit impossible to break. Hers was the love of criminals, the love of blood and passion, *de fuego y de polvora, de muerte y de vida!*

Soon, she became in demand. La Gitana would do the castanets and the zapateo for you and weave herself into the fabric of your soul.

And he, he was there to take his ten percent, which mounted to twenty, thirty, and forty percent if you take into account the coke she bought for him on the road, by train, by bus, by plane.

He made a scene when she flirted with a steward serving her coffee. He threatened to open the exit door and go flying out, thirty thousand feet over Utah—his home state, he said. Never felt at home in Utah.

And once in Washington state, she found herself a closeted apple picker. Family man with ten children, all lonely in the bar holding his Miller Draft. He begged her to stay in Washington, but the other "he," you know, the man with the "do," confronted the sweaty, sensual apple picker. Threatened him with exposing his secret among the apple grapevines—someone pulled a knife, and La Gitana had to expose her false titties to the blade of the knife, coming between the men to break up the fight.

Oh, after awhile he only wanted her to dance for him alone, and it became obvious that *she* had a "he" problem. That he would eventually ruin her career, that he would ruin her reputation as a reputable tramp, and that she would no longer be welcomed anywhere. But she told the world, "He comes with me, or I don't perform." And so the nightclub owners tolerated him because La Gitana would not have it any other way.

And the day came when, like so many other young men around her, she became ill. La Gitana could no longer continue to dance as she once did. She could no longer pay her electrolysis bills, let alone health care. But he . . . Oh, he was nowhere to be found! The day after her diagnosis was revealed, he went traveling again, seeking new talent elsewhere. The entire women's chorus of Bulgaria is now said to be his discovery—it's filled with drag queens!

And that's why he is no longer by her side. For months she has languished in this hospital bed. . . . For months she has hoped for his return.

Tonight, my friends, La Gitana has thought to herself, "Fuck him," and returned to you instead. You, the adoring public. You who've held firm for the return of . . . *[Coughs]*

They said it couldn't be done. Why couldn't she just stay in her hospital room? Why couldn't she just take her AZT with Zima and sleep tonight? Why couldn't she just stay home and count the aftershocks? No, instead, La Gitana *insists*—as her ancestors did—to perform until that final moment, that grand moment when the last breath passes through her ruby red lips. She's a stubborn one, this gypsy tramp—*esta puta gitana asquerosa y muy tramposa! Y ya está aqui*—in her soldout performance. There will be no extensions. . . .

She will look around at her adoring public, and then she will say, "Thank you; thank you. I am La Gitana, and tonight I will dance for you, and I will dance for the thousands that no longer dance among us. And I will dance for that empty chair that symbolizes 'him,' he who has no excuses for his absence. . . . Allow me this final breath—this final indulgence—so that I might live eternally, so that I might love and be loved again.

"As I deserve it, for I am not just any other *puta sinvergüenza asquerosa.* I am the Spanish pearl of Fuentevaqueros. I am the treasure that washed onto these shores. A blast from the past. The Spanish jewel blazing deep in the soul of old California. I am the daughter of Andalucian Moors, princess of old Arabian nights, cousin of the great sensual poets, whom I will join upon my demise.

"I am La Gitana!

"And for you, my *gran* ZAPATEO!" *[She warms up to a loud gypsy yell as she dances her life away.]*

Return of the
Gay Little Immigrant That Could

[This is a year later. FEDERICO is a bit more mature now, less naive.]

Knock, knock, knock. Hello . . . it's me. I'm back. Remember me? I'm Federico.

Last year, you refused to open the door for me. Well, I'm still around and I have not forgotten you, *pendejo!* Hello, I know you're in there. You come to my country and make all those promises, and now that I come here, you threaten to call the INS, the LAPD, and the NEA.

Look, I'm not going to go away just like that. There are millions of gay immigrants behind me, and they're all coming to California. Sooner or later. There is no place to hide. What happened to the colonies in space you say we populate? You and I?

You helped me believe in the future, and when I came to L.A., I expected open doors. I expected a checking account without charges.

I expected love. *Amor. Ay, el amor.* You disappointed me, *hijo de la gran puta.*

Look, let me tell you—and I know you're in there snuggling up to your southern Methodist wife. I have a job now. I work for the great Orange Bag Company of Los Angeles. We stand by the freeway and sell the greatest, juiciest *naranjas* for only a dollar a bag. I am up to fifty or more a day. I and my friend Joey live in the best shelters in town. For the upper crust of the homeless—Venice, Santa Monica—with a view of the ocean!

And I believe I have come to Los Angeles in the best of times. This city is on the verge of many great things! And if you open that door, *pendejo,* you will hear it! It's in the air, like the birds that fly from Argentina to San Juan Capistrano. We're like swallows. We serve the purpose: to spread our wings and let the shit fall where it may.

So, you see, I survive whether or not you help me, whether you like it or not, and whether I'm legal or not. I am an immigrant. I am the future of this great country of ours. They call me Federico, the gay little immigrant that could.

I'm here to stay. . . . Get used to it!

NAOMI WALLACE

In the Heart of America

EDITOR'S INTRODUCTION

ONE COMMON MOTIF running throughout this collection is that of the exciting new play by a gifted American playwright that has to travel to London to make its name. This is odder and sadder when the play contains a profound critique of aspects of American society. Unlike the British, Americans have problems with such critiques. American theatergoers tend to believe that plays should offer their audience pats on the back, not slaps in the face. Part of the Broadway success of Tony Kushner's *Angels in America* can be explained by the fact that ultimately the play does not call for change but forgiveness. Instead of offering the audience a challenge, it offers them a blessing. Naomi Wallace's *In the Heart of America* isn't so easy on us.

Wallace, a protégé and friend of Tony Kushner, shares her mentor's gift for combining wildly disparate elements into an exciting theatrical stew. *In the Heart of America* centers on a series of violent moments: the My Lai massacre, led by Lieutenant William Calley; the Gulf War, in which the slaughter was carried out by sophisticated technology that separated the killer from his victims and thus from the human outcome of his assault; the maiming of a young Palestinian-American girl's foot by children acting out the racial hatred they learned from their parents; and the murder of Remzi, a young American soldier of Palestinian descent, by his fellow soldiers because he was caught having sex with his male lover. Remzi's murder is Wallace's fictionalized version of the murder of gay sailor Allen Schindler in Tokyo by a fellow sailor.

Remzi's sister, Fairouz, seeks out the reason for Remzi's disappearance in order to deal with her own deeply mixed feelings about her brother, whom she loves but also hates for not stopping the children from crippling her. Remzi deeply wanted to be accepted as an American, but his race and sexual orientation made that acceptance impossible. Fairouz finds Remzi's lover, Craver Perry, in a motel in Kentucky and forces him to confess what happened to Remzi. Craver tells her:

> Remzi said to me the first time he kissed me, "What are you now, Craver Perry? A White Trash River Boy Who Kisses Arabs and Likes It?" I said, "I'm a White-

Trash-River-Boy-Arab-Kissing Faggot." And the rest, as they say, is history. Remzi
was, as they say, history, too.

FAIROUZ: Remzi is dead, isn't he?

CRAVER: I said he was history. That's something else.

Remzi will remain history as long as his story is told, and Craver will continue to
tell it: "Talking about it might keep me alive." Characters don't die in Wallace's play.
They continue to haunt those who loved them or killed them. And what killed
them is the name calling that is even part of lovemaking. *In the Heart of America* is
filled with epithets that express the way we expel people from the mainstream. The
violence is just the logical extension of the name calling. This is a world in which
only the names of weapons are spoken with tenderness and open eroticism.

In the Heart of America is peopled with haunted, haunting characters. Fairouz,
obsessed with recovering her brother; Craver Perry, literally upside down after
watching his lover be brutally murdered; Lue Ming; eternally haunting Boxler; the
dead soul of William Calley, who still teaches soldiers how to kill and who has the
most frightening lines in the play: "I was born a human being, you know. But one
can't stay that way forever. One has to mature."

Remzi tells Craver, "Love can make you feel so changed you think the world is
changed." He's wrong. The world hasn't changed, and Craver and Remzi must be
brutally punished for their outrage against American militarism and masculinity.
"Faggot" is still the worst epithet demanding the worst punishment. Craver sur-
vives because he doesn't fight back: He watches the soldiers kill his lover the way
Remzi watched the children maim his sister. Silence, passivity, is survival, but it is
also spiritual death.

In the Heart of America is harsh and wise. Its critique of American militarism,
racism, and homophobia is suffused with compassion, and the characters are rich
and endearing. At the heart of the play, after all, is a love story, which, like drama's
great love stories, ends tragically shortly after the consummation. I had the pleasure of seeing this fine play at the Bush Theatre in London. The Bush offers the
first presentation of some of the best contemporary drama. It is a tiny theater on
top of a pub. The audience is pressed together in ways that violate any notions of
comfort or privacy. The stage is tiny. The acting must be honest, for the audience
can literally reach out and touch the actors. In this tiny space, Naomi Wallace's
play held its audience spellbound. Wallace writes brilliantly for actors, and the
performances of Zubin Varla and Richard Dormer as Remzi and Craver were two
of the most moving I have seen in years.

AUTHOR'S INTRODUCTION

I write plays that I hope will disturb the public, yet disturb it in such a way that it
will want to come back for more. And even though I believe that theater must en-
tertain above all else, this entertainment should be challenging and dangerous. I

myself am most impassioned by a theater that puts us all at risk. I am not as interested in answers as I am in questions. When a playwright gives an audience an answer, the story is, in a way, finished, closed down. I am interested in conflict, questions, contradictions, and the different possibilities for the transformation of ourselves and our communities.

War and love. In a state of war as in a state of love, the familiar world is turned upside down, belief systems and values are put to the test, and the body becomes central, vulnerable. Whereas war is intent on destroying the body, love has the capacity to reconstruct or rediscover the body's sensuality. Conflicting loyalties arise during war: The body that loves is also the body that kills. So what might happen when two soldiers, one Palestinian American, the other "white trash" from Kentucky, fall deeply in love in the midst of war and the only language they are allowed is a language of mass destruction, a language of violence?

In many ways the Gulf War was presented by the mainstream media as an act of love, an honorable project to protect, defend, and restore peace and democracy. This act of love and its consummation (which is now recognized as the largest bombing campaign in the history of the world) were equal to dropping seven times the equivalent of the atomic bomb that destroyed Hiroshima. The second largest bombing campaign was against Vietnam, Laos, and Cambodia.

Although there are differences between the wars in the Gulf and Vietnam, what connects them is not only the B-52 bombers but also the racism used to define both the Vietnamese and the Iraqis, the linguistic processes through which an entire people is dehumanized in order to make its killing more acceptable. "Gooks" and "sand niggers" are easier to destroy than living bodies of flesh and bone. And the same dehumanization that is used against our supposed enemies is then often turned against us, or those of us who are not white enough, straight enough, or American enough to be considered loyal to the cause.

I am not interested in identities and their exclusive oppression; rather I am interested in what connects the situation of individuals within systems of oppression. In writing a love story between two servicemen, I wanted to explore the links between homophobia and racism within an institution—the military—that lies at the very core of U.S. society and that embodies what theorist bell hooks would call white supremacist, patriarchal, capitalist values. Two crucial political events of recent years inform the play. First, the U.S. war against Iraq saw the affirmation of the United States as the sole superpower and global cop, setting new precedents for warfare and intervention abroad and acquiescence and censorship at home. And second, the issue of gays in the military, which inaugurated Bill Clinton's presidency and backsliding, was represented to mainstream America as the undermining of U.S. might and right—gays and lesbians being the symbols of the general degradation of North American culture—just as it seemed to represent to progressive folk a beginning, though small and ambiguous, of a debate about the values and contradictions within our society.

Theater can be a space for what Alan Sinfield calls "cultural dissidence": a place to disrupt the cultural amnesia that denies historical resonance and obscures interlocking oppressions, the foregrounding of which might help build a common ground of resistance. The domination and destruction of the body are central to oppression. How do the body's sensuality and sexuality survive in the face of a system (be it the military or late capitalism) intent on destroying them? How do we continue to love and resist in the face of oppression?

Photo by Bruce McLeod

PRODUCTION HISTORY AND RIGHTS

In the Heart of America was originally presented in North America as a workshop production at the Long Wharf Theater, November 1994. Arvin Brown, artistic director; M. Edgar Rosenblum, executive director. The production was directed by Tony Kushner.

The play was first presented in the United Kingdom by the Bush Theatre, London, August 1994. The production was directed by Dominic Dromgoole.

Application for performance of any kind should be made, before rehearsals begin, to Carl Mulert, The Joyce Ketay Agency, 1501 Broadway, Suite 1910, New York, NY 10036. In the United Kingdom, inquiries should be directed to Rod Hall, A. P. Watt Ltd., 20 John St., London WCI-N2DR.

NAOMI WALLACE

In the Heart of America

Give birth to me again . . . Give birth to me again that I may know
in which land I will die, in which land I will come to life again.

—Mahmoud Darwish

Cast of Characters

CRAVER PERRY: Early 20s. Kentuckian.
REMZI SABOURA: Early 20s. Arab American from Georgia.
FAIROUZ SABOURA: Mid-20s. Remzi's sister.
LUE MING: 30s. Vietnamese.
BOXLER: 40s. U.S. lieutenant.

Setting

A motel room in Kentucky, a military camp in Saudi Arabia, another room, the Iraqi desert. The present and past.
   The setting should be minimal and not realistic.

Act One

SCENE ONE

[Lights up on CRAVER doing a headstand. After some moments we notice FAIROUZ standing in the shadows watching.]

FAIROUZ: He sent me a horn in a box. It was a ram's horn.

CRAVER: He is a funny guy.

FAIROUZ: Do you laugh at him?

CRAVER: *[Gets to his feet]* What did you say your name was?

FAIROUZ: I don't laugh at him.

CRAVER: What's your background? He's never clear where he's from.

FAIROUZ: Can you tell me how he's doing?

CRAVER: I told you over the phone I haven't heard from him in months.

FAIROUZ: You are his best friend.

CRAVER: I'm sorry to hear that.

FAIROUZ: Where is he? *[Beat]* Mr. Craver.

CRAVER: Perry. Mr. Perry. Craver's my first name. C.R.A.V.E.R. How did you get my address?

FAIROUZ: Remzi wrote in a letter. . . .

CRAVER: I hardly know him.

FAIROUZ: He wrote: "Craver and I are never separate."

CRAVER: People get lost. Call the Army.

FAIROUZ: I did.

CRAVER: *[Does another headstand]* This kid over in Saudi taught me how to do this. It's not keeping your legs in the air; it's how you breathe. See? You got to push the air up through your lungs and into your feet. Then your feet will stay up, float like balloons.

FAIROUZ: Can Remzi do that? Walk on his hands like you?

CRAVER: *[Stands]* Remzi had no balance.

FAIROUZ: He wrote me that he loved you.

CRAVER: And who do you love?

FAIROUZ: I threw it out. The ram's horn.

CRAVER: We must have bought a dozen horns while we were over there, but not one of them was good enough to send her. He wrote her name on the inside of it. F.A.I.R.O.U.Z. Fairouz. That was the name he wrote.

FAIROUZ: It had a bad smell.

CRAVER: Fairouz isn't anything like you.

FAIROUZ: Horns make noise.

CRAVER: He said she was like a flower.

FAIROUZ: I don't like noise. Remzi knows that.

CRAVER: No, he said she was like milk, sweet, fresh milk.

FAIROUZ: He likes to race. Did he race with you? He's not fast, but he won't believe it.

CRAVER: Fairouz would have appreciated his gift.

FAIROUZ: Do you expect me to beg you?

CRAVER: Know what we call Arabs over there?

FAIROUZ: I'm not afraid of you, Mr. Perry. When I find out, I'll be back. *[She exits.]*

CRAVER: *[Calls after her]* Fairouz! *[Beat]* He was my friend.

SCENE TWO

[CRAVER asleep, worn out. A figure of a woman, an apparition or perhaps something more real, enters. CRAVER wakes.]

CRAVER: Are you looking for him, too?

LUE MING: I might be. Who?

CRAVER: Remzi. Remzi Saboura.

LUE MING: Are you Mr. Calley?

CRAVER: No. I'm not.

LUE MING: Oh my. I'm in the wrong house.

CRAVER: How did you get in?

LUE MING: I was honing in on a small jewelry store in Columbus, Georgia. Is this Georgia?

CRAVER: Kentucky. Motel 6.

LUE MING: And you're not Calley?

CRAVER: Are you Chinese?

LUE MING: Oh no. I was born in Hanoi.

CRAVER: What are you doing here?

LUE MING: I've never left my country. I'm a real homebody.

CRAVER: You speak good English.

LUE MING: Haven't tried it before, but it's going nicely, isn't it?

CRAVER: What do you want?

LUE MING: He's about five foot ten, red in the face, and likes colorful fish. He should be in his fifties by now.

CRAVER: I'm not Calley. I can't help you.

LUE MING: Who are you?

CRAVER: Craver Perry.

LUE MING: What do you do?

CRAVER: Not much right now. I'm . . . on leave.

LUE MING: Ah. An army fellow. Where were you stationed in Vietnam?

CRAVER: Vietnam? I wasn't in Vietnam. I was in the Gulf. In Saudi. In Iraq.

LUE MING: How can they fight in Vietnam and the Gulf at the same time?

CRAVER: We're not fighting in Vietnam.

LUE MING: Of course you are. Why just yesterday my grandfather was out in the fields trying to pull a calf out of the mud. The rains. So much rain. You flew over with your plane and bang, bang, bang, one dead cow and one dead grandfather.

CRAVER: I've never even been to Vietnam.

LUE MING: Of course you have.

CRAVER: The Vietnam War ended over fifteen years ago, lady.

LUE MING: Are you sure?

CRAVER: Positive.

LUE MING: Who won? My God, who won?

CRAVER: You did.

LUE MING: Oh, I wish I could have told Grandpa that this morning. *[Beat]* So I missed the house and the year. But not the profession. How many gooks have you killed?

CRAVER: I don't kill gooks; I kill Arabs.

LUE MING: Really? Arabs?

CRAVER: Not just any Arabs, Iraqi Arabs. Saddam Arabs. But that war is over now, too.

LUE MING: Who won?

CRAVER: We had a kill ratio of a thousand to one.

LUE MING: Oh my! *[Beat]* What's it like to kill a woman?

CRAVER: I never killed anyone.

LUE MING: Such modesty! In my village alone you killed sixteen people, seven pigs, three cows, and a chicken.

CRAVER: I never killed anyone in my life. I never got that close.

LUE MING: Does it feel the same to shoot a cow in the back as it does to shoot a man in the back?

CRAVER: Get the fuck out of my room.

LUE MING: I can't leave now! I think we're falling in love. *[Caresses his face]*

SCENE THREE

[A year earlier in the Saudi desert. CRAVER and REMZI are in positions to sprint.]

REMZI: I get more traction running on this sand.

CRAVER: Get on your mark.

REMZI: Like a streak of light I'll pass you by, Craver. Just watch.

CRAVER: Get set!

REMZI: You just watch me.

CRAVER: Go!

REMZI: Wait! Wait! Cramp. Shit.

CRAVER: Bad luck to get beat before we start.

REMZI: I'm going to visit the village where my parents were born. When I get my first leave. Want to come with me?

CRAVER: Nope.

REMZI: Don't like to be seen with Arabs. Look. I've got more money than you. You're broke and I'm Arab. That about evens it out, doesn't it?

CRAVER: The CBU-75 carries eighteen hundred bomblets, called Sad Eyes. Sad Eyes.

REMZI: What do you think it's like . . .

CRAVER: One type of Sad Eyes can explode before hitting the ground.

REMZI: . . . to kill someone?

CRAVER: Each bomblet contains six hundred razor-sharp steel fragments.

REMZI: I wonder what I'll feel like after I do it?

CRAVER: It's nothing personal. We're not just here to get them out of Kuwait but to protect a way of life.

REMZI & CRAVER: Flawed it may be, but damn well worth protecting!

CRAVER: Those poor bastards are so brainwashed by Saddam, they need to kill like we need oxygen.

REMZI: When I went in for the interview, the recruiter asked me was I against taking another person's life.

CRAVER: If you are, you could fuck up an entire war.

REMZI: I just went in for the interview to piss my mother and sister off. The recruiter said, "What you need, son, is all right here." He looked at me and I looked back. Then he said something that changed my life: "The army will give you a quiet sense of pride."

CRAVER: "A quiet sense of pride." *[Beat]* I'm not going to die.

REMZI: I am.

CRAVER: It's hot here. Why does it have to be so hot here? Can't we just turn the sun up a few degrees and roast those motherfuckers! All these weeks with our ass frying in the sun, crawling through the sand like mutts, and the drills, drills, drills. Tomorrow might be the real thing. *[Beat]* We've got eight types of guided bombs.

REMZI: I wonder if you'll see it.

CRAVER: There's the GM-130, an electro-optically or infrared two-thousand-pound powered bomb. See what?

REMZI: How I die.

CRAVER: Then there's the GBU-10 Paveway ll, a two-thousand-pound laser-guided bomb based on an Mk 84.

REMZI: Let's say I'm lying over there, dead as can be, and then you see it's me, from a distance. But you still have to walk over to my body to check it out. So, how would you walk?

CRAVER: We've got Harm missiles, Walleyes, Clusters, and guided antitanks.

REMZI: Craver. This is something important I'm talking about. Let's say I'm you and I see me lying up ahead, dead. I stop in my tracks. I'm upset. We were friends and I've got to cross the thirty or so feet between us. *[Does a "walk" over to the imaginary dead body]* No. That feels too confident.

CRAVER: And you wouldn't feel confident because . . .

REMZI: Because I'd be thinking: "That could just as easily be me lying there as him."

CRAVER: Right. So maybe you'd do it like this. Kind of . . . *[Does "his walk" up to the imaginary "body"]*

REMZI: That's too careful.

CRAVER: Yeah. And too scared. I mean I might be feeling in a pretty nice way, thinking about being alive and not quite as dead as you.

REMZI: You've got a point there. You might be feeling pretty okay.

CRAVER: And fucking lucky too cause the blood's still rolling through my veins.

REMZI: Something like this maybe. *[Does another "walk," a sort of combination of his others]*

CRAVER: Yes! That's it! That's it! Let me try. Okay. I see you up ahead of me, twenty feet, maybe thirty, and I want to get closer to you. . . . Why do I want to get closer if you're dead and I know it's you? I mean there's nothing else to figure out then, is there?

REMZI: Because . . . I'm your friend and you'd rather be the one to report my death than some jerk who doesn't know I exist.

CRAVER: Right. So here I go.

REMZI: Get on your mark.

CRAVER: Get set.

REMZI: Go!

CRAVER: *[Copies REMZI's walk, but not quite as well]* That didn't feel right.

REMZI: Your shoulders are too tight. Loosen up. See it before you, my body up ahead.

CRAVER: How did you die?

REMZI: This Iraqi we shot dead isn't dead. He's almost dead, but he's got just enough strength to fire one more time. When I turn my back—bang!—he shoots me.

CRAVER: Where?

REMZI: In the neck.

CRAVER: Got it.

REMZI: So there I am in the sand, a bullet in my neck.

CRAVER: And it's hot. A fucking hot day and the sun is pissing a hole through my fucking hot head.

REMZI: Exactly and I'm dead.

CRAVER: But I'm alive.

REMZI: And glad to be that way.

CRAVER: But you were my buddy. We were friends. . . . Just friends or good friends?

REMZI: Pretty good friends.

CRAVER: Pretty good friends.

REMZI: Right. And now you have to cross the distance between us.

CRAVER: About thirty-five feet.

REMZI: And then you do it. The walk. The shortest and most important walk of your life. And you have to believe you can do it, with dignity in your stride, power, and, above all, a quiet sense of pride.

CRAVER: I'm ready.

REMZI: So am I.

[They link arms and walk in unison.]

SCENE FOUR

[Fairouz is also practicing a walk.]

FAIROUZ: Keep your chin in the air at all times. As though your chin has a string attached to it that is pulling it up.

[Lue Ming appears and walks in unison behind her. Fairouz doesn't yet notice her.]

No, a hook is better, a hook in your chin like a fish. Beauty lesson number seven: walking with grace.

LUE MING: It's all a matter of balance.

FAIROUZ: Not you again. I told you I don't know Calley.

LUE MING: Your friend Craver said you might know.

FAIROUZ: He's not my friend.

LUE MING: Are we still in Kentucky?

FAIROUZ: Yes.

LUE MING: American boys are so interesting! Full of secrets. All roads lead through him. My road. Your road. Dominoes in the dark.

FAIROUZ: Have you tried the other motel, across the street?

LUE MING: Calley's a soldier. A lieutenant. Of Charlie Company. A unit of the Americal Division's 11th Light Infantry Brigade. Very light. So light some thought he was an angel when he came home.

FAIROUZ: How do the women walk in your country?

LUE MING: Not as upright as we'd like. Hunched over a bit most of the time.

FAIROUZ: Show me.

LUE MING: *[Shows her]* The lower a body is to the ground, the less of a target.

FAIROUZ: I can't move without making noise. Clump, clump, clump. My mother always wanted me to walk with what she calls "presence." When I was in the fourth grade, I had to walk home from school.

LUE MING: Show me. How you walked home from school.

FAIROUZ: It was only three blocks. *[She walks again.]*

LUE MING: Yes. I think I remember it now.

[Now they are both practicing their walks.]

FAIROUZ: There were some older children in the seventh grade. Two boys and a girl. They stopped me on the sidewalk. They wanted me to take off my shoes.

LUE MING: You should meet my mother; she has one foot.

FAIROUZ: To see the toes.

LUE MING: She stepped on a mine on her way for a piss.

FAIROUZ: Not the toes, but the hooves. They said I had hooves for toes. Devil's feet.

LUE MING: It was March 16, 1968.

FAIROUZ: Devil's feet.

LUE MING: Why? You weren't even born then, were you?

FAIROUZ: *[Chants]* Devil's feet. Devil's feet.

LUE MING: Devil's feet?

FAIROUZ: Yes. *[Chants]* Fairouz has Devil's feet.

LUE MING: *[Chants]* Dirty Arab Devil, you go home.

FAIROUZ: *[Chants]* Dirty Arab Devil, you go home!

LUE MING: Get her shoe. Pull off her shoe.

FAIROUZ: Hold her down and pull off her shoe!

FAIROUZ & LUE MING: *[Chants]* Dirty Arab, dirty Arab, you go home!

FAIROUZ: Remzi! *[Beat]* Remzi.

LUE MING: Arab! Slope! Dink!

FAIROUZ: No. They didn't call me that: slope.

LUE MING: Thought I'd throw it in. Slope. Dink. Gook.

FAIROUZ: Gook I've heard of.

LUE MING: The Philippines War. It was used again for Korea and then recycled for Vietnam. How did they get your shoe off?

FAIROUZ: I can't remember. I can figure the distance from right here, where we're standing, to the center of the earth, but I can't remember just how the shoe came off.

LUE MING: But it did come off? And when they saw you didn't have Devil's feet, did they let you be their friend?

FAIROUZ: A happy ending? It was for them. I think they were scared of me. Afterwards, they weren't.

LUE MING: And now you have a Devil's foot?

FAIROUZ: It does look a bit like a hoof now. The bone's curved wrong. Do you know what's happened to my brother?

LUE MING: I think we met each other once, but we were headed in different directions.

FAIROUZ: My God, where? Where did you see him?

LUE MING: I don't know anymore. We passed each other in a rather bad storm, and he reached out and touched my sleeve. Then he was gone.

FAIROUZ: Thank God. He's alive.

LUE MING: I didn't say that, my dear.

FAIROUZ: *[Not listening]* He's alive!

SCENE FIVE

[A year earlier. REMZI and FAIROUZ are talking. FAIROUZ is polishing his combat boots.]

FAIROUZ: You're becoming a stranger.

REMZI: Look. I'm sorry about the occupation and that you don't feel you have a homeland, but I do. And it's here. Not over there in some never-never land.

FAIROUZ: I hardly recognize you.

REMZI: Iraq invaded a sovereign country. That's against international law.

FAIROUZ: International law? Ha! Your own land is overrun, occupied, slowly eaten up—

REMZI: *[Mocks]* village by village, orchard by orchard. Decades and decades of U.N. resolutions . . .

FAIROUZ: And no one's ever smacked a Desert Shield on those bastards!

REMZI: There's just no parallel.

FAIROUZ: There's always a parallel. Did Mother ever tell you how she broke her hip before she came to America?

REMZI: She fell down when she was running away from the soldiers. . . .

FAIROUZ: No. She was running towards the soldiers.

REMZI: I've heard this so many times it's a sweet little lullaby that could rock me to sleep. So Mother saved Father and they broke her hip with a rifle butt. Crack, crack. Bone broke. Hobble, hobble for the rest of her life. What do you expect me to do, hobble around for the rest of my life? You're so serious. Open your mouth and laugh for a change. You used to do that, remember? Get out of the house. Throw a party. Go to the Burger King on the corner and order some fries. *[Beat]* You're an American girl. Enjoy it.

FAIROUZ: I'm an Arab woman.

REMZI: You've never even been there.

FAIROUZ: Neither have you!

REMZI: If you walked into our village today, they'd tar and feather you.

FAIROUZ: Fuck you. I'd put on a veil.

REMZI: The veil's not the problem. You haven't been a virgin since you were thirteen.

FAIROUZ: How dare you!

REMZI: I'm sorry.

FAIROUZ: I was at least fourteen!

   [They laugh.]

Mother still says to me: "The honor of a girl is like a piece of glass. If it's broken, you can never glue it together again."

REMZI: Why don't you tell her the truth?

FAIROUZ: It's my truth. Not hers. You hardly know her and she lives five minutes away!

REMZI: I can't talk to her.

FAIROUZ: Learn Arabic.

REMZI: No. She should learn English. She's been here over twenty years.

FAIROUZ: She speaks English. She just won't.

REMZI: Not until the day of liberation, right? You're still doing the shopping for her, aren't you?

   [FAIROUZ doesn't answer.]

You should move out.

FAIROUZ: In the stores, for years, she'd lift me in her arms and whisper in my ear, "Chubbes."

REMZI: "Chubbes."

FAIROUZ: And I would say, "Bread." "Halib" and I would say, "Milk."

REMZI: "Halib."

FAIROUZ: She's our mother.

REMZI: You were going to be a nurse, a doctor, or something. Get your degree. Get a job. I want a quiet life. As an American citizen. That's good enough for me. Beats living in the past.

FAIROUZ: An American citizen. What is that? This government pays for the guns that force us off our land.

REMZI: Allah, spare me! Jesus Christ. It's not my land. I'm not into redrawing maps or being trapped in the minds of crusty grandparents.

FAIROUZ: We're your family.

REMZI: Some family. More like a selection of Mesopotamian ruins.

FAIROUZ: Why don't you learn a little something about—

REMZI: About ruins?

FAIROUZ: the Intifada?

REMZI: What? They're finally letting the women out of their houses to throw stones.

FAIROUZ: We throw stones. We run unions. We go to prison. We get shot.

REMZI: Oh, martyrdom! Why don't you get out of the house and throw a few stones around here? You've got a big mouth, Fairouz, but your world is this small. I'm sick of being a hyphen: the Palestinian, the gap between Arab-American. There's room for me here. Where I have my friends.

FAIROUZ: Ah, yes. Your friends. You tell your friends I was born that way.

REMZI: You're going to blame me that no one wants to marry a girl with a gimpy foot.

FAIROUZ: My foot is deformed, but my cunt works just fine!

REMZI: You have a mouth full of dirt, sister. What is it you want from me?

FAIROUZ: What I want? *[She speaks some angry lines to him in Arabic.]*

REMZI: Gibberish, Fairouz. Save it for the relatives.

[FAIROUZ speaks another line of Arabic to him.]

I'm not a refugee. It's always somewhere else with you, always once removed. I am not scattered.

FAIROUZ: If I could go to war with you, I'd shoot my enemies first; then I'd shoot the ones who made them my enemies.

REMZI: Enemies. Always the enemies.

FAIROUZ: There are three kinds of people. Those who kill. Those who die. And those who watch. Which one are you, Remzi? Which one are you? I know. I know which one you are, don't I?

REMZI: Go to hell. I was a kid. A child. You'll never let it go, will you?

FAIROUZ: I just don't want you to join up without knowing that sometimes I still hate you.

SCENE SIX

[A year earlier in the Saudi desert. REMZI and CRAVER are doing jumping jacks. BOXLER enters.]

BOXLER: That's enough. Take a rest.

REMZI & CRAVER: Yes, Lieutenant.

BOXLER: At ease.

CRAVER: Thank you, sir.

BOXLER: No sirs and thank-yous. We're equal when I say at ease. Where are you girls from? Haven't seen you around.

CRAVER: Echo Company A, 2, 3, sir.

REMZI: Those fatigues you have on. I don't think I've seen those kind before.

BOXLER: Special Forces.

CRAVER: I can smell the mothballs.

BOXLER: I like a sense of humor. *[To REMZI]* Where are you from, babe?

REMZI: The States.

BOXLER: I mean, where are your parents from?

REMZI: My father died when I was just a kid. My mother never told me where she was from.

BOXLER: Now that's not nice. . . . Parents owe the knowledge of their roots to their sons. A root must know its origins. You, my son, are a root living in the dark without a compass, and you have no idea what kind of tree is going to sprout forth from your skull. I'd say, American Indian, maybe. No. Could be your mommy is from Pakistan. Then again, could be South of the Border. It's hard to tell these days.

REMZI: Yes. It is.

BOXLER: But never mind. We're all family here, aren't we?

CRAVER: Do you know about the Sad Eyes, sir?

BOXLER: Boxler's my name. And of course I know about the Sad Eyes. I've seen them on the faces of many a soldier who comes back without his buddy at his side.

CRAVER: The weapon. Sad Eyes is a weapon.

BOXLER: That's what I love about war. The creativity of it. *[Beat]* Shall we?

CRAVER & REMZI: Ready, sir.

BOXLER: *[As he speaks, he takes out a blindfold and puts it on. He gets to his knees.]* Now, let's say you have a situation. A delicate situation. You've taken an Iraqi prisoner. He has a secret and you need to get this secret without breaking international law, the Geneva Constrictions, etc. Prisoners must be treated humanely. Please tie my hands behind my back.

[No response]

Do as I tell you. Use your handkerchief.

[REMZI does so.]

Alright. Interrogate me.

[Neither CRAVER nor REMZI responds.]

– Bang, crash! Rat-tat-tat-tat! Howl! There are bullets flying all around you. This camel jockey knows where the reserve forces are located, and if they aren't destroyed, you and your buddies are doomed. *[Beat]* Interrogate me!

REMZI: What's your name? I said: What's your name? He won't talk, Craver. What do we do?

BOXLER: Be firm.

CRAVER: Tell us your name, shit bag, and we'll go easy on you.

[No response]

Give him a push.

BOXLER: That's an idea. Go on.

[REMZI pushes him, but not hard.]

That's a start.

[CRAVER does so, but harder.]

You two Barbies, you think just because you push me around a little I'm going to spill my guts? You're nothing but piss-ants with one hand tied behind your back.

[CRAVER shoves him and he falls over.]

REMZI: One hand tied behind our backs?

[He strikes BOXLER. CRAVER strikes him, too.]

BOXLER: You two dandelions aren't getting anywhere. Hey baby doll, yeah you, the one with the dark skin, are you a half-breed?

REMZI: No. But you are. *[REMZI kicks him in the stomach.]*
You fucking sand nigger.

BOXLER: From what I can see of your face, you're a sand nigger yourself.

[REMZI kicks him again.]

What a farce: A sand nigger killing sand niggers.

[REMZI keeps kicking until BOXLER lies still. Some moments of silence.]

REMZI: Sir? Did I hurt you, sir?

[BOXLER doesn't move.]

CRAVER: Oh shit.

[REMZI and CRAVER free BOXLER's wrists and eyes. BOXLER springs to his feet, unharmed.]

BOXLER: *[To REMZI]* That was good. For a first time. *[Suddenly he punches REMZI in the stomach.]*
Pity is what you leave behind you, son, back home, tucked under your pillow with your teddy bear and girly magazine. Now get to your feet, you stinking Arab.

[REMZI starts to get up, but BOXLER pushes him over with his foot. REMZI attacks BOXLER, but BOXLER restrains him.]

That's it. That's it. Now hold onto it! Hold onto that anger. Stoke it, cuddle it, and when the right moment comes, take aim and let it fly. A soldier without anger is a dead soldier.
CRAVER: What about me, sir?
BOXLER: What about you?
CRAVER: How do I get that anger when I need it?
BOXLER: Where are you from?
CRAVER: Town of Hazard. Kentucky. Sir.
BOXLER: Let me see your teeth? Hmmm. Trash, are you?
CRAVER: Yes, sir.
BOXLER: Joined up because you couldn't get a job.
CRAVER: Yes, sir.
BOXLER: Father dead?
CRAVER: Yes, sir. The mines, sir.
BOXLER: Burned to a crisp in an explosion?
CRAVER: Suffocated. His lungs, sir.
BOXLER: A pity you weren't with him when he died.
CRAVER: It was like something sawing through wood. His breathing, sir. I couldn't stand to hear it. But the company wouldn't let him retire. He kept working. For the money, sir. We had to tie him into his chair to keep him at home.
BOXLER: Shat right there in his chair, did he? And you let your mother clean up his mess. Never offered her a hand. Tsk, tsk. Went out with your friends and got drunk on Pabst Blue Ribbon. But one night you came home early and he was still sitting there, tied to his chair. Your mother was passed out on the couch.
REMZI: Sir, this is ridicu—

BOXLER: *[Interrupts]* Yes, it is, isn't it? Because Craver then leaned over and said into his father's ear: "I'm sorry, Dad. I am so sorry." And do you know, Remzi, just what his father did to show his acceptance and respect for his prodigal son? He pissed. Right then and there. Pissed where he sat, and Craver didn't even know it until he looked down and saw he was standing in it. The piss soaked through his shoes, right into his socks.

CRAVER: When he went into the mines, he was my father. When he came back out, he was something else. I couldn't love something else.

BOXLER: And you were out fucking some pretty little box in the back of his Ford pickup truck the night he drew his last, painful breath. You shot your cum the moment his heart stopped.

REMZI: *[To CRAVER]* Don't listen to him, Craver.

CRAVER: That's where you're wrong. I didn't come. I never came.

BOXLER: And why not? *[Beat]* What was the problem? Are you a funny little boy, one of those ha-ha little boys?

CRAVER: What are you going to do about it? Report me? I'll break your fucking neck.

REMZI: Let's get out of here, Crave.

BOXLER: *[To CRAVER]* My, my. I can call your father a broken down, coal shit-ting, piss poor excuse for the American dream, and you don't bat an eye, but when I detect that you're a bit on the queer side . . .

REMZI: Craver?

[CRAVER suddenly turns on REMZI, knocks him down, and begins to choke REMZI.]

Craver! Fuck! Craver!

BOXLER: *[Whispers]* Faggot. Shit-fucker.

REMZI: Stop it!

BOXLER: Sodomite. Fairy. *[Beat]* Feel it? Feel it inside you, Mr. Perry? Now grab hold of it.

[CRAVER stops choking REMZI.]

Catch it. Hold it like a bullet between your teeth. And when the right moment comes, when you've spotted your enemy, let it rip, my son. Let it rip. But re-member, aim is everything and unbridled anger is of no use to you. It's like crude oil: worthless without refinement. But you've got to know where to direct it. Out there, my friend.

[CRAVER helps REMZI to his feet.]

Out there, in Indian territory, beyond the sand dunes where the camels lie in wait. Think of them as culprits in the death of your father. If the ragheads hadn't shot our buffalo, we could have swapped them for their camels, and then we wouldn't have needed the coal mines to begin with, and your father would have worked in an auto factory, and he'd still be alive today.

CRAVER: That's not how it happened. *[Beat]* Sir.

BOXLER: You can give his death any reason you want. Facts are not infallible. They are there to be interpreted in a way that's useful to you. Why, your president does it, and he is no smarter than you. President Johnson says—

REMZI: President Bush.

BOXLER: Whatever the hell his name is, he said: "Our troops . . . will not be asked to fight with one hand tied behind their back." As you did in Vietnam. *[Begins to laugh]*

Do you know how many tons of bombs we're dropping on Vietnam? Four million six hundred thousand. It's awesome, isn't it?

REMZI: This is a different war, sir.

BOXLER: The tonnage dropped by the Allies in World War II was only three million. Now, my hands won't be tied behind my back when we go into Panama City. Operation Just Because, it will be called.

CRAVER: It was called Operation Just Cause. Just Cause.

REMZI: That was in '89. In December.

BOXLER: I'll be driving a tank there. They promised me I could drive a tank this time. The only nuisance is that crunching sound under my treads. A crunching sound, like this. *[Makes the sound, shivers]*

Civilians have so little consideration.

CRAVER: You were never in Panama, sir.

REMZI: There were no civilian deaths to speak of.

BOXLER: But not to speak of, I'd say about three thousand. Now, when we went into the barrios of Grenada . . .

REMZI: Just where haven't you been, sir?

CRAVER: To hell. He hasn't been to hell, but he's on his way there.

BOXLER: Oh, there you're wrong. I stood outside the gates for a very long time. In rain and snow, fire and brimstone, but they wouldn't let me in. I don't know why they won't let me in.

[We hear LUE MING's voice offstage calling.]

LUE MING: Fairouz! Fairouz!

BOXLER: Now we're ready for lesson two: how to handle women in combat.

[Lue Ming calls: "Where are you?" in Vietnamese]

BOXLER: Hear it?

[Remzi and Craver do not hear it. Boxler begins to slink away.]

Can't you hear it? Poor hound. She's still after me. Still sniffing at my tracks.

FAIROUZ: *[Offstage, calling]* Remzi! Remzi!

SCENE SEVEN

[FAIROUZ is blindfolded. She moves about the dark stage carrying small paper lanterns. Throughout the scene LUE MING will move about the stage, taking up different positions in relation to FAIROUZ, sometimes surprising FAIROUZ with her voice, now here, now there.]

FAIROUZ: I can see through it anyway.

LUE MING: This is how we must operate: able to pinpoint the enemy even though we are almost blind. Night vision. Strategy where there should be none.

FAIROUZ: Like a bat?

LUE MING: If you like. Now. Think past the obstacles, that which hides your objective. Map out the lie of the land as you remember it and have never seen it.

FAIROUZ: And forget the motel carpet?

LUE MING: Hands up! Don't you know there's a war on? Keep your head. Look for what is not there.

FAIROUZ: Imagine the land I can't see.

LUE MING: Once, an American soldier called himself my brother.

FAIROUZ: Sounds like a friendly war.

LUE MING: In the first years the soldiers gave us toffee and boiled sweets.

FAIROUZ: By the rice paddies? In Saigon?

LUE MING: Tu Cung, actually. By the coast. *[Beat]* Rush always gave me gum, Juicy Fruit gum. He called me his little sis. Once he gave me a ribbon to put in my hair. I had very long hair, beautiful, thick hair that I wore in a braid down my back. *[Beat]* But one day Rush didn't bring any gum, and he took out his knife and cut off my braid.

FAIROUZ: Was it a slow knife? Serrated are slow.

LUE MING: Oh no, it was a quick knife, a Rush knife, and he strapped my hair to the back of his helmet. His friends laughed and laughed. Rush looked so very silly with his camouflage helmet on and this long black braid hanging down his back.

FAIROUZ: It was only hair.

LUE MING: I'd be careful if I were blindfolded.

FAIROUZ: I like it. I could go anywhere in the world right now, and to do it I wouldn't have to lift a finger.

[From the shadows, we hear the sound of REMZI's footsteps.]

LUE MING: Or a foot.

FAIROUZ: I'm four hundred thirty miles from home. This is the first time I've been outside of Atlanta. The first time I've flown in a plane.

LUE MING: I despise flying. It puts my hair in a tangle.

FAIROUZ: Could you get a message to Remzi?

LUE MING: Your brother's not accepting messages these days.

FAIROUZ: I'm sorry, but I don't have time for your lost braid. What's done is done. My brother is alive, and we must think about the living and wait for my brother to send word. *[Beat]* I'm sick of waiting. And I can't stop waiting.

LUE MING: Those who wait burn.

SCENE EIGHT

[FAIROUZ and REMZI a year earlier]

FAIROUZ: Did you get the vaccines you needed?

REMZI: Yesterday.

FAIROUZ: Then everything's in order?

REMZI: All set to leave. The big adventure awaits me. Little brother goes to war.

FAIROUZ: When we were small, the children from our school would come to our house to have a look at my funny foot. You made them pay a dime each time they had a look.

REMZI: I split the profit with you, fifty-fifty.

FAIROUZ: It was my foot.

REMZI: It was my idea.

FAIROUZ: I used to lie awake at night, for years, dreaming of ways to kill you. I thought: "If I kill him, there will be no one to hate." I was investing my hatred in you. It was a long-term investment. Really, I think you owe me some thanks.

REMZI: For hating me?

FAIROUZ: Yes. Then you wouldn't be surprised by the hate of the world.

CRAVER: *[Offstage]* Remzi! Remzi!

[CRAVER, offstage, and "somewhere else," calls REMZI's name and REMZI exits. LUE MING enters.]

FAIROUZ: Listen to me. You don't have the right balance. I do. You see, I love you, but I hate you too. I have to. Tightly, tightly. As though at any moment either of us could slip off this earth. Are you listening to me?

LUE MING: *[Answering as REMZI]* Yes, I am, Fairouz. I'm listening.

FAIROUZ: Go say good-bye to Mother. She's in her room and she won't come out. She says they'll kill you. Just like they killed father.

LUE MING: That was an accident and you know it. He fell onto the lily pads and into the pond and drowned.

FAIROUZ: His face was messed up. As though he'd been hit many times.

LUE MING: Water can do that to a face.

FAIROUZ: I've told Mother that, Remzi. Over and over I've told her that it's the Iraqis you're going off to fight, but she keeps saying *[speaks in Arabic and then translates]* "They'll kill him. The Yankees will kill him." Silly old woman. She's all mixed up.

SCENE NINE

[A military camp in Saudi Arabia. REMZI is sitting alone and reciting.]

REMZI: *"Tabun." "Mawid." "Zbib, trab ahmar, dibs."*

[CRAVER enters. He listens to REMZI awhile.]

Maya, zir, foron.
CRAVER: Sounds like you had a good leave.
REMZI: *Zbib, trab ahmar, dibs.* Raisins. Red soil. Molasses.
CRAVER: Really? How amazing. . . .
REMZI: I went to visit my father's village. On the western side of the Hebron Mountains. Al-Dawayima. According to my mother, there were 559 houses there.
CRAVER: I didn't know you were back.
REMZI: Tall grasses, wild flowers, scrubs. That's all that's there now. Dozers have flattened the houses.
CRAVER: When did you get back?
REMZI: I went to the refugee camp nearby, but I couldn't speak the language. I could point, though.
CRAVER: We went on alert a couple of times. Lucky we didn't start without you.
REMZI: A Palestinian farmer explained to me that there are three varieties of fig suitable for preserving: *asmar, ashqar, abiyad.* The black fig, the blond, and the white. Craver. I was a tourist there. An outsider.
CRAVER: You're a Palestinian.
REMZI: One old woman took me in for coffee because I didn't know anyone and had nowhere to go. She called me "Yankee Palestina." These people lose their homes. They live in poverty, and they're the enemies of the world. *[Throws CRAVER a bag of figs]* I brought that for you.
CRAVER: Nice you remembered I existed. I think of the three, I'm the white fig variety. How do you say it?
REMZI: *Abiyad.*
CRAVER: Yeah. *Abiyad. [He tastes a fig.]* These are nasty.
REMZI: You're not eating them right. You don't just plug them in your mouth like a wad of chewing tobacco. You've got to eat them with a sense of purpose. *[REMZI eats one.]* With a sense of grace.

[CRAVER picks out another one.]

CRAVER: With a quiet sense of pride?
REMZI: Exactly.

[CRAVER eats it.]

CRAVER: Nastier than the first one.

REMZI: No. Look. You're gobbling.

CRAVER: Why didn't you buy me a souvenir, like a nice little prayer rug?

REMZI: Eating is like walking. My sister taught me that. There's a balance involved. You have to eat the fig gently. As though it were made of the finest paper. *[Puts a fig in his own hand.]* Look. I'll put the fig in my hand, and without touching my hand, you pick it up. Gently.

[CRAVER starts to use his fingers, but REMZI stops his hand.]

With your mouth. *[Beat]* Go on. See if you can do it.

[CRAVER leans down to REMZI's open hand and very carefully and very slowly lifts the fig from REMZI's hand. CRAVER holds the fig between his lips.]

Now take it into your mouth. Slowly. *[REMZI helps the fig inside CRAVER's mouth.]*

Slowly. There . . . Well. How does it taste now?

CRAVER: *[After some moments of silence]* Did you take a lot of pictures?

REMZI: On the streets of Atlanta I've been called every name you can think of: pimp, terrorist, half-nigger, mongrel, spic, wop, even Jew-bastard. And to these people in this camp it didn't matter a damn that I was some kind of a mix. Some kind of a something else, born someplace in a somewhere else than my face said. Or something like that. Do you know what I mean?

CRAVER: *[Sincerely]* Haven't any idea.

REMZI: So. What's on for tomorrow?

CRAVER: Drills. Red alert. Stop. Go. Stop. Go.

REMZI: Every day it's anyday now.

CRAVER: I just want it to start.

SCENE TEN

[LUE MING and FAIROUZ rehearsing for FAIROUZ's travels. LUE MING is wearing REMZI's boots.]

LUE MING: Your shoulders are too tight. That's what they look for. Tight shoulders, pinched faces.

FAIROUZ: My face isn't pinched.

LUE MING: If you're going to find your brother, you have to cross borders. But not with sweat on your upper lip. Try it again.

Not a care in the world. Right at home. *[LUE MING assumes the posture of an immigration officer.]* Passport? Hmmm. North American?

FAIROUZ: Yes, sir.

LUE MING: Tourist?

FAIROUZ: Yes.

LUE MING: How long?

FAIROUZ: Most of my life, sir.

LUE MING: *[Speaks as herself]* Don't be perverse. *[Speaks as officer]* First time out of the United States?

FAIROUZ: Yes.

LUE MING: Relatives here?

FAIROUZ: Yes. I mean, no. I mean I do, but they

LUE MING: *[Interrupts]* Just what do you mean, Miss . . . Saboura?

FAIROUZ: My parents were born here.

LUE MING: Here? Born here?

FAIROUZ: Yes.

LUE MING: You mean right where I'm standing? *[She lifts her feet and looks under them.]*

FAIROUZ: *[Looks at LUE MING's boots]* Yes. *[Beat]* Where did you get those?

LUE MING: Do you think they're stuck to my shoes?

FAIROUZ: I know those boots. What?

LUE MING: Your parents. Do you think they're stuck to my shoes?

FAIROUZ: I don't understand.

LUE MING: I assure you it was an accident. One minute they're alive and well; the next minute they're under my shoes.

FAIROUZ: My brother is lost.

LUE MING: Lucky man.

FAIROUZ: I'm Palestin . . .

LUE MING: Don't say it! Don't say it! It's like a bee that flies into my ear and fornicates there.

FAIROUZ: Don't you think you're overdoing it?

LUE MING: You must be prepared for them to throw anything at you. *[Plays officer again]* Purpose of your visit?

FAIROUZ: Your ruins.

LUE MING: Yes. Lots of ruins. I like ruins. Your voice reminds me of one. Are you sad? Are you missing someone close to your heart? Pull up your shirt. I don't have all day.

[FAIROUZ raises her shirt.]

Education?

FAIROUZ: Doctor. I haven't finished the degree.

LUE MING: Ah, a person who quits?

FAIROUZ: I plan to go back.

LUE MING: You can't go back to Al-Dawayima. There's no place to go back to. *[Beat]* So you're Arab?

FAIROUZ: American.

LUE MING: American?

FAIROUZ: Arab.

LUE MING: Make up your mind!

FAIROUZ: I'm a Palestinian-Arab-American. From Atlanta. Sir.

SCENE ELEVEN

[FAIROUZ enters CRAVER's motel room.]

FAIROUZ: Did he talk to you about his visit to the Territories?

CRAVER: Not a word.

FAIROUZ: He never likes to learn anything new.

CRAVER: Ever heard of the Beehive? It's the ultimate concept in improved fragmentation. It spins at high velocity, spitting out eighty-eight hundred
fléchettes.

FAIROUZ: Fléchettes?

CRAVER: Tiny darts with razor-sharp edges capable of causing deep wounds.

FAIROUZ: What is a deep wound? How deep exactly?

CRAVER: To the bone. You should leave now.

FAIROUZ: I got a letter from the army.

CRAVER: Know the DU penetrator? Cigar-shaped, armor-piercing bullets. The
core of the bullet is made from radioactive nuclear waste.

FAIROUZ: They say he's missing.

CRAVER: When fired, the DU's uranium core bursts into flame. Ever had forty
tons of depleted uranium dumped in your backyard?

FAIROUZ: Not in action, just missing.

CRAVER: Things get lost. People

FAIROUZ: Get lost. But why not you? Why didn't you get lost?

CRAVER: Because I fell in love. In our bunkers at night, Remzi used to read the
names out loud to us, and it calmed us down. He must have read that weapons
manual a hundred times. All those ways to kill the human body. Lullabies. It
was like . . . they were always the same and always there and when we said them
to ourselves, there was nothing else like it: Fishbeds, Floggers, and Fulcrums.
Stingers, Frogs, Silkworms, Vulcans, Beehives, and Bouncing Bettys.

FAIROUZ: Did you love my brother?

CRAVER: I can't remember.

FAIROUZ: But you can. You will. Remember!

CRAVER: I remember . . . what my first . . . favorite was: the Buff. B.U.F.F. The Big
Ugly Fat Fellow, it can carry up to sixty thousand pounds of bombs and cruise
missiles.

FAIROUZ: Alright, let's try something more simple.

CRAVER: It has survived in frontline service for three generations.

FAIROUZ: Not about numbers this time, but about flesh.

CRAVER: It has an engine thrust of thirteen thousand seven hundred fifty pounds and a maximum speed of five hundred ninety-five mph. It's slow, but it's bad.

FAIROUZ: If you could give his flesh a velocity?

CRAVER: The Buffs, better known as B-52s, won the Gulf War. Not the smarts. Not the smarts.

FAIROUZ: Or a number, what would it be?

CRAVER: Ninety-three percent of the bombs dropped were free falls from the bellies of Fat Fellows.

FAIROUZ: If you could give his flesh a number?

CRAVER: Only seven percent were guided, and of these half-wits, forty percent missed their targets.

FAIROUZ: A number that's short of infinity? Was that your desire for him?

CRAVER: Forty to forty-five percent of the smarts . . . they missed. . . .

FAIROUZ: Something short of infinity?

CRAVER: They missed their targets.

FAIROUZ: Did you or did you not fuck him?

CRAVER: That [beat] is a lot of missed targets.

FAIROUZ: Okay. Mr. White Trash Likes Arab Ass, yes? Is it good? Is it sweet like white ass? Do you find it exotic?

CRAVER: I'm not that kind of a soldier.

FAIROUZ: He could be a bastard, my brother. But if you fucked him and then hurt him in any way, I'll tear your heart out.

CRAVER: Remzi never said he had a sister with a limp. His sister, he said, she walked like a princess.

FAIROUZ: Was he gentle with you? Sometimes when we were children, he would soak my foot in a bowl of warm water, with lemon and orange rinds. He would blow on my toes to dry them. He thought if he cared for my foot, day by day, and loved it, that somehow it would get better. [Beat] What was it like to kiss him?

CRAVER: After the Buffs it was the GR Mk-1 Jaguar with two Rolls Royce Adour Mk 102 turbofans. A fuselage pylon and four wing pylons can carry up to ten thousand pounds of armaments. . . .

[REMZI now "appears." FAIROUZ moves away and watches, as though watching CRAVER's memory.]

REMZI: The Jag can carry a mix of cannons, Smarts, and gravity bombs. And get this—maximum speed: mach 1.1.

CRAVER: Then there's the brain of the electronic warfare central nervous system: the E-3 Sentry, Boeing.

REMZI: If there ever was an indispensable weapon, it is the E-3 AWACS, capable of directing U.N. forces with tremendous accuracy. Improvements include:

CRAVER: A better Have Quick radar jamming system and an upgraded JTIDS. Able to manage hundreds of warplanes airborne at any given moment.

REMZI: At any given moment?

CRAVER: Any given moment.

REMZI: How about now?

CRAVER: We could go to jail. It's illegal in the Army.

REMZI: So are white phosphorous howitzer shells. So are fuel-air explosives.

CRAVER: We don't decide what gets dropped.

REMZI: Would you kiss me if I were dead?

CRAVER: Why would I kiss you if you were dead?

REMZI: Would you kiss me if I were alive?

CRAVER: I had a thing for the Sentry jet, but how long can love last, after the first kiss, after the second, still around after the third? I dumped the Sentry jet and went on to the Wild Weasel, F-4G. Like a loyal old fire horse, the Weasel was back in action.

REMZI: Have you ever touched the underbelly of a recon plane? Two General Electric J79-15 turbojets.

CRAVER: If you run your hand along its flank, just over the hip, to rear end, it will go wet. Not damp, but I mean wet.

REMZI: Have you ever run your face over the wing of an A-6 Intruder or opened your mouth onto the tail of a AV-8B Harrier II? It's not steel you taste. It's not metal.

CRAVER: Ever had a Phoenix missile at the tip of your tongue? Nine hundred and eighty-five pounds of power, at launch.

[CRAVER moves to kiss REMZI, but REMZI moves away.]

FAIROUZ: Is that how you kissed him?

CRAVER: I kissed a girl for the first time when I was twelve. She had a mouth full of peanut butter and jelly and that's what I got. Have you ever seen an airplane take off vertically? That's what I was when I kissed Remzi, like the AV-8B Harrier II, straight up into the air, no runway, no horizontal run, but VTO, vertical takeoff.

FAIROUZ: Why don't you say it?

CRAVER: One Rolls Royce turbojet going up, engine thrust, twenty-one thousand pounds, maximum speed:

FAIROUZ: Please. Just say it.

CRAVER: Forever. Remzi said to me the first time he kissed me, "What are you now, Craver Perry? A White Trash River Boy Who Kisses Arabs and Likes It?" I said, "I'm a White-Trash-River-Boy-Arab-Kissing Faggot." And the rest, as they say, is history. *[Beat]* Remzi was, as they say, history, too.

FAIROUZ: Remzi is dead, isn't he?

CRAVER: I said he was history. That's something else.

FAIROUZ: How can this be funny to you?

CRAVER: If you saw your brother lying dead in the sand, just what would you say to him? Imagine it. There he is. Dead on the sand. A bullet in his neck.

FAIROUZ: Bled to death?

CRAVER: Maybe. What would you do?

[FAIROUZ touches his face.]

Like that? Would you touch Remzi like that? What if he didn't have a face? What if his face were gone, too?

[She kisses CRAVER on the cheek.]

That would take a lot of guts if he didn't have a face.

FAIROUZ: What was it for? You're of no use to me. Just a dead brother now. Zero. No more Remzi to hate. No more Remzi . . .

CRAVER: . . . to love. That's right. Do you think we're doing it, too, falling in love?

FAIROUZ: *[Moves away from CRAVER]* Would Remzi like that? *[Beat]* Do you like to watch, or do you like to kill? You haven't tried dying yet, have you? Perhaps you should.

CRAVER: There's nothing wrong with your foot.

FAIROUZ: You're kind. I see why Remzi was so attached to you.

[REMZI enters, unobserved by either of them. He holds her foot.]

My brother was the kind that watched. Is he the other kind now, Mr. Perry? The dead kind? I think I am going to scream.

[CRAVER backs away, watching the two of them as though he is seeing them both in the past.]

REMZI: *[Talking to her gently]* Just once more.

FAIROUZ: I can't. I can't.

REMZI: You've got to do it, or you'll never walk right. Just once more.

FAIROUZ: Just once more. Only once more. Will it be better then?

REMZI: Soon. It will be better soon.

[REMZI twists her foot, and she lets out a sound of pain that is part scream and part the low, deep sound of a horn.]

Act Two

SCENE ONE

[LUE MING appears. She summons up the Gulf War: the sounds of jets, bombs, guns. The war sounds continue through the following invocation.]

LUE MING: My sweet. My love. Come out from your hiding. Oh, my little angel, my tropical fish. Swim to me through the corridors of air. I am waiting for you. Come home. Come home. *[Beat]* Yes. Yes. It's you.

[The war sounds stop. BOXLER appears.]

It is always, only you, could ever be you.
BOXLER: Boxler.
LUE MING: Is that it now, Boxler?
BOXLER: I have nothing to say to you.
LUE MING: You're looking so well. So robust. So alive. And happy?
BOXLER: When I'm training my girls.
LUE MING: And what do you teach them?
BOXLER: Are you enjoying your visit?
LUE MING: Some of your cities make me feel right at home. Burned out, bodies in the street, the troops restoring order. They're so much like Vietnam.
BOXLER: You're Vietcong, aren't you?
LUE MING: I hear your record sold over two hundred thousand copies. You're a pop star.
BOXLER: That was thirty . . . twenty-five . . .
LUE MING: Twenty-one years ago. Just how much time did you get?
BOXLER: I got labor for life, but three days later I was out of the stockade, courtesy of President Nick. Then I got thirty-five months in my bachelor pad at Fort Benning with my dog, my mynah bird, and my tank full of tropical fish.
LUE MING: Could you sing it for me? That song? *[Sings the following to the tune of "The Battle Hymn of the Republic"]*

> *My name is Rusty Calley*
> *I'm a soldier of this land!*

BOXLER: I'm a hero, you know. I'm a hero and you're a dead gook.
LUE MING: Don't try to sweet-talk me. It won't work.
BOXLER: They took care of me. Friends in high places. I have a jewelry store and a Mercedes. I have a lot to be grateful for.
LUE MING: Have you missed me terribly?
BOXLER: I'm sorry, but I can't place you.
LUE MING: Take a look at my face, closely.
BOXLER: Nope.
LUE MING: You'll remember the walk. There is no one in the world who walks like Lue Ming. *[She walks.]*
BOXLER: Sorry.
LUE MING: How is it I can remember you and you can't remember me?
BOXLER: What's done is done.
LUE MING: And what's done is often done again and done again.

SCENE TWO

[REMZI and CRAVER are watching the bombs over Baghdad from a long distance away. We hear the muffled thuds of the bombs, and we see beautiful flashes of light far off.]

REMZI: One, two. And there. Three. Look at it. Cotton candy. Carnival. Dancing. Craver. You're missing it. That one! *[Beat]* "And all the king's horses and all the king's men . . ."
CRAVER: "Couldn't put Humpty together again."

[An even bigger flash of lights. CRAVER joins him. They both watch.]

REMZI: Do you think he really wanted to be whole again?
CRAVER: Who?
REMZI: The egg.
CRAVER: What?
REMZI: Do you think he wanted to be put back together?
CRAVER: How the hell should I know what an egg wants?
REMZI: I should be dead, but I'm not.

[They see an awe-inspiring explosion.]

CRAVER: *[Sings]* Happy birthday, Baghdad.
REMZI: I think he was tired of being a good egg.
CRAVER: Make a wish.
REMZI: Yeah. A birthday.
CRAVER: If you sit out in the dark, they light up all around you. Like that. Back in Hazard. Just like that. All over the sky. Fireflies. There—
REMZI: That first time.
CRAVER: And then gone. There—
REMZI: Like. It was like—
CRAVER: And then gone.
REMZI: I was a window and you put your hand through me.

SCENE THREE

[BOXLER and LUE MING]

BOXLER: You're not bad looking.
LUE MING: I know.
BOXLER: But I could never touch you. I mean, really touch you. I mean, I know you are human, but well. *[Beat]* I was a child once. Hard to believe, isn't it? I had

blocks and crayons, and when it snowed, I'd open my mouth to catch the flakes on my tongue. I had a favorite blanket. I liked most to roll the corner of it into a little point and stick it in my ear. Then I'd fall asleep. All the sounds around me were muffled and soft.

LUE MING: My three-year-old daughter had a blanket made from two scarves my mother sewed together.

BOXLER: I had a father I loved and a mother I loved, and then I went to school.

LUE MING: Show me what you teach the boys. Show me.

BOXLER: My teacher made us sit in a formation, with the whitest faces up front in the first row, then the second and third row for the olive skins and half-breeds, and the fourth and fifth rows for the dark ones.

LUE MING: Remember, you have a situation. *[She puts on a blindfold.]* You've captured a Vietcong, and you need to know the whereabouts of the others. Now be polite. You're an American soldier and that means something.

BOXLER: Did you know they made bumper stickers with my name on it?

LUE MING: You know who I am.

BOXLER: *[He pulls her hair.]* Shut your squawking, bitch. *[Calls]* Hey, you two troopers. Over here on the double.

   [REMZI and CRAVER enter.]

Remzi, what's the best way to make a woman talk?

CRAVER: The, 'dozers are clearing the area, sir.

BOXLER: Get on with it. What 'dozers?

REMZI: We're mopping up.

BOXLER: I said, Make her talk!

CRAVER: Can you tell us where Saddam's minefields are?

BOXLER: This is Vietnam, son.

REMZI: We're in Iraq, sir.

BOXLER: This is Panama City!

CRAVER: We have the Dragon M-47 assault missile, sir. Couldn't we use that instead?

BOXLER: Duty is face-to-face confession, son. Between two people. You and this prisoner. Well, go on. Take down your pants.

CRAVER: Sir?

BOXLER: Take down your pants. *[To LUE MING]* Suck him.

LUE MING: *[To CRAVER]* Haven't we met before?

BOXLER: Suck him or I'll cut your head off.

   [CRAVER unzips his pants. Lue Ming begins to sing a Vietnamese lullaby.]

Jesus. Can't you even give her something to suck?

CRAVER: It's the singing, sir.

BOXLER: Remzi. Go get her kid. It's in the hut.

REMZI: What hut, sir? We're in the middle of a desert.

BOXLER: Get her fucking kid and bring it here, or I'll cut his dick off.

REMZI: What kid, sir?

BOXLER: What kid? There's always a kid.

LUE MING: The child is right here. In my arms.

[They all look at LUE MING.]

REMZI: We're moving out. Now, sir.

CRAVER: Remzi.

REMZI: Let's go.

[They exit. Silence.]

LUE MING: I so much prefer it like this. The two of us. Alone.

SCENE FOUR

[A U.S. military camp somewhere in the Iraqi desert. REMZI and CRAVER are stunned, worn out.]

REMZI: Ancient Mesopotamia.

[CRAVER begins to whistle to the tune of "Armor Hot Dogs." Then REMZI joins him.]

CRAVER: *[Sings]* Hot dogs. Armor hot dogs. What kind of kids eat Armor hot dogs?

REMZI: *[Sings]* Fat kids, sissy kids, kids that climb on rocks.

CRAVER: *[Sings]* Tough kids, skinny kids, even kids with—

REMZI & CRAVER: *[Sings]* . . . chicken pox! Love hot dogs. Armor hot dogs. The dogs kids love to bite.

CRAVER: I always loved that song when I was a kid.

REMZI: It made me feel included.

CRAVER: Yeah.

REMZI: Which kid were you—the fat kid?

CRAVER: The tough kid.

REMZI: Of course.

CRAVER: Some of those fuckers were still moving.

REMZI: Right here, where we're sitting, long ago they gave us the zero and the wheel.

CRAVER: Civilians.

REMZI: Irrigation and organized religion and large-scale trade.

CRAVER: But there are no civilians in Iraq.

REMZI: Laws and cities and schools. *[Beat]* That was in 2000 B.C.

CRAVER: Bad fucking luck.

REMZI: The first poet known in history.

CRAVER: Those pilots took whatever bombs they could get their hands on, even the clusters and five-hundred pounders.

REMZI: A woman called Enheduanna.

CRAVER: Imagine dropping a five-hundred-pound bomb on a Volkswagen! Every moving thing. Terminated. Thirty fucking miles of scrap metal, scrap meat. All scrapped. *[He lets out a howl that is half celebration and half terror.]* And I've never seen guys dig that fast. Forty-nine holes.

REMZI: They were going home. We shot them in the back. There are laws regarding warfare.

CRAVER: You're going to get out of the truck this time.

REMZI: I can't.

CRAVER: Yes, you can and I'll make you.

REMZI: Don't ask me to do it, Craver. I'm warning you.

CRAVER: But I have to. Get out of the truck this time and walk along the road with me. Get out of the truck this time and help me. Help me.

REMZI: No.

CRAVER: Someone has to do it.

REMZI: But not you!

CRAVER: Fuck off.

REMZI: What was it like, you son of a bitch? To carry a man's leg?

CRAVER: We were ordered to pick up

REMZI: *[Interrupts]* To carry a man's leg when the man is no longer attached?

CRAVER: To pick up the pieces and put them in the holes. The dozers covered the pieces we found with sand.

REMZI: Is that what you think we're doing, burying them?

CRAVER: We buried them.

REMZI: We're covering them up. So no one will ever know. I saw you, Craver. I saw you.

CRAVER: It was like the limb of a tree. No. It was like the branch of a tree. That's how heavy it was. I said to myself, "Craver, you're not carrying what you think you're carrying. It's just a piece of tree. For the fire. And you're out in your backyard in Hazard, Kentucky, and he's still alive, my father, and my mother still laughs, and we're having a bar-b-que. And I can smell the coals."

REMZI: One of the bodies I saw . . . it was very . . . burned. In one of the vans. For a minute I thought. Well. He looked like . . . Maybe it was the sun on my head. I don't know. *[Beat]* I put my finger inside his mouth. I wanted to touch him someplace where he wasn't *[beat]* burned.

CRAVER: Touch me.

REMZI: Every fucking time it tastes different with you. No.

CRAVER: You didn't try and stop it, did you? *[Shouts]* Did you?

[Some moments of silence]

REMZI: Why are we here *[beat]* killing Arabs?

CRAVER: For love? Say it's for love. Don't say for oil. Don't say for freedom. Don't say for world power. I'm sick of that. I'm so fucking sick of that. It's true, isn't it? We're here for love. Say it just once. For me.

REMZI: We're here for love.

[They kiss.]

SCENE FIVE

[BOXLER appears with a black box. LUE MING stands watching him in the shadows. BOXLER speaks to the audience.]

BOXLER: Trust me. I'm the man with the box. The amnesty box. And this time I'm in . . . Iraq. Is that right? *[Beat]* This box you see before you is a very special box. It's a common device we use here within the military, a receptacle in which soldiers can relieve themselves of contraband, no questions asked. Would you like to drop something in it? You can't take those bits and pieces home with you. No, no, no. I've already made the rounds with the other troops. You aren't alone. *[Lifts the lid just a bit but then slams it shut]*

What distinguishes this particular box is its stench. Now some soldiers are more attached to their souvenirs than others; in one instance, a severed arm was discovered on a military flight leaving the base for Chicago. One might assume that someone somewhere would be disciplined for anatomical trophy hunting, but no, not this time. Lucky, lucky. Are you listening? I'm ready for hell, but they won't have me, and that's where they're wrong. *[Beat]* All that nasty shit, it took place all the time, before I even killed my first one. But they weren't interested then. And then when they were—bingo—there I was. *[Beat]* Yes, I did it. I never denied it.

[LUE MING steps forward.]

LUE MING: March 16, 1968. Charlie Company . . .

BOXLER: A unit of the Americal Division's 11th Light Infantry Brigade entered

LUE MING: Attacked.

BOXLER: Attacked an undefended village on the coast of Central Vietnam and took the lives

LUE MING: Murdered.

BOXLER: And murdered approximately five hundred old men, women, and children. The killing took place over four hours. Sexual violations . . .

LUE MING: Rape, sodomy.

BOXLER: Anatomical infractions.

LUE MING: Unimaginable mutilations.

BOXLER: Unimaginable. Yes. By the time I went to trial, public opinion was in my favor. T-shirts, buttons, mugs. One company wanted to put my face on a new cereal.

LUE MING: And my daughter?

BOXLER: It's over now. They say it's over.

LUE MING: The past is never over.

BOXLER: The war is over.

LUE MING: Which one?

BOXLER: Do you have anything you want to put in the box?

LUE MING: Can I take something out?

BOXLER: It's supposed to be a one way thing.

LUE MING: Give the box to me. Give the box—

BOXLER: *[Interrupts]* I can't do that.

LUE MING: Give the box to me, or I'll hunt you across this desecrated world forever. *[Beat]* You owe me a favor.

> *[He hands it over to her. She opens the lid and feels about inside. She pulls out her braid.]*

It's my braid. My braid!

BOXLER: Can we call it quits?

> *[LUE MING looks at him but doesn't respond.]*

SCENE SIX

[REMZI and FAIROUZ the night before he leaves for the Middle East. FAIROUZ is tickling him.]

REMZI: Stop it. Get off of me! Stop it!

FAIROUZ: I'm going to tickle you until you pee in your pants. What will the other soldiers say?

> *[REMZI wrestles her off and now tickles her.]*

REMZI: You're so jealous. You can't stand me leaving.

FAIROUZ: Let's meet up in the Territories.

REMZI: You'll have to come out of the house!

FAIROUZ: We could look for the village where we might have been born. We could go exploring, find relatives, take photos, and—

REMZI: *[Interrupts]* If I get a leave, I'm going to go somewhere . . . fun. With my buddies. *[Beat]* Hey. But I'll tell you what. I am going to send you back something very special.

FAIROUZ: Send something for Mother, too.

REMZI: Maybe I'll even fall in love over there and bring somebody home with me. They do that in wars. Come back with lovers and wives.

FAIROUZ: If you fall in love, will you let me meet him?

[Silence some moments]

REMZI: Now you're going to be punished for your foul and lecherous tongue! *[He grabs her foot and begins to tickle it.]*

FAIROUZ: Not that one, you fool! I can't feel it.

REMZI: *[Playfully]* Oops. Sorry!

[He grabs her other foot and tickles it.]

FAIROUZ: Stop it. Stop it!

[He quits.]

Now go on or you'll miss your bus.

[He starts to say something, but she kisses him and shuts him up.]

Nothing more. Just go. Go on.

[He exits.]

Get out of here!

[LUE MING appears. FAIROUZ talks to her as though she were REMZI.]

No. Wait a minute. . . . It doesn't matter now. . . . We were children then. Are you listening to me? I'm thinking of leaving, too, you know. Perhaps I'll make a trip, all on my own. *[Laughs]* Yes. I might even start a clinic out there, at the edge of the world. You don't believe me? Well, you just wait. When I—

LUE MING: *[Interrupts]* Fairouz. I'll be back in a few months. Don't do anything rash. Just wait till I get back.

FAIROUZ: Those who wait, burn. *[Knowing now that it is LUE MING]* They won't send home the body.

SCENE SEVEN

[FAIROUZ and CRAVER are in his motel room.]

FAIROUZ: The Army won't send home the body.

CRAVER: What's it matter? It's just a body. It's not him.

[Split scene: REMZI and BOXLER elsewhere on stage. BOXLER ties REMZI's hands and blindfolds him. LUE MING stands watching.]

FAIROUZ: I want to see his body. It belongs to us.

CRAVER: It. It. Just what the fuck are you talking about? He's gone. I don't want anything to do with it.

[FAIROUZ's foot hurts her.]

FAIROUZ: I think I twisted it again.

CRAVER: You should see a doctor. Let me see.

FAIROUZ: I don't usually show men my foot unless I take my pants off first.

[CRAVER takes a look at her foot.]

It doesn't smell very good, does it? Remzi used to crush grass, and dandelions, sweet clover, sometimes even the wings of colorful insects, all together in a bowl. He was quite a medic.

LUE MING: *[To REMZI]* Devil's feet, devil's feet, devil's feet.

CRAVER: May I?

FAIROUZ: You want to kiss my foot?

CRAVER: Yes.

REMZI: *[Chants with a deadpan voice]* Fairouz Saboura has devil's feet.

FAIROUZ: Because you want to make it better?

LUE MING: *[Chants]* Dirty Arab Devil, you go home!

FAIROUZ: Or because I told you he used to do that?

REMZI: *[Chants]* Dirty Arab Devil, you go home!

LUE MING: *[Chants]* Get her shoe. Pull off her shoe.

CRAVER: Both.

REMZI: *[Chants]* Hold her down and pull off her shoe.

CRAVER: For both reasons.

FAIROUZ: Alright.

[CRAVER leans to kiss her foot.]

REMZI: No!

[FAIROUZ pulls her foot away from CRAVER.]

FAIROUZ: Don't.

[REMZI cannot get loose. He is "seeing" again his sister being beaten.]

REMZI: Get the fuck off her, you motherfuckers!

FAIROUZ: Remzi!

BOXLER: *[To REMZI]* We had an Iraqi prisoner. I stuck the knife in just below the sternum.

CRAVER: I won't hurt you.

BOXLER: *[To REMZI]* And I slit him all the way down.

REMZI: All of you! Back off!

BOXLER: I pulled his rib cage wide open—

REMZI: Leave her alone!

BOXLER: . . . and stood inside his body. I said:

REMZI: Fairouz!

BOXLER: Hey boys, now I'm really standing in Iraq.

CRAVER: I promise you, I won't hurt you.

[FAIROUZ lets CRAVER kiss her foot; then she kicks him.]

CRAVER: Bitch.

REMZI: Get away from her!

[FAIROUZ laughs.]

CRAVER: Fucking . . . Arab whore.

[FAIROUZ approaches CRAVER. She is holding a hammer. He is on his knees before her.]

REMZI: Get away from her. I'm warning you!

FAIROUZ: Take a look, Craver. This isn't a B-52. This isn't a B.U.F.F. This is a hammer. I could do to your face what they did to my foot.

CRAVER: Go on then. You fucking gimp. Go on. Do it! Hit me!

[She raises the hammer to hit him but then puts the back of the hammer under CRAVER's chin to bring him to his feet.]

Hit me, you fucking cunt! Please. Please. Hit me!

[She runs the hammer over his cheeks.]

FAIROUZ: How do you remember him now? *[She presses the face of the hammer into his mouth and moves it sexually.]* Like this?

REMZI: No!

CRAVER: No.

[REMZI goes "unconscious." CRAVER pushes the hammer away. FAIROUZ and CRAVER are alone.]

A plague. A flood. An ice age. That's what I expected when it was over and I got back here. An earthquake. Something that would rip this country wide open. Something apocalyptic. Eighty-eight thousand tons of explosives dropped. That country is like a body with every bone inside it broken.

FAIROUZ: How did he die?

CRAVER: Every single bone. We tried. Day after day, but there were too many pieces. We couldn't get them all. Do you know how many pieces make up the human body? Two, three hundred thousand. *[Beat]* Dead. Maybe half of them civilians. We bombed the sewers, the electricity, the water. They'll die in the thousands because of bad water. Just bad water.

FAIROUZ: Give me an answer.

CRAVER: They came for us. Both of us.

FAIROUZ: But you're still alive.

CRAVER: The question here isn't how many feet were between Remzi and me. It could have been thirty feet. Or twenty-five. I think it was more like twenty.

FAIROUZ: Tell me.

CRAVER: I had practiced it with him. I got it down just right. Do you want to see how I walked? *[CRAVER does his "walk" for her as she watches him.]* Are you watching me? *[He continues his "walk."]*

SCENE EIGHT

[BOXLER and LUE MING alone]

BOXLER: I remember you. I think I do. Is that what you want? An apology? Why didn't you just say so? Hey. Really. I'm sincerely sorry. I've always been sorry. Besides, I wasn't completely heartless. You didn't know I shot your kid because I shot you first.

LUE MING: You said you'd let her live if I did what you wanted. You couldn't get it up. That's why you killed us both.

BOXLER: I had a war on my mind.

LUE MING: What is it like to kill a child?

BOXLER: You're sick.

LUE MING: I have to know.

BOXLER: It's simple: A bit of . . . a clump of . . . a piece of . . . *[Beat]* a piece of the future is alive and then it isn't.

LUE MING: Were you ever in love?

BOXLER: Oh yes. Long ago. I was born a human being, you know. But one can't stay that way forever. One has to mature. *[Beat]* Maybe it was you I fell in love with. I mean, it could have happened, couldn't it?

[He kisses her. She does not respond.]

LUE MING: Why wasn't one time enough?

BOXLER: Because I wanted to kiss you again. Naturally.

LUE MING: Why did you have to shoot her twice? Three times? Just to make sure?

BOXLER: Just to make sure, I did it four times. And shooting a child, if you must know, is rather exceptional. It's like shooting an angel. There's something religious about it.

LUE MING: I woke up after you and your troops were gone. I woke up with my child in my arms. A dead child weighs so much more than a live one. I carried

her back to the village. When I was well again, I continued my work with the Vietcong. I was one of their top commanders. I searched for you everywhere. Everywhere. With more passion than one would a lost lover. But I never found you.

BOXLER: Just how did you die?

LUE MING: I can't remember. How long have you been dead?

BOXLER: Calley is still alive and well in Georgia. Only I've run out on him. I'm his
soul. Calley's dead soul.

LUE MING: His soul?

BOXLER: Yes, his soul, and I'm homeless.

LUE MING: I don't believe in souls.

BOXLER: Neither do I, but here I am. I go from war to war. It's the only place that
feels like home. I didn't kill your daughter. Calley did. I was inside him, looking
out, but I didn't do it. I didn't pull the trigger.

LUE MING: You watched.

BOXLER: What else can a soul do but watch? We're not magicians.

LUE MING: Are you suffering?

BOXLER: I can't suffer. I can't and it hurts me.

LUE MING: Is it terrible?

BOXLER: It tears me apart.

LUE MING: How long will this go on?

BOXLER: World without end.

LUE MING: Delightful. More than I'd hoped. *[Beat]* But I want you to make a
sound for me.

*[Split scene: FAIROUZ is watching REMZI and CRAVER, who don't "see" her
watching.]*

BOXLER: No.

LUE MING: You owe it to me.

FAIROUZ: *[Calls]* Remzi.

BOXLER: I don't know what you're talking about.

FAIROUZ & LUE MING: The sound—

FAIROUZ: . . . you made inside you. Not the second time.

LUE MING: Not the third or fourth. But the first time you died.

BOXLER: The first time I died.

LUE MING: Yes.

BOXLER: That would be sometime in November, 1967. There was an old man. He
was wounded. He wouldn't have made it anyway. I threw him down a well.

REMZI: *[To CRAVER]* I couldn't say it any louder. I whispered her name. *[Whis-
pers]* Fairouz.

CRAVER: *[Whispers]* Fairouz.

REMZI: There were five of them.

FAIROUZ: Go on.

BOXLER: I threw him down a well. An old man. I heard his head go crack against the stone wall and then splash.

REMZI: One of the boys had just come out of woodshop. He'd been making an end table for his mother for Christmas. He had a hammer.

CRAVER: You were a kid, Remzi.

BOXLER: I was a child once. Did you know that? I liked to run naked and jump up and down on the bed. I had a bath toy. A blue bath toy. I can't remember what it was.

REMZI: They got one of her shoes off. Then the sock. I stood behind the bushes and watched.

CRAVER: You looked out for yourself. That was right.

REMZI: I was afraid that if I tried to stop them, they'd do the same to me.

CRAVER: Shhhhhhhhh.

BOXLER: I threw him down the well. And I heard a crack. I heard a splash. I heard a crack and a splash and I died.

CRAVER: You were just a kid.

[CRAVER and REMZI kiss and CRAVER takes off REMZI's shirt.]

FAIROUZ: You were just a child.

BOXLER: When I killed him, I died, though I didn't make a sound when I died. My body just turned and walked back into the village to finish the rest of the job.

LUE MING: But I heard it. I heard the splash. And I heard you die.

FAIROUZ: Do you want to know what it sounds like?

LUE MING: What it sounds like to go on living and the child in your arms is so heavy and she is dead and you are dead and I am dead but—

FAIROUZ: We just keep living.

BOXLER: Forever and ever.

LUE MING: It sounded like this:

*[LUE MING, BOXLER, and FAIROUZ open their mouths to scream, "No."
Their screams are deafening and mixed with the sound of thundering jets.
REMZI and CRAVER look up at the jets above them, which are awe inspiring.]*

SCENE NINE

[CRAVER and FAIROUZ in his motel room. CRAVER is still holding REMZI's shirt.]

CRAVER: That's beautiful. Sad Eyes. The CBUs were prohibited weapons, like the napalm, cluster, and fragmentation. But Sad Eyes. Who would have had the heart to try and stop a weapon named Sad Eyes? Eyes like his. Not sad, really. But confused. Or furious. Or scared.

[REMZI appears as a vision. CRAVER speaks to him.]

The first time we made love, we were so scared and I started to cry. It was a first time for both of us and it hurt. You leaned over me and kissed the back of my neck and you said over and over:

REMZI: You are my white trash and I love you.

CRAVER & REMZI: You are my white trash and I love you.

CRAVER: They caught us together, out behind the barracks. They were lower ranks. Just kids. Like me. Kids who grew up with garbage in their backyards. Kids who never got the summer jobs, who didn't own CD players. They knocked us around. After awhile, they took us to a room. Handed us over to an upper rank. There was a British officer and an Iraqi prisoner in there, too, and they were laughing and saying, "Sandnigger. Indian. Gook." *[Beat]* Remzi. Well. He went wild. He jumped one of those officers. I was standing there. I couldn't move. I couldn't. . . . Then somebody hit me over the head and I went out. *[Beat]* The first time I came to, the prisoner was down and he kept waving his arms like he was swimming, doing the backstroke, and Remzi was there and I could hear his voice, but it was like trying to see through a sheet of ice. *[Beat]* My head was spinning and it was snowing stars. In that room. In the middle of the biggest bunch of hottest nowhere in the world and it was snowing stars and Remzi in the center of it and this one officer or maybe it was two and there was a knife and the Iraqi had stopped moving—I think he was dead—and they were all over him and having a good time at it. Like kids in the snow. *[Beat]* Do you want to know how you died, Remzi?

REMZI: Friendly fire.

CRAVER: One of them had his arm around my neck, choking me, while another one held you down. I shouted for you to stay down but you wouldn't stay down. Each time he knocked you down you stood up. He hit you in the mouth so many times I couldn't tell anymore what was your nose and what was your mouth. *[Beat]* What did you call the other soldiers when you first joined up?

REMZI: Family.

CRAVER: When I woke up, I took him in my arms. The blood had stopped coming out. *[Beat]* Five foot . . . eleven inches. That's how tall you were. I used to run my hand up and down your body like I was reading the bones.

REMZI: I wanted to travel every place on your body. Even the places you'd never been. Love can make you feel so changed you think the world is changed.

CRAVER: Up till then, we'd survived the war.

REMZI: *[To CRAVER. Whispers]* What are you?

FAIROUZ: *[To CRAVER]* What are you?

REMZI: *[Louder]* What are you, Craver?

CRAVER: *[Whispers]* What are you? What are you? *[Shouts]* What are you, Craver?

[REMZI says the following words with CRAVER, beginning with "Indian."
REMZI's words are spoken just a fraction sooner than CRAVER's.]

CRAVER: I am a white trash,
CRAVER & REMZI: Indian, sand nigger, brown trash, Arab, gook boy, faggot
CRAVER: *[To FAIROUZ]* from the banks of the Kentucky river.

SCENE TEN

[REMZI as a vision, as a child, making a "mix" for FAIROUZ's foot. FAIROUZ watches him as though from a long distance. CRAVER listens from the shadows.]

FAIROUZ: He and I. We were never children. We were pieces of children. After that. But what is a piece of a child?
REMZI: Grass. Black pepper. Gold. From a gold crayon.
FAIROUZ: Sweetness doesn't last. Bitter lasts. Bile lasts. I am looking. Yes. I am looking for him.
REMZI: Pancake syrup. Lots of that.
FAIROUZ: And I don't want to find him. Not now. Not tomorrow. But I'm looking. *[CRAVER exits.]* I don't want him to come back to me as him, but as a boy wearing my face. *[Beat]* Where you ended, I began.
REMZI: Ready, Fairouz? *[Calls]* Are you ready? *[To himself]* This one's just right. Won't sting.
FAIROUZ: And the sand. I can't sleep because of it. Everywhere. Inside my pillow. Inside my sleep. I'm walking. Walking and calling for you. But the sand slides below my feet, stopping me, keeping me in place. And the wind throwing handfuls. But then in the distance. I see. Something. Dark. Moving. Moving toward me.
REMZI: Eggshells. Mint.
FAIROUZ: And it seems hours, years, until I can see. What. Yes. That it's a child. Five or six. A boy. The wind has torn small pieces from your body. With each step you take toward me, you are less whole. When we reach each other, you are almost transparent.
REMZI: It's too dry. *[Calls]* Bring me some water.
FAIROUZ: Almost nothing left. I know I must say your name. Now. But I can't. There's no sand in my mouth. No wind. But I can't say it.
REMZI: *[Calls]* Are you coming?
FAIROUZ: I can't. Say it. And then you're moving away from me, moving back. I open my mouth. To say it. I say: Fairouz.
REMZI: *[Calls]* Fairouz.
FAIROUZ: My own name. Not yours. And in that moment, the sun drills brilliant through your chest. And then you are. Gone.

SCENE ELEVEN

[CRAVER and FAIROUZ in his motel room]

FAIROUZ: The ram's horn. Why did he send me the ram's horn?

CRAVER: He carved your name on the inside. It took him three hours to do it. His sister would have appreciated it. You should have given it to her.

FAIROUZ: I am his sister.

CRAVER: Yes. You are. *[He does a headstand.]*

FAIROUZ: Why do you do that?

CRAVER: I'm training my balance.

FAIROUZ: Remzi had no balance.

[CRAVER comes out of the headstand.]

CRAVER: No?

FAIROUZ: He said balance could be a bad thing, a trick to keep you in the middle, where things add up, where you can do no harm.

CRAVER: Remzi said that?

FAIROUZ: No. But he might have. *[Beat]* I'll go wherever I need to go. I won't leave them in peace.

CRAVER: Remzi said you were the best sister any brother—

FAIROUZ: *[Interrupts him]* Don't. Please. *[Beat]* It's terrible, isn't it? To be freed like this. *[Beat]* Are you going to talk?

CRAVER: I'm going to try.

FAIROUZ: But what is it for?

CRAVER: It might keep me alive. Talking about it might keep me alive.

FAIROUZ: I mean the ram's horn. What is it for?

CRAVER: He said.

[REMZI appears and gets into position to race.]

REMZI: I want to race.

CRAVER: He said, If you blow on it, it will make a noise.

REMZI: I haven't had a good race in almost . . .

CRAVER: You're on! *[Joins REMZI. Gets down in a starting position to run with him.]* Motherfucker. Ready? *[CRAVER is in two realities now and speaks to both REMZI and FAIROUZ with ease.]*

FAIROUZ: A noise.

REMZI: I'm going to beat you this time!

FAIROUZ: Alright.

CRAVER: On your mark.

FAIROUZ: Will it be loud?

REMZI: I'm going to pass you by so fast, I'm going to "bang," disappear right in front of you!

CRAVER: *[To FAIROUZ]* Fucking loud. *[To REMZI]* Get set?

REMZI: You just watch me.

FAIROUZ: Fucking loud. I like that.

REMZI: Just watch me!

FAIROUZ: Goddamn, fucking loud!
CRAVER & REMZI: Go!

[As the two men move to run, the lights go black.]

Selected Bibliography

BOOKS

Augustin, Ebba, ed. *Palestinian Women: Identity and Experience*. London: Zed Books, 1993.

Bennis, Phyllis, and Michel Moushabeck, eds. *Beyond the Storm: A Gulf Crisis Reader*. New York: Olive Branch Press, 1991.

Bilton, Michael, and Kevin Sim. *Four Hours in My Lai*. New York: Viking, 1992.

Boyne, Walter. *Weapons of Desert Storm*. Ill.: Signet Special, 1991.

Chomsky, Noam. *The Fateful Triangle: The United States, Israel, and the Palestinians*. Boston: South End Press, 1983.

Chomsky, Noam, and Edward S. Herman. *Manufacturing Consent: The Political Economy of the Mass Media*. New York: Pantheon Books, 1988.

Clark, Ramsey, and others. *War Crimes: A Report on United States War Crimes Against Iraq*. Washington, D.C.: Maisonneuve Press, 1992.

Cleaver, Richard, and Patricia Myers, eds. *A Certain Terror: Heterosexism, Militarism, Violence, and Change*. Chicago: American Friends Service Committee, 1993.

Darwish, Mahmoud. *Music of the Human Flesh: Poems of the Palestinian Struggle*. London: Heinemann, 1980.

Edelman, Bernard. *Letters Home from Vietnam*. New York: Norton, 1985.

Giannou, Chris. *Besieged: A Doctor's Story of Life and Death in Beirut*. London: Bloomsbury, 1991.

Gittings, John, ed. *Beyond the Gulf War*. London: CIIR, 1991.

Janz, Wes, and Vickie Abrahamson, eds. *War of the Words: The Gulf War Quote by Quote*. Minn.: Bobbleheads Press, 1991.

Khalidi, Walid, ed. *All That Remains: The Palestinian Villages Occupied and Depopulated by Israel in 1948*. Washington, D.C.: Institute for Palestinian Studies, 1992.

Murphy, Jay. *For Palestine*. New York: Writers and Readers Press, 1993.

Peters, Cynthia, ed. *Collateral Damage: The "New World Order" at Home and Abroad*. Boston: South End Press, 1992.

Said, Edward W. *After the Last Sky: Palestinian Lives*. New York: Pantheon Books, 1986.

———. *Covering Islam: How the Media and the Experts Determine How We See the Rest of the World*. New York: Pantheon Books, 1981.

Shaheen, Jack G. *The TV Arab*. Bowling Green, Ohio: Bowling Green State University Press, 1984.

Shilts, Randy. *Conduct Unbecoming: Gays and Lesbians in the U.S. Military.* New York: St. Martin's Press, 1993.

Tucker, Judith E., ed. *Arab Women: Old Boundaries, New Frontiers.* Bloomington: Indiana University Press, 1993.

Young, Elise G. *Keepers of History: Women and the Israeli-Palestinian Conflict.* New York: Teachers College Press, 1992.

PUBLICATIONS

The Guardian (U.K.)

The Independent (U.K.)

Lies of Our Times

M.E.R.I.P.

The Nation

The New Statesman and Society

New York Times

Out Now

Z Magazine

About the Book and Editor

Created for general and scholarly audiences alike, this volume offers ten of the best recent plays by and about gay men, all of which have been successfully produced and critically acclaimed in the United States and England. The playwrights, who reflect multicultural origins ranging from Anglo to African American and Latino, have crafted powerful and insightful depictions of the roles gay men play in gender politics.

Each play is explosive, politically and socially relevant, and enlightening, whether it be Martin Sherman's much-praised *A Madhouse in Goa* or the avante-garde Pomo Afro Homos' *Dark Fruit*. The first to offer such a diversity of voices, this collection also crosses generational borders. Included are two of the first and most important modern gay playwrights—Martin Sherman and Peter Gill—as well as exciting younger dramatists who have emerged in the "gay nineties."

Illustrating the sexual politics and events that have swirled through mainstream society since the Stonewall rebellion in the 1960s—AIDS, homophobia, transgendering, discrimination, violence—these plays offer essential and direct articulation of the human lives involved. Each of these plays in its own unique way deeply investigates the pain, sorrow, joy, and beauty of being gay in a predominantly heterosexual world.

JOHN M. CLUM is professor of English and professor of the practice of drama at Duke University. He is the author of *Acting Gay: Male Homosexuality in Modern Drama* (Columbia) and coeditor of and contributor to *Displacing Homophobia: Essays in Gay Male Literature and Culture* (Duke). He has written two books on American playwrights for the Twayne United States Authors Series and contributed numerous essays to journals and volumes on twentieth-century drama and gay literature and culture. He is also the director of over sixty professional and university dramatic and operatic productions and the writer of a number of one-act and full-length plays.